THE BUSINESS STUDENT'S GUIDE TO SUSTAINABLE MANAGEMENT

Principles and Practice

THE BUSINESS STUDENT'S GUIDE TO SUSTAINABLE MANAGEMENT

Principles and Practice

Edited by

PETRA MOLTHAN-HILL

Greenleaf
PUBLISHING

© 2014 Greenleaf Publishing Limited

No part of this publication may be reproduced, stored in a retrieval system, or transmitted, in any form or by any means, electronic, mechanical, photocopying, recording or otherwise, without the prior permission in writing of the publishers, except in the case of brief quotations embodied in critical reviews and certain other non-commercial uses permitted by copyright law.

Published by
Greenleaf Publishing Limited
Aizlewood's Mill, Nursery Street
Sheffield S3 8GG, UK
www.greenleaf-publishing.com

Printed and bound in the United States of America by Edwards Brothers Malloy

Cover by LaliAbril.com

British Library Cataloguing in Publication Data:
A catalogue record for this book is available from the British Library.
ISBN-13: 9781783531202 [paperback]
ISBN-13: 9781783531387 [hardback]
ISBN-13: 9781783531219 [PDF ebook]
ISBN-13: 9781783531394 [ePub ebook]

We do not inherit the Earth from our Ancestors, we borrow it from our Children

Anon.

In a finite world you cannot have infinite desires,
Money really does grow on trees!
Though we are tethered to the Earth from death to birth
We can fill the universe with our hopes and dreams.

Jerome Baddley

Sustainability is about protecting our options. This requires a new economic paradigm that allows humans to live and work in ways that can be maintained for decades and generations without depleting or causing harm to our environmental, social and economic resources.

Bob Doppelt, *Leading Change toward Sustainability*, 2nd edn (Sheffield, UK: Greenleaf Publishing, 2010), page 40

Contents

Adding core topics to the curriculum

Bringing it all together

Foreword

Stand in front of a group of people, and ask them if they think the way that we live now is sustainable, and you are unlikely to get one person thinking that this is the case. Those same people will start to think 'well we need to do something then', yet our education systems are mostly set up to feed graduates straight back into our already acknowledged unsustainable society and systems. Thankfully groups of students are starting to see this. Research carried out over the past four years has consistently shown that there is a demand from students to learn about sustainability at university. We have also seen students of economics walking out of their lectures in protest at the continued focus on what they see as unsustainable economic models, and in their place they are developing their own curriculum, targeted at what they believe is relevant to building a more sustainable society.

Students of business and related studies have an extremely important role to play in building a more sustainable society. The way that business is done shapes our society's interactions with the environment and with seemingly distant communities. Our business students of today are the business leaders of the future, and a path towards a more sustainable future requires business leaders who can, and choose to, make decisions through a sustainability 'lens'. It is therefore imperative that the business and related subjects curriculum helps our students develop not only greater sustainability knowledge, but also the values and skills to make business part of the solution.

This book is therefore incredibly timely. It is targeted at both staff and students themselves, giving students the materials to link sustainability to the courses, irrespective of the content of the curriculum they are presented with. It also provides a true treasure chest of materials to support staff wanting to integrate sustainability into their teaching. The book provides a vast array of material to help develop teaching at a whole range of scales, and provides support to staff and curriculum developers on ways to effectively embed sustainability in the curriculum. The material is not just useful to people in business schools, but also to those involved in wider scale curriculum change, and those looking to make links between different disciplines. This book is far more than a 'how to' guide: the range of ideas and inspiration it provides really leaves little excuse *not* to do what we can to make our curriculum fit for graduates who will need to lead the change for a fairer and more sustainable society.

Dr Zoe Robinson
Director of Education for Sustainability, Keele University
March 2014

INTRODUCTION

1

The structure and purpose of this book

Petra Molthan-Hill

Sustainability issues are relevant to all organisations of all sizes and in all sectors. Increasingly, organisations themselves are demanding sustainability literacy skills for a wide range of roles and responsibilities. If learners can gain these skills they are therefore improving both their own employability as well as their ability to contribute to making their future workplace and society more sustainable. Yet despite this, and an ever-growing emphasis on employability within the education sector, there are currently few examples of sustainability literacy being addressed across the curriculum in mainstream education.

Robinson 2009: 130

This book is written for undergraduates who are studying for a business or management degree and want to know the part played by **sustainability in the subjects they are studying, for example marketing**. It is also a textbook for lecturers wishing to embed sustainability into their subjects. Furthermore, a business school aiming to embed sustainability across its curriculum will find lots of inspiration for each subject, and later in the next chapter, an overview on how to do it systematically.

The book covers **all main subjects** taught in a business or management degree, from accounting to human resources to corporate strategy. It can be used in two different ways: either by selecting a chapter in one subject area, such as economics or operations, and adding it to an existing 'conventional' module, usually towards the end of the first year or whenever students have been introduced to the subject in question, or by using the whole book as a textbook for a core module or a final year elective in order to include the sustainability dimension in all subjects of management studied up to that point. For this purpose, the book offers 36 ready-made seminars, three for each subject, but enough to cover a year-long module on sustainability in business. As a student you can also choose to read the matching chapters after you have finished your core modules or in order to get some inspiration for research projects or your assessment. You might also decide to read it in your final year of study to fill the gaps and to increase your employability, or just because you want to be a responsible manager in the future. Whatever the approach is, it is important that you as a student have a basic understanding of the subject, such as supply chain, before you can make use of the seminars included in this book. So you might want to read this book in addition to the core texts in your modules. If lecturers want to integrate more than the three suggested fully developed seminars per subject, there are on average five additional teaching ideas provided in each chapter to enrich their modules. If you as a student want to learn more about the subject you will also find further reading in each chapter and often interesting movies. Special attention has been given to offer a variety of teaching methods, from role-play to case studies to artwork.

Each chapter is divided into five parts:

- **Chapter brief:** Each chapter starts with a chapter brief which outlines for you the learning outcomes and content of the chapter.

- **Core text:** Here you will find an introduction to the key definitions and concepts to be studied in the subject concerned, which are later applied in the seminars.

- **Three fully developed seminars (for a taught session of approximately 50–60 minutes):** Each of these seminars is ready to be delivered without further preparation. They can also be studied independently by you as a student. We recommend, however, that they are used in a group, as an exchange of ideas and understanding would be beneficial. Most seminars can be broken down into different exercises so that shorter activities can also be chosen. The three seminars in any one subject area use different learning methods, e.g. one artwork, one a game, one a case study.

- **Additional teaching material and ideas:** This section in each chapter offers short summaries of additional ideas for teaching/ self-study such as movies or websites. Most of them are designed for additional seminars/tutorials of about 60 minutes in length, but some larger activities are also suggested, such as consultancy projects, which could cover a whole term/module.

- **Further reading:** Here you will find on average five recommendations for deepening your knowledge in this area. Each book or article recommended is summarised in a short paragraph outlining the key benefits for the reader.

- **Solutions manual/teaching aid:** A PDF offering further guidance for lecturers on how to embed sustainability into their discipline, as well as additional teaching material, suggestions for assessment and pedagogical advice on how to use the material offered in this book, can be obtained from the publisher. If you would like a copy, please visit www.greenleaf-publishing.com/studentsguide.

Overview of the book

In **Chapter 2**, some of the **key concepts** used in this book and in sustainable management are briefly introduced. Guidance and a **framework on how to embed sustainability into management/business education** are offered. Anyone tasked with embedding sustainability into the curriculum of a business school will find ideas about the various approaches they can take and how it can all be combined together.

Chapter 3 is dedicated to the introduction of definitions of sustainable management. It is structured differently, as you are encouraged to explore your own interpretation of sustainability and sustainable management.

It encourages you as the reader to think about sustainability, using activities and 'seminars' to support engagement and sense-making. This is not the standard introduction to a textbook, but has been adopted here because we are dealing with uncertainty and a complex problem. In this context, the approach adopted (which encourages you to explore and make sense of sustainability and management in this context for yourself) is more sustainable and ethical than 'inflicting' definitions and prescribed vocabulary on you, as someone wanting to learn more about this area and take action as a result.

The definition of sustainable management we have used throughout this book is based on the **triple bottom line** as conceptualised by Elkington (1997). Elkington suggested a focus on **people, planet and profit** in that order of importance. These three dimensions are now commonly used in sustainable management and are often referred to as the social, environmental and economic dimensions of sustainable management. **Chapter 4** is dedicated to the exploration of this concept, discussing each dimension in turn and addressing the question of how these three dimensions of sustainability—social, environmental and economic—can be balanced.

In the **following chapters** the core subjects taught in a business or management course for undergraduates are covered and suggestions are made as to how sustainable management can be taught in accounting, economics, human resources, marketing, operations management, supply chain management and corporate strategy.

In addition, two further topics have been chosen which could form part of a year-long module or could be added to an existing module. Both are considered by the editor to be two of the major sustainability challenges that are faced today. One relates to the area of environmental sustainability: greenhouse gas management **(Chapter 12)**. The other relates to the area of social sustainability: corporate peacemaking **(Chapter 13)**.

The **fourteenth and final chapter** is dedicated to systems thinking. Here the main questions are how you as a future manager can handle a complex system like an organisation/business, and how you can link together all the subjects learned separately.

References

Elkington, J. (1997) *Cannibals with Forks: The Triple Bottom Line of 21st Century Business* (Oxford, UK: Capstone Publishing).

Robinson, Z. (2009) 'Greening Business: The Ability to Drive Environmental and Sustainability Improvements in the Workplace', in A. Stibbe (ed.), *The Handbook of Sustainability Literacy: Skills for a Changing World* (Totnes, UK: Green Books): 130-36.

2

A new framework for embedding sustainability into the business school curriculum

Petra Molthan-Hill

In this chapter some of the **key concepts** used in this book and in sustainable management are briefly introduced. Students might find it useful if they want to understand some of the underlying concepts or deepen their knowledge. However, this chapter is mainly written for lecturers and other staff members as **guidance and a framework on how to embed sustainability into management/business education**. Anyone tasked with embedding sustainability into the curriculum of a business school will find ideas about the various approaches they can take and how it can be all combined together. The following questions will be addressed:

- What structural approaches can be been taken by business schools to embed sustainability into the curriculum? (More a question of *how* it is taught rather than *what* is taught.)

- What should be taught/studied? What have been identified as core skills and knowledge in sustainable management?

> To facilitate this decision-making, a **new conceptual framework** for embedding sustainability into the business and management curriculum will be suggested. This framework can be used to assess the current status of how well sustainability is embedded in a business school and how it could be developed further.

The first question to be addressed is how sustainability can be embedded in the structure of a business school. Godemann *et al.* (2011) developed a matrix to distinguish between the different approaches adopted by business schools (see Fig. 1).

In the first quadrant, the '**piggyback**' approach, the business school will add some sustainability-related material to an existing module, such as a case study with a sustainable focus, a framework used in sustainable management such as the life-cycle assessment (see Chapter 9), or some suggestions for further reading. The material in this book can be used for such a 'piggyback' approach, as lecturers/business schools can choose to add one or more of the suggested seminars to an existing module. A student reading this book might also choose this approach and read a chapter on sustainable marketing in addition to what has been covered in a marketing module, for example. The 'piggyback' approach is a good starting point as it does not require much effort to integrate sustainability in this way. However, in the long term it would be better to embed sustainability throughout each module, so that related concepts can be integrated where they belong in the 'core teaching'. For this purpose the following chapters of this book offer additional teaching material and further reading.

The next approach, '**digging deep**', is also an easy way to implement sustainability, as it is normally easier to offer a new elective/option than to change the existing curriculum. The content in this book can be used in this way, so that business schools can offer a 'Sustainable Management' option in addition to their existing portfolio. In such a case all 36 seminars in this book can be offered in a year-long module. Or business schools could choose to offer, for example, a module on 'Greenhouse Gas Management' using the material in Chapter 12, so that some students are 'digging deep' in this area and developing a special expertise that will

Figure 1: Matrix to illustrate integration of sustainability.

	Existing structures	New structures
Narrow curricular	*Quadrant 1* Piggyback Integration of sustainability within existing structures by adding sustainability to individual sessions of courses or modules	*Quadrant II* Digging deep Integration of sustainability through new stand-alone modules
Broad curricular	*Quadrant III* Mainstreaming Integration of sustainability within existing structures but with the emphasis on a broader cross-curricular perspective (entire curriculum)	*Quadrant IV* Focusing Integration of sustainability though new cross-disciplinary offerings such as sustainability-related courses which are required for all business school students and new programmes

Source: Adapted from Godemann *et al.* (2011), based on Rusinko (2010).

help them in the jobs market, given that graduates with this expertise are so sought after (Lacy *et al.* 2010). Even though this approach has its benefits, students may still not choose this option and therefore will not develop sustainability literacy, a skill set each student should acquire as shown below.

The preferred approach for the application of this book is the third approach, '**Mainstreaming**'. Each core subject would add the appropriate sections of this book to its teaching, so the seminars on sustainable marketing would be integrated into the marketing module, the one on environmental economics into the economics module, and so on. Initially they could just be added at the end of the first year for example, but it is recommended that this should be developed further and that sustainability should be fully integrated into the core curriculum in every part where it belongs. It is important that this mainstreaming approach should be co-ordinated to some extent. For example, it would not be good for the 'triple bottom line' to be introduced several times, once in accounting, once in human resources and so on. It might be beneficial, therefore, to have some general introductions to sustainability (our Chapters 3, 4 and 14) at the beginning of the first year and then build on these in the following core modules. Some aspects of the sustainability literacy approach (Stibbe 2009) could be included in this general introduction: more on this later.

The fourth quadrant, '**Focusing**', also addresses the broad curriculum, but requires new structures to be established. An example could be an online course offered to students from all disciplines, introducing them to the main principles of sustainability as applied to different disciplines such as law, business, science or psychology. At Nottingham Trent University we offered such a 'Sustainability in Practice' certificate in the 2013/14 academic year, with the focus on sustainability and food. In the online sessions students could access this topic via their own discipline, but they could also learn how 90 other disciplines would approach the same topic of food and sustainability, from astrophysics to equine studies to psychology. One of the benefits of such an approach is that students realise how their own discipline relates to all the others, and that common sustainability challenges can be only solved when disciplines work together. This specific certificate is optional, and is therefore more linked to the 'Digging deep' approach, but it could be made obligatory and would then be an illustration of a 'Focusing' approach.

Goworek and Molthan-Hill (2013) have demonstrated how these different dimensions can be integrated in a business school, and have given many practical examples for each of the different approaches described above.

A new framework for embedding sustainability into the business school curriculum

Although the Godemann *et al.* (2011) matrix is helpful for making decisions on *how* sustainability can be integrated into the curriculum, it is less so on *what* should be taught. Sustainability-related teaching **content** needs to differentiate further between general sustainability knowledge (such as climate change), specific sustainability action strategies in business (subject-specific knowledge), and sustainability literacy skills, which are transferable and competency based.

Figure 2: Proposed new framework for embedding sustainability into the business school curriculum.

	Integrated approach		Specialist approach			Trans-disciplinary approach		
Narrow (Modules)	Subject-specific knowledge	Sustainability literacy skills (e.g. systems thinking)	Subject-specific knowledge	Additional sustainability knowledge	Sustainability literacy skills	Subject- and trans-disciplinary specific knowledge	Sustainability literacy skills (e.g. systems thinking)	Practical application (e.g. to business)
Broad (whole curriculum)								
Required	General sustainability knowledge (needs to be offered whatever the approach, might build on previous education, e.g. school)							
Optional (can be decided for students)	Philosophical assumptions and values reflection							
Required	Strategic decision-making: graduate attributes, learning outcomes, quality process, key decision-makers							

Source: Developed from Godemann *et al.* (2011) and Rusinko (2010).

These different categories have therefore been integrated into a new framework, shown in Figure 2, suggesting how to embed different aspects of sustainability into the curriculum, how it could be taught and what could/should be taught. These new dimensions are explained further in the remaining parts of this chapter.

Sustainability-related knowledge

In the past, teachers and lecturers taught and tested **lexical knowledge of sustainability-related** topics such as which animals are threatened by extinction or which pesticides are harmful. According to Bodenstein *et al.*'s (1997) study about the relationship between environmental knowledge and consumer decisions, a good lexical environmental knowledge merely indicates a consumer's educational background (particularly in science subjects) and their newspaper reading habits, and does not give any indication of whether they will engage in activities to improve environmental or social problems. Instead they insisted that students/consumers need to have action-specific knowledge. In their study involving German consumers, their lexical environmental knowledge and their engagement, they were able to highlight that 80% could answer questions related to lexical environmental knowledge, but only 30% could name at least one ecological brand or company, even though 71% claimed that they cared a lot about the environmental friendliness of products.

Another study about climate change also illustrates clearly how important specific knowledge about appropriate alternative actions appears to be needed for environmentally friendly behaviour. Kempton *et al.* (1996) analysed the environmental perception of five different American subgroups back in 1996. At that point in time the interviewees were linking global warming to ozone depletion; they claimed that energy efficiency and reduced energy consumption had no impact on the greenhouse effect. This study also suggested that action-oriented knowledge depended on specific knowledge of the causes of a particular environmental problem. Translated into our topic, for example, business students would need to have a basic understanding of climate change. They would also need to know what **causes** climate change and how to apply this to a business context. Furthermore they would then need to know which **action**

strategies they can employ as future managers and employees to address these issues. We have followed this three-step approach in Chapter 12: the students learn first about the science of climate change and what causes climate change; in the next step they link it to the impact business has on climate change; and finally they are taught action strategies for how to reduce a company's greenhouse gas emissions.

The focus of the other chapters of this book is to teach these action strategies in business, so students will learn tools and techniques for how to integrate sustainability into marketing, for example. We call this **subject-specific knowledge**. If readers are interested in increasing their general (lexical) understanding of sustainability-related topics such as the sustainability of food, a very good starting point is Robertson's (2014) *Sustainability Principles and Practice*, although here less attention has been given to action strategies, which readers need to find or develop through other resources.

Subject-specific knowledge can be taught in various ways as suggested in Godemann *et al.*'s (2011) matrix: do students learn about sustainability accounting, for example, in an option or in a core module? If in the core module, will it come at the end or will it be integrated throughout the module right from the beginning?

In addition, students need to understand topics such as GHG (greenhouse gas management) in a company. As Chapter 12 shows, GHG management covers corporate strategy, operations, accounting and marketing, so it cuts across different subject areas. Students need to have a basic understanding of how this applies to their subject, or to the profession they will choose for their career.

However, using the analogy of IT, everybody in today's society needs to know the basics, but we also need specialists. This applies even more to sustainability. Everyone needs to understand the basics, but some need to have specialist knowledge. Therefore a business school should teach the basics of GHG, for example, to each student, but also offer some the chance to become specialists by offering a year-long module on GHG management. In our chapter about GHG management we have made different suggestions for lecturers/business schools who want to introduce GHG management as a specialised stand-alone module.

Sustainable literacy

Several authors (Stibbe 2009; Courtice and Van der Kamp 2013) have indicated that subject-specific knowledge alone will not be sufficient to develop managers who can deal with sustainability challenges appropriately. In the first *Handbook of Sustainability Literacy*, Stibbe (2009: 10f) illustrated the different aspects of sustainability literacy and defined the term as follows:

> This book uses the term Sustainability Literacy to indicate the skills, attitudes, competencies, dispositions and values that are necessary for surviving and thriving in the declining conditions of the world in ways which slow down that decline as far as possible. Gaining practical skills requires a form of learning which goes beyond memorising and repeating facts. It requires active learning, a broad term used to refer to self-reflection, self-directed enquiry, learning by doing, engagement with real life issues, and learning within communities of practice.

Several aspects of sustainability literacy have been included in this book, such as materials awareness: the ability to expose the hidden impacts of materials on sustainability (Watson 2009), commons thinking (Kenrick 2009) and ecological intelligence (Sterling 2009). In this introduction we will reflect on **three key sustainability literacy skills as applied to management and business: systems thinking, values reflection and philosophical assumptions in business**. Other skills have been integrated in individual chapters without making them explicit; a whole list of these skills can be found in Stibbe's (2009) handbook. Furthermore, Robinson (2009: 131f) pointed out:

> It is essential that learners are introduced to 'real world' examples and case studies. This could involve, for example, engagement with local organisations and employers or their own institutions by conducting informal environmental audits for them, or researching the activities of larger organisations to expose environmentally damaging practices and to identify paths for improvements.

Our experience has also been that students benefit from solving problems in the 'real world' and society benefits from it too—**throughout the book you will find different projects as undertaken by our students**, normally in the 'additional teaching material' section. If you are interested in developing something similar, you can find more information in the teaching aid mentioned on page 4; in some cases, direct contact details are provided in the chapter itself, such as for the strategic management project in Chapter 11.

Systems thinking

Systems thinking is seen as a fundamental concept in sustainability (Robertson 2014; Stibbe 2009; Clayton and Radcliffe 1996), and a system is often defined as a 'coherently organised set of elements' (Meadows 2008: 188). Robertson (2014: 4) defines it further:

> A property of every system is that its identity is always more than the sum of its parts. The Earth itself is a system, made of many other nested and interrelated systems; the biophysical world is an intricate and multi-layered web, a complex, three-dimensional network of interconnected systems.

Schoemaker (2008) criticises business schools/lecturers for opting to teach well-defined problems and frameworks without offering support in how to deal with the 'messy ambiguities of the real world'. Systems thinking encourages acceptance of the complexity of the world and suggests **ways of dealing with the massive amounts of information and interconnectedness**. As it is such an important concept in sustainable management, it is not only embedded in many of the chapters through this book, but also further explored in its own right in Chapter 14.

Worth mentioning here as a way of integrating systems thinking into the curriculum is to offer a computer simulation game such as Meadow's (2001) *Fish Banks Ltd*. During this three-hour game, students are asked to run fishing companies with the aim of maximising profit for their shareholders. In addition to the original game we have added some features, such as 'press announcements' from Greenpeace highlighting fish decline and recommendations for fishing quotas from the European Union. We have also added interaction between the 'companies' (i.e. groups of students), such as a meeting of the 'trade organisation', in which they have to discuss the possibility of a quota. In all games we have played so far at Nottingham Business School, and previously at Manchester Business School, students were so focused on their profit that first they overfished the 'deep sea' (where the profit is higher) before then turning to the coastal area to overfish there. Sometimes there is one company which attempts to act in a more sustainable manner, but they have never been able to persuade their colleagues to do likewise. If students decide to agree on a quota at all, they normally do so too late in the game when fish stocks have already declined beyond repair. Normally, at this point in the game, the company which has had the highest profit and the biggest shipping fleet will block any agreement. The collapse of the whole fishing industry appears to be something of a revelation for students, as is the calculation of the reasonable amount of money the companies could potentially have made while still maintaining their industry by fishing at a sustainable level, as revealed in the debrief. At this point, concepts such as 'systems thinking' and 'sustainable management' are also explained in relation to the game.

Values reflection

Another skill students need to develop in business education is to reflect on their values or to even realise that values feature in all business-related models. Several authors (MacIntyre 1981; Watson 2003; Verhezen 2010; Trapp 2011) highlight the fact that managers are reluctant to talk about the moral dimensions of their work, or might insist that they try to be objective when it comes to business decisions, separating business interest from their own or other people's values.

Bird and Waters (1989: 73) label this phenomenon the 'moral muteness of managers':

> Many managers exhibit a reluctance to describe their actions in moral terms even when they are acting for moral reasons. They talk as if their actions were guided exclusively by organizational interests, practicality, and economic good sense even when in practice they honour

morally defined standards codified in law, professional conventions, and social mores. They characteristically defend morally defined objectives such as service to customers, effective co-operation among personnel, and utilization of their own skills and resources in terms of the long-run economic objectives of their organizations.

Molthan-Hill (2014a) proposes that there is no value-neutral way of doing business, rather it is a conflict between established values, which are framed as objective, and new or different values such as environmental protection, which are framed as ethics. Jones (1991: 380) points out that managers/business students need to be able to identify the moral aspects of any business decision they have to make: 'a person who fails to recognise a moral issue will fail to employ moral decision-making schemata and will make the decision according to other schemata, economic rationality, for example'.

This is especially true when it comes to considering environmental or social values in a business decision: here, often a bureaucratic, resource-orientated approach will be chosen. As Crane and Matten (2010) point out, all stages, not only the first one in the ethical decision-making process, are influenced by the issue's moral framing; the most important aspect of moral framing being the language in which moral issues are presented. The problem, they observe, is 'that many people in business are reluctant to ascribe moral terms to their work, even if acting for moral reasons, or if their actions have obvious moral consequences' (p. 153). Therefore, business students need to be enabled to identify the moral dimensions of normal business activities and decisions. In our experience, students tend to highlight business problems, but have difficulty defining the underlying values or even acknowledging them. Furthermore, we often get the impression that students do not feel so comfortable talking about ethical issues. This was also observed by Bird and Waters (1989: 78) in relation to managers, suggesting that the latter need to learn how to express themselves in moral terms:

Managers also shun moral talk in order to not expose their own ethical illiteracy. Most managers neither know nor feel comfortable with the language and logic of moral philosophy. At best they received instruction in juvenile versions of ethics as children and young adults in schools and religious associations. They have little or no experience using ethical concepts to analyse issues. They may more readily and less self-consciously use some ethical terms to identify and condemn obvious wrongdoings, but do not know how to use ethical terms and theories with intellectual rigor and sophistication to identify and resolve moral issues.

Therefore, students need to learn mature moral language as part of their sustainability skills set, in order to participate in the moral business discourse. They need to learn the appropriate words and concepts, but they also need to learn how to apply these concepts in the business world. Finally, the 'moral neutrality' of the business world needs to be questioned in the classroom (and maybe not only there ...). A discussion about the morality of ends and the morality of means within the business world needs to become the centrepiece of any sustainability study, so that students reflect on their own values and decide for themselves which of them they consider applicable to the business world. Any module could start with a reflection on the values to be integrated into this subject area: for example, for accounting this could mean that the first session would discuss what needs to be included in a report to give a 'true' picture of the company. Should we focus only on financial values? Why? Should we give a financial value for environmental impacts and, if yes, how and also how much? In this sense every subject would start with a philosophical discussion as also outlined in the next section. In this book, ethics is integrated into each chapter, but often not explicitly. Sometimes students will be asked to express their own values as, for example, in Chapter 3.

Philosophical assumptions in business

Values reflection is part of understanding philosophical assumptions. Often lecturers and students are not aware that the different business concepts and tools being taught have different underlying philosophical assumptions. In order to include sustainability, we can either involve students in the philosophical discussion of what should form part of a sustainably designed business system, or lecturers can decide what the philosophical assumptions are, and whether to make it make it explicit to students or not—as in the current system.

In his article 'Behind Global System Collapse: The Life-Blind Structure of Economic Rationality', McMurtry (2012) complains that 'social life standards to rationally regulate choices to cohere with life support systems are blinkered out' of the common understanding of 'economic rationality' (p. 50). In his opinion, this so-called '"rationality" rules out everything required for a healthy and flourishing human life' (p. 52). He recommends instead a 'life-coherent rationality' which is judged by 'consistency with and satisfaction of organic, ecological and social life requirements' (p. 56).

Our proposed new framework on how to embed sustainability into a business school curriculum suggests an optional module in business philosophy (see Fig. 2). Here students might discuss the underlying philosophical assumptions of an existing business system. I remember vividly how, in my first year of studying business as an undergraduate in Germany, the lecturer asked us to compare one of our (Western) economics books with one published in the GDR (German Democratic Republic) that introduced a planned economy. It became obvious that even the concept of 'demand' (and supply) could be phrased very differently, depending on the underlying philosophical assumptions!

The aim of such a module could not only be the analysis of existing frameworks and concepts, but also to design new concepts and tools while 'structuring what is to be preserved' (Habermas 1984: 398). With regard to environmental issues, it would also allow room for discussions on how environmental and social issues could become part of such new concepts and tools.

For example, economic sustainability has been commonly defined as securing the profitability of a company in the long term (Crane and Matten 2010). However, according to Molthan-Hill (2014b: np):

> it might be better to define it similar to the German understanding of survival, so that the company has to survive financially even when they integrate social and environmental issues into their strategic decision-making. Or to search for a different concept of 'economic rationality' combining the German and British approach as a starting point.

The three dimensions of sustainability—social, environmental and economic—could be assessed, and tools could be created showing how to balance them in our business system. This is the approach taken in some of our chapters. This discussion about philosophical assumptions could be also the starting point in any discipline for reflection on the existing tools in business—for example in marketing or operations—in order to improve or redesign them.

Philosophical questions are only discussed in some chapters of this book. If business schools/lecturers/students want to integrate philosophy and values reflection further in their teaching/learning, a good starting point would be Molthan-Hill 2014b, Crane and Matten 2010 or Fisher *et al.* 2012. There are also some recommendations in the teaching aid that accompanies this book (details of how to acquire it are on page 4).

Mission, strategy and key decision-makers

Fundamentally our proposed new framework requires a clear commitment from the senior management of business schools, especially deans, in order to offer or even embed sustainability into the curriculum. This should start at university level. For example, Nottingham Trent University has since 2010 promoted graduate attributes in sustainability, which have been a key driver for change not only in the business school but throughout the university. Furthermore, a business school should preferably integrate sustainability into its mission and its strategy. Ryan and Tilbury (2013) have also shown how the quality assurance and quality enhancement system could support and promote sustainability teaching throughout courses and modules. The position of a sustainability co-ordinator could be created to work with course and module leaders on how to embed sustainability into their modules, as well as co-ordinating all such efforts so that students do not carry out the same case study over and over again. Finally, a study by the European Foundation of Management Development and the Academy of Business in Society, which interviewed 131 deans and 136 faculty respondents, suggests that key decision-makers, such as the head of undergraduate studies, can help (or hinder) the process if they provide leadership in shaping and implementing their institution's sustainability-related agenda and objectives (Morland-Painter *et al.* 2014). Engaged staff can add to existing modules or courses, as in the 'Piggyback' approach mentioned earlier. However, 'Mainstreaming' can be only achieved if key decision-makers support the integration of sustainability in all modules and courses. This book offers enough material to achieve that, and our proposed new framework as presented in Figure 2 will help the appropriate decisions to be made.

Conclusion

To summarise, our proposed new framework includes all the dimensions discussed above in addition to those suggested by Godemann *et al.* (2011):

- General sustainability knowledge, such as climate change

- Subject-specific knowledge, such as tools for sustainable marketing

- Specialised knowledge, such as environmental management systems

- Sustainability literacy skills, such as systems thinking instead of a myopic view

- Understanding of values underpinning management, so that the integration of values reflection forms the basis of management education

- Philosophical assumptions in business, which can be discussed with students or decided for them (optional), with in either case these underlying assumptions being made transparent for students

- Engagement with business, so that students solve 'real life' problems for business and society

- Strategic decision-making: mission, strategy, and quality assurance process all aligned and supported by key decision-makers.

When developing an approach for a business school/course/module, our proposed new framework enables the following **core questions** to be addressed:

- *How* will it be embedded?

- *What* should be taught?

- Will it comprise subject-specific knowledge, general sustainability-related knowledge and/or sustainability literacy skills?

- Will the students solve 'real life' problems?

- Do the structures and strategies and key decision-makers support the decisions taken?

Further reading

Murray, P. (2011) *The Sustainable Self: A Personal Approach to Sustainability Education* (London: Earthscan).

> This book contains numerous worksheets to build sustainability literacy or to facilitate learning about a particular aspect of sustainability.

Stibbe, A. (ed.) (2009) *The Handbook of Sustainability Literacy: Skills for a Changing World* (Totnes, UK: Green Books).

> Thise book has been mentioned several times in this chapter and contains individual essays on topics such as carbon capability and systems thinking, which may be useful for general reading or as a base for learning activities. In particular, Zoe Robinson makes specific suggestions for business in 'Greening Business: The Ability to Drive Environmental and Sustainability Improvements in the Workplace' (pp. 130-36).

Weybrecht, Giselle (2013) *The Sustainable MBA: A Business Guide to Sustainability*, 2nd edn (Chichester: John Wiley & Sons).

> If you want to integrate more tools and concepts into your modules, you will find rich material in Weybrecht's book. It is also organised around the core subjects and offers tools in line with the MBA curriculum. *The Sustainable MBA* can be used to supplement our teaching material and ideas presented here; alternatively, some of our teaching ideas can be also adapted to the MBA and Master's curriculum in order to broaden the variety of the tools offered in *The Sustainable MBA*.

References

Bird, F., and J. Waters (1989) 'The Moral Muteness of Managers', *California Management Review* 32.1: 73-88.

Bodenstein, G., A. Spiller and H. Elbers (1997) *Strategische Konsumentscheidungen: Langfristige Weichenstellungen fuer das Umwelthandeln: Ergebnisse einer empirischen Studie, Diskussionsbeitraege des Fachbereichs Wirtschaftswissenschaften, 234* (Duisburg, Germany: Gerhard-Mercator-Universitaet).

Clayton, A.M.H., and N.J. Radcliffe (1996) *Sustainability. A Systems Approach* (London: Earthscan).

Courtice, P., and M. Van der Kamp (2013) *Developing Leaders for the Future: Integrating Sustainability into Mainstream Leadership Programmes*, working paper of the Cambridge Programme for Sustainability Leadership, commissioned by the Academy of Business in Society.

Crane, A., and D. Matten (2010) *Business Ethics: Managing Corporate Citizenship and Sustainability in the Age of Globalization* (Oxford, UK: Oxford University Press).

Fisher, C., A. Lovell and N. Valero-Silva (2012) *Business Ethics and Values* (Harlow, UK: Financial Times Prentice Hall).

Godemann, J., C. Herzig and J. Moon (2011) 'Approaches to Changing the Curriculum', paper presented at the *ISIBS Workshop: Session II*, University of Nottingham, UK, 20–21 October 2011.

Goworek, H., and P. Molthan-Hill (2013) 'Embedding CSR within the Undergraduate Business Curriculum: The Development of a Sustainable Organisation Module', in J. Ahmad and D. Crowther (eds), *Education and Corporate Social Responsibility: International Perspectives* (Bingley, UK: Emerald Publishing).

Habermas, J. (1984) *The Theory of Communicative Action. Volume 1: Reason and the Rationalization of Society* (London: Heinemann).

Jones, T.M. (1991) 'Ethical decision making by individuals in organizations: an issue-contingent model', *Academy of Management Review* 16: 366-95.

Kempton, W., J.S. Boster and J.A. Hartley (1996) *Environmental Values in American Culture* (Cambridge, MA: The MIT Press).

Kenrick, J. (2009) 'Commons Thinking: The Ability to Envisage and Enable a Viable Future through Connected Action', in A. Stibbe (ed.), *The Handbook of Sustainability Literacy: Skills for a Changing World* (Totnes, UK: Green Books): 51-57.

Lacy, P., T. Cooper, R. Hayward and L. Neuberger (2010) *A New Era of Sustainability: UN Global Compact–Accenture CEO Study 2010*, www.accenture.com/ SiteCollectionDocuments/PDF/Accenture_A_New_Era_of_Sustainability_ CEO_Study.pdf, accessed 31 March 2014.

MacIntyre, A. (1981) *After Virtue: A Study in Moral Theory* (London: Duckworth).

McMurtry, J. (2012) 'Behind Global System Collapse: The Life-Blind Structure of Economic Rationality', *Journal of Business Ethics* 108.1: 49-60.

Meadows, D.H. (2008) *Thinking in Systems: A Primer* (White River, VT: Chelsea Green).

Meadows, D.L. (2001) *Fish Banks, Ltd: Game Administrator's Manual* (Durham, NH: University of New Hampshire).

Molthan-Hill, P. (2014a) 'The Moral Muteness of Managers: An Anglo-American Phenomenon? German and British Managers and their Moral Reasoning about Environmental Sustainability in Business', *International Journal of Cross Cultural Management*, forthcoming.

—— (2014b) 'Making the Business Case: Intercultural Differences in Framing Economic Rationality Related to Environmental Issues', *Critical Perspectives on International Business*, forthcoming.

Morland-Painter, M., E. Sabet, P. Molthan-Hill and H. Goworek (2014) 'A Systemic Approach to Embedding Sustainability and Ethics into Management Education Globally: Is There Unity in Diversity?', paper to be presented at the *EBEN* conference, Berlin, Germany, 12–14 June 2014.

Murray, P. (2011) *The Sustainable Self: A Personal Approach to Sustainability Education* (London: Earthscan).

Robertson, M. (2014) *Sustainability Principles and Practice* (Oxon, UK: Routledge).

Robinson, Z. (2009) 'Greening Business: The Ability to Drive Environmental and Sustainability Improvements in the Workplace', in A. Stibbe (ed.), *The Handbook of Sustainability Literacy: Skills for a Changing World* (Totnes, UK: Green Books): 130-36.

Rusinko, C.A. (2010) 'Integrating Sustainability in Management and Business Education', *The Academy of Management Learning and Education* 9.3: 507-19.

Ryan, A., and D. Tilbury (2013) 'Uncharted Waters: Voyages for Education for Sustainable Development in the Higher Education Curriculum', *The Curriculum Journal* 24.2 (special issue: *Education for Sustainable Development as the DESD Approaches 2014: What Have We Achieved and Ways Forward?*): 2-13.

Schoemaker, P.J.H. (2008) 'The Future Challenges of Business: Rethinking Management Education', *California Management Review* 50.1: 119-39.

Sterling, S. (2009) 'Ecological Intelligence: Viewing the World Relationally', in A. Stibbe (ed.), *The Handbook of Sustainability Literacy: Skills for a Changing World* (Totnes, UK: Green Books): 77-83.

Stibbe, A. (ed.) (2009) *The Handbook of Sustainability Literacy: Skills for a Changing World* (Totnes, UK: Green Books).

Trapp, N.L. (2011) 'Staff Attitudes to Talking Openly About Ethical Dilemmas: The Role of Business Ethics Conceptions and Trust', *Journal of Business Ethics* 103.4: 543-52.

Verhezen, P. (2010) 'Giving Voice in a Culture of Silence: From a Culture of Compliance to a Culture of Integrity', *Journal of Business Ethics* 96.2: 187-206.

Watson, M. (2009) 'Material Awareness: The Ability to Expose the Hidden Impact of Materials on Sustainability', in A. Stibbe (ed.), *The Handbook of Sustainability Literacy: Skills for a Changing World* (Totnes, UK: Green Books): 137-43.

Watson, T.J. (2003) 'Ethical Choice in Managerial Work: The Scope for Moral Choices in an Ethically Irrational World', *Human Relations* 56: 167-85.

Weybrecht, Giselle (2013) *The Sustainable MBA: A Business Guide to Sustainability*, 2nd edn (Chichester: John Wiley & Sons).

3

Introducing issues of sustainability

Richard Howarth

This chapter encourages you to **think about sustainability** and uses activities and seminars to support your engagement and discourse. This is not the standard introduction to a textbook. It is adopted because we are dealing with uncertainty and a complex, and wicked, problem. This approach (which encourages you to explore and make sense for yourself of sustainability and management in this context) is more sustainable and ethical than 'inflicting' definitions and/or prescribed vocabulary on you as the reader and someone wanting to learn answers and/ or 'technical knowledge' about this area and take action as a result.

> The mind is not a vessel that needs filling,
> but wood that needs igniting.
>
> *Plutarch*

Since this is a textbook, it might be a reasonable to expect to find definitions and answers in this introduction. However, and while there is engagement with how one may infer and/or interpret definition(s) in Seminar 3, this chapter neither starts with nor offers specific definitions or answers. Instead it introduces a series of frameworks which can be brought to bear when considering management and managing sustainability (including the approaches offered in this book).

As what is offered is not what is expected, it would be unfair to go further without providing some introduction to the thinking behind a chapter that introduces and encourages *thinking* about (and thinking *around* and *through*) sustainability. This approach is taken because of the recognition that, as we progress through our education and continued learning in life, we come to terms with understanding that increasing complexity means that there are few obvious answers (or 'truths'). Simple definitions, which might be regarded as fixed, taken for granted or 'known', can be seen as 'vessel filling' and, if unchallenged, may be dangerous. This is particularly so in the context of sustainability as a complex, and wicked, problem.[1]

There is another reason too, which is illustrated when considering the following quotation attributed to Einstein:

> The world as we have created it is a product of our thinking. It cannot be changed without changing our thinking.

The above might be seen as a self-evident 'truth'. However, we not only need to change our thinking, we need to be able to articulate that new thinking. If we cannot create and share new thinking our problems will not be solved.

The agenda for this chapter is, therefore, set around the embrace of how we articulate and use ideas about sustainability. Transposing these to 'learning objectives', they are:

- To investigate the idea of 'sustainable' in context (e.g. a case business, businesses, etc.)
- To consider how this idea gets used
- To recognise how words impact on thinking, action and feeling
- To reflect on what people think, do and feel in response to the language used in 'sustainability'

1   'Wicked' (and complex) as per Rittel and Webber (1973).

- To think about the differences between using 'management systems' to control—or using **values** to guide—decision-making and action

The 'ignition' is exploration, and the argument for this approach is that learning how to explore and use the terms is more sustainable, and ethical, than 'inflicting' definitions, prescribed vocabulary, answers and/or 'technical knowledge' upon the reader. Specialist vocabularies will be acquired within each of the chapters in the book but here our intention is broader. The activities and the few commentaries that follow within this chapter now lead your journey and discovery.

Sustainable businesses or sustainable business?

Before setting out to explore ideas and concepts, it seems appropriate to understand the way in which we think about society, business, the environment or our ecology. In doing this, the ambiguity and playfulness of words is also illustrated.

- **Ambiguous** because words do not have fixed meanings: different groups, different professions and different disciplines have different meanings attached to the same word, as each chapter here makes clear
- **Playful** because we can often set up something of an ambiguity and learn from examining and 'playing' with it

Reading 'sustainable business or sustainable business?' is clearly a nonsense because we have no sense of context for each part—either side of the 'or'. How then can the question be made sensible? What might be thought of to create distinct meaning in the two parts?

'Sustainable businesses or sustainable business' is a small clue that implies some new and differing context(s) and a mutually exclusive choice of one or the other. The distinct choice becomes between business*es* which are sustainable or a form of business which is sustainable within the confines of social and ecological obligations, constraints and so on.

Seminar 1 is, therefore, set up to give an opportunity to examine this.

Suggested seminars

Seminar 1: Exploring what is 'sustainable'

This seminar sets two main explorations: what is sustainability and how is it spoken of? There are also subsidiary issues of who is doing the speaking and who they might be speaking to, and these are picked up later in this chapter.

More than the other seminars in this chapter, Seminar 1 will require some careful thinking about research and what sense is being made too. Where to go to find information *and* how to decide whether that information is credible and reliable are particularly important. The work here may lead to some interesting sources and the reference sheet overleaf offers some guidance on the sorts of things to look for and use, and so on.

Activity

1. Identify, read and interpret documents, materials, videos, etc., that would help you understand whether the case business you have selected (or has been given to you) is a 'sustainable business'.

2. Prepare a discussion note to be presented (i.e. to your class colleagues, or other audience) which:
   a. Articulates how sustainable business can be, and is, interpreted in the context of the case business
   b. Demonstrates your consideration of the contextual use of 'sustainable business'
   c. Presents your specific argument based on your investigation of sustainable business in context

This activity works best as a tutor facilitated seminar, prepared for in advance (as outlined above) and organised around, for example:

- A group discussion
- A debate format

- A 'series' of presentations

Alternative formats, which may be useful for the more adventurous, also include:

- Role-play: media interviews
- Presentation to a shareholder AGM
- Web-based discussion board

If the work is facilitated, your tutor may indicate in what way the business is to be considered sustainable (linked to 2c above) or they may give you free choice.

If you are working outside a classroom then it is recommended that you work with someone else and prepare for, and share, your discussion notes and reflect as below.

As a guideline the reading, researching and preparation for the discussion should take 2–3 hours but may, depending on individual motivation and engagement, take longer.

If organised around a formal class activity, it will take about 55 minutes and, depending on the specific approach selected, allow:

- 40 minutes in total for presentation(s), the debate element or group discussion(s)
- 15 minutes for reflection and 'setting down' of outcomes and post-discussion/presentation thoughts in pairs

Reference sheet

This reference sheet is intended offer guidance on the activity and the sort of information available. In addition to searching for and selecting information relevant to the business and/or perspective you have been allocated or chosen, you will also need to pay attention to, and interpret, the 'credibility' of the information. As you move on with the activity, your work here and your engagement with the area, your view/frame of what is, or is not useful and/or credible, is likely to shift too. Your ability to arrange and rearrange your understanding and interpret your shifting frames, and the sense made and given, is thus important.

Whatever business you choose, the task is the same. Namely to investigate sustainable business in context and to argue whether *the business* is a sustainable business or a sustainable business! How you will argue (and support this) will depend on your arrangement of the information (and evidence) accessed and the sense made of it.

In doing this, you may seek to consider and explore different perspectives such as:

- How powerful the business's product(s) are in generating and regenerating sales revenue: what is, for example, the 'secret' in sustaining the/a customer relationship?

- The ecological impacts of the selected business: is it a sustainable enterprise from the perspective of, for example, the focus of activity, how issues are identified and/or managed and so on?

In terms of sources, you will want a good range and you may consider, for example:

- Encyclopedia-style entries:
  - e.g. on Wikipedia

- Examples of the business and/or its product(s) in its market/marketing context:
  - e.g. in an online or 'bricks and mortar' context
  - e.g. via promotions and adverts (including those which are not 'sponsored' or parodies of 'official' adverts)

- Examples of what the company is saying

- Examples of what, for example, stakeholders and others are saying

The key will be your consideration of the specific and contextual use of the term (or terms) and how you articulate, argue and evidence your position as a result. Remember though, specifically when discussing and debating this with others, we (you) will need to remain open-minded as to how others have also interpreted (or will interpret) sustainable business. After all, we are not seeking a specific 'definition' of what is sustainable business here. Rather we are investigating, considering and exploring how the term is used in context (i.e. of the case business). How we do this and how we arrange our argument and 'position' are key to the outcomes of the activity too.

Commentary: thinking through 'sustainable'

Seminar 1 is designed for you to engage in your own research, to find sources and come to some understanding of those sources and the things they have to say. You will probably notice how *business* dominates the results of any web searches that you have made. This is either because (a) business is very proactive in promoting its message or because publishers and consulting houses are using digital media to place their message about helping companies to 'manage' their image and sustainability credentials.

Equally, pressure groups, lobby groups and individuals post blogs and materials that seek to challenge 'big business(es)'. What is to be recognised and acknowledged here is how and why we may interpret (and understand) these arguments, the different positions in these arguments and our (and their) arrangement and modelling of them.

These multiple points of view are possible because different 'theories' of how the world is (or ought to be) are behind them. The sustainable businesses or sustainable business dichotomy is set up because there is an implicit contradiction between the theory of business and the theory of sustainability posed.

It might be that seminar discussions reflect this but that does not mean such a thing has to be true. From a 'management' perspective, for example, Drucker (1994) set out the idea that each business is based upon 'the theory of the business', which business leaders should 'take out and shake down' every now and then, to make sure it is not out of date.

Drucker's article suggests an 'image' of a business model that views products in a marketplace which, in turn, is located within a broader social structure or social system. Drucker's warning is that change(s) can occur in the broader social system and these may not be detected by a business focused on, for example, market share or market performance. He gives examples of businesses that have let their 'theory of the business' be overtaken by events, so much so that the assumptions their value creation process is based upon, and the way it was supposed to work, are no longer valid.

Drucker gave one of the earliest discussions of what has become known as a business model. Business models have been described in literature in many ways (e.g. Baden-Fuller and Morgan 2010), but what is key for all of them is:

How does a business

- Create value?

- Deliver value?

- Appropriate, keep or distribute that value?

Sustainability seems to apply to the viability of a business model. That is to say, whether the business can continue to 'add value' to resource inputs and deliver that to customers or clients. Can it continue to operate its business model? This may have been at the core of Drucker's writing.

The broader meaning of sustainability (and what is sustainable business) includes, therefore, the systemic consequences of business activities in a really holistic sense. Frequently these are cited as consequences for stakeholders, communities and the environment, but how these are identified, interpreted, understood, assigned and arranged will also clearly be important and influential.

Seminar 2: Considering how 'sustainable' is used

The activities associated with Seminar 1 have brought us to consider, and give exposure to, different uses of the word 'sustainable' and the term 'sustainable business'. A single word is likely to have different interpretations and meanings in use and in context too.

What is also proposed is that we have different words in use too, and this is what we seek to investigate and uncover here by considering the meaning(s) of the following four terms:

- Sustainable

- Sustainably

- Sustainability

- Sustainability management

Essentially, how do you understand these words and how do you (and others) use them?

Activity

Prepare a flip chart which articulates/depicts your understanding of each of the following:

- Sustainable
- Sustainably
- Sustainability
- Sustainability management

The flip chart may be in any form but, for example, the following forms may be useful:

- A mind map
- A collage of pictures
- Drawings
- Quotations or annotations around a product
- Business or business model

The flip chart must, however, indicate:

- What it is (what the word refers to)
- How you do it (this may seem strange, but how do you 'do' sustainable)
- Why do it, why engage with it

This activity works best as a tutor facilitated seminar, prepared for in advance (as outlined above) and organised around a group discussion.

The flip chart is for discussion around a table rather than presentation. Although it is not necessary to use flip chart pens it is a good idea to use strong colours so that the flip chart (and its contents) can be photographed and used/shared later.

If organised around a formal class activity then allow 55 minutes, arrange the class into small groups (4–6 in each group) and allow:

- 40 minutes in total for each participant to share their flip chart. This should be arranged so that all participants share 'sustainable' in turn, then share 'sustainably', then the next and so on.
- 15 minutes for each group to collect a shared (consensus) meaning of each work/phrase on a new page per word/phrase.

Orientations (optional/supplementary activity)

In addition to the previous activity, it is also useful to consider your orientation(s) towards the different uses of 'sustainable'. This may be undertaken at the same time as the activity related to the different uses of 'sustainable', or may form part of the focus for reflections on the work, your seminar experience(s) and so on.

Essentially, you would need to use the elements in each of your flip charts to explore your reaction to or engagement with each use of 'sustainable' in turn. As before there are different ways you can approach this activity (e.g. through a mind map). Whatever approach is adopted you will need to embrace (and uncover) what you think, do and feel related to each of the uses and the 'elements' you have identified linked to the term(s).[2] The table below gives an overview of how this can be done, and whether you actually 'fill in' the table or not is up to you (or your tutor). Note that recording your thoughts via the table would be useful for capturing your thoughts/sense and also later reflection(s).

The example here is based on coffee and, possibly, the use of different coffee 'machines':

Flip chart	Element	What I think	What I do	What I feel
[Living] sustainably	Recycling	Good idea, takes space in kitchen!	Conform to local authority regime	It is a pain, inadequate
	Coffee	Becomes a 'lifestyle' statement. Coffee makers are excessive	Do not drink outside home much. Use simple cafetière, compost grounds	Sad!
	etc			
Sustainability	Market			
	Environment			
	Stakeholders			
etc				

---

2   An 'element' is, for example, a line on your mind map, an item on your collage, a comment/annotation on your business model, a node/item on your rich picture, etc.

Commentary: thinking around 'sustainable'

The seminar is designed to encourage a deeper dialogue about the meanings of these words and the way in which you (and others) respond to them. In doing this, we engage with what happens in our thinking as we engage in thinking about and working with them. For example, 'sustainably' is an adverb and requires some process (an activity or set of activities) to be done sustainably. An adverb characterises **how something is done**. It is this 'structure' and 'process' idea that leads to the three aspects we ask for on each flip chart:

- What is it?
  - Structure: a thing which we speak of ...

- How do we do it?
  - Process: activities and sequences of activity, the ongoing flow ...

- Why do it?
  - The cause–effect relation which is our purpose. We do 'A' to achieve 'B' ...

Gregory Bateson, an anthropologist and cyberneticist, expressed real concern that we separate 'structure' (named concepts, ideas, words as labels for events) from 'processes'. *Angels Fear* (Bateson and Bateson 1987) is a careful examination of the way in which we represent our universe in words and ideas and how mistakes and errors flow from misrepresentation. For example, it is very likely that a process description (how you do it) for 'sustainability management' is very different from 'sustainably'. And there are important implications of such differences in description.

The first is that we act on the detailed description of how to do it: this is the level of know-how. 'Knowing how to do something' can be tacit or explicit (both forms are important).

- Tacit 'know-how' is unchallenged and taken for granted: *it is a 'just do it' thing*

- Explicit knowledge or 'know-how' is where we have clear ideas of 'how' and 'why' we do things: *there is reasoning*

Patterns of social interaction emerge out of the way we do things in the everyday—moment to moment. Interaction comes largely from tacit know-how. Projects and enterprise comes from more explicit forms of know-how (although too often these are taken for granted rather than made explicit and debated!).

Bateson was concerned that too often the explicit know-how was based upon inaccurate descriptions of 'nested systems'. In an example of this, he carefully discusses the control process for room temperatures in a house (Bateson and Bateson 1987: 37-42). He points out that in normal ways of speaking (describing) we think of the thermostat as being the control, but systemically this is an error. There are other active agents within the system, that is to say the householder and other residents. Any of these individuals may set the bias on the thermostat and so could be seen as the control ... But these individuals do not act in isolation: they act and interact with their expectations of weather conditions and anticipated ambient temperatures, and so on.

If we wish to 'understand' the energy consumption and performance of a household, we therefore have to think about, engage with and seek to interpret the social system, as well as the 'technical' performances of the property, heating system, weather patterns and weather forecasting.

The second element of Seminar 2 (orientations and engagement) is a first step in understanding how individuals (and you) are engaged and involved in 'sustainability' in a proactive or reactive sense. Whether that is a conscious (explicit) commitment or a tacit participation in what goes on is important for you to uncover and recognise.

Seminar 3: Why 'sustainable'?

Watson (1994) identified a number of meanings of the term 'management', three of which concern us here:

- A body of knowledge

- A profession

- An activity or process

How do these meanings influence an understanding of sustainable management or sustainability management or managing sustainably?

- **Seminar 1** examined how 'sustainable' is used in different ways with very different connotations. The exercises contrasted sustainable business(es) and sustainable business.

- **Seminar 2** explored how we use the vocabulary around 'sustainability'. For example, sustainable management might mean 'managing sustainably' and suggest the redefinition of 'management' so that it becomes more legitimate and inclusive. Such a perspective might be much more supportive of stakeholders and their interests than a traditional and narrow sense of management as a proxy for shareholder interest. However, 'sustainability *management*' has a very different flavor; it suggests that sustainability is an outcome of the management process. There is a body of knowledge and technique for creating sustainability. The pattern is one of engaging in a process to achieve a purpose or an outcome and that in turn is a step towards a higher outcome (purpose). So sustainability management, operating in reverse, is a set of processes and outcomes that (logically) deliver sustainability. The issue of concern is how, or from where, the ideas used to create the logic are derived.

Activity

For this activity you should search for visualisations of the notion/concept of 'sustainability' (a good source for a collection of these is http://computingforsustainability.com/2009/03/15/visualising-sustainability/). You should then select three to five specific visualisations and critique each in turn (and in relation to each other as necessary). In so doing, you should explain any problems or concerns that may arise in reading and reflecting on them and your work in this chapter to date. The focus here is on what sense you might make of them and how you (and others) react to, or engage with, the representation(s).

Essentially, this activity is a semiotic deconstruction, or reconstruction, of each visualisation and/or diagram as a device (with a focus on the meanings made). In this sense, your work should seek to identify:

- What is being 'managed'?

- Who is doing the 'managing'?

- How is 'it' being managed?

- Why is 'it' being managed this way?

This activity works best as a tutor-facilitated seminar, prepared for in advance (as outlined above) and organised around a small group discussion with commentary on each diagram.

If organised around a formal class activity, allow 55 minutes and arrange the class into small groups (4–6 in each group). Depending on progress and the number of diagrams to be used allow:

- 40 minutes in total for each participant to share their commentary on each visualisation/diagram in turn and their reflections on 'managing' sustainability in the context of the above question prompts

- 15 minutes for each group to select a diagram (or elements of diagrams) and explain how it helps to make sense of sustainability and management in this context

The/a tutor should also encourage further individual reflection in order to ensure that understanding and sense is 'set down' (this will be particularly useful before, and following, reading and engaging with the content and activities included in the chapters that follow).

Commentary: making sense of 'sustainable'

Some organisations have systems which are designed to ensure excellence. Some have processes which are designed to facilitate doing things excellently.

- Is there a difference between these and a consequential difference in the organisation?

This seminar is designed to enable you to explore a similar notion. Not only that, but also to encourage you to explore who is empowered and who is disempowered by the theories and words that are used within the given scheme (and the logic which underpins it).

The exercises are predicated on ideas of making sense, and using interpretive schema, to enable shared action. Weick (1995) sets out an argument that we rely on verbal cues to 'make sense' of things. That is, what we think is based upon the words and ideas that we have available and the way in which we are used to hearing them used.

Billig (1996) also introduces a notion of foreground and rear ground. We pay direct and immediate attention to things which are foregrounded (for example, some businesses foreground their work on economic welfare of communities in the supply chain) and we are less aware of things which are rear-grounded (the materials and complexity of environmental impacts of, for example, a product and/or technology).

Placing things in the foreground, or rear ground, of attention is a key political and language-based skill. Understanding the way in which we respond to different words is also important.

Is managing sustainably (in a sustainable way) the same or different from sustainability management? When ideas of sustainable management are routinised, systematised or institutionalised there are very real consequences for participants within those institutions and the wider 'system'.

Later chapters introduce these concepts and discuss them from particular perspectives, frequently foregrounding particular things as significant.

Our purpose, in this last seminar, was to encourage you to try to 'step back' and understand the systemic consequences. In doing so, you will bring to bear some critical thinking grounded in your enquiring and sense-making.

References

Baden-Fuller, C., and M.S. Morgan (2010) 'Business Models as Models', *Long Range Planning* 43: 156-71.

Bateson, G., and M. Bateson (1987) *Angels Fear* (New York: Hampton Press).

Billig, M. (1996) *Arguing and Thinking: A Rhetorical Approach to Social Psychology* (Cambridge, UK: Cambridge University Press).

Drucker, P. (1994) 'The Theory of the Business', *Harvard Business Review* (September–October 1994): 95-104.

Rittel, H., and M. Webber (1973) 'Dilemmas in a General Theory of Planning', *Policy Sciences* 4: 155-69.

Watson, T. (1994) *In Search of Management: Culture, Chaos and Control in Managerial Work* (London: Routledge).

Weick, K. (1995) *Sensemaking in Organisations* (London: Sage).

4

Integrating the three pillars of sustainability: social, environmental and economic

Seraphina Brown and Aldilla Dharmasasmita

This chapter introduces the idea of sustainability as being constructed from social, environmental and economic elements. It also explores these elements as being fundamentally linked, and why this is important for business. Approaching sustainable business from each of the three perspectives, this chapter provides three seminars detailing the importance of integrating sustainability.

In this chapter, you will learn to:

- Understand the **triple bottom line** and what it means for business

- Appreciate the applied principles of sustainability and why they are fundamental to business

- Recognise the fundamental linkages between social, environmental and economic pillars of sustainability in a business framework

Hitchcock and Willard (2009: 3) express that sustainability in business can be understood as 'a **framework** for making sense of what is happening in the world so that you can foresee changes and take action before they happen'. Sustainability therefore forces you to observe the relationships between social, economic and environmental trends. The three pillars of sustainability are often depicted as three circles of an overlapping Venn diagram (for example, Figure 1), emphasising the importance of the links between social, environmental and economic sustainability.

The use of '**sustainable business**' has seen a steady uptake across the literature (Michel *et al.* 2011), and its further application looks set to increase into the future. In fact, Dermondy (2010) explains the need for students to come to their own mutual understanding of what sustainability is. In her development of a 'Greener Marketing' module, Dermondy stresses the need for students to 'share their thoughts on their understanding of sustainability and thus their perceptions of greener marketing' (Dermondy 2010: 12).

It is important to underline that, in recent years, there has been a move away from dictionary definitions of sustainability to more reflexive understandings which link closely to personal values and observation

Figure 1: The three pillars of sustainability.

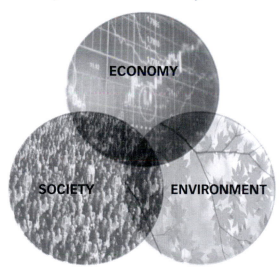

Source: Adapted from Parkin *et al.* (2003).

of the world around you. Dermondy (2010: 12) explains in reference to a mutual comprehension of sustainability:

> Usually a shared broader understanding emerges that embraces notions of corporate and individual citizenship, changing consumption patterns, social capital, personal values-driven behaviour, politics and legislation, the fair distribution of economic, environmental and social assets, and proactive personal and collective responsibilities—wrapped within an organisational and individual behavioural context that includes fairly traded products and services, reduction in energy usage, increasing use of public transport and decreasing use of cars, local organic food, reducing food miles, ecotourism, and non-supermarket shopping.

Sustainability and the triple bottom line

The classic understanding of sustainability in a business context is expressed in Elkington's (1997) *Cannibals with Forks*, in which the idea of the **triple bottom line (TBL)** is introduced. This is the quintessential account of the importance of sustainability and business. Elkington expresses 'sustainability' for a new millennium, suggesting that, in the past, it has been understood as an attempt to harmonise the traditional financial bottom line with an environmental agenda. He suggests that it is essential that businesses look towards a new horizon of a triple bottom line, involving not only economic prosperity and environmental quality, but also social justice. Therefore, Elkington asks that businesses look not only to their 'bottom line', or the account of profit and loss of their business, but also measure in some shape or form the societal impacts of their operations, and gauge the impact on the planet by how environmentally responsible it has been. In this way, the TBL scheme of thought illuminates the concept of three pillars of sustainability in a business context.

Elkington breaks down the three tenets of sustainability into **people, planet and profit**. Note the order: Elkington is implicitly suggesting that businesses should follow this mandate of importance, rather than the (almost) exclusive focus on profit seen to characterise much of business thought in popular imagination up until recently. Additionally, *Cannibals with Forks* represents a reversal in the way transparency of business is imagined: companies are now not just held accountable by industry and government regulators, but just as often environmentalist and media campaigns. Elkington also suggests that business leaders look beyond their own shareholder interests to consider the importance of **stakeholders**, or those that can be argued to have some effect on, or be affected by, a business. This can therefore include not only shareholders, but customers, suppliers and employees. A secondary group of stakeholders, traditionally exempt from business thought, includes governments, local communities and the wider public.

TBL has, since the publication of *Cannibals with Forks*, seen much traction in both the academic and business communities. Its philosophy and practice have been examined and promoted by many in the business community. One example is Fisk's (2010) *People, Planet, Profit* which borrows straight from Elkington's tripartite mantra and, directly addressing business leaders, not only offers them the opportunity to ameliorate the concerns of customers to 'do the right thing', but also appeals directly to those who want to grow but in more responsible ways. Willard's *The Sustainability Advantage* (2012), supported by a foreword from Elkington, provides one of the first quantifications of the efficacy of the business case for TBL. These accounts go beyond the *why* business leaders should pursue sustainability, important at the start of the millennium, to *how* to implement it from thought, through action, to progress. Since the early 2000s, sustainability strategies have become even more relevant to corporate success (Willard 2012).

Nevertheless, TBL is renowned enough to have also collected a wealth of criticism. The main critique levelled at TBL is that, despite its pretensions, sustainability does not fit neatly into the business case as Elkington would suggest, and that there is no standard of measurement for the 'non-traditional' social and environmental elements. Robins (2006) contends that the difficulty of quantifying the people and planet elements casts doubt on whether TBL really is a bottom line.

Despite these contentions, the fact remains that TBL has enjoyed a large and receptive audience in the business community. Elkington

(1997: 73) notes that it is difficult to measure progress against TBL as the pillars of society, environment and economy are 'in constant flux, due to social, political, economic and environmental pressures, cycles and conflicts. So the sustainability challenge is tougher than any of the other challenges in isolation.'

Elkington highlights that, while the path may not be easy and will be easily obscured, sustainability is well worth pursuing, and TBL is an excellent way to begin to ask the questions of your business that sustainability demands.

Positive thought, positive action

Business is uniquely positioned in the sustainability frontier in that it not only can be a powerful force of positive change in and of itself, but can also influence consumers to change behaviour in positive ways (Fisk 2010). Elkington (1997) suggests that, throughout the 21st century, businesses much more than governments or NGOs (non-governmental organisations) will be in the driving seat of society and leading future change. Laughland and Bansal (2011) concur that the new business-as-society paradigm will require the efforts of organisations across sectors. Traditionally, people have associated sustainable business with names such as Ben & Jerry's, The Body Shop and Patagonia. For example, Ben & Jerry's is known for its environmental co-ordinators which produce monthly progress reports (Epstein 2008). Positive case studies beyond these 'usual suspects' must be effectively communicated.

KPMG's *Survey of Corporate Responsibility Reporting* (2013) is recommended reading for anyone with an interest in the increasing importance of sustainability in business. The report provides a snapshot of the rates of CR (**corporate responsibility**) reporting across nations and sectors, and examines some emerging trends. CR reporting, or CSR (**corporate social responsibility**), has been seen to be closely associated with sustainability. However, CSR has also been suggested to be more aligned with fulfilling shareholder values rather than societal or environmental values (Bockstette 2013). One important finding is that many of the world's largest companies are now using CR reporting, to understand sustainability and embed it within business strategy:

> Almost all the world's 250 largest companies report on CR. Of those that do, 9 in 10 use their reports to identify environmental and social changes that impact the business and its stakeholders. Eight in 10 report that they have a strategy to manage the risks and opportunities. Seven in 10 report that these changes bring opportunities for the innovation of new products and services. An enlightened, but I suspect growing, minority of around one third also report opportunities to grow their market share and cut costs. Where these companies lead, others will follow. The direction of travel is clear. (KPMG 2013: 9))

This demonstrates how sustainability has now gone beyond an optional extra in corporate strategy. The majority of companies surveyed indicate sustainability has gone beyond improved resource efficiency and waste management towards a wide-angle-lens perspective, where sustainability allows a business to understand its impact on wider society and the environment.

Additionally, only one in ten companies that report on CR publish results as an **integrated report** according to KPMG (2013). This impacts upon integrating sustainability as there seems to be acceptance across the board that integrated reporting is the next destination of CR reporting. In South Africa, where integrated reporting has become mandatory, KPMG suggests it is a very effective way towards more integrated management (KPMG 2013). This means embedding a management system where all of its processes have an explicit sustainability focus, dimension or at least an understanding. This is fundamental to sustainable business, as top-level co-operation is one of the most important elements for ensuring real, positive change in business thought and practice (Hitchcock and Willard 2009). Elkington (1997: 70) agrees that 'some of the most interesting challenges are found not within but between the areas covered by economic, social and environmental bottom lines'.

Thus, understanding the interactions between discernible pillars of sustainability, and the feedback to business, will be crucial in the next few decades as businesses seek to embed sustainability more thoroughly into operations and processes.

KPMG report that only one third of firms are using the knowledge created in compiling CR reports to grow their market share and cut costs. This concurs with the *MIT Sloan Management Review* report (2011) which divided companies into sustainability embracers and cautious adopters according to their perceptions of sustainability. In order to realise a market advantage that sustainability can reveal, this report details that embracer companies have a number of features in common. This includes aggressively driving sustainability both top–down and bottom–up, involving a strong management element and effective internal communication. Also, creating measurement systems to build upon improvements is important. Embracers establish baselines and create assessment methods in order to quantify success towards sustainability. Finally, embracers move ahead of the curve, viewing acting first despite ambiguity as a way to create data and beat competition. Therefore, in embracing sustainability, leading companies are shaping the agenda and producing real results.

For growth to cease, development must accelerate

Approaching sustainability from each of the three elements, seeking to understand the fundamental linkages between the sustainability pillars in order to develop a holistic understanding of business and sustainability, is a great way to understand sustainability overall.

Overemphasis on any of the elements of sustainability is detrimental to the achievement of strong sustainability. For businesses, people, planet and profit should not be viewed as separate entities, but instead as being intimately intertwined (Elkington 1997). Looking at the big picture, Hitchcock and Willard (2009) argue that without a healthy economy, unemployment is high, creating a whole host of societal problems; and governments no longer have the revenues to handle increased social ills. If the provision of a healthy environment is ignored, the foundations of the economy are often undermined, and human health and wellbeing are negatively affected. Thus: 'Holding the other realms hostage to one ultimately backfires' (Hitchcock and Willard 2009: 9). In this way, it is possible to discern how sustainability differs from environmentalism. Sustainability aims to optimise all three pillars, without inflicting cost on any one element. It becomes necessary to look at the relationships between social, environmental and economic pillars in business to fully incorporate sustainability in business.

Figge *et al.* (2002) advocate the use of a BSC (balanced scorecard) as a tool to incorporate environmental and social management within the general management of a firm. The BSC methodology was developed in the early 1990s to counter ideological problems of short-termism in management accounting (Kaplan and Norton 1992). The purpose of the BSC as a tool is to formulate a hierarchic system of strategic objectives (Figge *et al.* 2002). BSC offers significant scope in terms of sustainability, as it allows the incorporation of elements of environmental and social sustainability integrally into financial thought. As previously indicated, for businesses to generate sufficient traction in sustainability, it is necessary that performance improves in all three dimensions of sustainability simultaneously. While conflicts between the three performance categories inevitably occur, practically businesses should seek to achieve improvements across the board. What differentiates the BSC as a corporate sustainability performance tool is the opportunity to incorporate environmental and social factors (as being notoriously difficult to quantify) into mainstream business thought and activity. This offers three major advantages: first, sustainability management that is economically sound is resilient and not deemed extraneous in times of economic crisis, but fundamental. Second, Figge *et al.* (2002) argue that sustainability management that contributes to economic objectives helps a business orientate itself towards competitors, and provides a positive example of success. Finally, the top–down integration of environmental and social factors ensures that corporate sustainability management considers all three facets of sustainability (ibid.), which is crucial for understanding the overlapping elements of sustainability and the ways they are important for a business's strategy.

In summary, for sustainability to be valuable to both the organisation and its stakeholders, it must be integrated into the way a company does business (Epstein 2008). Not only is it damaging to view sustainability in terms of just one of its pillars, it is difficult to achieve strong sustainability in business without achieving the balanced success of social, environmental and economic goals that are thoroughly understood as fundamentally linked. Without understanding this, the progress of sustainable businesses will likely stagnate.

Challenges of sustainable integration

Many have made good progress through reporting on sustainability, but it is unlikely that any company has fully integrated or achieved sustainability (Epstein 2008). Understanding the barriers to sustainability and its successful integration in a business context also deserves consideration.

One of the main detractions concerning the incorporation of social, environmental and economic metrics in the path to sustainability is that sustainability does not fit neatly into 'the **business case**'. Sustainability improvements often demand that investments are made to ensure success, but these investments are often based on long-term and intangible rewards (Laughland and Bansal 2011). Additionally, the payback period for sustainability-related investments often exceeds that required to approve projects, and initiatives are treated as stand-alone rather than integral (ibid.). This is complicated by the difficulty in directly comparing financial short-term gains to value-creating long-term impacts. However, the *MIT Sloan Management Review* (2011) report details that sustainability-related spending has survived the recession, with almost 60% of companies suggesting they have increased their investments since 2010. Thus, enthusiasm for sustainability is growing across all sectors, demonstrating that companies view sustainability as a necessary investment of capital, rather than a medium of short-term returns.

Molthan-Hill (2014) highlights the Anglo-American bias in the use of the phrase 'the business case' to infer that environmental improvements or considerations are extraneous to the activity of business in British mangers. In comparison, their German counterparts are more likely to refer to the business rationality of 'survival' and thus more fluently integrate environmental and sustainability concepts into their business thought. It is important to consider these linguistic and cultural attributes in the attitudes to sustainability many possess.

CSR has been suggested to be the latest in a series of management fads, failing to convince customers of genuine motives but instead reminding them of ethical appeasement. It has been suggested also that 'social responsibility' was too flimsy a concept to generate any interest with business leaders (Elkington 2014). Looking at sustainability as a new form of value demanded by society and effective businesses boosts the resilience and applicability of the term in corporate circles. Understanding sustainability in this way represents a new horizon for businesses, and demonstrating that the most effective and long-lasting sustainability solutions derive from all three parts of sustainability is important. This is supported in Devinney's (2009: 54) argument that the TBL is a 'template that should be applied more rigorously and consistently across ... all studies'.

Finally, Laughland and Bansal (2011) detail that business leaders are hesitant about communicating about sustainability to their employees and colleagues in a genuine manner, and managing expectations in terms of progress. Hitchcock and Willard (2009) suggest that many of today's employees want to work for a company that shares their values, citing the finding that 92% would be more inclined to work for a company that was known for being environmentally friendly (Mattioli 2007). Sustainability is a broad enough canvas to encompass most people's concerns, be they local or global, social or environmental, and thus can help infuse even the most mundane jobs with meaning (Hitchcock and Willard 2009). A major missing link in sustainable business concerns how to incorporate sustainability performance targets into employee incentives (see Chapter 7 for a fuller discussion of sustainability and human resources). Nevertheless, by motivating and communicating sustainability goals to an organisation effectively, it is possible to embed sustainability strategy holistically and sow the seeds for innovation across all three pillars of sustainability. The *MIT Sloan Management Review* (2011) report supports this, indicating that being authentic and transparent in talking about sustainability is fundamental to convincing employees, shareholders and the wider public of the depth of meaning behind sustainability claims.

There is plenty of reason for optimism concerning the state of sustainability in business. Sustainability is also spurring collaborative management solutions, where business leaders are working within and between their sectors to share innovation. The potential for the successful fusion of business and sustainability goals remains great.

Ecosystem services and business

This section will detail a new and exciting way business has managed to draw upon all three pillars of sustainability to implement improvements internally and for wider society.

'Businesses have an unrivalled ability to mobilise human, physical and financial capital, often manage large land holdings, and draw on resources and supply products that impact a wide range of ecosystems' (Armsworth *et al.* 2010: 235). Nevertheless, as expressed above, incorporating environmental thinking into business considerations is perceived as notoriously difficult, despite the fact that improving environmental and social sustainability can often provide new value to a business. Biodiversity is usually understood as an external environmental constraint on business activities (Houdet *et al.* 2012), but business is beginning to notice that the threat posed by biodiversity loss goes beyond the reputational. A total of 27% of global CEOs interviewed by PwC expressed concern about the impacts of biodiversity loss on their business growth (TEEB 2010). Payment for ecosystem services creates an opportunity for the successful inclusion of sustainability and ecosystems provision into business strategy.

ES (ecosystem services) can be defined as services provided by the natural environment that benefit people (HM Government 2013). For example, this includes benefits such as resources for basic survival (such as air and water), social, cultural and educational benefits, and support for a strong healthy economy through raw materials for industry and agriculture (Defra 2010a). These services are essential to life on Earth: the impact of pollinating insects is estimated to be worth £440 million to UK agriculture. This means that farmers and those further up the supply chain accrue £440 million in financial benefits from the actions of insects such as bees. If these insects disappeared tomorrow, agricultural crops would not propagate, and the ramifications of this would be felt throughout the agricultural economy. Humans would also have to devise new ways in which to pollinate crops manually in the absence of this ecosystem service. Therefore, ecosystem services can be defined as any benefit man derives from nature.

Some of these ecosystem services can be given an estimate of value, or contribution to the economy. However, many of the services provided by the natural environment are very difficult to value, despite being fundamental to life as we know it. Consider, for example, the task of valuing the benefits that trees bring across the planet. We know trees provide multiple benefits, such as capturing carbon, providing the basis for forest ecosystems, and value to society in the form of wood. To capture the entirety of this value to different communities across the world would be immensely difficult. It would also be complicated to place a monetary value on the benefits of biodiversity. Costanza *et al.* (1997) have estimated the contribution of the entire biosphere of the Earth at $16–54 trillion per year (for reference, global GNP is calculated to be $18 trillion per year), thus the contribution of nature's services to the economy and society is huge. Many of nature's services also benefit society as a whole, rather than an individual or organisation. Therefore, with weak incentives for protection, markets fail to fully value ES as a whole (RELU 2012), leading to an ecosystem becoming damaged or depleted.

PES (payments for ecosystem services) offer a new opportunity to business, in that they bring economic thinking and a market mechanism into the provision of ES. PES are voluntary market transactions between buyers and sellers (beneficiaries and providers) of ES. In this way PES involve a business paying another party to protect an area of land where it provides an obvious benefit to the company. One of the best-known examples of this is New York City paying for water services in the upper catchments of a river. The programme to conserve the forests in this region, the preservation of which provides clean water, was estimated at US$1.5 billion. Installing a water filtration plant would have cost $8–10 billion in comparison (Defra 2010b). The non-financial benefits of this example include improved natural environment and reputational gain. Because there are clear benefits for both groups, this should incentivise sustainable management (RELU 2012). The ES approach offers business

Figure 2: Linkages between ecosystem services and human wellbeing.

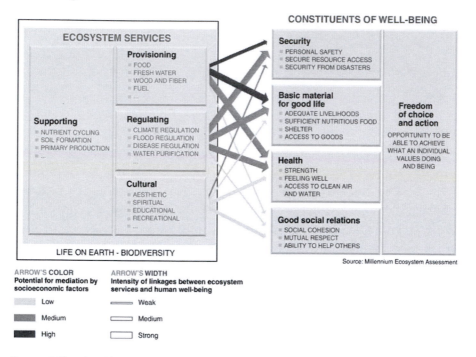

Source: Millennium Ecosystem Assessment, www.grida.no/graphicslib/detail/linkages-between-ecosystem-services-and-human-well-being_83bb, image credit Philippe Rekacewicz, Emmanuelle Bournay, UNEP/GRID-Arendal.

the opportunity to link environmental improvements to human wellbeing. Figure 2 details the strength of links between elements of ES, such as the provision of food, and elements of human wellbeing, such as adequate livelihoods and sufficient nutritious food. Therefore, businesses using an ecosystems approach effectively have the opportunity to combine a strategic business improvement with environmental and social goals, thereby working towards all three pillars of sustainability. An ES methodology also offers an integrated approach to sustainability in which business, environment and society benefits are intimately linked.

PES approaches in developing countries have demonstrated their capacity to help alleviate poverty and conserve natural resources as part of a single top–down scheme (RELU 2012). One example of this in agricultural supply chains is the case of coffee. Coffee is one of the most valuable legally traded export commodities in the world, and is grown across many of the world's most biodiverse regions (Ricketts *et al.* 2004). Seminar 1 provides more detail on the linkages between ES and business, using a case study of Starbucks.

In conclusion, the ES approach offers business a new way of embedding social and environmental sustainability into strategy and observing tangible results. There is an observable gap between the breadth of academic literature published on ES valuation and the ramifications of PES schemes, and information available to decision-makers within business seeking to establish local ecosystem markets (RELU 2012). Clear guidance to show how it works in practice would ease uptake for business leaders. Key business players promoting ecosystems thinking, such as Starbucks, have a clear role to play in this. Done correctly, businesses can derive economic benefit from looking at operations in the context of a wider ecosystem (ibid.), most especially those in the agriculture, water or food retail industries where links to ecosystems are strong and often globally widespread.

Social sustainability and business

This section of the chapter will focus on the social dimension of sustainability, and the importance for business to recognise the significant role that society and business play in affecting one another. Magis and Shinn (2009: 1) state that 'sustainability is premised on *systems theory*, stipulating that society, the environment and the economy are **interrelated constituents of a larger system**. The system can only remain viable to the extent that *each of the constituents functions properly.*' This highlights the notion that business and society do need each other for survival and prosperity.

Several academics have approached the social dimension from two different angles: **socio-efficiency** and **socio-effectiveness** (Hockerts 1999; Figge and Hahn 2001). Socio-efficiency can be termed as the relationship between a company's value added and impact on the society, and the impact can be both positive, for example the creating of work, and negative, such as work accidents and human rights abuses. However, Dyllick and Hockerts (2002) argue that its concern is predominantly with increasing economic sustainability and, although valuable, it only leads to relative improvements of society which can be limited to a micro-scale. Socio-effectiveness, the authors further contend, is when 'Business conduct should be judged not on a relative scale but rather in relation to the *absolute positive social impact a firm could reasonably have achieved*' (p. 138; our italics). Henceforth, what needs to be considered is the **overall impact** of business on its society.

Waage *et al.* (2005: 1149) contend that social sustainability 'span[s] from labour conditions and wages through access to natural resources-based needs (e.g. food, water), to socioeconomic resources (health, informational/educational, financial) etc'. The authors further state that social aspects of sustainability relate to 'not only to what employees are paid, but also to how the product, and production process, affects the parameters of people's lives (e.g., access to the full range of resources—natural, informational/educational, health, financial, etc.)', and that businesses need to look beyond the company, i.e. consider not just the employees but all the stakeholders who can be affected, such as the community directly impacted and the society as a whole that can be indirectly affected by the company's processes. On both a macro- and micro-level, businesses need to ask themselves some of the questions listed in Figure 3, in order to help them address social sustainability in their processes.

While it can be argued that business addressing social sustainability is voluntary and that it is difficult to police business's impact on society, there has been an increase in initiatives to address such issues, such as the International Labour Organization (www.ilo.org) and the Universal Declaration of Human Rights (www.un.org/en/documents/udhr/). This is due to the fact that there have been numerous cases whereby companies have faced legal claims for negligence or exploitation from the community in which they are operating. Examples include the aboriginal communities in northern Alberta, Canada being negatively affected by the oil sands development in that area (Droitsch and Simieritsch 2010), and the collapse of the Rana Plaza garment factory in Bangladesh, which was part of the supply chain for several high-street fashion stores (Burke 2013).

Although cases such as these are on the increase, there are also businesses that address social sustainability in their processes, and some of them have not only received positive attention, but have also been

Figure 3: A company's framework for social sustainability.

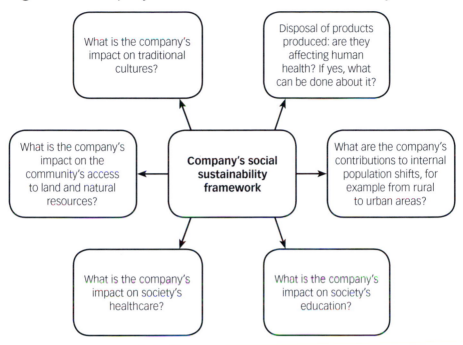

Source: Adapted from Waage *et al.* (2005).

labelled as 'pioneers' or 'champions' in their sector. Examples are Heineken leading the alcohol industry in the fight against alcohol abuse (Wills 2013) and the Shared Interest Society helping farmers in developing countries through its ethical and co-operative micro-financing (Beavis 2013).

Social sustainability concepts and practices are on the rise, and it makes perfect business sense for companies to integrate social issues in their overall strategy, as this can not only improve the company's brand but also increase its legitimacy to operate. Furthermore, evidence has shown that if businesses address their impact on society, this can have a positive knock-on effect on the environment, which in turn can ultimately lead to a more progressive economic sustainability (Porter and Kramer 2011).

Business and sustainability: what does it mean?

The economic element of sustainability arose from economic growth models that assessed the limits imposed by the carrying capacity of the Earth (Crane and Matten 2010). The Brundtland definition of sustainability emerged from this line of thought: 'development that meets the needs of the present without compromising the ability of future generations to meet their own needs' (UNCED 1987). The implications of economic sustainability on business activity and ethics occur on different levels. The first, narrow understanding of sustainability in business focuses on the economic performance of the company and the maintenance of a business model that secures the long-term economic performance of the company. This recognises the need to focus on strategies which lead to longer term rise in share price, market share or revenue, rather than short-term emphasis on profits (ibid.). A broader, more holistic understanding of economic sustainability, Crane and Matten (2010) argue, would be the company's ideological stance on the economic framework upon which it is embedded. One way to interpret this could be a business engaging in **tax avoidance** or evasion. While the latter violates the law, the former is possible through subtle accounting tricks or the use of tax havens. Nevertheless, the reluctance of a business to pay into the political institutional environment upon which its success is based is economically unsustainable (ibid.). A notorious example to emerge in recent years is the case of Starbucks. A four-month investigation by Reuters found that, despite Starbucks making over £3 billion in sales in the UK since 1998, it had paid only 1% corporation tax. Additionally, it had reported losses for the last five years, thereby paying no corporation tax, yet had reported to shareholders that it was profitable (BBC 2012a). Despite protesting that they operated to the letter of the law, this was met with mass public criticism, with Starbucks backpedalling a few months later and releasing the statement: 'We have listened to the feedback from our customers and employees, and understand that to maintain and further build public trust we need to do more' (BBC 2012b).

Barford and Holt (2013) have written on the rise of **tax shaming**, with the recession making the public increasingly aware of what they perceive as **tax injustice**. This can have an unquantifiable and lasting effect on a brand's hard-won appeal. The public is also increasingly aware of the capabilities of multinational corporations to evade tax obligations, which has been promoted as 'sound business practice', while many companies without an international arm are not able to avoid paying large tax bills. It was detailed earlier in this chapter how Starbucks has made great efforts to consider an ecosystems perspective as a way in which to embed all three pillars of sustainability into its sourcing and purchasing decisions. However, the failure of Starbucks to fully incorporate the three elements of sustainability thinking into the entire organisation has resulted in a scandal in the UK, inflicting possibly permanent damage to its brand and the way its customers perceive its sustainability efforts. These are the risks involved in the unequal treatment of sustainability priorities at different times, in different global locations.

Seminar 3 takes its cue from Crane and Matten's (2010) more nuanced definition of the business role of economic sustainability, which includes the company's attitudes towards—and impacts upon—its economic (and social and environmental) basis. This mirrors Hitchcock and Willard's (2009) understanding of the use of sustainability for business: as a framework for making sense of what is happening in the world, enabling you take action and foresee change. Crane and Matten (2010) also suggest an important understanding for business is that sustainability is about systems maintenance, i.e. ensuring that our actions as humans do not interfere with the long-term viability of the biotic system. Business sustainability therefore has strong links to systems theory, which seeks to understand 'problems' as being embedded in particular organisational structures, cultures and business environments (see Chapter 14 for further discussion). Nevertheless, the tripartite model of sustainability remains pre-eminent, as it arises from an understanding that not only is it impractical, but it is also sometimes impossible to address the sustainability of the natural environment within a business framework without also considering social and economic aspects (Crane and Matten 2010).

An important dimension of sustainability is that of intergenerational equity: equality between one generation and another. This also has important implications for geographically distant populations, and thus the role of globalisation in business is important. Globalisation has accentuated the homogenisation of ethics across the globe. This means that business faces the same ethical questions worldwide, and it is in emerging economies and developing nations where questions of business ethics are most pertinent (Crane and Matten 2010). It also makes a business's activities across the world much more transparent to the observant role and thus holds a business accountable. A consideration of social justice in the developing world is often deeply embedded in environmental justice. Take, for example, the accusations levelled against Apple and the pollution problems in its supply chain. In 2011, it emerged that many of Apple's factories in China were chronically out of compliance with environmental regulations:

> factories discharging toxic metals such as copper and nickel at levels that breach international safety standards, factories ignoring the health concerns of local communities, and problems with the disposal of hazardous waste. (Xiaoping 2011)

Additionally, Apple's own key performance indicators have no measures related to environmental responsibility, ignoring environmental demands placed on suppliers (ibid.). This is a recurring problem: a recent article detailed the push from the Western consumer groups China Labor Watch and Green America to get Apple to stop exposing its Chinese workers to harmful chemicals. They suggest that using substances such as n-hexane and benzene is 'now causing severe illness' and, by refusing to change to safer alternatives, Apple are saving a 'shockingly small amount of money' (Gibbs 2014). These ethical contrasts are increasingly visible to the Western consumer, making business accountability an important vehicle for sustainability throughout the supply chain.

Nevertheless, sustainability cannot be managed exclusively as a **public relations** strategy. Reputational benefits are not the only advantages companies can derive from pursuing sustainability, and stakeholders expect any communication a company produces expressing its efforts towards sustainability to be consistent with results. No organisation has managed to become fully sustainable—this is perhaps an impossible task. Instead, a company's focus should be on conceiving a sustainability framework, modelling social, environmental and economic performance, and using this as an opportunity to create real value for multiple stakeholders. Simultaneously, this model of corporate sustainability challenges managers to understand the complex interrelationships between economic, environmental and social performance (Epstein 2008). It is important to go beyond the 'usual suspects' of business sustainability, and champion those who innovate in their sector. One way to increase the visibility of sustainability efforts in the business sector is through awards schemes, such as *The Guardian*'s Sustainable Business Awards, which aim 'not just to give trophies, but to drive change' (*Guardian* 2014).

The award categories include communicating sustainably, waste and recycling, employee engagement and sustainable business leader of the year. This not only promotes and rewards the role of sustainability in business, but also provides a database of sustainable innovation and inspiration, making the concept of more approachable to the wider business community.

Conclusion

An excellent way to summarise the contemporary landscape of sustainability and business is expressed by Porter and Kramer (2011), in the creation of '**shared value**'. This focuses on the connections between societal and economic progress, expressing that businesses have the potential to

Figure 4: Corporate thinking and sustainability.

Pre-2000	2000–2005	2006–2010	Since 2010
'It's not a problem'	*'It is a problem'*	*'Let's solve the problem'*	*'It's an opportunity to create shared value'*
Let's ignore or understate the problem	Let's minimise the problem and throw some money at it to show we're contributing	We need to add costs to fix the problem	We can lower costs, grow revenues, or differentiate our value proposition by addressing social problems
Let's minimise our responsibility		We need to report transparently on our results	
Philanthropy is about personal values	CSR and philanthropy is about corporate reputation	We can use our core business capabilities to find solutions	Even social problems we don't usually affect pose opportunities

Source: Molthan-Hill (2014) adapted from Porter and Kramer (2011).

create the next wave of global growth (see Fig. 3). Shared value is created through a company enhancing its competitiveness, while simultaneously advancing the economic and social benefits of the community in which it is embedded. As expressed above, there is plenty of scope to include environmental thinking in business sustainability. The purpose of a corporation needs to be redefined as creating shared value, rather than just creating profit (ibid.). In this fashion, sustainability is and will be integral to businesses and reshape their relationships with society and the environment.

Suggested seminars

Seminar 1: Starbucks, impact investment and ecosystem services

Learning outcomes:

- Explore the **triple bottom line** with reference to the case study, and understand how all three elements are inextricably linked

- Relate the efficacy of **impact investment** to sustainability and encourage consideration in other areas of business

- Understand the motivations of businesses in ensuring a scheme that covers all three pillars of sustainability

Background

Across the globe, over 25 million people are directly dependent on growing coffee for a living. The frontier of coffee-growing is expanding into some of the most important and sensitive biodiverse regions. Also, the market for coffee is often volatile, with farmers suffering from the falling price of coffee. This damages the livelihoods of farmers who aim to cultivate high-quality coffee using traditional shade-grown techniques that have proven biodiversity benefits (Prickett 2005). Non-traditional production practices do not require the presence of trees, and thus are detrimental to the surrounding tropical ecosystem, as well as requiring the regular application of pesticides which have their own environmental impacts. Farmers who are priced out of the market are often tempted to convert to growing coca (for cocaine), exposing the community to violent and unstable cartels and contributing to the global problem of drugs trafficking (Oxfam 2005). This trend threatens not only the long-term availability of high-quality coffee, but also the integrity of local and sensitive ecosystems, and the overall wellbeing of communities that depend on it for an income, thereby addressing all three pillars of sustainability.

The opportunity to address this was identified in 1998 with the co-operation of Starbucks and Conservation International, an NGO with a focus on international biodiversity conservation. This first collaboration involved a field project in the southern state of Chiapas, Mexico, as Starbucks sought to source shade-grown, ecologically sound, premium coffee (Prickett 2005). Starbucks subsequently partnered with Verde Ventures, a programme founded in 2001 as a key component in the development of Conservation International's sustainable economies model (Conservation International 2014). Verde Ventures represents an important change in that they seek to advance the role of SMEs (small and medium-sized enterprises) in the coffee-growing trade. SMEs employ local people, giving communities a personal and economic stake in protecting their own natural resources. Despite their significant economic role in developing nations, many SMEs suffer from lack of access to financing, which not only means they are economically unstable, but also that SMEs are increasingly unable to invest in their own growth or adopt sustainable business practices (ibid.). Considering the potential to contribute towards both improvements in ecosystem health as well as human wellbeing (while providing a high-quality product), access to finance is paramount.

This model also offers a hands-off approach, as opposed to direct intervention, which allows human wellbeing goals to be delivered and allows the community ownership of its sustainable growth. In addition to a focus on habitat conservation, Verde Ventures offers training and education programmes focusing on environmentally preferential agricultural practices, for example in developing a community-run tree nursery adjacent to coffee crops. Verde Ventures also aims to promote the role of women in the community, furthering their education and facilitating their role in the business of both producing and marketing coffee and other native plants which offer health benefits (ibid.).

Starbucks made the decision to increase its farmer loans to $20 million by 2015 (ibid.). Based on the success of their investment with Verde Ventures, Starbucks also developed green coffee-sourcing guidelines to incorporate its environmental and social standards into worldwide purchasing criteria. In 2012, Starbucks ethically sourced 93% of its coffee, and aims to increase this to 100% by 2015 (Starbucks 2014).

Activity 1

You are asked to form groups of no more than five. Using the diagram below, each group will address one of two perspectives with reference to the Verde Ventures case study. List the benefits of Starbucks's impact investment programme either:

1.   From the point of view of the CEO of Starbucks, or

2.   From the point of view of the recipient farm managers

Write on the diagram where you think a benefit would lie. For example, the farmer's ability to access funding, ensuring financial security may be an economic benefit. Allow 10 minutes to discuss and compare results. Ideas may be, for example, strictly social or socioeconomic, or could address all three facets of sustainability.

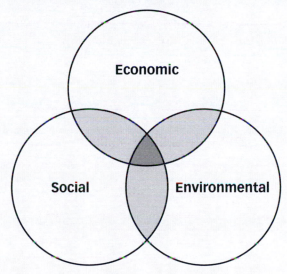

Activity 2

Remaining in groups, consider the following questions. Write down answers and then compare them as a class:

1.   What could have happened without the investment? What driving market forces can be identified?

2. Starbucks is looking to invest $20 million with Verde Ventures by 2015. Is this a small amount considering the size of the company? Is there need to invest more?

3. Can you assess that real change has occurred and, if so, how?

4. Is sustainability an effective mechanism to understand why and how change should occur with reference to the case study? Consider:

   a. Which side benefited more from the investment: Starbucks or the recipient community?

   b. Is sustainability a political tool?

Activity 3

On your own, write down examples of any other areas of business practice in which impact investment (also known as socially responsible investment) can be especially effective, and why you think this is. Consider the sustainability advantages and disadvantages.

Seminar 2: Monsanto and social impact

Learning outcomes:

- Differentiate between the concepts of 'socio-efficiency' and social sustainability

- Be aware of the impacts that social issues can have on the environmental and economic aspects of business

- Understand the role that social sustainability plays in the value chain of business's processes

This seminar focuses on the social aspect of sustainability, and the impact it can have on the environmental and economic dimension of a business.

Activity 1 (10 minutes)

1. As a collective seminar/tutorial group discuss some of the effects, that you may have read recently, that business has had on society, be it positive or negative. Divide your answers into a 'Negative' category and a 'Positive' category.

2. What are some of the areas that business has had influence on? For example, are they wages, healthcare, education, training?

3. Have any of these areas directly or indirectly impacted on the environment? What about the economy?

Activity 2 (20 minutes)

In groups of three, read the case study below individually:

Monsanto and India (adapted from Shiva 2013)

Monsanto India's website uses phrases such as 'Improving farmers lives' [sic], 'apply innovation ... help farmers' and 'innovative ... agricultural company', alongside pictures of smiling, prosperous farmers from the state of Maharashtra, India. However, Monsanto has a part to play in the epidemic of farmers' suicides in India resulting from the company's growing control over cotton seed supply: **95% of India's cotton seed is now controlled by Monsanto**.

Control over seed is the first link in the food chain because seed is the source of life. When a corporation controls seed, it controls life, especially the life of farmers.

Monsanto's domineering control over the seed sector in India, and globally, can be a cause of alarm. This is what connects farmers' suicides in India to *Monsanto v. Percy Schmeiser* in Canada, to *Monsanto v. Bowman* in the US, and to farmers in Brazil suing Monsanto for $2.2 billion for unfair collection of royalty.

Through patents on seed, Monsanto has become the 'Life Lord' of our planet, collecting rents for life's renewal from farmers, the original breeders.

Patents on seed are illegal because putting a toxic gene into a plant cell is neither 'creating' nor 'inventing' a plant. These are seeds of deception—the deception that Monsanto is the creator of seeds and life; the deception that while Monsanto sues farmers and traps them in debt, it pretends to be working for farmers' welfare, and the deception that GMOs (genetically modified organisms) feed the world. GMOs are failing to control pests and weeds, and have instead led to the emergence of superpests and superweeds.

The entry of Monsanto into the Indian seed sector was made possible with a 1988 Seed Policy imposed by the World Bank, requiring the government of India to deregulate the seed sector. Five things changed with Monsanto's entry: first, Indian companies were locked into joint ventures and licensing arrangements, and concentration over the seed sector increased. Second, seed which had been the farmers' common resource became the 'intellectual property' of Monsanto, for which it started collecting royalties, thus raising the costs of seed. Third, open pollinated cotton seeds were displaced by hybrids, including GMO hybrids. A renewable resource became a non-renewable, patented commodity. Fourth, cotton which had earlier been grown as a mixture with food crops now had to be grown as a monoculture, with higher vulnerability to pests, disease, drought and crop failure. Fifth, Monsanto started to subvert India's regulatory processes and, in fact, started to use public resources to push its non-renewable hybrids and GMOs through so-called public–private partnerships.

An internal advisory by the agricultural ministry of India in January 2012 had this to say to the cotton-growing states in India: 'Cotton farmers are in a deep crisis since shifting to Bt cotton. The spate of farmer suicides in 2011–12 has been particularly severe among Bt cotton farmers.'

The highest acreage of Bt cotton is in Maharashtra and this is also where the highest farmer suicides are. Suicides increased after Bt cotton was introduced: Monsanto's royalty extraction, and the high costs of seed and chemicals have created a debt trap. According to the government of India data, nearly 75% of rural debt is due to the purchase of raw materials such as seeds. As Monsanto's profits grow, farmers' debt grows. It is in this systemic sense that Monsanto's seeds are seeds of suicide.

Now, as a group, fill in the diagram below with impacts that you think Mosanto can have on India, the farming sector in India, and the community in general:

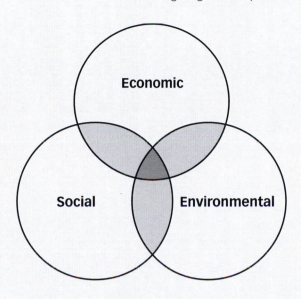

Activity 3 (20 minutes)

Still in your groups, complete the table below based on the Monsanto case study. Note that there can be more than one stakeholder in each group:

Social exposure of a business		
	Stakeholders	Claim/issue
Internal		
Along the value chain		
In the local community		
Society as a whole		

Seminar 3: Marketing and sustainability motives

Learning outcomes:

- Progress understanding of economic sustainability beyond traditional perceptions to include social and environmental elements

- Encourage students to build upon their own understanding of **brand sustainability** in a holistic fashion

- Reflect upon student's own understandings of sustainability and how the three elements are linked in a business context

This activity asks students to consider the importance of marketing in communicating sustainability, both in terms of actions and objectives. It examines the role of sustainability in business as a tool for foresight, which studies impacts upon business through a sustainability lens, and allows for an understanding of effects on overall business strategy. Finally, students are asked to reflect upon their own perceptions of the role of sustainability in business, and draw their own conclusions about how a company communicates its impacts and intentions.

Activity 1

In pairs, think of businesses that promote themselves as pursuing a sustainability agenda.

1. Discuss, as a group, why you have chosen particular organisations. What risks do organisations face by not pursuing sustainability to some extent?

2. On your own, draw a simple mind map. Consider the challenges faced by businesses looking to pursue sustainability: why are more companies not sustainable? List as many reasons as you can.

3. Discuss in pairs: what risks organisations face by not pursuing sustainability to some extent?

Activity 2

Consider one of the businesses identified in Activity 1, where you think sustainability issues have an important feedback on the financial security of a company.

1. Draw a three-by-three table. Label it 'People' and 'Planet' down the left, and 'Positive' and 'Negative' across the top, like so:

[Company]	Positive	Negative
People		
Planet		

2. In pairs, think of as many sustainability issues as you can that affect your company. Consider whether they are perceived as positive or negative impacts, and if they would be considered social or environmental effects. Try to write something in each of the four boxes.

3. Draw a circle underneath the table labelled 'Profit', and add arrows between the most important sustainability issues and the Profit bubble. You can draw thicker arrows, to represent a stronger linkage, like so:

[Company]	Positive	Negative
People		
Planet		

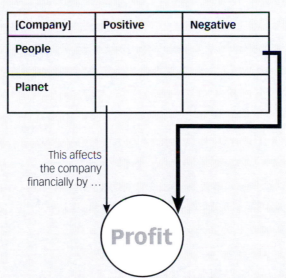

This affects the company financially by …

Profit

4. Write next to the arrow how you believe a particular sustainability issue has a feedback on the economic health of your organisation. These might be business oriented or customer oriented.

5. Discuss your findings as a group. Is there agreement on what sustainability issues have the biggest impacts?

Activity 3

Get the whole group to stand up, and divide yourselves into two. Consider the following question: 'Do you believe a brand prepared to use sustainability as a tool of self-promotion and a way to market its products should be congratulated for doing so?'

1. One team is asked to agree with the question, and the other to disagree.

2. Promote a spokesperson from each team. Discuss, as a team, why you believe you are right.

3. Each spokesperson will state three points supporting their point of view.

4. After this discussion is finished, ask if anyone would like to switch sides.

Below is a short example of Activity 2 to illustrate the activity, using a theoretical case study.

Company A is a privately owned multinational cosmetics company with many outlets on high streets across the UK, and an increasing number around the globe. Company A prides itself on ethical and environmental campaigning, together with rejection of animal testing along its supply chain. This company offers many products that are preservative free and/or packaging free, as well as all products being vegetarian friendly, with a large number of vegan products.

Company A places emphasis on reducing its environmental impact, including sourcing materials that are produced in a sustainable way. It also emphasises the need to re-use over recycle, and encourages customers to return empty packaging to stores rather than traditional disposal methods.

However, Company A has attracted criticism for environmental and ethical hypocrisy, from opening stores in countries with poor human rights legacies through to failing to address energy conservation in its many stores around the globe. A large amount of bad press has been generated by a dissatisfied cohort of former employees complaining about the lack of an effective human resources department.

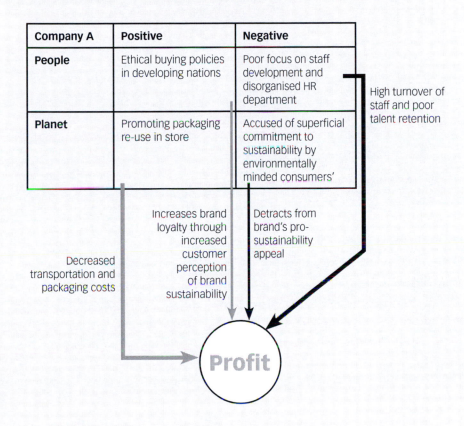

Company A	Positive	Negative
People	Ethical buying policies in developing nations	Poor focus on staff development and disorganised HR department
Planet	Promoting packaging re-use in store	Accused of superficial commitment to sustainability by environmentally minded consumers'

High turnover of staff and poor talent retention

Decreased transportation and packaging costs

Increases brand loyalty through increased customer perception of brand sustainability

Detracts from brand's pro-sustainability appeal

Profit

Additional teaching material and ideas

The Oxfam Coffee Chain Game

www.oxfam.org.uk/~/media/Files/Education/Resources/The%20
coffee%20chain%20game/Coffee%20Chain%20Game.ashx

This is an excellent group activity which highlights discrepancies in profit at both ends of the coffee supply chain. It details the market pressures felt by those in the coffee industry, and the trickle-down effect of low coffee prices on developing nations. This game helps players to understand the different protagonists in the coffee supply chain and their influence on determining a fair price. It also develops negotiation skills. It can be played within an hour, including debriefing. We modified it slightly by giving the 'roasters' the power to lead the discussion and determine the price if there is disagreement. This makes the game more challenging and reflects real-life negotiation as depicted in the film *Black Gold*.

Black Gold

www.imdb.com/title/tt0492447/

This film makes an excellent follow-up to either the coffee chain game above or to Seminar 1. This feature-length documentary film focuses on the contrast between struggling African coffee farmers and successful multinational coffee companies. It is an astute insight into the daily reality of those in developing nations struggling to get a reasonable price for an excellent product, and a hearty endorsement of Fairtrade.

The UN Global Compact Dilemma Game

More information available at: www.kpmg.com/DK/da/nyheder-og-indsigt/nyhedsbreve-og-publikationer/publikationer/advisory/csr/Documents/Presentation-UNGC-Dilemma-game-.pdf

This activity is ideal for more advanced business students looking to get a better grasp of sustainability issues and the trade-offs involved as a manager. It highlights dilemmas within human rights, labour rights, environment and anti-corruption, and considers how to negotiate these, encouraging players to create a more inclusive and sustainable marketplace. The game aims to close the gap between commitment and action in a business context.

The Sustainable Organisation Simulation Game

The Simulation Game is packaged into a portable two- or three-day workshop where students first get an overview of how sustainability adds value to the company. Using a case study of a live organisation, students apply for various leadership positions to lead either the whole company as CEO (or another board member) or as functional heads with the aim of embedding sustainability in their respective areas. Students acting as functional heads have to build convincing business cases and present these to the board, demonstrating how such proposals seek to add value to the organisation as well as how they sit alongside and/or support other functional proposals. Students acting as board members have to work on the strategic alignment of all functional areas and exercise responsible leadership. It could be offered as a two-day weekend class if space is otherwise limited. The final presentations could be assessed or the workshop could be taught on a 'pass/fail' basis or without assessment. More information can be obtained from petra.molthan-hill@ntu.ac.uk.

The sustainability balanced scorecard

Seminar 3 is a good starting point for understanding how sustainability fits into the business case. However, it can be useful to go into more detail and the use of a BSC (balanced scorecard) methodology is a good way to do this. Figge *et al.* (2002) detail the application of a sustainability balanced scorecard, an activity that can be extended across two or three sessions as a group project. Students can profile a business in detail using online resources, dividing the company's perspectives into the financial perspective, the customer perspective and the internal process perspective. The purpose of the BSC is to formulate a hierarchic system of strategic objectives, derived from these perspectives. This is an excellent way to embed sustainability perspectives into business thought rather than as an extra activity.

Managing sustainability

This is a term-long module where students act as consultants to a given desk-based company. They have to assess their 'own' company on how they address social, environmental and economic sustainability and give recommendations on how to improve these three areas. In every session they are taught one of the concepts of sustainability as given in this book and have to apply it directly to their 'own' company. The exercises are so designed that they also understand how the different functions within a company relate to each other, so it is a good module to connect various core modules while simultaneously applying sustainability concepts. Further information can be obtained from petra.molthan-hill@ntu.ac.uk.

Further reading

Crane A., and D. Matten (2010). *Business Ethics: Managing Corporate Citizenship and Sustainability in the Age of Globalisation* (Oxford, UK: Oxford University Press).

> An excellent entry-level textbook about the world of business ethics. This covers the foundation of business ethics, applying understandings to each of a corporation's major stakeholders. It details the role of sustainability in ethical business and why it is important. *Business Ethics* also looks at sustainability reporting and sustainability share indexes and why they are an excellent way to look into the future of business and sustainability.

Elkington, J. (1997) *Cannibals with Forks: The Triple Bottom Line of 21st Century Business* (Oxford, UK: Capstone Publishing).

> The quintessential read for understanding the importance of integrating all three elements of sustainability in business, and why the triple bottom line is important in this. While some of the claims about lacklustre attitudes to sustainability may feel a little dated, Elkington's book remains a worthwhile read and provides a solid understanding of the business case for sustainability from the ground up.

Fisk, P. (2010) *People, Planet, Profit: How to Embrace Sustainability for Innovation and Business Growth* (London: Kogan Page).

> This borrows directly from Elkington's (1997) tripartite mantra. Comparing the approach of many different companies from different sectors around the world, and their sustainability achievements, this book sets out the ase to business leaders why embracing sustainability is not only the right thing for society and

the environment, but also the right thing for their business. It also provides a wealth of case studies and practical examples of sustainability in action.

KPMG (2013) *The KPMG Survey of Corporate Responsibility Reporting 2013*, www.kpmg.com/Global/en/IssuesAndInsights/ArticlesPublications/ corporate-responsibility/Documents/kpmg-survey-of-corporate- responsibility-reporting-2013.pdf, accessed 28 March 2014.

> Recommended reading for students, academics and business professionals alike, this report details the current state of corporate responsibility publishing throughout the world and examines current trends. It details the growth in the number of countries and sectors producing corporate responsibility documents and the important implications for sustainability. Additionally, it describes the need for integrated reporting and the feedback this would have in implementing sustainable management strategies.

TEEB (The Economics of Ecosystems and Biodiversity) (2010) *The Economics of Ecosystems and Biodiversity: Ecological and Economic Foundations* (London: Hardback).

> This introduces the concept of ecosystem services and their use in a business context. The report demonstrates how businesses can align their actions in relation to biodiversity along with other corporate responsibility initiatives. It draws attention to the global economic benefits of biodiversity and its increasing importance as a field of interest in the next few decades. TEEB highlights that businesses have a crucial role in halting biodiversity loss, that can also have benefits for the company.

Websites

www.ethicalconsumer.org/

> This offers comparisons of companies' ethical and environmental intentions and monitors the progress of a large number of companies, aiming to make global business more sustainable and transparent through consumer pressure.

www.theguardian.com/sustainable-business/series/sustainability-case-studies

> A fantastic collection of sustainable business case studies, and an excellent way to understand sustainable business today, or to add quick case studies for your essays. Considers areas such as society, carbon and communicating sustainably.

https://plana.marksandspencer.com/

> 'We're calling it Plan A because we believe it's now the only way to do business.' Marks & Spencer are proud advocates of embedding sustainability top– down, throughout the whole business. The website provides information on how they are achieving this and their progress towards sustainable goals.

References

Armsworth P.R., A.N. Armsworth, N. Compton, P. Cottle, I. Davies, B.A. Emmett, V. Fandrich, M. Foote, K.J. Gaston, P. Gardiner, T. Hess, J. Hopkins, N. Horsely, N. Leaver, T. Maynard and A. Shannon (2010) 'The Ecological Research Needs of Business', *Journal of Applied Ecology* 47: 235-43.

Barford, V., and G. Holt (2013) 'Google, Amazon, Starbucks: The rise of tax shaming', BBC News, 21 May 2013, www.bbc.co.uk/news/magazine-20560359, accessed 21 March 2014.

BBC (2012a) 'Starbucks "paid just £8.6 million UK tax in 14 years"', BBC News, 16 October 2012, www.bbc.co.uk/news/business-19967397, accessed 21 March 2014.

—— (2012b) 'Tax: Starbucks in talks with UK's Revenue and Customs', BBC News, 2 December 2012, www.bbc.co.uk/news/business-20573208, accessed 21 March 2014.

Beavis, L. (2013) 'Shared Interest: Investing in a Fairer World', *The Guardian*, www.theguardian.com/sustainable-business/shared-interest-investing-fairer-world, accessed 30 March 2014.

Bockstette, V. (2013) 'CSR: why there's a difference between shared values and shared value', *The Guardian*, www.theguardian.com/sustainable-business/blog/csr-difference-between-shared-values-shared-value, accessed 28 March 2014.

Burke, J. (2013) 'Bangladesh factory collapse leaves trail of shattered lives', *The Guardian*, www.theguardian.com/world/2013/jun/06/bangladesh-factory-building-collapse-community, accessed 29 March 2014.

Conservation International (2014) *Verde Ventures 2*, www.conservation.org/global/verdeventures/vv2/pages/default.aspx, accessed 20 March 2014.

Costanza, R., R. d'Arge, R. De Groot, S. Farber, M. Grasso, B. Hannon and M. van den Belt (1997) 'The Value of the World's Ecosystem Services and Natural Capital', *Ecological Economics* 25.1: 3-15.

Crane, A., and D. Matten (2010). *Business Ethics: Managing Corporate Citizenship and Sustainability in the Age of Globalisation* (Oxford, UK: Oxford University Press).

Defra (2010a) *What Nature Can Do for You: A Practical Introduction to Making the Most of Natural Services, Assets and Resources in Policy and Decision Making*, http://archive.defra.gov.uk/environment/policy/natural-environ/documents/nature-do-for-you.pdf, accessed 28 March 2014.

—— *Payments for Ecosystem Services: A Short Introduction*, http://archive.defra.gov.uk/environment/policy/natural-environ/documents/payments-ecosystem.pdf, accessed 28 March 2014.

Dermondy, J. (2010) 'Evaluating Greener Marketing', in C. Roberts and J. Roberts (eds.), *Greener by Degrees: Exploring Sustainability through Higher Education Criteria* (Cheltenham, UK: University of Gloucester): 12-20.

Devinney, T.M. (2009) 'Is the Socially Responsible Corporation a Myth? The Good, the Bad, and the Ugly of Corporate Social Responsibility', *The Academy of Management Perspectives* 23(2): 44-56.

Droitsch, D., and T. Simieritsch (2010) *Canadian Aboriginal Concerns with Oil Sands: A Compilation of Key Issues, Resolutions and Legal Activities*, www.pembina.org/pub/2083, accessed 8 February 2012.

Dyllick, T., and K. Hockerts (2002) 'Beyond the Business Case for Corporate Sustainability', *Business Strategy and the Environment* 11: 130-41.

Elkington, J. (1997) *Cannibals with Forks: The Triple Bottom Line of 21st Century Business* (Oxford, UK: Capstone Publishing).

—— (2014) *From the Triple Bottom Line to Zero*, www.johnelkington.com/activities/ideas.asp, accessed 16 March 2014.

Epstein, M.J. (2008) *Making Sustainability Work: Best Practices in Managing and Measuring Corporate Social, Environmental and Economic Impacts* (Sheffield, UK: Greenleaf Publishing).

Figge, F., and T. Hahn (2001) 'Sustainable Value Added: Measuring Corporate Contributions to Sustainability', in *Conference Proceedings on the 2001 Business Strategy and the Environment Conference in Leeds* (Shipley, UK: ERP Environment): 83-92.

Figge F., T. Hahn, S. Schaltegger and M. Wagner (2002) 'The Sustainability Balanced Scorecard: Linking Sustainability Management to Business Strategy', *Business Strategy and the Environment* 11: 269-84.

Fisk, P. (2010) *People, Planet, Profit: How to Embrace Sustainability for Innovation and Business Growth* (London, UK: Kogan Page).

Gibbs, S. (2014) 'Apple urged to stop using harmful chemicals in factories', *The Guardian*, 12 March 2014, www.theguardian.com/technology/2014/mar/12/apple-harmful-chemicals-factories-labour, accessed 22 March 2014.

Guardian, The (2014) 'The Guardian Sustainable Business Awards 2014', *The Guardian*, www.theguardian.com/sustainable-business/gsb-awards, accessed 23 March 2014.

Hitchcock, D., and M. Willard (2009) *The Business Guide to Sustainability: Practical Strategies and Tools for Organisations*, 2nd edn (London: Earthscan).

HM Government (2013) *Guidance: Ecosystem Services*, https://www.gov.uk/ecosystems-services, accessed 28 March 2014.

Hockerts, K. (1999) 'The Sustainability Radar: A Tool for the Innovation of Sustainable Products and Services', *Greener Management International* 25: 29-49.

Houdet J., M. Trometter and J. Weber (2012) 'Understanding Changes in Business Strategies Regarding Biodiversity and Ecosystem Services', *Ecological Economics* 73: 37-46.

Kaplan, R., and D. Norton (1992) 'The Balanced Scorecard: Measures that Drive Performance', *Harvard Business Review* (January–February 1992): 71-79.

KPMG (2013) *The KPMG Survey of Corporate Responsibility Reporting 2013*, www.kpmg.com/Global/en/IssuesAndInsights/ArticlesPublications/corporate-responsibility/Documents/kpmg-survey-of-corporate-responsibility-reporting-2013.pdf, accessed 28 March 2014.

Laughland, P., and M. Bansal (2011) 'The Top Ten Reasons why Businesses Aren't More Sustainable', *Ivey Business Journal*, http://iveybusinessjournal.com/topics/social-responsibility/the-top-ten-reasons-why-businesses-arent-more-sustainable#.Uy7ZR4XROsh, accessed 14 March 2014.

Magis, K., and C. Shinn (2009) 'Emergent Principles of Social Sustainability', in J. Dillard, V. Dujon and M.C. King (eds.), *Understanding the Social Dimension of Sustainability* (New York: Routledge): 15-44.

Mattioli, D. (2007) 'How Going Green Draws Talent, Cuts Costs', *Wall Street Journal*, http://online.wsj.com/news/articles/SB119492843191791132, accessed 28 March 2014.

Michel, J., Y. Shen, A. Aiden, A. Veres, M. Gray, J. Pickett, D. Hoiberg, D. Clancy, P. Norvig, J. Orwant, S. Pinker, M. Nowak and E. Aiden (2011) 'Quantitative Analysis of Culture Using Millions of Digitised Books', *Science* 14.331: 176-82.

MIT Sloan Management Review (2011) *Sustainability: The 'Embracers' Seize Advantage*, http://c0426007.cdn2.cloudfiles.rackspacecloud.com/MIT-SMR-BCG-sustainability-the-embracers-seize-advantage-2011.pdf, accessed 28 March 2014.

Molthan-Hill, P. (2014) 'Making the Business Case: Intercultural Differences in Framing Economic Rationality Related to Environmental Issues', *Critical Perspectives on International Business*, forthcoming.

Oxfam (2005) *The Coffee Chain Game*, www.oxfam.org.uk/~/media/Files/Education/Resources/The%20coffee%20chain%20game/Coffee%20Chain%20Game.ashx, accessed 18 March 2014.

Parkin S., F. Sommer and S. Uren (2003) 'Sustainable Development: Understanding the Concept and Practical Challenge', *Engineering Sustainability* 156.ES1: 19-26.

Porter, M.E., and M.R. Kramer (2011) 'Creating Shared Value', *Harvard Business Review* (January–February 2011): 62-77.

Prickett, G. (2005) 'Business Industry Perspectives on the Findings of Millennium Ecosystem Assessment', www.maweb.org/documents/document.706.aspx.pdf, accessed 19 March 2013.

RELU (Rural Economy and Land Use programme) (2012) *Enhancing the Environment through Payment for Ecosystem Services*, www.relu.ac.uk/news/policy%20and%20practice%20notes/39%20PES/PES.pdf, accessed 28 March 2014.

Ricketts, T.H., G.C. Daily, P.R. Ehrlich and C.D. Michener (2004) 'Economic Value of Tropical Forests to Coffee Production', *PNAS* 101.34: 12579-82.

Robins, F. (2006) 'The Challenge of TBL: A Responsibility to Whom?', *Business and Society Review* 111.1: 1-14.

Shiva, V. (2013) *The Seeds of Suicide: How Monsanto Destroys Farming*, www.globalresearch.ca/the-seeds-of-suicide-how-monsanto-destroys-farming/5329947, accessed 31 March 2014.

Starbucks (2014) *Responsibly Grown Coffee*, www.starbucks.co.uk/responsibility/sourcing/coffee, accessed 20 March 2014.

TEEB (The Economics of Ecosystems and Biodiversity) (2010) *The Economics of Ecosystems and Biodiversity: Ecological and Economic Foundations* (London: Hardback).

UNCED (United Nations Conference on Environment and Development) (1987) *Our Common Future* (Zurich, Switzerland: Conches).

Waage, S.A., K. Geiser, F. Irwin, A.B. Weissman, M.D. Bertolucci, P. Fisk, G. Basile, S. Cowan, H. Cauley and A. McPherson (2005) 'Fitting Together the Building Blocks for Sustainability: A Revised Model for Integrating Ecological, Social and Financial Factors into Business Decision-Making', *Journal of Cleaner Production* 13(12): 1145-63.

Willard, B. (2012) *The Sustainability Advantage: 7 Business Case Benefits of the Triple Bottom Line* (Vancouver, Canada: New Society Publishers).

Wills, J. (2013) 'Heineken: leading the fight against alcohol abuse', *The Guardian*, www.theguardian.com/sustainable-business/heineken-leading-fight-alcohol-abuse, accessed 30 March 2014.

Xiaoping, X. (2011) 'Apple wakes up to Chinese pollution concerns', *The Guardian*, 4 October 2011, www.theguardian.com/environment/2011/oct/04/apple-chinese-pollution-concerns, accessed 22 March 2014.

EMBEDDING SUSTAINABILITY INTO CORE SUBJECTS

5

Sustainability reporting

Christian Herzig and Biswaraj Ghosh

This chapter is seeking to:

- Enhance appreciation of non- or extra-financial reporting and the different forms it can take

- Foster understanding of the content and design of sustainability reporting

- Impart awareness of the key reasons why companies develop sustainability reports and websites

- Develop knowledge about recent developments (e.g. guidelines and regulatory frameworks) and the capability of evaluating their role in enhancing transparency and accountability

- Impart awareness of some problems in sustainability reporting

---

Introduction

This chapter introduces the evolution and advancement of corporate reporting beyond financial information as a way to communicate corporate policies, performances and impacts regarding the environment and society to a broad range of stakeholders. The chapter begins with a historical perspective detailing the growth of and drivers for different forms of non- or extra-financial reporting. This includes some observations on national and international regulations as well as sustainability reporting frameworks. Particular focus is placed on two initiatives, the **GRI (Global Reporting Initiative)** and **IR (integrated reporting)**. Then, perspectives and reasons are outlined which aim to explain the existence of sustainability reports and the use of the Internet for sustainability reporting. The chapter concludes with a reflection on some problem areas associated with sustainability reporting.

Developments

In Europe, a number of companies started publishing **social reports** in the 1970s. With these reports companies informed their stakeholders about the company's activities, products and services, and related positive and negative social impacts. This new type of report also included new social accounting techniques such as the value-added statement, which presents the added value generated by an organisation and how it is appropriated to the contributors of the value; hence a way to show how the value was created and attributed to a larger number of stakeholders (e.g. employees, the state, creditors) rather than just the shareholders. The emergence of these new forms of accounting and reporting can be seen in the light of rising income levels at that time which shifted the focus of society and politics to objectives such as quality of life, while at the same time the negative effects of quantitative economic growth and a Tayloristic organisation of production processes were evaluated critically in society. The rise in social reporting in the 1970s is often seen to be the first development of non- or extra-financial corporate reporting (although it was preceded by the disclosure of employee and community issues within annual reports for many decades: Guthrie and Parker 1989). However, by the end of the 1970s, social reporting was already in decline again. Among the reasons for this decline were an inadequate target group orientation; a mismatch between the information interests of most stakeholders and social reports that were often scientifically designed and remote from the reality of most people's lives; a misuse of social reporting as a public relations tool, which reduced its reliability and credibility; an insufficient integration of social and financial reporting; and the positive economic and political development of Europe, with job movements to the services sector and improved working conditions (Dierkes and Antal 1985; Hemmer 1996; Herzig and Schaltegger 2011).

Various incidents of environmental catastrophe occurred in the late 1980s and 1990s (e.g. Schweizerhalle, Sandoz, Switzerland; Griesheim, Hoechst AG, Germany), and companies were scrutinised for being responsible for these environmental disasters. In response to the increased pressure for greater transparency and accountability, companies, in particular those operating within environmentally sensitive industries, started to publish **environmental reports** to explain to stakeholders how the organisational activities impacted on the natural environment (e.g. through air and water emissions, types and amounts of wastes, etc.) and how these impacts would be managed. The environmental reporting activities were partly forced by new laws (compulsory reporting) and partly voluntary. Overall, environmental reporting superseded to a large extent the early social reporting activities of companies. Until the end of the last millennium, the number of environmental reports and the attention they received in the media and society increased significantly, and their average quality improved—from initially being primarily green glossaries and one-off reports—to more comprehensive environmental reports published on a regular (e.g. annual) basis (Herzig and Schaltegger 2011). An example of a voluntary approach to environmental reporting is the European Union EMAS (Eco-Management and Audit Scheme). The scheme, which has recently become an internationally applicable standard, acknowledges companies that manage and improve their environmental performance and document their respective achievements through publicly available environmental statements, a specific form of an environmental report (www.emas.eu).

Succeeding years saw different attempts to integrate environmental and social issues within corporate reporting (e.g. safety, health and the environment reports). Since the mid-1990s, and increasingly towards the end of that decade, the attention shifted towards **sustainability reports** (e.g. Kolk 2004). Sustainability reports reflect companies' claims to depict an overall picture of their ecological, social and economic sustainability activities and performance, and to inform stakeholders as to how and to what extent these corporations contribute to sustainable development (Herzig and Schaltegger 2011). One of the earliest examples is Shell's so-called 'three Ps' report (*People, Planet & Profits*), published in 1999, the title of which already reflects a multidimensional reporting style. In certain industrial sectors the number of stand-alone sustainability reports nowadays exceeds those of environmental reports—in particular if one also considers that companies use various alternative titles for their reports with which they endeavour to demonstrate their wider responsibility to society (e.g., 'corporate (social) responsibility report', 'corporate citizenship report' or 'report to society'). Similarly with environmental statements, there is a trend towards more integrated reporting (BMU 2007). In practice, many of these reports are still published as stand-alone publications (KPMG 2011). Compared to social reporting in the 1970s (where emphasis was placed on employee-related issues and value creation for various stakeholders), social aspects within sustainability reports are nowadays often more globally and also more comprehensively dealt with, in terms of moral and ethical questions of sustainable development (e.g. child labour in the supply chain, human rights, poverty alleviation, gender issues and trading relationships).

A growing body of international and national guidance documents for sustainability reporting has evolved in recent years to support companies in developing reports and communicating externally their social, environmental and economic performance and impacts in order to satisfy the information needs of interested stakeholder groups (UNEP *et al.* 2010; Adams and Narayanan 2007; Leipziger 2010). The most generally accepted and universally applied **sustainability reporting framework** is probably that provided by the **GRI (Global Reporting Initiative**; www.globalreporting.org). It was developed through an international multi-stakeholder consultation process (involving representations from businesses, civil societies, academia and public institutions worldwide) and comprises reporting guidelines (the most recent, fourth version is called G4), sector guidance and other resources such as templates for a basic GRI report, checklists or a GRI content index. The gradual advancements in the GRI guidelines since their first inception in 2000 are substantiated by a number of requirements including: to remove any ambiguity in the interpretation of concepts and principles; to better allow companies to improve their understanding of material issues to be included in sustainability reports; to include additional disclosure requirements as gathered from the stakeholder consultative method; and to reach harmonisation with other major published guidelines or initiatives including Integrated Reporting (see further below). GRI's reporting principles focus on defining two aspects of reporting. First, the principles relate to what should be included in the report, i.e. they define the **content of the sustainability report**. Second, the principles prescribe ways to enable companies attain a **standard quality for sustainability reporting**. In essence, the GRI principles attempt to standardise sustainability reporting and ensure relevant, useful and timely information that truly reflects the organisations' sustainability activities and supports stakeholder decision-making.

Besides stand-alone sustainability reports, **extended financial reports and integrated (business) reports** have received more attention in recent years. Mainly driven by the increasing interest of investors and analysts as well as regulatory requirements for sustainability disclosure, there has been more focus on selected environmental (and social) aspects of corporate performance in financial reports in recent years. In Europe, the implementation of the EU Accounts Modernisation Directive with the reformed law regulating the balance sheet (EU 2003) has forced shareholder companies to include non-financial performance indicators, specifically environmental and labour-related indicators, in the prognosis reports included in their annual reports. Further evidence for the heightened attention given to the regulation of **extended annual reporting** in European and other countries may be seen in France for example, where since 2001 listed companies are required to publish an integrated annual report (incorporating environmental, social and governance disclosures around 30 topics, which increased to 42 topics in 2013) and South Africa where, according to the King III Code on Corporate Governance, companies listed on the Johannesburg Stock Exchange have been required to produce a report which integrates financial and sustainability performance (or explain why they do not) since 2010. Overall, disclosure of sustainability issues has become the subject of a growing body of regulations (UNEP *et al.* 2010). According to a study by UNEP and others (2010), approximately two thirds out of 142 country standards, identified in 30 selected countries and related to some form of sustainability reporting, can be classified as mandatory. For a long time, however, most of these regulations have been limited to companies of a certain (usually large) size, state-owned or listed companies, or companies that are significant emitters of pollution. However, most recent developments show that this is going to change. For example, the French regulatory framework for integrated reporting was revised to deepen the level of non-financial information in annual reports and extend the applicability to large private companies or subsidiaries of foreign companies (and add new requirements of third-party verification). By January 2016, all unlisted companies with an annual revenue of €100m or more and staff of 500 or more will be affected by what is currently seen to be one of the strongest stances yet taken by any country to enhance transparency on environmental, social and governance issues in annual reports (Ernst and Young 2012). At the European level, similar changes have been proposed within the Fourth and Seventh Accounting Directives (dealing with corporate annual and consolidated financial statement and related report preparation) (EC 2013, 2014). The suggested amendments to current accounting regulations would require several thousand companies in Europe to report on non-financial aspects in their annual reports.

Another recent initiative to enhance **IR (integrated reporting)** is the IIRC (International Integrated Reporting Council) which was co-founded by GRI and the Prince's Accounting for Sustainability Project (and other international partners) in 2010 (www.theiirc.org). This encompasses a multi-stakeholder approach that brings in the views of investors, civil society organisations, accountants, regulators, businesses and standard-makers who share a common perspective on the importance of communicating to the users of reports how value is created. IIRC defines the framework as an instrument for companies to concisely communicate 'about how an organisation's strategy, governance, performance and prospects, in the context of its external environment, lead to the creation of value over the short, medium and long term' (IIRC 2013: 7). It can be seen as an attempt to enable companies to demonstrate to interested stakeholder groups: first, the connections between corporate strategy, governance, financial, social and environmental policies and performances; and second, simultaneously to establish the ability of such companies to create and sustain value. The framework that was introduced only in December 2013 does not prescribe any methods for measuring performance or key performance indicators, but comprises seven principles that subscribing organisations need to abide by and eight aspects that need to be included in the report. The following videos introduce the initiative in a simple and easy-to-understand format.

- HRH The Prince of Wales introduces IR and its significance: www.youtube.com/watch?v=BIVWxmqGs9M

- Susanne Stormer, Vice President—Corporate Sustainability, Novo Nordisk (a global healthcare company headquartered in Denmark), briefly explains Novo Nordisk's journey towards IR: www.youtube.com/watch?v=fUocAfqmm1o

Internet-based reporting

While there has been a constant increase in publishing sustainability reports (see, for example, what is probably the world's largest online database for sustainability reports at www.corporateregister.com), the limitations of printed reports have encouraged companies to turn to the more expansive possibilities provided by the Internet. Greater use of the Internet for sustainability reporting is often attributed to its advantages in **providing more sustainability information** and **increasing information accessibility and comprehensibility** (Adams and Frost 2006; Herzig and Godemann 2010). With the media-specific linking possibilities and the use of the HTML format, reporting is for example no longer limited by the number of printed pages. A large quantity of information, including historical company information and links to other information sources related to the company or to other organisations, can be offered online without necessarily overwhelming the reader. The Internet allows a company to present an integrated view of different aspects of sustainability, and allows interested stakeholders to select, from a large information database, that information which is of specific interest to them. Moreover, the Internet offers possibilities such as 24-hour accessibility, addressee-specific information tailoring and distribution, individual access for stakeholders, and a combination of different media elements such as words, figures, images or videos (Isenmann 2005). Finally, the range of communication possibilities through stakeholder engagement and **dialogue in online sustainability reporting** extends much further than in printed sustainability reports (Unerman and Bennett 2004; Unerman 2007). While in printed reports stakeholder dialogue mainly takes place prior to production and the results of these stakeholder engagement processes can be documented in the reports, dialogue-based online relationships can include various forms of interaction (mutual asynchronous forms such as mail-to functions or discussion forums as well as mutual synchronous forms such as chats, audio or video-conferencing) (Herzig and Schaltegger 2011).

However, there are also several disadvantages to using the Internet. Some stakeholders tend to be excluded from the Internet or hindered in their use of it. Information on websites can be changed without warning and the assurance of web content is difficult. Traditional printed reports are thus often said to enjoy a higher degree of credibility among users than the Internet. Moreover, some stakeholders and their reading situations may still favour a printed report. Thus, their combined use is usually recommended as the primary means of communication. On the other hand, considerations to encourage a wider application of EMAS by reducing the costs of publishing environmental statements has raised a debate about the necessity of printed reports. Also, in practice some companies have abandoned printed reports completely and now solely focus on Internet-based sustainability reporting (e.g. Adidas or E.ON UK).

Perspectives

Why do companies engage in sustainability reporting? A widely recognised motive underlying sustainability reporting is the **business case for sustainability**. Perceived benefits and pressures of social and environmental reporting, as observed by Spence and Gray (2007) in their UK study, include business efficiency, market drivers, reputation and risk management, stakeholder management, internal champions and mimetic motivations—each viewed as expressing ideas on the legitimate mores of business and yet forming a part of an overall business case (see also Bebbington *et al.* 2008; Burritt and Schaltegger 2010).

Another widely accepted motive for sustainability reporting is that it is a way of assisting companies in **managing threats to organisational legitimacy** (Deegan 2002). The link between sustainability reporting and the establishment, maintenance or repair of legitimacy has been investigated in a large body of accounting research (e.g. Milne and Patten 2002; Neu *et al.* 1998; O'Donovan 2002).

Several researchers (e.g. Milne *et al.* 2009; Adams and Frost 2006; Deegan and Rankin 1996; Neu *et al.* 1998; O'Donovan 2002; Wiseman 1982) have noted a potential lack of relationship between environmental and social disclosure and performance. The so-called '**performance–portrayal gap**' (Adams 2004) reflects a way to measure the level of accountability of organisations by comparing a company's ethical, social and environmental performance disclosures with information obtained on the company's performance from other sources. This concept has been used to demonstrate that reporting is likely to assist management both in controlling the perceptions of stakeholders and in seeking legitimacy and/or reputation rather than in enhancing stakeholder accountability for the real impact of companies' activities on society. Concern about the predominance of the business case perspective has thus been raised, deflecting attention from social change and current problems to be addressed in sustainability reports to the benefit of increased corporate reputation of powerful elites that steer society in a direction that reinforces their own dominance (Welford 1998; see also Brown and Fraser 2006; Cooper and Owen 2007).

To confront managerial capture of the social and environmental agenda and to reveal possible contradictions between a company's self-presentation, on the one hand, and stakeholder perspectives, on the other, the concept of **shadow reporting** has been put forward (Gray *et al.* 1997; Dey 2007). Shadow accounting can be viewed as a technology that collects and compiles, makes visible, represents and communicates evidence from external sources including newspaper articles, NGO (non-governmental organisation) reports, direct testaments from workers, ex-employees, trade unions, suppliers, public pollution registers, etc., in order to reveal contradictions between what companies disclose in their corporate reports and what they suppress, problematises companies' activities and provides additional insights into environmental and social impacts associated with these activities (Dey *et al.* 2011). It is important to note that such corporate shadow accounting can be understood as an attempt to challenge corporate reporting and move away from an organisation-centred perspective of sustainability reporting through the use of independent but not necessarily objective sources (Dey *et al.* 2011).

Some problem areas

In addition to the rhetoric of sustainability and the performance–portrayal gap addressed in the previous section, reporting on sustainability is associated with further problems. First, sustainable development is a **contested concept**. Its meaning can vary according to the context in which business operates and is dynamic in that its meaning, application and use has changed over time. This makes recording and reporting on sustainability difficult. The fact that it overlaps with other concepts (such as 'corporate social responsibility' or 'corporate citizenship') adds to this complexity, and the fairly fast and often changing terminology applied to non- or extra-financial reporting initiatives is equally unhelpful. Owen and O'Dwyer (2008) see a tendency for 'corporate responsibility' to displace 'sustainability' and 'social and environmental' while, more recently, 'environmental, social and governance' seems to have become the term of choice (UNEP *et al.* 2010).

Another problem related to the concept of sustainable development is reflected in the observation that sustainability reports often focus on *performance* measurement (e.g. the amount of waste water and air emissions) and leave out the *impacts* of corporate activities (e.g. information about the condition of the surrounding environment of the organisation) which can be more material to stakeholders than the usually more narrowly defined performance aspects (Herzig *et al.* 2011). Is the legal corporation perhaps the **wrong entity** to report on sustainability and demonstrate accountability for material social and environmental impacts? As Gray (2006a: 73) states, 'precise, reliable statements of organisations' sustainability are oxymorons. Sustainability is a planetary, perhaps regional, certainly spatial concept and its application at the organisational level is difficult at best.' An interesting alternative approach in this regard is presented by the Italian reporting concept of 'bilancio sociale territoriale', which aims to integrate various protagonists within a region ('territoriale') and reflects a commitment to report on impacts more broadly.

Sustainability reports have also been criticised for being non-specific, because they are aimed at a diffuse and excessively wide group of potential readers. The **lack of target group orientation** is associated with the risk of creating an information overload. The term 'carpet bombing syndrome' (SustainAbility and UNEP 2002) illustrates the fact that some companies have 'flooded' their readers with increasingly extensive sustainability reports—noted by some, but in practice mostly read by only a few. In addition to that, environmental, social and economic aspects of organisational activities have so far been considered primarily in an additive, rather than integrative manner in reports—failing to recognise and mention possible and actual conflicts and challenges embodied in companies' approach to sustainability (Gray 2006b; Herzig and Godemann 2010).

Although guidance on managing the reporting and stakeholder engagement process is given through guidelines and standards published by various national and international bodies (in the UNEP *et al.* 2010 study in 30 selected countries a total of 50 standards, codes and guidelines with some form of voluntary sustainability-related reporting guidance have been identified), Adams and Narayanan (2007) stress that these documents differ in terms of the extent to which they are concerned with the interest of business and the views and needs of a broad range of stakeholders. There remains a **tension between using reporting guidelines as a legitimating exercise** (to report the minimum required in such guidelines) and demonstrating accountability for views and needs of a broad range of stakeholders. Given that some guidelines focus on the needs of business and prescribe report content at the expense of concern with processes of stakeholder engagement, they conclude that 'without mandatory reporting guidelines focusing on processes of reporting and governance structures, some companies will continue to produce reports which leave out impacts which are material to key stakeholder groups' (Adams and Narayanan 2007: 83).

For many years, there has been a lively debate about the role governments should play in sustainability reporting. Some researchers have called for governments to put in place at least a **minimal regulatory**

framework in order to overcome the incompleteness of voluntary non-financial reporting and the reluctance of a vast majority of companies to make any kind of sustainability disclosure (among others, this include a large number of medium-sized, non-listed enterprises). This would prevent companies from conveying a misleading view of their activities and seeking to manage public impressions in their own interest through the provision of false information (Adams and Narayanan 2007; Gray 2006b). In contrast, sceptics have often questioned whether regulations (alone) can have a significant impact on both corporate accountability and the quality of sustainability information published in reports (Owen *et al.* 1997; Schaltegger 1997), or stressed that command and control regulation may not only be costly but also stifle innovation (Buhr 2007). Concern has been raised about a '**too simplistic view**, according to which the regulation of environmental reporting would prevent all the short-comings of voluntary environmental disclosures' (Larrinaga *et al.* 2002: 737). In their analysis of the Spanish environmental disclosure standard, Larrinaga *et al.* (2002) conclude that at a minimum more participation in the form of discursive dialogue is needed for the development of regulation and the effective enforcement of legislation (see also Owen and O'Dwyer 2008). In recent years, **smart regulations** have become more prominent, and consider voluntary and mandatory reporting to be a spectrum rather than conflicting positions, and that regulations (by a variety of institutional bodies such as governments, accounting regulators or securities regulators) are used to best effect when designed as complementary approaches which enhance the sharing of relevant information (Buhr 2007).

Other concerns associated with sustainability reporting include the limited comparability of ecological and social performance information published in sustainability reports (resulting from data collection and presentation practices which can vary over time or between companies), a low quality of data published in reports (e.g. due to a lack of measurement capability), and the limited contribution that current assurance practices in sustainability reporting can make to promoting greater transparency and true accountability to the stakeholders (due to ambiguities and inconsistencies in current approaches to sustainability assurance, e.g. independence and degree of thoroughness of audits) (see Owen and O'Dwyer 2008; O'Dwyer 2011).

General introduction to the seminars

The three seminars can be undertaken separately or as a series of seminars in the order presented below. In the following sections, you will find general information about the role-play, activities and a brief of the case company (relevant for all seminars), before more specific instructions for each seminar are given. While you can work on the activities of Seminars 1 and 2 using the materials given in the textbook and the *Unilever Sustainable Living Plan: Progress Report 2012* (Unilever 2012), Seminar 3 includes an online evaluation of Unilever's sustainability website and thus should be carried out in a computer laboratory or with the help of laptops/tablets.

Role-play and activities

Food Business Reform is a sustainability consulting company whose mission is to constructively engage with companies operating in the food sector with the aim of encouraging greater levels of social responsibility, transparency and accountability. Your team has been retained to advise Unilever on their reporting aspects as part of their ongoing contract between Unilever and Food Business Reform.

Your team's task is to critically assess the extent to which Unilever's SLP (*Sustainable Living Plan*) report and the company's website succeed in fully demonstrating transparency and accountability for the company's impact in terms of promoting sustainable development.

Company background

A common household name in the 21st century, Unilever was formed in the 1930s by the merger of its founding companies, which in turn had their origins in the late 18th century. Most of us recognise Unilever as a major player within the FMCG (fast-moving consumer goods) sector, with over 400 different products ranging from soaps and hygiene products to food products. Familiar brands such as Dove, Pond's, Knorr, Pureit and Axe that are all part of a portfolio available to a wide range of customers globally.

During its 80-year journey, Unilever has witnessed several negative world events including the Great Depression, the Second World War and the hard economic environments of the 1970s marked by rising inflation. Nonetheless, with the expansion of the world economy and the rise in the standard of living in Western Europe during the late 1950s, alongside the emergence of new opportunities in other parts of the world slowly welcoming economic reforms, Unilever made steady progress through acquisitions and new market entries, and continued to extend its product portfolios until the late 1970s. From the 1980s to the late 1990s, however, owing to a change in strategy and emphasis placed on core products in its portfolio, Unilever gradually withdrew most of its existing product ranges. With the advent of the 21st century, Unilever's priorities have been to focus on the uncertainties of the modern world that have become the 'new normal', in addition to meeting the needs of the modern world consumer base (Unilever 2012: 4).

To account for the uncertainties and pressures emanating from social, environmental and economic issues of the modern world, Unilever developed 'the Compass' in 2009 that shapes their business strategy and model supplemented by the SLP in 2010. The Compass and the SLP drive the activities shaped around Unilever's vision and purpose statements:

- **Unilever vision statement**: 'Double the size of the business, whilst reducing our environmental footprint and increasing our positive social impact. We will lead for responsible growth, inspiring people to take small everyday actions that will add up to a big difference. We will grow by winning shares and building markets everywhere.' (Unilever 2012)

- **Unilever purpose statement**: 'To make sustainable living commonplace. We work to create a better future every day, with brands and services that help people feel good, look good and get more out of life. Our first priority is to our consumers—then customers, employees, suppliers and communities. When we fulfil our responsibilities to them, we believe that our shareholders will be rewarded.' (Unilever 2012)

Unilever uses both the web platform and printed reports to communicate their sustainability commitments to a wide range of stakeholders. Links to the *Unilever Sustainable Living Plan: Progress Report 2012* (Unilever 2012) and the corresponding online information are provided in the seminar material.

Suggested seminars

Seminar 1: Sustainability reporting principles

This chapter has introduced the GRI G4 guidelines as one of the most generally accepted and widely applied reporting frameworks. Using the principles on reporting content and quality presented in Table 1, students are asked to evaluate how Unilever addresses the reporting principles of the GRI.

Activity 1 (30 minutes)

Work in small groups and critically examine the content of the *Unilever Sustainable Living Plan: Progress Report 2012* (printed copy or PDF from http://unilever.com/images/USLP-Progress-Report-2012-FI_tcm13-352007.pdf) according to the principles described above. Each group concentrates on two or three of the principles and presents its results to the class. Discuss to what extent the report accommodates the ten principles.

Activity 2 (15 minutes)

Did you encounter any challenges when evaluating the report according to the principles? Which principles, if at all, did you find more difficult to assess than others?

Activity 3 (10 minutes)

Can you imagine any tensions or challenges which companies such as Unilever might face when trying to follow all principles?

Table 1: G4 reporting principles of the GRI.

Report aspect	Principle	Explanation and examples (questions to verify if principles have been followed)
Content	Stakeholder inclusiveness	The organisation should identify its stakeholders, and explain how it has responded to their reasonable expectations and interests. Examples: Does the report contain information on the stakeholder engagement process, if any? Are the process and outcomes from the engagement explained? Does the report explain whom the organisation considers as stakeholders and report on how it responds to their expectations and interests?
	Sustainability context	The report should present the organisation's performance in the wider context of sustainability. Examples: Has the organisation reported on how its sustainability engagements relate to its organisational strategic contexts, policies, risks and uncertainties in the longer term? Is there an attempt made to relate organisational sustainability performance or impact to the broader sustainability context— at local, regional or national levels?
	Materiality	The report should cover aspects that: • Reflect the organisation's significant economic, environmental and social impacts; or • Substantively influence the assessments and decisions of stakeholders Examples: Does the report focus on those opportunities and risks which are most important to stakeholders, the economy, environment and society, or to the reporting organisation (i.e. consider those economic, environmental and social impacts that cross a threshold in affecting the ability to meet the needs of the present without compromising the needs of future generations)?
	Completeness	The report should include coverage of material aspects and their boundaries, sufficient to reflect significant economic, environmental and social impacts, and to enable stakeholders to assess the organisation's performance in the reporting period. Examples: Does the report contain significant material events that occurred both internally and externally during the reporting period for all entities within the organisation? Does it specify any future uncertainties or foreseeable events that might occur in the short or long term?

(continued…)

Report aspect	Principle	Explanation and examples (questions to verify if principles have been followed)
Quality	Balance	The report should reflect positive and negative aspects of the organisation's performance to enable a reasoned assessment of overall performance. Examples: Has the report provided an unbiased view of the organisation's performance and impact? Are there any omissions of unfavourable or negative aspects of the organisation's performance and impact?
	Comparability	The organisation should select, compile and report information consistently. The reported information should be presented in a manner that enables stakeholders to analyse changes in the organisation's performance over time, and that could support analysis relative to other organisations. Examples: Is there sufficient data or information to compare the organisation's current performance with its past performances? Is it possible to gauge the performance against the objectives set out?
	Accuracy	The reported information should be sufficiently accurate and detailed for stakeholders to assess the organisation's performance. Examples: Does the report indicate how the data or information reported has been obtained, i.e. explains the data-gathering process? Does it indicate if the data is actual or estimated?
	Timeliness	The organisation should report on a regular schedule so that information is available in time for stakeholders to make informed decisions. Examples: Does the report indicate the time-frame it relates to? Are the key indicators or events discussed in the report recent and aligned to the reporting period? Is the reporting schedule consistent and regular?
	Clarity	The organisation should make information available in a manner that is understandable and accessible to stakeholders using the report. Examples: Does the report contain significant, easily accessible and understandable information for stakeholders who are aware of the organisation's activities to make decisions?
	Reliability	The organisation should gather, record, compile, analyse and disclose information and processes used in the preparation of a report in a way that they can be subject to examination and that establishes the quality and materiality of the information. Example: Is there an assurance statement?

Compiled from the guideline available at https://www.globalreporting.org/resourcelibrary/GRIG4-Part1-Reporting-Principles-and-Standard-Disclosures.pdf.

Seminar 2: Comparing external views with a company's self-presentation on sustainability

As part of your assessment of the report's transparency, your consulting team has conducted an online search for external media coverage about Unilever and how impacts associated with its activities are perceived by stakeholders. The coverage includes reports about the company or the sector published by critical stakeholder groups such as NGOs or consumer or trade associations, and similar documents such as newspaper articles or contributions to social media (e.g. blogs). You have found the following information:

1. **An online petition on Change.org** (www.change.org/petitions/unilever-stop-using-unsustainable-palm-oil)

Focus: raw materials, biodiversity

'Palm oil is produced by the slashing and burning of rainforests. This is driving many species, including orangutans, close to extinction. It is also the source of huge amounts of carbon emissions … Unilever, please consider using sustainable ingredients. Although perhaps more expensive for you, they are much better for our planet!' (the petitioner).

'To:
Paul Polman, CEO
Unilever, Media Relations
   I am giving up Unilever products and will spread the word so that others can be informed and will also stop buying products made with palm oil. Unilever needs to use sustainable palm oil immediately. This cannot wait years, things need to change and it has to happen now!
   Sincerely,

[Your name]'

2.   Interview with a Business and Community Foundation employee (India) (www.civilsocietyonline.com/pages/Details.aspx?180)

Focus: health and safety, environmental damage, supply chain, workplace, sustainable living

'Earlier this year in Delhi, Hindustan Unilever (HUL) presented a progress report under the Unilever Sustainable Living Plan. The audience was specially invited and consisted of reporters, NGOs and representatives of other companies ... HUL is remembered here for causing mercury poisoning. In 2001 HUL's thermometer factory at Kodaikanal, in Tamil Nadu, dumped 7.4 tonnes of glass waste contaminated with mercury behind its factory near the Pambar Shola forest. Campaigns by Greenpeace and the Palni Hills Conservation Council resulted in the factory being closed.'

'Amita Joseph of the Business and Community Foundation (BCF), which works closely with managements across industries, says while HUL is ambitious about its business targets, it is surprisingly modest when it comes to its social concerns. It talks about a few hundred villages here and a few hundred farmers there ... Joseph worries that the mercury pollution and its aftermath does not find mention in HUL's sustainability report. Joseph attended the presentation on the report and raised several questions. She says the answers she has got from the HUL management are either vague or show that very little is being done.'

'While sales and profits have soared, Hindustan Unilever remains rather modest and unambitious with regard to water use, labelling, workplace injuries, livelihood enhancement and agricultural outreach.'

'Well, given the fact that most of the company's products—soaps, shampoos, detergents—are water dependent, Unilever's Vitality Foundation expects to reach only 180 villages that too by 2015. In 2010 it provided free drip irrigation to just 25 farmers with one acre each! These farmers work with their suppliers. By 2015, Unilever aims to reach drip irrigation to 1,000 farmers in a country that has 550 million farmers.'

'NGOs do better. A single NGO I know reaches 1,200 villages with 75 mobile health units. Unilever talks of reaching 800 farmers with five mobile health clinics. Compared with their ambitious business targets their CSR [corporate social responsibility] targets are really rather modest.'

'The company talks about optimizing distance travel, increasing the height of trucks so that they can carry heavier loads. This, in a country where overloading causes serious road accidents. There is no strategy for reducing pollution or road accidents by training drivers. They don't use the railways for transportation.'

'I did ask them for more details on this glorified women's initiative. I wanted to know how much the women earned. Nitin Paranjpe (HUL's CEO and managing director) replied that each Shakti Amma earned INR1,000. That's all! This in a company where 40% of their products are consumed in the "fast growing markets of rural India", and their CEO is one of the highest paid with a salary of INR7.5 crore'.

'In Kodaikanal the company refuses to take full responsibility for remediation of the contaminated site. In Dharwad, the illegal closure of its factory and dismissal of workers continues to simmer. In Doomdooma at its tea estate it tried to smash the workers' union. All these issues should have been made clear in the report.'

3. **Trade Union Perspective** (www.foodmanufacture.co.uk/
    Business-News/Unilever-repels-attack-on-job-cuts)

Focus: employment

'Unilever has defended itself against trades union claims its green business strategy may be sustainable for profits, but not for jobs.' An industrial relations outfit (Unilever Euro Works Council) claims that Unilever has cut as many as 70,000 jobs over the last decade in Europe. The outfit further pointed out the closure of eight Europe-based factories since 2010.

4. **Online News Article** (www.theguardian.com/sustainable-business/
    blog/unilever-labour-practices-vietnam-oxfam-report)

Focus: supply chain, workplace

- 'Wages insufficient to make savings or support dependants, with instances of workers unable to eat adequate diets or afford to keep children in school.

- Suppliers and managers unclear about Unilever's codes of conduct, in some cases only accessible in English.

- Workers too scared to voice grievances or engage in freedom of association.

- Factory workers employed by a third party on much poorer terms and conditions.

- Suppliers with employees working illegal overtime hours.'

'Any such labour issues could be dealt with by a grievance hotline or the trade union. However, neither were used nor trusted. There is only one state-run trade union in Vietnam, and it is dominated by senior managers. Similarly, the workers feared that the grievance hotline would simply go straight to the management and put their job at risk. "We dare not raise our voice through the union leaders because they are paid by the company, they are the company's people," said one worker. Conditions for those employed temporarily, by a third party, or by suppliers, were even worse. Globally, the number of people directly employed by Unilever decreased by nearly a half (45%) from 295,000 employees to 164,000 between 2000 and 2009. However, the report states: "The work of 131,000 people did not disappear. According to Unilever, in 2009 this work was being done instead by 86,000 people that were outsourced and/or under temporary contracts." ... At one supplier, employees worked four hours' overtime a day, six days a week, for 10 months: well in excess of a legal national limit of 200 hours a year. Another said that offering excessive overtime gave it a competitive advantage.'

Activity 1 (25–30 minutes)

Compare and contrast the information above with the environmental and social accounts provided by Unilever in *Unilever Sustainable Living Plan: Progress Report 2012*. Discuss to what extent the company's self-presentation covers the issues raised by various stakeholders. How does your appraisal influence your evaluation of the extent to which Unilever succeeds in demonstrating transparency and accountability for the company's impact in terms of promoting sustainable development?

Activity 2 (20–25 minutes)

If you have discovered a divergence between Unilever's reporting practice and the views and statements of external stakeholders, what could be the reasons for this?

Additional activity for participants who have attended Seminar 1 (10 minutes)

Are the materials above helpful when evaluating the extent to which Unilever follows the GRI principles of reporting quality and content? If yes, how?

Seminar 3: The use of the Internet for reporting on sustainability issues (computer laboratory session)

You have advised Unilever on their sustainability reporting practice and they have welcomed your critical evaluation of the *Unilever Sustainable Living Plan: Progress Report 2012*. They believe that they can benefit from further exploration of the strengths and weaknesses of their approach to reporting and have assigned a new task to you. Given the increased importance attributed to Internet-based technologies for sustainability disclosure, Unilever wants to review the way in which they use the Internet for improved (i) provision, (ii) accessibility and (iii) comprehensibility of sustainability information as well as for (iv) more dialogue-orientated approaches to sustainability reporting.

Activity 1 (25 minutes)

Work in groups. Each group should critically examine the Unilever sustainability website (http://unilever.com/sustainable-living/) in one of the four dimensions detailed earlier in the chapter—provision, accessibility, comprehensibility and dialogue—by which the Internet-based reporting system can stand out against the print-based reporting system. Use the list of criteria presented in Table 2 and share your findings with the class. Which areas are covered well and which are not? Suggest the use of Internet features that you think would aid one's understanding and evaluation of the sustainability performance of the company.

Table 2: Criteria for evaluating Unilever's sustainability website.

A. Provision of sustainability information

A.1 Download service for sustainability report(s)

Level	Download service for one or more sustainability report(s) (PDF)	Unilever score
0	No download service	
1	Download service for current sustainability report	
2	Additional download option for previous sustainability report(s)	

A.2 Archive of additional sustainability information

Level	Archive which allows additional sustainability information (e.g. brochures, code of ethics, previous sustainability websites) to be downloaded	Unilever score
0	No archive function	
1	Archive of sustainability information (<12 months)	
2	Archive of sustainability information (>12 months)	

A.3 Updates of sustainability information

Level	Updates of sustainability information	Unilever score
0	No updates of sustainability information or update >6 months	
1	Last update(s) of sustainability information within 4–6 months	
2	Last update(s) within <3 months	

A.4 Sustainability newsletter/e-mail notification

Level	Newsletter and/or e-mail notification on sustainability issues	Unilever score
0	No newsletter or e-mail notification on sustainability issues	
1	E-mail notification (e.g. on publication of a sustainability report)	
2	Newsletter with sustainability information (standardised or adaptable to specific interests of stakeholders)	

B. Accessibility of sustainability information

B.1 Links from the company's homepage to the sustainability area ('sustainability gateway')

Level	Number of clicks required to get from the company's homepage to the sustainability area of the company website	Unilever score
0	Sustainability is not mentioned on the company's homepage or it needs >4 clicks	
1	2–3 clicks	
2	1 click	

B.2 Links from the sustainability report to the company's sustainability website

Level	The way in which the reader of a sustainability report (print/PDF) is guided towards additional sustainability information on the company website	Unilever score
0	No link made to the company website	
1	General link given to the sustainability area of the company website	
2	Specific (context-sensitive) links given to the places where additional sustainability information can be found on the company website	

(continued…)

B.3 Links from the annual report to the company's sustainability website

Level	The way in which the reader of an annual report (print/PDF) is guided towards additional sustainability information on the company website	Unilever score
0	No link made to the company website	
1	General link given to the sustainability area of the company website	
2	Specific (context-sensitive) links given to the places where additional sustainability information can be found on the company website	

B.4 Search function

Level	Function to search for sustainability information on the company website and/or specifically in the sustainability area	Unilever score
0	No search function available	
1	Search function available but cannot include or exclude the content of certain type of documents (e.g. PDFs)	
2	Search function also allows the inclusion or exclusion of the content of certain type of documents (e.g. PDFs)	

B.5 Site map

Level	Extent to which the site map contains sustainability information	Unilever score
0	No site map available	
1	Sustainability is mentioned in the site map of the company website, but without itemisation	
2	Site map (either on the company website or in the sustainability area of the company website) includes itemised levels of sustainability	

B.6 Navigation through sustainability indices

Level	Sustainability indices which display sustainability terms and concepts, and connect these to the corresponding information on the company website via hyperlinks	Unilever score
0	No index available	
1	Sustainability index available with terms and concepts defined by the company (key word index)	
2	Use of a sustainability index from an external organisation (e.g. GRI Index)	

C. Comprehensibility of sustainability information

C.1 Internal links

Level	Hyperlinks within the sustainability area of the company website and/or to other areas of the company website (e.g. investor relations, products)	Unilever score
0	No internal hyperlinks	
1	Internal hyperlinks are made but only in some instances	
2	Internal hyperlinks are made in most instances	

C.2 External links

Level	Hyperlinks in the sustainability area of the company website which guide users to external websites	Unilever score
0	No hyperlinks to external sources and organisations related to sustainability	
1	Hyperlinks to external sources and organisations related to sustainability are made but only in some instances	
2	Hyperlinks to external sources and organisations related to sustainability are made in most instances	

C.3 Sustainability glossary

Level	Glossary which explains sustainability terms	Unilever score
0	No sustainability glossary	
1	Sustainability glossary can be reached indirectly (>1 click)	
2	Sustainability glossary can be reached from each page and/or contains hyperlinks to the place in which the term is found (with 1 click)	

C.4 Use of multimedia

Level	Use of multimedia elements to elaborate on sustainability issues	Unilever score
0	No use of multimedia	
1	Static pictures	
2	Animation, video or audio elements, interactive tools	

(continued…)

C.5 Display of sustainability data

Level	Static or adaptable display of sustainability data	Unilever score
0	No display of sustainability data	
1	Static display of sustainability data	
2	Interactive (adaptable) display of sustainability data (e.g. with regard to type of indicator or time-frame)	

D. Sustainability online dialogue

D.1 Contact possibility

Level	Possibility of contacting people responsible for sustainability-related topics	Unilever score
0	No contact possibility	
1	Non-personal contact (e.g. anonymous contact form or e-mail address)	
2	Personal contact (named people for general request regarding sustainability or for specific sustainability topics)	

D.2 Feedback possibility

Level	Possibility of providing feedback on sustainability-related aspects	Unilever score
0	No feedback possibility	
1	Simple feedback possibility (e.g. polls with one question)	
2	Extensive feedback possibility (e.g. online survey)	

D.3 Dialogue offerings on the company website

Level	Dialogue offerings between stakeholders and the company (or among stakeholders themselves)	Unilever score
0	No dialogue offerings	
1	Discussion forums, chats or blogs without specific topics	
2	Topic-specific discussion forums, chats or blogs	

D.4 Use of social media

Level	Extent to which social media is used to communicate about sustainability issues	Unilever score
0	No use of social media	
1	Use of social media tools to communicate about sustainability in general	
2	Use of social media tools to communicate about specific sustainability topics	

Adapted from Herzig and Godemann (2010).

Activity 2 (10–15 minutes)

The list of criteria is not meant to be exclusive and comprehensive. Can you think of any additional criteria? Please suggest at least one additional criterion for each of the four dimensions. Does Unilever use this feature that you have suggested or have you encountered the use of this technology on any other (sustainability) website before?

Activity 3 (10–15 minutes)

Note that the reporting principles of the GRI are expected to help in defining what should be included in the sustainability report and attaining an appropriate level of reporting quality. How do you think the Internet can complement or potentially compromise these objectives? Reflect on individual principles.

Additional activity for participants who have attended Seminar 2 (10 minutes)

In Seminar 2, we discussed gaps between, on the one hand, Unilever's self-presentation on sustainability and, on the other, statements and viewpoints of external stakeholders. What role does or could the Internet play in this regard?

Additional teaching material and ideas

1. Please refer to the comments made in the short video which can be found at: http://bcove.me/kb9puj3b. In what ways do you think that sustainability reporting may enhance transparency both within the organisation and externally? Do you think the benefits derived from transparency suggested in the interview can be truly achieved by sustainability reporting? You may want to refer to the concept of shadow reporting and the critique of the performance–portrayal gap introduced in this chapter.

2. Small and medium-sized enterprises (SMEs) constitute a large part of our economies and—in total—account for much of businesses' social and environmental effects. Please reflect on the specific characteristics of SMEs and what that might mean for the sustainability reporting practices of these types of organisations. Compare the G4 guidelines with the *High 5!* handbook which was specifically developed for SMEs. How do they differ from each other?
   a. **GRI G4 guidelines:** https://www.globalreporting.org/reporting/g4/Pages/default.aspx
   b. *High 5!*: www.triple-innova.de/images/stories/publications_eng/high5_final.pdf

3. As multinational companies operate within and across various national boundaries characterised by differences in cultural, socio-economic and political contexts requiring diverse approaches to engage in sustainability, how (if at all) is it possible to incorporate and consider such differences in a consolidated global sustainability report? Will such an attempt not result in leaving out national-level or even significant local-level issues concerning sustainability and stakeholder needs, i.e. compromising accountability to local stakeholders?

4. This chapter has argued that the use of the Internet for sustainability reporting will increase in relevance. In practice, reporting strategies of companies include various combinations of print and Internet or exclusively focus on one of the two. Which strategy would work most effectively from your point of view?

5. The conflation of corporate governance, financial and sustainability reporting has recently been reinforced by the move towards IR. Watch the following short videos and make notes on aspects that you believe are important:

    a. http://bcove.me/tooa78tk

    b. www.bancaforte.it/video/le-sfide-dell-and-039-integrated-reporting-RB61380n

    c. http://bcove.me/fun23x4u

    d. http://bcove.me/2emm7p7y

    Working in small groups, discuss the following: Is there a need for IR or is it just another reporting fad? Will IR enhance the value of reporting for both internal and external stakeholder needs? If at all, do you find any merit of IR in permitting stakeholders to better appraise how sustainable an organisation is both financially and otherwise? Lastly, will the IR initiative weaken the progress of GRI or other recognised frameworks?

Further reading

Godemann, J., and G. Michelsen (eds.) (2011) *Sustainability Communication. Interdisciplinary Perspectives and Theoretical Foundations* (Dordrecht, Netherlands: Springer).

> This handbook gives a broad overview of theoretical frameworks and methods associated with the concepts of sustainability communication and reporting. These refer to, for example, sociological and psychological aspects, media and communication theories as well as constructivism. In the last part of the handbook, 'Practice of Sustainability Communication', links to climate change and biodiversity communication, sustainable consumption and stakeholder participation are introduced and explained.

Gray, R.H., C. Adams and D. Owen (eds.) (2014) *Accountability, Social Responsibility and Sustainability: Accounting for Society and the Environment* (Upper Saddle River, NJ: Pearson).

> This textbook is a must for students who want to gain comprehensive views on the developments in accountability, social responsibility and sustainability theories and practices and their relevance for socio-environmental and financial issues. This in-depth and nuanced guide to the topic represents a critical account of the tensions between the way in which organisations are controlled and their greater responsibility and accountability to society.

Hopwood, A., J. Unerman and J. Fries (eds.) (2010) *Accounting for Sustainability: Practical Insights* (London: Routledge).

> This book provides a great starting point for students who intend to gain rich insights on the different tools and techniques that companies use to advance their sustainability agenda and embed sustainability in their decision-making and reporting. The book features case studies from eight organisations including HSBC, Sainsbury's, Novo Nordisk and BT, providing practical guidance to professionals and students alike.

Owen, D., and B. O'Dwyer (2008) 'Corporate Social Responsibility: The Reporting and Assurance Dimension', in A. Crane, D. Matten, A. McWiliams, J. Moon and D. Siegel (eds.), *The Oxford Handbook of Corporate Social Responsibility* (Oxford, UK: Oxford University Press): 384-409.

> This book chapter provides an overview of corporate social and environmental reporting while at the same time presenting a critical evaluation of corporate reporting practice. The chapter also offers a critical account of the contribution assurance can make to enhanced transparency and true accountability to stakeholders of companies.

Schaltegger, S., M. Bennett and R. Burritt (eds.) (2006) *Sustainability Accounting and Reporting* (Dordrecht, Netherlands: Springer).

> This compilation of papers offers an exploration of conceptual developments and applied cases in the area of sustainability accounting and reporting. In Part 3 of the book you will find a selection of contributions examining external accounting frameworks and benchmarking. This book also offers valuable insights into links between strategy, measurement and information management, and between accounting and reporting.

Songini, L., A. Pistoni and C. Herzig (eds.) (2013) *Accounting and Control for Sustainability*, Studies in Managerial and Financial Accounting, vol. 26 (Bingley, UK: Emerald Publishing).

> The edited book explores new challenges and prospects in sustainability accounting research. Topics include the disclosure practice of SMEs, determinants of corporate social responsibility disclosure, and water accounting and accountability.

Unerman, J., J. Bebbington and B. O'Dwyer (eds.) (2014) *Sustainability Accounting and Accountability*, 2nd edn (London: Routledge).

> This authoritative textbook covers the key subject areas and issues currently under discussion in the field of sustainability accounting and reporting. Areas examined include, for example, the assurance of sustainability reports, silent and shadow reports, integrated reporting, and sustainability reporting in the public sector. Written by internationally renowned authorities, this book provides probably at present the most comprehensive and contemporary account of the theory and practice of sustainability reporting.

References

Adams, C. (2004) 'The Ethical, Social and Environmental Reporting–Performance Portrayal Gap', *Accounting, Auditing & Accountability Journal* 17.5: 731-57.

Adams, C., and G. Frost (2006) 'Accessibility and Functionality of the Corporate Web Site: Implications for Sustainability Reporting', *Business Strategy and the Environment* 15: 275-87.

Adams, C., and V. Narayanan (2007) 'The "Standardization" of Sustainability Reporting', in J. Unerman, J. Bebbington, and B. O'Dwyer (eds.), *Sustainability Accounting and Accountability* (London: Routledge): 70-85.

Bebbington, J., C. Larrinaga, and J.M. Moneva (2008) 'Corporate Social Reporting and Reputation Risk Management', *Accounting, Auditing and Accountability Journal* 21: 337-61.

BMU (Bundesumweltministerium) [German Federal Ministry for the Environment] (2007) *EMAS: Von der Umwelterklärung zum Nachhaltigkeitsbericht* [EMAS: From the Environmental Statement to the Sustainability Report] (only available in German; Berlin, Germany: BMU).

Brown, J., and M. Fraser (2006) 'Approaches and Perspectives in Social and Environmental Accounting: An Overview of the Conceptual Landscape', *Business Strategy and the Environment* 15.2: 103-17.

Buhr, N. (2007) 'Histories of and Rationales for Sustainability Reporting', in J. Unerman, J. Bebbington and B. O'Dwyer (eds.), *Sustainability Accounting and Accountability* (London: Routledge): 57-69.

Burritt, R.L., and S. Schaltegger (2010) 'Sustainability Accounting and Reporting: Fad or Trend?', *Accounting, Auditing and Accountability Journal* 23.7: 829-46.

Cooper, S.M., and D.L. Owen (2007) 'Corporate Social Reporting and Stakeholder Accountability: The Missing Link', *Accounting, Organizations and Society* 32.7–8: 649-67.

Deegan, C. (2002) 'The Legitimising Effect of Social and Environmental Disclosures: A Theoretical Foundation', *Accounting, Auditing and Accountability Journal* 15: 282-311.

Deegan, C., and M. Rankin (1996) 'Do Australian Companies Report Environmental News Objectively? An Analysis of Environmental Disclosures by Firms Prosecuted Successfully by the Environmental Protection Authority', *Accounting, Auditing and Accountability Journal* 9.2: 50-67.

Dey, C. (2007) 'Developing Silent and Shadow Accounts', in J. Unerman, J. Bebbington and B. O'Dwyer (eds.), *Sustainability Accounting and Accountability* (London: Routledge): 307-26.

Dey, C., S. Russell and I. Thomson (2011) 'Exploring the Potential of Shadow Accounts in Problematising Institutional Conduct', in S. Osbourne and A.

Ball (eds.), *Social Accounting and Public Management: Accountability for the Common Good* (Abingdon, UK: Routledge): 64-75.

Dierkes, M., and B. Antal (1985) 'The Usefulness and Use of Social Reporting Information', *Accounting, Organizations and Society* 10: 29-34.

EC (European Commission) (2013) *Proposal for a Directive of the European Parliament and of the Council Amending Council Directives 78/660/EEC and 83/349/EEC as Regards Disclosure of Non-Financial and Diversity Information by Certain Large Companies and Groups*, http://eur-lex.europa.eu/legal content/EN/TXT/?uri=CELEX:52013PC0207, accessed 4 April 2014.

—— (2014) *Disclosure of Non-Financial Information by Certain Large Companies: European Parliament and Council Reach Agreement on Commission Proposal to Improve Transparency*, http://europa.eu/rapid/press-release_STATE-MENT-14-29_en.htm, accessed 4 April 2014.

Ernst & Young (2012) *How France's New Sustainability Reporting Law Impacts US Companies*, www.ey.com/Publication/vwLUAssets/Frances_sustainability_law_to_impact_US_companies/$FILE/How_Frances_new_sustainability_reporting_law.pdf, accessed 4 April 2014.

EU (European Union (2003) 'Directives 2003/51/EC of the European Parliament and of the Council of 18 June 2003 Amending Directives 78/660/EEC, 83/349/EEC, 86/635/EEC and 91/674/EEC on the Annual and Consolidated Accounts of Certain Types of Companies, Banks and Other Financial Institutions and Insurance Undertakings', *Official Journal of the European Union*, 17 July 2003: 16-22.

Godemann, J., and G. Michelsen (eds.) (2011) *Sustainability Communication. Interdisciplinary Perspectives and Theoretical Foundations* (Dordrecht, Netherlands: Springer).

Gray, R.H. (2006a) 'Does Sustainability Reporting Improve Corporate Behaviour? Wrong Question? Right Time?', *Accounting and Business Research* 36.1: 65-88.

—— (2006b) 'Social, Environmental and Sustainability Reporting and Organisational Value Creation? Whose Value? Whose Creation?', *Accounting, Auditing and Accountability Journal* 19: 793-819.

Gray, R., C. Dey, D. Owen and S. Zadek (1997) 'Struggling with the Praxis of Social Accounting: Stakeholders, Accountability, Audits and Procedures', *Accounting, Auditing and Accountability Journal* 10.3: 325-64.

Gray, R.H., C. Adams and D. Owen (eds.) (2014) *Accountability, Social Responsibility and Sustainability: Accounting for Society and the Environment* (Upper Saddle River, NJ: Pearson).

Guthrie, J., and L.D. Parker (1989) 'Corporate Social Reporting: Emerging Trends in Accountability and Theory', *Accounting and Business Research* 19: 343-52.

Hemmer, E. (1996) 'Sozialbilanzen. Das Scheitern einer gescheiterten Idee' [Social reporting. The Failure of a Failed Idea], *Arbeitgeber* 23: 796-800.

Herzig, C., and J. Godemann (2010) 'Internet-Supported Sustainability Reporting: Developments in Germany', *Management Research Review* 33: 1064-82.

Herzig, C., and S. Schaltegger (2011) 'Corporate Sustainability Reporting', in J. Godemann and G. Michelsen (eds.), *Sustainability Communication. Interdisciplinary Perspectives and Theoretical Foundations* (Dordrecht, Netherlands: Springer): 151-69.

Herzig, C., J. Moon, M. Halme and M. Kuisma (2011) 'Report of Company Self-Presentations', *FP7 CSR Impact Project*, http://csr-impact.eu/documents/documents-detail.html?documentid=4, accessed 4 April 2014.

Hopwood, A., J. Unerman and J. Fries (eds.) (2010) *Accounting for Sustainability: Practical Insights* (London: Routledge).

IIRC (International Integrated Reporting Council) (2013) *The International (IR) Framework*, www.theiirc.org/wp-content/uploads/2013/12/13-12-08-THE-INTERNATIONAL-IR-FRAMEWORK-2-1.pdf, accessed 5 April 2014).

Isenmann, R. (2005) 'Corporate Sustainability Reporting. A Case for the Internet', in L. Hilty, E. Seifert and R. Treibert (eds.), *Information Systems for Sustainable Development* (Hershey, PA: Idea Group): 164-212.

Kolk, A. (2004) 'A Decade of Sustainability Reporting: Developments and Significance', *International Journal for Environmental and Sustainable Development* 3: 51-64.

KPMG (2011) *KPMG International Survey of Corporate Responsibility Reporting 2011*, www.kpmg.com/Global/en/IssuesAndInsights/ArticlesPublications/corporate-responsibility/Documents/2011-survey.pdf, accessed 16 June 2014.

Larrinaga, C., F. Carrasco, C. Correa, F. Llena and J.M. Moneva (2002) 'Accountability and Accounting Regulation: The Case of the Spanish Environmental Disclosure Standard', *European Accounting Review* 11: 723-40.

Leipziger, D. (2010) *The Corporate Responsibility Code Book* (Sheffield, UK: Greenleaf Publishing).

Milne, M.J., and D.M. Patten (2002) 'Securing Organizational Legitimacy: An Experimental Decision Case Examining the Impact of Environmental Disclosures', *Accounting, Auditing and Accountability Journal* 15.3: 372-405.

Milne, M.J., H. Tregidga and S. Walton (2009) 'Words Not Actions! The Ideological Role of Sustainable Development Reporting', *Accounting, Auditing and Accountability Journal* 22.8: 1211-57.

Neu, D., H. Warsame and K. Pedwell (1998) 'Managing Public Impressions: Environmental Disclosures in Annual Reports', *Accounting, Organizations and Society* 23.3: 265-82.

O'Donovan, G. (2002) 'Environmental Disclosures in the Annual Report: Extending the Applicability and Predictive Power of Legitimacy Theory', *Accounting, Auditing and Accountability Journal* 15.3: 344-71.

O'Dwyer, B. (2011) 'The Case of Sustainability Assurance: Constructing a New Assurance Service', *Contemporary Accounting Research* 28.4: 1230-66.

Owen, D., and B. O'Dwyer (2008) 'Corporate Social Responsibility: The Reporting and Assurance Dimension', in A. Crane, D. Matten, A. McWiliams, J. Moon and D. Siegel (eds.), *The Oxford Handbook of Corporate Social Responsibility* (Oxford, UK: Oxford University Press): 384-409.

Owen, D., R.H. Gray and J. Bebbington (1997) 'Green Accounting: Cosmetic Irrelevance of Radical Agenda for Change', *Asia-Pacific Journal of Accounting* 4: 175-98.

Schaltegger, S. (1997) 'Information Costs, Quality of Information and Stakeholder Involvement', *Eco-Management and Auditing* (November 1997): 87-97.

Schaltegger, S., M. Bennett and R. Burritt (eds.) (2006) *Sustainability Accounting and Reporting* (Dordrecht, Netherlands: Springer).

Shell (1999) *The Shell Report 1999: People, Planet & Profits – An Act of Commitment* (London: Royal Dutch/Shell Group of Companies).

Songini, L., A. Pistoni and C. Herzig (eds.) (2013) *Accounting and Control for Sustainability*, Studies in Managerial and Financial Accounting, vol. 26 (Bingley, UK: Emerald Publishing).

Spence, C., and R.H. Gray (2007) *Social and Environmental Reporting and the Business Case Research Report 98* (London: Association of Chartered Certified Accountants).

SustainAbility and UNEP (2002) *Trust Us. The Global Reporters. 2002 Survey of Corporate Sustainability Reporting* (London: SustainAbility).

Unerman, J. (2007) 'Stakeholder Engagement and Dialogue', in J. Unerman, J. Bebbington and B. O'Dwyer (eds.), *Sustainability Accounting and Accountability* (London: Routledge): 86-103.

Unerman, J., and M. Bennett (2004) 'Increased Stakeholder Dialogue and the Internet: Towards Greater Corporate Accountability or Reinforcing Capitalist Hegemony?', *Accounting, Organizations and Society* 29: 685-707.

Unerman, J., J. Bebbington and B. O'Dwyer (eds.) (2014) *Sustainability Accounting and Accountability*, 2nd edn (London: Routledge).

Unilever (2012) *Unilever Sustainable Living Plan: Progress Report 2012*, http://unilever.com/images/USLP-Progress-Report-2012-FI_tcm13-352007.pdf, accessed 15 June 2014.

UNEP (UN Environment Programme), KPMG Advisory NV, GRI (Global Reporting Initiative) and Unit for Corporate Governance in Africa (2010) *Carrots and Sticks: Promoting Transparency and Sustainability. An update on Trends in Voluntary and Mandatory Approaches to Sustainability Reporting*, https://www.globalreporting.org/resourcelibrary/Carrots-And-Sticks-Promoting-Transparency-And-Sustainbability.pdf, accessed 15 June 2014.

Welford, R. (1998) 'Corporate Environmental Management, Technology and Sustainable Development: Postmodern Perspectives and the Need for a Critical Research Agenda', *Business Strategy and the Environment* 7.1: 1-12.

Wiseman, J. (1982) 'An Evaluation of Environmental Disclosures Made in Corporate Annual Reports', *Accounting, Organizations and Society* 7.1: 53-63.

6
Environmental economics

Rosa Maria Fernandez

In this chapter you will learn about the interactions between the economy and the environment and how economists try to solve the puzzle of giving the right value to our environmental resources so that sustainable development can be achieved. At the end of this chapter you will be able to:

- Identify basic concepts related to environmental economics. Bearing in mind that economics is the discipline that studies the efficient allocation of scarce resources which have alternative uses, environmental economics will be the area of the discipline focused on the efficient allocation of natural resources and environmental goods and services, taking into account the requirements for sustainable development.

- Get a reasonable knowledge of the policies and instruments more widely used to tackle environment-related issues, from the point of view of the necessary incentives for producers and consumers to change to more sustainable behaviour.

- Distinguish the methods used to give a monetary value to environmental goods and services, including an introduction to waste management as one of the policies for which these methods could be applied.

- Discuss in an informed way the influence of international trade on the environment.

Introduction to environmental economics

The classical study of economics did not use to pay attention to the interactions between the economy and environmental resources. The focus, considered narrow by many (Pearce and Turner 1990), was on the balance between supply and demand for products and services needed to achieve an equilibrium level of production and its corresponding market price.

The production process was conceived as a linear one, from which goods and services were obtained for consumption, or capital assets were created to be part of the capital stock that ultimately would be used to produce more goods and services. From those goods and services consumed we get different levels of utility or satisfaction, and that was the end of the chain.

The problems with this view come from the fact that, on the one hand, for any production process it is necessary to use some inputs and, as it happens, some of those inputs are natural resources (fuels, raw materials, water etc). On the other, both production and consumption generate some sort of waste, and even natural systems generate their own waste, for instance, the leaves falling from trees. That waste goes back into our environment unless it is recycled and introduced into the system again, so we can have waste in form of CO_2 into the atmosphere, plastic bags on a landfill, or chemical products in a river, to give a few examples. Besides, as human beings, we do not only appreciate those natural resources used in a production process, we give a positive value to the fact that we can contemplate their beauty or that we can visit them for leisure, like a national park. So when we use the environment as a waste sink, the impact on society will be a negative amenity.

Figure 1: The circular economy.

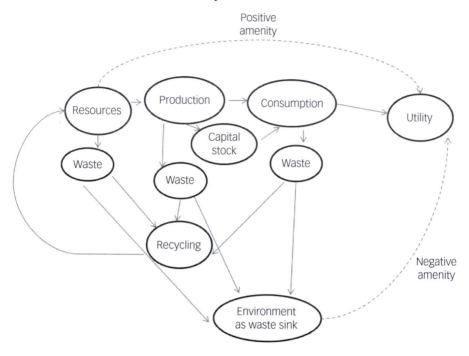

Source: Author's elaboration, adapted from Pearce and Turner (1990).

All these interactions define the economy as a circular process instead of a linear one (see Fig. 1) and we should be aware of the consequences of not being careful and exceeding the environment's assimilative capacity. This assimilative capacity can be defined as the ability of the environment to adapt to changing conditions and keep performing the functions that it is supposed to perform in order to keep ecosystems in balance (Beder 1996).

The best way to make economic agents (producers, consumers and governments) behave in an environmentally friendly way is to make them pay for all the resources actually used and for all the damage they impose on them. But in order to do that, it is necessary to assign a monetary value to natural resources in order to incorporate that value into the costs of production and into the market price of goods and services. This is not always possible with natural resources because property rights are not well defined in most cases, and they have characteristics of what we call public goods: they are non-rival and non-excludable (Hanley *et al.* 2001).

If the use made of our resources does not take into account the negative consequences that we impose on others, then there is a divergence between the costs that society will suffer and the private costs that we are accountable for. This difference is what we call **externality**, and it exists when 'the consumption or production choices of one person or firm enters the utility or production function of another entity without that entity's permission or compensation' (Kolstad 2009: 91).

This definition has a negative connotation and immediately makes us think of greenhouse gas emissions, water contamination, the health risks of passive smoking, etc. But externalities can also be positive, and we can find ourselves enjoying the benefits of actions taken by someone else without paying for them. A typical example is vaccination against an infectious disease (Perman *et al.* 2011). If you receive a vaccination you are protected against the disease and so are the persons around you—family, friends and work colleagues—in the sense that they will not get it from you and so you will be contributing to cost savings on the health system of your community.

But we are more interested in the negative externalities because they lead to potentially threatening conditions for human life sooner or later, and it is understandable that authorities try to prevent possible negative effects on large population groups.

You will learn in the next section about the different policies and instruments used to correct externalities, focusing on pollution as the most typical case.

Instruments for pollution control

Having mentioned some of the characteristics of environmental resources, the fact that we cannot assign them a market price as with other goods and services creates what we call a market failure, with externalities being the most visible consequences. Governments may try to intervene in the market to correct a market failure, but sometimes it is government behaviour (giving subsidies to polluting activities or not

Figure 2: Socially efficient production.

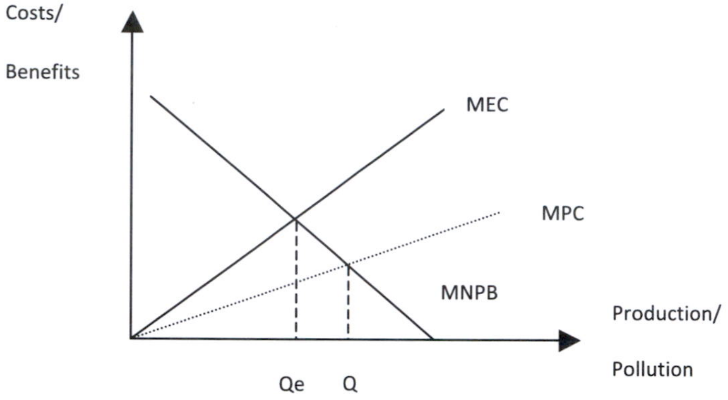

Notation: MNPB = marginal net private benefits; MPC = marginal private costs; MEC = marginal external costs; Q = excessive level of production; Qe = socially efficient level of production (equivalent to socially efficient level of pollution).

Caveat: Although straight lines have been drawn, this is just a simplification and in reality we would have curves with different shapes and changing slope. The slope of the MEC curve would be different depending on the type of pollutant we are considering and the damages that it may cause. A steeper curve would indicate a high level of damage coming from relatively small amounts of the pollutant. We could also represent the Marginal Social Cost curve, which would be the sum of MPC and MEC.

Source: Author's elaboration, adapted from Turner et al. (1994).

taxing them sufficiently) that creates the failure (Tietenberg and Lewis 2009). It is not clear sometimes if public authorities are capable of managing natural resources more efficiently than markets.

The purpose of intervention is to make the polluter internalise the externality (Lesser et al. 1997) or, in other words, to apply a full-cost pricing so that when paying for goods or services the usage of all the resources is included. If that purpose is achieved, the result will be a socially efficient level of production, with its equivalent socially efficient level of pollution, reached at the point where the benefits that are obtained from one extra unit of production are equal to the damages that producing that extra unit will impose on society. In economic terms, this will be the point where the MNPB (marginal net private benefits) are equal to the MEC (marginal external costs) (Turner et al. 1994), as shown by point Qe in Figure 2.

There are two approaches that can be used when implementing measures for pollution control. The most commonly used until recently is called **command and control**, because government imposes a measure, usually a technological standard (BATC/BATNEEC: Best Available Technology not entailing excessive Costs) and commands all the firms in the industry to adopt it (Perman *et al.* 2011). If the standard is exceeded then firms will have to pay a penalty or charge. This approach directly uses the regulatory power of governments and does not take into consideration the fact that different firms have different cost structures, and that what for one firm can be easily achievable and even cheap, may be totally unaffordable for another firm. This is one of the reasons why this approach is not considered cost-efficient.

The other approach involves using the market through economic incentives (Kolstad 2009), and then we have several **market-based instruments**. We will explore here the ones acknowledged as most efficient.

Market-based instruments take into account the different cost structures of each firm so that they can adjust to the instrument and make decisions about reducing their level of pollution or not, depending on what it is more cost-effective for them. If their costs for reducing pollution (called abatement costs) are higher than what they would have to pay to the government for excessive pollution (tax per unit of pollution), or if their costs are higher than what they should pay under a regime of authorised limited pollution (a permits system), then they will pay. Otherwise (costs of abatement lower than the tax or the price of permits) they will reduce pollution. Please observe that in this case there is no imposition of one level of production for the firm as with the command and control approach.

The first of the market-based instruments are **environmental taxes**, also called pollution taxes, green taxes or pigouvian taxes (after the economist Arthur Pigou). They can take several forms, but in general we talk about a uniform tax per unit of pollution (Pearce and Turner 1990). If the tax is established correctly, it will be at a level where the costs of reducing one more unit of pollution (MAC: marginal abatement costs) equalise the damage imposed to society by that extra unit (MSD: marginal social damage), as shown by point Qe in Figure 3. This will be equivalent to the equilibrium point described previously (MNPB = MEC).

Figure 3: Internalisation of externalities through taxation.

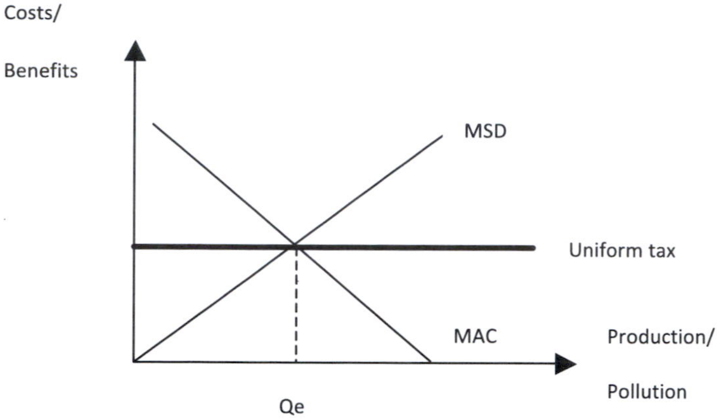

Source: Author's elaboration, adapted from Perman *et al.* (2011).

Alternatively to taxes, governments can approve the use of a system of **marketable permits**. Several countries have been using this system with relative success, though it is controversial as detractors question if it is ethical to buy the right to pollute. But given the fact that the European Union is using it through the ETS (European Emissions Trading Scheme), its acceptance by authorities can be considered widespread (Perman *et al.* 2011).

The rationale behind a permit system relies on authorities establishing a maximum amount that can be emitted of one particular pollutant (for instance CO_2), which is called a ceiling or cap. Once this level is fixed, they distribute permits to the firms according to their individual level of emissions and then firms can trade the permits freely in the market (hence the inclusion among the market-based instruments). This means that if a firm does not use all its permits because it is reducing its level of emissions, it can go to the market and sell its surplus of permits to those firms who are not so efficient in reducing pollution and need more permits than those they were initially allocated.

If the market is efficient, the price of the permits will be indicative of their scarcity, and that will incentivise firms to adopt cleaner technologies to reduce pollution, because that should be cheaper than buying permits (Turner *et al.* 1994).

However, there are two issues associated with this system. The first has to do with how governments decide on the ceiling and then on how many permits to assign to each firm. It is usually based on information coming from the historical level of emissions, what is called grandfathering (Hanley *et al.* 2007), which can lead to an over-allocation of permits. The other issue has to do with the way permits are distributed to each firm. It can be done for free (as it has been the case with the European ETS) or through an auction system. It is quite obvious that if permits are distributed for free and there is an excessive number in the market to trade, the price is not going to be high enough to incentivise firms to go greener.

The last market-based instruments to be mentioned here are **subsidies**. Their use responds to the idea that industries should be paid to reduce pollution so that they can get enough resources to acquire more efficient equipment. In this case the subsidy will be received only if the firm manages to reduce pollution to a certain threshold and not otherwise. But there are problems associated with the philosophy of subsidies. The main one has to do with the fact that even if they can be effective at firm level, the reduction in costs that the subsidy would involve could have a 'call effect' and attract more firms into the market, ultimately causing the total emissions level to increase (Pearce and Turner 1990).

None of the systems is perfect and there are many issues associated with information costs and administrative costs. You will analyse those problems in Seminar 1.

One of the main problems that we have mentioned with regard to environmental resources and environmental degradation has to do with the difficulties in giving them a monetary value, so in our next section you will see some of the techniques used to try and overcome these difficulties.

Environmental valuation techniques

There are many methods that economists can use to try and assign a value to environmental goods and services. Before doing that, it is necessary to decide which type of value will be part of the **total economic value** of the

goods and services. With environmental resources this is not an obvious thing to do because, as we mentioned earlier, we have use values
(derived mostly from utilisation on production processes) and non-use
values (derived from the pleasure that the mere existence of the good
gives us). Even in the case of using those environmental goods and services, it is not certain that the usage will have an economic purpose,
such as in the case of using coal for the production of energy; and we
may find satisfaction (value) coming from visiting a natural park and
spending a relaxing day there (recreational purpose). The issue comes
from the fact that when no direct income is obtained, the other values
tend to be ignored or not taken into account (such as biodiversity conservation or carbon absorption). These use and non-use values may play
against each other when deciding between preservation or exploitation
(for instance when deciding whether to keep a forest untouched or start
logging to sell the timber and get a profit). Most techniques only allow
calculation of the use values, and for some of these a monetary value
will prove difficult to be assigned, which means that in the end the value
assigned to environmental resources is not going to be complete.

One of the most common techniques for environmental valuation is
the **contingent valuation method**. It uses surveys to ask people about
their willingness to pay for the implementation of one particular environmental project. As it is based on people's stated preferences it incorporates the non-use values of the environmental resources concerned.
Issues associated with this method specifically derive from the fact that
it relies on people's answers, which may not be accurate or may be biased
due to lack of information, a survey that has been incorrectly designed,
or a population sample that does not cover the relevant geographical
area or group affected, among other reasons (Mitchell and Carson 1993).

Hedonic pricing, however, tries to extract the value of an environmental resource (for instance air quality) from the influence that changes
on the quality of that resource create on the value of marketed goods,
such as land prices or wages. In this sense, this method is classified as a
revealed preferences approach (since the changes on market will reflect
the actual preferences of consumers). Statistically speaking, the hedonic
pricing regression equation will end up giving us the demand curve for
the environmental good, resource or service under consideration. The
type of question being answered with this method, for instance, is how

much would the price of a house change if it is close to a dirty river or a clean one (Kolstad 2009)?

Applications of this method also help to indicate to an employer how much should they should pay in terms of wage premium or wage differential to those employees who undertake riskier jobs. This is going to be conditioned on one side by the levels of risk aversion of each person, which will be different, and on the other side by the cost to each employer of implementing safety measures that would reduce those risks. A more controversial application is to calculate what is called the **value of a statistical life**, where the objective is to ascertain the amount that people are willing to pay to avoid a risk by the probability of death from that risk (Lesser *et al.* 1997). Not everyone considers it appropriate to put a monetary value on human life, but it is not the purpose of this chapter to enter that particular debate.

The final method we are going to mention, though obviously not the last one available, is called the **travel cost method**. As the name suggests, it tries to find out the willingness to pay for recreational activities at natural areas like a forest, a beach or a national park, together with the willingness to pay for changes to the opportunities to undertake those activities, all of which require a trip in order to arrive to the area in question. Travelling to recreational sites requires time (opportunity cost in terms of the salary that we are not earning) and money (transport costs, etc.). By finding out how many times people visit one particular site and for how long, and how much they spend on the trip, we estimate the demand for the site. Obviously, this is not straightforward and we need to take into account many variables, such as the existence or not of alternative places or activities (Hanley *et al.* 2007). Common sense indicates that the more expensive a place becomes to visit, the less often it will be visited (demand will decrease). This method is another example of the revealed preferences approach. The results obtained can then be used to calculate entrance fees to the site, which will in turn contribute to the preservation of the natural environment.

Giving a monetary value to environmental goods or services is not easy, but if at least we can get some sort of idea, we will be able to undertake, for instance, cost–benefit analysis to decide if it is worthwhile or not to implement a particular project; or to decide which are the best policy measures that can be taken to protect the environment, like the taxes, permits or command and control measures discussed in the previous section. This value can also be used to form part of the natural capital stock of a country, which should be one of the indicators most commonly used to determine a country's level of success in terms of economic growth, and of its capacity to grow in the future (Hanley *et al.* 2001).

An example of policy decision making: waste management policies

One of the policies for which environmental valuation techniques can be used is that of municipal waste management. We need to acknowledge the fact that waste generation has been increasing over time in developed societies up until very recently (just see Eurostat data: http://ec.europa.eu/eurostat/waste), as an accompanying effect of economic growth, and, as would be expected, the type of waste has also been evolving, so the way to treat that waste necessarily has to be adapted.

Our environment has a large assimilative capacity, as we have already mentioned, but the amounts of waste generated and accumulated and the nature, sometimes particularly damaging, of that waste make it necessary to adopt policies to make behaviour more sustainable. Surprisingly, most policies focus on how to dispose of the generated waste and on recycling instead of on trying to reduce the amount that is initially generated (Turner 1995).

Once waste is generated, policies can only focus on how to dispose of it. It makes sense, then, that the initial group of policies needs to be dedicated to avoiding or minimising the risk of illegal disposal. Options within this group can include patrolling or surveillance with the aim to catch fly-tippers, adding a severe penalty or fine for those found guilty. The problems with this option arise from the fact that it may be expensive to implement and it is difficult to determine the adequate level of penalty. Alternatively, the government could increase the number of places available for legal disposal, but again this would not be optimal since the initial problem is the limited amount of land available for these purposes (OECD 2011).

When the issue to be tackled has to do with the consequences of legal disposal we must bear in mind the external effects resulting from the different alternatives for disposal. Using a landfill site obviously has environmental and health impacts in terms of the substances that go into the atmosphere or those contaminating the soil. It is common to find landfill taxes which try to prevent an excessive use of the site (HMRC 2012). This would involve reducing the amount of waste generated or searching for alternatives to disposal, such as re-use, recycling or incineration with energy production.

Existing policies are usually focused on the production side of the economic activity, since this is what initially generates a product that will result on waste. Subsidising the use of recycling materials or commanding their use in a minimum percentage could decrease the amount of waste arriving at landfill sites. Whichever option is chosen by policy-makers, they will apply a cost–benefit analysis to the process in order to give weight to the advantages and disadvantages of each alternative. Hedonic pricing or contingent valuation could be methods used for this cost–benefit analysis but, for instance, if we are going to consider the distance between the place where the waste is generated and the place where it is going to be disposed of, the travel cost method can be part of the analysis. You will work on these possibilities in Seminar 2.

International trade and the environment

The final section of this chapter tries to answer questions such as: Is international trade good for the environment? Do gains from trade liberalisation get outweighed by damage to the environment? What is the environmental impact of transporting goods internationally?

If we already know that production processes create negative externalities why would it be desirable to get involved in international trade? There are many theories trying to explain why countries trade, from the absolute advantage of Adam Smith and the comparative advantage of David Ricardo, to the Heckscher-Olhin factor endowment theorem (Perman *et al.* 2011).

One of the main concerns of international trade with regard to the environment has to do with the suspicion that when developed countries adopt more stringent environmental regulations, pollutant activities move to less developed countries where those regulations are very basic or do not even exist. The assumption is that regulation will increase production costs and will negatively affect industrial competitiveness. This is what it is known as the **pollution haven hypothesis** (Kolstad 2009).

On the other hand, there are theories suggesting that countries will specialise in the production processes of those factors in which they are more abundant. If that is the case, countries more abundant in capital will focus on capital-intensive industries and countries abundant in labour will focus on labour-intensive industries. The follow-up of that rationale, known as the **factor endowment hypothesis**, will lead us to think that capital-intensive industries are more pollutant than labour-intensive ones. This comes from the idea that heavily pollutant industries (paper, steel, chemicals, etc.) need large amounts of capital investment to start working. And the evidence (Cole and Elliot 2005) seems to suggest that developed countries will be more abundant in capital and developing countries more abundant in labour so, in this case, more pollutant activities will concentrate in developed countries.

Several studies have tried to identify which of the two hypotheses is prevalent (Antweiler *et al.* 2001; Cole and Elliot, 2003) but the results are inconclusive. They do it through the analysis of the three identified effects of trade over environment. These can be classified as follows (Grossman and Krueger 1991; Brock and Taylor 2005):

1. **Scale effect:** With trade liberalisation there is better or easier access to markets and this is supposed to contribute to economic growth. The scale effect aims to measure the increase in pollution associated with the growth of the economy (scaled up) compared to the increase in levels of economic activity, while keeping constant the mix of goods and the production techniques used. As a result, this is supposed to have a negative effect on environment.

2. **Composition effect:** When there is trade liberalisation, the mix of goods produced is likely to change so the size and importance of the different economic sectors in the country or economy under consideration will be modified. Depending on which production factors

the economy is more abundant in, and thus which type of industry it has specialised in, the effect on the environment can be positive or negative (if the country becomes more oriented towards dirtier industries).

3. **Technique effect:** This makes reference to the change in production methods that is associated with trade liberalisation. One of the assumptions made about trade is that it increases the levels of income per capita. If that is the case, it then becomes apparent that consumers will demand products that are of higher quality and less environmentally damaging. As a result of consumer demand, producers will need to change their production processes and, furthermore, if governments become responsive to such a demand for better environmental quality, they will approve more stringent and environmentally friendly regulations. This will encourage producers to innovate and offer less pollutant goods and services. In this regard, the technique effect will have a positive effect on the environment (Jaffe *et al.* 1995).

Additionally, another theory also builds on the idea of the influence of environmental regulation, but in this case arguing that it will enhance innovation and increase companies' competitiveness, so it will contribute positively to economic growth. Under this idea, known as the **Porter hypothesis**, firms would not move from developed countries to developing ones just to save costs (Porter and Van der Linde 1995; Palmer *et al.* 1995).

In reality, what we have is the influence of many factors on trade and decision-making processes, so there is no fixed or easy answer to the questions that we previously formulated. The best answer would include a complete study of all the levels of welfare of all the countries involved, and would quite likely start with 'It depends …' (Managi *et al.* 2009).

Suggested seminars

Seminar 1: Instruments for pollution control

The purpose of this seminar is further analysis of the possible measures for pollution control that a regulator or government can implement. Focusing on taxes and permits, by the end of this seminar you will be able to put yourself in the position of a regulator who has to make a decision about which type of policy will be more efficient for reducing pollution when operating under uncertainty, something that resembles reality much more closely than the theoretical approach that has been described so far.

One of the main difficulties for a government in implementing policies for pollution control has to do with the lack of information, particularly with regard to companies' marginal abatement costs (defined as the cost of reducing one additional unit of pollution). It is for this reason that an ongoing dialogue usually takes place between regulators and firms, but sometimes firms can adopt strategies to try to reduce the amount of money they pay for their pollution levels.

Activity 1

Review with your classmates the basic concepts related to pollution control instruments:

- Externality

- Marginal external cost

- Abatement

- Market-based instruments

- Command and control measures

Activity 2a

Work in groups.

Scenario 1: Each group will be an oil company established close to a river in a European country (e.g. France) with the ability to find out which approach a regulator is going to take to reduce pollution. The groups will have to decide what would be their behaviour if they find out that the regulator is going to implement a pollution tax. Using Figure 4, say which would be the costs you would try to make the regulator believe you have (MACs) compared to the real ones (MACr). Consider your answer using Figure 3 earlier in this chapter.

Figure 4: Stated versus real marginal abatement costs.

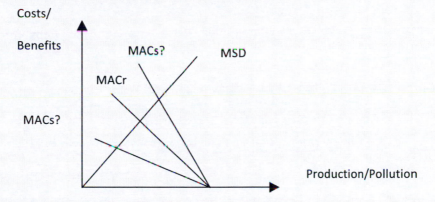

Source: Author's elaboration, adapted from Perman *et al.* (2011).

Scenario 2: You are the same company that you considered for Scenario 1 but, in this case, what would be your answer if you pre-empt that the government is going to establish a permit system?

Scenario 3: Some groups can play the role of the regulator/government and then answer the following question: Which would be the preferred measure for the government to adopt if the uncertainty in the information comes from not knowing which are the marginal social damages? Draw the relevant diagrams to show which policy would be better (taxes or permits) depending on the steepness of the marginal social damage curve.

Activity 2b

Using the groups created for the previous scenarios, groups acting as the company and groups acting as the regulator will be paired so that they actually undertake a negotiation. After a few minutes you will have to come to an agreement as a result of the negotiation and explain which variables you took into consideration for the final decision.

In order to solve these questions you will have to remember what has previously been explained in this chapter: an instrument for pollution control will be efficient if it can be established at the point where the marginal abatement costs are equal to the marginal damage costs, since at this level we would achieve a socially efficient level of production and pollution. So this is the level at which a uniform tax should be implemented, or the cap for the number of permits should be fixed in the case of a tradable permits system.

The problem is that the regulator cannot be certain about what this point could be.

Clarification for scenarios 1 and 2: As a company decision-maker, you would be interested on minimising your costs and having to pay a tax or buy permits would increase those costs, so your strategy in your conversations with the regulators will be to try and make them fix the tax at the lowest level possible, or to assign you as many permits as possible at the cheapest price. Bearing that in mind, you need to make a decision about what to tell the regulators with regard to your marginal abatement costs. Will you make them believe that they are higher or lower than the real ones?

Clarification for scenario 3: For the regulator, the problems do not end here. The other curve for which information is required, in order to decide which policy to implement, is the marginal social damage curve. How to calculate the damages that society can potentially suffer derived from a pollution problem or any other type of environmental disaster is quite complicated and in many cases the damage is related to the type of pollutant we are considering.

For scenario 3, you will have to incorporate different options for the marginal social damage curve (steeper or flatter curve) with the uncertainty about the marginal abatement cost curve. Your goal is to determine which instrument will be more efficient even if you cannot establish it at the optimal level, by looking at which of them gives you a result that is closer to the socially optimal outcome.

Seminar 2: Waste management and environmental valuation

The aim of this seminar is twofold. On the one hand, to have a better understanding of the problems that waste generation can cause and, with that in mind, to try to formulate the best waste management policies possible. On the other hand, to try and apply the methodology of cost–benefit analysis and determine which are the pros and cons of each policy option, figuring out which would be the most appropriate environmental valuation technique to use in the calculations required.

When we described the interactions between the economy and the environment, we saw that one of the main roles that our environment plays is that of waste sink. But what if we generate so much waste that the environment cannot cope with it?

Pre-seminar work

Watch the video *Pyramids of Waste: The Light Bulb Conspiracy* (2010, 52 minutes duration, www.youtube.com/watch?v=Vil6uAxqEOY). Based on the problems identified in the video, consider your own ideas about how to improve waste management policies and promote recycling in order to prevent problems associated with excessive waste generation. Those ideas will be discussed during the seminar.

Activity 1

Make a list of all the proposals and try to identify the costs and benefits associated with each of them. Based on the different costs and benefits, work in groups to decide which would be the policy that as experts you would recommend to the government.

Activity 2

Assuming that at least five different options have been identified, again work in groups trying to determine which valuation technique, or combination of techniques, could be used to obtain those costs and benefits for each of the options.

Seminar 3: Is trade good for the environment?

The aim of this seminar is to try and determine up to which point international trade affects the environment and, as a consequence of this, the general welfare of a society, where both developed and developing (or less developed) countries are taken into consideration.

At the end of the seminar you will be able to identify the contradictory points of view about the role of environmental regulations on international trade and on a country's competitiveness.

Pre-game activity

Review the basic concepts related to environmental regulations and trade:

- Scale, technique and composition effects
- Pollution haven hypothesis
- Porter hypothesis

Game

Divide your classroom into two groups. Each group will play the role of a country, one of them a developed country and the other a developing country. The initial assumption is that both countries produce a good whose production is highly pollutant (e.g. steel) and that most of the consumption is done by the developed country.

The purpose of the game is to analyse the decision-making process to see if the implementation of environmental regulation in developed countries leads to the creation of pollution havens (as defined previously in this chapter) in developing countries. The 'developed country' group will have to decide what is better for that country, in terms of production, consumption, environmental degradation and welfare in general. The 'developing country' group will have to make the same kind of decisions for that developing country.

We are going to assume that the two countries are open to international trade, which means in our case that they trade between each other and without anyone else.

The rationale behind the decision-making process needs to use the basic economic theory of supply and demand, and you can do this with the help of diagrams. Try to imagine that your two countries are the only countries in the world, so world welfare will depend on what happens in both countries. Represent the initial supply curves of each of the countries, assuming that the developing country is going to be producing more than the developed country from the beginning. The sum of both supply curves will give the world supply and, in conjunction with the demand curve, you will find equilibrium stating the quantity of the good produced and the world price for that good.

Case 1: If the developed country implements an environmental tax for the production of the polluting good that we are considering, **how would the supply curve of the developed country move, assuming that it increases the production costs**? The 'developed country' group should work on this answer, as they are only concerned about what happens in their own territory.

According to that move, both groups should look at **what happens to the worldwide equilibrium**, and then the 'developing country' group will have to check **how this affects the level of production in the developing country**.

Bearing all these changes in mind, the next step will be to **analyse the possible changes in welfare levels**. Again using concepts from basic economic theory, each of the groups should be able to identify, for their type of country, the changes in consumer and producer surpluses.

Both countries should look at the following question: What happens with welfare at the worldwide level?

Case 2: If the implementation of the tax is considered to increase the production costs in one country, the movement of the supply curve will have one particular direction. But what happens if we see (as one of the theories was indicating) that the tax boosts innovation and increases the productivity of the country that implements that tax (the developed country in our case)? Each of the groups will have to analyse, from their country's perspective, what would happen with welfare levels in this case ('developed country' group to work on developed country welfare; 'developing country' group to work on developing country welfare; both groups to work on world welfare)?

Additional teaching materials and ideas

Better Business Game

www.bitc.org.uk/services/advisory-services/our-services/
better-business-game

This interactive game provides options for different worlds, more or less inclined towards a sustainable future. You will be allocated a budget for a business plan, and you will have to decide how much to spend in different areas, including renewable (or not) energies, local suppliers, etc. According to the decisions made, the game will produce an outcome letting you know if your company will be successful in the medium/long term in the three areas that count for sustainability: economic, ethical and environmental. This helps you understand the importance of how taking sustainable decisions now will create a successful company in the future. You can play the game as many times as you want, choosing different worlds and types of behaviour. It may be possible that you need an agreement to access the game completely.

Natural resource management

This is a topic that usually accompanies environmental economics so, if time allows, some tips about sustainable exploitation of natural resources could be introduced. Fisheries are a good example of renewable resources and any mineral can be used to illustrate a non-renewable resource. Forestry management is also highly appropriate, comparing the results of public management with those of private management.

The European Common Fisheries Policy (http://ec.europa.eu/fisheries/cfp/index_en.htm) provides a good description of the different instruments being used to try and avoid the disappearance of some species, and to promote sustainable fishing without destroying employment.

Most of the books mentioned in the references list contain a chapter, or part of chapter, providing information useful in preparing materials in this area.

An activity connected to this could be for students to identify an example of a national park or equivalent from their own countries, if such exists, sharing with the rest of the class how they are managed in each case: for instance, if the number of visits per year is limited or the entrance is restricted or prohibited during particular periods; if they charge an entrance fee, and in that case, how much they charge; etc. The idea is to compare different management options and, in light of the conditions of the site, suggest possible changes.

A real case of environmental valuation

Most of the literature uses as an example of contingent valuation the case of the Exxon Valdez oil spill in 1989 (see e.g. Lesser *et al.* 1997). To find out if contingent valuation has been used again, or if a mix of methods is now being used, students could try to find out how compensation for environmental and economic damage was calculated for the Deepwater Horizon oil spill in 2010. This will help them to understand the use of valuation techniques in practice, instead of thinking of them as something theoretical and abstract. Using a relatively recent case will help to create a connection and hopefully increase their interest in undertaking some research. The fact that the case was widely covered in the media will make easy to find information and it will be possible to start a discussion about the long-term effects of the spill.

Blame matrix

This interesting title enables the topic of transboundary pollution to be introduced. Looking at EMEP (European Monitoring and Evaluation Program) data (http://emep.int/mscw/index_mscw.html), you will see how air pollution can move from country to country. The idea is to prevent problems like acid rain from occurring. The blame matrix transforms a vector of emissions into a vector of depositions and, going beyond the concept itself, the need for international co-operation in this area can be outlined. It can be mentioned that public policies are focused on reducing the social costs associated with acid rain and, within this framework, how co-operation should be promoted instead of the defence of self-interests. This would involve some knowledge of game theory and the concept of the Nash equilibrium, with co-operative and non-co-operative solutions, so it would not be suitable for first-year undergraduate students. On a more basic level, games using maps to roughly calculate where emissions that originated in one country can end up may contribute to students' participation, particularly if the class/lecture/

seminar has students of different nationalities. They can use their countries as the subject of the game: for example, imagine that you have the 28 EU countries and data from EMEP indicates that most of the pollution originating in Germany is finally deposited in France; or that most of the pollution originating in the UK is deposited in Greece. Students can calculate which country 'sends' more pollution out of its borders and which is the one being most damaged by other countries' pollution.

Weak sustainability versus strong sustainability

These controversial ideas can be seen in the context of how appropriate GDP (gross domestic product) or GNP (gross national product) are as indicators of a country's success. In connection with this, the role of capital stocks in economic growth could be explained, and then the different types of capital that should be considered: man-made capital, human capital and natural capital, all capable of being depreciated. Natural capital will be the key concept for distinguishing the two points of view about what sustainability is and the importance of keeping at least a minimum stock of resources to allow production in the future, and thus economic growth. Discussion could be achieved by asking students questions such as: Is it possible to replace all the natural capital with man-made capital?

Project XL

Information about this project can be obtained from the website of the US Environmental Protection Agency (www.epa.gov/projectxl/). The project scheme (eXcellence in Leadership) started in 1995 and pilot initiatives were accepted up to 2002. The idea behind the project was to allow business and communities to have more flexibility regarding the implementation of measures to protect the environment, in order to reach the most cost-effective options. Students will be able to see data on the different projects, participating companies, local or state governments, if there is any project still ongoing, etc. This can be used as complementary information when talking about market-based instruments and their flexibility in comparison with command and control measures for pollution control.

Further reading

Folmer, H., H.L. Gabel and H. Opschoor (eds.) (1997) *Principles of Environmental and Resource Economics: A Guide for Students and Decision-Makers*, repr. (1st edn 1995; Cheltenham, UK: Edward Elgar).

> This book provides a basic introduction to environmental and natural resource economics, covering the main concepts and policies and also placing particular emphasis on companies' behaviour, from their involvement in the policy-making process to the adoption of environmental management practices as part of corporate strategies to gain market share, responding to consumer demands for environmental quality. Though written a good number of years ago, it can help the understanding of the basic rationale for policy introduction for the protection of environmental resources and the correction of market failures that cause environmental damage.

Helm, D., and C. Hepburn (eds.) (2009) *The Economics and Politics of Climate Change* (Oxford, UK: Oxford University Press).

> This book summarises the economic instruments and policy approaches used so far to tackle climate change, outlining the uneven and sometimes disappointing results obtained, and suggesting alternatives for targets or areas of focus. It highlights the need for international co-operation and gives examples of what has been done by the European Union but also in countries outside of Europe. The difficulties on reaching agreements both to mitigate and adapt to the consequences of climate change, an issue with potentially wide implications worldwide and which constitutes a risk to the possibilities of a sustainable future, reinforces the need for international intervention instead of national or regional approaches.

Jordan, A.J., and A. Lenschow (eds.) (2008) *Innovation in Environmental Policy? Integrating the Environment for Sustainability* (Cheltenham, UK: Edward Elgar).

> This book provides a good overview of the way that environmental concerns have been progressively introduced in the policy decision-making process across different countries, in and outside of Europe, the rationale behind it and the difficulties in getting real progress and positive outcomes from measures implementation. Policy-makers face many challenges, associated both with uncertainty and with reluctance to change, as well as with sometimes divergent interests when it comes to priorities at the time of deciding which policy should be chosen and which sectors should be affected.

Mallon, K. (ed.) (2006) *Renewable Energy Policy and Politics: A Handbook for Decision-Making* (London: Earthscan).

> One of the many initiatives designed to make our society lower carbon and more sustainable is the promotion of renewable energies as the best alternative to fossil fuels. This book outlines the different policies that could be used to

enhance this option and make it work from both environmental and economic points of view. It identifies the stakeholders who are mainly affected by the decision-making process, and presents several case studies at country level that could be used as examples: Germany, Spain, United States, United Kingdom, India and Cambodia. It would be interesting to investigate how the situation might have changed since this book was written, in light of the international economic crisis for each of these countries.

Stavins, R.N. (ed.) (2012) *Economics of the Environment: Selected Readings*, 6th edn (New York: Norton).

This book includes a selection of papers by some of the most renowned experts in the area of environmental economics, setting out their points of view on many of the issues surrounding environmental economics, natural resources, sustainability, climate change economics and policies, and corporate social responsibility, among others. Sometimes responses to, and criticism of, previous papers is included, which could initiate an enriching discussion process to ascertain with which of the expressed positions the reader most identifies. The papers included cover a good number of years, which also facilitates the observation of changes in approach to the same issues over time.

References

Antweiler, W., B.R. Copeland and M.S. Taylor (2001) 'Is Free Trade Good for the Environment?', *American Economic Review* 91.4: 877-908.

Beder, S. (1996) *The Nature of Sustainable Development*, 2nd edn (Newham, Australia: Scribe).

Brock, W.A., and M.S. Taylor (2005) 'Economic Growth and the Environment: A Review of Theory and Empirics', in Philippe Aghion and Steven Durlauf (eds.), *Handbook of Economic Growth*, (San Diego, CA: Elsevier): 1749-821.

Cole, M.A., and R.J.R. Elliot (2003) 'Determining the Trade Environment Composition Effect: The Role of Capital, Labour and Environmental Regulations', *Journal of Environmental Economics and Management* 46.3: 363-83.

—— (2005) 'FDI and the Capital Intensity of "Dirty" Sectors: A Missing Piece of the Pollution Haven Puzzle', *Review of Development Economics* 9.4: 530-48.

Folmer, H., H.L. Gabel and H. Opschoor (eds.) (1995) *Principles of Environmental and Resource Economics: A Guide for Students and Decision-Makers* (Cheltenham, UK: Edward Elgar).

Grossman, G.M., and A.B. Krueger (1991) *Environmental Impacts of a North American Free Trade Agreement*, Working Paper No. 3914, National Bureau of Economic Research, www.nber.org/papers/w3914.pdf, accessed 16 June 2014.

Hanley, N., J. Shogren and B. White (2001) *Introduction to Environmental Economics* (Oxford, UK: Oxford University Press).

—— (2007). *Environmental Economics in Theory and Practice*, 2nd edn (Basingstoke, UK: Palgrave Macmillan).

Helm, D., and C. Hepburn (eds.) (2009) *The Economics and Politics of Climate Change* (Oxford, UK: Oxford University Press).

HMRC (HM Revenue and Customs) (2012). *A General Guide To Landfill Tax: Notice LFT1* (London: HMRC).

Jaffe, A.B., S.R. Peterson, P.R. Portney and R.N. Stavins (1995) 'Environmental Regulation and the Competitiveness of U.S. Manufacturing: What Does the Evidence Tell Us?' *Journal of Economic Literature* 33 (March 1995): 132-63.

Jordan, A.J., and A. Lenschow (eds.) (2008) *Innovation in Environmental Policy? Integrating the Environment for Sustainability* (Cheltenham, UK: Edward Elgar).

Kolstad, C.D. (2009) *Environmental Economics* (Oxford, UK: Oxford University Press).

Lesser, J.A., D.E. Dodds and R.O. Zerbe (1997) *Environmental Economics and Policy* (New York: Addison-Wesley Educational Publishers Inc.).

Mallon, K. (ed.) (2006) *Renewable Energy Policy and Politics: A Handbook for Decision-Making* (London: Earthscan).

Managi, S., A. Hibiki and T. Tsumuri (2009). 'Does Trade Openness Improve Environmental Quality?', *Journal of Environmental Economics and Management* 58 (2009): 346-63.

Mitchell, R.C., and R.T. Carson (1993) *Using Surveys to Value Public Goods: The Contingent Valuation Method*, 3rd printing (Washington, DC: Resources for the Future).

OECD (Organisation for Economic Co-operation and Development) (2011) 'Waste Generation, Recycling and Prevention', in *Greening Household Behaviour: The Role of Public Policy* (Paris, France: OECD Publishing): 81-95.

Palmer, K., W.E. Oates and P.R. Portney (1995) 'Tightening Environmental Standards: The Benefit–Cost or the No-Cost Paradigm', *Journal of Economic Perspectives* 9.4 (Autumn 1995): 119-32.

Pearce, D.W., and R.K. Turner (1990) *Economics of Natural Resources and the Environment* (Baltimore, MD: The Johns Hopkins University Press).

Perman, R., Y. Ma, M. Common, D. Maddison and J. McGilvray (2011) *Natural Resource and Environmental Economics*, 4th edn (Harlow, UK: Addison-Wesley).

Porter, M.E., and C. Van der Linde (1995) 'Toward a New Conception of the Environment–Competitiveness Relationship', *Journal of Economic Perspectives* 9.4 (Autumn 1995): 97-118.

Stavins, R.N. (ed.) (2012) *Economics of the Environment: Selected Readings*, 6th edn (New York: Norton).

Tietenberg, T., and L. Lewis (2009) *Environmental and Natural Resource Economics*, 8th edn (Boston, MA: Addison-Wesley).

Turner, K. (1995) 'Waste management', in H. Folmer, H.L. Gabel and H. Opschoor (eds.) (1995) *Principles of Environmental and Resource Economics: A Guide for Students and Decision-Makers* (Cheltenham, UK: Edward Elgar): 440-66.

Turner, R.K., D.W. Pearce and I. Bateman (1994) *Environmental Economics: An Elementary Introduction* (Hemel Hempstead, UK: Harvester Wheatsheaf).

7

Human resources management: supporting sustainable business

Elaine Cohen

Sustainable HRM (human resources management) is a combination of two elements: (1) **leveraging HR (human resources) tools and processes to support sustainable business objectives**, and (2) **performing HR sustainably**, that is, in a way which creates an organisational culture that is ethical, respectful and inclusive, invests in the development of employees and empowers them to engage at the maximum level of their capabilities (Cohen *et al.* 2012).

This chapter will help students understand the roles of HR teams in supporting sustainable business and the responsibility of HR teams to perform HR sustainably.

The learning outcomes of this chapter are:

- Students will be able to describe how HR supports sustainable business and the connection between HRM and sustainability

- Students will be able to understand examples of the way HR practices affect society and possible ways to integrate social and environmental considerations into

HR processes in order to improve the social and environmental impacts of business

- Students will be able to know where to find more information and examples of good practice in the area of sustainable HRM.

Sustainable HR as part of sustainable business

Leveraging HR Tools and processes to support sustainable business is the extension of the HR business partnership role which the HR function has been aspiring to fill in the past decade or so. Rather than HR being the 'voice of the employees' or the 'instrument of management', or both, the more precise role of HR is to enhance organisational capability, by understanding what the business needs and what people, knowledge, skills and culture need to be in place to deliver those needs. As more and more companies today adopt strategies for sustainable business, so the HR understanding of how their role as not only business partner, but as sustainable business partner, needs to evolve. This of course assumes that HR understands what sustainable business is and how it differs in approach from business as usual as we have always known it.

The key attributes that distinguish sustainable business from business-as-usual are acceptance of **accountability for impacts on people, society and the environment**, and a willingness to **engage with stakeholders**, both internal and external, to ensure both an understanding of their expectations and an assessment of the way business impacts their lives in a range of different ways. Every business has an impact, whether it is a company which is small or large, local or global, private or public. (By the way, this applies not only to for-profit companies: this is equally relevant for not-for-profit organisations, public agencies and even governments.) By employing people, serving customers, erecting buildings, inhabiting offices, using transportation, manufacturing products, developing and marketing a product range or providing a service—every company has an impact on those around them.

In determining the appropriate business strategies to deliver growth and profit the bottom line, sustainable thinking demands consideration of both social and environmental needs, in addition to economic needs. Many such strategies require the active participation of the HR function in order to engage employees in their pursuit. By erecting a new manufacturing plant in accordance with 'green' principles and using, say, renewable energy sources such as solar power, a plant will both be more cost-efficient through the long term and have a much lower negative impact on climate change, avoiding the use of carbon-intensive fossil fuels. Undertaking such activity requires employees who have the skills and knowledge to design and implement green practices. Research has shown that by investing in employee health and wellbeing, beyond the minimum requirements of law, a business will reap the benefits of improved employee motivation and productivity while contributing to a healthier and more vital society (HBR 2010). By investing in community development activities, a business will make reputation gains which will serve its long-term ability to attract and retain investors and customers, while strengthening the fabric of the local community from which it also draws resources.

Sustainability is based on fundamental elements of **good governance, ethical conduct and compliance with the law**, while going beyond compliance with the law to generate additional opportunities to mitigate business risk, enhance business reputation and take advantage of new business developments. In adopting a sustainability strategy, companies contribute not only to the sustainability of the planet but also to their own sustainability as businesses. This approach is changing the way businesses develop strategy, take decisions, execute processes, engage with employees, consumers, external pressure groups and communities, and respond to the diverse expectations of all these groups in this fast-moving, transparent age of business. This requires not only a strategy for sustainable business but also a **culture** that supports strategy delivery.

The fundamental ability to deliver a strong sustainable business strategy lies with a company's leadership and is embodied in its **values, culture, capabilities and communications**. This means embedding a **sustainability-enabled culture** in all parts of the organisation. Business leaders need to ensure that employees, the group which most influences a business's results, and which is most directly influenced by the employment practices of the business, understands, engages with and proactively advances the sustainability agenda.

The broader HR role in sustainability

HR teams are **critical partners** in making this happen. This means that HR must understand and engage with the new rules of business sustainability and align its support accordingly (Cohen 2010). For example, in a business which wishes to develop a new line of products marketed to women, a culture of **women's empowerment** within the business must be present for optimal results to be achieved. It can be argued that selling to women requires an understanding of women's needs and habits in relation to a particular product range. It is extremely challenging, if not impossible, for a business to succeed in marketing to women if women are not valued and empowered in the workplace. Helping to create **an inclusive culture** is a key role of the HR function which, in this case, can support the achievement of specific business objectives. Not only this, but there is a ripple effect in the local community when women are empowered (WEP 2012).

Another example might be the process of achieving energy efficiencies as businesses work towards being part of a low-carbon economy. Many companies have found that the formation of '**green teams**' in the business assists in generating awareness of energy savings, and recycling of waste among employees. Although they may be formed from volunteers within the business, green teams still require a framework of operation and a set of guidelines for ensuring they both deliver results as well as engage employees at different levels. In some cases, this might require specific training of employees, including green team leaders, or a broader communications process within the company. These are the tools that the HR function can provide and, in fact, HR is best positioned to provide such team-working frameworks and processes. Green teams not only help a company to reduce its costs and environmental impacts, but also engage employees in activities which enable them to experience additional purposeful contribution in the workplace. This has been correlated to increased retention, motivation and engagement (IESE 2013).

Not only this, but there is again a ripple effect in the community. As employees learn the benefits of **environmental efficiencies in the workplace**, they may take this learning home and apply similar practices in their homes. This saves them money and also reduces the environmental burden of private energy consumption and waste, etc.

Further, in today's 'war for talent', existing and potential **employees are searching for meaning** in their work, beyond receiving a salary slip at the end of each month (Ulrich and Ulrich 2010). Research from Universum's employer branding study in France, for example, showed that among more than 26,000 students there was an overwhelming response in favour of **CSR (corporate social responsibility)-oriented workplaces** (see Fig. 1). HR managers cannot afford to ignore this movement towards meaning.

Further research has shown that CSR 'enhances a corporation's reputation for prospective employees by increasing organizational attractiveness and firm familiarity, but also influences incumbent employees' (Gond *et al.* 2010).

Therefore, the role of HR in helping businesses become more sustainable can be demonstrated in different ways, and requires an understanding by HR leaders and team members of **sustainable business priorities**.

Figure 1: Importance placed by French students on companies with active CSR policies and practices when choosing an employer.

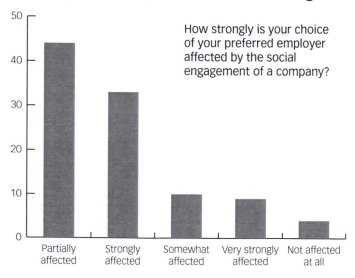

Source: Employer Branding Today (2011).

Performing HR sustainably

Equally as important as supporting business objectives is the way HR performs its traditional functions so that, even in cases where sustainable business strategy has not been specifically articulated, **HR remains accountable for its impacts on society and the environment**. The implications on society of HR decisions in almost all aspects of HR work can be far-reaching, well beyond the primary considerations of business growth and profitability. Closing a factory, for example, and laying off employees may have extensive implications for the social and economic wellbeing of a local community. While HR considerations may not be enough to prevent closure, the way in which the HR leadership defines strategies to communicate, execute plans and support employees through a life-changing event can make a critical difference to individuals and families within the community. Sustainability, in this sense, means that HR takes into account these implications when formulating HR policies, plans and programmes.

Traditional core HR functions include recruitment and retention, training and development, compensation and benefits, organisational

Figure 2: Examples of the connection between HR policies and social and environmental impacts.

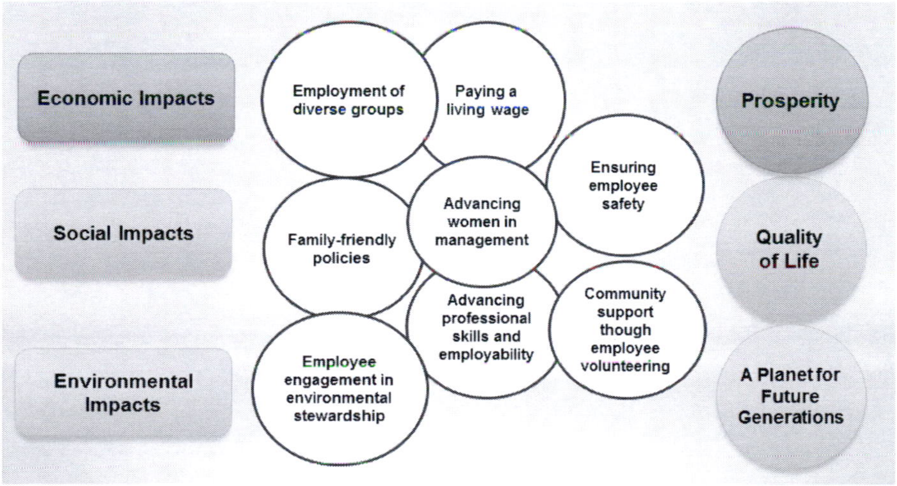

development and internal communications. HR has an inherent accountability to consider the **broader implications of HR decisions** not only on employees, but also on employee families, communities, economies and society in general (see Fig. 2).

By recruiting a **diverse workforce**, which is inclusive of different ethnic groups in society, or ensuring the recruitment of local nationals into key roles rather than expatriating managers for short time periods, HR plays a role in strengthening the fabric of local society. By investing in the employability of individuals in the organisation, and helping them manage their own careers, HR supports a more robust economy in today's society where 'jobs for life', once a key promise of many companies, can no longer be guaranteed. By paying a fair wage, or what is often called a '**living wage**', HR makes a difference by helping to reduce poverty in countries of operation and encouraging **investment back in the community**. By providing benefits such as health insurance and wellness programmes, HR contributes to a healthier society and reduces the burden of healthcare costs on economies and societies.

In so many ways, the decisions made by HR departments have potentially far-reaching, short- and long-term consequences for society, beyond the considerations of an individual company and its employees. While HR cannot be expected to single-handedly solve all of society's problems and inequalities, a **sustainable HR function understands the impacts it creates** and considers these broader needs when formulating policies.

Sustainable HR metrics

Performing HR sustainably can be measured in many ways. In almost all cases, a correlation can be established between HR performance and business outcomes and value generation. The specific correlation in each company may be a little different, but in general, the connection is not only possible, but imperative, in order to establish the financial value to the business of sustainable HRM. Table 1 shows some examples of the HR contribution and the aspects of business value that can be calculated. BT, for example, reports sick pay costs as a business value metric relating to employee health and safety (BT plc 2014).

Table 1: Examples of HRM metrics and connection to business outcomes and value.

HRM role	HRM objective	HRM metric	Business value
Values and ethics	Employees understand and behave in line with corporate values	Percentage of employees trained in values and ethics	Mitigation of risk due to unethical behaviour by employees. Improved corporate reputation and trust
		Percentage of employee responses in survey showing employee support company values	
Recruitment	Recruitment is based on diversity principles	Percentage of employees recruited by gender and by minority groups	Improved business results, innovation and customer satisfaction
Compensation	Compensation is driven by equal opportunity for men and women	Ratio of base salary men to women	Lower HR costs due to turnover, improved motivation and trust
	Compensation is linked to sustainability performance	Number of employees with sustainability targets in annual work-plans	Improved execution of sustainable business strategy
Wellbeing	Employees are fit to contribute to their maximum capability	Percentage of employees who engage in a corporate wellbeing program	Reduced business health costs, lower absenteeism, improved productivity
		Percentage improvements achieved in employee wellbeing (health, stress, diet etc)	
Development	Diverse employees are given opportunities to advance	Percentage of women in management positions	Improved business results, innovation and customer satisfaction
		Percentage of minorities in management positions	
	Employees understand and act in line with sustainability strategy and principles	Percentage of employees trained in sustainability	Improved execution of sustainable business strategy
Engagement	Employees enhance corporate community relations	Percentage of employee volunteers	Employee engagement, reputation benefits, enhanced community relationships
	Employees contribute to improving environmental impacts	Percentage of employees participating in 'green' activities	Energy and materials costs reductions

© Elaine Cohen, 2014.

Opportunities for sustainable HR management

Beyond fulfilling traditional roles as mentioned above, HR has an opportunity to use tools provided by a sustainable business approach to **engage employees in sustainable practices**. These are practices not typically undertaken by HR managers, and may include supporting environmental stewardship through **green team** development, or encouraging employee volunteer programmes in the community. For example, one telecommunications company, ECI Telecom, engages employees in environmental awareness through competitions which engage hundreds of employees and their families. In the ECI Telecom 2012 *Sustainability Report*, ECI displays photos from a 'green camera' competition in which employees of the company's Indian subsidiary participated (ECI Telecom 2013). **Raising awareness** is the first step in changing practice. In the US, the US Postal Service reports massive business savings through recycling, waste reduction, energy conservation and more through the activities of employee green teams throughout its US operations (USPS 2013).

Employee volunteering programmes

Employee volunteering is an opportunity to do more than simply give back to the community. The business benefits to be gained from **employee volunteer programmes** include increased employee satisfaction, motivation and loyalty, as well as innovative opportunities for employees to gain new experience and enhance their skills. For example, the healthcare company GSK (GlaxoSmithKline) reports a 47% higher rate of promotion among volunteers who have participated in the company's PULSE volunteer programme (Korngold 2014: 122). GSK, as well as other companies such as IBM and Intel, maintains extensive volunteer programmes which involve sending employees outside of the organisation for weeks or even months to participate in volunteer activities to support social causes, often in emerging economies. The overriding experience of these employees is one of **learning, personal growth and development,**

leadership, communication and team-working skills which they bring back to benefit the business. Many employee volunteers keep journals, such as the GSK PULSE volunteer blog (http://gskpulsevolunteers.com), in which they record their experiences, thus helping to improve the company's reputation as well as advancing internal benefits, for example. In other cases, companies maintain many different types of volunteering programmes from a one-day annual corporate event for all employees, to ongoing local activities in different operating locations.

Whatever the nature or scale of volunteering activities, they universally contribute to motivation and skill development. HR must be a partner in developing such programmes in a way which meets both community needs and also strategic HR needs.

Human rights

Management of **human rights** is not something HR managers traditionally tend to consider as part of their job description. Most HR managers are conversant with labour laws or have in-house legal counsel. But human rights in a company's supply chain often goes beyond the minimum requirements of law, especially if a company is operating in emerging economies where legal frameworks are less developed or minimally enforced. As an HR function in a business whose extended responsibility includes those employees in its supply chain, HR must consider ways of supporting good HR practice beyond the traditional boundary of the organisation chart. In this way, for example, Nike conducts HR workshops for suppliers in its supply chain in Asia, recognising that an advanced approach to human resources can make the difference in reliable and responsible supply and overall sustainability of the business (Nike 2013). Ensuring a supply chain free from child labour, forced labour, human rights abuses and discrimination has now also become part of the role of HR management and goes beyond traditional relationships with suppliers and outsourcing vendors based on procurement contracts focusing on price, quality and service. For example, many companies have established ethical sourcing policies which require suppliers to commit to maintaining human rights and employee rights in their companies. HR management has a role in assisting in the establishment, implementation and control of such practices.

Employee wellness

Beyond the requirement of compliance with health and safety laws, which is often an operational responsibility and not an HR responsibility, there exists great opportunity for HR management in **advancing employee wellness in the workplace**. Wellness and wellbeing are concepts which are not usually mandated by law but which can help organisations save on healthcare costs, protect business continuity and improve employee morale and productivity, while also improving their impacts on society. Large companies such as Unilever, Johnson & Johnson and Caesars Entertainment have advanced **employee wellbeing programmes**, including **employee health risk assessments**, and have found that the return on investment is significant. Caesars Entertainment, for example, quotes saving upwards of $2.5 million per year through voluntary participation of employees in the company's wellbeing programme, while reducing health risks such as cholesterol, high blood pressure and glucose (diabetes) in double percentage points (Caesars 2013). The Caesars Entertainment wellness programme has 85% employee participation and provides incentives to employees who look after their own health in the form of healthcare costs savings and gifts. Ultimately, the organisation derives great benefit in employee productivity, and the burden of healthcare investment to local economies is reduced significantly.

This type of programme is clearly within the framework of the HR role, which can provide tools, processes and internal communications to help the programme succeed. In addition to the internal and external benefits, this is also an area in which the HR function can demonstrate a direct contribution to the business bottom line, a perfect match of sustainability and business objectives.

Summary

The above examples show how HR can leverage its core competencies in any company to support sustainable business objectives and perform HR sustainably. In doing so, HR must be concerned not only with the business objectives defined by management and employee needs, but also with the **wider impacts of HR decisions** and performance on **communities and the environment**. The essence of this approach is for HR managers to understand the concepts, principles and strategy of **sustainable business** and to recreate HR management processes in a way that leverages HR capabilities for the broader good, not only of the company and its employees, but also of society as a whole.

Suggested seminars

Split into teams of two. Each team selects a sustainability report published within the past year by an organisation of your choice. These are freely available to download from the corporate websites of companies that report on sustainability. Each team should analyse the report and identify all the disclosures relating to employees and human resources practices. Formulate answers to the questions listed below.

Report analysis questions

1. What aspects of human resources practices are referenced in the report?

2. Of all the human resources elements disclosed by the company, which would be the most important for you and why, if you were:
   a. A shareholder in the company?
   b. An employee of the company?
   c. A potential recruit?
   d. A family member of an employee of the company?
   e. A local city council official in a city where a number of the company's employees are located?

3. Review commonalities and differences in the way companies report on human resources aspects of their sustainability performance. What can you infer from the content and style of their disclosures about the organisational culture of the company?

4. Review whether the disclosures related to human resources and organisational development are linked to the business performance of the company, and if so, state in what ways. What metrics connect HR performance to business results?

5. Have these disclosures increased your level of trust in this company?

6. Would you want to work for this company?

After you have answered these questions in your teams, get together as a group and review your findings. Consider the differences and similarities, and the elements which have inspired greater trust in the company as a result of their sustainability disclosures.

As a group, agree on the top five characteristics of HR sustainability reporting that you feel are essential to any sustainability report on HR practices.

Seminar 2: Sustainable organisation culture

In a sustainable organisation, as in any organisation, the underlying culture can be both a reflection and a predictor of sustainable business results. In a sustainable organisation, values are emphasised as part of the organisation's way of operating, communications are frequent and intensive, and individuals feel instilled with a sense of purpose and are empowered to make a difference. More than concerned with their specific roles and direct business results, they are conscious of their responsibilities to society and the environment, and the impacts which result from the things they do and the way they do them. These impacts are felt both internally and externally. In the sustainable organisation, values must offer a certain common ground to enable the wide engagement of employees in a shared culture which continues to respect and celebrate the diversity of individuals.

It is always difficult to assess how people understand and prioritise values and therefore what is necessary in order to motivate and frame common behaviours driven by shared values. Describing values in visual terms is often an excellent way of demonstrating alignment, or otherwise, with the values which underpin a sustainable business.

In this seminar, participants have the opportunity to create a visual expression of the way they see sustainable organisations add the values that helped them become sustainable.

This seminar requires teams of four, working together. The tools required are large 1 m² canvases (on easels if possible), paints and paint-brushes.

Each team should collaborate to create their portrait entitled 'The Ideal Sustainable Company'. No more than 40 minutes should be allocated to creating the portrait.

Once all the portraits are complete, each team should present its picture to the other teams, explaining the different elements in the image and why priority has been given to certain elements. Following the presentations, a group discussion should address the following questions:

1. What were the common visual elements in the portraits?

2. What were the values that stood out as the most significant in all the portraits?

3. Did different visual elements portray the same values or different values? What does this tell us about the way values can be embedded in organisations?

4. What does this exercise tell us about the values that we see as important for sustainable organisations? Would we have created different portraits 20 years ago? Are any of these visual elements used in employer branding or companies that you are aware of?

5. Did the process of creating the canvasses engage team members in discussion about the relative importance and prioritisation of different values for sustainable organisations? Would this be a useful exercise to conduct within company teams?

Seminar 3: Case study—diversity and inclusion

Read the following case study. Engage in a discussion and respond as a group to the questions at the end of the case study.

Diversity and inclusion

You are the HR manager of a supermarket chain which has been expanding rapidly in your country and is poised for overseas expansion in the coming years. You know that the ability of the company to expand depends on a constant stream of recruitment of the right quality people at all levels in the organisation. In fact, you have specific recruitment objectives which are more challenging than at any time in the past. You are very aware of the 'war for talent' and the fact that there is great competition for good people, especially university graduates. After talking with colleagues in the market, you and your HR team realise that you must proactively seek out innovative ways to attract new talent to your company. You believe that this means leveraging your reputation for sustainability more effectively during the recruitment process, as well as broadening your recruitment channels and reaching out proactively to a more diverse range of candidates from different backgrounds and minority groups.

Typically, diversity has not been a focus of your company and no special efforts have been made to increase diversity. In fact, this is not something that you and your HR team have focused on in any way in the past. Your workforce is predominantly led by males, while most of the unskilled roles are performed by women (e.g. check-out cashiers, shelf-stockers, cleaners, etc.). The population barely includes people with disabilities and ethnic groups in the population are not significantly represented.

In order to compete effectively in the 'war for talent', you believe your company must significantly rethink the way it recruits and who it recruits, in order to exploit fully the potential talent available in the market. Not only must the company now learn to recruit in a more diverse way, the organisation must be able to take diverse candidates on board successfully and enable them to progress within the company over time. You charge yourself with delivering a plan to attract, recruit, advance and retain diverse candidates to meet the targets defined by your CEO within three years:

- 25% of the workforce (currently 10%) should be sourced from diverse groups
- 20% of management (currently 5%) should be women
- 5% of management should be from diverse groups (currently zero)

It won't be easy!

Questions for discussion

1. Who is affected by this situation and what is the impact on them? List all the relevant internal and external stakeholders and implications for them in this change in policy.

2. What tools does the HR manager have to increase diversity in recruitment processes? Which new channels can the HR manager open up? How do recruitment processes need to change?

3. What sort of organisational culture is necessary in order to attract, recruit and retain more diverse people? What needs to be done to ensure the right culture is in place? Which key HR processes and tools are required?

4. Which tools does the HR manager have to measure the impact of this change in policy on the business results, organisational culture, employees, local communities and the local economy? Which performance indicators should be developed to measure success?

Output required

1. State the top three actions you recommend the HR manager should advance during the next 12 months.

2. Explain why these are the most important things you should do.

3. Explain the role of the CEO and other managers in supporting this programme.

Additional teaching material and ideas

Made in Dagenham

www.imdb.com/title/tt1371155/

This movie is a dramatisation of the 1968 strike at the Ford Dagenham car plant, where female workers walked out in protest against sexual discrimination. There are several important elements in this movie which relate to the nature of power relationships in the workplace and the strength and courage it takes to drive change in support of human rights at work. While this scenario may seem rather outdated, the challenges of women in achieving equal rights are still relevant today in many workplaces, not to mention the challenges of other groups such as the LGBT (lesbian, gay, bisexual, transgender) community. This movie can be the basis for a discussion about what needs to change in order to ensure that equal opportunity and equal rights become reality in all workplaces, and whose responsibility it is to fight for those rights.

BITC Competency Map

www.bitc.org.uk/services/learning-bitc/cr-practitioner-competency-map

This is a tool for CSR and HR managers. It provides a tool to better understand and develop the required behaviours of CSR managers, and includes a guide for HR managers to understand these behaviours so that they can develop programmes to encourage such behaviours in the organisation. The map provides case studies of how companies have used the competency map. The map can be a useful tool to teach approaches to CSR and the ways in which HR can support effective CSR and sustainability development in the organisation.

GRI (Global Reporting Initiative) Sustainability Disclosure Database

http://database.globalreporting.org/

This is a repository of sustainability reports from around the world, updated as reports are published. HR managers, seeking to understand the way in which sustainable HRM is reported, may search the database by company, sector or even by specific performance indicators and review how sustainability and HRM topics are practised and reported by companies, providing both interesting insights and ideas as well as performance benchmarks against different metrics. The GRI database can be used as a basis for setting exercises to develop an understanding of sustainable HRM transparency.

UN Global Compact

www.unglobalcompact.org/

The UN Global Compact is a voluntary framework for responsible business based on ten principles which have been accepted by thousands of business organisations around the world. Seven of the ten principles have a clear link to HRM and HR process as they relate to upholding human rights, labour rights and maintaining an ethical culture which opposes corruption. The UN Global Compact is rich with information, reports and tools which can assist business in understanding the issues and developing management approaches and can be used in designing learning exercises in different areas of sustainable HRM.

Anita Roddick, *Business as Unusual: My Entrepreneurial Journey—Profits with Principles* (Roddick 2005)

www.anitaroddick.com/books.php

This book was not written specifically as a management teaching book in sustainable HRM. However, it is immensely readable and chronicles the experiences and conflicts inherent in developing a business based on social and environmentally responsible values. The book can be used as a basis for discussion about the ways in which socially responsible businesses create cultures in which values thrive and the challenges that business leaders face in selecting and developing employees.

Further reading

Cohen, E. (2010) *CSR for HR: A Necessary Partnership for Advancing Responsible Business Practices* (Sheffield, UK: Greenleaf Publishing).

> The HR department can and should play an important role in CSR. This book is designed to assist practitioners in understanding how CSR is changing the HR function. It outlines the implications of the growing importance of CSR for different HR functions, examines how HR can help embed CSR and proposes the infrastructure needed. Effectively, *CSR for HR* is a guide for HR professionals in how to adopt a CSR approach to HRM.

Cohen, E., S. Taylor and M. Muller-Camen (2012) *HRM's Role in Corporate Social and Environmental Sustainability* (Alexandria, VA: Society for Human Resource Management).

> This report begins by examining the critical role HRM plays in sustainability and the HRM tools available to embed sustainability strategy in the organisation. The second section introduces a road map to sustainable HRM. It outlines global business approaches to sustainability, labour standards and specific aspects of sustainable practice such as employee volunteering, employer branding and green HRM. Finally, the report explores the new HR skills required for practising sustainable HRM and the applicability of sustainable HRM in different types of organisations.

Savitz, A. (2013) *Talent, Transformation and the Triple Bottom Line* (San Francisco, CA: Jossey-Bass).

> Employees are central to creating sustainable organisations, yet they are left on the side-lines in most sustainability initiatives along with the HR professionals who should be helping to engage and energise them. This book shows business leaders and HR professionals how to: motivate employees to create economic, environmental and social value; facilitate necessary culture, strategic and organisational change; embed sustainability into the employee life-cycle; and strengthen existing capabilities and develop new ones necessary to support the transformation to sustainability.

SHRM (Society for Human Resource Management) (2011) *Advancing Sustainability: HR's Role* (Alexandria, VA: Society for Human Resource Management).

> The majority of organisations in the US are engaged in some form of sustainable work practices and, of those that have calculated the return on investment, almost half have reported a positive outcome. This research is based on a 2010 survey of 728 HR professionals in the US. Other noteworthy findings were that the three key drivers for these activities were contribution to society, competitive financial advantage and environmental considerations. Moreover, one of the most important positive outcomes from sustainability initiatives was improved employee morale. In this report, you will find examples and case studies from a range of organisations and sustainable workplace practices.

Ulrich, Dave, and Wendy Ulrich (2010) *The Why of Work* (New York: McGraw Hill).

> This book, while not specifically focusing on sustainable HRM, is certainly a precursor to the creation of an organisation in which sustainable principles form part of the culture. Drawing attention to the 'meaning' of work, and the reasons employees become motivated and engaged, beyond the pay slip, this is an enlightening, easy-to-read volume of how HR can support a purposeful culture and why this is important.

References

BT plc (2014) *Better Future Report*, www.btplc.com/Betterfuture/BetterBusiness/BetterFutureReport/Keyperformanceindicators/Default.aspx, accessed 29 March 2014.

Caesars Entertainment Corporation (2013) *2012 CSR & Sustainability Report*, www.caesars.com/corporate/reports.html, accessed 29 March 2014.

Cohen, E. (2010) *CSR for HR: A Necessary Partnership for Advancing Responsible Business Practices* (Sheffield, UK: Greenleaf Publishing).

Cohen, E., S. Taylor and M. Muller-Camen (2012) *HRM's Role in Corporate Social and Environmental Sustainability* (Alexandria, VA: Society for Human Resource Management).

ECI Telecom (2013) *Sustainability Report*, www.ecitele.com/abouteci/AboutECIDocs/ECI-Telecom-Sustainability-Report-2012.pdf, accessed 29 March 2014.

Employer Branding Today (2011) *French Affection for CSR Employers*, www.employerbrandingtoday.com/blog/2011/04/21/french-affection-for-csr-employers/, accessed 29 March 2014.

Gond, J.P., A. El-Akremi, J. Igalens and V. Swaen (2010) *Corporate Social Responsibility Influence on Employees*, www.nottingham.ac.uk/business/ICCSR/assets/muihqmluwosf.pdf, accessed 31 March 2014.

HBR (*Harvard Business Review*) (2010) 'Employee Wellness Programs', http://hbr.org/2010/12/whats-the-hard-return-on-employee-wellness-programs/ar/1, accessed 29 March 2014.

IESE (2013) 'Corporate Volunteering', Expatriatus blog, http://blog.iese.edu/expatriatus/2013/11/23/corporate-volunteering-what-does-the-latest-research-say, accessed 31 March 2014.

Korngold, Alice (2014) *A Better World, Inc.: How Companies Profit by Solving Global Problems* (New York: Palgrave Macmillan).

Nike (2013) *Nike Responsibility*, www.nikeresponsibility.com/report/content/chapter/manufacturing, accessed 29 March 2014.

Roddick, Anita (2005) *Business as Unusual: My Entrepreneurial Journey—Profits with Principles* (Chichester, UK: Anita Roddick Books)

Savitz, A. (2013) *Talent, Transformation and the Triple Bottom Line* (San Francisco, CA: Jossey-Bass).

SHRM (Society for Human Resource Management) (2011) *Advancing Sustainability: HR's Role* (Alexandria, VA: Society for Human Resource Management).

Ulrich, Dave, and Wendy Ulrich (2010) *The Why of Work* (New York: McGraw Hill).

USPS (2013) *Green Teams Help U.S. Postal Service Save Millions*, http://about. usps.com/news/national-releases/2013/pr13_015.htm, accessed 31 March 2014.

WEP (Women's Empowerment Principles) (2012), *Making the Connections: Women, Corporate Sustainability and Sustainable Development*, http:// weprinciples.org/files/attachments/37.pdf, accessed 31 March 2014.

8

Sustainable marketing

Helen Goworek

In this chapter you will learn about ways in which businesses can conduct their marketing activities more sustainably and how we can harness our power as consumers to reduce sustainability impacts. After reading this chapter you will be able to:

- Relate marketing theory to sustainability

- Understand how the key aspects of marketing are linked to sustainability

- Examine recent academic and industry developments in this field, in terms of both theory and practice

- Understand how marketers and consumers can lower their sustainability impacts

---

Introduction

This chapter aims to give an overview of contemporary developments in sustainable marketing. This topic is viewed from two perspectives: first, the marketing of products and services which are sustainable, and second, using marketing techniques which are in themselves sustainable. Literature on sustainable marketing is relatively limited and recent, with most of the key books on this topic having only been published since 2009 (e.g. Arnold 2009; Belz and Peattie 2009; Dahlstrom 2011; Martin and Schouten 2012). However, earlier ground-breakers were writing journal articles about the topic more than a decade ago (e.g. Carrigan and Attalla 2001), thereby sowing the seeds for more recent research. Those researching into sustainable marketing tend to be marketing consultants currently working in the field (e.g. Arnold 2009) or academics dispersed across various global regions.

Marketers have always been inspired by a wide range of different disciplines and the interdisciplinary nature and systemic thinking of sustainability therefore lend themselves well to marketing's eclectic mix of influences, drawing as it does from the fields of sociology, accountancy, finance, political science, design, geography and psychology. Marketing has a key role to play in a business's approach towards sustainability, since it is the main interface between the organisation and consumers (Martin and Schouten 2012). However, it should be acknowledged that a tension exists between marketing's goal of encouraging consumption and sustainability specialists' aim to reduce consumption of resources. Nevertheless, sustainability has become a significant issue for consumers, especially during the 21st century, and sustainable consumer behaviour has therefore become a key area of interest within the marketing literature, making it the focus of various studies (e.g. Wrigley 2008; Joergens 2006). Annual sales of ethical products in the UK have increased substantially, more than tripling between 1999 and 2012 from £13.5 billion to £47.2 billion (Co-operative Bank 2012).

Sustainable marketing is defined by Martin and Schouten (2012: 10) as 'the process of creating, communicating and delivering value to customers in such a way that both natural and human capital are preserved or enhanced throughout'. There is some crossover between sustainable marketing and **social marketing**, which aims to change consumers' behaviour for the benefit of society in general. However, social marketing's roots are in health campaigns and it more often applies to governmental policies and promotional strategies to encourage behavioural change (Belz and Peattie 2012), than it does to commercial strategies. A subsection of sustainable marketing is **green marketing**, since it concentrates only on environmental sustainability, and this is described by Dahlstrom (2011: 5) as 'the study of all efforts to consume, produce, distribute, promote, package and reclaim products in a manner that is sensitive or responsive to ecological concerns'. Dahlstrom exhorts governments, non-governmental organisations, consumers, retailers, manufacturers and service firms to engage in green marketing due to a variety of factors (Dahlstrom 2011):

- Environmental benefits
- Support for developing economies
- Consumer benefits
- Strategic benefits for organisations
- Product benefits
- Production process benefits
- Supply-chain benefits

This chapter's seminar content will draw both from students' business knowledge and their experiences as consumers. The key points are based on the standard marketing mix framework: product, price, promotion (marketing communications) and place (distribution channels). Though more contemporary marketing paradigms such as relationship marketing have emerged (see below), the marketing mix is deemed as being suitable for framing such a complex subject, since business students are very likely to have prior knowledge of it, thus allowing them more scope for the exploration of relevant sustainability issues. Overall, this chapter will review ways in which marketers can address sustainability issues in both their everyday practice and longer term strategy.

Sustainable marketing strategy and planning

Creating a marketing strategy is usually the responsibility of marketing managers or directors, derived from the corporate strategy that is usually devised by an organisation's senior management team. In order for marketing strategy to be effective it needs to be aligned closely with the overall corporate strategy and the strategies of other divisions within the organisation such as finance, procurement, human resources management, design and logistics. The inclusion of a sustainable approach within the corporate strategy can facilitate the development of a marketing strategy that recognises the significance of lessening the company's sustainability impacts. This type of strategy, that takes the long-term impacts of products and services into account, is referred to as **societal marketing** (Blythe 2009). It has now become standard practice for retailers, as well as many companies in other sectors, to incorporate CSR (corporate social responsibility) policies into their corporate strategies, thus making societal marketing (a close relation to social marketing) more widespread, as long as those policies are implemented in practice. Since the **marketing planning** process includes an audit of the environment in which the organisation operates, incorporating both external and internal factors, this is an ideal situation in which sustainability can be taken into account.

Of the **PESTEL factors** (political, economic, societal, technological and legal) that are investigated by marketers when assessing the **macro-environment**, ecological issues are the most obvious factors to examine in relation to sustainability. However, a broader approach can be taken by recognising that each of the PESTEL macro-environmental areas can also be considered in terms of sustainability. For example, technological advances can be used to make products and processes more environmentally sustainable. Innovative digital technology such as design software or 3D printing are

Figure 1: Stratasys desktop 3D printer (left) and *Crania Anatomica Filigre* 3D-printed artwork by Joshua Harker (right).

Source: Courtesy of Stratasys (left) and Joshua Harker (right).

becoming more widely accessible (see Fig. 1) and can lessen the wastage and use of materials for prototypes, with the extra advantage of speeding up the process. Nevertheless, these technologies usually reduce sustainability impacts, rather than removing them, since fossil fuels are needed to operate them, such as the energy and plastic involved in the 3D printing. 3D printing has applications for art, prototyping and production (see artwork by Joshua Harker in Fig. 1), and is even being used to construct a house in Amsterdam at the time of writing, using a bioplastic made from 75% plant oil blended with microfibre (Nield 2014).

The other key model used in the formulation of marketing strategy is the **SWOT** (strengths, weaknesses, opportunities and threats) analysis. This is another opportunity for marketers to incorporate sustainability issues within their strategies, by acknowledging sustainable approaches used by the company as strengths and considering areas where sustainability could be improved as weaknesses. Outside the organisation, opportunities to develop more sustainable practices, products and services can be reviewed, as well as considering threats to the organisation's capacity to operate in a sustainable manner. When marketing plans are devised to put strategies into practice they can have a substantial impact on customers, the environment and society in general, as discussed below. Marketing strategies usually begin with STP (**segmentation, targeting and positioning**). Segmentation divides consumers into groups with similar needs and characteristics. Organisations can then target these selected market segments by devising an appropriate marketing mix which aims to place the company, brand or product in a particular position in the consumer's mind. Encouraging consumers to perceive sustainability as an integral component of a brand's market position is becoming a key feature of many STP strategies.

Sustainable consumer behaviour

CB (consumer behaviour) is the study of who buys and what, how, when, where and why they buy (Jobber 2010). The consumption of products and services clearly has significant sustainability impacts, with its effects stretching well beyond the realms of marketing and business. Traditional CB models are predicated on the notion that marketers should seek to increase sales of products and services and consequently a need exists for contemporary models that take sustainability issues into account. One of the most widely used CB theories is the CDP (**consumer decision process**). Developed by Engel, Kollat and Blackwell (1968), the theory is based on the assumption that consumers follow a series of logical, rational steps when making consumption decisions.

Consumer decision-making

The CDP model originally included five phases: problem recognition, information search, evaluation of alternatives, purchase and post-purchase use. Tellingly, this version was inspired by earlier models of buyer behaviour in industrial markets (Robinson *et al.* 1967; Webster and Wind 1972) which did not acknowledge the disposal of products after the purchase decision. Unfortunately, this version of the model is often included in marketing textbooks, whereas a more recent adaptation with further steps developed by Blackwell *et al.* (2001) includes consumption, post-consumption evaluation and divestment stages (see

Figure 2: The CDP (consumer decision process) model.

1. Need recognition

2. Information search

3. Pre-purchase evaluation of alternatives

4. Purchase

5. Consumption

6. Post-consumption evaluation

7. Divestment

Source: Adapted from Blackwell *et al.* (2001).

Fig. 2). This updated model allows marketers to reflect on the longer term impacts of their products on the environment, yet it still has the potential to address sustainability issues more fully, e.g. by including more sustainable options in the 'evaluation of alternatives' phase.

However, it has been recognised that consumers do not always make rational decisions, which has led to the development of a different theory. Rather than viewing consumer decision-making as initiated by the recognition of a problem, the theory of **experiential consumer behaviour** acknowledges that consumerism can be led by hedonistic values, with consumers being motivated by pursuit of the enjoyment inherent in making purchase decisions (Holbrook and Hirschman 1982). There appears to be a prevailing view in many societies that consumption equals success, leading to conspicuous consumption where purchases are displayed ostentatiously and shopping being viewed as a leisure activity. These attitudes towards purchasing are frequently stimulated by marketing activity to persuade shoppers to spend more, a situation which is unsustainable as it leads to unnecessary usage of raw materials, particularly fossil fuels that are used in the manufacture and delivery of products. This can also cause extreme behaviour such as compulsive shopping and shoplifting, a trend which has been termed 'consumer misbehaviour' by Tonglet (2002).

Market segmentation in terms of sustainability

Market segmentation is traditionally based on consumers' **demographic, psychographic, geographic** or **behavioural** characteristics. Demographics are factual details about consumers such as age, psychographics are aspects of lifestyle and behavioural segmentation groups consumers by their frequency of use of a product or service, e.g. a loyal customer or occasional purchaser. In recent years, market segmentation categories have been developed that are based primarily on the sustainability of consumers' behaviour. An example of this is the *Framework for Pro-environmental Behaviours* developed for the UK government (Defra 2008). The framework categorises consumers into seven different groups from the sustainability-orientated 'positive greens' through to the opposite extreme:

1.   Positive greens

2.   Waste watchers

3. Concerned consumers

4. Sideline supporters

5. Cautious participants

6. Stalled starters

7. Honestly disengaged

Figure 3 describes the characteristics of each of these categories and positions them in terms of their willingness and ability to act in a sustainable manner. This type of model assists marketers in identifying, understanding and consequently responding to customer requirements, thus enabling sustainable CB by the provision of products and services to allow more sustainable purchase decisions to be made. It is anticipated that the proportion of the population in each category will change with the passage of time and be dependent upon the location of the market.

Studies have been conducted to investigate consumers' lack of willingness to purchase products with low sustainability impacts. For example,

Figure 3: A framework for pro-environmental behaviours.

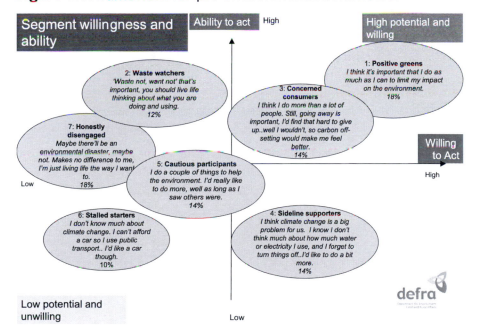

Source: Defra (2008).

according to Eckhardt *et al.* (2010: 426) 'many consumers profess to want to avoid unethical offerings in the marketplace yet few act on this inclination ... the market share held by green products is abysmally low'. Although people do not appear to wish to be viewed as behaving unethically, there is a disconnect between their behaviour and their professed opinions. Some people did change their behaviour but they were exceptions. All respondents in Eckhardt *et al.*'s (2010: 434) research offered justifications for unethical behaviour and the authors concluded:

> The nature of the rationales suggests that simply making information available to consumers about the ethical nature of their purchases, or even using moral appeals to try and invoke behavior change, will not likely engender anti-consumption of unethical or irresponsible brands ... Strong emotional appeals rather than rational or moral appeals may have a better chance of making the luxury of consumer ethics more appealing and the case for action more compelling.

Another study in this area compared **sustainable consumption** patterns across different sectors. McDonald *et al.* (2009: 141) found that sustainability criteria are used inconsistently across product sectors:

> For example, the same consumer may prioritise environmental criteria in his/her purchase of FMCGs [fast-moving consumer goods], consider them when buying white goods or flights, but ultimately sacrifice them in favour of availability or convenience, and not take them into account at all during the purchase of small electrical products. Equally, consumers focus on different green or ethical criteria in different product sectors.

CB is already a complex area that marketers are seeking to understand with the assistance of various methods including **consumer neuroscience** (Serrano and de Balanzo 2011), and issues of sustainability and ethics add a further dimension of complexity to these issues that researchers have yet to unravel fully.

Sustainable products and brands

There is a lack of consensus about what constitutes sustainable products and brands. The terms 'green' and 'eco' have been widely applied to products but since they have no precise definition it's not clear to consumers whether they are made entirely of renewable resources or simply have less impact on the environment than competing merchandise. Martin and Schouten (2012: 140) define a **sustainable brand** as being 'economically enduring and its associations in the minds of customers and other stakeholders rightfully include social justice and ecological sustainability', thereby aligning such brands with the triple bottom line.

Certain brands are inherently sustainable, having been built on sustainable values, such as the Body Shop and Howies. Other brands and retailers take a more limited approach to sustainability by offering a small selection of environmentally friendly or Fairtrade products, such as Puma's cradle-to-cradle certified InCycle products which are all either biodegrable or recyclable (Puma 2014). Most of the major car brands have incorporated improved fuel efficiency and more sustainable design into a selection of their cars in recent years, including Volkswagen's Blue Motion models and hydrogen fuel cell cars from Hyundai and Toyota. The automotive industry clearly has a huge amount of scope for improvement in terms of its impact on the environment and it is now becoming standard practice for concept cars to include more sustainable features. Many major brands and retailers, such as Nike and Marks & Spencer, are now seeking to incorporate sustainable values within their brand images. This trend is likely to have been prompted by criticism from pressure groups and consumers against major brands, which escalated during the 1990s. Various studies suggest that a socially responsible approach to business could be related to strong business performance. For example, Martin and Schouten (2012: 139) state that 'a study by Interbrand finds a correlation between CSR and brand value' and Waddock and Graves (1997) find a positive link between CSR and financial performance.

Sustainable products can be environmentally or socially sustainable and some brands combine both aspects, e.g. People Tree garments are manufactured only by Fairtrade companies, as well as being made from materials such as organic cotton. Handmade cosmetics retailer Lush sells 'charity pots' of hand and body moisturiser in its stores, donating

Figure 4: Charity pots from Lush incorporate both environmental and social sustainability.

Source: Courtesy of Lush.

the selling price (minus sales tax) to charity (see Fig. 4). The lotion contains organic ingredients and is socially sustainable through offering grants from its proceeds to groups in the UK and overseas that aim for long-term positive change to human rights, the environment and animal protection, with some of the groups being featured on the recycled/recyclable pots. Sustainable products have been criticised for being unfashionable in previous decades but many now combine strong design with sustainable materials as they need to be fit for purpose, offering functional and aesthetic properties alongside sustainability. Environmentally sustainable products can take various forms, being made of materials which are recycled, recyclable, re-used, repurposed or a combination of more than one of these aspects. For example, From Somewhere designs clothing from pre-consumer waste fabric from luxury brands, thus saving it from disposal, and Freitag makes durable messenger-style bags from recycled truck tarpaulins. Durability is perhaps a less conventional way of viewing sustainable products, by manufacturing them for longevity rather than disposability (Cooper 2010). Products and services can therefore have sustainability built into them via various processes and choices of materials, with marketers and designers being central to sustainable decision-making. These products can be 'choice edited' by retailers and brands to include an offer to customers that only consists of environmentally and socially sustainable products, such as Sainsbury's decision to only include Fairtrade cotton in its own-label T-shirt range.

Sustainable integrated marketing communications

Sustainable IMC (integrated marketing communications) can be viewed from two main perspectives: the promotion of sustainable products and services and promoting products and services using sustainable methods. A key IMC issue is that overstating the sustainable values of products has led to accusations of **greenwashing** against the brands that sell them. This seems to have made many companies somewhat reticent about making claims that reveal the sustainable nature of products. Consequently, consumers can find it difficult to discover which products and brands they could purchase to enable them to lessen their sustainability impacts, yet they would be willing to receive more information to allow them to do so (Fisher *et al.* 2008).

Since IMC involves two key levels of communications, corporate communications at the parent company level and brand/product communications, two different sets of stakeholders need to be addressed. At the corporate level, messages about the company's sustainability policies need to be communicated in ways that will engage stakeholders such as shareholders, the press and industry while reassuring them that the company retains financial sustainability. Because consumers may be oblivious to the existence of parent companies such as Unilever or Procter & Gamble, they require more specific messages about the practicalities and aesthetics of products and brands that they purchase. There is a danger that more sustainable products can be viewed as being weaker than their standard counterparts, referred to as 'sustainability liability' (Luchs *et al.* 2010), and it is therefore important to stress the stronger aspects of such products, without resorting to greenwash, using a careful balance of providing sufficient information without exaggerating claims.

There has been a tendency in recent years to move away from relying on the 'hard sell' of broadcast and print advertisements, towards digital advertising and 'soft sell' forms of promotion such as online PR (**public**

relations) and **word-of-mouth** (Meerman-Scott 2007). Facilitated by the Internet, these methods could be considered to be more sustainable than using printed promotional material, although clearly computers may use fossil fuels as an energy source, whereas print media can be both renewable and recyclable. RM (**relationship marketing**) is viewed as an alternative method of engaging with consumers, rather than focusing on the marketing mix. Derived from B2B marketing, as well as from traditional relationships between tradespeople and customers, RM is defined by Blythe (2013: 368) as 'the practice of concentrating on the lifetime value of customers rather than their value in the single transaction'. Building up this longer term relationship often involves personalised communication being sent to consumers via direct marketing messages. **Direct marketing** can now be distributed more sustainably and economically by e-mail, thus saving on paper, printing, postage and distribution associated with traditional mailshots (Goworek and McGoldrick in press). Word-of-mouth communication can now be distributed more rapidly than in previous generations through the use of social media. While this can benefit companies in terms of the efficiency and reach of their own PR, the messages spread by consumers via social media and user reviews on third-party websites such as TripAdvisor are beyond the control of companies. It is therefore now increasingly important that consumers receive clear, reliable and transparent information about the sustainability of products and services.

Sustainable pricing

As consumers seek to purchase more products, under the pressure of marketing stimuli and peer groups, retailers and brands may seek to reduce prices to fulfil their customers' desire to buy more products. This can lead to the production of an excessive amount of products that not only use up valuable raw materials, but can also lead to more pollution from manufacturing as well as increased landfill waste in the divestment phase. Reduced prices are also central in problems concerning social sustainability, with competitive prices driving manufacturers to pay low wages and offer poor working conditions. Problems with low prices are not restricted to the cheaper, so-called 'value' end of the mass market. This is illustrated by the tragic Rana Plaza factory collapse in Bangladesh in 2013, which resulted in more than 1,000 deaths and many injured victims. Products were manufactured in the building not only for low-priced retailer Primark but also middle mass-market companies Inditex and Mango, among others. Therefore, paying a mid-level retail price for a product is no guarantee that it has been made by operatives with good employment conditions, and the purchase price does not indicate the cost price that has been paid by the retailer to the supplier. Fortunately, minimum wages have been increased in Bangladesh since the disaster, yet this is no guarantee that all of their factories will give pay rises (Thomasson 2014) and it does not address safety issues or in any way compensate for the devastation and loss of life which has occurred. Consequently, at New York Fashion Week in February 2014, activists projected photos of victims of the Rana Plaza disaster onto the Lincoln Center to publicise the real price of non-socially sustainable fashion (Malik Chua 2014).

An obvious issue with the pricing of sustainable products and services is that they are frequently perceived as being more expensive than standard items. This can be the case when, for example, products or their components are organic, leading to lower yields for land in comparison to produce grown using pesticides, as well as payment for the process of organic certification. Similarly, premiums paid to farmers for **Fairtrade** goods or socially responsible donations to the community where products are manufactured inevitably add extra costs. However, a sustainable approach to business also has the potential to reduce costs, e.g. by eliminating waste, or using recycled products or more fuel-efficient transportation.

High costs may also be associated with sustainable products because many have been introduced at the higher end of the market, as is usually the case with new innovations, and products can consequently become more cost-effective when they reach the mass market, due to achieving economies of scale. Through advance planning, it is possible for the costs associated with sustainability to be 'designed out' of products, e.g. incorporating solar panels into buildings during construction is more economical than adding the panels at a later stage. Manufacturers are able to calculate more realistic product costs by considering their full impact on the environment, using **life-cycle assessment**, defined by Dahlstrom (2011: 137) as 'accounting for production and processing as well as resource energy, usage, emissions and waste'. Consumers have the option to act in a more environmentally sustainable way by voluntarily paying an additional price for products or services by using **carbon offsetting**. This can be used when paying for flights, for example, to contribute towards reforestation to offset the CO_2 emitted by the aviation fuel.

Sustainable distribution channels

Distribution channels for products and services have several facets relating to environmental and social sustainability issues: the use of materials in the selection of products they offer (as covered earlier); the use of materials to construct the retail environment; and the social sustainability of employees in manufacturing, transportation, warehousing and retailing. Although all types of organisation can address sustainability, retailers are uniquely positioned in the distribution chain at the nexus between suppliers and consumers, interacting directly with both of these stakeholder groups and thus being able to exert a strong influence upon their sustainability impacts. There were 287,000 retail outlets in the UK in 2012, employing 3 million workers and selling £321 billion worth of goods, worth 20% of the country's GDP (gross domestic product) (BRC 2014), thus showing the significance of the retail sector to the economy. **Etailing** (online retailing) has become a key part of the retail market and this is growing further through the widespread use of mobile devices (mtailing).

Since it acts as a filter between suppliers and consumers, as well as being the largest source of private sector employment, retailing is the industry which can have the greatest potential impact upon society and its ability to behave sustainably, possibly even more so than any other societal group. The industry's main body, the BRC (British Retail Consortium), has played an active part in improving retailers' sustainability impacts, e.g. by developing 'A Better Retailing Climate' in 2008 as its sustainability policy to guide retailers, with the involvement of businesses worth more than half of the retail market by value (BRC 2009). This followed on from the 'Plan A' sustainable retailing policy being published the previous year by the UK's leading clothing retailer, M&S (Marks & Spencer 2007).

The following list proposes techniques that can be used by retailers to exert a positive influence on sustainable practice:

- Encouraging suppliers to behave more sustainably in the ways that they source, manufacture and deliver products (see Chapter 10)

- Choice editing by sourcing and selling products that offer only environmentally and socially sustainable choices to consumers (see above)

- Minimising energy consumption in distribution and in stores or offices

- Sustainable store design (or sustainable etailing/mtailing in the case of online retailers)

- Minimising disposal of waste, particularly to landfill

- Recycling or using recycled/repurposed materials in products, stores and offices

- Educating and enabling consumers to behave more sustainably

Retailers could educate their customers by offering sustainability guidelines online or in store for their customers to act upon, to alter ingrained habits. Each of the tactics listed above has financial implications for retailers, but they are not all negative, as many could be implemented at relatively low cost or be instrumental in reducing costs, e.g. through lowering energy consumption. Implementing these techniques could decrease the possibility of legislation or regulations regarding sustainability being imposed on retailers in the future (Goworek *et al.* 2012). However, many companies may welcome the introduction of legislation to ensure a more 'level playing field' among competitors.

Conclusion

The consequences of living unsustainably have been represented by the film business in the form of disaster movies (Blincoe 2009), thus potentially making consumers feel helpless to act. Rather than presenting the world as hurtling inevitably towards the apocalypse, more positive motivation can be given to consumers with examples of positive scenarios in which sustainable behaviour could potentially avert such a crisis. In higher education, business and marketing academics can create and disseminate such scenarios via curricula, assignments and placement/employment opportunities. Marketing academics can benefit from working alongside colleagues in different disciplines to develop curricula which address sustainability, since 'interdisciplinarity will be an important vehicle for driving transformation and will demonstrate that success does not simply derive from specialisation and narrowness' according to Phillips (2009). The topic of sustainable marketing has begun to be addressed in academic journals in the fields of marketing and ethics but there is scope for this to become a discipline in its own right or, as this chapter seeks to demonstrate, sustainability can be integrated throughout the marketing curriculum. Marketing educators have numerous opportunities to encourage others to behave more sustainably within their institutions and as consumers, such as:

- Seeking out literature on sustainable marketing to incorporate into module reading lists, post on intranet pages, order for the library and share with colleagues in their own departments and at other universities

- Passing on information to encourage sustainable CB in students who are in other departments

- Facilitating opportunities for staff to meet to discuss sustainable marketing issues

- Encouraging the formation of student groups interested in sustainability and marketing, e.g. by booking rooms for them to meet in

- Disseminating information to friends and relatives about behaving more sustainably as a consumer

- Generally encouraging the purchase of products which have low sustainability impacts

Businesses usually act in response to sales figures, complaints and negative publicity, and therefore consumers also have the potential power to encourage marketers and businesses in general to behave more sustainably through the following actions:

- Buying products which have low sustainability impacts, to encourage businesses to offer more of them in future

- Buying less products overall but selecting goods which are more durable

- Asking questions of businesses about sustainability, e.g. whether they sell Fairtrade merchandise or use palm oil

- Contacting companies to complain when their ranges of sustainable products are limited or non-existent

- Posting reviews about products or services in relation to their sustainability on companies' websites or third-party review websites

- Contacting the media about experiences with businesses in relation to sustainability

In conclusion, the **extended marketing mix**, or 'seven Ps', can be applied to services marketing, with the addition of people, physical environment and process. It could be argued that alternatively, the three Ps of the triple bottom line, 'people, planet and profit', could be added to the traditional marketing mix to make a new seven Ps framework for the sustainable marketing of products and services.

Suggested seminars

Seminar 1: Sustainable products

In this seminar you will investigate your own behaviour in relation to sustainability and the products you buy.

Activity 1 (15 minutes)

Working in pairs or small groups, list some specific examples of your own sustainable practice relating to the products you buy when shopping, e.g. buying durable goods, choosing products made from renewable, recycled or repurposed materials and recycling products afterwards. You can also include sustainable practices you've heard of other people using or you could create new ideas.

Activity 2 (10 minutes)

Now describe and discuss some of the things you do where the sustainability impacts could be improved, e.g. where you send used materials to landfill or purchase products from unsustainable sources.

Activity 3 (30 minutes)

Consider what influenced (or could influence) you to adopt the practices in Activity 1. What are the barriers to you behaving more sustainably when you are shopping, consuming or disposing of products, in relation to the outcomes of Activity 2? Make suggestions of ways in which these barriers could potentially be removed. For example, this could involve policy changes by retailers, your university/college, companies, the government and you or your peer group. As a result of this discussion, specify three key suggestions for removing barriers to consumers behaving more sustainably. Place these suggestions on a flip chart or visualiser and discuss them with the rest of the seminar group.

Seminar 2: Sustainable consumer behaviour exercise

In this seminar you will investigate your behaviour as a consumer in relation to sustainable consumption.

Activity: Sustainable CB focus group (55 minutes)

Split the seminar group into teams of around eight to ten students. One person in each team should be appointed as a moderator and another should take on the role of note-taker, leaving six to eight people to take part in a focus group. The briefing for the activity should take up to five minutes. The moderator needs to manage the discussion without offering their own views, so as not to influence the group's perceptions, keeping the discussion on track. Group members should be allowed to offer their opinions and all of them should be drawn into the conversation at some point (except for the note-taker).

The moderator should introduce the topic of sustainable CB and read the questions below to the group, allowing each question to be explored by the participants. Prompts can be used to extend the conversation. Each group should discuss the issues in these questions for around 30 minutes. The note-taker should make notes on the key points of the discussion, to summarise participants' views. It's not essential for each group to get to the end of all of the questions, as long as there has been interaction and debate about sustainability issues between the group members. The lecturer can observe part of each group's discussion and may wish to support the moderator in ensuring that all participants become involved in the conversation.

After the group discussions, the next ten minutes should be taken up with feedback by the note-taker and moderator of each group, summarising the views of the participants to the whole seminar group and noting where the groups had responses in common with each other. This could include the written notes being shown on a visualiser or overhead projector. In the final ten minutes the whole seminar group should be drawn together by the lecturer and asked to offer views on the potential implications of the findings for manufacturers and retailers.

Discussion group questions

The questions have been adapted from those used within a study funded by Defra (Fisher *et al.* 2008) to establish the public's understanding of sustainable clothing consumption. The full report and appendices are available to download online at: http://randd.defra.gov.uk/Default.aspx?Menu=Menu&Module=More&Location=None&Completed =1&ProjectID=15626 (see Appendices p. 35 in the report).

Introduction by moderator

This discussion session is about the sustainability impacts of clothing. We will discuss how you obtain your clothes, how you look after them and what you do when you no longer need them. We want to encourage you to be open and honest with your contributions and feel free to disagree, but please respect the fact that other people are entitled to hold different views from you by only speaking one at a time. Also we will aim to enable everyone to contribute equally to the discussions. What you say is to be considered confidential within this seminar group.

Key questions

1. **Obtaining clothes:** First of all, we're going to talk about buying clothes. What kind of information informs your clothing purchasing decisions (e.g. adverts, magazine articles, brochures, seeing new clothes on friends)?

2. Do you feel that you usually buy clothes having recognised a need for some or for the pleasure of shopping?

3. Do you always buy your own clothes or do your family or partner ever buy them for you?

4. What kind of clothes would you think of as 'sustainable' and why? Does anything influence your decisions about which clothes are sustainable? (Use these prompts if needed: brand, fabric (e.g. organic), durability and manufacturing conditions.)

5. Do any of you buy sustainable clothing? If so, can you give some examples (e.g. sustainable brands and fabrics)?

6. **Clothing use and maintenance:** Next we want to consider issues to do with washing, drying and caring for your clothes. What are the

usual elements in your laundry routine? (Prompt if necessary by asking whether they sort, wash, dry and iron or dry clean.)

7. Do you separate different types of items (e.g. colours and fabrics)? If not, why?

8. Do you always use a washing machine or sometimes hand wash?

9. Which machine wash temperature do you use and why?

10. How do you dry your clothes? (Prompts: tumble drying, line drying, using an indoor clothes airer.)

11. If you normally use a tumble dryer, what are your reasons for doing this? Do you consider the money or energy involved in using it?

12. Do you or anyone else in your household ever repair clothes? If not, what puts you off doing this? (Prompts: lack of skill, equipment or time or it's cheaper/easier to replace them.)

13. **Disposing of clothes:** What influences how long you keep clothing? (Prompts: it's gone out of fashion, worn out or a poor fit.)

14. What sort of clothes do you put in the rubbish bin? What do you do with other types? (Use prompts if needed, e.g. give to a charity shop or jumble sale, put it in a clothing recycling bin/bank, give it away to friends or family, take it to a clothes exchange party, sell it via a car boot sale, eBay, Amazon, etc.)

Seminar 3: Sustainable retailing exercise

This seminar will focus on the ways in which retailers can behave more sustainably.

Working in small teams of two to four students, select a bricks-and-mortar retailer that you believe has the potential to improve its sustainability impacts. This could be one which is already improving its sustainability impacts or one which does not seem to have done this at all. This retailer could be selected at the previous seminar so that students have the opportunity to visit one of the company's branches beforehand and to look for ideas of good practice in terms of sustainability in other organisations. Teams may all choose the same retailer or different ones. The lecturer may wish to show this one-minute video about Timberland's sustainable store design at the start: http://community. timberland.com/Earthkeeping/Sustainable-Store-Design.

Activity 1 (10 minutes)

Each team should establish areas in which the retailer has room for improvement in terms of behaving sustainably. This could fall into two main areas:

- Store environment (e.g. energy use in lighting and heating, as well as the sustainability of materials used in the store's fixtures)

- Products and services (e.g. the availability of environmentally sustainable or Fairtrade products)

Activity 2 (45 minutes)

For up to 30 minutes you should discuss ways in which the retailer can improve its sustainability impacts in these respects. See the section on 'sustainable distribution channels' for inspiration. You can use good practice from other organisations to give you some ideas and the financial viability of your suggestions should be taken into account. Suggestions from each team should be presented informally to the rest of the seminar group for ten minutes, through verbal discussion or through a list of ideas on a flip chart or visualiser. For the last five minutes, as a result of the discussion, the seminar group should sum up the key ways in which retailers in general can improve their sustainability impacts.

Additional teaching material and ideas

1. Apply the CDP model (Fig. 2) to shopping for organic vegetables. Consider each one of the model's stages and decide whether it is relevant to this type of purchase. Suggest ways in which the model could be adapted to take sustainability into account, e.g. by removing or renaming any of the seven stages or adding in one or more new stages.

2. Sustainable Brands conferences take place in San Diego and London. Delegates can attend in person but it is also possible to register to watch a live stream of these events, with selected footage available on the organisation's website at: www.sustainablebrands. com/library_search/results/taxonomy%3A65. Watch an extract of 30 minutes or more from a recent Sustainable Brands conference and discuss the possible effects on brands of these issues.

3. The Centre for Sustainable Design (CfSD) at the University of the Creative Arts (UCA) in Surrey, UK, provides a wide range of resources and links relating to innovative design, sustainable marketing and sustainable supply chains: http://cfsd.org.uk/projects/. Assess which of these resources you would recommend marketers to use to encourage more sustainable practice in their organisations.

4. Watch this video about Nike recycling trainers, then investigate the criticism that has been levelled at the company by ethical campaigners in the past, using an Internet search. Assess the effectiveness of Nike's subsequent initiatives to enhance their sustainability credentials: www.nikereuseashoe.com/

5. Describe the current marketing mix of a retailer that you consider to have a weak reputation in terms of sustainability. Amend aspects of any of the four elements (product, price, promotion, place) to devise a more sustainable marketing mix for this business, with each of the four areas working together compatibly.

6. Read and watch the information presented here by 3D printing companies: www.3dprintingnews.co.uk/ and www.stratasys.com/corporate/about-us. Working in teams, suggest ways in which 3D printing could be used to help businesses lessen their sustainability

impacts, giving specific examples where this technique could be applied, e.g. in prototyping and manufacturing.

7. Pressure groups such as Labour Behind the Label have criticised retailers for a lack of transparency about where their products are sourced and the employment conditions in which their operatives work. Discuss potential reasons why retail businesses don't usually reveal this information to consumers and consider the effects that being more transparent about their sources could have on their products, pricing and promotion.

Further reading

Allwood, J.M., S.E. Laursen, C.M. de Rodriguez and N.M.P. Bocken (2006) *The Present and Future Sustainability of Fashion and Textiles in the UK* (Cambridge, UK: University of Cambridge Institute for Manufacturing; www.ifm. eng.cam.ac.uk/resources/sustainability/well-dressed/).

> This extensive report covers a wide range of issues in relation to sustainability in the fashion and textiles industry and can be considered a standard reference for this business sector in the UK. You will find a selection of interesting facts and figures relating to the production, selling and consumption of textiles, e.g. we consume approximately two million tonnes or around 35kg per person of textiles each year, costing us about £20 per kg.

Belz, F.M., and K. Peattie (2012) *Sustainability Marketing: A Global Perspective*, 2nd edn (Chichester, UK: Wiley and Sons).

> This seminal text offers an in-depth exploration of sustainability marketing and the ways in which it can address socio-ecological problems. It begins by discussing key marketing issues in the 21st century and a framework for sustainability marketing then covering values, marketing strategies, CB and the marketing mix, with the final part predicting the future of sustainability marketing.

Dahlstrom, R. (2011) *Green Marketing Management* (Andover, UK: South-Western Cengage).

> This textbook covers a wide variety of issues exploring the relationship between environmental sustainability and marketing, with an emphasis on the significance of value and a good selection of case studies on well-known brands. Key sections include the consumption–environment interface and providing value via sustainable marketing strategies, as well as green marketing and sustainability reporting. The book is original in providing a macroeconomic view of

energy consumption, pertaining to households, the services sector, the transportation sector and industry.

Harrison, R., T. Newholm and D. Shaw (2005) *The Ethical Consumer* (London: Sage).

> This edited compilation offers a series of perspectives from various authors on the ways in which consumers can behave ethically, as well as considering the barriers to this behaviour. The book discusses how consumers can act as voters, the impact of campaigners, consumers' beliefs and decisions, corporate disclosure and challenges for ethical markets.

Martin, D., and J. Schouten (2012) *Sustainable Marketing* (Upper Saddle River, NJ: Prentice Hall).

> This definitive textbook by academics from the University of Portland, US, comprises all of the aspects you would expect to find in a standard marketing textbook, viewed from a sustainability perspective, forming a comprehensive guide to the topic with innovative cases and a broad range of academic references.

References

Allwood, J.M., S.E. Laursen, C.M. de Rodriguez and N.M.P. Bocken (2006) *The Present and Future Sustainability of Fashion and Textiles in the UK* (Cambridge, UK: University of Cambridge Institute for Manufacturing; www.ifm. eng.cam.ac.uk/resources/sustainability/well-dressed/, accessed 25 October 2012).

Arnold, C. (2009) *Ethical Marketing and the New Consumer* (Chichester, UK: Wiley).

Belz, F.M., and K. Peattie (2009) *Sustainability Marketing: A Global Perspective* (Chichester, UK: Wiley).

—— (2012) *Sustainability Marketing: A Global Perspective*, 2nd edn (Chichester, UK: Wiley).

Blackwell, R.D., P.W. Miniard and J.F. Engel (2001) *Consumer Behavior*, 9th edn (Mason, OH: Thomson South Western Publishing).

Blincoe, K. (2009) 'Re-educating the Person', in A. Stibbe (ed.), *The Handbook of Sustainability Literacy: Skills for a Changing World* (Totnes, UK: Green Books): 204-208.

Blythe, J. (2009) *Principles and Practice of Marketing*, 2nd edn (Andover, UK: South-Western Cengage).

—— (2013) *Consumer Behaviour*, 2nd edn (London: Sage).

BRC (British Retail Consortium) (2009) *A Better Retailing Climate*, www.brc.org. uk/brc_show_document.asp?id=4195&moid=7261, accessed 20 October, 2013.

—— (2014) *Stats and Facts*, www.brc.org.uk/bis/default.asp?main_id=15, accessed 23 January 2014.

Carrigan, M., and A. Attalla (2001) 'The Myth of the Ethical Consumer: Do Ethics Matter in Purchase Behaviour?', *Journal of Consumer Marketing* 18.7: 560-78.

Cooper, T. (2010) *Longer Lasting Products: Alternatives to the Throwaway Society* (Farnham, UK: Gower).

Co-operative Bank (2012) *Ethical Consumerism Report*, www.co-operativebank. co.uk/servlet/Satellite?c=Page&cid=1169627027939&pagename=Corp/Page/ tplCorp, accessed 23 January 2014.

Dahlstrom, R. (2011) *Green Marketing Management* (Andover, UK: South-Western Cengage).

Defra (2008) *A Framework for Pro-environmental Behaviours*, http://archive. defra.gov.uk/evidence/social/behaviour/documents/behaviours-jan08-report. pdf, accessed 23 January 2014.

Eckhardt, G.M., R. Belk and T.M. Devinney (2010) 'Why Don't Consumers Consume Ethically?', *Journal of Consumer Behaviour* 9: 426-36.

Engel, J.F., D.T. Kollat and R. Blackwell (1968) *Consumer Behavior* (New York: Rinehart & Winston).

Fisher, T., T. Cooper, S. Woodward, A. Hiller and H. Goworek (2008) *Public Understanding of Sustainable Clothing*, http://randd.defra.gov.uk/Default.aspx?Me nu=Menu&Module=More&Location=None&Completed=1&ProjectID=15626, accessed 30 November 2013.

Goworek, H., and P.J. McGoldrick (in press) *Retail Marketing Management: Principles and Practice* (Harlow, UK: Pearson).

Goworek, H., T. Cooper, T. Fisher, S. Woodward and A. Hiller (2012) 'The Sustainable Clothing Market: An Evaluation of Potential Strategies for UK Retailers', *International Journal of Retail & Distribution Management* 40.12: 935-55.

Harrison, R., T. Newholm and D. Shaw (2005) *The Ethical Consumer* (London: Sage).

Holbrook, M., and E. Hirschman (1982) 'The experiential aspects of consumption: Consumer fantasies, feelings and fun', *The Journal of Consumer Research* 9.2: 132-39.

Jobber, D. (2010) *Principles and Practice of Marketing*, 6th edn (Harlow, UK: McGraw Hill).

Joergens, C. (2006) 'Ethical Fashion: Myth or Future Trend?', *Journal of Fashion Marketing and Management* 10.3: 360-71.

Luchs, M.G., R.W. Naylor, J.R. Irwin and R. Raghunathan (2010) 'The Sustainability Liability: Potential Negative Effects of Ethicality on Product Preference', *Journal of Marketing* 74: 18-31.

Malik Chua, J. (2014) 'Activists project Photos of Rana Plaza Victims at New York Fashion Week', *Ecouterre*, 7 February 2014, www.ecouterre.com/activists-project-photos-of-rana-plaza-victims-at-new-york-fashion-week/, accessed 10 February 2014.

Marks & Spencer (2007) *Plan A*, http://plana.marksandspencer.com/about, accessed 12 February 2008.

Martin, D., and J. Schouten (2012) *Sustainable Marketing* (Upper Saddle River, NJ: Prentice Hall).

McDonald, S., C. Oates, M. Thyne, P. Alevizou and L.A. McMorland (2009) 'Comparing Sustainable Consumption Patterns Across Product Sectors', *International Journal of Consumer Studies* 33: 137-45.

Meerman-Scott, D. (2007) *The New Rules of Marketing and PR* (Hoboken, NJ: Wiley and Sons).

Nield, D. (2014) 'A full-size 3D house is under construction in Amsterdam', *Digital Trends*, 30 March 2014, www.digitaltrends.com/cool-tech/full-size-3d-printed-house-construction-amsterdam/#!B0tJq, accessed 31 March 2014.

Phillips, A. (2009) 'Institutional Transformation', in A. Stibbe (ed.), *The Handbook of Sustainability Literacy: Skills for a Changing World* (Totnes, UK: Green Books), 209-14.

Puma (2014) *Sustainability*, https://brand.puma.com/bringmeback, accessed 23 March 2014.

Robinson, P.J., C.W. Faris and Y. Wind (1967) *Industrial Procurement* (New York: Allyn and Bacon).

Serrano, N., and C. de Balanzo (2011) 'Neuroscience and Communication Strategy: Redefining the Role of the Unconscious', *Tripodos*, Universitat Ramon Llull, www.raco.cat/index.php/Tripodos/article/view/247474, accessed 20 March 2014.

Thomasson, E. (2014) 'Inspections highlight safety risks at Bangladesh factories', Reuters, 10 March 2014, www.reuters.com/article/2014/03/10/us-bangladesh-inspections-idUSBREA2914920140310?feedType=RSS, accessed 24 March 2014.

Tonglet, M. (2002) 'Consumer Misbehaviour: An Exploratory Study of Shoplifting', *Journal of Consumer Behaviour* 1.4: 336-54.

Waddock, S.A., and S.B. Graves (1997) 'The corporate social performance–financial performance link', *Strategic Management Journal* 18.4: 303-19.

Webster, F.E., and Y. Wind (1972) *Organizational Buying Behavior* (New York: Prentice Hall).

Wrigley, P. (2008) 'Ethics Must Stay High on the Agenda', *Drapers*, 27 November 2008, www.drapersonline.com/news/ethics-must-stay-high-on-the-agenda/1936268.article#.U5HEvhsU_IU, accessed 27 November 2013.

9

Sustainable operations management

Maggie Zeng

Sustainability has long been on the agenda of many organisations. However, many of the sustainability initiatives lack cohesion, with little thought given to long-term operations practice. Most organisations take a fragmented, reactive approach to comply with regulation by launching their green credentials. This chapter will look at three sustainable operations management concepts: life-cycle assessment, sustainable product design and 'lean and green' manufacturing, and show how organisations can capture significant value by integrating sustainability into their operations management agenda.

On completion of this chapter, students should be able to:

- Understand the difference between traditional operations management and sustainable operations management
- Discuss the contribution that sustainable operations management can make to business efficiency
- Identify sustainable operations management practices in different organisations

Introduction

OM (operations management) can be defined as 'the activity of managing the resources which produce and deliver products and services' (Slack *et al.* 2010: 4) and is thought of as the 'engine room' of any organisation. It focuses on the activities, decisions and responsibilities of design, purchase, production, distribution and delivery of products and services. Many innovative operational approaches such as TQM (total quality management), BPR (business process reengineering), JIT (just-in-time) and lean manufacturing have been introduced by the Japanese automotive industry since the 1980s to help them obtain and maintain a competitive edge. Traditionally, OM's primary objectives were mainly to focus on cost, quality, speed, dependability and flexibility (Slack *et al.* 2010). However, it was recognised that profitability was not the sole element in a company's long-term success (Hay *et al.* 2005) and traditional OM's performance objectives should be complemented by environmental criteria (Jimenez and Lorente 2001).

OM's main concern is how systems handle the delivery of a firm's product or service, but the underlying tenet of sustainable OM is the adherence to the idea that efficient and successful OM goes hand-in-hand with recognising the firm's impact on the environment. From a different perspective, the concept of sustainability is a modern, environmentally savvy version of traditional lean manufacturing ideas towards operating an efficient organisation (Haanaes *et al.* 2011). The problem lies in that many firms view sustainability as an extra cost or burden that correlates negatively with returns, so they are reluctant to embrace it fully. However, ample evidence has revealed that there are many opportunities for competitive advantages and increased profits by engaging in sustainable operations management initiatives (Funk 2003). For example, Johnson & Johnson successfully completed more than 60 energy reduction projections, which represented $187 million in capital investments, and it fully expects to reduce its annual CO_2 emissions by 129,000 metric tonnes and at the same time provide an internal rate of return of almost 19% (Cheeseman 2012). Many other industries such as textiles, automotive and agriculture are fighting a green competition that ranges from racing to launch sustainable products, to a battle over what constitutes a sustainable product in the first place, in order to gain first mover advantages. In the coffee industry, for example, many companies are competing to define the benchmarks for 'sustainable coffee'. While the Audubon Society and Transfair focus on pesticides used, worker's housing and bird conservation, others such as Starbucks and Nestlé highlight the fair trade and create value for society (Unruh and Ettenson 2010b).

Mihelcic *et al.* (2003: 5318) defined sustainability from OM's perspective: 'the design and operation of human and industrial systems to ensure that humankind's use of natural resources and cycles do not lead to diminished quality of life due either to losses in future economic opportunities or to adverse impacts on social conditions, human health and the environment'. They emphasised that this definition requires clear metrics in order to make decisions on the efficacy of any decision about the resulting sustainability. Kleindorfer *et al.* (2005) also proposed a similar definition of sustainable OM as a set of skills and concepts that enables organisations to structure and manage their products and services to result in returns from its capital investment without compromising not only the legitimate needs of internal and external stakeholders, but also the needs of future generations.

So sustainable OM is not just about the usual process of the introduction of raw materials through completion delivery, but also more environmentally aware issues such as design, development, and by-product and waste disposal. It should be kept in mind that operation decisions that influence a firm's ability to sustain itself and its surroundings often go hand-in-hand with traditional OM schools of thought, and so this chapter will take a closer look at three sustainable OM concepts: lifecycle assessment, sustainable product design and 'lean and green' manufacturing. Each will be illustrated through case studies to demonstrate how OM can be used to contribute to an organisation's sustainability goals.

Life-cycle assessment

> Life Cycle Assessment is a process to evaluate the environmental burdens associated with a product, process, or activity by identifying and quantifying energy and materials used and wastes released to the environment; to assess the impact of those energy and materials used and releases to the environment; and to identify and evaluate opportunities to affect environmental improvements. The assessment includes the entire life cycle of the process, product, activity or service system, encompassing extracting and processing raw materials, manufacturing, transportation and distribution, use, reuse, maintenance, recycling and final disposal. (SETAC 1993)

LCA (life-cycle assessment), often referred to as 'cradle to grave' assessment, was developed as an analytical tool, is practised globally and has been standardised by ISOs 14040 and 14044. By following the course of all inputs (e.g. processing of raw materials, use of energy, water and fuel) and outputs (e.g. consumer products, waste to landfill, CO_2 emissions, heat and energy loss), this system will enable companies to assess and identify the environmental impacts of a product or activity over its entire life-cycle.

A fully comprehensive LCA should include every material component and process to assess both their direct and indirect impacts. This data is then placed in a hierarchy based on its impact category, i.e. global warming, acidification, carcinogens, etc. By implementing LCAs, firms are able to systematically organise complex data from comprehensive environmental, economic and social categories as well as identifying the trade-offs between the three sustainability pillars, life-cycle stages, impacts, products and generations throughout the product's entire life-cycle (Seliger *et al.* 2003). For example, Figure 1 provides a life-cycle assessment for a pair of jeans focusing on the effects of resource extraction, manufacturing, packing, logistics and the end of life of the jeans, where they are either reused or end up in a landfill.

Levi's is a pioneer in the clothing industry having conducted an LCA in 2007, and sustainability has been embedded in the company's policy

Figure 1: Life-cycle assessment for a pair of jeans.

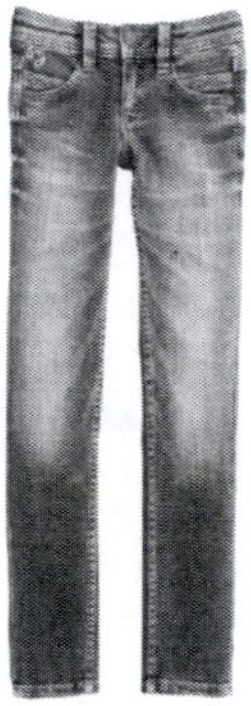

Cotton	Water, pesticides, herbicides, fertiliser, energy use
Spinning	Energy consumption, dust, waste material
Dying/weaving	Chemical use, dyes, waste water, energy
Other materials	Zips, button, label, rivets
Garment production	Material waste, ethical labour condition, energy use
Packaging	Plastic packaging
Transport	Different transportation modes, energy consumption, gas emission
Use, care and maintenance	Water, wash chemical, energy consumption
End-of-life	Landfill, re-use, unravelling into fibres

Source: Adopted from Thorpe (2012).

and operations practice (Thorpe 2012). For example, Levi's identified that a pair of jeans consumed 919 gallons of water during its lifetime and 49% of water usage was during the early stages when the denim was still in its cotton, plant form. In other words, just under half the amount of water it will be exposed to occurs during its raw material stage, and this led Levi's to educate its farmers in China, India, Brazil and other places on how to grow cotton with less water and how to process the stonewashing of jeans without using any water at all. Levi's later joined the Better Cotton Initiative, a non-profit organisation, in 2009, with the aim of reducing the negative environmental impact of clothing manufacturers. A 'green wash initiative' was also launched in order to encourage consumers to wash their jeans less and to wash in cold water to further reduce water consumption.

Tropicana undertook a LCA and found that rather than its carbon footprint being mainly due to the transportation of heavy juice containers, evidence showed that it was actually the agricultural inputs needed to grow its oranges (Martin 2009). This has now changed the company's attitude towards how to reduce its carbon footprint: rather than focusing on the fuel efficiency of its distribution vehicles, it now concentrates on sustainable agricultural practices, i.e. reduced fertiliser use. The information provided by LCAs can be a valuable insight into alternative ways of cutting costs and waste, raising profits, gaining a competitive advantage and improving operations practices, while at the same time reducing environmental impact. In addition, by identifying the source and relative magnitude of environmental impacts, this data can shape the innovation agenda. It highlights fertile areas that are ready for improvement, and can help drive the outcomes of competing new ideas.

Sustainable product design

Sustainable product design is an approach whereby the design stage of a product is intended to be more sustainable (Kaebernick *et al.* 2001). By doing this there is equilibrium between the demands of the environment, social responsibility and economic needs while still demonstrating the traditional product requirements, e.g. quality, market, technical, cost issues, etc. We have to accept the reality of the business environment: it has always been about profit and companies need profit for their continued existence, so the move towards a more sustainable approach will not occur overnight. However, with a gradual integration of environmental requirements into the product development process at every stage, this will eventually bring about a new ethos within businesses and companies will no longer see sustainability as a harbinger of extra restraints or extra costs, but maybe they will see it as a way of entering a new market and a way of opening up new and alternative revenue streams (Unruh and Ettenson 2010b).

Traditionally, taking into account environmental demands was viewed as a necessary evil, bringing with it extra restraints and costs, and as a result environmental assessments were usually conducted during the latter stages of the development process. This means that they were not integrated into existing development activities, which would naturally increase costs thus completing the self-fulfilling prophecy. Companies that legislate for sustainable product design are able to reduce their environmental impact at the design phase and experience fewer disruptions in disposals later on. This enables the company to clear up the possible causes of environmental impact rather than merely masking the symptoms (Fuller and Ottman 2004). There are several different strategies that can be employed to design products more sustainably:

- **Economic use of materials:** This involves using less material or the re-use or recycling of nature resources as a material input for a product. H&M launched 'The Conscious Collection' in 2001, in which all the items, including blouses, T-shirts, dresses and trousers, were made from organic linen, polyester recycled from PET bottles, textile waste and Tencel (Dishman 2013). This was also demonstrated by Nike who redesigned some of its footwear to have mechanically locking soles, meaning no glues or solvents were used in the production system (Nike 2013).

- **Design for ease of repair/disposal:** This approach focuses on design for dismantling, re-use and recycling (Unruh and Ettenson 2010b). For example, Nike introduced insertable booties and removable logos which, together with the mechanically locking soles, make its shoes easy to dismantle and further simplify the recycle process (Nike 2013). In May 2003, Herman Miller launched the Mirra task chair, the first product to be designed for sustainability. Its fabric was made from 96% annually renewable material and is completely compostable at the end of its useful life (Dunn 2007).

- **Life-cycle design:** This is a technique to enable firms to understand the process from the beginning of production to the end of consumption, and the resulting environmental impact (Unruh and Ettenson 2010b). Companies therefore need to consider all design processes, from the concept to manufacturing, packaging options and transportation, and finally use and disposal of products. The Swedish retailer, IKEA, is replacing its wooden pallets with recyclable paper pallets that are lighter, thinner and cheaper to use. The paper pallet is 90% lighter than a wooden pallet and IKEA is able to save 10% of its transportation cost (Funk 2003). Xerox adopted a programme of asset recycle management that takes back leased copiers to recondition and reassemble them into 'new' machines through a remanufacturing process. It was estimated in 1995 alone that this programme saved Xerox $300–400 million in raw materials, labour and waste disposal (Hart 1997).

- **Innovative environmental product design:** This is a sustainability-driven design that balances both customers' expectations as well as the needs of the environment (Unruh and Ettenson 2010b). Such sustainability-driven innovative product designs help firms to redefine their market scope and drive more economic returns (Unruh and Ettenson 2010b). Toyota is one of the pioneers who introduced the Prius, their hybrid car, which was able to take advantage of technological advancements that allowed cars to run on electricity as well as traditional petrol, thus reducing the CO_2 emissions (Unruh and Ettenson 2010b). Other competitors, such as Mercedes-Benz and BMW, have also followed this trend by launching their own versions of the hybrid model (Unruh and Ettenson 2010b). The German company, QMilk, turned spoiled milk into biotextile fabric that competes with cotton. The soft fibre is 100% biodegradable, created only with renewable resources, produces zero waste and can be used to make clothing and home textiles (Visser 2012). Many other innovative designs such as biomimicry, nanotechnology and 3D printing are emerging as new ways to tackle resource scarcity. For example, one of the plastic filaments used in 3D printing is polylactic acid, which is made from renewable resources such as corn starch or sugar cane. Many organisations are eyeing up 3D printers as a means of revolutionising their manufacturing processes and addressing the triple bottom line of people, planet and profit (Maxey 2014).

Yet, implementing a sustainable product strategy can be challenging due to misconceptions about cost versus benefits. Product design is the natural and best place to implement sustainable design as it causes the least amount of disruption to businesses. Many firms engage in widespread sustainable product design to optimise natural resource efficiencies, reduce cost, simplify the operational process and stimulate innovation. Proactively embracing a sustainability strategy will allow organisations to gain a competitive edge over their rivals.

Lean and green manufacturing

Following *The Machine that Changed the World* (Womack *et al.* 1990), Womack and Jones (1996) introduced the Western world to *Lean Thinking* by addressing the revolution in manufacturing production systems presented by the Toyota production system. Compared to traditional 'mass production' manufacturing systems epitomised by batch-and-queue methods, lean systems focus on just-in-time, waste elimination, value stream and continuous improvement. Empirical evidence shows that companies that adopt the lean manufacturing philosophy are also benefiting the environment by becoming more resource and energy efficient through pollution prevention, waste reduction and recycling opportunities (King and Lenox 2001; Bergmiller and McCright 2009).

Because lean focuses on reducing non-value-added activities and producing only the amount of a product that is needed, systematic improvements combine well with sustainable operations. Lean results in an operational and cultural environment highly conducive to the minimisation of waste and pollution, thus providing an excellent platform for environmental management tools such as LCAs and design for environment (Simon and Mason 2003). Boeing has been implementing lean manufacturing practices throughout its commercial aeroplanes divisions since 1996. Implementing this manufacturing approach enabled Boeing to reduce the amount of energy and raw materials used, together with the costs associated with non-product output, and much of this reduction can be translated into environmental improvements (Ross & Associates Environmental Consulting 2000). For example, energy savings result from improved space utilisation, decreased transportation and a reduction in product defects, while raw material saving can be achieved by use of less space, better inventory control, decreased scrap rates and decreased usage of lubricants and sealants. This was embedded in Boeing's organizational culture, meaning that employees strive to improve the value stream and eliminate unnecessary waste.

Lean practices are aimed at providing the right materials at the right time, to support manufacturing needs by focusing on reducing excess inventories of raw or work-in-process materials that are not immediately consumed by the production cycle. Significant reductions in waste material delivered to landfill have come about through cell-based manufacturing processes that signal a pull for materials based on demand of a product. This has also led to a reduction in raw materials consumed. By using this process-focused approach, managers have the luxury of adopting a more holistic view regarding change. Both lean and green focus on minimising waste and time resulting in an improvement in quality of the product. The former considers waste as no value to the customer, and the latter considers it as the extraction and subsequent disposal of resources at a rate and in a form which is environmentally sustainable. The belief is that all companies can make minor operational changes that will exponentially reduce costs and improve sustainability (Florida 1996).

An example of a lean management approach is Marks & Spencer: it undertook its 'Plan A', with the aim of reducing energy consumption by 25% by 2012. This was achieved through the accumulation of small adjustments: by switching from 90-watt to 75-watt light bulbs in all its UK food stores, for example, they found that their lighting costs dropped by 17%, and similar improvements were made with their refrigeration and air conditioning requirements (Nichols 2013). Lean and green practices share common goals and values, so this collaboration could also stretch to non-manufacturing companies. Which company would not welcome a reduction in waste (be it time, energy or resources) that leads to rising profits, as well as developing the maturity to embed environmental responsibility within its processes? The implementation of lean and green practices would lead to companies being more competitive and environmentally friendly.

It is imperative for companies to explore ways to improve their productivity in order to maintain their competitive edge. Many organisations have been striving to improve efficiency and productivity through sustainable operations management, such as life-cycle assessment, sustainable product design, and lean and green manufacturing practice. It is evident that by adding environmental criteria as part of an operation's performance objectives help firms to reduce waste, improve efficiency, drive innovation, shorten product lead time and establish both tangible and intangible value. Companies that fail to capture this opportunity will face increased regulatory and social pressure, while those that embrace it and master it will enjoy competitive advantages and gain more market share (Haanaes *et al.*, 2011)

Suggested seminars

Seminar 1: Life-cycle assessment

This seminar provides a set of activities for the teacher to use LCA techniques to encourage students to take a more proactive attitude towards sustainable operations and not perceive them as an extra cost or restriction.

Activity 1 (10 minutes)

1. During a student's typical day can they identify opportunities to carry out sustainable practices, i.e. ethical food consumption, turning off the lights, food recycling, using a bike rather than driving.

2. Students then can compare the differences and discuss them with their peers.

Activity 2 (40 minutes)

1. Students are divided into different groups, and required to apply and analyse the LCA for two products: a carton of orange juice from a supermarket and a cup of coffee sold in a coffee shop.

2. Students are then encouraged to draw the LCA maps for the orange juice and a cup of coffee on the white board and compare and contrast the differences.

3. Students are required to discuss how organisation can benefit from conducting an LCA for these two products.

Seminar 2: Sustainable operations management

The seminar will give students an overview of how sustainability is practised and executed through OM within different organisations. This seminar inclued online evaluation of company websites and should therefore be carried out in a computer laboratory or with the help of laptops/tablets.

Activity 1 (30 minutes)

Students are allocated into four groups and will choose two different companies from the following list (each company can only be selected by one group).

- IKEA
- Dell
- Walmart
- Levi's

- Brita
- GE
- BP
- Marks & Spencer

By conducting online research of their chosen companies, the students will need to discuss how they are working towards the goal of sustainability through their respective OMs and answer the following two questions:

1. Does sustainable operations management constrain or drive your selected organisations' profitability?

2. What are the benefits that could be derived from running sustainable OM for your selected organisations?

Activity 2 (20 minutes)

Each group then summarises (maybe on a poster) their findings or each group could produce a mini-presentation based on their findings. Alternatively, their posters could be displayed and students are free to look at the other groups' work.

Seminar 3: Lean and green practices

The aim of this seminar is for students to understand that both lean and green practices share common goals and that the principles could also be adopted by non-manufacturing organisations.

Activity 1 (5 minutes)

Students are required to identify which statements from the list below are lean or green.

- Faulty product
- Excessive water usage
- Employee engagement
- Extra copies, unnecessary/excessive reports
- Excessive resource usage
- Excessive power usage
- Unnecessary movement of product
- Process efficiency
- Continuous improvement
- Batch-processing transactions
- Pollution

Activity 2 (20 minutes)

Students are required to take a tour of their university and note down their observations:

- What are the evidences of green practices within the campus?
- Can you see any evidence of lean practice?

Activity 3 (25 minutes)

Students will then need to categorise their observations of green and lean practices into two categories and put on Post-it notes on the board, where two overlapping circles are drawn as shown below.

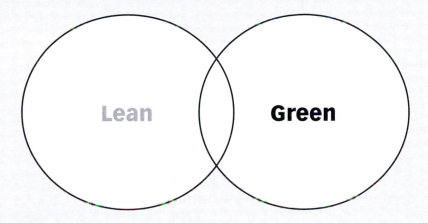

Students will then compare the similarities between lean and green within a university context by answering the following questions:

1. What is the evidence that this university is a sustainable one?

2. Are there any overlapping characteristics between lean and green universities?

3. What are the benefits of being a lean and green university?

Additional teaching material and ideas

Product design game

Activity 1: Students are required to undertake a mini investigation involving products in their everyday life to explore and identify the most and least sustainable product design, and then to discuss their reasoning.

Activity 2: Students are then encouraged to identify the best way for the least sustainable product design to be improved.

Case study

An article from the *MIT Sloan Management Review*, 'The Mini-Cases: 5 Companies, 5 Strategies, 5 Transformations' (Fromartz 2009), provides students with a range of case studies to rethink how companies could utilise OM to achieve their goal of becoming a sustainable organisation. Students can be divided into five groups with each group allocated one case. Students can then discuss within their groups, and then with the whole class, to compare and contrast the differences and similarities among the five cases.

A video clip

There are a variety of clips available, e.g.:

- www.youtube.com/watch?v=ehA2H0Rmpdo (a good example of sustainable food product design)

- www.youtube.com/watch?v=r9ejG83lrX4 (an example from McDonald's about sustainable food packaging design)

Activity 1: This virtual aid will help students to gain more understanding of what constitutes sustainable product design.

Activity 2: Students are divided into teams. Their brief is to choose a target company and select one of their products and make a pitch to that company on ways of improving sustainable product design.

Activity 3: Winners will be selected by a 'Dragon's Den' style presentation with teachers playing the role of board members who will make a decision based on the quality and originality of the students' pitch.

Application of concepts to a real-life organisation

Students are to play the role of a professional consultant for a local company and advise it on ways of solving the sustainability operations challenge. In 2013, I held a **sustainability essay competition** and involved Cheltenham Racecourse as the project sponsor. The managing director of the racecourse was invited as a guest speaker and gave a presentation to the students on the current status of the racecourse and its main operations sustainability challenges. Many of the students had previous employment experience of working for the racecourse so had already developed a good level of understanding of its business operations. The students were required to adopt the role of consultant and provide solutions to the challenges mentioned, with a £500 prize awarded to the student who offered the best solution.

Reflective workshop presentation

Students are to prepare a reflective presentation where they are able to elaborate on how their attitudes towards sustainable OM have changed by the end of the workshops. Students are to use the concepts and examples covered during the programme, and they are encouraged to seek out evidence from a range of business practices that go beyond what was covered in class. They will need to elaborate on how their individual and collective approaches to sustainability have now evolved.

Further reading

Haanaes, K., B. Balagopal, M.T. Kong, I. Velken, D. Arthur, M.S. Hopkins and N. Kruschwitz (2011) 'New Sustainability Study: The "Embracers" Seize Advantage', *MIT Sloan Management Review* 52.3 (Spring 2011): 23-35.

> By conducting surveys and interviews with more than 3,000 business executives and managers located around the world, this articles provide a good collection of evidence showing how organisations view sustainability as part of their 'core competence' through operations management execution. Organisations that embrace sustainability concepts see benefits derived from their sustainability-driven management in the ability to cut cost, process improvement and product innovation.

Lubin, D.A., and D.C. Esty (2010), 'The Sustainability Imperative', *Harvard Business Review* (May 2010), 42-50.

> This article discusses the varied ways sustainability could be incorporated into an OM context. It offers examples of how companies focus on cost and risk reduction and over time develop sustainability strategies for value creation. It maps out four positions an organisation could adopt to match sustainable product/service offerings with strategic executions.

Rothenberg, S. (2007) 'Sustainability Through Servicizing', *MIT Sloan Management Review* 48.2 (Winter 2007): 83-91.

> This article uses different examples of how companies have taken advantage of a business model that allows for growth by educating society to switch from high to low consumption of its products. Examples show that by adopting a low product consumption business model, companies can make their business more profitable by focusing on services that extend the efficiency and value of their product.

Unruh, G., and R. Ettenson (2010a), 'Growing Green: Three Smart Paths to Developing Sustainable Products', *Harvard Business Review* (June 2010): 94-100.

> This article offers a holistic and practical framework for integrating sustainability product design strategies into an organisation's business portfolio. It provides a good range of case studies to illustrate the three steps of green growth (accentuate, acquire and architect) as part of a company's business activities and offering to assist managers in crafting a sustainable business strategy.

Unruh, G., and R. Ettenson (2010b), 'Winning in the Green Frenzy', *Harvard Business Review* (November 2010): 110-16.

> This article offers a framework based on in-depth case studies to show how organisations can differentiate their businesses, offering and bolstering a company's reputation by shaping its sustainable OM standards in the industry. Four sustainability strategies (adopt, co-opt, define and break away) were discussed in detail to ensure the organisation would win the green competition and seize the business opportunities.

References

Bergmiller, G.G., and P.R. McCright (2009) 'Are Lean and Green Operations Synergistic?', paper presented at the 2009 Industrial Engineering Research Conference, Miami, FL, May 2009.

Cheeseman, G.M. (2012) 'Johnson & Johnson Makes Progress Toward Its Sustainability Goals', www.triplepundit.com/2012/07/johnson-johnson-makes-progress-sustainability-goals/, accessed 11 August 2013.

Dishman, L. (2013) 'Inside H&M's Quest for Sustainability In Fast Fashion', www.forbes.com/sites/lydiadishman/2013/04/09/inside-hms-quest-for-sustainability-in-fast-fashion/, accessed 11 December 2013.

Dunn, C. (2007) 'Herman Miller's Approach to Sustainable Design', www.treehugger.com/sustainable-product-design/herman-millers-approach-to-sustainable-design.html, accessed 15 December 2013.

Florida, R. (1996) 'Lean and Green: the Move to Environmentally Conscious Manufacturing', *California Management Review* 39.1: 80-105.

Fromartz, S. (2009) 'The Mini-Cases: 5 Companies, 5 Strategies, 5 Transformations', *MIT Sloan Management Review* (October 2009), 51.1: 41-45.

Fuller, D., and J. Ottman (2004) 'Moderating Unintended Pollution: The Role of Sustainable Product Design', *Journal of Business Research* 57.11: 1231-38.

Funk, K. (2003) 'Sustainability and Performance', *MIT Sloan Management Review*, 44.2: 65-70.

Haanaes, K., B. Balagopal, M.T. Kong, I. Velken, D. Arthur, M.S. Hopkins and N. Kruschwitz (2011) 'New Sustainability Study: The "Embracers" Seize Advantage', *MIT Sloan Management Review* 52.3 (Spring 2011): 23-35.

Hart, S.L. (1997) 'Beyond Greening: Strategies for a Sustainable World', *Harvard Business Review* (January/February 1997): 66-76.

Hay, R.L., R.N. Stavins and R.H.K. Vietor (2005) *Environmental Protection and the Social Responsibility of Firms: Perspectives from Law, Economics and Business* (Washington, DC: Resources for the Future, RFF Press).

Jimenez, J., and J. Lorente (2001) 'Environmental Performance as an Operations Objective', *International Journal of Operations and Production Management* 21.12: 1553-72.

Kaebernick, H., M. Anityasari and S. Kara (2001) 'Re-use or Recycling of Industrial Products, a Technical and Economic Model for Decision Support', paper presented at 8th International Seminar on Life Cycle Engineering, Varna, Bulgaria, 18–20 June 2001.

King, A., and M. Lenox (2001) 'Lean and Green? An Empirical Examination of the Relationship between Lean Production and Environmental Performance' *Production and Operations Management* 10.3: 244-57.

Kleindorfer, P.R., K. Singhal and L.N. Van Wassenhove (2005) 'Sustainable Operations Management', *Production and Operations Management* 14.4: 482-92.

Lubin, D.A., and D.C. Esty (2010) 'The Sustainability Imperative', *Harvard Business Review* (May 2010): 42-50.

Martin, A. (2009) 'How Green is My Orange', *The New York Times*, www.nytimes.com/2009/01/22/business/22pepsi.html, accessed 11 August 2013.

Maxey, K. (2014) '3D Printer Filament Recycling is Super Green', www.engineering.com/3DPrinting/3DPrintingArticles/ArticleID/7273/3D-Printer-Filament-Recycling-is-Super-Green.aspx, accessed 11 March 2014.

Mihelcic, J.R., J.C. Crittenden, M.J. Small, D.R. Shonnard, D.R. Hokanson and Q. Zhang (2003) 'Sustainability Science and Engineering: The Emergence of a New Metadiscipline', *Environmental Science and Technology* 37.23: 5314-24.

Nichols, W. (2013) 'How M&S is Making Sustainability Pay: Part One', www.businessgreen.com/bg/feature/2286363/how-m-s-is-making-sustainability-pay-part-one, accessed 11 December 2013.

Nike (2013) 'Through the Years: Nike's History of Sustainable Innovation', *The Guardian*, www.theguardian.com/sustainable-business/nike-history-sustainable-innovation, accessed 11 December 2013.

Ross & Associates Environmental Consulting (2000) 'Pursuing Perfection: Case Studies Examining Lean Manufacturing Strategies, Pollution Prevention and Environmental Regulatory Management Implications', www.epa.gov/lean/environment/pdf/perfection.pdf, accessed 11 December 2013.

Rothenberg, S. (2007) 'Sustainability Through Servicizing', *MIT Sloan Management Review* 48.2 (Winter 2007): 83-91.

Seliger, G., A. Buchholz and U. Kross (2003) 'Enhanced Product Functionality with Life Cycle Units', *Proceedings of the Institution of Mechanical Engineers, Part B, Journal of Engineering Manufacture* 217.B9: 1197-202.

SETAC (Society of Environmental Toxicology and Chemistry) (1993) 'Guidelines for Life-Cycle Assessment: A Code of Practice', SETAC workshop in Sesimbra, Portugal, 31 March–3 April 1993.

Simons, D., and R. Mason (2003) 'Lean and Green: Doing More with Less', *ECR Journal* 3.1: 84-91.

Slack, N., S. Chambers and R. Johnston (2010) *Operations Management*, 6th edn (London: Pearson Education).

Thorpe, L. (2012) 'Levi Strauss & Co: The Levi style with a lot less water', *The Guardian*, www.theguardian.com/sustainable-business/levi-rethinking-traditional-process-water, accessed 11 August 2013.

Unruh, G., and R. Ettenson (2010a), 'Growing Green: Three Smart Paths to Developing Sustainable Products', *Harvard Business Review* (June 2010): 94-100.

—— (2010b) 'Winning in the Green Frenzy', *Harvard Business Review* (November 2010): 110-16.

Visser, M. (2012) 'Fabric Made of Milk Waste', www.design-4-sustainability.com/materials/72-fabric-made-out-of-milk-waste, accessed 29 August 2013.

Womack, J.P., and D.T. Jones (1996), *Lean Thinking: Banish Waste and Create Wealth in Your Corporation* (New York: Simon & Schuster).

Womack, J.P., D.T. Jones and D. Roos (1990) *The Machine that Changed the World: The Story of Lean Production* (New York: Harper Collins Publishers).

10

Sustainable supply chain management

Peter Lund-Thomsen and Lynn Oxborrow

In this chapter, you will be given an overview of the some of the key challenges related to the theory and practice of sustainable supply chain management. After having read the chapter you should be able to:

- Provide a short definition of sustainable supply chain management

- Briefly describe the historical background for the rise of sustainable supply chain management as an important topic in the study of sustainability management

- Discuss some of the main dilemmas related to the practice of sustainable supply chain management, including both social and environmental sustainability

---

The concept of supply chain management

In general terms, **supply chain management** can be defined as 'the management of upstream and downstream relationships with suppliers and customers to deliver superior customer value at less cost to the supply chain as a whole' (Christopher 2011: 3). In this context, **upstream** to **downstream** represents the predominant flow of materials from their source to finished goods or services at the point of distribution, while information flows in both directions. The discipline of supply chain management therefore incorporates numerous business functions ranging from product design to procurement, facilities management, production, logistics, marketing, finance and distribution. Trends in supply chain management have seen a rapid growth in **outsourcing**, where organisations commission a third-party supplier to carry out a specific activity; **off-shoring**, where such activities are undertaken in a different country from the sourcing organisation; and consequently **global sourcing**, where the supply chain spans different countries (Slack *et al.* 2013). Together with the growth in consumerism across the globe, these developments have resulted in more supply chain activity, made more complex by its global nature, and consequently with greater opportunity to impact upon social, environmental and economic sustainability issues.

Citing the Danish Council for Corporate Social Responsibility (2010: 5), we can state that **sustainable supply chain management** is related to the dialogue that companies 'have with their suppliers in order to prevent violations of fundamental human rights and international environmental standards'. To this definition of sustainable supply chain management, we could also add that companies need to ensure that violations of international labour standards and environmental codes do not take place at suppliers' production sites. **International labour standards** here refer to issues such as securing workers the minimum wage, reasonable working hours and overtime payment, the right to collective bargaining, freedom of association, and health and safety at supplier factories. **Environmental codes** include managing product stewardship, production and logistics throughout the supply chain to minimise the negative impacts of using energy, materials, water and harmful substances, while reducing emissions and waste.

The emergence of sustainable supply chain management can be traced back to the rise of global supply chains in the 1980s and 1990s, as a response to various technological and socioeconomic developments. First, international trade had been liberalised substantially through various rounds of free trade negotiations in what is today known as the **World Trade Organization**. Organisations such as the World Bank and the International Monetary Fund had also played key roles in convincing developing country governments that they needed to privatise many state companies and deregulate their national economies (Haufler 2001). In turn, this helped multinational companies not only sell their products in developing countries, but also to set up their own factories or source from local supplier firms that could meet their production, price, timing, and delivery requirements (Gereffi 1999). At the same time, labour costs had gone up in the developed world and environmental regulation been tightened in the 1970s and 1980s, making many retailers and supermarkets look for alternative and cheaper sources of supply in developing countries or countries in transition. In addition, the reduction in air-fare prices and the emergence of the Internet facilitated the rapid growth of global supply chains linking dispersed consumers and importers in the developed world with suppliers, contractors and workers in developing countries (Haufler 2001).

Social sustainability in the supply chain

Our focus in this section will be on the **social aspects** of sustainable supply chain management—i.e. the question of how the **working conditions** of those labouring in supplier factories in developing countries may be improved over time. The concern with the social aspects of supply chain management can be traced back to the early 1990s when a series of media exposés highlighted issues of child labour, forced labour, poverty wages, excessive overtime and general exploitation of workers in the supply chains of some of the world's most famous brands such as Nike and Levi's (Greenberg and Knight 2004). These companies mostly specialised in the branding, marketing and distribution of consumer goods through outlet stores in Europe and the US, but sourced from complex networks of suppliers in developing countries (Bair and Palpacuer 2012).

With the growth of global supply chains in the 1990s and early parts of the new millennium, fears were also increasing that an international social and environmental race to the bottom might be occurring. In relation to the social aspects of sustainability, the nightmare scenario was that well-paid, well-regulated jobs with high levels of social security in

Europe and North America were now outsourced to countries in Latin America, Asia and Africa whose governments might not care about the wellbeing, health and safety of their workforce (Khara and Lund-Thomsen 2012).

These developments sparked concerted campaigns by trade unions, student organisations, media outlets and NGOs (non-governmental organisations) against the exploitation of workers in developing countries in order to produce cheap goods for Western consumers (Bair and Palpacuer 2012). To respond to these allegations—and protect their **brand value**—many high-profile Western importers started developing so-called **corporate codes of conduct**, ethical guidelines which specify the social and environmental conditions under which goods and services are to be produced at supplier factories in developing countries. Corporate codes of conduct will typically state that suppliers must employ workers on a regular contract, that workers must be paid the minimum wage and for any overtime work, that no child labour is employed, and a host of other similar criteria. Western importers often 'borrow' these criteria from international labour standards as specified in the conventions of the ILO (**International Labour Organization**), an agency of the United Nations entrusted with protecting the rights of workers worldwide (Lund-Thomsen 2008).

By 2006, different scientific and policy-oriented studies highlighted that the outcomes of implementing corporate codes of conduct—at best—brought about mixed results when it came to ensuring that a social race to the bottom did not take place in developing country export industries (Barrientos and Smith 2007). On the one hand, the implementation of corporate codes of conduct appeared to help factory-based workers by ensuring that they were paid the minimum wage, received overtime payment, and that fewer occupational health and safety accidents took place within supplier factories. On the other hand, codes of conduct appeared to make little or no difference when it came to guaranteeing that workers were free to join trade unions or that they could collectively bargain with their employers in order to improve their work conditions. At the same time, many workers were not really covered by codes as they tended to work further upstream in the supply chain. For example, women and child workers would often be employed in semi-formal workshops or labour at home outside the purview of Western multinational companies that mainly sought to keep track of work conditions at the level of their **first tier suppliers** (ETI 2006).

At the same time, the aforementioned academic and policy studies also highlighted that Western multinational companies tended to use **purchasing practices** and corporate codes of conduct that contradicted one another (Barrientos and Smith 2007). For example, a Western retailer's procurement staff might ask a supplier to reduce its prices or face the risk of losing an order. At the same time, the retailer's sustainability department might ask the same supplier to increase worker's wages or at least ensure that workers were not cheated of the wages that they had rightfully earned (ETI 2006). Moreover, some Western importers were only able to place orders at certain periods of the year in response to changing seasonal demand in the West. This would often result in employment insecurity in developing country export industries where first-tier suppliers tended to hire and fire workers in response to the level of orders that they received from their buyers. Alternatively, suppliers might subcontract work to smaller suppliers whenever orders were available in order to avoid national labour laws stipulating that workers had to be offered more permanent contracts if they laboured in factory settings (Khara and Lund-Thomsen 2012). Finally, international retailers were criticised for placing orders at the last minute, thus compelling their suppliers in developing countries to force their employees into doing excessive overtime work. As a result, the outcome was often that suppliers had to devise innovative, but perhaps also counterproductive, strategies if they were to stay in business. For example, suppliers might instruct their workers in what to tell the social auditors that were employed by Western importers to check work conditions in these factories. For instance, workers might be instructed to say that they received the minimum wage and were paid for their overtime work if they wanted to retain their jobs (Responsible Purchasing 2006).

Examples such as these also highlight the difficulties and complexities inherent in sustainable supply chain management. Often there are trade-offs between commercial and social considerations which are not easily reconciled. At the same time, even well-intended corporate codes of conduct might do more harm than good to workers in instances where they are implemented without due consideration for **local social and environmental circumstances** (Lund-Thomsen 2008). For instance,

Western retailers may stipulate that their suppliers are not allowed to employ children as part of the workforce. However, if strictly enforced, suppliers may feel compelled to fire children working in their factories (e.g. garment and shoe factories), leaving these child labourers and their families with even less income than before. This could possibly force children into even worse types of occupation such as prostitution or bonded labour. Such examples illustrate that implementing **'global' ethical guidelines** of companies in **'local contexts'** often requires considerable knowledge of the context in which the supplier is operating, the ability to handle dilemmas, and the ability to devise concrete, practical solutions to real-life challenges faced upstream in the global supply chain in developing countries (Lund-Thomsen and Lindgreen 2013). We suggest that you as a student try to explore how to handle such dilemmas in Seminars 1–3 below.

Environmentally sustainable supply chain management

Srivastava (2007: 54-55) defines **green supply chain management** as 'Integrating environmental thinking into supply-chain management'. Achieving a sustainable supply chain has become a multidisciplinary task, encompassing relationships, networks, channels and partnerships (Srivastava 2007) throughout the sourcing, process and delivery of goods and services to the final consumer.

There is a lack of consensus regarding the key **drivers** to instituting a sustainable supply chain. These are variously attributed to market forces (Seuring and Muller 2008), customer buying power, such as retail or public sector (Sharma *et al.* 2010; Preuss 2009), government regulations (Jones *et al.* 2008) or consumers demanding better environmentally driven products and services, especially those espoused through corporate value statements. Meanwhile, there are also counter-arguments such as linking green products and services to market failure due to the perception of their being too expensive and functionally or aesthetically inferior (Ginsberg and Bloom 2004).

Sustainable supply chain initiatives can be implemented in two broad ways. Often they are imposed on suppliers, perhaps as a result of legislation, strategic objectives or codes of conduct of powerful brands and retailers. Alternatively, introducing new and innovative sustainability solutions into the supply chain depends on relationships, sharing of information and working to common goals (Vachon and Klassen 2006), and suppliers are more likely to adopt improvements if they have good relationships with the customers who request those improvements. Implementing a successful sustainable supply chain therefore requires marketing and purchasing functions working together (Sharma *et al.* 2010), senior management buy-in, a supportive organisational culture and inter-functional co-operation (Krause *et al.* 2009), with a wider set of performance objectives beyond economic measures (Seuring and Muller 2008). Some generic supply chain concepts such as network design, logistics management, waste minimisation and order fulfilment strategies can help to achieve sustainable supply chain management (Liu *et al.* 2012; Sharma *et al.* 2010).

Network design determines **location choices** for key facilities and the way that goods are moved between them, hence impacting upon supply chain sustainability in a number of ways. One of the key arguments regarding the location of manufacture, warehousing and distribution facilities is the **local–global** argument. Using more local supply as an alternative to offshore outsourcing is controversial, as there are also social costs to changing sourcing decisions, costs are often considered to be prohibitive and in some developed economies the local infrastructure has declined in traditional industries. In the automotive industry, suppliers are often clustered close to the final assembly plant which reduces the transportation impact of just-in-time delivery, an important factor as deliveries can be required every few hours. Meanwhile, in the food industry, **build-to-order** based on information sharing with local suppliers reduces unsustainable surplus production and **food miles**—the distance travelled by components and goods within global supply chains. However, Soler *et al.* (2010) suggest that adding value by using local suppliers is often in conflict with prevailing procurement legislation which hampers the local supply agenda (Preuss 2009) in favour of impartiality. For an alternative discussion about the value of local and more distant supply see Brindley and Oxborrow (2014).

Distance and network design in turn impact upon **logistics**—the planning, control and implementation of moving goods and exchanging information throughout the supply chain, or getting the right product, to the right place, at the right time (SBC 2003). The consensus is that transporting goods less often, in larger volume, is more cost effective as well as being less environmentally damaging, but may not complement contemporary supply chain models such as just-in-time and the fulfilment of online orders. The trend for **consolidation** is increasingly evident in global shipping, with a growing number of super-ships that can carry more freight, use more sustainable power sources and reduce the cost per item shipped (Mangan *et al.* 2012). However, these huge ships can only operate in the world's largest ports and so consolidation also involves developing **hub and spoke** models of storage, transport and distribution along the supply chain, to feed the major shipping routes and offload and redistribute goods into local distribution systems. In integrated supply chains, this role is often outsourced to specialist 3PL (**third-party logistics**) providers able to introduce the latest technology for warehouse and distribution management, as well as helping to identify opportunities for the sharing of resources between compatible clients. A 3PL provider might enable a Christmas gift company and a garden centre chain with different seasonal peaks to share their warehouse facilities, or suppliers to an automotive plant to share transport for just-in-time delivery. Another example would be filling the base of a truck with heavy bottles and cans of beverage to supply the catering trade, and then using space above to '**top stow**' light items such as crisps (SBC 2003).

Choice of **mode of transport** (road, rail, air or sea-freight, etc.), fuel-efficient vehicle designs, reducing vehicle emissions and switching to alternative fuels can also help to reduce the environmental impact of logistics—see the IKEA case study in Seminar 3. In spite of all of these efforts, there are still occasions when goods are flown to their destination in order to enhance responsiveness and reduce **lead-time** for fashion or perishable items, or to compensate for delays that have occurred elsewhere in the supply chain and meet delivery deadlines.

Waste reduction, which includes over-ordering of materials, or over-production of components and finished goods, requires input from marketing to produce consistent, stable demand (Chan *et al.* 2012). However, where there is uncertainty, for example because of seasonality or fashion, solutions such as close proximity supplier hubs, exchange of personnel with suppliers and shared plans for new product implementation help keep suppliers abreast of market trends, react more responsively and avoid oversupply. However, as is the case with social sustainability, there are often **trade-offs** or conflicting outcomes between commercial and sustainability objectives or between the various participants. Indeed, sustainability may be an **order qualifier**, enabling suppliers to compete for business in a given context, but the prevailing **order winner**, or decisive selection criterion, is often cost (Cousins *et al.* 2008). Chan *et al.* (2012) suggest that the cost imperative in a sustainable supply chain should be reflected through lean thinking or waste minimisation, rather than exploitative cost reduction.

The **reverse supply chain** is a growing phenomenon in sustainable supply, as legislation, cost pressure and shortage of materials make it more viable for all kinds of recycled items to find their way back into the supply chain—sometimes as completely different products—in a phenomenon known as **cradle-to-cradle** design (Lovins 2008). The reverse supply chain can be defined as collecting and moving goods from their normal end-of-life for the purpose of capturing value from waste, re-use or refurbishment, or managing their disposal (see Mehrmann 2008). The reverse supply chain can encompass the collection of packaging materials for re-use, of materials for integration into new products, or obsolete or surplus products to be disassembled into constituent parts. It can also include reclaiming fuel, water or waste to be recycled or used in energy generation. Some recycled goods, particularly valuable metals, are exported to global manufacturing locations for sorting, reprocessing and reintegration into new products; others, such as clothing, find a second-hand market in developing economies. However, the supply chain for these processes has to be designed, just like any other.

Companies in the supply chain have the ability to conduct their businesses sustainably through consideration of the triple bottom line: financial, environmental and social sustainability. Suppliers and buyers can therefore improve their approaches to sustainability via:

- Reducing CO_2 output

- Recycling and effective waste management

- Using renewable resources

- Selling ethical products such as organic and Fairtrade
- Providing facilities for communities linked to their suppliers and outlets
- Sustainable logistics/reduced movement
- Reducing wasteful production/processing
- Changing consumption values

Suggested seminars

Seminar 1: Nike and the dilemmas of social sustainability in Sialkot, Pakistan[1]

Nike is one of the world's most famous sports brands and, in the early 1990s, started sourcing football (soccer) products. From the mid-1990s and onward, Nike sourced all of its footballs from one supplier, Saga Sports, in Pakistan. Football stitching, the most labour-intensive aspect of football manufacturing, was carried out exclusively by hand, and 75% of all hand-stitched footballs were manufactured by the 390 small and medium-sized manufacturers in the Pakistani town of Sialkot.

However, machine stitching of footballs was invented in China in the late 1990s, and Chinese football manufacturers could produce large volumes of medium-quality training footballs and lower quality promotional footballs, and do it more quickly than their Pakistani counterparts. Nike began to source footballs from China in the early 2000s. Nike was also concerned about the potential risk of having child labour employed in its football supply chain in Pakistan. Whereas footballs in China tended to be stitched inside factories, in Pakistan manufacturers used large networks of subcontractors to outsource the football-stitching process to designated stitching centres in the villages around Sialkot. Workers from nearby homes would gather in the stitching centres, for males or females, where they could stitch footballs within a designated building or controlled space, and where it was possible to monitor the production process for child labour and workers' rights.

In 2006, Nike decided to cut its ties with Saga Sports because of labour rights transgressions and the unauthorised outsourcing of football stitching from stitching centres to home workers. Immediately after Saga lost the Nike contract, around 7,000 male and female stitchers lost their source of income as Nike tried to switch its entire sourcing of footballs to

1 This seminar is mostly based on the findings presented in Lund-Thomsen and Coe (2013).

China. However, Nike soon realised that the Chinese manufacturers were not willing or able to meet Nike's entire demand for hand-stitched balls as they did not possess the technological capability to stitch high-quality, hand-stitched match balls and because higher wages in China made the production of hand-stitched footballs in China financially unviable.

Instead Nike re-entered Sialkot, with a new supplier called Silverstar. Under Nike's new production and CSR (corporate social responsibility) philosophy it was decided that all football stitching had to take part inside the Silverstar factory so that children could not become involved in football stitching. All football stitchers were to be paid the minimum wage, they had to be paid for overtime work, and they would receive a higher wage if they managed to stitch more than four footballs per day, the daily quota required by workers within Nike's production regime. Stitchers were also to be provided with health and social insurance (including pension benefits and compensation in case they were laid off). In addition, the football stitchers inside Silverstar were to receive training in workers' rights and to arrange elections inside the factory where workers could freely elect their own representatives. Finally, monitoring of production and work conditions would be undertaken on a weekly basis by Nike's agent in Pakistan—a sourcing company, Matrix Sourcing.

You are now part of a consultancy team that has been asked to undertake an impact assessment of Nike's new production and CSR approach in the Silverstar factory, identifying how aims are being met and whether there are any unintended consequences of Nike's new policies. As part of the impact assessment you interview Nike's sourcing and CSR personnel, the Silverstar management team, Matrix Sourcing, PILER (Pakistan Institute of Labor and Education Research) and the UK-based labour rights consultancy Just Solutions, and conduct 60 interviews with Silverstar football stitchers, divided equally between those working in factories, stitching centres and at home. These interviews are undertaken in the village homes of individual stitchers with the help of local (Punjabi-speaking) interpreters. Undertaking these interviews outside the factory premises enables workers to speak freely without being influenced by their managers.

Your interviews with Nike, Silverstar, Matrix, PILER and Just Solutions indicate that Nike's new production and CSR policy is working as intended. However, your own observations at the Silverstar factory and the worker interviews tell a different story:

- You observe 400–500 all-male football workers—and your worker interviews indicate that male relatives do not allow female football stitchers to commute to and work in the factory in case they are sexually harassed. Instead female household members are expected by their male family members to undertake childcare and household chores at home.

- Workers do not appear to be paid the full minimum wage, are not receiving any extra payments for exceeding the target of four footballs per day and they have not all received the full compensation owed to them because the factory is in financial trouble. Some 50–60% of the original 1,200 male stitchers employed at the factory have been laid off, and since the financial crisis Nike is only sourcing 20–25% of the target 300,000 footballs per month. In order to stay financially afloat, the Silverstar management has no other option but to cut workers' wages.

- Workers report that their representatives have been elected in a free and fair way, but they lack the authority to help workers if their wages have not been paid in full. The representatives are mostly poor and easily intimidated by Silverstar management. However, as the football stitchers have attended the PILER training on workers' rights under Pakistani labour law and Nike's code of conduct, they are now able to calculate their own wages and have started striking whenever anyone's wages are not paid in full. This causes the Silverstar management to lose thousands of dollars every time production is stopped and workers have now been paid at least some of the money owed to them.

Now answer the following questions:

1. How do Nike's CSR requirements affect workers and households in the football manufacturing industry of Sialkot?

2. What trade-offs are evident in the football manufacturing supply chain?

3. What could companies like Nike do better to balance their commercial needs with the needs of the workers and communities involved in football manufacture?

Seminar 2: Ten questions to ask footwear and garment companies

In this seminar, you are asked to make an initial, desk-based assessment of whether an importing company in a developed country is using sustainable supply chain management practices. The toolkit includes ten questions that allow you as a student or learner to find out whether a given importing company, for example, a retailer or a supermarket, is in compliance with ethical procurement policy. Select a company and try to find out whether they live up to Oxfam Australia's ethical procurement policy. The ten questions are summarised below and can be downloaded in full from https://www.oxfam.org.au/explore/workers-rights/resources-for-students/.

1. Does the company have a supplier code of conduct to guide suppliers through the implementation of human rights for their workers?

2. If the company has a code of conduct, is it publicly available? Is the implementation of the code of conduct being audited by a third party? Is the audit process transparent and reports available?

3. Does the company publish a list of its suppliers and their locations? Oxfam sees this as a way to achieve supply chain transparency so that other groups can check working conditions. Would the company consider doing this?

4. Are core ILO conventions ratified in the countries where the company's suppliers are based? This should give workers the right to freedom of association.

5. Does the company have a good system to audit factory conditions? Some commercial auditing causes concerns, so instead Oxfam Australia recommends that local unions and NGOs are involved in any verification process of factory conditions. Workers should be interviewed away from their place of work, so that they can speak more freely and anonymously, and discuss whether they are being treated fairly.

6. Are production workers paid a living wage, rather than a legal minimum wage? NGOs and trade unions can help companies to determine a living wage standard.

7. Do the suppliers' workers enjoy freedom of association and the right to collective bargaining? Can workers join a trade union? Workers should be interviewed away from their place of work, so that they can speak more freely and anonymously.

8. Does the company know how many workers have joined a workplace union? How well do workers know their rights? Local unions can often send in representatives to inform workers of their rights.

9. Can workers register a confidential workplace complaint? Are any complaints followed up and resolved in a timely fashion?

10. Do production workers have permanent contracts and job security?

Seminar 3: Resolving the trade-offs between commercial and sustainable supply chains

The issue of location choice is addressed by IKEA who, working with a group of Polish suppliers, reconfigured their supply chain so that two suppliers assumed a co-ordinating role over 26 others and took on the management of centralised distribution facilities. This meant that the suppliers collectively could make more frequent deliveries of smaller batches, which enhanced stock availability in-store, while also taking advantage of more efficient transportation using the local rail network (Bestlog n.d.). IKEA are also known for reducing transport volume by designing products that take up less space, volume and weight, such as jug-shaped watering cans that stack more easily, or flat-packed furniture to be assembled by the consumer (Mangan *et al.* 2012).

Activity 1

Research the supply chain management practices of IKEA and their code of conduct (IWay). See Bestlog (n.d.) and Ikea.com for a starting point. Alternatively you can do this exercise with a company of your choice.

Activity 2

1. With reference to the case study, complete the following table to contrast the key objectives of commercial and sustainable supply chain management.

2. Identify where there are trade-offs (conflicting priorities) and give examples that illustrate your answer.

3. Discuss how companies like IKEA can manage, overcome or remove such trade-offs to improve the sustainability of their supply chain.

	Commercial supply chain	Sustainable supply chain
Skill level	Skilled, specific logistics support	
Demand pattern	Relatively stable, predictable	
Language	English, commercial	
Network design	Configured to optimise structure and locations	
Strategic objectives	Maximise profit, reduce cost, return on investment	
Technology	State-of-the-art systems, information sharing	
Innovation focus	Process is focused on standardised supply chain	
Execution time-frame	Varies due to market conditions	
Infrastructure	Modern, well-maintained	
Product/service design	Standardisation, modularisation	
Stakes	Customer satisfaction, profitability	
Control	Centralised control	

Additional teaching material and ideas

'Where from?' ice-breaker

This is a way to encourage students to get to know each other and learn more about sustainable supply chains. In pairs or threes, examine labels in the clothes you are wearing, the snacks in your cafeteria or the contents of your bag. Map where each of your items has come from, and then identify any aspects of sustainability that might relate to the items and their supply chains, such as transport, packaging, materials, production processes, waste or recycling, skills, working conditions, etc. The groups can compare notes by presenting their most interesting and surprising 'finds'.

The Buying Game

The **Buying Game** is an online game developed by the UK charity Traidcraft and the Chartered Institute of Purchase and Supply. The game helps interested learners to improve their knowledge of the everyday realities faced by farmers, workers and communities in developing countries and the social aspects of sustainable supply chain management, enabling practitioners to improve the way they purchase so that low-income producers and workers can improve their livelihoods and conditions of work. The game asks learners to answer a series of questions about how they would buy an imaginary product called a 'dimble' that is produced in the developing world and sold to consumers in the West. There are six scenarios in which the buyer must make purchasing decisions and identify the consequences—whether positive or negative—further up the supply chain for local producers, workers and communities in developing countries.

The Buying Game is most usefully played in groups of two, each with a laptop. Their experience of having played the game can then be discussed in a plenary setting at the end of the session. The Buying Game can be accessed and played free of charge at www.thebuyinggame.org/

Short videos

If you prefer to watch video material, the following provide a short introduction to environmental sustainability in the supply chain:

- **www.greenconduct.com/news/2011/10/23/video-future-supply-chain-2016/** features supply chain practitioners from some of the world's leading corporations discussing how they can balance environmental and commercial pressures in their supply chains

- **http://greenconduct.com/news/2011/10/23/video-green-supply-chain/** illustrates how the supply chain can adopt more environmentally friendly practices, featuring the reverse supply chain of a carpet supplier

As an alternative, this BBC radio feature, recorded on board a Maersk Line super-ship, discusses aspects of global trade, logistics networks, sustainability in shipping technologies and supply chain security: www.bbc.co.uk/iplayer/episode/p00r3qlt/One_Planet_Sustainability_on_the_High_Seas/.

Case study resources

The European Platform for Supply Chain Management Best Practice was established by the European Logistics Association to promote supply chain efficiency and sustainability. The website www.elabestlog.org provides numerous case studies covering all aspects of logistics and supply chain improvements in many different industries.

Topics for debate

The trade-off choices between commercial and sustainable pressures in the supply chain provide fertile territory for class debate. Topics to explore could include:

- Is it possible to have sustainable fast fashion?

- Local or global: evaluate the social and environmental impact of importing fresh food.

- Reverse logistics in the clothing industry: who benefits from exporting second hand clothes from the West to developing economies?

Further reading

For an easy-to-read introduction to sustainable supply chain management, we suggest that you read the Danish Council for Corporate Social Responsibility (2010) guidelines, which provide comprehensive guidelines about dealing with suppliers and setting standards.

Alternatively, a practical guide to help you understand the environmental challenges that businesses face in the supply chain is available from the New Zealand Sustainable Business Council (SBC 2003). This identifies a range of environmental issues at all stages of the supply chain and gives examples of business initiatives.

If you are interested in getting an overview of some more recent developments in the field of sustainable supply chain management from an academic and policy-oriented perspective, the article by Lund-Thomsen and Lindgreen (2013) might be of help to you.

If you are interested in knowing more about how to work practically with solutions to ethical dilemmas that arise in the context of sustainable supply chain management, you should have a look at the document *Buying Matters*, produced by the UK-based NGO Traidcraft (Traidcraft, 2006).

For a case study in alignment between sustainable supply chain management and the marketing function, read Brindley and Oxborrow 2014. The case shows how a university catering department addressed a marketing challenge by redesigning the supply chain.

References

Bair, J., and F. Palpacuer (2012) 'From Varieties of Capitalism to Varieties of Activism: The Anti Sweatshop Movement in a Comparative Perspective', *Social Problems* 59.4 (November 2012): 522-43.

Barrientos, S., and S. Smith (2007) 'Do Workers Benefit from Ethical Trade? Assessing Codes of Labour Practice in Global Production Systems', *Third World Quarterly* 28.4: 713-29.

Bestlog (n.d.) *Reconfiguration of the Supply Chain Structure: Ikea Case*, www.elabestlog.org/node/272, accessed 15 June 2014.

Brindley, C., and L. Oxborrow (2014) 'Aligning the Sustainable Supply Chain to Green Marketing Needs: A Case Study', *Industrial Marketing Management* 43: 45-55.

Chan, H.K., H. He and W.Y.C. Wang (2012) 'Green Marketing and its Impact on Supply Chain Management in Industrial Markets', *Industrial Marketing Management* 41.4: 557-62.

Christopher, M. (2011) *Logistics and Supply Chain Management* (London: FT Prentice Hall).

Cousins, P., R. Lamming, B. Lawson and B. Squire (2008) *Strategic Supply Management: Principles, Theories and Practice* (London: FT Prentice Hall).

Danish Council for Corporate Social Responsibility (2010) *Guidelines for Sustainable Supply Chain Management*, http://samfundsansvar.dk/file/319140/guidelines_for_sustainable_supply_chain_management_februar_2011.pdf, accessed 2 April 2014.

ETI (Ethical Trading Initiative) (2006) *ETI Code of Labor Practice: Do Workers Really Benefit?* (Brighton, UK: University of Sussex, Institute of Development Studies)

Gereffi, G. (1999) 'International Trade and Industrial Upgrading in the Apparel Commodity Chain', *Journal of International Economics* 48.1 (June 1999): 37-70.

Ginsberg, J.M., and P.M. Bloom (2004) 'Choosing the Right Green Marketing Strategy', *MIT Sloan Management Review* 46.1 (Fall 2004): 79-84.

Greenberg, J., and G. Knight (2004) 'Framing Sweatshops: Nike, Global Production, and the American News Media', *Communication and Critical Cultural Studies* 1.2 (June 2004): 151-75.

Haufler, V. (2001) *A Public Role for the Private Sector. Industry Self-regulation in a Global Economy* (Washington, DC: Carnegie Endowment for International Peace).

Hill, T. (2005) *Operations Management*, 2nd edn (Basingstoke, UK: Palgrave Macmillan)

Jones, P., D. Comfort and D. Hillier (2008) 'Moving Towards Sustainable Food Retailing', *International Journal of Retail and Distribution Management* 36.12: 995-1001.

Khara, N., and P. Lund-Thomsen (2012) 'Value Chain Restructuring, Work Organization and Labour Outcomes in Football Manufacturing in India', *Competition and Change* 16.4 (October 2012): 261-80.

Krause, D., S. Vachon and R. Klassen (2009) 'Introduction and Reflection on the Role of Purchasing Management', *Journal of Supply Chain Management* 45.4: 18-25.

Liu, S., D. Kastriratne and J. Moizer (2012) 'A Hub and Spoke Model for Multi-Dimensional Integration of Green Marketing and Sustainable Supply Chain Management', *Industrial Marketing Management* 41: 581-88.

Lovins, L. Hunter (2008) 'Rethinking Production', in Worldwatch Institute, *State of the World 2008: Innovations for a Sustainable Economy* (New York: W.W. Norton): 38-40.

Lund-Thomsen, P. (2008) 'The Global Sourcing and Codes of Conduct Debate: Five Myths and Five Recommendations', *Development and Change* 39.6 (November 2008): 1005-18.

Lund-Thomsen, P., and N.M. Coe (2013) 'Corporate Social Responsibility and Labour Agency: The Case of Nike in Pakistan', *Journal of Economic Geography*, http://joeg.oxfordjournals.org/content/early/2013/12/16/jeg.lbt041.full.pdf+html, accessed 30 May 2014.

Lund-Thomsen, P., and A. Lindgreen (2013) 'Corporate Social Responsibility in Global Value Chains: Where Are We Now and Where Are We Going?', *Journal of Business Ethics*, http://link.springer.com/article/10.1007%2Fs10551-013-1796-x#page-1, accessed 30 May 2014.

Mangan, J., C. Lalwani, T. Butcher and R. Javadpour (2012) *Global Logistics and Supply Chain Management*, 2nd edn (London: Wiley).

Mehrmann, J. (2008), *Reverse Logistics in Supply Chain Management*, www.improvementandinnovation.com/features/article/reverse-logistics-supply-chain-management/.

Preuss, L. (2009) 'Addressing sustainable development through public procurement: the case of local government', *Supply Chain Management: An International Journal* 14.30: 213-23.

SBC (Sustainable Business Council) (2003) *Business Guide to a Sustainable Supply Chain: A Practical Guide*, www.sbc.org.nz/resources-and-tools/guides/sustainable-supply-chain.

Seuring, S., and M. Muller (2008) 'Core Issues in Sustainable Supply Chain Management: A Delphi Study', *Business Strategy and the Environment* 17: 455-66.

Sharma, A., G.R. Iyer, A. Mehrotra and R. Krishnan (2010) 'Sustainability and Business-to-Business Marketing: A Framework and Implications', *Industrial Marketing Management* 39: 330-41.

Slack, N., A. Brandon-Jones and R. Johnston (2013) *Operations Management* (Harlow, UK: Pearson).

Soler, C., K. Bergstrom and H. Shanahan (2010) 'Green Supply Chains and the Missing Link between Environmental Information and Practice', *Business Strategy and the Environment* 19.1: 14-25.

Srivastava, S.K. (2007) 'Green Supply Chain Management: A State of the Art Literature Review', *International Journal of Management Reviews* 9.10: 53-80.

Traidcraft (2006) *Buying Matters—Consultation: Sourcing Fairly From Developing Countries* (London: Traidcraft).

Vachon, S., and R. Klassen (2006) 'Extending Green Practices Across the Supply Chain', *International Journal for Operations and Production Management* 26.7: 795-821.

11

Developing sustainably responsible strategies in business

Mathias Schüz

This chapter provides the reader with a better understanding of how companies can assess their strategic options for business development in order to comply with demands from different environments. For this, it clarifies the deeper meaning and interrelation of fundamental terms such as sustainability, responsibility and ethics. Furthermore, it discloses the significance of sustainably responsible activities for the long-term success of business strategies. Participants of this course can:

- Learn how to gain a competitive advantage by developing sustainable strategies that cope with the different challenges of economic, social and ecological issues

- Develop strategies that cope with threats and exploit opportunities by applying strengths and compensating for weaknesses

- Understand the deeper meaning of responsibility, sustainability and ethics

- Check whether a strategic option is in compliance with demands for sustainable corporate responsibility

---

Introduction

All living beings have to respond to challenges in order to survive, and human beings cultivate the planet in order to survive. Technological and scientific advances, as well as economic efficiency, allow nature's power and resources to be exploited strategically. Meanwhile, the risks inherent in this have become highly visible while outweighing the opportunities in many regards. Short-term gains are a trade-off for losses on the social and environmental front.

Countless problems, disasters and catastrophes caused by the corporate world, such as those ascribed to Foxconn in China's supply industry (Hick 2012; SACOM 2012; NN 2012; ts/dpa 2012), Monsanto in India's agriculture, Lehman Brothers in the financial industry, BP in the Gulf of Mexico and Tepco in Fukushima, have broadened the minds of many business leaders as surveys (Lacey *et al.* 2010; KPMG 2011; PwC 2010) and trend research (Ernst & Young 2012) have proven (Schüz 2012: 8). Companies have recognised that gaining a long-term competitive advantage is only possible if one has respect for the interests of all the stakeholders involved and for the greater whole of nature. Otherwise, they might lose their stakeholders' trust, an important precondition for successful business and a core purpose of sustainable strategic management. Furthermore, they might destroy the basis of existence in the present and future for their own and future generations (Stead and Stead 2013: 9ff).

Consequently, companies' understanding of responsibility has undergone a paradigm shift from being purely aligned to the financial interests of shareholders to having a **triple responsibility** encompassing economic, social and environmental dimensions. Furthermore, they have learned to respond to the consequences of their activities for **future generations**, i.e. acting sustainably, incorporating a time dimension of corporate responsibility.

Together, these four dimensions of corporate responsibility comprise SCR (**sustainable corporate responsibility**), illustrated by a model developed by Schüz (2012). How can SCR be applied when developing business strategies? This chapter outlines a practical approach to integrating SCR into strategic management lessons.

First, it addresses why and how strategies and SCR can be integrated into the **open system** of a company. Second, it explains the different key terms, scopes and degrees of SCR. Third, it links the SCR model to typical models of strategic management such as PESTEL (political, economic, societal, technological, ecological and legal), Michael Porter's 'Five Forces' and SWOT–TOWS (strengths, weaknesses, opportunities and threats) analyses. Finally, three seminars use a case study to give students the opportunity to apply the tools for developing sustainably responsible strategies which are efficient enough for economic survival, while at the same time being acceptable to different stakeholders and consistent with an environmental agenda. Each seminar can be completed by undergraduate students in an hour, having been introduced to the topic as taught at the School of Management and Law at Zurich University of Applied Sciences, Switzerland.

Strategic planning and SCR in the corporate world

The purpose of business strategies is to gain a **competitive advantage**. How can one develop those strategies? There are many different approaches, concepts, frameworks and methods that advise on how to develop business strategies and how to make decisions.

For the reasons set out above, whatever top managers decide on as their business strategy, it should be sustainably responsible towards the justifiable demands of nature and of **stakeholders**. This increases the opportunities for profitability, stakeholder **trust** and the needs of the greater whole. They are interdependent. The following **systemic view of companies** reveals the inner link between strategic management and corporate responsibility, since both are exploratory **heuristic research models for reasonable courses of action** in complex and dynamic environments.

Systemic view of companies

Like ecological systems, companies are **viable** when they (a) maintain their identity for generations (**self-preservation**), (b) co-operate with other systems (**co-preservation**), and (c) adapt to their changing environments (**preservation of the whole**). They preserve themselves by exchanging **matter**, **energy** and **information**. They use limited resources such as materials, people and skills (input) in order to create valuable products or services (output), which external systems are willing to pay for. This transformation process is profitable so long as income exceeds costs (Schüz 1999: 116ff; Stead and Stead 2013: 21; Blackmore *et al.* 2012).

However, there are many areas where the **risk of failure** needs to be considered. All activities are aimed at creating a particular outcome, but often have unforeseen consequences too. To what extent an organisation is able to be aware them depends on its intrinsic culture, which functions similarly to a sensory system in natural organisms. Due to its members' respective **virtues** or **vices** it might filter out environmental information. For instance, the vice of **greed** ignores the needs of customers and other stakeholders and consequently provokes their resistance. Thus, profit-driven companies often have a one-sided view of their environment and correspondingly adopt narrow-minded strategies. In contrast, the virtues of **trustworthiness** and **openness** gain stakeholders' **trust** and lead to better relationships with them. Companies with **integrity** create value for everyone. Profit-driven companies only care about economic performance indicators such as share prices or credit ratings, while those with integrity also take social and ecological indicators into acount, such as consumer complaints or dwindling natural resources. Thus, strategies based on virtues involve corporate structures, processes and behaviour that respond more adequately to the demands of diverse stakeholders.

Kotter and Heskett (1992), who empirically researched and compared **corporate cultures**, found that they were either '**adaptive**' or '**non-adaptive**' to environmental needs and changes. The former react sensibly and fit in well within the business context: their strategies and practices respond sustainably to changing markets and new business opportunities and threats. The latter ignore all the signals and are just focused on protecting their status: if anything, they are confused by complaints about socially or environmentally insensitive behaviour. For the most part, their **input filters** accept only self-affirming and economic feedback, and so they tend to be seen as 'reactive', 'risk averse', inwardly focused and 'bureaucratic' (Kotter and Heskett 1992: 44). Over long periods they might fail to deliver excellent performance, unless their competitive advantage is based on fraudulent activities, or on monopolistic or oligopolistic cartels. An example of the latter might be the commodity provider, Glencore. Economically it is very successful due to its strong position in the market, but it is often faced with complaints, be they unjustified or legitimate, about its negative impact on the working conditions of its suppliers or its irreversible exploitation of nature (Harvey and Pidd 2011).

One could say that corporate virtues or vices respectively open up or close down a company's filter system for interacting with its environment. In either case, they are the company's responsibility. If it chooses to ignore or suppress this responsibility, it might face expensive (even life-threatening) **feedback from authorities** or other stakeholders. In order to minimise such risks and to increase the chances of success, business managers are therefore advised to use **sustainably responsible strategies** when planning their businesses. These strategies should encourage all employees to act more responsibly, which will then overcome the company's negative aspects and move it towards more virtuous behaviour, which will in turn be more acceptable to the majority of stakeholders involved. Actions with negative consequences are viewed as breaches of duty and usually provoke resistance in those affected, who might charge the company for compensation as a result. Such reactions should be borne in mind when planning strategically to secure a company's income in the long term.

Figure 1 depicts the company as an open system **creating value** step by step from input to output. A well-formulated vision or mission statement might focus all employees' efforts in one particular direction, while the strategy defines the milestones by which the vision could become reality and preshapes the structure and processes of the organisation, which in turn influences organisational behaviour and results in more efficient and effective output.

Figure 1: The company as an open social system.

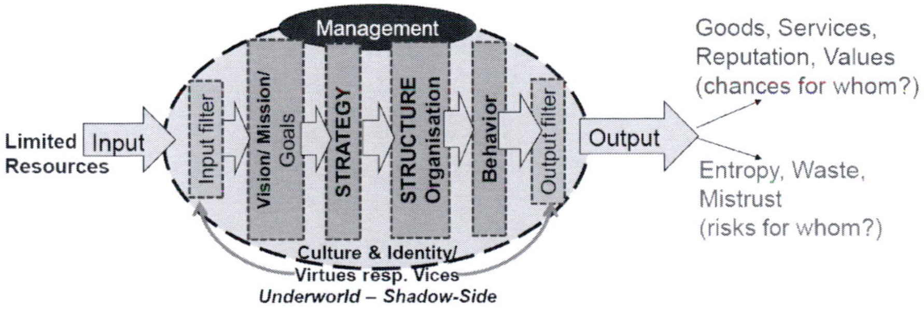

Source: Derived from Rieckmann (2000: 76).

From a systemic perspective, then, the success of a company depends on how it responds to environmental demands. In so doing, its strategy becomes a rational concept of how to prevail in the market. Before we discuss how a company can be sustainably responsible, the next section describes the typical stages in the development of a systemic strategy.

Stages of systemic strategy development

In order to meet environmental challenges successfully, a structured approach to the strategy of all organisations is recommended. One convincing 'formula' for identifying '**strategic options**' is to choose a particular **direction** and then select an appropriate strategy **method** (Johnson *et al.* 2005: 340). The direction can initially be derived from **Ansoff's matrix** for product and/or market development (ibid.: 354ff), and then from strategic recommendations proposed by a SWOT–TOWS analysis. The methods that a company can follow range from 'organic growth' to 'mergers and acquisitions' and 'strategic alliances' (ibid.: 359).

Although the choice of Ansoff matrix and methods encompasses sustainable responsibility issues, for reasons of space this chapter will concentrate on strategic development using a SWOT–TOWS analysis. The following steps in the strategic management process can be taken:

1. The organisation's **vision and mission** have to be defined. They depict the desired future and provide the main purpose and focus for the strategy (Crawford 2005), something that applies to all activities within the organisation. In addition to principal business activities, they might consist of key objectives, beliefs, values and stakeholders (Dobson *et al.* 2004). However, they will only provide a focus for organisational behaviour if senior management lead by example and **'walk the talk'**. Otherwise such declarations can easily backfire, as demonstrated by the example of **Tepco**, the Japanese energy provider. In September 2010, the firm released its new *Vision 2020*, which made a commitment to 'value social trust', 'open the way to the future' and 'maximize human and technological potential' as three 'Management Policies for the direction of our business'. Furthermore, it promised 'to ensure energy security, [and] deliver stable supplies of low-cost, eco-friendly electricity' (Tepco 2010). Six months later, a nuclear catastrophe took place at Tepco's Fukushima power plant.

2. The company's **external environment (or context)** has to be analysed, and what responses are provoked by **threats** and **opportunities** (Boddy 2008: 84, 245f). It can be analysed (a) in the industry-specific micro-environment or (b) in the general macro-environment. Porter's 'Five Forces'—substitutes, barriers to entry, bargaining power of customers and suppliers as well as that of competitors (ibid.: 93ff)—characterise the former, while the PESTEL frameworks differentiate between six macro-environmental spheres: the political, economic, societal, technological, ecological and legal (ibid.: 96ff). Tepco ignored many of the external threats and opportunities, such as the environmentalists' recommendations that it should build 30m tsunami protection walls along the shore. Instead, to save money, it only built the wall 6m high (Redaktion 2012).

3. The **internal environment (or context)** has to be analysed as to whether its elements reveal, in comparison with its competitors, strengths and weaknesses along Michael Porter's **'value chain'** (Porter 1985: 36-47). These represent the company's ability to run its business profitably and the related consequences responsibly (Boddy 2008: 248f). After the explosion at Tepco's nuclear plant in Fukushima, many weaknesses (compared to its competitors) came to light: the company had adopted a strict focus on shareholder value and low safety standards, engaged in corrupt practices with officials, and ignored individual, social and environmental integrity.

4. The entrepreneurial risk, the opportunity to either lose or secure income, has to be identified by combining the external and internal environments with the following question: How far do the internal strengths and weaknesses allow the company to deal with threats and exploit opportunities? The answers can be derived from (a) a SWOT analysis and (b) the **TOWS framework** for developing strategic recommendations. The latter considers the different combinations of strengths ($S_{1,2,\ldots}$) and weaknesses ($W_{1,2,\ldots}$) with the identified opportunities ($O_{1,2,\ldots}$) and threats ($T_{1,2,\ldots}$), resulting in a list of recommendations (Weihrich 1982). Tepco could have addressed its low safety standards (W) and the threat from the global anti-nuclear movement (T) by upgrading its safety installations to the standard used by a competitor engaging in best practice (WT strategy).

Figure 2 depicts the open system of a company within its different external and internal environments. It clarifies the interdependencies between internal capabilities and external influences. At this point it should be noted that the term '**environment**' encompasses all the external or internal surroundings of a company with which it exchanges material, energy or information. For example, in the case of the 'ecological environment' such resources are provided by nature. Internal environments are built by employees who may, for example, put all their efforts into realising the company's goals or who may, on the other hand, withdraw their good will for certain possibly vindictive reasons.

5. However, each of the strategic recommendations derived from the TOWS framework has to be checked in terms of whether it is acceptable according to the checklist of the SCR model. Only then can strategists select and prioritise suitable recommendations. The final decision depends on the company's capabilities and the resources at its disposal.

Since steps 1 to 4 are established tools of strategic management practice they are not discussed in detail here, but they are applied directly in the Frog case study seminars below, together with sustainable responsibility

Figure 2: The company systemically embedded in its different environments.

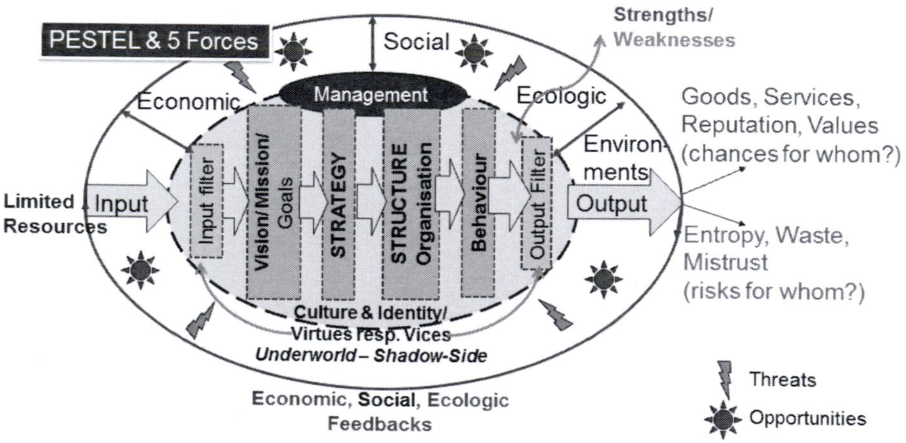

Source: Derived from Rieckmann (2000: 76).

issues. The SCR model and checklist mentioned in step 5 will be introduced in the next section.

A holistic model for sustainable corporate responsibility

The SCR checklist is based on the SCR model published in Schüz (2012). This model outlines in depth what responsibility means and how far it can be adopted in the business world.

The structure of responsibility

The term '**responsibility**' describes the relationship between an acting subject S causing **consequences** $C_{1,2 \ldots m}$, which are assessed by **authorities** $A_{1,2 \ldots n}$ as positive or negative (Picht 1969: 319). The structure of any responsibility is depicted graphically in Figure 3. A subject, be it an individual or a company, is responsible for the intended and unintended consequences of its activities towards different authorities.

Authorities such as stakeholders evaluate a company's activity as responsible or irresponsible, praising or condemning it. Their verdicts differ due to their **different value systems** and their view of the

Figure 3: The structure of responsibility.

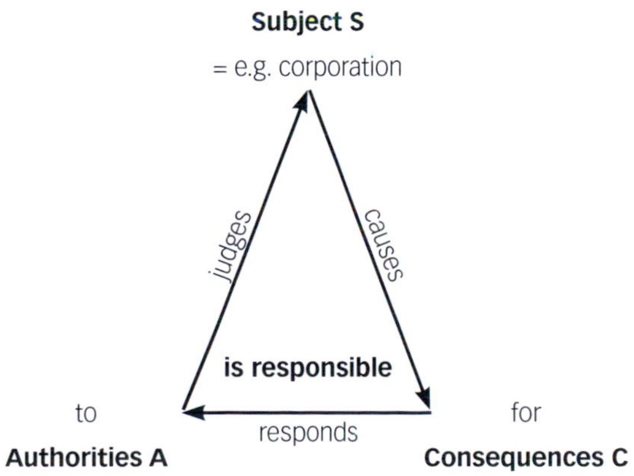

Source: Schüz (2012: 9).

consequences. A magistrate in court might decide to let someone off for a crime, while people with a vested interest, or even the wrongdoer's own conscience, might deem their actions to have been irresponsible. Shareholders usually evaluate disasters differently from other stakeholders, so one can therefore consider responsibility as a **construction** with different solutions (Bayertz 1995: 4).

For instance, the explosion at Tepco's nuclear power plant in Fukushima can be seen as an act of nature beyond human control, because it was caused by a tsunami. Consequently, the operating company can be absolved from blame. But further investigations showed that Tepco had neglected cracks in the cooling system for economic reasons. Instead, it had bribed safety officials to ignore the faults. Neglected duties of care, mismanagement and corrupt practices for the sake of maximising profit were therefore jointly responsible for the catastrophe, with tremendous social and environmental implications. As a result, 'the public has targeted Tepco, Japanese politicians, nuclear experts and the media, which has promoted the myth of safe nuclear plants for the past 50 years', as Satoko Kogure, a freelance journalist based in Japan, stated (Kogure 2012). From his point of view, Tepco and its executives should be held responsible for the disaster, while the Japanese government still tries to exculpate them. This example shows how responsibility is a variable term, depending on how one assesses consequences and which authority is accepted.

The triple corporate responsibility

But what should corporate responsibility comprise? It is important to distinguish three dimensions of responsibility, each ranging from narrow to broad.

As mentioned above, companies are open systems embedded in their economic and social spheres as well as within their own ecological environment, with which they can exchange resources. In the long run, they can only survive when they co-operate with other systems (such as those represented by stakeholders) to fit into the greater whole of their different environments: in other words, when they find their ecological niche or the fundamental meaning of their existence. Thus, **corporate health** can only be sustained when physical, social and mental resources are exchanged fairly.

Figure 4: Corporate responsibility as a feedback loop with its environments.

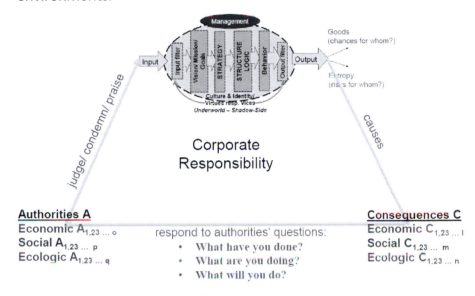

Source: Derived from Rieckmann (2000: 76).

Instead of acting in a purely selfish manner, a company should pursue **'enlightened self-interest'** (Ikerd 1999) and take on responsibilities that gain the trust of stakeholders, assuring low **transaction costs**, creating willingness to co-operate in the long term, and protecting its own conditions for existence. Hence, besides economic responsibility, the dimensions of social and ecological responsibilities are fundamental for sustaining long-term survival.

The three dimensions have to be balanced, because at first glance they often appear to be conflicting. Social and ecological engagement seems to harm economic results. But this is an investment which yields returns through stakeholder co-operation in general, especially in terms of customer loyalty. If they are not integrated, the neglected environments **have a negative impact on stakeholder confidence** in the company, thus causing high economic losses.

Consequently, one can **define** (see Fig. 4) **corporate responsibility** as the following: a manager or a company acts responsibly when they are **responding** (a) to the consequences of their actions; (b) to the authorities **economically** by being profitable to shareholders, **socially**

Figure 5: Triple corporate responsibility.

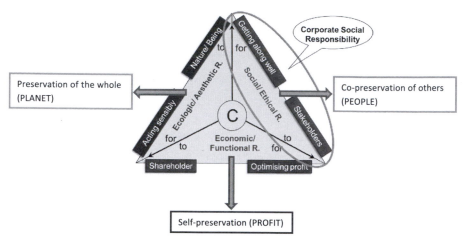

Source: Schüz (2012: 10).

by getting along well with all stakeholders, and **ecologically** by acting responsibly towards the natural world. By responding to shareholders, self-preservation is achieved; by responding to ethical demands, co-preservation with stakeholders is enabled; and by responding to 'nature' or 'being', preservation of the whole is achieved (Schüz 1999: 76 f). Figure 5 outlines the triple corporate responsibility with its different consequences and authorities.

The triple corporate responsibility model is not identical to John Elkington's concept of the **triple bottom line** (1997). While the latter values the output of a company as, for example, worked out in the Global Reporting Initiative (GRI 2012) or used by rating agencies such as SAM (2012), the former also tackles the root causes in order to improve corporate behaviour. For example, Shell and other companies have defined their corporate responsibility according to the '**three Ps**' of people, planet and profit. They emphasise that these three responsibilities have to be balanced to a large extent, in order to achieve sustainable development (Shell 2012). How far and how seriously the three dimensions of responsibility are considered, or concretely implemented, is not proven just by generating a lot of publicity about them. Only practice shows whether the social and ecological dimensions serve as fig leaves or whether they are truly respected in the daily running of the business.

Corporate economic responsibility and functional approaches

The economic dimension of sustainable corporate responsibility assures the **profitability** of a company. It delivers the right means to an end in order to ensure survival. All existing business administration techniques enable the organisation to **function** and to secure the necessary income to allow all costs to be covered **efficiently**. The purpose is to avoid losses and to gain profits through efficient and effective products and services. In this case the company functions profitably and is able to preserve itself.

Corporate social responsibility and ethics

Corporate social responsibility can be related to the three main traditional ethical concepts: the '**ethics of goods**', or utilitarian ethics, assesses the consequences as beneficial or damaging; the '**ethics of duties**', or deontological ethics, defines the authority asking for the fulfilment of ethical duties; and the '**ethics of virtues**', or virtue ethics, strengthens the company's ability to take responsibility (Schüz 1999: 174ff).

The **utilitarian** ethicists calculate the '**greatest good for the greatest number**' (Jeremy Bentham). An action is ethically good when all of its consequences result in more pleasure (happiness) to all concerned than suffering. Thus, Tepco might send 100 employees into the radioactive containment in order to clean it up. Although the workers will be subjected to a higher risk of getting cancer and of suffering from it, millions of residents nearby will see it as a good thing. To avoid arbitrariness the consequences should be discussed from the standpoint of all stakeholders involved.

Deontological ethicists might not assess this action as ethically good, because they see it as a breach in the duty to protect human dignity. According to Immanuel Kant's **categorical imperative**, no human being should be treated only as a means to an end. Workers sacrificing their life for others should only do this autonomously and not as a result of being blackmailed with the threat of losing their jobs.

Virtue ethics strengthens the actors' ability to avoid selfish behaviour and to act virtuously. This means the company should develop corporate virtues and with them an ethical culture, in which the employees are able to act ethically. Virtuous behaviour is willing and able to be discussed in public, while those engaged in selfish actions would normally seek to avoid publicity. Public assessment and comparisons will also highlight the **best-practising** company. Although Tepco's *Vision 2020* made

Figure 6: Corporate social responsibility and ethical approaches.

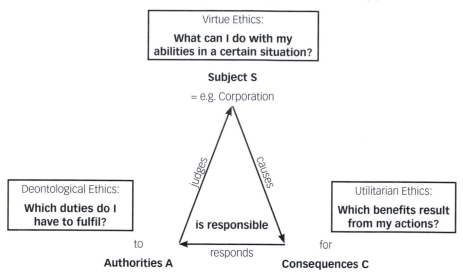

Derived from Schüz (2013: 42).

a general announcement of its 'social and environmental initiatives and new values', these did nothing to prevent the ultimate maximum credible accident in Fukushima. Obviously, it was not specific enough and not meant to be carried out in practice.

As shown in Figure 6, the three ethical concepts are not mutually exclusive, but do ultimately **complement** each another when linked to the issue of responsibility (Schüz 1999: 174ff).

Corporate ecological responsibility and aesthetics

Most of the current debate still reduces ecological issues to social responsibility (Mey *et al.* 2007). The point is made that NGOs (non-governmental organisations) such as Greenpeace are responsible for defending global ecological issues. Thus, it would suffice to negotiate with them in order to meet nature's needs. However, there are many risks in simply delegating ecological issues to NGOs rather than finding one's own solutions. Shell's **Brent Spar** case exemplifies this. Greenpeace condemned the deep-water disposal of the North Sea oil storage tank as not being environmentally friendly, although it turned out to be the best option. Instead, the NGO (ab)used the issue by fighting for highly expensive and environmentally questionable on-shore disposal, in order to attract new sponsors for its organisation. Ecological responsibility cannot be delegated to a third party: it has to be addressed directly by the company responsible.

Furthermore, ecological responsibility should refer to **aesthetics** in order to make mankind aware of those activities that are beneficial to nature and those that are harmful. Aesthetics appeals to us to act sensibly by using all our senses and reason, as well as inspiring us as to what to strive for and what to avoid. Concretely, Braungart and McDonough's initiative of 'cradle to cradle' (2002) broadens our understanding of what is advantageous and meaningful for the whole planet. It seeks to fully reintegrate whatever man produces into the cycles of nature, a challenge for 'corporate environmental management' (Schaltegger *et al.* 2003).

Scopes of triple responsibility

Each dimension of the triple corporate responsibility model has a different **scope** in terms of how far responsibility is concretely taken. Three steps for each are proposed following Jean Piaget (1932) and Lawrence Kohlberg (1971):[1] (a) the narrow scope of responsibility, striving for **selfish** benefit, (b) the medium or mid-scope striving for mutual or **reciprocal** benefit, and (c) the broad scope striving for **universal** benefit.

According to Figure 7, the scope of responsibility of each dimension can be expressed differently: economic responsibility can range from self-interest and company interest through to the common good; social responsibility can range from egocentric and anthropocentric through to a biocentric orientation; and environmental responsibility can focus from the useful through the regional right up to a global scale. Detailed explanations of these categories (Schüz 2012: 12f) are beyond the scope of this paper.

---

1   Jean Piaget discovered that as children grow they show different stages of moral development (1932). Lawrence Kohlberg continued Piaget's research with adults. Both defined three main stages of ethical behaviour: the 'preconventional', 'conventional' and 'postconventional' (Kohlberg 1971: 163ff). While preconventional moral behaviour is more egoistically responsive to sanctions and appraisals, conventional morality is based on social convention and reciprocity. Only at the postconventional level is the actor oriented to universal principles based on autonomy, as opposed to law and order which might represent only particular interests.

Figure 7: Different scopes of responsibility.

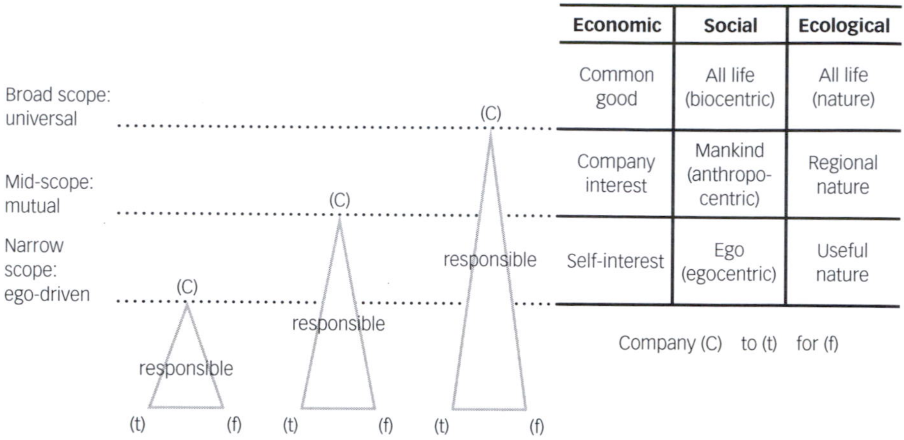

	Economic	Social	Ecological
Broad scope: universal	Common good	All life (biocentric)	All life (nature)
Mid-scope: mutual	Company interest	Mankind (anthropocentric)	Regional nature
Narrow scope: ego-driven	Self-interest	Ego (egocentric)	Useful nature

Company (C)   to (t)   for (f)

Source: Schüz (2012: 11).

The concept of sustainable corporate responsibility

The triple corporate responsibility model described so far still excludes the whole issue of **sustainability**. While the different scopes of the former are more related to space (e.g.: How far does responsibility reach on this planet?), the latter introduces the dimension of **time**. Time becomes a factor when one starts to consider how long responsible actions should last or be sustained. Because of its worldwide dissemination, we can refer to the term 'sustainability' as it was defined in 1987 by the **Brundtland Commission**: 'Sustainable development is development that meets the needs of the present without compromising the ability of future generations to meet their own needs' (Brundtland 1987). In short, it declares that we should not create a disadvantage for **future generations** without explaining whether this includes future generations of non-human species such as animals and plants (the **biocentric** approach) or whether this only takes the future of human beings into account (the **anthropocentric** approach). Moreover, it does not define what disadvantage means. Does it mean securing their survival or—more strongly—that they should have the same life chances as us?

Combined with our model of responsibility, it is now quite easy to illustrate all the different ranges and scopes. The **model** of sustainable corporate responsibility (Fig. 8) is shown as a **clock** with three different **clock faces** representing the triple corporate responsibility. The three

Figure 8: Model of sustainable corporate responsibility.

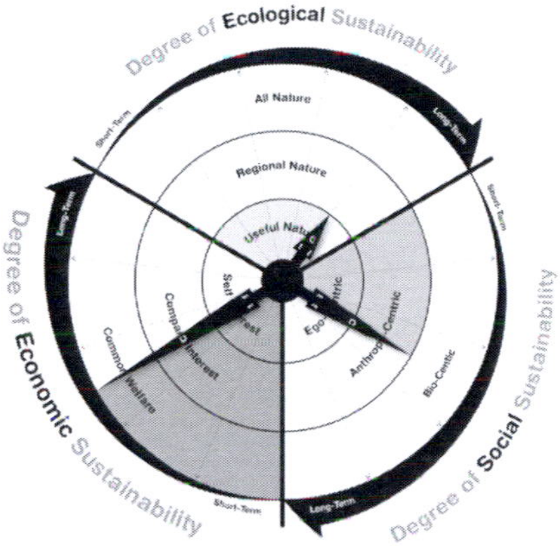

Source: Schüz (2012: 12).

clock hands are used to indicate the time period as well as the scope of responsibility achieved: the longer they are the larger scope they represent. The further the hands move round the clock, the more sustainable the responsibility is; in other words, the more the impact on future generations is considered. Like the different scopes, the range of the respective **degrees of sustainability** is divided into three steps: short term, mid-term and long term.

Within the economic dimension, the short-term oriented entrepreneur sees only the success of today without reflecting on the consequences for tomorrow or the wider future. According to its *Vision 2020* (2010), Tepco hoped to 'realize [the] sustainable growth of our Group and share the fruits of our achievements with society'. Instead, it ended up sharing with society the fruits of a contaminated environment caused by its profit-driven business. Another example might be the self-interested entrepreneur thinking of their great-grandchildren inheriting the company, without any respect for the future generations of other human beings, not to mention other species. Also, investors such as day-traders or hedge-fund managers can be very short-term oriented.

However, being highly sustainable does not automatically imply a short scope in responsibility, for some family businesses (or investment groups such as Berkshire Hathaway) can be really long-term oriented.

The strategic importance of SCR

In all scenarios, the SCR model sets the **benchmark** for sustainably responsible strategies. It alerts businessmen to the essential dimensions of their responsibility with its possible scopes and ranges, and allows us to outline the **responsibility profiles** of typical companies (Fig. 9). Furthermore, it facilitates comparison with best-practice companies and/or the gap between the actual responsibility profile and that to which a company might aspire. The latter helps companies to define their own strengths and weaknesses regarding SCR, which in turn facilitates a better SWOT analysis. Last but not least, the SCR profile can also be used by companies to assess their own decisions based on the SCR checklist, which allows us to illustrate the SCR characteristics of those businesses.

In addition to these benefits, a checklist (see Worksheet 5 below) referring to the dimensions of SCR helps to verify whether a strategic option complies with the intended SCR standards or not. One can answer the questions and weigh up the positives and negatives, which then serves as a guide to companies in their decision whether to adopt this particular option. Additionally, it is an excellent basis upon which to discuss your own results with those of colleagues. The main aim is to achieve considered and reasoned strategic decisions with better consideration of consequences, duties to be fulfilled and virtues pursued, according to the corporate culture the company has set out to achieve.

Figure 9: The responsibility profiles of typical organisations.

Case A: **Economistic family enterprise** considering social and ecological responsibility and future generations only when it serves its own offspring and long-term profitability

Case B: **Fundamentalist nature protection organisation** privately sponsored and relying on volunteers for its activities, reglecting social needs

Case C: **Pragmatic-idealistic pharmaceutical company** primarily claiming to 'improve and preserve human life': when this is fulfilled profits follow automatically

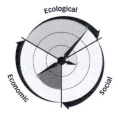

Source: Derived from Schüz (2013: 31).

General introduction to the seminars

The following three seminars use a case study to assist in the development of a sustainably responsible strategy. Strategic options will be assessed on the basis of whether they are acceptable in terms of sustainable corporate responsibility. After the case study, external and internal influences will be analysed in Seminar 1, while a SWOT–TOWS analysis helps to develop strategic options in Seminar 2. The compliance of these options with SCR criteria will be assessed in Seminar 3.

Case study

The narrative is based on a real case, but has been anonymised and modified for teaching purposes in order to focus on sustainable corporate responsibility issues. The purpose of the case is to develop **sustainably responsible strategies** for Frog AG in order to resolve its difficult situation. Students should read it carefully and apply their understanding in a series of three seminars, which help progressively to develop strategic options which fulfil sustainably responsible demands from both social and environmental perspectives.

The Frog AG case study

The German company, Frog AG, has been successfully producing shoe polish, leather-care products and cleansing agents for more than 80 years. Although highly reputable, Frog has recently run into a crisis. For some years, Frog has been selling shoe sprays which probably cause serious health problems. Especially after using it in confined spaces, customers have complained of respiratory problems, dizziness, skin rashes, serious headaches and nausea, symptoms which sometimes persist for several days.

Dr Sprayman, Frog's CEO, admits to his personal strategic consultant, the freelancer Dr Pestel, that until now the board and the management have not been paying much attention to the customers' complaints. They have discussed the situation in board meetings, but not introduced any measures to address the problem. They did not even take any action when the company doctor reported some cases in which employees in the production unit had noticed various health problems in connection with the shoe spray. The executives simply did not want to compromise the sales of this successful and profitable product.

Meanwhile, the editor of a prominent business newspaper has obviously received some insider information about the senior management's attempts to keep the issue quiet. The journalist concerned has started his own research into the case. Police reports have been compiled, and the state attorney has started an investigation. Consumer organisations, health authorities and medical doctors have begun to warn the public about using the spray in confined spaces. Environmentalists have started a campaign against sprays in general due to their effect on the ozone layer. As a result, even the biggest discounter in the German-speaking market has just announced a product recall.

Frog employees are now regularly receiving enquiries from worried customers without being able to answer them. They therefore pass these questions on to the board, demanding transparency about the real risks of the leather spray. Moreover, after Frog AG's shares slumped sharply, the rumour of an imminent takeover by an American company (a so-called 'black knight') shatters Frog's management and the market. In return, some major shareholders have announced their intention to defend the company against the hostile takeover bid.

During preliminary meetings Dr Sprayman has mentioned Frog's Ecoclean department, led by Dr Vinegar, which researches and develops new product lines made from pure plant extracts. But Dr Vinegar is regarded as an introvert and is unpopular with his colleagues because of his distant and peculiar behaviour. Dr Sprayman himself considered Dr Vinegar's ideas to be impractical and not marketable. Consequently, he cut Ecoclean's budget considerably, and the board has even been considering closing the department down.

Coincidentally, Dr Pestel has heard one of Ecoclean's market researchers complaining about the bad image that Dr Vinegar's product ideas have inside the company, despite their huge market potential.

Now, Dr Pestel is asked by Dr Sprayman whether he is willing and able to develop restructuring proposals for Frog AG. He is supposed to develop strategic options for coping with the present crisis and for leading the company to a sustainable future. Now it is up to you to support Dr Pestel by carrying out the following tasks, using the attached worksheets, in order to develop strategic options for Frog AG.

Suggested seminars

Seminar 1: External and internal influences (60 minutes)

This seminar will guide you through the different steps needed to lead Frog AG in the direction of a more sustainably responsible business. Please read the case study above carefully. Then you are asked:

1. To formulate a brief vision/mission statement for the new Frog AG (use Worksheet 1).

2. After you have finished the brief vision/mission statement, analyse Porter's 'Five Forces' and the relevant environmental spheres according to the PESTEL scheme. Focus on the related threats and opportunities for Frog AG with regard to SCR issues (use Worksheet 2).

3. Work out Frog's strengths and weaknesses with regard to SCR issues by using Porter's value chain (use Worksheet 3).

Seminar 2: SWOT–TOWS analysis (60 minutes)

4. Use the results of Activity 1 to identify the most challenging threats and opportunities (derived from the Porter's 'Five Forces' analysis and the PESTEL analysis in Activity 2) and most important strengths and weaknesses (derived from Porter's value chain-analysis in Activity 3 and the case study) and develop strategic options and recommendations with the help of a SWOT–TOWS analysis (use Worksheet 4).

5. Prioritise them according to Frog's capabilities with regard to its culture, available resources and market situation.

Seminar 3: SCR compliance (60 minutes)

6. Check the acceptability of your two highest priority recommendations to determine whether or not they comply with the SCR model (use Worksheet 5).

Worksheets for Frog case

The following worksheets support you as you go through the different activities outlined above.

Worksheet 1: Frog AG's vision and mission statement

A vision is an **image of a desired future**. It should be understandable, catchy, ambitious, attractive, motivating, exceptional and trend-setting, and also create enthusiasm. Ideally it gives purpose and identity, and enhances performance. In the 19th century, for example, Gottlieb Daimler had the vision of a motorised humanity moving much faster and more comfortably 'on land, on water and in the air'. Out of this he derived his mission to build and sell cars. In this sense a mission statement is derived from the vision and defines what purpose an organisation serves, as well as its broader goals, and how its activities should taken forward. It is 'the framework or context within which the company's strategies are formulated' (Hill and Gareth 2008: 11). With this in mind, formulate a brief vision/mission statement for the new Frog AG. This could be also complemented by a symbol, an image or a picture outlining the desired future:

....

....

....

....

Symbol/picture:

Worksheet 2: Frog AG's market and environments

Frog AG operates within the framework of its (a) micro-economic market and (b) macro-environments.

1. Analyse **Porter's 'Five Forces'** for Frog AG: which force is Frog confronted with (give an example for each) after its (negative) SCR issues came to the attention of the media? Fill in the following chart, including the respective forces outside the boxes.

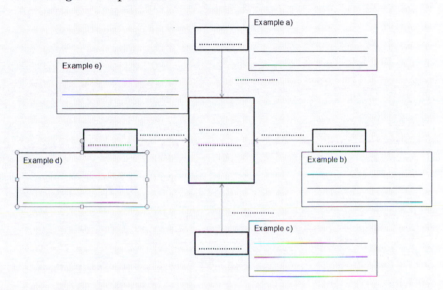

2. Analyse Frog's macro-environment using the PESTEL framework. Note: Consider only those factors which have an impact on Frog AG and cover SCR issues:

Political issues	
(Macro-)economic issues	
Socio-cultural issues	
Technological issues	
Environmental issues	
Legal issues	

Worksheet 3: Frog AG's value chain

The following diagram is adapted from Porter and Kramer (2006) and has integrated the role of corporate culture as an important input and output filter for sustainably responsible activities. The original value chain with relation to social responsibility is available as part of the additional teaching material (see page 4).

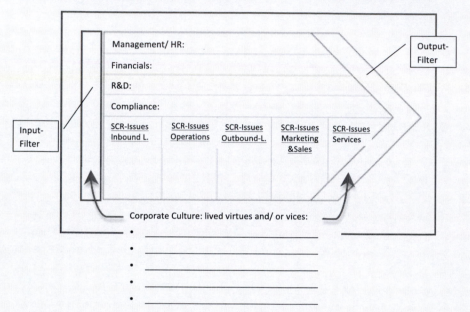

Worksheet 4: Frog AG's new strategic options based on a SWOT–TOWS analysis

external factors TOWS Analysis of FROG Case internal factors	Opportunities (O): O1: O2: O3:	Threats (T): T1: T2: T3:
Strengths (S): S1: S2: S3:	**S/O strategies:** S__/O__: ....:..................... ....:..................... S__/O__: ....:..................... ....:.....................	**S/T strategies:** T__/O__: ....:..................... ....:..................... T__/O__: ....:..................... ....:.....................
Weaknesses (W) W1: W2: W3:	**W/O strategies:** W__/O__: ....:..................... ....:..................... W__/O__: ....:..................... ....:.....................	**W/T strategies:** W__/T__: ....:..................... ....:..................... W__/T__: ....:..................... ....:.....................

Select the two most important and feasible strategic options (regarding FROG's available resources and capabilities):

1. ....

2. ....

Worksheet 5: Frog's compliance check with SCR

Checklists are useful tools for decision-makers (Fisher and Lovell 2009: 139f; Collins 2012: 159). First, formulate the issue to be checked as a question, e.g.: 'Should I switch to planting genetically modified seed on my farm?' Second, go through the questions related to the SCR dimensions. Determine whether the SCR factor is acceptable (+), unacceptable (–), or neutral (0). If the overall acceptability level is high (i.e. scores more + than –), the proposed action is sustainably responsible, if it is not (more – than +), the proposed action may not be sustainably responsible.

Sustainable corporate responsibility (SCR) criteria for accepting (yes = +) or rejecting (no = –) the action:	SCR factor (see below)*	+/0/–
I. Economic dimension—functional responsibility		
1. **Efficiency:** Are the necessary resources available? Do I have the means to accomplish the proposed action? In other words: am I doing things right?		
2. **Fair exchange:** By going ahead with this action, will I give at least as much as I will take?		
3. **Effectiveness:** Is this action profitable, i.e. am I doing the right things?		
II. Environmental dimension—aesthetic responsibility		
4. **Self-reflection:** Will the action give me an overall sense of wellbeing?		
5. **Reflection on meaning/cradle-to-cradle test:** Can the waste generated by my action be effectively reintegrated into the natural cycle?		
6. **Integrated reflection:** Will my action respect the common good?		
III. Social dimension—ethical responsibility		
7. Virtue ethics (average value of 'a' and 'b')		
a. **Light-of-day test:** Would I feel good (+) or bad (–) if others (my friends, family, colleagues or the public) knew about my action/decision?		
b. **Golden mean of moral virtue:** Could the action in question be seen as virtuous (i.e. as the golden mean between two extreme vices) and thus become a good example or even be declared best practice?		

Sustainable corporate responsibility (SCR) criteria for accepting (yes = +) or rejecting (no = –) the action:	SCR factor (see below)*	+/0/–
8. Utilitarian ethics (average value of 'a' and 'b')		
a. **Considering the consequences:** ** What are the consequences of my action for stakeholders: more beneficial (+) or more harmful (–)?		
b. **Stakeholder discourse test:** Has there been a (fictitious or real) discourse with the major stakeholders concerning the proposed action and has this discourse been fair and transparent?		
9. Deontological ethics (average value of 'a' and 'b')		
a. **Compliance:** Does the action comply with the law and with the company's established vision/mission/value statements?		
b. **Universal applicability and dignity test (categorical imperative):** Can the action become a universal principle or does it violate the dignity of those affected?		
Number of +: _____ Number of –: _____ Result: Is the action responsible based on the principles of SCR? Yes: ☐ No: ☐		

*   The factor is based on the scope and sustainability of the corporate responsibility sought by the company in accordance with the following table (cf. figure on the right):

Sustainability scope	Short term 1	Mid-term 2	Long term 3
a) Small	1	2	3
b) Medium	2	4	6
c) Large	3	6	9

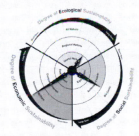

The acceptability of a proposed action increases considerably (e.g. by a factor of 9) if its scope of responsibility and 'degree of sustainability' are larger.

**   The activity 'Getting an overview of consequences', described in 'Additional teaching material and ideas' below, can be used to find out more about utilitarian ethical calculations.

How the positive and negative points are awarded depends on the individual decision-maker. Since such decisions are rarely made alone, it makes sense to ask all decision-makers to go through the checklist separately and compare and discuss the individual results afterwards.

The table raises decision-makers' awareness of the side-effects, repercussions and long-term effects of an action as well as of a potential evaluation by various entities.

Those using the table must be aware that a negative answer to one of the questions may result in an automatic rejection of the action in question, for instance if Question 9a is answered negatively and certain requirements, such as the UN Global Compact principles, are taken as absolute. Since they target corrupt behaviour, the proposed action in the above example automatically leads to the action having to be rejected. The checklist is particularly useful when dealing with dilemmas in which both the rejection and the acceptance of an action might be seen as responsible.

Additional teaching material and ideas

Developing virtues

Virtues characterise an ethically good person or company. Thus, corporate virtues constitute the character of a good corporate culture. Once developed they enable individuals or organisations to take on ethical responsibility more effectively according to their capabilities. Virtues can be developed and trained like muscles in a physical body. They shape one's behaviour towards others.

To find out more about virtues, see *The Power of Action Values* (Schlager 2012), in which Silvia Schlager defines 80 of them and also shows what one's behaviour looks like without them. Furthermore, Schlager lists all of them in the form of rating scales (0% to 100%). Thus, readers can estimate the percentage by which these virtues are expressed individually or in their organisation.

Students working their way through these lists familiarise themselves with virtues and identify those they want to develop (challenge virtues) or those which are already traits of their character (strength virtues). A company's specific virtue profile characterises the actual or desired corporate culture, and indicates which virtues should be part of staff training in order to achieve the desired corporate culture.

This further activity supports the answer to Question 7b in the SCR checklist (Worksheet 5).

Getting an overview of consequences

Taking on responsibility means getting an overview of the intended and unintended consequences of one's activity. Only when the consequences for all concerned have been weighed up, to see whether they are more beneficial or harmful, can one can accept or refuse the activity as good or bad according to utilitarian ethics. A rough utilitarian assessment of all consequences of an action can be conducted by using the following table with the following example: Shall we bribe an official who has gambling debts in order to be awarded a state contract or not?

This further activity supports the answer to Question 8a in the SCR checklist (Worksheet 5).

List of all affected stakeholders	Beneficial consequences (e.g., bribing an official)	Harmful consequences (e.g., bribing an official)
Politician	Can pay back his/her debts	Risk of being caught
Company	New contract	Penalty in case of discovery
Employee	Job security	
Customer		Receives lower quality because bribe must be refinanced
Competitor		Loses out despite possibly better product range
Competitor's employee		Risk of loss of job security
...	...	...
...	...	...
...	...	...
First result: **Based on utilitarian ethics, bribing an official causes more harm than benefit**	**Bribing an official is generally beneficial:** **3 x (+)**	**Bribing an official is generally harmful:** **5 x (–)**

Understanding ethical duties

Besides defining consequences, ethical responsibility is an important authority regarding duties to be followed, such as what one should do or what one should desist from doing. By saying that one has to treat every human being not only as a means but also as an end, Immanuel Kant's categorical imperative laid the foundations for such an ethical duty. This imperative also postulates that one must respect the dignity of all human beings. In this respect, it represents an 'anthropocentric' ethic (centred around human beings).

The UN Global Compact (www.unglobalcompact.org) is the most widespread and accepted catalogue of duties that corporate responsibility should comply with, according to several surveys. Discuss with your colleagues the ten principles of the UN Global Compact and how far they apply Kant's categorical imperative. Which principles do not comply with it? Which principles go beyond anthropocentric duty? How could one formulate a 'biocentric' (centred around all living beings) categorical imperative?

Sustainable responsibility at your university

Use the SCR model to check how far your university's courses and activities—teaching, research, further education, facilities, food, etc.—respect and apply sustainable responsibility. Which responsibility profile would you suggest for your university? Use the SCR checklist to get a deeper insight into sustainable responsibility activities. Try to develop recommendations as to how your university could improve its SCR profile.

Strategic management project

To provide practical experience of sustainable responsible activities, the study programme could give students social and or environmental assignments which have real impact. Such fieldwork programmes were successfully executed by students from the International Management study programme at the School of Management and Law at Zurich University of Applied Sciences, Switzerland.

In groups of four to six, they took on a predefined assignment, contracted by the supervisors with NGOs, companies or start-ups, or they selected their own project. For example, in 2013 the students:

- Introduced and organised a new waste recycling system in Ghana together with a local university.

- Raised funds for Syrian refugees, and collected and prepared medical equipment and clothes to be transported to relevant areas.

- Organised fundraising events for an orphanage in Nigeria.

- Investigated the shadowy side of the supply chain for leather production and proposed a socially and environmentally clean supply chain to a luxury leather bag producer. The company was then able to use its environmentally friendly track record in subsequent marketing campaigns.

- Developed a strategy for transferring Swiss experience in organic agriculture to China.

Students were not only tasked with doing the practical work to complete these assignments, but they also had to strategically plan and execute their projects, integrating the economic, social and ecological impact and working out how to address this impact. Furthermore, they had also to write reports (around 50 pages), where they described the efficiency and effectiveness of their sustainably responsible activities.

Further information can be obtained from mathias.schuez@zhaw.ch

Further reading

Braungart, M., and W. McDonough (2002) *Cradle to Cradle: Remaking the Way We Make Things* (New York: North Point Press).

> This classic in new ecological thinking and acting in business highlights how mankind could ideally develop an economy without any waste. Instead, all waste generated by one product should be used as a resource for other products, inspired by the way nature produces no waste but rather has closed cycles of life where one living being uses the output of other living beings as an important resource for survival (i.e. cradle to cradle).

Cannon, Tom (2012) *Corporate Responsibility: Governance, Compliance and Ethics in a Sustainable Environment*, 2nd edn (Harlow, UK: Pearson).

> This critical view on diverse issues of corporate responsibility, with many practical recommendations and case studies, allows leaders to strategically develop organisations, integrating social and ecological environments for successful business.

Collins, Denis (2012) *Business Ethics: How to Design and Manage Ethical Organisations* (Hoboken, NJ: Wiley).

> This book provides the reader with a broad overview of the most important issues of business ethics and delivers many organisational recommendations that allow ethics to be implemented in daily business life.

Porter, Michael E., and Mark R. Kramer (2006) 'Strategy and Society: The Link between Competitive Advantage and Corporate Social Responsibility', in *Harvard Business Review* (December 2006): 78-91, http://efnorthamerica.com/documents/events/ccc2008/Mark-Kramer-Keynote/Strategy-Society.pdf, accessed 15 March 2014.

> This article thoroughly eliminates the prejudice that social responsibility is an obstacle for profitability in business. Moreover, it includes many business opportunities which have yet to be exploited. The authors show how to use strategic planning in order to gain a competitive advantage.

Sandel, Michael J. (2009) *Justice: What's the Right Thing to Do?* (New York: Farrar, Straus and Giroux).

> The Harvard philosopher gives an excellent introduction to the established theories of ethics. With many examples it introduces the different ways one can evaluate actions as ethical or not. The introduction of utilitarian, deontological and virtue ethics is especially useful in terms of gaining a deeper understanding of the ethical responsibility that represents one dimension of the SCR model.

References

Bayertz, K. (1995) 'Eine kurze Geschichte der Herkunft der Verantwortung', in K. Bayertz (ed.), *Verantwortung: Prinzip oder Problem* (Darmstadt, Germany: Wissenschaftliche Buchgesellschaft): 3-71.

Blackmore, C., J. Chapman and R. Ison (2012) *Systems Thinking: Understanding Sustainability*, The Open University, http://openlearn.open.ac.uk/mod/oucontent/view.php?id=405678, accessed 26 September 2012.

Boddy, D. (2008) *Management: An Introduction*, 4th edn (Harlow, UK: Pearson).

Braungart, M., and W. McDonough (2002) *Cradle to Cradle: Remaking the Way We Make Things* (New York: North Point Press).

Brundtland Commission (1987) *Our Common Future: Towards Sustainable Development*, Chapter 2, World Commission on Economic Development (WCED), www.un-documents.net/ocf-02.htm, accessed 24 September 2012.

Cannon, Tom (2012) *Corporate Responsibility: Governance, Compliance and Ethics in a Sustainable Environment*, 2nd edn (Harlow, UK: Pearson).

Collins, Denis (2012) *Business Ethics: How to Design and Manage Ethical Organisations* (Hoboken, NJ: Wiley).

Crawford, D. (2005) *The Balanced Scorecard and Corporate Social Responsibility: Aligning Values for Profit*, www.greenbiz.com/news/2005/10/23/balanced-scorecard-and-corporate-social-responsibility-aligning-values-profit, accessed 25 September 2012.

Dobson, P., K. Starkey and J. Richards (2004) *Strategic Management: Issues and Cases* (Oxford, UK: Blackwell).

Elkington, J. (1997) *Cannibals with Forks: The Triple Bottom Line of 21st Century Business* (Oxford, UK: Capstone Publishing).

Ernst & Young (2012) *Six Growing Trends in Corporate Sustainability: An Ernst & Young Survey in Cooperation with GreenBiz Group*, www.greenbiz.com/sites/default/files/1112-vey1315117_CCaSS_SixTrends_FQ0029_lo%20res%20revised%203.7.2012.pdf, accessed 24 September 2012.

Fisher, C., and A. Lovell (2009) *Business Ethics and Values: Individual, Corporate and International Perspectives*, 3rd edn (London and New York: Prentice Hall).

GRI (Global Reporting Initiative) (2012). *Reporting Guidelines*, https://www.globalreporting.org/resourcelibrary/G3.1-Sustainability-Reporting-Guidelines.pdf, accessed 24 September 2012.

Harvey, F., and H. Pidd (2011) 'Glencore is in dark ages compared with rivals, says NGO boss', *The Guardian*, 19 July 2011, www.theguardian.com/business/2011/may/19/glencore-in-dark-ages-says-ngo-boss, accessed 22 January 2014.

Hick, M. (2012) 'Children Found Working in Foxconn iPhone Factory', *Huffington Post*, www.huffingtonpost.co.uk/2012/01/17/children-found-working-in-iphone-foxconn-factory_n_1209953.html, accessed 25 September 2012.

Hill, C.W.L., and R.J. Gareth (2008) *Strategic Management: An Integrated Approach*, 8th rev. edn (Mason, OH: South Western Educational Publishing).

Ikerd, J. (1999) *Rethinking the Economics of Self-Interests*, http://web.missouri.edu/ikerdj/papers/Rethinking.html, accessed 27 September 2012.

Johnson, G., K. Scholes and R. Whittington (2005) *Exploring Corporate Strategy*, 7th rev. edn (Harlow, UK: Pearson Education).

Kogure, S. (2012) *A Lesson Not Yet Learned*, www.ibanet.org/Article/Detail.aspx?ArticleUid=6c2935ff-c51d-4254-a334-4f5fbc5667d4, accessed 26 September 2012.

Kohlberg, L. (1971) 'From Is to Ought', in T. Mischel (ed.), *Cognitive Development and Epistemology* (New York: Academic Press): 151-235.

Kotter, John P., and James L. Heskett (1992) *Corporate Culture and Performance* (New York: The Free Press).

KPMG (2011) *KPMG International Survey of Corporate Responsibility Reporting 2011*, www.kpmg.com/Global/en/IssuesAndInsights/ArticlesPublications/corporate-responsibility/Documents/2011-survey.pdf, accessed 16 June 2014.

Lacy, P., T. Cooper, R. Hayward and L. Neuberger (2010) *A New Era of Sustainability: UN Global Compact–Accenture CEO Study 2010*, www.accenture.com/SiteCollectionDocuments/PDF/Accenture_A_New_Era_of_Sustainability_CEO_Study.pdf, accessed 31 March 2014.

Mey, S., G. Cheney and J. Roper (eds.) (2007) *The Debate over Corporate Social Responsibility* (Oxford, UK: Oxford University Press).

NN (2012) 'Foxconn: Suizide bei Mitarbeitern', *Die Welt kompakt*, www.welt.de/print/welt_kompakt/print_wirtschaft/article109439140/Foxconn-Suizide-bei-Mitarbeitern.html, accessed 25 September 2012.

Piaget, J. (1932) *Le jugement moral chez l'enfant* (Presses Universitaires de France).

Picht, Georg (1969) 'Der Begriff der Verantwortung', in *Wahrheit—Vernunft—Verantwortung: Philosophische Studien* (Stuttgart, Germany: Klett): 318-42.

Porter, Michael E. (1985) *Competitive Advantage: Creating and Sustaining Superior Performance* (New York: The Free Press).

Porter, Michael E., and Mark R. Kramer (2006) 'Strategy and Society: The Link between Competitive Advantage and Corporate Social Responsibility', in *Harvard Business Review* (December 2006): 78-91, http://efnorthamerica. com/documents/events/ccc2008/Mark-Kramer-Keynote/Strategy-Society.pdf, accessed 15 March 2014.

PwC (2010) *CSR Trends 2010*, www.pwc.com/ca/en/sustainability/publications/ csr-trends-2010-09.pdf, accessed 25 May 2012.

Redaktion (2012) *Wie oft muss Tepco in Fukushima die eigene Inkompetenz beweisen bevor eingeschritten wird?*, www.planet-burgenland.at/2012/06/08, accessed 2 October 2012.

Rieckmann, Heijo (2000) *Managen und Führen am Rande des 3. Jahrtausends*, 2nd edn (Frankfurt, Germany: Peter-Lang).

SACOM (2012) 'New iPhone, Old Abuses: Have Working Conditions at Foxconn in China Improved?', 20 September 2012 http://sacom.hk/reportnew-iphone-old-abuses-have-working-conditions-at-foxconn-in-china-improved/, accessed 17 June 2014.

SAM (2012) *Company Assessment*, www.sam-group.com/int/sustainability-services/company-assessment.jsp, accessed 25 September 2012.

Sandel, Michael J. (2009) *Justice: What's the Right Thing to Do?* (New York: Farrar, Straus and Giroux).

Schaltegger, S., R. Burritt and H. Petersen (2003) *An Introduction to Corporate Environmental Management: Striving for Sustainability* (Sheffield, UK: Greenleaf Publishing).

Schlager, Silvia (2012) *The Power of Action Values: 80 Values as a Foundation for a Constructive Change* (Vienna, Austria: Eutonia).

Schüz, M. (1999) *Werte—Risiko—Verantwortung: Dimensionen des Value Managements* (Munich, Germany: Gerling Akademie Verlag).

—— (2012) 'Sustainable Corporate Responsibility: The Foundation of Successful Business in the New Millennium', in *Central European Business Review* 2 (2012): 7-15, http://cebr.vse.cz/cebr/article/view/34, accessed 14 January 2014.

—— (2013) *Grundlagen der ethischen Unternehmensverantwortung*, SML Essentials No. 1 (Zurich, Switzerland: vdf-Hochschulverlag der ETH).

Shell (2012) *Sustainable Development*, www.shell-livewire.org/business-library/ employing-people/management/sustainable-development, accessed 25 September 2012.

Stead, J.G., and W.E. Stead (2013) *Sustainable Strategic Management*, 2nd edn (Sheffield, UK: Greenleaf Publishing).

Tepco (2010) *Vision 2020: Medium to Long-term Growth Declaration*, press release, 13 September 2010, www.tepco.co.jp/en/press/corp-com/release/10091301-e. html, accessed 25 January 2014.

ts/dpa (2012) *Foxconn-Arbeiter sterben fürs iPad*, www.manager-magazin.de/ unternehmen/it/0,2828,druck-824713,00.html, accessed 25 September 2012.

Weihrich, Heinz (1982) 'The TOWS Matrix: A Tool for Situational Analysis', *Long Range Planning* (April 1982): 54-66, www.usfca.edu/fac-staff/weihrich/docs/ tows.pdf, accessed 15 December 2013.

ADDING CORE TOPICS TO THE CURRICULUM

12

Climate change and greenhouse gas management

Aldilla Dharmasasmita, Ellie Kennedy, Helen Puntha and Richard Holmes

---

This chapter introduces the global challenge of climate change as it relates to business activity, with specific focus on business approaches to GHG (greenhouse gas) management. It considers some risks and opportunities to organisations both of managing and not managing their emissions, and discusses the key steps for business organisations to identify and measure their GHG emissions, to help them be more efficient in their processes and in some cases lower their production costs.

The aim of this chapter is to facilitate your understanding of:

- The concept of GHGs
- The effects of business on climate change, specifically GHG emissions
- How climate change might affect business
- How organisations can identify and quantify their GHG emissions
- The steps business organisations can take to manage their GHG emissions in line with or beyond legislation

---

Introduction

Sustainability has many facets and the first that comes to many people's minds is environmental. This chapter will focus on **climate change**, a key sustainability challenge which relates chiefly to the environment but has widespread and critical implications for social and economic sustainability. Climate change is a subject of widespread controversy and debate. A 2013 landmark report by the United Nations Climate Panel stated that scientists are 95% certain that climate change is man-made (IPCC 2013). Some of the effects of climate change include increased temperatures ('**global warming**'), **rising sea levels**, and **extreme weather** including cyclones, storms, droughts and **flooding**, as shown in Figure 1. Such effects change global ecosystems and bring serious environmental, social and economic consequences to individuals, communities, nations and business organisations. Such consequences include environmental

Figure 1: Some of the effects of climate change.

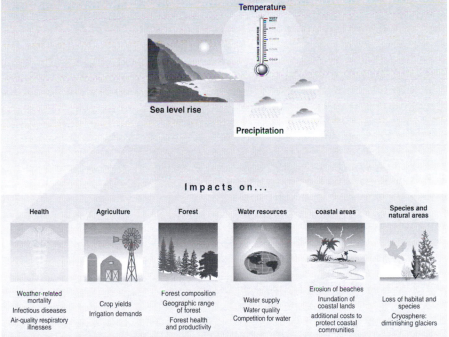

Source: United States environmental protection agency (EPA), www.grida.no/graphicslib/detail/potential-climate-change-impacts_035a, image credit Philippe Rekacewicz, UNEP/GRID-Arendal.

degradation, food shortages, loss of human and other life and the break-down of socioeconomic systems. Consequences specific to business organisations might include increased financial risk, higher commodity costs and broken supply chains (Davenport 2014), as well as lost work capacity and reduced labour productivity (IPCC 2014). Organisations are already experiencing some direct effects of climate change: for example, in 2004 water shortages in India led to Coca-Cola losing an operating licence and in 2008 four Nike factories in Thailand were temporar-ily shut down due to flooding (Davenport 2014). Climate change may actually offer some business opportunities in the short term such as for those with expertise in geoengineering technologies as documented by McKenzie Funk (2014). However, as Funk himself states, 'At 6 degrees warming, there are almost no winners. Winners are just for the short term' (quoted in Hartigan Shea 2014). The reality, then, is that business organisations need to consider and manage the long-term sustainability of their activities beginning with, but not limited to, their greenhouse gas emissions. This chapter focuses on some key challenges of doing this and discusses some possible approaches and methods.

One of the main ways business organisations, like individuals, contrib-ute to climate change is through production of **GHGs (greenhouse gases)** which cause the atmosphere to retain heat (the '**greenhouse effect**'). Organisations emit GHGs through heating and cooling office spaces, use of electronic equipment, transport, business travel and manufacturing processes (Lingl *et al.* 2010). Figure 2 depicts the sources of GHG emis-sions globally.

Under the Kyoto Protocol (UN 1998), industrialised nations have com-mitted to reducing their GHG emissions and many business organisations are taking steps to manage their GHG emissions in line with or beyond regulatory requirements. Organisations may work on reducing their '**car-bon footprint**'. CO_2 is the main contributor to climate change hence the term '*carbon* footprint'. A carbon footprint, however, does encompass all six GHGs caused by human activity, as illustrated in Figure 3. The amount of a carbon footprint is the total amount of emissions produced by an individual, an organisation, a country, etc., as measured in CO_2e or 'carbon dioxide equivalent' (sometimes called 't CO_2e', i.e. tonnes of CO_2 equivalent). The footprint is calculated by converting the amounts of the various GHGs into equivalent amounts of CO_2 based on their GWP

Figure 2: Global GHG emissions in 2004 by source.

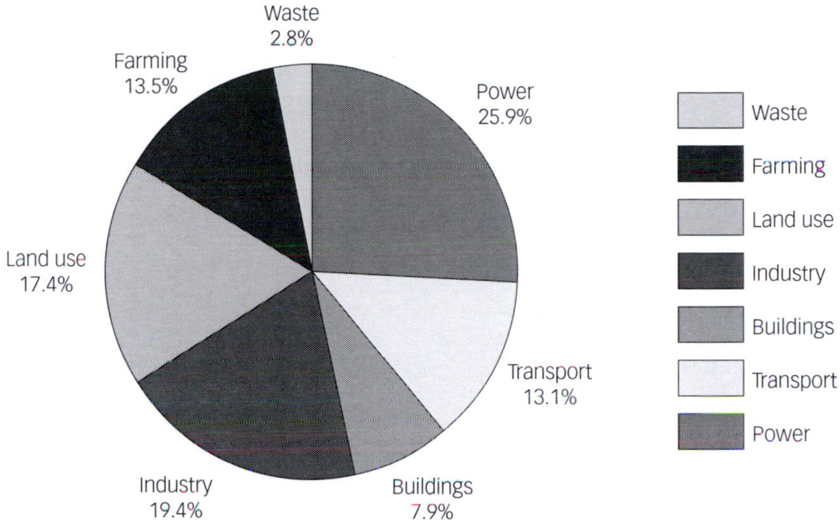

Source: IPCC, Working group 1 (2007), www.grida.no/graphicslib/detail/greenhouse-gas-ghg-emissions-by-source-2004_f7cc, image credit IAASTD/Ketill Berger, UNEP/GRID-Arendal.

Figure 3: The six major man-made GHGs and the common sources of their emissions.

Carbon dioxide (CO$_2$)		
Main contributor to climate change, especially through deforestation, the burning of fossil fuels (e.g. oil, gas and coal), and other changes in land-use.		
Methane (CH$_4$)		**Nitrous oxide (N$_2$O)**
Produced naturally when vegetation is rotted in the absence of oxygen or when burnt. However, the majority is released through cattle farming, production of oil and gas, and landfills.		Released by chemical fertilisers and the burning of fossil fuels.
Hydroflourocarbons (HFCs)	**Perflourocarbons (PFCs)**	**Sulphur hexaflouride (SF$_6$)**
In essence chemical by-products, and also used in some refrigeration equipment.	Manufactured and chemical compounds used in various medical and other applications.	Manufactured compound used in specialised applications, e.g. insulation for high-voltage electrical equipment.

Source: Adapted from Lingl *et al.* (2010).

(100-year global warming potential). Once aware of their carbon foot-print, organisations may choose to go **carbon neutral** (reducing or offset-ting their CO_2 emissions to zero) or **climate neutral** (encompassing the whole spectrum of GHGs). **Mandatory carbon reporting** came into force in the UK in October 2013. Under the Companies Act 2006 (Strategic and Directors Reports) Regulations 2013, all quoted companies must report their annual GHG emissions within their directors' report.

Greenhouse gas management

In order to reduce their impact on the climate, business organisations first need to be able to identify the sources of their **GHG emissions**. Some of these are obvious (for example, the amount of electricity used in a fac-tory), while others are less obvious (such as fuel used in employees' busi-ness travel). This exercise can be done through a **GHGMP (greenhouse gas management programme)**. Before any organisation undertakes a new venture it will want to assess the costs and benefits of doing so, such as by applying the SWOT (strengths, weaknesses, opportunities and threats) and/or PESTLE (political, environmental, social, technology, legal and economic) model (Porter 1980, 1985). The GHGMP is no different. While most organisations emit GHGs from similar areas of their business model, the extent to which GHG management will benefit them is very much particular to each business organisation. Assessing the business case is an important part of the decision-making process and is all the more vital if the decision-makers have yet to be convinced of the benefits of a GHG management programme within their organisation. Whether the business case is being assessed by key decision-makers or by someone who hopes to influence them, the issues to consider are the same.

The main benefits for organisations of managing GHGs include com-pliance with regulatory requirements, enhanced staff morale, potential costs savings, brand enhancement, accreditation from a respected veri-fier such as the Carbon Trust, impetus for innovation, and contribution to sustainability for individual and collective wellbeing and survival.

Table 1 presents the opportunities and risks for an organisation in implementing a GHG management programme. It is imperative that organisations assess themselves against the areas specified here (adapted from Lingl *et al.* 2010). To help decision-makers understand and address the risks and opportunities, such an assessment should explain how the risks identified apply specifically to the organisation concerned, and should also provide examples of how the issues might be addressed.

In order for companies to be successful in reducing their GHG emissions, they will need to quantify their targets. It can be helpful to follow the SMART principles coined by Doran (1981):

- **S**pecific: target a specific area for improvement

- **M**easurable: quantify an indicator of progress

- **A**ssignable: specify who will be responsible/accountable in doing it

- **R**ealistic: state what results can realistically be achieved, given the resources the organisation has available

- **T**ime-related: specify when the result(s) can be achieved

Setting targets using such a rubric helps an organisation to quantify what it is trying to achieve, and to identify how much effort will be necessary. Setting goals for the GHGMP will give the organisation something

Table 1: Examples of specific risks and opportunities.

Risks	Issues for business	Opportunities
Continued expenditure related to high fuel and energy costs	**Fuel and energy costs**	Cost-savings potential from reduced fuel and energy consumption due to reduction in GHG emissions
		Improved operational efficiencies, e.g. through better logistics management
Being the target of a public campaign, e.g. from pressure groups or consumers singling out companies that do not address how their business processes are impacting the climate	**Reputation**	Brand enhancement: showing leadership and/or initiative on climate change can increase positive visibility in the marketplace, which in turn can lead to increase in market share via competitive advantage

(continued...)

Risks	Issues for business	Opportunities
Increased challenges in recruiting and training new employees for companies with poor records on climate change Higher employee costs related to lower productivity and efficiency due to employee dissatisfaction with company's failure to take positive action	**Employees**	Attracting new employees who are looking for companies with strong sustainability programmes Motivating employees, building loyalty and promoting employee innovation with climate change action and programmes Enhancing employee wellness and increasing efficiency through measures that also save energy (e.g. use of natural light, or upgrades to heating, ventilation and air conditioning)
Carbon taxes and other measures leading to increased fuel and energy costs Requirements to meet energy efficiency standards for buildings and vehicles Limits on emissions due to international standard implementations such as the Kyoto Protocol	**Regulations**	Benefiting from government incentive programmes for voluntarily reducing GHG emissions Early movers may be able to influence and/or lobby policy-makers regarding future legislation Flexibility to choose a course of action—likely to be more cost-effective than if mandated
Losing customers/consumers who switch to competitors that are more GHG-focused	**Products, services and technologies**	Taking advantage of the growing demand for climate-friendly products and services, and customers/consumers who are more GHG aware
Exposure to high shipping costs due to higher fuel costs Costs of GHG-intensive production for suppliers being passed along to the company, unless the company initiated them	**Supply chain**	Managing transportation in the supply chain can reduce fuel consumption and GHGs Choosing suppliers with low-carbon products and services can reduce a company's upstream GHG emissions and reduce production costs
Shareholders are now more aware of climate change issues, and may demand specific measures for addressing these Shareholders' concern about climate change, risk exposure and company inaction can lead to a 'snowball' effect	**Investors**	Meeting corporate social responsibility goals Attracting new investors who want to invest in progressive, well-managed, and innovative companies

Source: Adapted from Lingl *et al.* (2010: 3).

definite to aim for and help it measure its success. Without a target it is highly likely that the organisation will lose focus, and ultimately not make any progress. Furthermore, by quantifying and measuring, the organisation can also address efficiency in its GHGMP. When setting the goals, organisations should ask themselves four questions:

1. How much will we reduce our GHG emissions? This needs to be clear and precise.

2. By when will we do it? A target date needs to be set, so that everyone in the organisation knows the deadline.

3. What year is the baseline? This means the year the new target will be compared to.

4. How does the goal align with overall strategy?

It is important to **integrate** the GHGMP strategy into the organisation's overall strategy because GHGMP affects the whole of the organisation, not just a department.

Examples of effective goal-setting are a catering company aiming to reduce its GHG emissions by 30% by 2017, and comparing that with the 2014 levels, or a bus company aiming to make its entire operations carbon neutral within ten years. Notice how precise these targets are: 30% for the catering company, or carbon neutral (i.e. zero emissions) for the bus company. Note also there is a clear deadline and a baseline set in each case: compare 2014 with the deadline 2017, or the deadline of ten years' time. These exact time-lines and targets can help the GHGMP team, or the whole organisation, to work towards a common goal.

Initiating a GHGMP does not require much in the way of resources, so the barriers or excuses at the beginning of the journey can be few. However, commitment from key decision-makers is fundamental if appropriate resources are to be allocated and goals officially endorsed. For all organisations someone has to be assigned responsibility for the overall GHGMP. For larger bodies this might be a team of people. Once an action plan is drawn up, more staff might be assigned responsibility to deliver the various actions, such as energy-saving improvements or recycling.

While many GHG management measures cost very little or nothing, making meaningful reductions will require some financial investment. Much of this investment can provide a good short-term return on investment and can be markedly better than returns from banks or shares, as illustrated by the following case study on 'Facelift Access Hire'.

Case study 1: Facelift Access Hire[1]

Facelift Access Hire is reaping the benefits of cutting its energy use, having reduced its carbon footprint by 403 tonnes year on year through a succession of simple yet effective changes. Examples of the changes include low-carbon vehicles, paperless communications, LED lighting and a new wood-fuelled boiler.

The company lends machinery and access platforms to some of the UK's most carbon-intensive industries. Nevertheless, it is eager to take responsibility for reducing its impact on the environment, as well as helping its customers along the way.

After researching how energy and resources were being used across every aspect of its business, Facelift introduced hard-hitting measures to generate radical energy savings without negatively impacting its bank account. The project was named 'Facelift Business Innovation'.

Starting on its transport fleet, the company upgraded its 26-tonne trucks, investing in more fuel-efficient vehicles. This resulted in diesel fuel savings of 4,550 litres per month. By opting for lighter Transit vans, Facelift saved a further 960 litres of diesel each month. The managing director also changed his car from a Porsche Cayenne to a Vauxhall Ampera, an extended-range electric vehicle, to help save fuel.

The company's future vehicle-sourcing policy will focus on low-carbon alternatives where possible, including hybrid, electric and lighter-weight vehicles.

In terms of renewable energy alternatives, Facelift decided to reduce its dependence on fossil fuels by installing a state-of-the-art wood boiler. The wood fuel is sourced from tree surgeons—who are among its customers—saving 22,000 litres of diesel oil per year.

1   Adapted from Earley 2013.

The company has also added movement sensors and LED lighting to its depots, ensuring much tighter control over its lighting and making an annual saving of £5,000.

The introduction of its new low-carbon equipment, the hybrid self-propelled boom, is set to save the company's customers 900 litres of diesel oil per week. This energy-saving opportunity will be communicated via the company's e-newsletter, *High Times*.

Elsewhere in the business, Facelift uses water more efficiently and tackles waste by installing waterless urinals, saving 200,000 litres of water per year.

The company also recycles electronic equipment and printer cartridges, and has switched to a paper-free communications policy (internally and externally), saving 16,000 kg of paper per year.

Facelift state that careful energy management is simply good for business. By reducing its energy consumption and cutting its carbon footprint, Facelift has freed up cash to invest in future business and sustainability innovations.

Measuring greenhouse gas emissions

Having decided to set up a GHGMP with goals and resources, it is essential for the organisation to measure and assess its current situation through an '**emission inventory**'. This is a vital step which needs to be undertaken by every business organisation regardless of their size, otherwise it will be very difficult for the organisation to quantify its success and maintain support from management. The emission inventory process involves recognising and categorising an organisation's major emission sources. These might include energy used by office buildings and factory plants, and emissions from the organisation's vehicles and air travel. Such data will be gathered in various ways, including through reviewing utility bills and interviewing colleagues about their commuting or business travel methods. The emissions identified are then quantified, usually in tonnes of CO_2e.

Figure 4: Example of inventory results of companies.

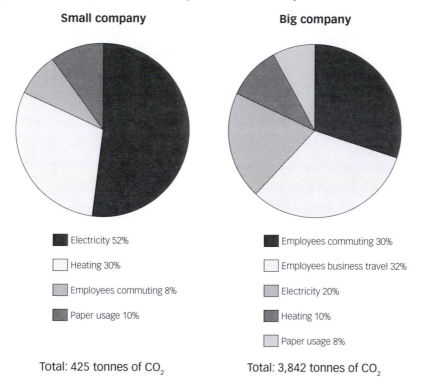

Small company

- Electricity 52%
- Heating 30%
- Employees commuting 8%
- Paper usage 10%

Total: 425 tonnes of CO_2

Big company

- Employees commuting 30%
- Employees business travel 32%
- Electricity 20%
- Heating 10%
- Paper usage 8%

Total: 3,842 tonnes of CO_2

The GHG emissions from an organisation are ideally assessed over a 12-month period. As well as documenting the total annual emissions it is useful for an organisation to have a percentage breakdown of emissions and to know the sources of those emissions. That way, management and the GHGMP team can prioritise actions to reduce them by targeting areas of greatest emissions first. Figure 4 illustrates what the resulting emissions breakdown might look like for two different business organisations.

Greenhouse Gas Protocol

For a business organisation to assess and quantify its emission sources, it should use the **GGP (Greenhouse Gas Protocol)**, which is the internationally agreed method for counting and reporting GHG emissions (UNFCCC 2014). It is important that the same approach is used by everyone involved, so that comparisons can be made between companies and over time. Lingl *et al.* (2010) set out four basic steps that companies can follow for their GHGMP:

1. Establish an emission boundary

2. Collect activity data

3. Calculate GHG emissions

4. Quality control

Establishing an emissions boundary is the first step of the protocol. Due to the complex nature of business organisations, it is not always possible to calculate all the emissions associated with their activity. It may be difficult or impossible, for example, to quantify the emissions of a business which has a complex supply chain or a complex organisational structure. To help with this, two boundaries need to be decided upon before emissions can be measured: organisational boundary and operational boundary. **Organisational boundary** means: Which part of the organisation is to be assessed? Is it all of the organisation or just a subsidiary? Will it be every site or just a single site? Having decided which part of the organisation is to be assessed, the organisation should establish the **operational boundary**, i.e. decide which sources of emissions are to be counted towards the overall GHG annual total.

For example, a furniture manufacturing company that has a head office, two office branches, two production sites, and outsourcing of delivery of finished furniture from warehouse to stores, needs to decide which sites to include in the emissions boundary. Each site is then further divided into activities such as amount of (office) paper used, company cars, raw materials, energy used, employee business travel, employee commute, etc. Once these boundaries have been established, the activity data can be collected for each selected activity for each site. From there, the organisation or the GHGMP team can decide which emission sources they would like to address—typically, this will be areas that can have the most impact on the organisation's processes, or ones that will save them the most money without negatively affecting the organisation's employees and/or processes.

In an ideal world all emissions associated with an organisation's operations would be assessed. However, it is often impractical to do this. According to the GGP, sources of emissions are placed in one of three categories, or the **three scopes of emissions** as shown in Figure 5a. Scope 1 includes the processes over which the organisation has the **most control**, for example fuel that the organisation generates itself to run manufacturing equipment (e.g. via solar panels). Scope 2 covers 'indirect GHG emissions' over which the organisation has **some control**, such as purchased electricity, heat or steam. Scope 3 involves the processes **outside the control of the organisation**, for example the disposal of its packaging by end users. Companies need to look at all three scopes in order to manage their GHG emissions effectively. Further illustrations of the three scopes can be found in Figure 5b.

When the emissions boundary has been established, the next step is to **collect related information** about each emission source within the boundary that has been mapped. This is called '**activity data**', defined as 'measurement of the activities that generate emissions' (Lingl *et al.*

Figure 5a: The three scopes of emissions according to the GGP.

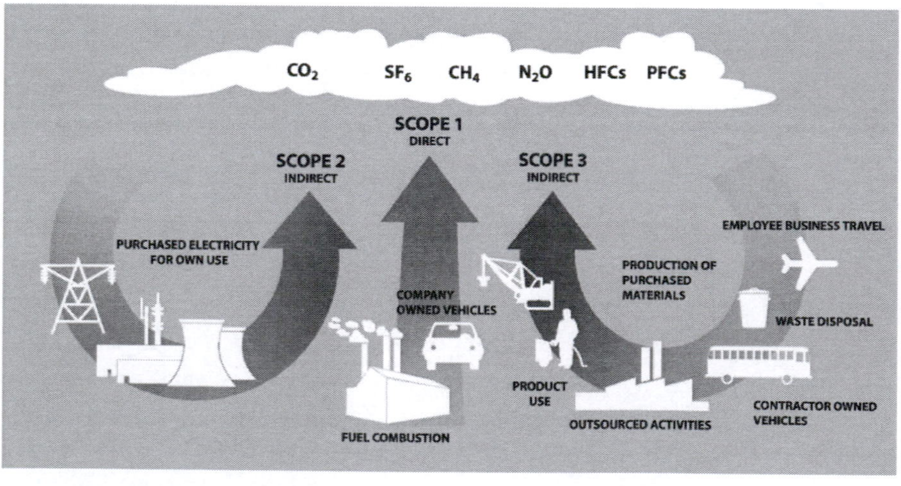

Source: New Zealand Business Council for Sustainable Development (2002: 10).

Figure 5b: Further examples of emissions scopes.

Scope 1: Direct GHG emissions (company-owned or controlled sources)	Scope 2: Indirect GHG emissions (purchased electricity, heat or steam)	Scope 3: Indirect GHG emissions (other sources)
Generation of own heat, steam and electricity	Purchased electricity (from a utility company)	Transportation of goods and materials in vehicles **owned or controlled by third parties** (e.g. shipping services)
Transportation of materials, goods, products, waste and employees in **company-owned or controlled** vehicles, planes, ships, etc.	Purchased heat or steam	Extraction and production of materials and products (e.g. paper/gypsum) purchased by the business
Emissions from chemicals, such as HFCs, used in refrigeration and air-conditioning equipment		Outsourced activities such as delivery, design, printing, etc.
Manufacturing and chemical processing (using machines that can be controlled by the company)		End-use and disposal of company products
Combustion of fuel in furnaces, boilers or generators		Transportation of people in vehicles owned or controlled by third parties (e.g. business travel and employee commuting on public buses/trains)
Fugitive emissions either intentionally or unintentionally released (e.g. leaks from equipment joints that can be repaired by the company)		Consumption of purchased electricity, heat or steam in a leased operation not owned or controlled by the company (e.g. company in a leased building where utilities are included in the rent)

Source: Adapted from Lingl *et al.* (2010: 12).

2010: 16). The emissions can be found on utility bills and equipment manuals. These emissions might be expressed, for example, as kilometres driven, kilowatts, or litres of fuel consumed.

This activity is the most time-consuming section in the development of a GHG inventory. This is due to the fact that most companies might not have recorded this information in a methodical way. However, ploughing through this process is vital for the successful implementation of a GHGMP.

As the success of an organisation's GHGMP is highly dependent on this process, accuracy is key: the data needs to be collected carefully and precisely, the calculation needs to be accurate. For areas where exact data is missing, the organisation or the GHGMP team needs to make

Table 2: Common sources of emissions: where information can be found and the units represented.

Source of emission	Where emission data can be found	Data units
Purchased electricity	Utility bills, online accounts of companies	kWh, MWh
Purchased heat	Utility bills, online accounts of companies	GJ, MWh, therms, BTUs, lbs of steam
On-site heat generation	Utility bills, storage tank logs, online accounts of companies, fuel purchase records and invoices	Litres, GJ, gallons, m^3, kg, BTUs, cubic ft, lbs
Company-owned vehicles	Fuel purchase records, fuel tank logs	Fuel type and amount (litres/gallons), or km/miles travelled and the vehicle make/model/year
Business travel (air)	Online calculators are available and can be used to find distances that flights have covered	Km/miles flown, or fuel used (in case of charter flights)
Business travel (vehicles)	Expense claims, accounting receipts	Fuel type and amount (litres/gallons), or km/miles travelled and the vehicle make/model/year
Employee commuting	Many employers use surveys to obtain information about how their employees travel to work. These surveys can be available online, or some small and medium-sized enterprises might prefer hard copies	Km/miles travelled and mode of transportation, of fuel type and amount depending on the type of vehicles used
Freight transport	Delivery invoices, shipping invoices	Kg/lbs/tonnes and km/miles transported, mode of transport (lorries, trucks, air, ship, rail)
Leased premises	In cases where tenants do not receive utility bills, calculations can be done based on the size of the premises	m^2 or sq. ft and the number of days the property has been leased
Fugitive emissions (refrigeration equipment, air-conditioning, pipelines, etc.)	Government and industry publications, equipment specifications/manuals	Varies

Source of emission	Where emission data can be found	Data units
Material inputs	Receipts of purchase, suppliers, life-cycle analysis	Varies
Outsourced services	Information needs to be obtained from suppliers or an organisation can collaborate with them to measure data	Varies

Source: Adapted from Lingl *et al.* (2010: 17).

calculated and realistic estimates. Table 2 shows some of the common sources of GHG emissions, where these emissions data can usually be found, and the common units by which they are represented.

When all appropriate data (activity data) has been collected, the next step is to **calculate all the emissions.** The universal formula is:

$$\textbf{(activity data) x (emission factors) = GHG emissions}$$

By using emission factors, the data that has been obtained can be converted into GHG emissions values, expressed in kilograms or tonnes of CO_2e. For example, using the emission factor for flights, it is possible to calculate that for one passenger to travel 17,000 km by plane from Birmingham, UK, to Sydney, Australia (www.worldatlas.com/), their GHG emission is:

$$\textbf{17,000 km x 0.11 kg } CO_2\textbf{/km = 1.87 tonnes } CO_2$$

The Defra UK emissions toolkit (Defra 2014) provides a more detailed illustration of the different types of emission factors which companies can use to calculate their GHG emissions. More helpful resources can also be found at the end of this chapter. In the UK, the governmental website **UK Greenhouse Gas Emission Statistics** (https://www.gov.uk/government/collections/uk-greenhouse-gas-emissions) provides data on estimated emissions by source and sectorial breakdown.

Quality control of the emissions inventory is key, if the GHGMP is to remain successful. The organisation, or its GHGMP team, needs to ensure that all data collected is reliable and recorded in a methodical way. This is to ensure that the correct analysis can be applied, problematic areas easily identified, appropriate and relevant recommendations can be made, and that the information can be shared with the public when applicable.

GHG management matrix

The GHG management matrix given in Table 3 is a tool which can help an organisation identify the current priority it attaches to GHG management. Matrices are often used as management tools to help organisations identify areas of weakness and show how they compare to others. As most organisations don't employ staff who specialise in carbon management, easy to use assessment tools can be very helpful.

Each of the issues covered in the matrix should be considered if GHG emissions are to be reduced. An organisation needs to take a structured approach with a policy and action plan to direct the work. Staff need to be trained and aware of the need to fulfil those actions with someone being given responsibility to ensure they are followed through. Finally, money should be invested in improvements and the effect of those improvements monitored.

Reducing greenhouse gas emissions and going carbon neutral

Having identified emissions sources across a whole organisation, quantified the emissions, and analysed the organisation's priorities and progress, an organisation is in a position to develop a robust and achievable GHGMP. Management may decide to reduce carbon or GHG emissions by an internally defined amount, or they may have an external target to meet—such as one set by government regulators—or they may wish to go beyond simple reduction and aim to become completely **carbon neutral**. Going carbon neutral can be defined as 'cancelling out the harm done to the earth's atmosphere by one type of greenhouse gas-generating human activity' (Murray and Dey 2009: 238). This means aiming for a net carbon footprint of zero.

Whatever its target, an organisation's emissions management plan is likely to combine **internal reductions** with a **carbon offset** programme (Carbon Neutral Co. Ltd 2014b). Internal reductions can be made by adjusting processes, activities and facilities. At home, this might mean, for example, switching off more lights and appliances when these are not

Table 3: GHG management matrix.

Level	Policy	Organising	Training	Monitoring	Communication	Investment
4	Energy policy, action plan and regular reviews with commitment from senior management	Fully integrated into senior management structure	Appropriate and comprehensive staff training tailored to identified needs	Comprehensive performance measurement against targets and reported to management	Communication of energy issues inside and outside the organisation	Resources routinely committed to energy efficiency
3	Formal policy but no commitment from top management	Clear line management accountability	Energy training for most staff	Weekly monitoring of all areas	Regular staff briefings and promotion	Energy-saving given same importance as other investments
2	Unadopted policy	Some delegation of authority but line management unclear	Ad-hoc internal training for selected staff	Monthly monitoring by fuel type	Promotion of energy saving in an organised fashion	Low- or medium-cost measures considered if short payback period
1	An unwritten set of guidelines	Informal, mostly focused on energy supply (i.e. cost of energy)	Some staff occasionally attend specialist courses	Invoice checking only	Ad-hoc informal promotion of energy efficiency	Only low- or no cost measures taken
0	No explicit energy policy	No delegation of responsibility for managing energy	No energy-related staff training provided	No measurement of energy costs or consumption	No communication or promotion of energy issues	No investment in improving energy efficiency

Start at bottom and work up ←

Source: Adapted from Carbon Trust (2013: 48).

being used. For a business example, see Case Study 2 for how one super-market has adjusted its internal energy use and significantly reduced carbon emissions.

Internal reductions, while vital, may not be sufficient by themselves to meet GHG reduction targets. In this case, an organisation can choose to offset some carbon emissions. **Carbon offset** is the process of reducing GHG emissions 'created by one party that can be purchased and used to balance the emissions of another party' (Lingl *et al.* 2010: 49). Individuals can also take part in carbon offsetting. For example, when booking a flight, you might be offered the opportunity to calculate your carbon footprint for that flight and pay an additional fee which will be invested in clean energy projects or tree-planting. In this way, your contribution to the carbon footprint of the flight you took is neutralised—or offset—by an equivalent amount of carbon reduction elsewhere.

From a corporate perspective, there are two approaches to carbon off-setting. The first is similar to the individual approach described above. An organisation which wants to go carbon neutral may find that it is still producing a certain level of carbon emissions even after all possible internal adjustments to processes and behaviours have been made. In this case, it may choose to offset the remaining emissions by investing in sustainable projects elsewhere, often in developing countries. In this way, an organisation can further reduce its impact on the climate by financing carbon-reducing projects which might otherwise not be funded.

The second corporate strategy of carbon offsetting is through trading **carbon credits** in a marketplace. Here, an organisation which has not met an emissions reduction target (usually one set by a government or in an international treaty such as the Kyoto Protocol) can 'buy' carbon credits from a company which has already exceeded that particular target. This strategy has been quite controversial: the main criticism is that carbon offsetting allows larger companies in particular simply to purchase offsets without making a real reduction in their GHG emissions, while for smaller companies purchasing carbon offsets means increased production costs (AltFuelsNow 2014; Lovell *et al.* 2009). It can also mean that industry as a whole is unlikely to exceed carbon reduction goals, as some of the biggest polluters can afford to avoid making significant reductions.

Case study 2: Sainsbury's[2]

J Sainsbury plc uses innovative technology to cut its carbon use and reduce its demand on the national grid. Less demand for peak electricity means less pressure on high-carbon reserve power stations, reducing the CO_2 footprint of not only the store but also the UK as a whole.

While reducing peak demand cuts carbon today, Sainsbury's is also mindful of the future. It is using its Hythe branch as a test bed to learn and prepare itself for a time when electrical availability, carbon intensity and the cost of power may differ across the day. A collaborative partnership with Imperial College and Grantham Institute for Climate Change has enabled accurate mapping of the energy use of complex operations. Specialist IT systems reduce Hythe's heating, ventilation and lighting systems at peak times, resulting in less strain on the local and national grid.

One example of an adjustment made by the store is the use of night blinds on chiller cabinets saving up to 140 kWh and £20 per week, significant when multiplied by over 1,000 sites, 52 weeks of the year. Chillers and freezers can be run slightly colder during the night and allowed to come to target temperatures during the day: this approach uses the same amount of energy but, importantly, is less carbon intense as the chillers are not drawing on peak electricity power.

The partnership has also looked closely at daylight hours and light intensity. This has resulted in lower lux levels being introduced at different times of day. Within six months, levels were reduced from 800 to 650 lux with a corresponding 12% energy reduction on Hythe's baseline. This innovation is now being rolled out to 89 stores.

Currently, the bakery ovens start at 3.30am and continue through the morning of peak electricity demand. But instead of relying entirely on the national grid and carbon-intensive power stations, Hythe can also switch to its own low-carbon supply.

On site, Hythe has a biofuel generator—the first of its kind that uses waste fat from Sainsbury's meat suppliers and cooking oil from its stores. Grid-monitoring equipment systems activate the biofuel generator during

2   Adapted from Fox n.d.

peak demand. In addition, the store has roof-mounted photovoltaic cells, as well as generating heat and hot water from a biomass boiler that uses waste wood.

The company has been impressed with the results so far: the store's target of a 60% reduction in energy use has been exceeded, as has its 50% decrease in carbon emissions. Judges from the *Guardian* Sustainable Business Best Practice Exchange thought the project has real potential to be scaled up and other retailers could learn a lot from this initiative.

Through partnering with academic institutions, Sainsbury's has developed new ways of thinking about energy, particularly electricity, and its use over time. Many of the improvements made at Hythe and other leading low-carbon stores are being replicated across the country. Despite an 8% increase in supermarket space, carbon emissions have reduced.

The work at Hythe is part of Sainsbury's £1 billion sustainability plan for the next eight years. This includes building new zero-carbon stores, as well as using proven and next-generation renewable technologies.

By 2030, the plan is to use renewable heat in the majority of its supermarkets, as well as converting all refrigeration systems to natural refrigerants. However, Sainsbury's is not just looking at its stores. It is also working with its suppliers to halve carbon emissions across all of their own-brand products by 2020.

Communication of the GHGMP

For a GHGMP to be effective, communication within the organisation is fundamental. Management needs to agree on the strategies to be implemented, and members of staff need to be kept aware of these strategies so that there is cohesiveness. Additionally, effective communication ensures that **greenwashing** can be avoided and the reputation of the organisation is not put at risk. The following factors of communication, adapted from Lingl *et al.* (2010), can help companies in their strategy of a successful GHGMP:

1. Developing an effective communications plan
    a. **Clear tasks of responsibility:** All members of staff who are involved, directly or indirectly, need to understand clearly their responsibility in relation to the GHGMP.
    b. **Methods of information obtained:** Ways that information is obtained within the organisation need to be communicated clearly to ensure that the quality of information is maintained.
    c. **Where and how information is communicated internally:** Examples include staff e-mails, team meetings, intranet.
    d. **Where and how relevant information will be communicated to the external audience:** Examples of this include the organisation website, sustainability report/annual report, customer newsletter, external conferences, advertisements, labels, etc.
    e. **Install reliable mechanisms to ensure clear and consistent communication:** Across the organisation, internally and externally.

The term 'greenwashing' is used when companies make false claims about their emissions management, use selective scientific data to downplay their negative effects on the environment, overstate the benefits of their 'green' programmes, or embellish their sustainability accreditations.

Greenwashing can also apply to:

- Advertising that uses images of nature, certain words, or even the colour green to evoke sustainability in consumers' minds, when the product itself may actually be toxic to the environment

- A company which spends more money on promoting its 'green' credentials than on its efforts to reduce its environmental impact

When you see a picture of a field or a forest on a product's packaging, what comes to your mind? Do you think of environmental responsibility? Or are you immediately suspicious?

The University of Oregon has created five criteria which you can use to spot and 'score' greenwashing in advertisements: www.greenwashingindex.com/about-greenwashing/.

f. **Create opportunities to receive feedback:** This needs to cover direct and indirect stakeholders, and continue to improve the GHGMP based on the feedback received.

g. **Responsibility must meet reporting requirements:** Mandatory in the case of government or voluntary GHG programmes, where applicable.

2. Principles of good communications

a. **'Inside out':** Communicate internally first! This ensures that all staff members who are directly involved with the GHGMP know the strategy that needs to be implemented, and the rest of the staff members are kept in the loop. In this way, there can be a uniform message delivered across the organisation.

b. **Authenticity:** Companies need to ensure that their actions are in line with their communication, i.e. 'do what you say you are doing/going to do'. Failure to do so will erode any trust that employees, customers and other stakeholders have in the organisation. A lack of authenticity can also be perceived as greenwashing.

c. **Be specific:** Provide detailed and precise information about GHG emissions so that appropriate steps can be taken to address them.

d. **Gain the right knowledge and proficiency required:** This is in order for companies to communicate the GHGMP effectively. Inaccurate and ineffective modes of communication can hamper even the best strategy for managing emissions.

e. **Obtain assurance from independent and accredited third parties:** Research by AccountAbility and Consumers International (2007) found that 70% of US and UK consumers felt more assured when companies had verifications and accreditation from recognised independent third parties in relation to their GHGMP. These accreditations also reassure other stakeholders such as the government, non-governmental organisations and the media.

f. **Seeing is Believing:** The more an organisation can 'show' what it is doing in its GHGMP, the better. Examples of these 'visuals' can include solar panels on an organisation's building, or a fleet of hybrid vehicles.

Conclusion

Climate change is already having catastrophic effects for individuals, communities, nations and business organisations. GHGs released by burning fossil fuels and other human activities are a major contributor to climate change. By managing these emissions, business organisations can contribute to the long-term sustainability of their operations and of the planet. All business organisations, regardless of their size, can address climate change by creating a coherent GHGMP and integrating it into their overall business strategy. This is especially important if they want to have a competitive advantage and maintain their legitimacy to operate. Although identifying and managing emissions may seem daunting, particularly for an organisation with a complex supply chain, there are tools and frameworks to help with this, some of which have been introduced in this chapter. Taking positive steps now can help organisations to reduce costs, improve staff morale, gain recognition for sustainable leadership and protect the Earth for future generations.

Suggested seminars

Seminar 1: Perspectives on GHG management

In this seminar, you will discuss how business activities can both contribute to and be affected by climate change. You will learn about carbon reporting—one possible strategy related to GHG management—and consider a variety of perspectives on this strategy, and on GHG management as a whole.

Activity 1: Effects of human activity on climate change (5 minutes)

There are six GHGs caused by human activity (IPCC 2007), listed below. Draw a line to match each gas with the business activity which typically causes it. One pair is highlighted as an example.

Greenhouse gas	Typical activity
Hydrofluorocarbons (HFCs)	Released by cattle farming, landfills, rice farming and the production of oil and gas
Carbon dioxide (CO$_2$)	Chemical by-products also used in some types of refrigeration equipment
Sulphur hexafluoride (SF$_6$)	Manufactured compound used in some specialised applications, like insulation for high-voltage electrical equipment
Nitrous oxide (N$_2$O)	Manufactured chemical compounds used for a variety of medical and other applications
Methane (CH$_4$)	**Emitted through burning of fossil fuels like coal, oil and gas, and also as a result of deforestation and other land-use changes**
Perfluorocarbons (PFCs)	Released by chemical fertilisers and burning fossil fuels

Bonus question: Can you think of a naturally occurring GHG? (Clue: it is the most abundant GHG in the earth's atmosphere.)

Activity 2: Effects of climate change on business (10 minutes)

1. Dr Celine Herweijer of PwC states that '[t]he Thai floods in 2011 wiped over £1.6 billion off Lloyd's of London's books and restricted the availability of some electronic goods' (Paddison 2013). Why do you think flooding in Thailand created a) financial losses for a UK company; and b) goods shortages for British consumers?

2. Look at Figure 1 in this chapter, which gives some examples of climate change. Work with a classmate to brainstorm the consequences of climate change on business organisations such as:

   • An international clothing retailer

   • A local greengrocer

   • An airline

   • A manufacturer of a product of your choice

   • A bank

Activity 3: Perspectives on GHG reporting (25 minutes)

While business organisations may be affected directly by climate change, they are also affected indirectly via government regulations such as emissions caps and environmental taxes. As carbon is the most prevalent greenhouse gas (see Figure 3 in this chapter), government policies often focus on measuring and reducing carbon emissions. Mandatory carbon reporting is one recent UK strategy for measuring carbon emissions.

1. Your tutor will assign you one of the roles below:

   • A 'Friends of the Earth' representative

   • A representative of Defra (the UK Department for Environment, Food and Rural Affairs)

   • A representative of the CDP (Carbon Disclosure Project)

   • The CEO of a quoted company

   • The CSR (corporate social responsibility) manager of a quoted company

   • The manager of an independent second-hand appliance shop

Mandatory GHG reporting

Since October 2013, all quoted companies (i.e. those listed on the London Stock Exchange) must publicly disclose their CO_2e emissions in their directors' report. This regulation includes the following requirements:

- A company must measure its GHG emissions using a suitable, widely recognised, independent standard such as the GHG Protocol Corporate Standard

- A company's report must cover emissions for all activities for which the company is globally responsible, including all relevant GHGs

- Reports should provide readers with a clear understanding of the operations for which emissions data has been reported; explanation should be provided where operations differ from those stated in the consolidated financial statement

- From the second year of reporting onward, emissions data from the previous report must be repeated alongside present year data

- Emissions must be expressed as an intensity ratio or ratios, e.g. emissions per unit of floor space or sales revenue

- Though not a regulatory requirement it is recommended that companies enlist an independent party to check the accuracy of their reporting

Defra estimates that the reporting will contribute to a reduction of 4 million tonnes of CO_2e emissions by 2021.

You can find out more about mandatory carbon reporting on the following websites:

- https://www.gov.uk/government/uploads/system/uploads/attachment_data/file/206392/pb13944-env-reporting-guidance.pdf

- www.carbontrust.com/resources/guides/carbon-footprinting-and-reporting/mandatory-carbon-reporting

Read the information opposite on mandatory GHG reporting and spend 10 minutes considering the perspective of your assigned role regarding mandatory GHG reporting. Imagine you are that person and what you think about the following:

- How do you view the relationship between GHG reporting and climate change?

- What do you think about the fact that GHG reporting is now mandatory for quoted companies?

- What will you gain/lose professionally from mandatory GHG reporting?

- What, if any, are the conflicts of interest/competing pressures for you in terms of your stance on GHG reporting? (Consider any conflicts of interest within your professional practice and any conflicts between your personal/professional stance.)

2. Compare your notes and ideas with others who have been assigned **the same role as you**. Based on the discussion, amend your notes as necessary.

3. Form mixed groups in which **all the different roles are represented**. Share your perspectives in turn within your group—speak as if you are that individual.

Activity 4: Discussion on perspectives (10 minutes)

Discuss as a class why different groups/individuals have different perspectives about carbon management.

Seminar 2: First steps to managing GHG emissions

In Seminar 1, you explored how business activities can both contribute to and be affected by climate change, and you considered different perspectives on carbon management. In Seminar 2, you will consider three scopes of emissions to explore how companies can map their GHG emissions in some detail.

Activity 1: Brief discussion (5–10 minutes)

To refresh ideas from Seminar 1 and consider some next steps, brainstorm in small groups or as a class:

- Why do business organisations try to reduce their carbon emissions?

- What might an organisation do to reduce its emissions?

- What are the potential risks and benefits of these actions for the organisation concerned?

Introducing the three scopes for measuring emissions

An organisation attempting to reduce its GHG emissions will be able to measure this reduction more effectively if it has a complete picture of the emissions produced. However, it can be difficult or impossible to

Figure 7: GHG emission scopes.

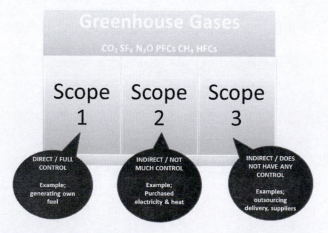

quantify an organisation's emissions, particularly where multipart supply chains or complex organisational structures are involved. Furthermore, some emissions associated with an organisation may be outside its control. To help measure an organisation's total emissions, it can be helpful to categorise emissions according to the amount of control the organisation has over them (see Fig. 7). For more detail, read (or reread) the part of this chapter on establishing an emissions boundary and look at Figures 5a, 5b and 5c.

Activity 2: Activities within each scope (3–5 minutes)

With a partner, suggest one or two additional business activities which may typically fall into each of the three scopes.

Identifying the three scopes for measuring emissions

The University of British Columbia (UBC 2012) is trying to minimise its greenhouse gas emissions. Below is a partial inventory of emissions for UBC's Vancouver campus: the right-hand column categorises the relevant activities according to the scopes of control.

Component	Usage data	GHG emissions (t CO_2e)	Scope (1, 2 or 3)
Paper	98,906 PKG	572	3
Ancillary buildings:[a] electricity	50,344,856 kWh	1,251	2
Staff air travel (including research and conference travel)		19,772	3
Natural gas direct use (core buildings)	84,004 GJ	4,214	1
Core buildings: electricity	156,491,863 kWh	3,887	2
Commuting		30,757	3
Natural gas direct use (ancillary buildings)[a]	94,859 GJ	4,758	1
Biomass facility (core and ancillary buildings)[a]	75,502 GJ	261	1
Building life-cycle		11,705	3
Solid waste		TBD	3
Total Campus emissions offset[b]			

[a] Ancillary buildings include student housing, conference, and athletics facilities.

[b] This table shows some of the campus emissions that were offset in 2012. For a full list, see UBC 2012 .

Activity 3: Categorising activities according to the three scopes (15–20 minutes)

Read through the Yum Scrum restaurant case study below, and, with a partner, identify which of its activities could be categorised under each of the three scopes.

Scope 1 (full control)	Scope 2 (indirect/less control)	Scope 3 (minimal control)

Case study: Yum Scrum restaurant

Yum Scrum is a restaurant in the UK Midlands that offers an 'all-you-can-eat' buffet. It is open seven days a week, from midday to 1am including public holidays. For lunch, served from 12pm to 5pm, the restaurant charges £9.90, while dinner, from 5pm to 1am, costs £16.99 excluding drinks. The company owns the building in which the restaurant is located. The talented chef produces food of good quality and the restaurant is popular with its customers—particularly students. Food is prepared in a kitchen and transported to the respective hot and cold buffet units, where diners serve themselves. Customers can also buy food to take away.

During its opening hours, the restaurant keeps the lights on constantly, including those in the lavatories. The same applies to the heating in the washrooms and dining area during the winter season. Consequently, the heat from the dining area has sometimes affected food quality. At off-peak times, the food on the cold buffet unit needs to be changed more frequently to avoid complaints (and possible lawsuits) from customers. This has resulted in increased production costs and food waste. Additionally, the management and some members of staff have noticed that the buffet units which keep the food warm have to remain switched on throughout the restaurant opening hours. Some staff take the initiative to turn the heat down or off during off-peak times, but not everyone does. The cost of keeping the buffet warm all day affects the restaurant's profit. In the beverage section, some members of staff make the extra effort to ensure that the refrigeration units where drinks are kept chilled are closed; however this can be quite a challenge during busy periods. There have been times when the refrigeration units are left ajar, especially during busy periods, without anyone noticing.

Where its supply chain is concerned, because of its high production costs Yum Scrum gets its ingredients from wherever the cheapest prices are offered. Hence, its suppliers can be from anywhere in the UK, and sometimes from Europe and beyond. Since negotiations sometimes need to take place face-to-face, management often travel to these areas to get the best deals. As long as its suppliers offer competitive prices, Yum Scrum is delighted to do business with them. However, topics such as sustainable fishing and farming are increasingly highlighted in the mainstream media, and the public are gradually becoming aware of these issues.

Yum Scrum has hired an external cleaning company to clean the premises after the restaurant has closed for the day. However, in order to cut costs, the cleaning company is only commissioned to clean the dining and buffet area twice a week. So far, there have been no complaints from customers about the restaurant's hygiene, and the management is happy to carry on with this arrangement. However, they are also considering how they can increase their profit margins. Additionally, new legislation on GHG emissions has meant that Yum Scrum restaurant will need to look into its practice and processes, in order to avoid paying a fine.

The staff and management are aware of rising energy costs and management discuss it verbally with staff on a regular basis. All staff are aware of what to do to save energy but no-one is in charge of this area. Energy consumption is checked against gas and electricity bills on a quarterly basis to ensure the company is not being overcharged. Although money is available for investment, only essential upgrades and maintenance are actually implemented, such as replacement of light fittings when they fail.

Compare your table with another pair's. Where you have different answers, discuss and try to support your point. Adjust your answer if the other pair's reason is more convincing.

Activity 4: Applying your analysis (15–20 minutes)

Based on your analysis of the Yum Scrum case study so far, work in small groups to discuss the following questions:

1. Which of Yum Scrum's activities would be easiest to change in order to reduce GHG emissions, and which would be most difficult?

2. Change in which areas(s) would have the greatest effect on total GHG emissions?

3. What particular strategies would you use to bring about change in your chosen area(s)?

4. Change in which area(s) would have the greatest effect on other areas of business, e.g. staff morale, public image, customer satisfaction?

5. What disadvantages might be created in other areas of scope by reducing the GHG in certain areas? For example, switching to gas power decreases GHG emissions but increases methane.

Use your notes from the discussion to make some recommendations and present them to the class.

Seminar 3: Managing GHG emissions— an organisational approach

In Seminar 2, you considered various sources of GHG emissions and organised these into three scopes based on an organisation's level of control over them. Seminar 3 introduces an organisational approach to managing these emissions. You will use a GHG management matrix to evaluate an organisation's current GHG management performance and use your findings to make appropriate recommendations.

Activity 1: Review (5 minutes)

Interview a classmate to find out what they have learned/remember about GHG management so far. Possible questions you could ask are:

1. Why is GHG management important?

2. If an organisation doesn't manage its GHG emissions, what are the main risks to a) the organisation; b) other stakeholders?

3. What are the three scopes of control within which GHG emissions can be measured?

The GHG management matrix

Earlier in the chapter you were introduced to the GHG management matrix. Go back and have another look. As you can see, the matrix has six columns: **policy**, **organising**, **training**, **monitoring**, **communication** and **investment**. Each one represents an area of management related to an organisation's ability to manage GHGs. You are going to apply this matrix to the Yum Scrum case study from Seminar 2.

Activity 2 (10 minutes)

Skim the Yum Scrum case study from Seminar 2 and/or review any notes you made on Yum Scrum. List the activities mentioned in the case study in the appropriate row of **column 2 only** in the table below (an example has been done for you):

Matrix category	Activity 2: Example of Yum Scrum activity	Activity 3: Effect on GHG emissions
Policy	Management aware of costs but no policy.	No policy means any measures will be implemented on an *ad hoc* basis without any overview or action plan. Opportunities will be missed.
Organising		
Training		
Monitoring		
Communication		
Investment		

Activity 3: Determining current emissions management performance (15 minutes)

1. Work in a small group and choose one area of management respon-sibility from the table above (your tutor might assign an area to you or ask you to choose one). Analyse Yum Scrum's activities in your assigned area to determine their effect on Yum Scrum's greenhouse gas emissions. For each activity, write a comment in the **right-hand column**.

2. Complete the rest of the table by asking other groups for information on their chosen areas of responsibility.

Activity 4: Using the GHG management matrix (15 minutes)

1. Your class will have a shared copy of the Greenhouse Gas Management Matrix. Work as a class to transfer your analyses of the various management areas onto the matrix. The ascending rows (0 to 4) represent increasing sophistication in the handling of the relevant issues. Working from the bottom up and taking each column in turn, tick the box which you feel best represents Yum Scrum's current performance in this area.

2. **Evaluating the organisation's overall performance:** The matrix shows the organisation's overall performance in GHG management in two ways: via a numerical score and via a line on a graph.

   - **Numerical score:** As a whole class, use the numbers in the left-hand column of the matrix to calculate Yum Scrum's overall score on GHG management. Read the information below explaining what the score means:

Your score	Comments (assuming relatively level graph)
0–8	You need assistance in developing GHG management in your organisation
9–16	You have developed the foundations for GHG management but need to expand the work on all levels
17–24	Very good, but even though you have achieved this you still need to work hard to maintain this position

   - Now that you've mapped the organisation's performance in each assigned area, look at the overall profile shown in the matrix. Join up the marks you've made in each category on the matrix to form a line (as you would find on a graph). This line shows the overall profile.

   The objective is to achieve a balanced improvement across the columns and reach as high a level as possible. Have a look at the example profiles and explanations below to help you understand Yum Scrum's performance.

Examples of profiles

High balanced

This shows a high degree of success but will require continued effort to maintain this position.

Low balanced

This could be the result of steady, considered progress or stagnation.

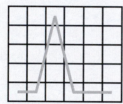

Peak

The efforts taken to reach the achievement at the peak of the graph could be wasted if the other areas haven't been developed to support it.

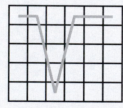

Trough

The lack of success in one area could hold back the success which has been achieved in other areas.

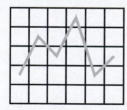

Unbalanced

The more unbalanced the approach, the more difficult it will be to perform well.

Activity 5: Analysing your results (5 minutes)

In small groups or as a whole class, look at the profile of Yum Scrum restaurant on the matrix. Compare Yum Scrum restaurant's profile with the examples above:

- Which does it most closely resemble?

- What are the implications of this result?

- What effect could a result in a particular category have on other categories? For example, how might a low score in the 'organising' category affect GHG management as a whole.

Follow-up activity

Use your findings and ideas from today's discussion to write up a report for Yum Scrum outlining the key points of its current GHG management and making some recommendations for improvement.

Additional teaching material and ideas

Risks, adaptation issues and prospects

- Read through the key risks, adaptation issues and prospects for the various continents as identified in IPCC 2014: 27-30.

- Choose an area of business where you have worked or are interested in working and consider the relationships between your business and climate change in terms of risks, adaptation issues and prospects.

- Discuss your thoughts with another student, preferably a student whose work or supply chain is based on another continent.

NB In addition to the IPCC document, you may wish to refer to the risks and opportunities listed in Table 1 earlier in the chapter.

Climate change and the case of the strawberry yogurt

Food production and consumption is an issue of critical global importance. The IPCC has stated with high confidence that 'all aspects of food security are potentially affected by climate change, including food access, utilization, and price stability' (IPCC 2014: 18). Imagine you are a producer of strawberry yogurt. Consider the relationships between your business and climate change at each stage of the food life-cycle namely: production, processing, distribution, retailing, consumption and waste. Consider:

- The likely sources of your three main ingredients: strawberries, sugar and milk

- How is your business affecting climate change and how is climate change affecting your business?

- The relationships between the different stages of the food life-cycle

Dimensions of action on climate change

Jonathan Rowson (2014) identifies seven dimensions for action on climate change: science, law, money, technology, democracy, culture, behaviour. Discuss in small groups how each dimension is relevant to how business organisations can help combat climate change. Then, rank the dimensions according to which you think is most important. Compare your answers with another group's.

Strong statements

Consider each of the following statements in turn and decide how strongly you agree/disagree with each one:

- Business is responsible for the world's environmental problems
- Trying to regulate climate change is like rearranging deckchairs on the *Titanic*
- Carbon offsetting is an effective way of halting climate change
- GHG management is anti-capitalist
- We can eat money
- Mandatory carbon reporting is harmful to business

Draw an imaginary line on the floor where one end of the line represents 'strongly agree' and the other end 'strongly disagree'. Stand at the point on the line where your agreement lies. Compare your position with those on each side of you and try to convince them of your point of view. Move to a different point on the line if you change your mind based on discussion. If you don't have space in the classroom to make a line do a show of hands or use online voting or a clicker system. At the end of the activity, reflect on which opinions you kept and which you changed, and why.

Emissions report

Choose an area of business where you have worked or would like to work, and list the main activities of that business. Skim the US Environmental Protection Agency's information on greenhouse emissions (www. epa.gov/climatechange/ghgemissions/gases.html) and list the likely main greenhouse gas emissions of that business area, based on your list of activities. Create a single PowerPoint slide to summarise your ideas.

Carbon neutrality

The University of St Andrews is trying to go carbon neutral (www.eauc.
org.uk/university_on_its_way_to_carbon_neutral_status).   Discuss   in
small groups the advantages and disadvantages of this and report back
to the group. You may wish to refer back to the risks and opportunities
listed in Table 1 and also the risks and adaptations identified by the
IPCC (2014).

Further reading

Websites

IPCC (Intergovernmental Panel on Climate Change), www.ipcc.ch
> The IPCC (Intergovernmental Panel on Climate Change) is the leading inter-
> national body for the assessment of climate change. Established by the UNEP
> (United Nations Environment Programme) and the World Meteorological
> Organization (WMO), it provides updated information on climate change from
> scientific perspectives, and the potential environmental and socioeconomic
> impacts. It currently has a membership of 195 countries, helping governments
> in their decision and policy-making.

The Science of Climate Change, www.bis.gov.uk/go-science
> The role of the Government Office for Science and its Adviser is to provide
> sound advice and recommendations to all levels of government, including the
> Prime Minister and Cabinet with regards to policy-making in relation to current
> scientific evidence related to climate change.

United Nations Environment Programme: Environment for Development, www.
unep.org/
> The UNEP is part of the United Nations system established for the environ-
> ment. It acts as a catalyst, advocate, educator and facilitator to promote the
> wise use and sustainable development of the global environment. UNEP's work
> comprises of strengthening institutions in relation to the management of the
> environment, assessing global, regional and national environmental trends and
> conditions, and developing global and national environmental mechanisms
> that can be utilised globally.

Publications

Berners-Lee, M. (2010) *How Bad are Bananas: the Carbon Footprint of Everything* (London: Profile Books).

> This informative and entertaining book provides information about the carbon footprints of a huge variety of products and activities while challenging beliefs and ideas about sustainability and sustainable living.

BSR (Business for Social Responsibility) (2007) *Beyond Neutrality: Moving Your Company Toward Climate Leadership*, http://bsr.org/reports/BSR_Beyond-Neutrality.pdf, accessed 20 May 2014.

> This report describes how companies can create business and social value by acting on climate change beyond reducing their internal carbon emissions, through the application of several resources including interviews with corporate practitioners and insights from BSR conferences, including the company round table 'Arriving at Strategic Policy Positions on Climate Change' held in May 2007 in conjunction with Yale University and Time Warner.

Carbon Neutral Co. Ltd (2014a) *Carbon Offset Project Types*, www.carbonneutral.com/knowledge-centre/carbon-offsetting-explained/project-types, accessed 20 May 2014.

> This introduces projects around the world in which companies are investing in order to offset some of their carbon emissions and make a positive change overall.

Greenhouse Gas Protocol (2004) *The Greenhouse Gas Protocol: A Corporate Accounting and Reporting Standard*, rev. edn, www.ghgprotocol.org/standards/corporate-standard, accessed 20 May 2014.

> This provides an international accounting tool for governments and businesses to manage their GHG emissions. The result of a long-standing partnership between the World Resources Institute and the World Business Council for Sustainable Development, the organisation provides the basis for business to begin their GHG management programme.

Lingl, P., D. Carlson and the David Suzuki Foundation (2010) *Doing Business in a New Climate: A Guide to Measuring, Reducing, and Offsetting Greenhouse Gas Emissions* (London: Earthscan).

> This book offers advice on how business organisations can reduce their impact on climate change and save money at the same time in easy-to-follow steps. It includes case studies of over 50 leading businesses and provides additional resources for businesses and other organisations looking to reduce their GHG emissions.

Schumacher, E.F. (1984) *Small is Beautiful: A Study of Economics as if People Mattered* (London: Abacus).

> This seminal text predates current understanding of the causes of climate change. However, it touches on many related subjects such as renewable energy sources and the use of natural resources.

Stibbe, A. (ed.) (2009) *The Handbook of Sustainability Literacy: Skills for a Changing World* (Totnes, UK: Green Books).

> The handbook contains chapters on carbon capability, systems thinking, greening business, etc., which may be useful for general reading or as a base for learning activities.

References

AccountAbility and Consumers International (2007) *What Assures Consumers on Climate Change: Switching on Citizen Power* (London: AccountAbility and Consumers International).

AltFuelsNow (2014) *Carbon Credits: Criticisms*, www.altfuelsnow.com/carbon/carbon-credits-criticisms.shtml, accessed 23 March 2014.

Berners-Lee, M. (2010) *How Bad Are Bananas? The Carbon Footprint of Everything* (London: Profile Books).

BSR (Business for Social Responsibility) (2007) *Beyond Neutrality: Moving Your Company Toward Climate Leadership*, http://bsr.org/reports/BSR_Beyond-Neutrality.pdf, accessed 20 May 2014.

Carbon Neutral Co. Ltd (2014a) *Carbon Offset Project Types*, www.carbonneutral.com/knowledge-centre/carbon-offsetting-explained/project-types,   accessed 20 May 2014.

—— (2014b) *Carbon Offsetting Explained*, www.carbonneutral.com/knowledge-centre/carbon-offsetting-explained, accessed 1 April 2014.

Carbon Trust (2013) *Energy Management: a Comprehensive Guide to Controlling Energy Use*, www.carbontrust.com/media/13187/ctg054_energy_management.pdf, accessed 1 April 2014.

Davenport, C. (2014) 'Industry awakens to threat of climate change', *The New York Times*, www.nytimes.com/2014/01/24/science/earth/threat-to-bottom-line-spurs-action-on-climate.html?_r=0, accessed 1 April 2014.

Defra (2014) *The Environment: Emissions*, http://laqm.defra.gov.uk/review-and-assessment/tools/emissions.html, accessed 28 February 2014.

Doran, G.T. (1981) 'There's a S.M.A.R.T. Way to Write Management's Goals and Objectives', *Management Review* 70.11: 35-36.

Earley, K. (2013) 'Facelift Access Hire: simple innovations for big energy savings', *The Guardian*, www.theguardian.com/sustainable-business/facelift-access-hire-innovations-energy-saving, accessed 28 February 2014.

Fox, N. (n.d.) 'Sainsbury's: working smarter, not harder', *The Guardian*, www.theguardian.com/sustainable-business/best-practice-exchange/sainsburys-working-smarter-not-harder, accessed 28 February 2014.

Funk, M. (2014) *Windfall: The Booming Business of Global Warming* (New York: The Penguin Press).

Greenhouse Gas Protocol (2004) *The Greenhouse Gas Protocol: A Corporate Accounting and Reporting Standard*, rev. edn, www.ghgprotocol.org/standards/corporate-standard, accessed 20 May 2014.

Hartigan Shea, R. (2014) 'Q&A: How to Make Money from Climate Change', *National Geographic*, http://news.nationalgeographic.com/news/2014/03/140307-climate-change-business-mckenzie-funk-windfall-science/, accessed 1 April 2014.

IPCC (Intergovernmental Panel on Climate Change) (2007) *How do Human Activities Contribute to Climate Change and How do They Compare with Natural Influences?*, www.ipcc.ch/publications_and_data/ar4/wg1/en/faq-2-1.html, accessed 1 April 2014.

—— (2013) 'Summary for Policymakers', in *Climate Change 2013: The Physical Science Basis. Contribution of Working Group I to the Fifth Assessment Report of the Intergovernmental Panel on Climate Change*, https://www.ipcc.ch/report/ar5/wg1/, accessed 1 April 2014.

—— (2014) 'Summary for Policymakers', in *Climate Change 2014: Impacts, Adaptation and Vulnerability. Contribution of Working Group II to the Fifth Assessment Report of the Intergovernmental Panel on Climate Change*, http://ipcc-wg2.gov/AR5/images/uploads/IPCC_WG2AR5_SPM_Approved.pdf, accessed 1 April 2014.

Lingl, P., D. Carlson and the David Suzuki Foundation (2010) *Doing Business in a New Climate: A Guide to Measuring, Reducing, and Offsetting Greenhouse Gas Emissions* (London: Earthscan).

Lovell, H., H. Bulkeley and D. Liverman (2009) 'Carbon offsetting: sustaining consumption?', *Environment and Planning* 41: 2357-79.

Murray, J., and C. Dey (2009) 'The Carbon Neutral Free for All', *International Journal of Greenhouse Gas Control* 3: 237-48.

New Zealand Business Council for Sustainable Development (2002), *The Challenge of Greenhouse Gas Emissions: The 'Why' and 'How' of Accounting and Reporting for GHG Emissions*, www.sbc.org.nz/__data/assets/pdf_file/0019/54901/Climate_Change_Guide.pdf, accessed 22 March 2014.

Paddison, L. (2013) 'Climate change: are companies prepared for the impact?', *The Guardian*, www.theguardian.com/sustainable-business/climate-change-companies-supply-chain-impact, accessed 1 April 2014.

Porter, M.E. (1980) *Competitive Strategy: Techniques for Analysing Industry and Competitors* (New York: The Free Press).

—— (1985) *Competitive Advantage: Creating and Sustaining Superior Performance* (New York: The Free Press).

Schumacher, E.F. (1984) *Small is Beautiful: A Study of Economics as if People Mattered* (London: Abacus).

Rowson, J. (2014) 'The seven dimensions for action on climate change', *The Guardian*, 14 February 2014, www.theguardian.com/sustainable-business/behavioural-insights/2014/feb/14/seven-dimensions-action-climate-change, accessed 20 May 2014.

Stibbe, A. (ed.) (2009) *The Handbook of Sustainability Literacy: Skills for a Changing World* (Totnes, UK: Green Books).

UBC (2012) *The University of British Columbia: GHG Inventory*, http://sustain.ubc.ca/campus-initiatives/climate-energy/ghg-inventory, accessed 22 March 2014.

UN (1998) *Kyoto Protocol to the United Nations Framework Convention on Climate Change, Dec. 10, 1997, U.N. Doc FCCC/CP/1997/7/Add.1, 37 I.L.M. 22*, https://unfccc.int/kyoto_protocol/items/2830.php, accessed 1 April 2014.

UNFCCC (2014) *Greenhouse Gas Inventory Data*, http://unfccc.int/ghg_data/items/3800.php, accessed 22 March 2014.

13
Stakeholder engagement and corporate peacemaking

Natalie Ralph and Ellie Kennedy

Stakeholder engagement is essential for sustainable business. In conflict-prone markets, most companies benefit from peace and stability, while violent conflict is detrimental to sustainability. This chapter proposes stakeholder engagement can support peacemaking in violent conflict through CPM (corporate peacemaking). CPM helps bring disputing parties together for peace talks to halt/prevent violent conflict. CPM can demonstrate corporate responsibility, build peace and good relations with and *between* stakeholders, and protect the company and its reputation. This chapter outlines concepts in stakeholder theory/engagement, and then illustrates how companies can conduct CPM by applying a framework of 14 interventions. A CPM case study in Colombia is presented, along with seminar plans (with more case studies and scenarios), additional activities and further reading. Students learn to: discuss concepts in stakeholder theory and CPM; understand various approaches to peace; identify stakeholders/conflict actors to engage; and apply the CPM framework to case studies and scenarios.

Introduction

Stakeholder engagement is essential for responsible, sustainable business in today's highly networked world. In conflict-prone markets, this chapter proposes, stakeholder engagement encompasses an added, critical role: supporting peace. Most companies benefit from peace and stability, while violent conflict is detrimental to sustainability for most businesses, the natural environment and social cohesion (Rodrigues 2007: 182-5). In a report by the UN Global Compact, the agency which engages business in the UN's international work, businessman Steve Killelea states:

> If the cost of reducing levels of violence in society was significantly lower than economic activity lost due to violence, would it not be fitting for businesses to engage with government and civil society to create peace in the markets in which they operate? (UN Global Compact 2010: 12)

A range of corporate actors are currently doing this. In 2013, over 60 companies and business associations formed the Global Compact's new international 'Business for Peace' platform. They seek practical ways to support peace, and to implement responsible business practices in conflict-prone markets (UN Global Compact 2013a, 2014). Sir Richard Branson, head of the Virgin Group of companies, along with the musician Peter Gabriel and former South African President, Nelson Mandela, created The Elders. The Elders brings together diplomatic leaders like the former President of Ireland, Mary Robinson to help catalyse peace processes in conflict-affected countries (The Elders 2014).

These examples demonstrate stakeholder engagement supporting peace and peacemaking. This may be termed, CPM (corporate peacemaking). CPM is proposed as a strategy for demonstrating proactive corporate responsibility, building peace and good relations with and *between* stakeholders, and protecting the company and its reputation. CPM helps to bring disputing parties in intra-state conflict together to participate in peace talks to prevent or halt violent conflict. Intra-state conflict may arise within or between communities, or between armed groups and/or the government.

This chapter provides key concepts in stakeholder theory and engagement as applied, in particular, to conflict-prone countries. Importantly, research on business and peace is a new and emerging field. Little is yet known regarding best practice in CPM. Research tends to be exploratory, and there are few published case studies. You must draw your own conclusions, carefully considering whether and how you, as a corporate manager, might apply CPM in different conflict situations.

Stakeholder engagement

In R. Edward Freeman's (2010: 52-3) book, *Strategic Management: A Stakeholder Approach*, originally published in 1984, this pre-eminent advocate of stakeholder theory defines stakeholders as groups or individuals who affect, or are affected by, the attainment of an organisation's goals. Stakeholders can include the full range of individuals/groups that companies may engage with, including shareholders, employees, customers, social justice and environmental non-governmental organisations (NGOs), suppliers, communities, the natural environment, governments and armed groups or terrorist groups when they substantially affect operations.

In the traditional managerial (or shareholder) model of the firm, owners (shareholders) are the primary group and management is responsible for prioritising maximised value for the owners. This is exemplified by Milton Friedman's (1962) famous declaration that the business of business is 'mak[ing] as much money for their shareholders as possible'. Contrary to this, the stakeholder model proposes that all those affected by the firm's pursuit of its goals must have their legitimate interest in the company acknowledged, and the firm must maximise value for these 'stakeholders'. Stakeholder theory can therefore be viewed as a normative theory advocating, to varying degrees, that firms are *morally obligated* to consider stakeholder interests (see Crane *et al.* 2013: 133-9; Phillips *et al.* 2003; Donaldson and Preston 1995). Where it falls short is that considering such interests may not necessarily mean these interests influence company decision-making.

Stakeholder theory can also be applied as an analytical tool to identify and manage stakeholders (Crane *et al.* 2013). A company should identify its stakeholders and their perceived interests and influence, have processes in place to engage stakeholder concerns, and aim to benefit both the company and stakeholder. Companies benefit from preserving their license to operate, gaining knowledge on issues from external actors, and improving long-term, innovative decision-making. Stakeholders benefit from promoting their needs and interests and, ideally, being able to do so in a co-operative rather than hostile manner (Fifka 2012; Freeman 2010: 52-82).

Standards like ISO 26000 and AA 1000 help companies develop strategies for stakeholder engagement and sustainability. Firms report publicly through such processes as those provided, for example, by the Global Reporting Initiative. Companies typically engage stakeholders through their sustainability or corporate social responsibility annual reports, community meetings, round-table discussions, partnerships and social media like Twitter (Hitchcock and Willard 2009).

Ignoring stakeholders' interests can damage a firm's reputation, share price and sales, while risking costly legal battles and disparaging campaigns by NGOs like Global Witness (www.globalwitness.org), whose campaigns on 'conflict diamonds and minerals' brought the practices of the global diamond and mining industries under scrutiny. They demonstrated how these natural resources are used by armed groups and corrupt political leaders to fund wars, with companies providing pathways to international markets.

Despite these risks, it can be difficult to assess how to prioritise stakeholders and to balance competing stakeholders' claims. Mitchell *et al.*'s (1997) seminal model assesses stakeholder 'salience' based on a stakeholder's power, legitimacy and urgency. Power is the ability to influence the company; legitimacy derives from having a legal claim or moral argument against the company; and urgency concerns how time-sensitive or critical a claim is. This model assists managers to prioritise stakeholders' claims, taking into account the dynamic, changing environment.

Stakeholder engagement in conflict-prone markets

In conflict-prone markets, companies can benefit from engaging stakeholders to promote peace and ensure the company does not cause or exacerbate conflict. The latter is important. Many companies have been accused of ignoring, manipulating or being complicit in the abuse of stakeholders such as local communities and political groups. Companies have either deliberately or unwittingly increased tensions over revenues, jobs or the destruction of local environments and livelihoods, allowed security personnel to respond violently to protesters, or provided revenues to undemocratic host governments that are used to buy weaponry to suppress civilians (Business & Human Rights Resource Centre 2014a; Swanson 2002).

Yet, civil society is increasingly powerful in demanding that companies address their negative social, environmental or political impacts on communities through conflict-sensitive business practices and respect for human rights (Business & Human Rights Resource Centre 2014b). Conflict-sensitive practices consider the conflict context, its actors and dynamics, and the interaction between any business intervention and its context. This helps to avoid negative impacts and maximise positive effects (Conflict Sensitivity Consortium 2014; International Alert 2005). Amid violent conflict, human rights cannot be enjoyed. Companies may therefore find that supporting peace processes to reduce violence is the most immediate way to halt human rights abuses.

Most companies benefit from peace, and a governance system that respects transparent and accountable government, a strong civil society and an independent judiciary system to maintain rule of law. They gain from strong infrastructure to support healthcare, education and transport. In contrast, the costs of conflict impede the operation of businesses by such practices as employee kidnapping, destruction of company installations, reduced production or closure of operations, raised international insurance premiums, and diminishing profits and employee morale.

Considering this, the following discusses CPM as a stakeholder engagement strategy for promoting peace.

Corporate peacemaking

Rather than focusing on domestic businesses, this chapter focuses on CPM undertaken by TNCs (transnational corporations), business organisations (with TNCs as members) or business leaders representing TNCs. When considering companies, characteristics such as company size, sector and ownership structure will influence how a company is able to support peacemaking.

It is important to distinguish CPM from CPB (corporate peacebuilding) and structural peacebuilding. CPB is the umbrella term for both structural peacebuilding and peacemaking. Structural peacebuilding addresses the underlying structural issues which cause grievance and conflict. These arise when society's socially constructed institutions, such as government, police and universities, provide some people with material resources, representation and a voice in matters affecting their wellbeing and status, while depriving others (Christie and Wessells 2008: 1957).

Structural peacebuilding by companies can include support for equitable economic and business development (such as jobs for youth and ex-combatants), democracy and good governance (for example, capacity-building for transparent local government), promoting human rights (such as those of indigenous groups or employees), disarmament and demobilisation programmes, and local environmental sustainability.

In contrast, direct physical violence requires *peacemaking* between conflict parties. Peacemaking concentrates on the political/diplomatic, relational and reconciliation aspects of peace work. It builds peaceful relations between conflict parties and communities, progresses peace processes and helps parties reach a peace agreement. Peacemaking is more critical at certain times, such as an immediate response for preventing fighting between belligerents.

The following presents a framework for peacemaking by corporate actors, outlining 14 interventions that they might potentially apply in intra-state conflict.

The 14-intervention corporate peacemaking framework

The 14-intervention CPM framework is the culmination of research on case studies of CPM, and a cross-fertilisation of concepts from business and peace theory, peace and conflict studies, conflict resolution, diplomacy and peace psychology (Ralph 2012, forthcoming).

The framework is an exploration of potential interventions only. Some interventions have been implemented by corporate actors, while others are hypothetical. Some interventions may only be effective in certain situations, or may only be supported by TNCs, while actually led by more traditional peace actors such as professional mediators, the UN or conflict resolution organisations. The framework is illustrated in Figure 1 in the form of a jigsaw puzzle, showing that this conceptual framework remains unfinished, possibly awaiting other interventions and pieces of the puzzle.

From collective action to shuttle diplomacy (Interventions 1–7)

Through **Intervention 1**, collective action between TNCs and/or with domestic businesses and civil society organisations, CPM gains credibility and influence. The Northern Ireland branch of the CBI (Confederation of British Industry), a non-party-political organisation promoting business interests, supported the (successful) peace processes in the 1990s to end the violence in Northern Ireland. To gain influence, the CBI partnered with other trade and industry organisations such as the Institute of Directors and the Hotel Federation (Banfield *et al.* 2006).

Applying **Intervention 2**, corporate actors focus on lobbying and advocacy with the conflict parties, public or other businesses to mobilise them to work towards peace. The Northern Ireland CBI's advocacy included writing *Peace: A Challenging New Era*, referred to as 'the peace dividend paper', which outlined an economic rationale for peace. Politicians and the media adopted the concept of a 'peace dividend' which then infused new momentum into the peace processes (Tripathi and Gündüz 2008; Nelson 2000).

Intervention 3 includes providing economic or industry advice that supports peace, either in the public realm (per the CBI example above)

Figure 1: The 14-intervention corporate peacemaking framework.

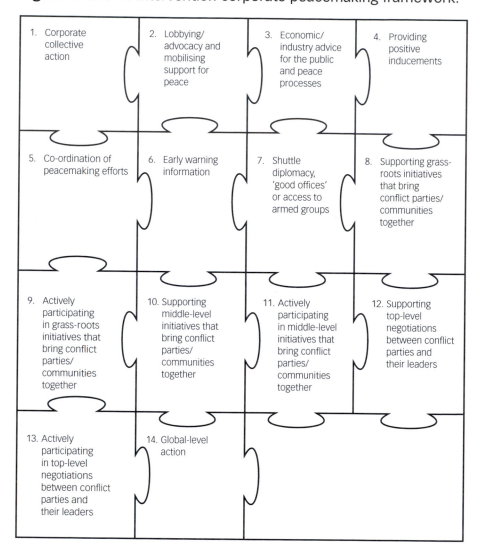

or in peace negotiations. In the early 2000s, oil TNCs provided reviews on oil exploration, production and revenue distribution for the peace negotiations attempting to end Sudan's north–south conflict. This culminated in the first civil war peace agreement which explicitly outlined how oil industry and revenue management would be organised to promote peace (Shankleman 2007).

By applying **Intervention 4**, corporate actors provide 'positive inducements' to enable or encourage the conflict parties to come to the negotiating table. This may include funding, transportation, equipment, accommodation, increased investment, aid or economic development projects. This intervention is controversial; transparency and compliance with law such as the UK Bribery Act 2010 will be crucial (Haufler 2001).

Intervention 5 includes corporate support or leadership for the (often lacking) co-ordination of activities by multiple peace actors in a country. The Colombian business organisation, FIP (Ideas for Peace Foundation), produced databases on Colombian peace negotiations to record and understand the roles of various peace actors, potentially facilitating co-ordination (FIP 2005; Sweetman 2009).

Applying **Intervention 6**, companies provide information for the early warning of conflict. An organisation could be funded or established to collate data from businesses located in conflict-prone areas to inform wider early warning systems (Sweetman 2009; Nelson 2000).

With **Intervention 7**, corporate actors conduct shuttle diplomacy, provide 'good offices' and/or provide access to armed groups to build trust between parties (Tripathi and Gündüz 2008; Nelson 2000). In Aceh, Indonesia, Juha Christensen, head of a Swedish pharmaceutical company with economic activities in Indonesia, used his contacts with key people to undertake shuttle diplomacy, relaying information between the Free Aceh movement and the Indonesian government. This assisted a peace agreement in 2005 that ended the civil war (Braithwaite *et al.* 2010; Iff *et al.* 2010).

Little is known about company interactions with armed groups, and the strategies businesses use when dealing with such groups. Greater research on this, and ways business can safely promote peace during such interactions, is needed. As Bardouille-Crema (2011) states, while some armed groups are predatory, many have strong links to local communities and often draw on community support ... In some cases, therefore, dialogue with armed groups can become a business necessity, both as part of an on-going context and stakeholder analysis and as part of normal due diligence and community engagement.

Grass-roots to global interventions (Interventions 8–14)

TNCs have international reach and their influence ranges from the global level to the national and local levels in a country. When discussing CPM activities that can be conducted at different levels of a society, the adaption of John Paul Lederach's (1997; see also Killick 2000) conceptual societal structure for building peace is beneficial.

Lederach conceives society as a pyramid, which includes the national, top-level peace process and its (relatively few) political leaders, mostly applying direct negotiations between leaders of warring parties. These negotiations aim for a ceasefire and peace agreement. The pyramid's base represents grass-roots communities and leaders and their often numerous yet less visible peace initiatives. In the middle-level are actors such as business leaders, academics and religious, ethnic and humanitarian leaders. Middle-level actors are well-placed to link grass-roots with top-level processes, and often have relationships with counterparts across the conflict divide (Lederach 1997). To represent all possible CPM activities, the apex here reflects global-level action.

Within a country, a TNC's executives may be middle-level leaders, but they can act at the top and middle levels of a society, and *support* grass-roots activity. Lower level company workers and managers acting at the grass-roots level in local communities would demonstrate grass-roots activity (see Figure 2).

Usually implemented by community leaders, grass-roots approaches **(Interventions 8 and 9)** use existing networks such as church associations. They build pressure from 'the people' to encourage peace processes. For example, a travelling 'Circus of Peace' in Mozambique used drama to explore the challenges of war, possible reconciliation, and conflict resolution skills (Lederach 1997: 52-55). Company workers could

Figure 2: Conceptual structure for corporate peacemaking.

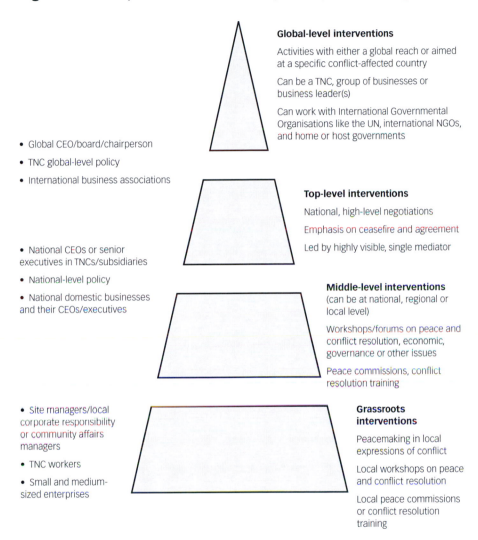

Global-level interventions

Activities with either a global reach or aimed at a specific conflict-affected country

Can be a TNC, group of businesses or business leader(s)

Can work with International Governmental Organisations like the UN, international NGOs, and home or host governments

- Global CEO/board/chairperson
- TNC global-level policy
- International business associations

Top-level interventions

National, high-level negotiations

Emphasis on ceasefire and agreement

Led by highly visible, single mediator

- National CEOs or senior executives in TNCs/subsidiaries
- National-level policy
- National domestic businesses and their CEOs/executives

Middle-level interventions
(can be at national, regional or local level)

Workshops/forums on peace and conflict resolution, economic, governance or other issues

Peace commissions, conflict resolution training

- Site managers/local corporate responsibility or community affairs managers
- TNC workers
- Small and medium-sized enterprises

Grassroots interventions

Peacemaking in local expressions of conflict

Local workshops on peace and conflict resolution

Local peace commissions or conflict resolution training

Source: Adapted from Killick's (2000) use of Lederach's (1997) conceptual pyramid of the societal structure for peacebuilding to demonstrate roles for business leaders.

initiate or support such activities with the additional support (including funding) of the company or a collective of companies.

Conflict resolution activities at the middle level of society (**Interventions 10 and 11**), such as behind-the-scenes conflict resolution workshops, can build relationships across society and prepare the ground for agreements between top-level leaders. In conflict resolution workshops, middle-level leaders are invited because of their knowledge of the conflict and proximity and influence with top-level decision-makers. Workshops do not replace formal, top-level negotiations but broaden participation in the peace process and encourage participants to analyse problems and seek creative solutions (Ralph and Conley-Tyler 2006; Lederach 1997). In the 1990s, to support peace negotiations in South Africa to end apartheid, the Consultative Business Movement, with international and domestic companies as members, organised forums on peace, development and the economy. These brought together societal leaders from across the conflict divide, often deeply suspicious of one another, and helped them to develop solutions and build trust (CBM 1997; Chapman and Hofmeyr 1994).

In national-level negotiations between conflict parties' top-level leaders (**Interventions 12 and 13**), corporate actors either support or actively participate by providing advice and mediation (see the Colombian and South African case studies below). Research into these potential interventions (Ralph forthcoming) is needed to identify best practice and ways to curb corporate interests negatively influencing peace negotiations. Corporate actors can underline they want a business-friendly environment but, beyond this, are neutral and support democratic, inclusive peace processes (Fourié 2006; CBM n.d.). To gain credibility, corporate actors can work as a collective with domestic businesses, or simply support the preparation of these negotiations (Intervention 12). This could include assisting logistics, administration, funding or capacity-building in peace-process design and mediation for the conflict parties (Nelson 2000).

When taking action at the global level (**Intervention 14**), corporate actors may promote peace generally, or within a particular country. Support could be given to international business associations, the UN, governments and others to promote peace. Richard Branson and the UN Global Compact's 'Business for Peace' platform demonstrate how corporate power and influence can be harnessed for peace at this global level.

This 14-intervention CPM framework is useful for examining existing corporate responses to intra-state conflict as well as considering potential future interventions by corporate actors. The following empirical case study applies the framework to examine CPM interventions in a long-standing conflict situation in Colombia.

Case study: Colombia

Colombia has suffered widespread violence for half a century. The main conflict parties are the Colombian government, paramilitary groups and the dominant Marxist guerrillas, FARC (Revolutionary Armed Forces of Colombia) and ELN (National Liberation Army). Both FARC and ELN are listed as terrorist groups by the US and European Union (Hallam 2013). Colombian citizens, both rich and poor, have been both the direct and indirect victims of this violence. During President Pastrana's administration (1998–2002), there was unprecedented participation in peace processes by international and Colombian business including through the peace-focused business organisation, FIP (Ideas for Peace Foundation) (personal conversation with A. Guáqueta, former Academic Director, FIP, 19 July 2008; Rettberg 2007, n.d.).

Illustration of CPM interventions

Corporate collective action and advocacy for peace

President Pastrana established a negotiating team to develop contacts with FARC. Four high-ranking Colombian business executives in turn held positions on the team. TNCs were linked to this business involvement via FIP, which was established in 1999 to provide advice on organising negotiations to the government team. TNCs comprised a number of FIP's founders, executive committee and membership: founders included, for example, the US oil company Occidental Petroleum Corporation, and the mining company Cerrejón (owned by BHP Billiton, Xstrata and Anglo American), while representatives on the executive committee included the brewer SABMiller. FIP's founders aimed to encourage broader business backing for peace negotiations, a commitment that continued to be a priority over the years (conversation with Guáqueta; Rettberg n.d.; Guáqueta 2006; FIP 2005).

FIP also partnered with the UN Global Compact and UK-based IBLF (International Business Leaders Forum) to organise events that brought TNCs that invested in Colombia together with civil society and government. The events aimed to support peace by finding ways to address social and economic issues within a conflict context (IBLF 2007).

Co-ordination of peacemaking efforts

As stated above, FIP recorded the roles of the many peace actors involved over the years, potentially facilitating co-ordination (FIP 2005).

Supporting top-level negotiations

FIP and its hired researchers provided technical and process advice to Pastrana's negotiating team for negotiations with FARC (conversation with Guáqueta). Through their leadership and membership in FIP, TNCs and domestic firms were able to support this intervention.

Nonetheless, by 2002, the peace talks had broken down for a number of reasons. For example, despite participating in the negotiations, FARC issued 'Law 002' demanding a 'peace tax' from wealthy Colombians who otherwise risked being kidnapped by FARC. This led to broad criticism of the peace process. Furthermore, disunity across the business sector as a whole, resulting from the connection of some firms to paramilitary groups and the illegal drugs trade, and from the weak representation of business in business associations, meant that no broad and unified business peace movement developed. In general, business was ambivalent towards both a peaceful solution to the conflict and organising itself as a force to shape the peace talks (Rettberg 2007; Guáqueta 2006; Arnson and Whitfield 2005). A new government in 2002 led by President Uribe replaced the peace talks with a decade-long, hardline military strategy. FIP continued its peace efforts by supporting **structural peacebuilding**, focusing on economic development, strengthening institutions and assisting internally displaced persons and ex-combatants (FIP 2005: 9-10).

However, negotiations began again in 2012 between the Colombian government (now under President Santos) and FARC. Similar talks may start with the ELN (Economist 2013; DFAT 2013; Hallam 2013). In late 2013, the UN Global Compact's local network in Colombia hosted the first ever country-level event of the 'Business for Peace' platform (Interventions 1 and 2). A panel, which included the president of FIP, highlighted 'the importance of public–private partnerships to generate solutions that foster peace'. Riding on the momentum of the current Colombian peace talks, the event held multi-stakeholder workshops and dialogues to identify strategies that business (such as Unilever Colombia) can implement to support the Colombian peace process, stability, and economic and social development (UN Global Compact 2013a).

Suggested seminars

Seminar 1: CPM and stakeholder engagement

In this seminar, you will learn to explain and use keywords associated with the topics of stakeholder engagement and CPM; you will learn to discuss issues associated with these topics from different value perspectives; and you will learn to differentiate between structural peace-building (such as economic interventions) and peacemaking (political/diplomatic interventions) in areas of conflict.

Activity 1

Thinking about stakeholder engagement in general, tell a partner:

1. What are stakeholders (give some examples)?

2. What is stakeholder engagement?

3. Why is this important for business?

Activity 2a

Figure 3 shows some possible stakeholders in a region of conflict (i.e. armed struggle). Discuss in small groups what effects armed conflict might have on each of the stakeholders (Two boxes are left blank for you to add your own suggestions for other stakeholders.)

Discussion point example: 'Armed conflict could create a lot of problems for **local government** because they are responsible for infrastructure, such as telecommunications and roads, and these can be destroyed and disrupted by violent conflict.'

Figure 3: Possible stakeholders in a region of conflict.

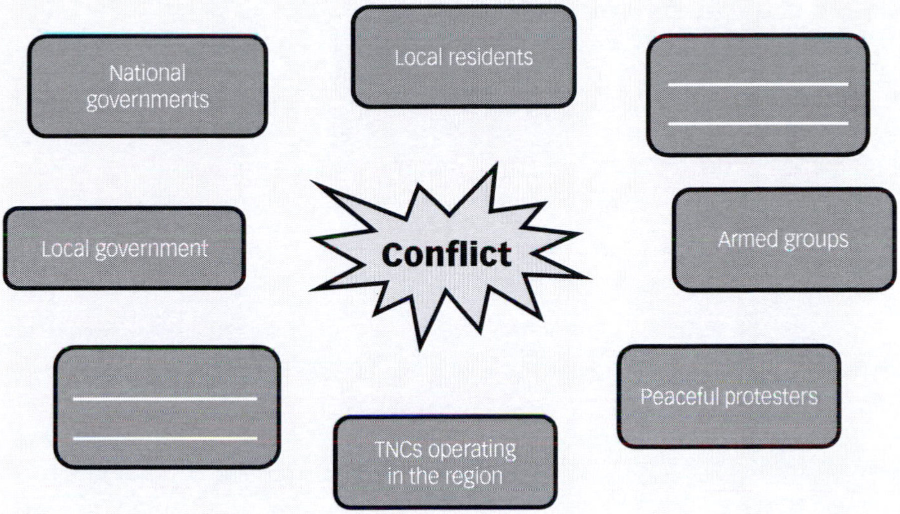

Activity 2b

In the previous activity, you considered the effects of conflict on stakeholders. However, stakeholders can influence situations as well as being affected by them. They are called stakeholders because their actions can also be driven by the *stake* that each *holds* in the situation. Thinking about the stakeholders you have been discussing, which ones might have a stake in exacerbating conflict and which might have a stake in promoting peace? Why?

Discussion point example: 'Local businesses are likely to want peace, as violence can make it difficult or dangerous for them to operate normally. However, some might have a stake in prolonging a conflict, such as businesses that provide food or entertainment to soldiers.'

Activity 3

TNC involvement in conflict can take different forms and have different effects. Read the three case studies below, all of which show examples of stakeholder engagement in conflict-prone areas. Identify which intervention(s) promote(s) peace and which exacerbate(s) conflict.

Case A: Elf Aquitaine in Congo

Congo-Brazzaville (Republic of Congo) is a major oil exporter. In 1997, forces loyal to President Pascal Lissouba clashed with forces loyal to former President Denis Sassou Nguesso. The French oil company, Elf Aquitaine (now Total), bought oil futures (the sale of future rights to oil reserves) and through this revenue allegedly helped *both* Sassou Nguesso and Lissouba obtain arms and equipment for their forces. After Sassou Nguesso overthrew Lissouba, Elf regained its dominant position in the country's oil industry (Ross 2012: 175-76; Swanson 2002).

Case B: Lonrho in Mozambique

Mozambique suffered civil war from 1975 until 1992. In the 1980s, following spiralling security costs, 'Tiny' Rowland, CEO of the mining TNC, Lonrho (now Lonmin), conducted shuttle diplomacy between the leaders of key groups in the conflict. Lonrho supplied one group with a jet to transport representatives to negotiations, and millions of dollars to enable it to transform into a political party and encourage the group to remain in talks. During difficult negotiations, Rowland organised meetings, gave advice and encouraged the leaders until they finally reached an agreement (Banfield *et al.* 2006; Wenger and Möckli 2003; Vines 1998).

Case C: Heineken in Rwanda

Violent conflict between the Tutsi and Hutu ethnic groups in Rwanda, including the 1994 genocide, forced the Hutu government's defeat and the formation of a coalition government. Although less severe, fighting continues, with former rebel soldiers active in the border regions. The Dutch brewing TNC, Heineken International, operates in Rwanda through its subsidiary Bralirwa. Bralirwa has adopted policies on ethics, environment, socioeconomic welfare and governance. The company generates economic growth, jobs and tax revenue. Bralirwa increases local economic development by incorporating local farmers into their supply chain, offering them a set price above market price, and enabling 5,500 farmers' families to join the national health insurance program. Bralirwa does not actively encourage political change, but supports equal human rights, and transparent, accountable politics (Andersson *et al.* 2011; Feil *et al.* 2008).

The Heineken case study above is an example of *structural peacebuilding*, while the Lonrho one is an example of *peacemaking*. Structural peacebuilding and peacemaking both take place in regions of conflict. Although these concepts are connected, they are not the same thing. To understand the difference, consider the following definitions:

- **Structural peacebuilding** involves helping to provide what a society needs in order to function fairly and effectively. This can include government capacity-building, equitable economic development, human rights promotion, environmental sustainability, and disarmament programs. Corporations can get involved by, for example, providing jobs for youth and ex-combatants, helping local development and environmental initiatives, and teaching their security forces about human rights.

- In contrast, **peacemaking** concentrates on the political/diplomatic, relational and reconciliation aspects of peace work. It builds peaceful relations between conflict parties and communities, progresses peace processes and helps parties reach a peace agreement.

Activity 4

Below are some activities that can promote peace. Work in groups to allocate each activity to the relevant category in the table below (an example of each has been filled in for you).

- Economic advice for negotiations
- Conflict resolution workshops
- Providing funds for new hospitals or schools
- Protecting the local environment
- Lobbying for peace
- Supporting mediation between disputants
- Offering fair employment terms
- Early warning information on rising conflict
- Creating jobs

Structural peacebuilding	Peacemaking
Helping local government be more transparent and accountable to its constituents	Supporting grass-roots initiatives that bring disputing communities together for talks

Activity 5

Discussion:

1. Based on what you have learned so far, to what extent do you think companies are likely to get involved in a) structural peacebuilding and b) peacemaking? Why do you think they get involved (or not) with these interventions? In what ways might their decision whether to get involved depend on the particular conflict?

2. Of the stakeholders in Activity 2, which would be easier/more difficult to engage with? What might be the benefits and dangers of engaging with each group? What additional considerations might companies take into account if considering engaging with armed groups?

3. Of the types of engagement discussed today, which are probably more difficult? How beneficial will each type of intervention be over the long term for both the company and the region's people?

Seminar 2: Applying the 14-intervention CPM framework

In this seminar, you will identify and discuss interventions from the 14-intervention CPM framework by means of examples. You will learn about corporate involvement in peacemaking in South Africa; and you will reflect on and critically discuss key aspects of corporate involvement in peacemaking.

It is recommended that you read the detailed explanation of the 14-intervention CPM framework in this chapter in preparation for this seminar.

Activity 1

Complete column 3 of the table below with ideas learned from the previous seminar and/or your own thoughts:

When operating in conflict-prone areas, companies can:	• do nothing	What are the risks and the benefits?
	• get involved in structural peacebuilding	Give a real or hypothetical example.
	• help with peacemaking	Give an example; what are the risks and benefits?

Activity 2

Before you read a case study on South Africa, what do you already know about the conflict and peace process in that country?

Discuss in small groups:

1. From 1948 to 1994, the South African political system was known as **apartheid**. What does this mean and why did many people object to it?

2. Have you heard of the following: P.W. Botha, F.W. de Klerk, Archbishop Desmond Tutu, Nelson Mandela, the ANC (African National Congress)? What do you know about them?

3. Some governments, businesses and individuals used **divestment** and **sanctions** to protest the South African political system? What do these involve and how do you think they affected South African businesses and international corporations with interests in South Africa?

4. What was the final outcome of this situation?

Activity 3

Read the case study below, which provides background information on the South Africa situation:

1. What information can you add to your previous discussion about South Africa's recent history; and

2. What was the CBM (Consultative Business Movement) and why was it formed?

Case study: Consultative Business Movement, South Africa

Apartheid, or racial segregation, in South Africa was enforced by the ruling party, the NP (National Party) between 1948 and 1994. The majority black population had few rights and Afrikaner minority rule was maintained. Apartheid led to resistance, violence and the killing of many black protesters. International protests and trade sanctions were established against South Africa, reducing investment and growth and forcing many TNCs to divest. In 1990, the NP President de Klerk agreed to negotiations. These led to democratic elections in 1994, the end of apartheid and the election of the ANC (African National Congress) with Nelson Mandela as leader.

In 1988, a group of businesspeople faced great danger when bringing together representatives of some domestic and international businesses in South Africa to form the CBM (Consultative Business Movement). The CBM was a non-party-political movement, led mostly by representatives of domestic businesses. Its objectives were peace, democracy, economic growth and the end of international sanctions. Many of the businesses realised they needed to participate in the peace processes to encourage negotiations, and to meet all political parties to ensure an inclusive peace process and the outcome of a business-friendly economy (Fourié 2006; CBM 1997, n.d; Ramwell 1993). As CBM members, TNCs supported peacemaking through their membership, roles on the CBM 'board', or actively participating in the CBM's peacemaking interventions. TNCs included Anderson Consulting, Arthur Andersen & Associates, Anglo American, Cadbury, Ernst & Young, Kellogg's, Siemens, Toyota, BP, Caltex Oil, Shell and Unilever (personal conversation with T. Eloff, former Executive Director, CBM, 28 August 2008; personal conversation with G. Hutchings, Director (Memberships), National Business Initiative, formerly CBM, 3 July 2008; CBM 1994, 1997).

Activity 4

Strategies used to engage stakeholders in conflict situations with the aim of bringing about peace can be called **interventions**. Before you complete the next activity, shut your book and, with a partner, try to guess some of the interventions which the CBM might have used, and not used, in this situation.

Activity 5

Table 1 is a list of the actual interventions used by the CBM in South Africa. Using the 14-intervention CPM framework described earlier in this chapter, identify which of the framework's interventions is illustrated in each point, and write in the relevant name and number. An example is done for you.

Table 1: CBM interventions in the South Africa peace process.

The CBM ...	Name(s) and number(s) of intervention(s) from the CPM framework illustrated here:
• Worked with the South African Council of Churches and Chamber of Business, unions, political parties, women's groups and NGOs to build pressure for talks	Intervention 1: Corporate collective action
• Took a non-partisan, inclusive approach, holding hundreds of meetings to meet separately the various groups that could help create peace	
• Maintained communication flows between the conflict's political parties, particularly when the negotiations stalled, to ensure the negotiations could continue	
• Organised regional and national forums addressing economic and development issues, providing advice throughout, and building consensus on solutions that could be fed into the national (top-level) negotiations	
• Supported the establishment of local dispute resolution committees, run by community leaders to mediate in local incidences of the violence	
• Helped to create regional dispute resolution committees, which mediated conflicts at the regional level, preventing violence from spreading and derailing top-level, constitutional negotiations	
• Donated financial resources	
• At least one TNC representative took a leadership role in a regional dispute resolution committee	
• Provided process and administrative support for the national negotiations negotiations between the top political leaders of the conflict parties	
• Actively participated in national negotiations: for example, John Hall, a CBM member and domestic businessman, was co-chair in initial peace talks alongside Archbishop Desmond Tutu	
• Observed the national negotiation process, identifying any stumbling blocks that could stall the process, and encouraged the parties to reach an agreement	

Source: Fourié 2006; Collin Marks 2001; Eloff 1999; CBM 1993, 1994, 1997; Chapman and Hofmeyr 1994; Ramwell 1993).

Activity 6

Return to your speculations on possible CBM interventions in Activity 4. How accurate were your guesses as to the strategies used?

Activity 7

To consolidate and reflect on what you have learned so far, jot down some thoughts on the following questions, and then debate them in small groups or in a whole-class setting:

1. Based on what you have learned so far, do you think companies should get involved in conflict mediation? Why/why not?

2. What key skills and knowledge might companies have that could help bring about a successful outcome (e.g. conflict resolution, facilitation, local knowledge, etc)?

3. In what situations should company representatives simply enable others to mediate, and in what situations might they take direct part in mediations?

4. How might companies approach mediation at grass-roots level differently from mediation at top levels?

5. Besides mediation, what else can company representatives do to support peace negotiations?

Seminar 3: Role-play—companies and stakeholders in Colombia

In this seminar, you will critically apply relevant interventions from the 14-intervention CPM framework to a conflict scenario. You will role-play a meeting between international companies, and create a proposal for corporate support of peacemaking.

Before you commence this seminar, you may find it useful to read and make notes on the Colombia case study earlier in this chapter.

Activity 1: Refresher quiz

Quiz a classmate on what you have learned about CPM so far. You can use the following questions as a guide, or make up your own:

1. What are the main differences between structural peacebuilding and peacemaking?

2. Name at least one company that has been involved in CPM and the region in which it has done this.

3. How many interventions from the 14-intervention CPM framework can you remember without looking at your book/notes?

4. What are the main reasons companies might get involved in CPM?

5. What are the main dangers for companies getting involved in CPM?

Activity 2

Research on Colombia. Later, you will role-play a discussion between companies operating in Colombia, about possible CPM interventions. To prepare for this, first read the case study on Colombia earlier in this chapter. Make notes on:

1. The background to the conflict (first paragraph of the case study)

2. Key details of the interventions which have been applied (remaining paragraphs).

Alternatively, if you have pre-read the case study before the seminar, take a few minutes now to refresh your memory by reading your notes and comparing them with a classmate's. Can your partner help add or clarify any points in your notes?

Activity 3: Role-play

A group of TNCs operating in Colombia has decided to work together to help promote peace in the country. Senior representatives from each TNC involved will meet and present their ideas to each other. Complete the steps below to prepare for, and carry out, the presentation, and engage in follow-up discussion.

Activity 3a: Work in groups. First, choose one of the companies below. Read the paragraph provided to learn about your company's activities in Colombia. (Alternatively, you may choose to act as another international company, representing a different sector such as the mining or oil industries, but the company must be one that exists in real life and operates or could potentially operate in Colombia.)

Nestlé

Nestlé is a Swiss food and beverage TNC providing products like baby foods, cereals, water and coffee. Nestlé states it creates shared value for society by helping consumers make the right nutritional choices, addressing a 'crisis' in fresh water globally, rural development, environmental protection, sourcing raw materials responsibly and respecting human rights in operations and supply chains (Nestlé 2013a). In Colombia, Nestlé purchases milk and coffee, for instance, from rural communities. The company works with around 4,000 dairy farmers and 10,000 people in the milk supply chain as milkers, rural workers, transporters and traders (Nestlé 2013b). It works with around 44,000 Colombian coffee farmers participating in a programme for sustainable coffee practices (Nestlé 2012).

Microsoft

Headquartered in the US, Microsoft develops and supports computer products and services such as Windows, Microsoft Office, Xbox and Skype. In Colombia, it is based in the capital, Bogotá. Microsoft states it acts as a good 'corporate citizen' by empowering youth, donating software to non-profit organisations, and providing technology to keep information flowing during humanitarian crises. It works responsibly by supporting environmental sustainability and human rights (Microsoft 2013a). Microsoft collaborated with the Colombian government and the Arhuaco indigenous people, who live in remote northern Colombia. Using a cloud-based solution and technologies based on customer relationship management, the Arhuaco can maintain their culture and environment by maintaining records of their people, lands and sacred places (Microsoft 2013b).

Coca-Cola

Headquartered in the US, Coca-Cola is a beverage company with over 500 brands. The company claims to support sustainability and social value by promoting wellbeing and responsible marketing (such as offering low- or no-calorie beverages, and transparent nutrition information); building stronger communities (for example, promoting women's economic empowerment, charitable contributions, and human and workplace rights); and protecting the environment (such as through climate protection and sustainable agriculture). In Colombia, Coca-Cola states it supports programmes that help children and education, and provide relief for the conflict's victims. It has funded the Colombian Foundation for Education and Opportunity to support victims of violence. Coca-Cola bottlers employ over 2,000 Colombians, distribute products to 500,000 retailers, and provide jobs through sales, marketing and shipping (Coca-Cola 2013a: 11, 2013b).

Activity 3b: Identifying key stakeholders. The table below lists some key stakeholders in the Colombia situation. Discuss and prioritise which of these stakeholders your company will engage with in your peacemaking endeavours.

1. What are their interests and influence in the conflict?

2. How might your company affect them and vice versa?

3. How might you prioritise their claims on your company's attention?

4. Which stakeholders should you definitely *not* ignore and why?

Possible key stakeholders mentioned in the case study	Other stakeholders to consider
FIP, IBLF, UN Global Compact and its Colombian local network	Local communities; local government; police; religious, human rights, environmental and labour groups; Colombian or international peace-focused NGOs; media; academia; Colombian government and other political parties; Colombian irregular armed groups; Colombian national and small businesses; other state governments and their embassies in Colombia

Activity 3c: Your group represents senior management at the Colombian headquarters of your chosen company. You have decided to work with other TNCs operating in the country to help make peace in Colombia. You are preparing a presentation for a meeting with these companies. Write a proposal in bullet points and prepare to present your proposal to representatives of these other TNCs. Include the following information:

1. Who are the key stakeholders where your company is concerned?

2. What interventions from the 14-intervention CPM framework will you use with each stakeholder (including ones which could bring your stakeholders together for peacemaking)?

3. How will you employ your chosen interventions?

4. Who in your company will carry out this work?

5. What expertise already exists in your company to carry out this work and what additional skills/training will be needed?

Activity 3d: Meet the representatives of the other companies and present your solutions to each other.

Activity 3e: Based on your group's proposal and the proposals of the other groups, discuss all together if it is possible for your companies to co-operate and form collective action to foster peace in Colombia.

Additional teaching material and ideas

Research report on Syria and corporate peacemaking

Research the recent conflict in Syria, either in groups or individually. You must identify the major conflict parties, their goals and interests, and any other stakeholders in the conflict that could affect a peace process. Choose an international company that is invested in Syria (or develop a hypothetical company). Then, identify your company's main stakeholders within Syria and internationally, and describe how your company might apply three or more interventions from the CPM framework, showing which stakeholders might be involved and how. You can either present the results of your research in a later seminar or write a report.

Films: *End Game* and *Blood Diamond*

1. Watch the film *Endgame* (Daybreak Pictures, 2009, www.youtube. com/watch?v=AlvJcaOplTs or www.imdb.com/title/tt1217616/). Can you identify aspects of corporate peacemaking in the film?

2. Watch the film *Blood Diamond* (Warner Bros, 2006, www.youtube. com/watch?v=OWi-WvBq6FU or www.imdb.com/title/tt0450259/). Identify the negative effects for a country of:
   a. having resources like diamonds; and
   b. corporate involvement in extracting or selling these resources.

3. Speculate as to how effective a structural peacebuilding initiative such as the Kimberley Process (www.kimberleyprocess.com) will be. The Kimberley Process introduced an international certification system for monitoring where rough diamonds originate from. This aims to stop the sale of diamonds from conflict-prone areas that are exploited by rebel groups and corrupt government officials, and sold via corporations to the public.

Richard Branson and The Elders

Research the work of The Elders, created partly by Richard Branson, and supported by Virgin Unite, the Virgin Group's non-profit foundation.

Much of The Elders' work aims to catalyse peace negotiations in countries. Watch the following videos:

- Richard Branson and Peter Gabriel share their thoughts on the founding of The Elders, www.youtube.com/watch?v=3HT90uVIIv0

- *What Is The Elders?*, www.theelders.org/about

See also the Virgin Unite website (www.virgin.com/unite) and especially *The Elders visit Washington and London* (www.virgin.com/unite/leadership-and-advocacy/elders-visit-washington-and-london).

Question: The Elders was created partly by Branson, an international business leader. What could other business leaders do to support peacemaking worldwide?

Your own corporate peacemaker

As a class, create your own hypothetical international company. Identify its name, sector, products/services, etc. Among its markets, your company operates in a country that suffers violent conflict sporadically between two groups. Divide the classroom into seven areas entitled:

- Products/services

- Marketing and advertising

- Political and external affairs

- Environmental initiatives

- Staff involvement

- Supply chain

- Global initiatives and relations

Individually, using sticky notes or flip-chart paper, write down your ideas for how your company could support peace in the country through each of these seven areas. Be as creative as you can! Then you can either:

- as a class, discuss the different ideas suggested; or

- individually, identify which idea is the best in each category (you could draw a star by the idea); as a class, bring together the best ideas (one from each category) and discuss how your company would draw the ideas together as a coherent strategy for the company.

The economy, trade relations and peace

How does assisting economic development and increased trade relations between disputing communities (structural peacebuilding) support peace? How can companies, both domestic and international, support peace in this way? Answer these questions, by researching one of the following initiatives:

- In Cyprus, the 'Economic Interdependence Project', implemented by the Peace Economics Consortium, fosters trade links between the divided Greek Cypriot and Turkish Cypriot communities, with the long-term potential goal of a unified Cyprus (see Peace Economics Consortium 2011).

- The Palestine International Business Forum (PIBF) is a Swedish business initiative, bringing together Palestinian, Israeli and Swedish businesspeople to counter the effects of the Israeli-Palestinian conflict and build Palestine's economic development (see www. pibf.net).

The Millennium Development Goals

By 2015, the eight MDGs (Millennium Development Goals) aim to meet targets including establishing universal primary education and halving extreme poverty. The MDGs have received substantial support from companies, countries and development organisations (UN 2014). Internationally, discussions have been held regarding what the new goals might look like post-2015. There is already support from some business circles for the inclusion of the goal of peace and stability (UN Global Compact 2013b). For businesses supporting the MDGs, this may mean their direct link to supporting peace.

Discussion: For companies supporting the MDGs post-2015, what might this mean if peace is included as a major goal? What might be the facilitators/obstacles to business support of this goal?

Institute for Economics and Peace teaching materials

The Institute for Economics and Peace (http://economicsandpeace.
org/education/tertiary) provides free education materials, including on
'Peace and Sustainability' and 'Peace and Economics' (focusing on tour-
ism and retail industries). You can also download modules which give
an innovative approach to peace and business issues.

Self-study activity

Identify a company that is/was involved with structural peacebuilding
or peacemaking in an area of violent conflict. What are/were the company's main strategies (interventions) and what have been the effects of
those strategies (so far)?

Further reading

Andersson, J.J., T. Evers and G. Sjöstedt (2011) *Private Sector Actors and Peacebuilding: A Framework for Analysis* (Stockholm, Sweden: International Council of Swedish Industry and The Swedish Institute of International Affairs).
   This resource gives a framework for examining the role of business actors in
   building peace, and case studies demonstrating the impact of some businesses.
   While there is a strong focus on structural peacebuilding (particularly economic roles), there is also innovative analysis of such CPM activities as 'dialogue', 'implementation of peace agreements' and 'reconciliation'.

Banfield, J., C. Gündüz and N. Killick (2006) *Local Business, Local Peace: The
Peacebuilding Potential of the Domestic Private Sector* (London: International
Alert).
   This book provides excellent research, case studies and practical approaches
   for domestic (local) business to understand and partake in both peacemaking
   and structural peacebuilding in conflict-prone areas. It is also useful for identifying potential peacemaking activities that could be undertaken by TNCs and
   ways TNCs could link with domestic businesses for peacemaking.

Fort, T., and C.A. Schipani (2004) *The Role of Business in Fostering Peaceful Societies* (Cambridge, UK: Cambridge University Press).
   Fort and Schipani outline how responsible business practices can foster peace.
   They discuss companies supporting 'Track Two Diplomacy', economic development, corporate social responsibility and external evaluation principles,

transparency and the rule of law, and a sense of community in the company and communities in which they operate.

Nelson, J. (2000) *The Business of Peace: The Private Sector as a Partner in Conflict Prevention and Resolution* (London: International Alert, Council on Economic Priorities and The Prince of Wales Business Leaders Forum).
Jane Nelson's ground-breaking work gives a solid overview of the key issues relevant to corporate involvement in peace efforts. Nelson discusses how a specific intervention by business is determined by a range of factors. These include the causes, stage and location of a conflict; the role, power and capacity of, and relationships among, the actors involved; and the type of industry, size, history and ownership of a company.

Sweetman, D. (2009) *Business, Conflict Resolution and Peacebuilding: Contributions from the Private Sector to Address Violent Conflict* (Oxford, UK: Routledge).
Derek Sweetman explores 'business-based peacebuilding', providing solid analysis and case studies on both domestic and international business, multiple industries, inter-state and intra-state conflict and both structural peacebuilding and peacemaking (although with less emphasis on the latter).

References

Andersson, J.J., T. Evers and G. Sjöstedt (2011) *Private Sector Actors and Peacebuilding: A Framework for Analysis* (Stockholm, Sweden: International Council of Swedish Industry and The Swedish Institute of International Affairs).

Arnson, C.J., and T. Whitfield (2005) 'Third Parties and Intractable Conflicts: The Case of Colombia', in C.A. Crocker, F.O. Hampson and P. Aall (eds.), *Grasping the Nettle: Analysing Cases of Intractable Conflict* (Washington, DC: US Institute of Peace Press): 231-68.

Banfield, J., C. Gündüz and N. Killick (2006) *Local Business, Local Peace: The Peacebuilding Potential of the Domestic Private Sector* (London: International Alert).

Bardouille-Crema, D. (2011) 'Business and Armed Non-state Actors', International Network for Economics and Conflict, 30 September 2011, http://inec.usip.org/blog/2011/sep/30/business-and-armed-non-state-actors-conflict-zones, accessed 10 February 2014.

Braithwaite, J., V. Braithwaite, M. Cookson and L. Dunn (2010) *Anomie and Violence* (Canberra, Australia: Australian National University EPress).

Business & Human Rights Resource Centre (2014a) *Business, Conflict & Peace Portal*, www.business-humanrights.org/ConflictPeacePortal/Home, accessed 10 February 2014.

—— (2014b) *UN 'Protect, Respect and Remedy' Framework*, www.business-humanrights.org/SpecialRepPortal/Home/Protect-Respect-Remedy-Framework/GuidingPrinciples, accessed 10 February 2014.

CBM (Consultative Business Movement) (1993) *Managing Change: A Guide to the Role of Business in Transition* (Johannesburg, South Africa: CBM).

—— (1994) *Information Update 15* (Johannesburg, South Africa: CBM).

—— (1997) *Submission to the Truth and Reconciliation Commission 1988–1994* (Johannesburg, South Africa: CBM).

—— (n.d.) *Consultative Business Movement* brochure (Johannesburg, South Africa: CBM).

Chapman, T.N., and M.B. Hofmeyr (1994) *Address Delivered on the Occasion of the Consultative Business Movement Receiving the Harvard Business Statesman of the Year Award* (Johannesburg, South Africa: Harvard Business School Club of South Africa).

Christie, D., and M. Wessells (2008) 'Social Psychology of Violence', in L. Kurtz (ed.), *Encyclopaedia of Violence, Peace, & Conflict* (Oxford, UK: Elsevier): 1955-63.

Coca-Cola (2013a) *Coca-Cola 2012/2013 GRI Report*, http://assets.coca-colacompany.com/44/d4/e4eb8b6f4682804bdf6ba2ca89b8/2012-2013-gri-report.pdf, accessed 30 May 2014.

—— (2013b) *The Facts: Coca-Cola Company and Colombia*, www.coca-cola-company.com/press-center/company-statements/the-facts-the-coca-cola-company-and-colombia, accessed 10 February 2014.

Collin Marks, S. (2001) *Watching the Wind: Conflict Resolution During South Africa's Transition to Democracy* (Washington, DC: US Institute of Peace).

Conflict Sensitivity Consortium (2014) *Welcome to the Conflict Sensitivity website*, www.conflictsensitivity.org, accessed 10 February 2014.

Crane, A., D. Matten and L.J. Spence (eds.) (2013) *Corporate Social Responsibility: Readings and Cases in a Global Context*, 2nd edn (London: Routledge).

DFAT (Australian Department of Foreign Affairs and Trade) (2013) *Colombia Country Brief*, www.dfat.gov.au/geo/colombia/colombia_brief.html, accessed 10 February 2014.

Donaldson, T., and L.E. Preston (1995) 'The Stakeholder Theory of the Corporation: Concepts, Evidence, and Implications', *Academy of Management Review* 20.1: 65-91.

Economist, The (2013) 'To The Edge and Back Again', *The Economist*, 31 August 2013, www.economist.com/news/

americas/21584384-hiccup-serves-confirm-government-and-farc-are-making-progress-edge-and, accessed 10 February 2014).

Elders, The (2014) *What is the Elders?*, http://theelders.org/about, accessed 10 February 2014.

Eloff, T. (1999) 'South African Business and the Transition to Peace and Democracy: From Honest Broker to Constructive Partner', in European Centre for Conflict Prevention & Global Partnership for the Prevention of Armed Conflict (ECCP and GPPAC), *People Building Peace* (The Hague, The Netherlands: ECCP and GPPAC).

Feil, M. *et al.* (2008) 'Bad Guys, Good Guys, or Something in Between?', *PRIF Reports* 84, www.hsfk.de/fileadmin/downloads/prif84.pdf, accessed 10 February 2014.

Fifka, M.S. (2012) 'The Impact of Socioeconomic and Political Factors on Stakeholder Dialog', in A. Lindgreen *et al.* (eds.), *A Stakeholder Approach to Corporate Social Responsibility: Pressures, Conflicts, and Reconciliation* (Burlington, VT: Gower): 5-24.

FIP (Ideas for Peace Foundation) (2005) *Ending the Internal Conflict in Colombia: A Peacebuilding Agenda* (Bogotá, Colombia: FIP).

Fort, T., and C.A. Schipani (2004) *The Role of Business in Fostering Peaceful Societies* (Cambridge, UK: Cambridge University Press).

Fourié, A. (2006) *A Brief Overview on the Role of the Business Sector During the South African Political Transition and Beyond*, presentation to The Aspen Institute Middle East Strategy Group, Washington, DC by the National Business Initiative, South Africa.

Freeman, R.E. (2010) *Strategic Management: A Stakeholder Approach* (Cambridge, UK: Cambridge University Press).

Friedman, M. (1962) *Capitalism and Freedom* (Chicago, IL: University of Chicago Press).

Guáqueta, A. (2006) 'Doing Business Amidst Conflict: Emerging Best Practices in Colombia', in J. Banfield, C. Gündüz and N. Killick (eds.), *Local Business, Local Peace: The Peacebuilding Potential of the Domestic Private Sector* (London: International Alert).

Hallam, M. (2013) 'Colombian Peace Talks Reopen in Cuba', *DW*, 3 October 2013, www.dw.de/colombian-peace-talks-reopen-in-cuba/a-17134517, accessed 10 February 2014.

Haufler, V. (2001) 'Is There a Role for Business in Conflict Management?', in C. Crocker, F. Hampson and P. Aall (eds.), *Turbulent Peace* (Washington, DC: US Institute of Peace Press): 659-75.

Hitchcock, D., and M. Willard (2009) *The Business Guide to Sustainability Practical Strategies and Tools for Organisations* (Oxon, UK: Earthscan).

IBLF (International Business Leaders Forum) (2007) *Dialogue on Business, Peace, Development and Human Rights in Colombia*, www.eldis.org/go/home&id=24725&type=Document#.UviIH7RtU8W, accessed 10 February 2014.

Iff, A., D. Sguaitamatti, R.M. Alluri and D. Kohler (2010) *Money Makers as Peace Makers? Business Actors in Mediation Processes*, Working Paper 2 (Bern, Switzerland: Swisspeace).

International Alert (2005) *Conflict-sensitive Business Practice: Guidance for Extractive Industries* (London: International Alert).

Killick, N. (2000) 'Adaption of Lederach's Triangle: A Role for People in Business', in J. Nelson, *The Business of Peace: The Private Sector as a Partner in Conflict Prevention and Resolution* (London: International Alert, Council on Economic Priorities and Prince of Wales Business Leaders Forum): 55.

Lederach, J.P. (1997) *Building Peace: Sustainable Reconciliation in Divided Societies* (Washington, DC: US Institute of Peace Press).

Microsoft (2013a) *Citizenship Report*, www.microsoft.com/about/corporatecitizenship/en-us/reporting/, accessed 31 May 2014.

—— (2013b) 'Microsoft Collaboration Preserves Biodiversity and Culture in Colombia', The Fire Hose Blog, http://blogs.technet.com/b/firehose/archive/2013/07/01/microsoft-collaborates-with-colombian-government-and-indigenous-people-to-preserve-biodiversity-and-culture, accessed 10 February 2014.

Mitchell, R.K., B.R. Agle and D.J. Wood (1997) 'Toward a Theory of Stakeholder Identification and Salience: Defining the Principle of Who and What Really Counts', *Academy of Management Review* 22.4: 853-86.

Nelson, J. (2000) *The Business of Peace: The Private Sector as a Partner in Conflict Prevention and Resolution* (London: International Alert, Council on Economic Priorities and The Prince of Wales Business Leaders Forum).

Nestlé (2012) *Nestle in Society*, www.nestle.com/asset-library/documents/library/documents/corporate_social_responsibility/nestle-csv-full-report-2012-en.pdf, accessed 10 February 2014.

—— (2013a) *Nestlé in Society: Creating Shared Value*, www.nestle.com/csv, accessed 10 February 2014.

—— (2013b) *Working with Dairy Farmers*, www.nestle.com/brands/dairy/dairycsv, accessed 10 February 2014.

Peace Economics Consortium (2011) *Economic Interdependence in Cyprus Current Assessment and Prospects for the Future*, report for the Economic Interdependence Project, Cyprus, www.transconflict.com/10/wp-content/uploads/2012/06/Cyprus_EconomicInterdependence.pdf, accessed 10 February 2014.

Phillips, R., R.E. Freeman and A.C. Wicks (2003) 'What Stakeholder Theory Is Not', *Business Ethics Quarterly* 13.4: 479-502.

Ralph, N. (2012) 'Corporate Social Responsibility: Applying Contact Theory and Mediation', in D.J. Christie (ed.), *Encyclopaedia of Peace Psychology* (New York: Wiley-Blackwell Publishers).

—— (forthcoming) *Transnational Corporations and Corporate Peacemaking* (Sheffield, UK: Greenleaf Publishing).

Ralph, N., and M. Conley-Tyler (2006) 'Companies as Peacebuilders: Engaging Communities Through Conflict Resolution', *University of Melbourne Legal Studies Research Paper* 196, http://papers.ssrn.com/sol3/displayabstractsearch.cfm, accessed 10 February 2014.

Ramwell, S. (1993) 'The Role of Business in Transition: A Supplement to The Star', *The Star* (South Africa), 17 June 1993.

Rettberg, A. (2007) 'The Private Sector and Peace in El Salvador, Guatemala, and Colombia', *Journal of Latin American Studies* 39.3: 463-94.

—— (n.d.) *Business Led Peacebuilding in Colombia: Fad or Future of a Country in Crisis?* (London: Crisis States Programme, Development Research Centre, London School of Economics and Political Science).

Rodrigues, M.V. (2007) 'Practical Nationalism and Global Duties of Justice', *South African Journal of Philosophy* 26.2: 176-89.

Ross, M.L. (2012) *The Oil Curse: How Petroleum Wealth Shapes the Development of Nations* (Princeton, NJ: Princeton University Press).

Shankleman, J. (2007) *Oil, Profits, and Peace: Does Business Have a Role in Peacemaking?* (Washington, DC: US Institute of Peace Press).

Swanson, P. (2002) *Fuelling Conflict: The Oil Industry and Armed Conflict*, Fafo-Report 378 (Oslo, Norway: FAFO Institute).

Sweetman, D. (2009) *Business, Conflict Resolution and Peacebuilding: Contributions from the Private Sector to Address Violent Conflict* (Oxford, UK: Routledge).

Tripathi, S., and C. Gündüz (2008) *A Role for the Private Sector in Peace Processes? Examples and Implications for Third-party Mediation* (Oslo, Norway: OSLO Forum Network of Mediators).

UN (2014) *Millennium Development Goals and Beyond 2015*, www.un.org/millenniumgoals/, accessed 10 February 2014.

UN Global Compact (2010) *Doing Business While Advancing Peace and Development*, www.unglobalcompact.org/docs/issues_doc/Peace_and_Business/DBWAPD_2010.pdf, accessed 10 February 2014.

—— (2013a) 'Business for Peace Kicks Off Local Network Event Series in Colombia', 30 October 2013, www.unglobalcompact.org/news/591-10-30-2013, accessed 10 February 2014.

—— (2013b) *Corporate Sustainability and the United Nations Post-2015 Development Agenda, Report to the UN Secretary-General*, www.unglobalcompact.org/docs/news_events/9.1_news_archives/2013_06_18/UNGC_Post2015_Report.pdf, accessed 30 May 2014.

—— (2014) *Business for Peace Participants List*, www.unglobalcompact.org/docs/issues_doc/Peace_and_Business/Business_for_Peace_Participants.pdf, accessed 10 February 2014.

Vines, A. (1998) 'The Business of Peace: "Tiny" Rowland, Financial Incentives and the Mozambican Settlement', in A. Vines and D. Hendrickson (eds.), *ACCORD 3: The Mozambican Peace Process in Perspective* (London: Conciliation Resources): 66-74.

Wenger, A., and D. Möckli (2003) *Conflict Prevention: The Untapped Potential of the Business Sector* (Boulder, CO: Lynne Rienner).

BRINGING IT ALL
TOGETHER

14

Systems thinking and sustainable management

Néstor Valero-Silva

This chapter will illustrate how systems thinking can contribute to understanding, communicating and addressing sustainability issues in management. It will also familiarise you with the main concepts used in systems thinking which might facilitate further research.

The learning outcomes of this chapter are to:

- Introduce the notion of systems (holistic) thinking in relation to other ways of thinking such as reductionism

- Lead to an understanding of the notion of system as a creation of the observer, i.e. as a personal and social construct rather than an as objective entity that exists 'out there' and yet to be discovered

- Introduce the main types of diagram commonly used in systems thinking and practice

- Appreciate how diagrams (including system diagrams) could contribute to thinking and acting in relation to managerial problems that have a dimension of sustainability

- Introduce the notion of 'long-lasting products' as a particular application of systems thinking in management

Introduction

Systems thinking challenged the long-held view that humans were intrinsically superior to other biological entities and were thus the 'masters' of nature. It also contributed to discrediting the assumption that the planet's natural resources were unlimited. Furthermore, it has been at the centre of recent attempts to understand and express the interconnectedness that exists between the natural and the social worlds (Meadows *et al.* 2006). In this sense, systems thinking has helped contemporary societies to improve their appreciation of the complex web of interactions between nature and human activities—and between different social groups. These include: the forecast of weather patterns and their impact on communities; the impact of deforestation on animals and air quality; the evolution and extinction of species; the spread of viruses and disease; and helping governments design and implement meaningful policies in relation to the conservation of natural resources, including attempts to eradicate disease and alleviate poverty.

Other specific areas of application include: economic modelling (Lietaer *et al.* 2012); international development and politics; negotiation; public sector management (Seddon 2010; Trochim *et al.* 2006); science, industrialisation and ecology (Capra 1997; Carson 1962; BBC 2014); ethics and sustainability (Fisher *et al.* 2013); business management and operational research (Jackson 2000; Mingers and White 2010); and, more recently, the development of information systems (Checkland 2002) and of the computer games and Internet-based industries.

It would be impossible to find a simple definition of the concept of 'systems thinking' that would fully address all of these areas of application, although the achievement of a useful approximation might start by considering the relationship between systems thinking and reductionism.

Systems thinking and reductionism

Systems thinking focuses on 'totalities' (wholes) when trying to understand and address the challenges faced by every organisation—see, for example, Churchman (1968), Jackson (2000) and Senge (2006). Instead of trying to solve problems—and problematic situations—in isolation, it assumes them to be embedded in particular organisational structures, cultures and business environments. Furthermore, some of these challenges could even be the unintended consequences of previous organisational policies.

ACME, a company that operates in a very competitive and cost-cutting environment, decided to reduce its costs by outsourcing production to developing countries. This was perceived as a very good, 'tried and tested', textbook strategy. However, the decision had disastrous consequences for the company's reputation, sales and overall competitiveness, when it was reported that overseas workers were grossly underpaid and overworked, and that pristine natural environments were being polluted with industrial waste generated by the company's production. The situation was tackled as a 'public relations' issue, in isolation, with a glossy new marketing strategy that soon backfired when a worker committed suicide by jumping from the roof of the factory. The company then decided to frame the situation as a legal and HR problem that needed 'decisive action', announcing that the facility would be closed. A long strike by the workers and painful redundancy negotiations with the foreign government followed, in the full glare of the press. In response, the company then decided to hire some PR consultants to manage the negative press reports. An international boycott resulted, promoted by angry consumers using social media.

The above example highlights the need for ACME to use a systems approach towards addressing the company's competitiveness. This way of thinking, which is also often called **holistic** or **systemic** thinking (von Bertalanffy 1969), could have helped ACME to include all of its operations and its environment (including the communities in which it operates) as part of their decision-making process. In this sense, adapting the organisation to its environment is at the centre of the 'contingency' and 'organic' approaches to management (Morgan 2006). Perhaps ACME could have followed a more successful long-term strategy involving a mixture of investing in product design, staff training and dealing with distribution and waste problems, rather than opting for a single 'textbook' solution in isolation.

The Foxconn scandal in China that engulfed several Western technology companies in 2012 (*Economist* 2012), and also BP's initial response to the Deepwater Horizon oil spill in the Gulf of Mexico in 2010 (BBC 2010), provide further case studies for analysis.

Conversely, an approach that compartmentalises the complexity and allows managers to focus on certain sections of the organisation (e.g. production), including some immediate interactions (e.g. levels of pollution on the immediate natural environment), is sometimes useful. The type of approach that focuses on a 'slice' of the whole organisation (or problem) is called **reductionism**. The importance of reductionism cannot be underestimated, as it has been successfully used to increase productivity (Taylor 2013), and to solve engineering and scientific problems. Many solutions, especially in science and engineering, can be found by following very well-established problem-solving methods that must be rigorously followed, step by step, in a very orderly and **systematic** manner (Descartes 1989; Kuhn 2012).

Reductionism must be used with caution as, on the one hand, it promotes specialisation; however, on the other, it may reinforce a 'silo mentality'—a criticism that has been levelled against business education! It may also render complex problems down to simple 'cause and effect' mechanisms, as it focuses on very small aspects of the overall situation. Sometimes, steps such as researching the best technological solution, conducting a robust analysis of the competition, commissioning a glossy sustainability report from a consultant, or developing the most advanced product do not, in isolation, guarantee success if there has been a failure to consider other factors.

However, as managers are eager to find immediate answers to the challenges they face, it is sometimes very difficult for them to take a **systemic** approach to understanding where and how the chosen 'slice' fits within the overall picture. Instead, on many occasions, managers opt for a quick solution, moving on to the next important issue and hoping for the best long-term outcome; time pressures, the unavailability of data, information processing limitations and lack of experience could all hinder the success of a holistic approach.

At this point, it could reasonably be asked how managers can take decisions and design policies if they should, ideally, begin by considering every element and every relationship inside and outside their organisations, including the natural, social and business environments. In the search for 'the whole', where do you stop? Where do you draw the line?

Boundary

An important tool in facilitating a systemic (holistic) approach to organisational challenges involves the use of boundaries in order to encapsulate the most important elements and their interactions, thus separating them from others considered less pressing.

A boundary is a differentiating device, an **artificial construct** that is not fixed, obvious nor natural. Boundaries may be useful, and they certainly facilitate understanding, debate and purposeful action; nevertheless, they are, as products of human perception, arbitrary. In other words, boundaries reflect particular interests and social (**power**) relations (Cooper 1986, 1992; Morgan 2006). Consequently, different stakeholders will define different boundaries in relation to the same set of issues or problems. Boundaries also operate as control mechanisms that simultaneously highlight, include, discriminate and exclude. To **define** what the boundary aims to represent, perhaps in words, could be very useful when trying to explore its rationale. Finally, boundaries are endlessly created and transformed by individuals in organisations.

> A CEO decides to call a meeting to discuss a pressing problem. They must choose which manager to invite, the agenda for the meeting and what information is needed. This involves the creation of a mental boundary around the problem. If one of the participants cannot attend the meeting, the CEO must again make a decision as to whether the meeting should go ahead without this person, or if the meeting should be rescheduled. It could be that the meeting had been scheduled on that particular date in the full knowledge that some managers could *not* attend! The relative importance of the presence of a particular manager (including the information and experience they could bring) at this meeting depends on the CEO's mental boundary—which is, in turn, related to the CEO's interests and objectives.

Boundaries are sometimes perceived as 'closed' with little or no interaction with elements outside (e.g. when a boundary is drawn around the components of a small machine to understand how it works). However, in most managerial situations boundaries tend to be 'open', as the interactions between the inside and the outside are considered important (von Bertalanffy 1969). For example, changes in legislation, the competition, people joining and leaving the organisation, new information and the social and natural environments may all be contributing factors (Checkland 2000).

As we have illustrated, perhaps the most important challenge for a senior manager is to use an appropriate boundary that would help them and their organisation to understand and address the challenges they face. This is particularly critical as every middle manager, every department and every subsidiary has its own agendas and interests. Some of these interests, although entirely legitimate, could be at odds with each other; also, if followed without appropriate checks, they could damage the whole organisation, as recent banking and stock market scandals have demonstrated only too well.

Furthermore, the same senior manager may need to use different boundaries when considering such factors as: short- and long-term perspectives; local, regional or international issues; and marketing, financial, operational and human resources initiatives. Finally, appropriate boundaries are also important when a business professional is considering their own career and work–life balance from the short, medium and long-term perspectives.

The environment

As we said earlier, although boundaries are very useful (and necessary) human constructs that allow us to focus on certain elements and interactions and to differentiate these from what lies in the 'background', they also reflect particular interests and social (power) relations. Furthermore, assuming these interests and power relations were absent, as everything has an effect on everything else—as Lorenz's (1972) 'butterfly effect' metaphor beautifully illustrated—it could be argued that we could talk only about one 'whole': the universe!

In this context, some scientists and business leaders think that the most important boundary worth considering must be placed around the planet Earth. This is also known as the **Gaia theory** (Lovelock 1979; 2006); this theory assumes the planet to be a dynamic collection of living and non-living elements that continuously interact with each other. The Gaia theory highlights how the planet has a series of highly complex self-regulatory mechanisms that, within certain parameters, support life. The mechanisms, which include evolution and natural selection (organisms **co-evolve** with their environment), weather patterns, extinction patterns and changes in composition of the planet's water, air and land, are found at the centre of contemporary understandings of sustainability, ecology and science.

By locating the boundary around the planet, the Gaia theory demonstrates how human activity could destroy the planet's self-regulatory mechanisms, thus threatening the possibility of life. Examples include uncontrolled pollution, nuclear waste, global warming emissions, misuse of pesticides (Carson 1962). overuse of antibiotics, deforestation, overfishing and population growth (Fisher *et al.* 2013).

The main point to highlight is that these threats do not, in the main, come from isolated actions—although a potential nuclear accident could create irreparable damage. Instead, they could be directly linked to **routine activities** found in families, communities, charities, commercial organisations and even schools and universities. Each of these activities contributes, to a degree and on a different scale, to the same overall and dangerous outcome. The acknowledgement of such risk has particularly been highlighted by initiatives to reduce household and industrial waste and increase recycling levels, to improve packaging design and transport logistics, and to reduce consumerism and 'planned obsolescence' (London 1932). The notion of individual and organisational 'carbon footprint' could be considered as an expression of these ideas (Berners-Lee 2010).

Consequently, when **companies and individuals** choose to focus exclusively on the elements and interactions more closely linked to their operations (either **spatially** or **temporarily**), without properly considering their natural, business and social environment, the long-term survival of their organisations could be at risk. Examples include:

- Pharmaceutical companies aggressively promoting the indiscriminate use of antibiotics to increase sales in the short term (after spending billions on their development) then these become ineffective as bacteria develop resistance

- Poor farmers destroying their land through small-scale yet relentless deforestation from collecting wood for cooking

- Large fishing fleets routinely using 'bottom trawling' methods only to collect a particular species of fish, and destroying the environment it needs to reproduce.

- Multinationals facing enormous fines that threaten their survival due to the accumulation of small 'savings' on health-and-safety measures that later cause deadly chemical and nuclear accidents (BP's Deepwater Horizon in 2010; the Fukushima nuclear disaster in 2011).

- The promotion of an uncontrolled risk-taking culture (reinforced by the payment of generous short-term bonuses) that produces great financial returns in the short term, and large-scale bankruptcies in the long term (Barings Bank in 1995; Enron in 2001; Lehman Brothers in 2008)

Having considered the notions of boundaries and of the environment (which has social, business, natural and temporal dimensions), we can now explore the notion of 'system'.

The system

The word 'system' means different things to different people. People often use expressions such as political systems, religious systems, payment systems and information systems. Even criminals, compulsive gamblers and stock market risk-takers talk about 'having a system'. The modern idea of system was first presented by Churchman (1968) and von Bertalanffy (1969), and further developed and applied by several philosophers, scientists and writers such as Bradbury (2005), Capra (1982; 1997), Carson (1962) and Jackson (2000).

- Systems are **dynamic** mental constructs that behave as if they have some **purpose**. For example, when we talk about organisations as systems, we sometimes indicate that they are created to serve a particular money-making, social or charitable purpose; we could say that mission statements reflect, to some extent, the organisation's purpose. However, some organisations could have different purposes, as perceived by different stakeholders, or decide to change their overall purpose as they rebrand themselves.

A university can be understood as a system to provide education; a system that produces knowledge and original research; an entertainment and socialising system for young people; a system that provides employment to academics, administrators and support staff; or a system that provides income for local businesses, employment to residents and tax revenue to local government.

- A system has an **owner**; in other words, every system reflects the views of its creator(s). Systems make sense to someone or to a particular group of people. In the above example, we can easily see that perhaps the system owners were students and their sponsors are academics, HR managers and local businesses. Furthermore, multiple systems may have the same owner, as individuals and groups have multiple—and sometimes contradictory—interests.

The development of the High Speed Rail system (HS2) between London and the north of England may be seen as a system to move a large number of people from A to B in a cost-efficient and timely manner (train operator); a system that promotes economic growth, employment and taxes (the Treasury); a system that threatens the ecology, scars beautiful landscapes and pollutes the countryside with emissions/noise and concrete/steel (certain environmentalists and landowners); a system that will provide employment and lucrative contracts (civil engineers, builders and train manufacturers); a complete misuse of financial resources that could be used for health and education (people located in areas not covered by the planned service, and/or worried about the levels of government debt); and finally, a very inefficient way to improve the country's infrastructure when other options could be cheaper (motorway builders and car manufacturers).

- As human constructs, either individual or social, systems reflect the **ethical values** of their owner(s). To suggest that boundaries are mechanisms that include and highlight also implies that they simultaneously exclude and send into the background. As it is impossible to consider every single actual or potential factor, the selection process required cannot be taken lightly.

Is it necessary to consider natural resources such as the quality of air or the availability of natural landscapes in the system that guides planning and decision-making? Should managers consider future generations, beauty and happiness? Is it the organisation's responsibility to consider these issues, or someone else's? Is it useful to express the relationships between different issues solely/mainly in financial terms and, if so, for what purpose? Shall we ignore or exclude anything that cannot easily be expressed in financial terms, or shall we create 'convenient' financial proxies? Is it acceptable for an organisation to relate to its environment mainly in terms of threats and opportunities?

Which stakeholders shall I consider or consult in my decision-making process?

Are local workers more important than those in far-away countries? Shall we equate following the law with being ethical and responsible?

Shall I focus my department on short-term financial gains, increasing my annual bonus, rather than on stability and surplus in the long term, as I am planning to leave the company in a couple of years?

- A system is a group of **components** (including elements and relationships) linked **in an organised manner**.

The **interaction** between bricks, mortar, steel and other materials constitutes a particular building—not these elements by themselves, stored in a warehouse. Furthermore, the same elements may be used to construct an office building or a bridge, if organised differently.

Conversely, if the materials are not of a certain quality, or are not available in sufficient quantities, the construction could either not be completed or would collapse.

Many business organisations have the same functional areas, operate in similar buildings, and have a comparable workforce; however, it is the interaction between these elements that makes them unique to each organisation.

- The **components are affected** by being included in the system, and are changed if they leave it.

Taking a fish out of the sea, interrupting its interaction with the seawater and with other creatures that give it sustenance, would cause its death. A very successful manager could become less successful in a different organisational culture, and vice versa. A medication (e.g. a pill) that has been unsuccessful in medical trials for its intended purpose, or that has been superseded by newer medications, may become a big earner when used for a different purpose or in a different market. A life-saving medication for some individuals can constitute a poison for others.

- Systems exhibit **feedback** mechanisms (Ashby 1956; Beer 1985; Wiener 1948). This is to say, the information about the outcome of a process is fed back to the beginning of the process to reinforce its action, or to slow it down. Examples of **positive** feedback, which could spiral out of control and even threaten the entire system, include the **snowball effect** (i.e. the reinforcing/amplifying effect that creates a snow avalanche) and the **vicious/virtuous circle** (Senge 2006: 81).

The arms race between the West and the former Soviet Union; the use of credit cards and pay-day loans to cover daily expenses (or to cover previous loans) that suck people into greater debt; the process of global warming; the link between customer satisfaction and future sales; and addictive behaviours to shopping and consumerism, are particular examples of positive feedback mechanisms.

There are other feedback mechanisms that tend to control, or dampen down, the overall process. Examples of this **negative** feedback include:

The biological processes used by the human body to keep its temperature constant; the use of electronic thermostats to start/stop central heating systems, cooling fans, fridges and freezers; the increase in interest rates to reduce borrowing; policies to reduce complaints to a certain manageable level; and efforts to reduce carbon emissions to internationally agreed levels.

- Systems have **inputs** and **outputs** (involving transformation processes), and may also exhibit **emerging properties**. Most systems interact with their surrounding environment as energy, information, money, raw materials, products and waste are transformed and exchanged. People also move across organisational boundaries as they join and leave an organisation. Contractors and consultants belong to more than one organisational system. Finally, systems exhibit properties that cannot be explained by analysing individual components, **emerging** instead from their interaction. This is what is meant by the famous expression attributed to the Greek philosopher Aristotle: '**the whole is greater than the sum of its parts**'.

Life is one of the most interesting emerging properties on the planet, which cannot be explained by analysing the functioning of a single organ, or a few organs in isolation—even though not all organs are required to keep a body alive! Happiness is another emerging property that governments around the world are trying to understand, measure and include in their long-term planning and investment.

Motivation, satisfaction, leadership, loyalty, reputation, culture, work–life balance and sustainability are also emerging properties routinely used in business studies.

Diagrams

Diagrams constitute effective tools to help managers understand, frame and communicate organisational problems and issues (as you can see in the 'system diagram' in Fig. 1). In this sense, diagrams are often selected through personal preference, familiarity and previous training. For example, flowchart diagrams (see Fig. 5) are routinely used to explain how to operate household appliances, and usually accompany self-assembly furniture. Managers who originally trained in finance and engineering may prefer flowcharts, while those trained in social sciences may prefer rich pictures (Fig. 3). As it is very easy to find examples and explanations of modelling diagrams on the Internet and in books (e.g. Waring 2010), the following list is intended to provide a general framework to use as a basis for further research. Please note that sometimes these diagrams are simply classified within what is known as 'soft systems' (qualitative; exploring) and 'hard systems' (quantitative; prediction), e.g. Checkland (2000).

Figure 1: A system.

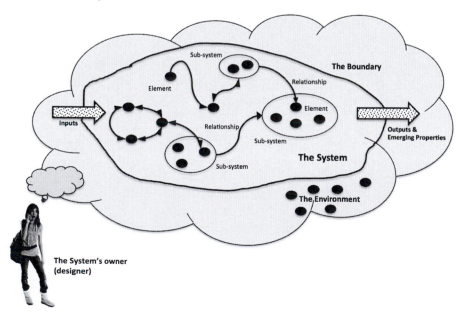

Figure 2: Spray diagram.

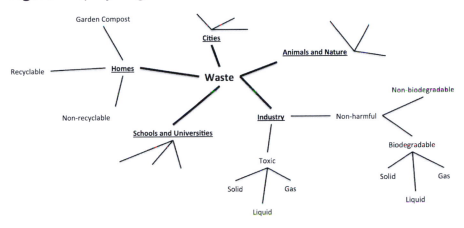

Figure 3: Rich picture.

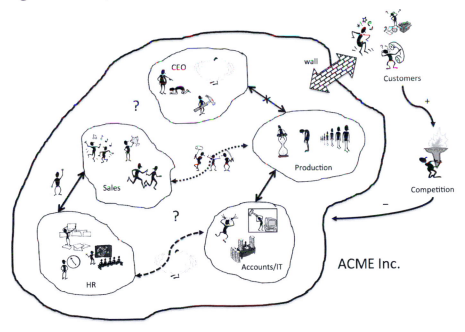

Diagrams for exploration, understanding, and brainstorming

Most of these diagrams begin at the centre of the sheet of paper and expand outwards. For example, Buzan's (2003) **spray diagram** (Fig. 2) expands from an initial element in a branch/tree manner; it is often used for note-taking as it can easily represent the structure of an argument. He also developed the **mind maps** used in brainstorming (Buzan 2003). **Fishbone diagrams** (Ishikawa 1956) are a variant commonly used in quality and lean management. There are several free and paid mind-mapping software applications available (e.g. FreeMind, WikkaWiki, iMindMap, Prezi).

Checkland (2000) developed **rich pictures** (Fig. 3), which are cartoon-like diagrams that show a great deal of information. They are excellent in addressing complex situations, as they can display numerical information (hard data), together with people's feelings and emotions (soft data). They also promote the sharing of opinions and perceptions in group activities where participants are asked to talk to each other and then to modify and enrich the diagram.

Diagrams that highlight connections

Such diagrams focus on the structure of the situation by highlighting connections between elements with circles and lines. Some show how certain elements influence others by including arrows, highlighting cause-and-effect and feedback processes. Examples include: **system, relationship, influence, casual-loop and 'organisational chart' diagrams**.

In terms of detailed analysis and quantitative model building, other diagrams go beyond showing just connectivity in order to include information such as whether an element influences positively or negatively another element (using plus and minus signs) as in **sign diagrams** (Fig. 4). Others focus on processes such as **input–output** (black-box) diagrams, while **decision sequence diagrams** and **flowcharts** (Fig. 5) are also used to give instructions, and in the early stages of computer games and engineering design.

Figure 4: Sign diagram.

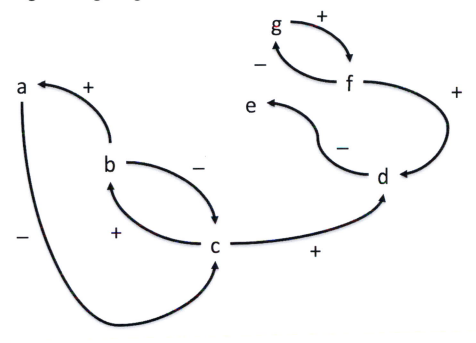

Figure 5: Flowchart.

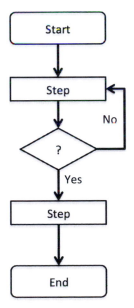

The future of systems thinking and management

Systems thinking has had a profound impact in the management sciences since the 1940s. During the Second World War, it was used to prevent U-boat attacks on the shipping of supplies and movement of troops from the US and Canada to the UK; to co-ordinate the logistic efforts involved in the movement of personnel, ammunition and supplies; and in the planning of both air defences and air raids. Immediately after the war, it played an important role in the post-war reconstruction of Europe and in Japan (Deming 1982; Ishikawa 1956), the development of welfare institutions such as the National Health System (UK), and in the socio-technical approaches pioneered by the UK's Tavistock Institute of Human Relations in the 1950s. Examples of Tavistock's approach include the study of technological change in mining companies in the UK (Trist and Bamforth 1951), and at Volvo in Sweden (Gyllenhammer 1977). The socio-technical approach aimed to reconcile human (individual/group) needs with technical efficiency. Systems thinking was also applied, although with different degrees of success, in the centralised economies of socialist and communist countries (Myant and Drahokoupil 2011).

Other important areas of application include the development of the total quality management, just-in-time and lean management movements (Deming 1982; Juran 1988; Ishikawa 1956). Management writers such as Beer (1985), Checkland (2000) and Jackson (2000) developed practical methodologies such as VSM (viable system model), SSM (soft systems methodology) and CST (critical systems thinking), respectively. Finally, Senge's (2006) *The Fifth Discipline* popularised systems ideas within an even wider audience.

More recently, these concepts have played a role in the development of Fairtrade and in the controversial 'carbon market mechanisms' (Fisher *et al.* 2013). Finally, it lies at core of current understandings regarding the impact on the environment of product design, packaging, transport, waste and consumption (Cooper 2010).

In this last area, and in relation to the notion of consumerism and **affluenza**, i.e. the compulsive acquisition of products and the discarding of still-functioning products in search of new models that offer the same or similar function, that systems thinking is at its most promising. It has became clear that any improvements in the manufacturing of 'greener' products would have no overall positive impact on the environment even if current levels of consumption were maintained. In fact, not only per capita consumption but also the number of consumers is continuously increasing worldwide. This is to say, 'green shopping/consumerism' and 'sustainable consumerism' are still consumerism! However, as the whole economic and social systems are dependent on current production levels, it is neither practical nor socially desirable to terminate all of the jobs and the economies built on the premise of unlimited growth and development.

Cooper (2010: 12) advocates instead a circular 'systems thinking' economic model, which:

> requires that the throughput of materials and energy be minimized by optimizing product longevity, reusing or reconditioning products and their components, and recycling—alongside other measures such as energy efficiency.

This economic model would be combined with the concept of 'slow consumption' (Cooper 2005):

> This approach is supported by increasing 'product lifespan', which involves improving production processes, creating skilled jobs in repair and maintenance work, consumer satisfaction, and second-hand markets. In sum, Cooper believes that the combination of 'longer life-spans' and 'slow consumption' (within a 'systems thinking' economic model) would provide an antidote to the notion of 'obsolescence' and should allow the economy to absorb lower levels of production (Fisher *et al.* 2013: 384).

Cooper's ideas provide an excellent example of the relevance of systems thinking in helping individuals, organisations and communities to understand, discuss, devise and implement new ways of living and of working that are 'sustainable' in the long term. In this sense, systemic thinking, with all its tools and diagrams, provides no definite answers; instead, it provides a starting point in the building of a more holistic and sustainable future.

Suggested Seminars

Seminar 1: Video on diagrams

The following Open University (Free Open Learning) video, *A Guide to Using Diagrams* (17:20 minutes duration), provides examples of various diagrams: www.youtube.com/watch?v=TQwA9krV8EA. The video will be presented in class.

The diagrams follow the analysis of a case study based on certain social and environmental issues (such as population growth and urbanisation) as experienced by the inhabitants of an island in the Mediterranean (0:00–2:30).

The video starts with a rich picture (at 2:33) produced by the island's inhabitants that is then translated into a spray diagram (at 6:30), a system diagram (at 9:45), an influence diagram (at 11:48) and a multiple-cause diagram (at 11:50).

You are asked to produce each of these diagrams following the examples provided in the chapter. Next, you can compare your results with those offered by the video. Please note that there is not a perfect diagram. You will be able to produce more complex diagrams with some practice. Finally, you could improve each diagram after watching the video.

This video can also be watched prior to attending the seminar, then played and discussed in class.

Seminar 2: Flowcharts

Flowcharts are some of the most commonly used diagrams in business and engineering. Their ability to convey information in a highly systematic manner and with very few elements makes flowcharts especially useful in explaining processes and to convey instructions. They are also frequently used in the design of websites embedded in the menu options offered to customers (usually in menus on the left-hand side of web pages), to design user manuals and to explain procedures. It is very easy to produce professional flowcharts as their building blocks are now included as 'autoshapes' in the drawing toolbars in Office-style software packages.

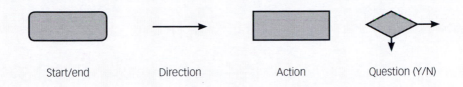

Start/end   Direction   Action   Question (Y/N)

Activity

Using the basic four elements above, select two processes from those listed below (including at least ten steps and five yes/no questions) and create a flowchart; do not forget to include **sustainable management** issues/considerations! Test your chart with the other members of a small group to see if it is clear. Select the best flowchart to present to class. This activity can also be completed during independent study and include doing some basic research on flowcharts and incorporating more types of elements (e.g. www.rff.com/flowchart_shapes.htm).

- Designing and implementing a policy to encourage employees to cycle to work

- Reducing the amount of printing at a university, including training, storage and IT support considerations

- Job hunting: from the initial decision to seek work to finding a permanent or temporary job

Seminar 3: Sales targets and their impact on corporate reputation—when does an incentive become a bribe?

The aim of this seminar is to illustrate the interaction between different elements and stakeholders in relation to a particular complex situation; highlight how porous organisational boundaries are; show the usefulness of the concept of emerging properties; reveal the unintended consequences of well-intended organisational policies (e.g. sales targets and bonuses); and discuss the 'usefulness' of the diagrams.

The final presentation will also illustrate how different individuals and groups might produce different diagrams and recommendations, highlighting the necessarily subjective nature of systemic thinking and practice. This seminar could be split into two sessions, if considered appropriate.

Activity

GSK (GlaxoSmithKline)'s top management has asked your group to provide an outline of the situation described below, followed by some basic suggestions towards addressing this crisis.

1. In groups of four or five students, read the case study and conduct some general research using the links provided and a general Internet search (this research could be done in advance of the class).

2. Identify the different stakeholders in this case study.

3. Each student must choose one of these stakeholders.

4. Each student will sketch a couple of diagrams to express the view of the chosen stakeholder. NB All students in the group must agree on what type of diagrams to use: for example, a system and an influence diagram, or a system and a rich picture.

5. Present the diagrams to the other members of the group, and then create two final diagrams combining the individual contributions.

6. What would be the general advice to GSK's top management that emerges from your two group diagrams?

7. Present to the class and general discussion.

Case study: GSK in China

GSK is a British pharmaceutical company with its headquarters in London. It is currently one of the largest prescription drug companies in the world. Its importance is related to its size, financial muscle, the tax revenues it provides, and to producing medications to alleviate the suffering of millions of individuals worldwide from common conditions such as asthma, cancer and diabetes.

According to the BBC and other media, GSK has recently been investigated by the Chinese government over allegedly bribing Chinese doctors to prescribe the firm's drugs. Other practices under the spotlight include paying doctors to give lectures at international conferences (including very generous hospitality and other incentives), and the perceived aggressive marketing techniques used by the company's sales representatives at doctors' surgeries. It is said that these 'sales and information' visits could make it difficult for health professionals to distinguish between marketing information and scientific information. Furthermore, GSK's use of individual sales targets and performance-related bonuses for its employees has also been criticised (these are human resource management techniques commonly used as an incentive to reward individual or group performance). Please note that other pharmaceutical companies have also faced similar and other criticisms, such as the use of live animals in drug development and testing, and the availability and quality of experimentation data (e.g. Goldacre 2012).

A selection of relevant stakeholders invited by the BBC and other media (e.g. *The Guardian*) to give their opinions on these issues include:

- Editor of the British Medical Journal: 'Doctors need independent, unbiased information about drugs'.

- Ben Goldacre (author of the book *Bad Pharma*): 'Doctors get a lot of their education about which treatment works best from the pharmaceutical industry itself—from doctors who have been paid to give lectures about which drug is best. This free education has been shown to be biased in research and it's non-trivial.'

- The BMA (British Medical Association) Head of Science and Ethics: 'Whilst we agree that GSK should not directly sponsor doctors' going to meetings, we are satisfied that they will continue to financially support education.'

More information:

- www.bbc.co.uk/news/business-25415485

- www.bbc.co.uk/news/business-23402154

- www.theguardian.com/business/2013/jul/24/
gsk-china-crisis-questions

Additional background information

https://www.gov.uk/government/publications/
bribery-act-2010-guidance

The UK government introduced the Bribery Act 2010, which aimed to improve corporate transparency and to fight corruption. One of the key elements of this Act is its near-universal jurisdiction, i.e. it allows for the prosecution of an individual or a company *with links to the UK*, regardless of where the crime was committed.

www.transparency.org.uk

Transparency International (UK) is a non-governmental organisation that challenges corruption worldwide. Its activities include producing research reports, campaigning and lobbying. Important reports include: *How to Bribe: A Typology of Bribe and How to Stop It*; *Corruption in the UK*; *Bribery in China: 10 Lessons form Recent Cases*; and *Global Corruption Report: Climate Change*.

Additional teaching material and ideas

1. Films

Several films on environmental and sustainability issues with a systems orientation could be used for class discussion and to provide examples of the relevance of the systems approach to management. A filmography chapter in Fisher *et al.* (2013: 549-63) is worth consulting for further material.

Students could be asked to use diagrams to illustrate and discuss each film's main topics, different viewpoints, sub-plots, and how relevant the stories are to their future professional practice, using systems concepts such as boundaries, feedback and emerging properties. A few examples are as follows:

Mindwalk (dir.: Bernt Capra, US, 1990, 1:52 hours duration)

This film is based on the book *Turning Point* written by Fritjof Capra. The first half of the film provides a very interesting and comprehensive story of the evolution of science *vis-à-vis* developments in Western society since medieval times. The second half is devoted to the evolution of systems thinking, highlighting its possible application in the fields of politics, conservation, science, technology and business ethics. The main characters, a nuclear scientist, a US presidential candidate and a poet, provide a very interesting debate on the pros and cons of this approach at the theoretical and at a practical level. Music by Philip Glass. The film is available on VHS and on the Internet. Duration: 1hr 52 min.

The Fight for True Farming (dir.: Eve Lamont, Canada, 2005, 1:30 hours duration)

A most interesting film, it provides an opportunity for farmers in Canada, the US and France to provide solutions acceptable to the social and environmental 'Scrooges' of factory farming. The roles of globalisation and agribusiness in the demise of traditional farms are discussed, while biodiversity and genetically modified crops also feature prominently.

Up the Yangtze (dir.: Yung Chang, China, 2007, 1:33 hours duration)

This is film is based on the largest hydroelectric dam in the world, built in China. As entire cities are being submerged and two million people displaced, luxury cruise ships take tourists on 'farewell' tours to see the legendary landscape before it is flooded. The film contrasts the experience of naïve and well-intentioned Western tourists with those of crewmembers native to the region.

An Inconvenient Truth (dir.: Davis Guggenheim, US, 2006, 1:37 hours duration)

Al Gore, former US vice-president and presidential nominee, presents an informative documentary on the dangers of global warming. It is taut, intelligent and darkly humorous.

Blood in the Mobile (dir.: Frank Piasecki Poulsen, Denmark, 2010, 1:25 hours duration)

We cannot live without our mobile phones, but their production has a dark and bloody side. Minerals used to make our mobiles come from mines in the eastern part of the Democratic Republic of the Congo, funding a brutal civil war responsible for around five million deaths, atrocious child labour and some 300,000 rapes in the last 15 years. It is a war that will continue as long as armed groups can trade the minerals. Director Frank Poulsen travels to Congo and gets access to its largest illegal tin mine, where enslaved children dig for days in narrow tunnels. He then tries to confront Nokia, the world's largest phone company. Are they and other mobile companies implicated in trading 'conflict minerals'? What do you think of Poulsen asking a small child to be his guide into the mines?

2. RSA Animate

www.thersa.org/events/rsaanimate

Short animations from the RSA (Royal Society for the Encouragement of Arts, Manufacturers and Commerce), based in London. Lectures and other material are also available at this site. The animations are excellent examples of the power of rich pictures and cartoons to convey complex information.

Crisis of Capitalism

www.thersa.org/events/rsaanimate/animate/
rsa-animate-crisis-of-capitalism

Students could be asked to spot the section when the notion of 'systemic risk' is mentioned then summarise the issues addressed up to that point.

Choice

www.thersa.org/events/rsaanimate/animate/choice

Explores the paralysing anxiety and dissatisfaction surrounding limitless choice. This short animation could also be linked to the concepts of consumerism, 'affluenza', and obsolescence.

3. Gaia theory

There are several resources on 'Gaia theory' available online (including James Lovelock's website, www.jameslovelock.org). A special edition of the *New Scientist* magazine devoted to this concept, including the views of its critics, can be found at www.newscientist.com/special/gaia.

4. Systems thinking diagrams

Examples of systems thinking diagrams can be found online: a web search with the words 'systems thinking diagrams' should provide many images to explore and discuss.

5. Sea wall 'eco-engineering' can help boost biodiversity

www.bbc.co.uk/news/science-environment-26034196

This piece of news from the BBC could be used to illustrate and discuss issues regarding the interaction between man-made structures and the natural environment. Emphasis could be placed on the fact that the scientists' proposals would not increase the cost of building these sea walls; also, consider the advantages of forming multidisciplinary teams to design and build these structures, as opposed to simply *managing* these projects as purely engineering jobs. System and influence diagrams could be produced to aid the discussion.

Further reading

Checkland, P. (2000) *Systems Thinking, Systems Practice* (London: Wiley) and Checkland, P., and J. Poulter (2006) *Learning for Action: A Short Definitive Account of Soft Systems Methodology, and Its Use for Practitioners, Teachers and Students* (London: Wiley).

> Peter Checkland's main contribution to systems thinking was the development of his SSM (soft systems methodology). As a former chemical engineer, his approach is both very clear and practical. These books provide many examples of how to develop rich pictures and how to progress from achieving a general understanding of a problematic situation to the development and implementation of recommendations for improvement.

Fisher, C., A. Lovell and N. Valero-Silva (2013) *Business Ethics and Values*, 4th edn (London: Pearson-Financial Times).

> This is a very popular book on business ethics written with a systemic flavour. It has a chapter devoted to corporate social responsibility and another on sustainability. It also contains a filmography chapter with over a hundred films (each with a short synopsis) that could be chosen as case studies for class discussions and essays, and personal/group independent study.

Jackson, M.C. (2000) *Systems Approaches to Management* (New York: Springer).

> This text provides a comprehensive summary of systems thinking in the management sciences. The main sections on functionalist, interpretive and emancipatory systems approaches include reviews of the main systems methodologies. Jackson not only provides a summary of the methodologies, but also an analysis of their strengths and weaknesses. It is written in a very clear and accessible style and is a good source of references for further study.

Morgan, G. (2006) *Images of Organization* (London: Sage).

> This book has become a classic on the study of organisations since its first edition in 1986. The idea of managers using metaphors in 'the art of reading' problematic situations is very powerful indeed. The first four metaphors, organisations as 'machines', 'organisms', 'brains' and 'cultures', are central to the understanding of how systems thinking is interwoven into the different management disciplines. The strengths and weaknesses of each metaphor are particularly important, as are the bibliographical notes provided at the end of each chapter.

References

Ashby, W.R. (1956) *An Introduction to Cybernetics* (London: Methuen).

BBC (2010) 'BP boss Tony Hayward's gaffes', BBC News, 20 June 2010, www.bbc.co.uk/news/10360084, accessed 20 October 2013.

—— (2014) 'Sea walls tweaks boost biodiversity', BBC News, 6 February 2014, www.bbc.co.uk/news/science-environment-26034196, accessed 6 February 2014.

Beer, S. (1985) *Diagnosing the System for Organizations* (Chichester, UK: Wiley).

Berners-Lee, M. (2010) *How Bad Are Bananas? The Carbon Footprint of Everything* (London: Profile Books).

Bradbury, R. (2005) *A Sound of Thunder and Other Stories* (New York: Harper Perennial).

Buzan, T. (2003) *Use Your Head (Mind Set)* (London: BBC Publications).

Capra, F. (1982) *The Turning Point: Science, Society, and the Rising Culture* (New York: Bantam).

—— (1997) *The Web of Life: A New Synthesis of Mind and Matter* (New York: Flamingo, HarperCollins).

Carson, R. (1962) *Silent Spring* (Boston, MA: Houghton Mifflin).

Checkland, P. (2000) *Systems Thinking, Systems Practice* (London: Wiley).

—— (2002) 'Information Systems and Systems Thinking: Time to Unite?', *International Journal of Information Management* 8.4: 239-48.

Checkland, P., and J. Poulter (2006) *Learning for Action: A Short Definitive Account of Soft Systems Methodology, and Its Use for Practitioners, Teachers and Students* (London: Wiley).

Churchman, C.W. (1968) *The Systems Approach* (New York: Delacorte Press).

Cooper, R. (1986) 'Organization/Disorganization', *Social Science Information* 25.2: 299-335.

—— (1992) 'Formal Organization as Representation: Remote Control, Displacement and Abbroviation', in M. Reed and M. Hughes (eds.), *Rethinking Organization* (London: Sage): 254-72.

Cooper, T. (2005) 'Slower Consumption: Reflections on Product Life Cycles and the "Throwaway Society"', *Journal of Industrial Ecology* 9.1/2: 51-76.

—— (2010) *Longer Lasting Products: Alternatives to the Throwaway Society* (Farnham, UK: Gower).

Deming, W.E. (1982) *Out of the Crisis* (Cambridge, MA: MIT Press).

Descartes, R. (1989) *A Discourse on Method and The Meditations* (London: Penguin Books).

Economist, The (2012) 'Apple and the American Economy', *The Economist*, 23 January 2012, www.economist.com/blogs/freeexchange/2012/01/supply-chains, accessed 23 November 2013.

Fisher, C., A. Lovell and N. Valero-Silva (2013) *Business Ethics and Values*, 4th edn (London: Pearson-Financial Times).

Goldacre, B. (2012) *Bad Pharma: How Medicine is Broken, And How We Can Fix It* (London: Fourth Estate).

Gyllenhammer, P. (1977) *People at Work* (Reading, MA: Addison-Wesley).

Ishikawa, K. (1956) *Guide to Quality Control* (Tokyo, Japan: JUSE).

Jackson, M.C. (2000) *Systems Approaches to Management* (New York: Springer).

Juran, J.M. (1988) *Juran on Planning for Quality* (New York: Free Press).

Kuhn, T. (2012) *The Structure of Scientific Revolutions: 50th Anniversary Edition* (Chicago, IL: University of Chicago Press).

Lietaer, B., C. Amsperger, S. Brunnhuber and S. Goemer (2012) *Money and Sustainability: The Missing Link* (Axminster, UK: Triarchy Press).

London, B. (1932) *Ending the Depression Through Planned Obsolescence*, http://upload.wikimedia.org/wikipedia/commons/2/27/London_(1932)_Ending_the_depression_through_planned_obsolescence.pdf, accessed 20 November 2013.

Lorenz, E.N. (1972) 'Predictability: Does the Flap of a Butterfly's Wings in Brazil Set Off a Tornado in Texas?', *American Association for the Advancement of Science 139th Meeting*, MIT, http://eaps4.mit.edu/research/Lorenz/Butterfly_1972.pdf, accessed 31 December 2013.

Lovelock, J. (1979) *Gaia: A New Look at Life on Earth* (Oxford, UK: Oxford University Press).

—— (2006) *The Revenge of Gaia: Earth's Climate Crisis and the Fate of Humanity* (New York: Basic Books).

Meadows, D., J. Randers and D. Meadows (2006) *The Limits of Growth: The 30-Year Update* (London: Earthscan).

Mingers, J., and L. White (2010) 'A Review of the Recent Contribution of Systems Thinking to Operational Research and Management Science', *European Journal of Operational Research* 207.3: 1147-61.

Morgan, G. (2006) *Images of Organization* (London: Sage).

Myant, M., and J. Drahokoupil (2011) *Transition Economies: Political Economy in Russia, Eastern Europe, and Central Asia* (Hoboken, NJ: Wiley)

Seddon, J. (2010) *Systems Thinking in the Public Sector* (Axminster, UK: Triarchy Press).

Senge, P.M. (2006) *The Fifth Discipline: The Art and Practice of the Learning Organization* (London: Random House).

Taylor, F.W. (2013) *The Principles of Scientific Management* (Scottsdale, AZ: Creative Space)

Trist, E.L., and K.W. Bamforth (1951) 'Some Social and Psychological Consequences of the Long-Wall Method of Coal-Getting', *Human Relations* 4.1: 3-38.

Trochim, W., D. Cabrera, B. Milstein, R. Gallagher and S. Leischow (2006) 'Practical Challenges of Systems Thinking and Modelling in Public Health', *American Journal of Public Health* 96.3: 538-46.

von Bertalanffy, L. (1969) *General System Theory: Foundations, Development, Applications* (New York: George Braziler).

Waring, A. (2010) *Practical Systems Thinking* (London: International Thompson Business Press).

Wiener, N. (1948) *Cybernetics* (New York: Wiley).

Acknowledgements

First of all, I would like to thank the authors of the different chapters for contributing to the book, for their enthusiasm and for their hard work on this in addition to their 'normal' workload!

I would also like the following colleagues for peer reviewing the chapters and for their very useful comments and suggestions: Alastair Allen (Nottingham Business School), Barbara Beeby (Manchester Business School), Craig Bickerton (NBS), Serena Brown (NBS), Alison Edmonds (MBS), Anne Keegan (NBS), Julie Rosborough (NBS), Roy Smith (Nottingham Trent University), Roy Stratton (NBS), Néstor Valero-Silva and, last but definitely not least, Fiona Winfield (NBS). Most of them also attended and contributed to our research day, where all authors presented their ideas for their chapters for the first time and we had very lively discussions about the content of the book. In addition I would like to thank the following colleagues for their help during this research day in shaping the chapters: Debra Easter (NTU), John Friedrichs (NBS), Sian Hancox (NBS) and Chris Hunt (NBS).

A big 'thank you' also to our students who tried and tested many of the ideas in this book! I would like to thank our NTU Green Academy Graduate Interns Serena Brown and Amy Scoins as well as my dear colleague Helen Goworek for all their feedback and ideas, for example, with regards to designing the cover for this book. I would like to extend a special thanks to Ellie Kennedy (NTU), who did not only contribute to two chapters but also helped other colleagues to improve their seminars.

It was a pleasure to work with Rebecca Macklin and her team from Greenleaf, thanks for the countless e-mails you answered patiently and with great expertise! I would also like to thank John Stuart for supporting the idea of this book wholeheartedly and making it happen. And to Zoe Robinson for writing the foreword and to Jerome Baddley and all the others who answered to my 'poem competition'.

A special thanks belongs to my husband Eric Molthan-Hill for taking the kids out so that I can work and for cooking me delicious Sunday dinners—our son Ansgar commented that he *has* to cook while Mummy is *allowed* to work—and to all three of them—Eric, Ansgar and Kiera—in supporting me generally!

And finally to the founder of my church Martin Luther who taught me about trust and hope in God by writing the following:

> Und wenn morgen die Welt unterginge, so wuerde ich heute noch ein Apfelbaeumchen pflanzen!

> [And if the world would end tomorrow, I would still plant an apple tree today.]

Although my sincere hope is that humankind will come to reason in time—in this hope I have written this book.

Biographies

Seraphina Brown is currently working in the field of sustainability and higher education at Nottingham Trent University. In her current role, she is responsible for embedding sustainability within the curriculum in the schools of Business, Law and Social Sciences, as well as having a key role in sustainability events at the university. She received her MSc in Environmental Management from the University of Nottingham, after having studied at undergraduate level for a BA in Archaeology and Geography.

Elaine Cohen is an expert and influential voice in the field of CSR (corporate social responsibility) and sustainability strategy, reporting and the CSR interface with HR (human resources) management. She is the author of three books on sustainable practice and reporting, including the first-ever book on CSR and HR (*CSR for HR: A Necessary Partnership for Advancing Responsible Business Practices*, Greenleaf Publishing, 2010). Elaine writes regularly for her *CSR Reporting* blog and other publications, and is a frequent chair and speaker at sustainability conferences. As the founder manager of Beyond Business Ltd (www.b-yond. biz), Elaine works with many clients around the globe. Elaine gained over 20 years of business experience in executive positions with Procter & Gamble and Unilever prior to founding Beyond Business Ltd in 2005. Elaine was selected as one of the 100 Top Thought Leaders in Trustworthy Business Behavior in 2014 and tweets as @elainecohen.

Aldilla Dharmasasmita has been teaching undergraduates and postgraduates in various modules, where sustainability has been fully embedded. She is also supervising students in greenhouse gas management consultancy projects. Her research interests are comparisons between institutional theories and the process of corporate social responsibility and sustainability. Currently, she also plays a key role in embedding and designing an innovative online pedagogy into the university's curriculum across all faculties (as part of an HEA initiative), the Sustainability in Practice Certificate. Aldilla received her full-scholarship MSc in Corporate Social Responsibility at the University of Nottingham and a BA(Hons) in Business with a major in Operations and Data Analysis at the Nottingham Trent University.

Dr **Rosa Maria Fernandez** is a teaching fellow at the University of Birmingham where she lectures in environmental economics and sustainable development. She has previously been an associate tutor in business ethics and sustainability at the University of Bradford, as well as visiting researcher at the University of Exeter (UK) and York University (Toronto), and lecturer in economics at UNED (National Distance Education University, Spain). She presented her thesis in 2010, on 'European Union and Climate Change: Main Economic Effects'. She has recently published articles related to climate change, energy policy and corporate social responsibility, which are her main research interests, using an interdisciplinary approach. She is a member of the Collaborative Research Network on the Governance of Sustainability promoted by UACES (University Association for Contemporary European Studies), and occasionally evaluates research projects for the COST initiative of the European Commission. Rosa is currently working on the design of a masters module on energy economics and policy for the Midlands Energy Group. She enjoys long walks and tries to discover as many new places as possible by visiting areas of special natural beauty.

Biswaraj Ghosh has recently started his fully funded PhD at the Nottingham Trent University having gained considerable experience as a research assistant while working on different academic projects at the Nottingham University Business School. He has also co-authored a book chapter for Springer Publications looking at comparative corporate social responsibility involving the UK and other countries. His current research focuses on investigating internal control mechanisms promoting sustainability in Anglo-Germanic country contexts. Previously, he obtained a full-scholarship Master's degree with distinction from the University of Nottingham having graduated with a first-class BA(Hons) degree in Finance, Accounting and Management from the same university.

Helen Goworek is a senior lecturer in marketing at Nottingham Business School, and a tutor at Loughborough University School of Business and Economics and the University of Leicester, where she teaches postgraduate marketing courses. She has a first-class BA(Hons) in Fashion Marketing and gained her Master's degree while working full time in industry for retailers such as Next, and for manufacturers supplying retailers including Marks & Spencer. She has worked both as a buyer and as a design manager, liaising with overseas suppliers in Europe and the Far East. She is the author of three books about the fashion business and retailing that have been translated into Spanish, Russian and Chinese. She has also written several book chapters and articles on retail buying, product development and sustainability, and she is completing a PhD by publication comprising these topics. Helen has participated in research projects into sustainable clothing funded by Defra. She is an external assessor at Regent's University, London, and collaborates on the Fashion Bridge project in Berlin. Outside work she enjoys reading about psychology, producing artwork, attending comedy shows and listening to dance music. She tweets as @creativemktng1.

Christian Herzig held academic positions at the Leuphana University, Lüneburg, and the University of Nottingham before he joined Nottingham Business School as Professor in Business and Sustainability. His research and teaching interests have also taken him to the Asia-Pacific region. He was a visiting research fellow at the University of South Australia, and he stayed for over a year in South-East Asia (Indonesia, Thailand, the Philippines and Vietnam) where he carried out an international capacity development and research project on environmental management accounting and resource efficiency. During his stay in the Emilia Romagna region of Italy he carried out a management project on the implementation of an ISO14001 environmental management system.

Short-term academic appointments include visiting lectureships at the Free University, Berlin, Germany and at the Marmara University, Turkey. Christian holds a PhD in Economic and Social Sciences, an MA in Business Administration and an MSc in Environmental Sciences.

Richard Holmes is a low carbon consultant for the design and operation of buildings via the CIBSE Chartered Institute of Building Service Engineers), an MEI (Member of the Energy Institute) and a chartered environmentalist. After ten years working for the UK Energy Saving Trust's advice network, the European Energy Agency network and a local authority carbon management team, Richard set up his own consultancy business (Third Stone Ltd) in 2005. He provides an advisory service to all users of energy from the construction industry to businesses and public sector organisations. He has delivered training presentations for the Building Research Establishment and is a lecturer in Nottingham Business School and Nottingham Trent University's School of Architecture.

Dr **Richard Howarth** is course leader of the BA(Hons) Management and Business Management (in-company) suite of courses at Nottingham Business School. He has previously worked in the area of corporate education and work-based learning, and with practitioners on environmental management, sustainability and risk-management focused courses. Richard is particularly interested in the representation and interpretation(s) of sustainability and how individuals and organisations can, and do, respond to the concept and problem. He has a DBA from Nottingham Business School, which focused on the engagement of managers of small and medium-sized enterprises in a supply-chain environmental management context.

Dr **Ellie Kennedy** is a learning and teaching officer at the Nottingham Trent University. In this academic development role, her primary focuses are assessment and feedback, learner-centred teaching approaches, and internationalisation of the curriculum. Prior to this, Ellie gained nearly 20 years' experience teaching in higher education, including lecturing on literature, culture and gender; tutoring international students in English for academic purposes; and teaching German language. She is also an editor of the *International Student Experience Journal*. Ellie has enjoyed collaborating with colleagues across the world on this project, and has learned a tremendous amount about sustainability.

Peter Lund-Thomsen is Associate Professor at the Copenhagen Business School and Visiting Professor at Nottingham Business School. His research focuses on the linkage between global value chains, industrial upgrading, and corporate social and environmental responsibility in developing countries. He theorises and empirically investigates how the corporate social and environmental responsibility policies of internationally branded companies are implemented in global supply chains, and how they affect supplier competitiveness, work conditions and the environment in the South. He also teaches courses to PhD, masters and bachelor students on this and related topics.

Dr **Petra Molthan-Hill** is Principal Lecturer in Business Sustainability at Nottingham Business School and, as NBS Sustainability Co-ordinator, is responsible for embedding sustainability and business ethics into the curriculum of the business school. At the moment she is also leading the Higher Education Academy Green Academy 'Food for Thought' Project for Nottingham Trent University, developing teaching methods on how to embed sustainability into various disciplines from business studies through medieval history to astrophysics. Her main research interest has been experiential learning methods and the integration of sustainability into the curriculum, but also the behaviour and sense-making of managers in cross-cultural comparisons. She has written her PhD, several articles (accepted for publication) and a book chapter about these topics. She also holds an MBA and a Master in Divinity. Outside work Petra loves hiking with her family in beautiful landscapes, music, dancing and novels about time travelling.

Lynn Oxborrow is director of the Future Factory project at Nottingham Trent University. Future Factory is supported by the European Regional Development Fund and has been helping small businesses to become more sustainable since 2009. In addition, Lynn teaches global supply chain management to undergraduate and postgraduate students at Nottingham Trent University. Her research interests focus on the textiles and clothing industry supply chain, and she has been involved in numerous projects to explore supply chain developments in the UK, US and European clothing industries. Most recently, Lynn has been involved in a project funded by the UK WRAP (Waste and Resources Action Plan) to identify ways to produce clothing that lasts for longer, and has undertaken research into sustainable supply chain management in the food industry. Lynn is working towards a DBA entitled 'A Study into Future Scenarios within the UK Apparel Supply Chain'. After studying Social and Political Science at the University of Cambridge, Lynn's interest in supply chain management was generated through her extensive experience of working in clothing retail management.

Helen Puntha is a research officer in the Centre for Academic Development and Quality at Nottingham Trent University where she gained her MSc in Social Science Research Methods. Her current work is in the areas of research informed teaching, assessment and feedback and sustainability in the curriculum. She is Deputy Lead of the University's Higher Education Academy Green Academy 'Food for Thought' Project and is a steering group member for the British Conference of Undergraduate Research. Outside of work she enjoys time with her children, Chinese brush painting, flamenco dancing, learning languages and anything written by Paulo Coelho.

Dr **Natalie Ralph** is a consultant for business, corporate social responsibility and corporate peacebuilding issues. She is currently working in Corporate Peacebuilders, a consultancy that assists businesses and organisations in the new and growing field of business, peace and human rights. Natalie has over ten years' research and practical experience on these issues, having worked alongside business within state government, civil society, academic and research organisations. Natalie has enjoyed working with the book's team and is looking forward to using the innovative teaching plans provided by all the book's authors.

Prof. Dr phil. **Mathias Schüz** is Professor for International Business and Responsible Leadership. with exploratory focus on corporate responsibility and business ethics, at the Center for Human Capital Management in the School of Management and Law at ZHAW (Zurich University of Applied Sciences), Switzerland. He studied physics, philosophy and pedagogics, and was trainee and key account manager at IBM. Together with the insurance entrepreneur Dr Rolf Gerling, he co-founded the Gerling Academy for Risk Research in Zurich and ran it for 14 years before becoming a senior lecturer at various universities, and finally professor at ZHAW. He has published numerous articles and books, such as one outlining a new philosophy of economy in German: *Werte—Risiko—Verantwortung. Dimensionen des Value Managements* [Values, Risk, Responsibility: Dimensions of the Value Management] (Munich, Germany: Gerling Akademie Verlag, 1999); another, published with two co-authors, deals with lies in management: *Lügen in der Chefetage* [Lies on the Executive Floor] (Weinheim, Germany: Wiley, 2007).

Dr **Néstor Valero-Silva** worked in the petrochemical and ceramics industries after graduating as a chemical engineer. Néstor then read for a postgraduate degree in HRM (human resources management) followed by an MA and a PhD in Management Systems at the University of Hull, UK. He held academic posts at the Universities of Hull and Lincoln before joining the Nottingham Business School. Néstor is a chartered member of the CIPD (Chartered Institute of Personnel and Development) and a fellow of the Higher Education Academy. His research interests emerged from his doctoral studies on systems thinking and management. He has explored and applied systemic thinking in the fields of business ethics (including CSR/sustainability/diversity), systems thinking and practice, HRM, social housing and information systems. He is a principal lecturer in HRM, and leads the Nottingham Business School's PhD Programme.

Dr **Maggie Zeng** is a lecturer in operations management at the University of Gloucestershire and teaches on a range of undergraduate, postgraduate and professional modules. Prior to joining the university, she was project adviser for several companies from a variety of UK industries. She is particularly interested in operations management, emerging strategies in the digital economy and sustainability. She also has a keen interest in developing innovative pedagogies and enriching student experiences.

Index

Note: Page numbers in **bold** indicate figures and tables.

Mental Health Issues and the Media

Our ideas about mental health and illness can be informed by personal experiences but are most often formed by the prevailing attitudes of society. A wide range of contemporary media helps create these attitudes and for all health professionals the ways in which they do so are of immediate concern. Health professionals need to:

- be aware of media influences on their own perceptions and attitudes
- take account of both the negative and positive aspects of media intervention in mental health promotion and public education
- understand the way in which we all interact with media messages and how this affects both practitioners and service-users

Mental Health Issues and the Media provides students and professionals in nursing and allied professions, psychiatry, psychology and related disciplines, with a theoretically grounded introduction to the ways in which our attitudes are shaped by the media. Covering the press, literature, film, television and the Internet, it also includes practical advice and recommendations on how to combat negative images for service-users, health care workers and media personnel.

Gary Morris is a Mental Health Nursing Lecturer working at the University of Leeds, UK, where he runs, amongst other courses, a taught module entitled 'Mental Health Issues and the Media'.

Mental Health Issues and the Media

An introduction for health professionals

Gary Morris

Routledge
Taylor & Francis Group

LONDON AND NEW YORK

First published 2006 by Routledge
2 Park Square, Milton Park, Abingdon, Oxon OX14 4RN

Simultaneously published in the USA and Canada
by Routledge
270 Madison Ave, New York, NY 10016

Routledge is an imprint of the Taylor & Francis Group, an informa business

© 2006 Gary Morris

Typeset in Times by
RefineCatch Limited, Bungay, Suffolk
Printed and bound in Great Britain by
MPG Books Ltd, Bodmin

British Library Cataloguing in Publication Data
A catalogue record for this book is available from the British Library

Library of Congress Cataloging in Publication Data
Morris, Gary, 1962–
    Mental health issues and the media : an introduction for health
professionals / Gary Morris.
        p. ; cm.
    Includes bibliographical references and index.
    1. Mental health.   2. Mass media in mental health education.
    3. Health in mass media.   I. Title.
    [DNLM: 1. Communications Media.   2. Mental Health.   3. Health
Knowledge, Attitudes, Practices.   WM 105 M876m   2006]
RA790.53.M67   2006
                                    362.2—dc22   2005023846

ISBN10: 0–415–32530–7 (hbk)
ISBN10: 0–415–32531–5 (pbk)
ISBN10: 0–203–358228 (ebk)

ISBN13: 978–0–415–32530–1 (hbk)
ISBN13: 978–0–415–32531–8 (pbk)
ISBN13: 978–0–203–35822–1 (ebk)

To

Lottie, William, Sam,

Daisy and Caitlin

Contents

Figures

Acknowledgements

I would like to acknowledge the support and assistance I have received from a number of people whose help has been vital to the process of writing this book.

First, I owe an immeasurable sense of gratitude to my wife Emily for her tireless support and insightful advice at every stage of this process. This has enabled me to maintain my levels of energy and enthusiasm as well as my focus for this work especially at times when it felt a struggle.

A massive thank you has to be extended to my colleague, Jack Morris, for his collaboration throughout, both in the development as well as the running of the taught module 'Mental Health Issues and the Media'. This has provided the impetus for this publication. This module has been offered on numerous occasions at the University of Leeds and has attracted an extremely wide number and eclectic range of students. Many of the issues addressed within this book are inspired directly through our frequent discussions and planning meetings concerning themes and frameworks for inclusion. It is clear to say that without the valuable support and experience that he has brought to this entire project, none of it would have progressed further than the initial contemplation stage.

I would also like to acknowledge the much-needed and experienced contributions I have received from Pauline Bispham, Marie Clough, Anna Davie, Ian Harrow, Steve Howarth and Peter Morrall. Their thought-provoking and stimulating contributions have provided me with fresh and inspired perspectives from which to revisit material.

I must also mention the excellent and supportive feedback received from the Taylor & Francis team throughout this project who notably include Stephanie Kerrigan, Amanda Lastoria, Margaret Lipscomb, Kirsty Smy and Edwina Wellham.

Finally, many thanks to all the students on the taught module for their invaluable assistance and challenging engagement with some of the themes developed within this publication.

1 The mental health–media relationship

What is this book about?

This book is primarily about a relationship. It addresses the ways in which we as individuals and collectively as a society interact with mental health issues and the extent to which this relationship is changed as a result of media exposure. What we know or how we feel about those who are categorised or labelled as 'mentally ill' is subject to continual change and is influenced by the type of information accessed and the degree of credibility afforded its source. The range of messages that carry mental health themes is vast and we are exposed on a daily basis to a plethora of themes through an ever-increasing selection of media. All of this plays a significant part in the construction of what we know or what we feel about issues connected with the topic of mental health and our ways of relating which may either be of a connecting or distancing type. This relates to the degree to which we are able either to connect with and get closer to understanding the inner world of those affected by mental health problems or to maintain a 'safe' but uninformed distance.

The first element of this relationship concerns what we know. Much of what we learn about the world around us comes from messages transmitted by the wide selection of media types available. We are literally bombarded with segments of information from the moment we wake until the time of finally retiring to bed. On a typical day this might include trawling through the paper, watching television, listening to the radio, visiting Internet sites, watching a film and reading a book as perhaps the more obvious means. We also engage with other media messages from formats such as advertising, stage production, the music industry and the world of art. All of these examples have multiple sub-divisions or genres that further widen the scope and variety of what is on offer. Ongoing advancements within telecommunications and digital television bring fresh new sources to add to this selection. It is important also to consider what is learnt indirectly or second-hand from others who have been exposed to media messages. The chain of communication can be extended to create a form of Chinese whispers with the authority of information being diminished with each successive link. It is hardly

surprising therefore that our understanding of mental health issues can end up wildly inaccurate or that it might prove difficult and confusing trying to discriminate between the various sources from which our knowledge originates.

These issues are all explored in detail throughout this book that is essentially (as Figure 1.1 illustrates) about a relationship. This namely concerns a tripartite relationship between: a) us as *individuals* (or collectively as a *society*); b) *mental health issues*; and c) the *media*. It addresses and examines the myriad of processes that play a part in this relationship and how all of those involved exert a degree of influence over the others. Each participant shares some of the overall responsibility as to the outcome of this relationship as we can, for example, place the blame upon the tabloid press for biased and insensitive reporting although disregard the fact that we as a society are aiding and encouraging this process by continuing to buy their products. Clearly, each of those involved has a distinctly different perspective and separate interests that influence the way in which they relate to certain aspects. It is the significance of these factors and the impact upon the overall relationship that forms the main focus addressed within this book.

In order to begin exploring these themes, it is important to look in detail at each of the following participants within this tripartite relationship: individuals/society; mental health issues; and the media.

Individuals/society

Definitions of the term *society* include:

> 'The institutions and culture of a distinct self-perpetuating group.'
> 'The totality of social relationships among humans.'
>
> (Dictionary.com 2005)

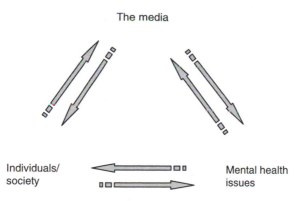

Figure 1.1 Tri-partite relationship.

'The fact or condition of being connected or related.'

(*Oxford English Dictionary* 2005)

What emerges strongly from these definitions is that *society* is primarily concerned with a set of relationships between its members with regard to what is shared. The term *society* can be regarded as a collective entity or broken down into separate components containing *individuals* or groupings of individuals. The Gestalt focus upon 'the whole' being more than the sum of its parts (Köhler 1947) fits very aptly here in that individuals in society should be seen not simply in fractional terms but as dynamic and influential components whose identity is formed through their interaction and relationships with others in 'the whole'. There are numerous sub-groupings or sets each representing differing values or beliefs. As individuals we naturally belong to a number of these sub-groups each of which has its own collective viewpoints and influences. The family provides us with our first significant group experience and is followed by others such as those encountered through schooling, leisure activities, religion, employment, political affiliation, health care and a potentially endless list of many others.

Individuals hold multiple roles, their relationships being governed by the different sub-groups to which they belong (Epting 1984). Within different contexts what is expected of us, how we perceive ourselves and how we respond will naturally vary. Within the family, for example, as a parent or partner we may have significantly different ways of interacting with others than we do at work with colleagues and employers. We are constantly modifying our thoughts, attitudes and behaviours in response to the accompanying feedback and reinforcers we are exposed to. This can be related to concepts such as social identity or personal identity as identified by Gripsrud (2002). The former relates to what we get from others' perceptions of us and the shared contexts that we are part of (e.g. culture, gender) and the personal identity being what makes us unique and distinguishable from others.

The component *individual/society* can therefore be regarded as a dynamic and multifaceted entity either regarded as a number of distinct and unique individuals, a varied set of sub-groupings or as a collective whole. The qualities and values held by this component therefore depend heavily upon specific experience and the range of pressures and influences which individuals or groups are exposed to.

Mental health issues

The term *mental health issues* is a vastly encompassing one having many different attributable meanings. We can consider the actual words themselves, which evoke wildly differing associations and interpretations. The strongest and most impactful of the three words here is undoubtedly that of '*mental*'. It is a word which, depending upon the context of its use, may have either positive or negative connotations. On the favourable side, the word *mental*

can be related to aspects such as *cerebral*, which denotes enhanced cognitive ability. This word may therefore evoke thoughts of individuals such as Einstein or Newton and signify qualities such as high levels of intelligence. These are esteemed and valued connections that afford a true sense of value and worth to whomever they are applied. At the opposite end of the spectrum is a far from flattering association. It is where the word *mental* is used as a form of derision, something that greatly undermines and reduces the credibility of the individual it is applied to. It is often used dismissively and seemingly unconcerned about a person's felt experience. When appearing in newspaper headlines it can drastically influence the impression given – for example, the *Daily Express*'s 'Bruno Put in *Mental* Home', or on another occasion, the *Independent*'s '*Mental* Patient Freed to Kill'. The use of words in this manner is commonly found within many media products and serves to reinforce negative attitudes held by the general public.

The wider term *mental health issues* can be looked at in two contrasting ways but is perhaps more commonly associated with that of *mental illness* over that of *mental well-being*. The former term carries a number of stereotypical associations including the exaggerated propensity for violence. This highlights a commonly held fear that those with mental health problems are unpredictable and more prone to aggressive acts than other members of the population (Morrall 2000a). Other negative connotations include the underlying assumption that the 'mentally ill' are unable to adequately care for themselves (Health Education Authority 1999). This brings about a pitying and disempowering approach, which diminishes an individual's sense of autonomy or choice. By contrast, the less applied connotation of *mental well-being* is associated with aspects such as campaigning and health promotion initiatives.

Another association is that of *mental health treatment*, something generally viewed with a sense of trepidation and fear, borne out of striking and lasting images seen in media examples such as in the film *One Flew over the Cuckoo's Nest* (Seale 2002). This type of portrayal is made more frightening by the strong sense of powerlessness attributed to those receiving care. Examples such as these reflect the destructive culture of institutionalised care outlined in some depth a few decades ago by the social researchers Goffman (1961) and Barton (1976). Clearly, many people's understanding of treatment is inaccurately fuelled by various impactful sources that do not properly convey the range and scope of current care approaches available. Fortunately there do exist within the media a variety of examples showing treatment as a caring process as evidenced in the films *Good Will Hunting* and *Ordinary People* that portray the helpful and enabling side of mental health care.

To conclude this section, another issue worthy of mention is the term *mental health legislation*. This covers a largely polarised set of opinions with, at one end of the spectrum, feelings that not enough control is being taken with unsupervised and 'unwell' individuals being left to roam the streets. At the other end, the proposals for added levels of constraint are viewed with

some concern, particularly with worries about the ways in which this might further breach and impinge upon an individuals' freedom. Proposed governmental changes in the Draft Mental Health Bill (Department of Health (DOH) 2004) enables people to be detained in hospital and given treatment against their will. While this is welcomed in some quarters in others it is greeted with suspicion and distrust. In particular, comments by the mental health charity Mind (2004a) express concerns regarding the wide range of people and types of treatment included within this new legislation providing for compulsory treatment and loss of liberty. The main argument being raised by mental health advocates concerns the availability of effective treatment and support over that of detention and exclusion (Mental Health Media 2004; Mind 2004a)

The media

The term *media* can be understood simply as a means of communication by organisations or individuals with a targeted audience. Messages are transmitted via a number of communicating channels and are interacted upon by a receiver primarily through the senses of sight and sound. Information is inputted in forms such as narrative (either printed or spoken), imagery (light, colour, appearance, expressions and gestures) or as sound (music and verbal exclamations).

A number of distinctions are made with regards to the term *media* including those of *mass media* and *new media*. The mass media may be understood simply as a communicating agent that can reach potentially large numbers of people in a diverse range of social settings (Devereux 2003). The concept here of wide reach is supported by McQuail (2005), who indicates the ability the *mass media* has in acting as a cohesive force connecting scattered individuals in a shared experience. This picture is changing with the advent of *new media* as the concept of an audience as a mass entity is becoming more fragmented in light of the greater number of media providers and products available. We can understand the term *new media* with regards to the recent technological developments within telecommunications that notably include the Internet and digital television services (Stevenson 2002).

The *media* itself is a communicating entity that has provided its audiences with forms of entertainment and education for many centuries. Historically this involved traditional forms such as art, writing and drama. The range of media types available changed rapidly especially with advancements in scientific and technological endeavours from the late nineteenth century onwards. There was a greater accessibility to the written word through the development of the printing press by William Caxton in 1477, commencing with the publication a year later of *Dictes or Sayengis of the Philosophres.* Nowadays, an almost limitless array of newspapers, magazines and books are published, geared towards every conceivable format or interest group.

The era of photography began with the announcement on 7 January 1839

of the development of the Daguerreotype, the first successful photographic process. The process consisted of exposing copper plates to iodine, the fumes forming a light-sensitive silver iodide. This led on to the search for animated or moving pictures with early inventions including the 'wheel of life' or the 'zoopraxiscope', where moving drawings or photographs were watched through a slit in the side. Modern motion picture making began with the invention of the motion picture camera in 1895, largely credited to the Frenchman Louis Lumière. Three decades later, *The Jazz Singer*, made in 1927, was the first feature length film to use recorded song and dialogue.

The birth of radio dates back to 1885 when Marconi sent and received his first radio signal. In 1924, John Logie Baird demonstrated a television system which transmitted an outline of objects and followed this a year later with an improved system which showed the head of a dummy as a real image. These achievements have continued to develop at a rapid pace with a virtual explosion in the number of channels now offered through cable and satellite services. This has been followed with the advent of digital television and radio services.

This brings us on to new media and in particular the birth of the Internet, whose origins date back to the 1960s with the development of a technology where strings of data were broken down and reassembled at their destination (LaBruzza 1997). This is complemented by further advances in telecommunication technology heralding an era of greater interactivity between the sender and receiver. The huge selection of media products now available does allow for much greater consumer choice although it poses problems with regard to examining the concept of audience reception because of the scale and complexity of the possible channels and sources involved (McQuail 1992).

Relationships

Having looked briefly at each of the participants in turn we can now focus our attention upon the relationship they have with each other leading towards an appreciation of the total relationship.

Society's relationship with mental health

This is an exceedingly complex relationship to describe and perhaps is better understood not by a single relationship but a set of multifaceted ones. Within society, there are many different ways in which mental health issues are encountered. Contact may be close or distant, informed or misinformed, personal or professional. We understand and react to those experiencing mental health problems as a consequence of what we know and what we feel. A core consideration regarding this relationship relates to *who* within the perspective of *society* is being considered. The following categorisations provide a useful means of exploring the very diverse range of vantage points

involved: personal experience; professional experience; *victims* of the mentally ill; the mentally ill as *victims*; and the inexperienced.

Personal experience

Personal experience of mental health problems might incorporate either one's own direct experience as a mental health service-user or as a carer to family and friends. This potentially will predispose those involved to being more informed and sensitive towards mental health issues than those without an appreciation of the actual reality of these experiences. Recognition of this leads to those with a direct understanding of the actual lived experience of mental health problems being afforded a greater sense of authority and credibility. This has led individuals and organisations such as Mind and Rethink to become actively involved in mental health campaigning and in providing a range of services, resources and support networks.

The nature of a person's experience and the eventual outcome will naturally have a significant impact upon how mental health issues are regarded. For instance, we can consider a range of experiences falling somewhere along a continuum from destructiveness at one pole towards survival at the other. People who have received good, supportive care and have been able to work through their problems and rebuild their lives will clearly have a different perspective than those who are, for example, actively depressed and feeling let down by agencies of care. The wide range of differing perspectives here can be verified through reviewing sources such as personal Internet sites which provide well-informed, helpful and informative sites alongside those that are overly subjective, wildly inaccurate and harmful.

Professional experience

For the purpose of this category, professional experience can be taken to incorporate not only those on a professional register but all the allied health care support personnel as well. Those involved in professional caring roles will have their own thoughts and feelings concerning those with mental health problems. Naturally there will in a number of cases be an overlap between this and the previous group where individuals have both a professional and personal experience of mental health issues. The nature of a person's clinical experience and the philosophy and approaches to care encountered is important. For example, some nursing homes caring for people with dementia utilise approaches to care reflecting a culture of paternalism believing that clients are to be 'looked after' and that carers know best what their needs might be. While in a number of instances representing well-meaning approaches to care, this approach, as highlighted by the work of Tom Kitwood and the Bradford Dementia Group, reduces personal choice and freedom and has a detrimental effect upon those concerned (Kitwood 1997). This opinion originates in some of the widely held stereotypes such as

the view that people with mental health problems are unable to care for themselves sufficiently. It is sharply contrasted by clinical approaches that demonstrate a greater focus upon family involvement, client-centred work and collaborative working relationships as advocated by a number of writers within the person-centred domain (Rogers 1961; Peplau 1988).

Victims of the 'mentally ill'

The descriptor here should be widened to encompass all those who feel themselves to be victims of those who are regarded as mentally ill irrespective of what the reality of the situation actually is. Obviously we have individuals who are clearly affected in tragic ways such as Jane Zito whose husband Jonathan was killed in a London tube station by Christopher Clunis, a man diagnosed with schizophrenia and with a long history of violence, institutional care and non-compliance with treatment programmes (Zito Trust 2005). We may also include other individuals here who have felt intimidated or uncomfortable regardless of the actual level of threat they have been exposed to. The reason for this is because of the way in which they feel about the mentally ill and any resultant response can be engendered irrespective of how others might regard or frame the same situation. Therefore the word *victim* can range from actual experience of physical or verbal abuse through to a feeling of insecurity or discomfort engendered by those with mental health problems. One of the core aspects here relates to how felt or perceived experience influences one's subsequent thoughts and behaviour. A useful frame of reference here is O'Connor and Seymour's (1990) model (see Figure 1.2) which addresses the relationship between feelings and behaviour.

The essence of this model is that of interaction where the behaviour of one person generates an internal feeling in the other which in turn influences their subsequent behaviour. For example, Person A is admitted to a mental health unit and feels lost, intimidated and frightened (*internal response*). He behaves

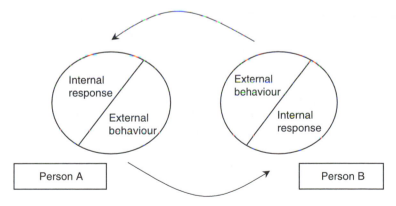

Figure 1.2 Internal response and external behaviour. Adapted from O'Connor and Seymour (1990).

by questioning and challenging staff in a somewhat forceful manner attempting to regain some feeling of control (*external behaviour*). This is interpreted as aggressive and intimidating by the health care professional (Person B), who feels threatened and uncertain (*internal response*). She reacts defensively and attempts to assert herself by outlining, rather more forcefully than necessary, the unit protocols regarding aggressive behaviour (*external behaviour*). This in turn reinforces the intimidated feelings of the client and the dynamic illustrated here continues to progress in a somewhat negative spiral.

The essence then of this category is of individuals who predominately feel either intimidated or antagonistic towards those with mental health problems. Their fears and lack of security are heightened and reinforced through continued media coverage of the negative kind where stigmatising and ill-informed portrayals can be found in abundance. It covers in particular the proliferation of media examples where mental health issues are associated with a sense of violence or dangerousness (Morrall 2000a).

The mentally ill as victims

This category includes those with mental health problems who perceive themselves in the role of victims. As with the previous category, the emphasis here is on a felt or perceived experience that may differ significantly from what is actually encountered. There are a number of negative reinforcements which help to shape this perception such as incidences of rejection and alienation felt from the general public; a relegation of roles or one's position within the family; or an abusive or disempowering experience of health care. As illustrated by Skinner (1974), an individual's behaviour is shaped and maintained by consequences as what happens afterwards will determine whether or not it will be repeated (being strengthened) or will stop (becoming weakened). As individuals with mental health problems fall into one of the main groups in society who encounter stigma (Bloch and Singh 1997) – and there are countless examples throughout history of them being badly treated and socially excluded (Wing 1978) – the feelings of victimisation are exacerbated. It is also heightened by the continued use of jargonistic and abusive terminology (e.g. 'loonies', 'psycho' or 'mentals') that has been freely used both within society and the media in what may be either a thoughtless or intentful manner (Wahl 1995; Philo 1996a).

The negative impact upon those with mental health problems who consider themselves to be *victims* either of a health care system or by their communities cannot be underestimated. This can be seen through Cooley's '*The looking glass self*' whereby a person's identity and self-concept is built primarily as a result of how others act and respond towards them (Cohen 1982). The impact of disempowering and rejecting approaches therefore by others can leave individuals within this category feeling marginalised, rejected and helpless. As Mind's (2000) *Counting the Cost* report highlights, negative public attitudes and stigmatising media portrayals serve to enhance a person's

feeling of isolation and lowered self-esteem. They are also subsequently less motivated towards seeking support because of the stigma surrounding mental health care.

The inexperienced (general or lay public)

This category includes those with little direct involvement or experience. The majority of what people within this grouping know about mental health issues is gathered second-hand, namely what has been related by others or extrapolated from the media. In a sense this might also include those with mental health problems as experience of any one specific mental health state does not necessarily mean that individuals will be more tuned into the experience of others. For instance, people suffering with depression or anxiety have a completely separate concept of what mental illness means when compared, for example, to the experience of altered cognition and delusional thought patterns encountered with schizophrenia. Finer distinctions may even be made within single mental health conditions as, for example, one person's experience of bereavement will be uniquely different to that of others. This is affected by factors such as the type of relationship held with the deceased (e.g. one of dependency) and the subsequent impact this has upon their role. Each person therefore has their own unique and distinctive experience and understanding as to what the term mental illness actually means. What needs recognising is the vast spectrum of difference encompassed within the term 'mental illness' instead of seeing everyone concerned as belonging to one collective 'mass' upon whom we attribute similar qualities, for example, potentially violent, 'mad', or unpredictable. Another aspect worthy of mention is the degree of hierarchy that exists with regard to mental health problems as distinctions and gradings are made between certain conditions. If looking for instance at the classifications of neuroses and psychoses, it is the former which tends to be perceived in general more sympathetically compared to the latter which is seen less favourably and with a greater degree of stigma being applied. This is evidenced clearly within newspaper headlines that treat conditions such as depression (e.g. 'Sad Kerry' – *The Sun*) very differently from those that fall within the category of psychoses where fear and mistrust are strongly reflected (e.g. 'I ate his brains . . . lovely' – *Daily Mirror*). The psychotic classification clearly lends itself to a more dramatic portrayal reflected in, although helping to build up, an inaccurate and unbalanced view among the general public. This creates the dichotomy which exists for some whereby some types of mental health problems are to be pitied whereas others are to be feared.

Misinformation and stereotypes can be so pervasive and powerful that we accept certain elements without question as representing the truth. In terms of collective learning, it is hard to separate out what has been learnt from credible and reliable sources and what has been obtained from other less reliable ones. We may feel so certain about particular issues (e.g. the danger

potential of those with mental health problems) that we are not swayed even when in possession of fuller and more accurate facts. This can be illustrated by reflecting back in time to an era when the certainty and belief that the world was flat led to much anxiety when setting sail in search of new lands. This erroneous belief was supported at the time by a good deal of 'reliable' evidence until being clearly disproved a number of years later. The way in which the mentally ill are viewed has changed enormously over the years and the concept of 'insanity' has been regarded as many things including an excess of bodily humours; an indication of moral weakness; demonic possession; a sign of witchcraft; a sense of feebleness; a response to environmental factors; or, as indicated by Thomas Szasz (1992) and R.D. Laing (1990), an experience which exists as a social construction. What is evident though is that despite the ever-changing connotations of the term mental illness, negative feelings and associations continue to proliferate in our thinking and treatment towards those concerned.

Society's relationship with the media

The relationship between society and the media can be regarded on a cyclical basis with each participant in turn exerting a sense of influence upon the other (see Figure 1.3). There is wide-ranging debate as to which is the more powerful agent within this relationship; societal attitudes or media depictions. One element, subject to much study over the years, relates to the impact that media exposure has upon people's subsequent attitude and behaviour. The prevailing view is that the mass media has a degree of power in effecting social change through the distribution among a population of opinion, beliefs, values and practices (McQuail 2005). A focus for many studies has been that of 'media effects' and the work of individuals such as Albert Bandura (1986) on social learning theory. This approach details the direct influence that exposure to modelled behaviour has and relates to aspects such as the reported increases in suicide attempts following scenes depicted in television dramas (Hawton *et al.* 1999). The media effects model has, though, been greeted with a fair degree of criticism over recent years because of the overly simplistic manner in which it has been applied and the lack of attention to various aspects whereby audience members are able to respond differently to media examples or come up with their own interpretations (Gauntlett 1995). It is interesting therefore to note Noble's (1973) findings which demonstrated that 6-year-old children exposed to violence on television discriminated

Societal attitudes   Media depiction

Figure 1.3 Societal attitudes and media depiction relationship.

between the different styles of production they were exposed to. Documentaries and more realistic scenes made them anxious whereas the more stylised and distanced scenes of violence proved stimulating regarding their play. Another view is that in some cases it might be cathartic to have some exposure to violent portrayals as evidenced by Feshbach and Singer's (1971) study whereby it was found that watching programmes with a violent content for some participants helped to control aggression by purifying them of such impulses. While acknowledging that media effects do not address the whole picture, there is no question that they do have some effect. While claims might be made by tobacco companies to the effect that the power of tobacco advertising does not directly encourage the uptake of smoking but merely influences brand choice, it is hard then to understand the huge increase in smoking in third world countries noted by organisations such as Action on Smoking and Health (ASH 2005) following major and sustained marketing campaigns. Likewise, many media professionals reject the notion that they are responsible for the perpetuation of harmful stereotypes, claiming that they merely mirror the values and beliefs of society (Bolton 2000). Whether we accept this statement or not there is certainly some strong evidence to suggest that stigmatising media coverage does have a detrimental effect upon creating the stereotypical and negative beliefs which are then being 'mirrored'. The core issue here is to do with responsibility and accountability for some of the destructive content being relayed by media groups and it is not acceptable to simply deflect criticism elsewhere. There is an appetite among the public for dramatic and sensational coverage as evidenced through ratings, box office receipts and sales circulation, but it is irresponsible to simply meet this need and perpetuate the debilitating impact this has upon those with mental health problems (Mind 2000). Although there are instances when drivers slow down through curiosity to look at a car crash it would clearly be tasteless to produce videos of real-life accidents to meet this perceived need. Likewise, media providers should be held to account for the output of insensitive and inaccurate material regarding mental health issues that continues to be produced in direct contravention of their own regulatory standards.

Conversely, the media are in a sense reflecting what are the current views and beliefs concerning mental illness. This is shown very clearly through historical examples where the type of portrayal reflects the thinking of that era. The range of variations of depiction concerning the term madness is vast and, as stated by Wing:

> Madness can stand for every variety of unreason from foolery to psychosis . . . [and] carries different meanings according to the epoch, the society, and the social group involved, and according to the interests and preconceptions of the person who is using it.

> (Wing 1978: 2)

Ancient views about madness predominantly had divine connotations with explanations of it being a punishment visited upon humankind by the gods (Porter 2002). An example can be found in the Old Testament (Deuteronomy 6: 5) which relates how Nebuchadnezzar is punished by God with the line 'the lord will smite thee with madness'. Early Greek attitudes towards mental health were derived from myths and epics. These again had divine connotations such as the visitation upon Heracles by the gods of a force which heralded his period of madness. We can also look at eighteenth and nineteenth-century literature and the reflection of generally held assumptions that madness was regarded as an extension of the female condition (Small 1996). The era of incarceration is well-represented by portrayals such as Hogarth's *Rake's Progress*, the films *Asylum* and *Bedlam*, and Ken Kesey's seminal *One Flew over the Cuckoo's Nest*, all of which powerfully reflected the thinking of their day. It is therefore not surprising with the advent of Community Care (following the Community Care Act (DOH 1990)) to find a greater selection of media examples which reflect the enhanced visibility of mental illness. This includes many instances of autobiographical writing, film portrayals or soap characters that portray more clearly the lived and felt experience.

The relationship between society and the media has a middle ground where these participants are seen to merge. Media providers can be seen as holding a duality of roles, in a sense sitting on both sides of the relationship by transmitting as well as receiving messages. Despite this there is a sense of separateness highlighted by McQuail's view that: 'The media constitutes a separate social institution within society, with its own rules and practices, but is subject to definition and limitation by the wider society' (McQuail 2000: 5). This is where media providers might stand outside their normal sphere of influence and set of values and beliefs and engage instead within the pressures, influences or expectations engendered by their media group. It is also a place where, for example, newspaper reporters might be swayed towards a particular style of narrative (irrespective of their own held views) because of its expected attractiveness to a group of readers.

The nature of the relationship between society and the media has to some degree changed with modern resources and new interactive technologies, in a sense bringing the two groups even closer together. Certainly, the present selection of media types offers almost unlimited choice with less direct influence being exerted by media providers upon a mass audience (McQuail 2005). It is a relationship determined by a number of factors such as lifestyle or the sub-groups that individuals belong to. The intensity or degree of interaction with various media types is worthy of exploration, particularly concerning the theme of active versus passive interaction. Media providers have a clear view in mind as to the needs or requirements of their targeted audience. We make choices as to which types of media we engage with or how we access them based upon issues such as the attractiveness of a given product or the extent to which our particular needs are met. Certainly some genres are specifically geared to a fast and impactful engagement (e.g. tabloid newspapers)

among their recipients compared to others that offer a more informed and detailed perusal (e.g. broadsheet newspapers). Daytime television, for instance, serves up a diet of soaps and chat shows which are geared towards a less involved interaction. Viewers are engaged through a fast turnover of themes and sub-plots and can quite comfortably follow programmes with only partial attention. Media types such as film are different whereby messages are presented as a collective and total package requiring a more involved and responsive degree of attention from their audience. New media brings with it a fresh degree of choice, especially with the potential for a fast accessibility of a wide array of resources.

Media providers spend considerable sums of money in studying the needs of their targeted audiences and seeking further ways of enhancing audience engagement with their products. An audience's requirements are multi-faceted and might either relate to their needs to be entertained for purposes of relaxation, stimulation and distraction or to be educated for reasons such as a desire to learn, satisfying curiosity, or being reassured. Increased com-petition and financial considerations place further pressures upon media groups to engage consumers. This leads to the use of techniques that make messages stand out from the background, such as powerful and emotive newspaper headlines or overly dramatic scenes in television shows.

The media's relationship with mental health issues

Media organisations are made up of individuals who belong to the same sub-groups in society as discussed earlier and naturally are prone to the same array of influences. A point worth highlighting here is that media personnel will naturally include those with personal experiences of mental health prob-lems (self, family or friends), health care providers, as well as those with little direct contact or experience. These individuals will clearly differ in their atti-tudes and feelings towards the mentally ill and can be found in varied groups within the broad classification which we know as *the media*. The particular mix of people within different organisations as well as the positions of power and influence held will determine the resultant relationship between the media and mental health issues.

There are various factors which have a bearing upon how mental health themes are covered and which can be looked at with regards to whose needs are primarily being addressed. This covers issues such as commercialism and mental health promotion.

Commercialism

What is clearly of great interest to various media providers is the realisation that 'madness' sells. Dramatic storylines such as Sarah's obsessional and violent infatuation with Martin Fowler in *Eastenders* or *Coronation Street*'s 'Mad Maya', the deranged solicitor, all help to keep viewers gripped and in

turn enhances television ratings. Likewise, the overdramatic psychopathic killer served up through numerous metamorphoses in the 'slasher' film genre
has proved exceedingly popular at the box office and encourages the production in some cases of multiple sequels (Wahl 1995). Other notable examples
can be found within the tabloid press where an over-dramatisation of stories
helps to create maximum impact on their readers and to sell papers. The issue
of commercialism therefore means that many pressures will be placed upon
media personnel to frame products in a certain way. The drive towards
impactful and profit-making media products means that the feelings and
sensitivities of the mentally ill are largely overlooked and that guidelines and
regulatory standards are ignored. There is clearly much pressure being
brought to bear from within the media industry itself from editorial staff,
producers and directors to produce material that enhances the commercial
appeal of the product being produced.

Health promotion

As addressed above it seems as if the predominant needs being met are those
of the media providers themselves. There is scope though to use various
media products as vehicles to carry health promotional material. There are a
number of notable examples both factual as well as fictional that help to
educate the public and challenge attitudes towards 'mental illness'. Initiatives such as the Royal College of Psychiatry's (RCP 2001) Changing Minds
campaign, media mental health awards and autobiographical writing all
help to raise awareness of the real issues connected with mental illness. It is
assisted by media products that reach large audiences, thereby gaining
heightened exposure for the issues being addressed. This might include a
mental health storyline depicted in television soaps such as that of the self-
harming storyline which appeared in *Hollyoaks*. While clearly providing a
sense of gain for the media provider, there is also a sense of what the
audience can learn about the lived experience and feelings of those involved.
The approach of education and promotion is furthered by *new media* products such as the Internet, which offer many opportunities for consumer
updating with fast, accessible access to information available (Christensen
and Griffiths 2000).

A notable development involves the degree of liaison being developed
between the media and professional/service-user groups. This incorporates
degrees of involvement from production of media products and consultancy
support through to the creation of guidelines or feedback to media groups.
Many of these groups, as can be seen with the Royal College of Psychiatry,
the British Psychological Society, Mind and Mental Health Media, all provide specific training for their members to get involved with the media. The
essence of all this is the mounting of a challenge to the overwhelmingly
negative depiction and stigmatising portrayal of mental health issues in the
media. The concept of liaison is vital as the channels of communication used

by various media providers are needed in order to achieve the highest levels of exposure possible.

Society, the media and mental health issues

Finally, we can draw all these participants together to gain a sense of the total relationship which can be regarded in terms of a connecting or a distancing type. This relates to ways in which we interact with mental health issues as a consequence of media exposure either by being drawn towards them and feeling more in tune with aspects involved or of being repelled and removed to a greater distance. The *connecting/distancing* framework will be addressed in some detail throughout this book as it plays a major part in influencing the ways in which subsequent messages are formulated.

Connectors

This in a sense forms what might be seen as the lesser evoked strand (versus its more familiar stigmatising opposite) although it can likewise have an extremely powerful resonance with its audience. It is here that we are drawn towards certain areas of understanding and experience that are normally held at some distance because of feelings of trepidation, anxiety, or simply lack of opportunity. What is clear is that, if engaged with, there are many occasions where connecting and more empathic relationships can be fostered.

Some of these examples incorporate the somewhat striking perspective of being *inside looking out*. This is where the audience member is invited to enter the inner world of thoughts and feelings of those experiencing mental health problems. It is potentially a place where much learning can take place as well as somewhere that may for some prove uncomfortable and difficult to stay with. An example of this might be found with the first-person narrative of the psychopathic killer Patrick Bateman as related in the book *American Psycho*. There are countless, wonderful opportunities to gain real degrees of insight that can be quite striking when compared with what was previously known or 'assumed' learning concerning mental health issues. Notable examples include the film *A Beautiful Mind* and the sense of extreme confusion regarding the distinction between fantasy and reality encountered by John Nash. The clever film structure ensures that we as the audience are also able to experience the visual hallucinations and are left feeling unsure as to what is real and what is not. Another example can be seen with the fragmented and disconnected thought processes conveyed in Doris Lessing's *Briefing for a Descent into Hell*. Again, it is presented through first-person prose which keeps the reader very closely engaged with the principal character and his steady reconnection with the world around him. Also, television soaps and dramas provide examples where familiar and liked characters encounter mental health problems. These examples provide the recipient with a journey towards a closer and more engaged

connection with how mental health issues are experienced by those most affected.

Distancers

This category contains by far the predominant number of mental health examples. It is where the emphasis for the audience is upon entertaining, shocking or exciting and messages are handled in thoughtless and somewhat insensitive ways with little attention given to how far they might stray from what is factual. Two particularly negative types of depiction are when the 'mentally ill' are presented either as violent figures to heighten dramatic tension, or as comic eccentricities to provide us with a sense of amusement. With regard to the former strand, examples such as the packaging of news stories provide us with numerous 'factual' associations which connect mental illness with a heightened propensity for violence. This is evidenced in the style of writing using jargonistic and emotive words and narrative (Philo 1996b). This connection is further reinforced through a steady stream of examples evidenced across all media types including television dramas (Wilson *et al.* 1999) or the extremely powerful and popular films *Psycho* and *The Silence of the Lambs*.

Comedy is another much-used vehicle for incorporating mental health themes in order to heighten an audience's sense of amusement. Mental health issues provide us with the full range of characterisations from the likeable eccentric, as seen in the cinematic examples of *Harvey* and *Arsenic and Old Lace*, through to the unlikeable or offensive, in particular Jim Carrey's character in *Me, Myself and Irene*. Perhaps the key distinction with these varied examples is the degree to which we are engaged in either laughing *at* or *with* those depicted as 'mentally ill'. However, whichever way we regard this issue, these stereotypical representations serve to perpetuate the sense of difference perceived between those with mental health problems and the rest of the population.

There are also considerations whereby recipients fluctuate between the states of connecting and distancing. One of the factors influencing the public's distancing response is that of reaching a place which feels less threatening or uncertain. We might be exposed for a short space of time to a person's lived experience although then opt to remove ourselves to a more comfortable distance. For example, the reading of an autobiographical account of a person's struggling with a life of sexual abuse has the potential to evoke feelings of sympathy and horror. It connects us with uncomfortable and distressing feelings as well as a sense of helplessness where it may be easier to detach from what we are being exposed to and psychologically move away.

Why the need for this book?

The need for this book is highlighted through numerous studies that indicate the predominantly negative depiction being portrayed by the media. An overwhelming array of stigmatising imagery and negative associations can be

found in media examples throughout history to the present day. This book fits within the current climate where a greater number of studies, campaigns and initiatives are being set up to challenge the negative representation and increase the positive promotion of mental health. These approaches are helping to replace some of the traditionally held, stereotypical ideas with more helpful and less alienating ones. Essentially, as addressed above, it brings us closer to the term *mental illness* in every respect, permitting us to actually gain a greater sense of what is involved. The need therefore is to appreciate how attitudes and understanding of mental health issues are shaped and fostered through exposure to varied media products. This involves examining the influences affecting both the sender (media provider) and the recipient (audience) and the nature of the resultant relationship with mental health issues, either of a connecting or distancing type.

The need to address how the media reflect and address mental health issues is clearly identified by a number of prominent studies and reports. Media representations of mental health issues would appear in the main to be increasingly portraying negative images and comment, and concerns about this have been expressed by many groups including governmental, professional and mental health service-user organisations (Health Education Authority 1999; Mind 2000; Mindout for Mental Health 2001a; Day and Page 1986). These all highlight the need for further attention and, despite some movement in the right direction, the media as a whole still requires a much greater emphasis upon positive promotion. It involves beginning to change the current picture to one which is more real, one that reflects what is really going on, such as the fact that the mentally ill are more at risk from the general public than vice versa.

The current picture does provide some heartening developments especially with regard to stigma minimisation and the media. Commissioned by the Department of Health, Mindout for Mental Health (2001a) is working closely with partners in the voluntary sector, the media, companies and youth and student organisations to combat the stigma and discrimination surrounding mental health. It includes:

- Running workshops for journalists and media professionals on portraying mental health issues in the media
- Producing a practical guide on mental health in the media for trainee journalists

This fits in with the positive mental health promotion urged by the National Service Framework (DOH 1999) standard which outlines: '[a need to] promote mental health for all . . . combat discrimination against individuals and groups with mental health problems, and promote social inclusion' (DOH 1999). A number of initiatives instigated by mental health professionals include the Royal College of Psychiatrists (2001) five years (1998–2003) anti-stigma campaign 'Changing Minds: Every Family in the Land'. One of the aims of

the Changing Minds campaign is to challenge the inaccurate representation of mental illness in the media and elsewhere, based on stigmatising attitudes and stereotypes, myths, misunderstandings and discriminatory attitudes.

There is some evidence of change as highlighted by studies carried out by the Health Education Authority in 1997 (*Making Headlines: Mental Health and the National Press*) and 1999 (*Media Mentality*) which provide a useful comparison. The 1997 study found 46 per cent of all mental health press coverage being about crime, harm to others and self-harm. Also, 40 per cent of daily tabloid articles contained stigmatising words like 'nutter' and 'loony'. The later study in 1999 found a continued fuelling of stigma although offered increased optimism with more favourable coverage and a growing interest in mental health issues being highlighted. An area though of core concern is that of suicide with numerous examples being cited when suicide attempts have been influenced by media messages. It is a theme focused upon in particular throughout this book.

This book aims to stimulate questioning regarding the messages that individuals are exposed to on a daily basis. It also strives to encourage the reader to stop and challenge where their information about mental health comes from and to question the credibility of the source. What is crucial to a person's learning about mental health issues is an ability to discriminate between what is accurate and what is not and to develop a more balanced understanding of the nature and experience of mental health problems.

Content summary

Chapter 2 The role of the media

This chapter begins by outlining the scope and range of media sources and presents the core communication model used – that of Berlo (1960). This model covers the flow of communication from a source (sender) to its targeted recipient (receiver). It is related to the concepts of media provider and audience member and addresses the range of influences that play a part in shaping the eventual message which is decoded by the person accessing the message. This is related to each part of the communication process with aspects such as regulatory guidelines, media type and recipient's predisposition to certain stimuli all being covered.

Chapter 3 Stigma, labelling and social exclusion

What is *bad* about various media types is summarised and covered in this section. It begins by defining stigma and then looking at related concepts such as labelling theory, deviance and social exclusion. The effects and consequences of these types of portrayal within the media are examined in detail with thought given to some of the reasons for their perpetuation by different media providers. In part this includes a look at factors such as commercial

considerations and a desire among the public to be able to engage with 'monsters' and have exposure with them in a safe way. Finally, thought is given to some of the means being employed to challenge and tackle the problem of stigma.

Chapter 4 The positive depiction of mental health issues through the media

This chapter presents a contrast to the previous one highlighting what is *good* about the media. The essence given here is that not all of the messages regarding mental health conveyed by the media are bad. Increasingly, the channels for communication within the media are also being used as vehicles for health promotion and education. It includes strategies such as the development of better liaison between media providers and mental health service-users. There is also a specific focus upon media products which enable recipients to connect and engage with the experience of mental illness as well as those that help to increase a person's understanding of the reality of mental health problems. Lastly, thought is given to some of the current initiatives being employed to maintain more progressive attitudes and approaches to the mentally ill.

Chapter 5 The press

This chapter explores the portrayal of mental health issues through the medium of news reporting. It focuses primarily upon the newsprint media with particular attention being given to the broadsheet and tabloid press as well as a look at magazine coverage. Regulation and guidelines that relate specifically to the news media are covered, such as the National Union of Journalists *Code of Conduct* (NUJ 1999) and the *Code of Practice* of the Press Complaints Commission (PCC 2005). What is interesting here is that despite some very clear guidelines concerning issues such as accuracy and discrimination, stigmatising and stereotypical reporting styles continue to proliferate. The framework of headlines, narrative and imagery is applied as a means of examining some of the broad differences between publication types.

Chapter 6 Literature

The depiction of mental health issues through the medium of literature is reflected upon here with the different publication types of autobiography, semi-autobiography and fiction being covered. It begins with a look at historical sources tracing the portrayal from ancient works by Homer and Virgil through to more contemporary writers such as Marge Piercy (*Woman on the Edge of Time*) and Iain Banks (*The Wasp Factory*). It addresses some of the core strengths offered by this particular medium including the ability to engage the reader more directly with the inner world of those experiencing

mental health problems. The clear distinction between examples depicting mental illness as a destructive entity and those which portray it as a survivable condition is also addressed.

Chapter 7 Film

This chapter reviews the medium of film and the very diverse range of examples being reflected. The framework of narrative, sound and imagery is used to explore the way in which mental health themes are handled. Cinematic depictions can be regarded as falling within the broad categories which regard the mentally ill as: killer; afflicted genius; and comic eccentric. These are covered in detail including thought as to the range of emotions (e.g. fear, sympathy and amusement) evoked for the viewer by these distinctly different variations. It also focuses upon historical themes which reflect the changing ways in which mental health care and the mentally ill have been viewed over the years.

Chapter 8 Television

This chapter begins by considering the broad range of television programming through which we are exposed to mental health issues. Although broadly falling within factual and fictional categories there are numerous genres appealing to many different audience types. Standards and regulations which play a part in governing what is shown on television are reviewed along with the various influences that lead programme makers into neglecting them and including discriminatory content. Attention is given to some of the ways in which viewers' perceptions are shaped through the wide variety of positive and negative imagery they are exposed to. There is also discussion given to the extent to which programmes balance the aspects of entertainment and education, especially given the pressures to promote and protect audience viewing figures.

Chapter 9 The Internet

This chapter provides an opportunity to look at a modern and rapidly developing media source, that of the Internet. A major strength of this facility is the accessibility and ready availability of material providing advice, guidance and information. The scope is almost limitless covering a number of quality sites run by professional groups and user-carer organisations as well as a range of unregulated and poorly constructed ones. The quality varies greatly from those that are informative to those that are misleading. Some of the attempts at providing markers of quality are reviewed including examples of kitemarking and various frameworks for rating sites. Other aspects covered include the coverage of suicide, future implications for the health care relationship and the potential offered by online therapy.

Chapter 10 And . . .?

This section draws the key themes together looking at the implications and significance for those involved with different media sources as well as health care providers. It looks at ways in which further progress can be made in improving the depiction of mental health issues across all media types. Some of the core frameworks used throughout this book are revisited and considered with regards to ongoing development. These are the themes of connecting; educating and exposure. Essentially it relates to ways in which better relationships can be fostered between society and the topic *mental health*.

2 Media sources and the role of the media

Introduction

This chapter is about the flow of communication from a media source to its audience. It addresses the multiplicity of processes and influences that play a part in shaping the message which is finally received. Numerous aspects come into play regarding each stage of the communication process from the initial processing and framing of information to be sent out, the channel along which it is transmitted and its eventual reception and decoding. In a number of cases the message sent out may alter significantly to the one which is received. The reasons for this, such as the differing perspectives between sender and receiver, will be examined later on in detail.

We have on the one hand a sender or transmitter of information and on the other a recipient. The message relayed between them, in the context of this book, relates to mental health content. This subject matter can be very powerfully emotive with opinions being very clearly divided dependent upon expectations and experience. For example, a group of people might watch the film *Me Myself and Irene* yet differ wildly in how they receive it with some finding it 'entertaining' and 'hilarious' while others regard it as 'insulting' or 'totally misleading'. Of significance within this process are the reasons behind the media provider's intentions and subsequent packaging of their product as well as the audience member's personal viewpoint and interpretation of the received messages. These issues are all addressed in detail using Berlo's (1960) communication model (see Figure 2.1) as the framework for examining the flow of data from one source to another.

The core components of Berlo's (1960) communication model are:

- referent (the stimulus which begins the communication process)
- sender (the initiator of contact)
- message (information or data which is sent or expressed)
- medium (channel) (the vehicle for transmission of messages)
- receiver (recipient and interpreter of message sent)
- and feedback (response to sender).

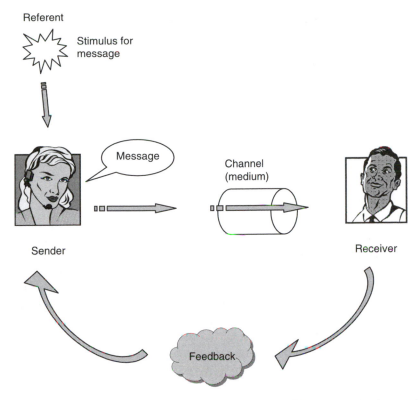

Figure 2.1 The communication process. Adapted from Berlo's communication model
(1960).

Referent

The referent refers to the stimulus or purpose for any given communication
process (Berlo 1960). In this case the needs of the media provider or alternatively those of the consumer can be seen as constituting the main driving
force. What these needs are will clearly differ and there may be a strong
feeling of conflict between these two groups. It is therefore hard to ascertain
the degree to which the needs and requirements of each are being satisfied.
We can also consider the pressure or influence from other parties whereby
media messages are carried on behalf of external sources and organisations
such as political parties, advertisers, lobbyists, businesses, social action
groups and government departments (McQuail 1997). The following
addresses the media provider's requirements concerning commercial and
therapeutic gain as well as the consumer's need for entertainment or
education.

The media provider's need

The term *media provider* here is a vastly encompassing description which includes a diverse collection of individuals. Tension may obviously exist at this stage between the different needs of those involved such as the consummatory and instrumental tension identified by Berlo (1960). For instance, a tabloid journalist might seek recognition as a credible writer (consummatory intention) by producing a clear and honest article yet is pressured by the editor who is concerned with sales (instrumental intention) to adopt a jargon-filled and moralistic style of writing.

For the *media provider* as a group entity, one of the prime factors relating to the inclusion of mental health material relates to financial considerations. The inclusion of mental health content adds an extra touch of drama that has an influence upon box office takings, television ratings, as well as newspaper and book sales. 'Madness' as a topic is both fascinating and compelling and has proved immensely attractive to many different audiences. This provides media organisations with strong incentives to include mental health content even though it may result in poor quality products. Wahl (1995) reflects this point with the example of the many 'slasher' films being made with multiple sequels, each seemingly worse than the preceding one because of the tendency of investors to repeat what has proved profitable in the past.

It is also worth noting the manner in which the referent for mental health coverage is 'located' by some media providers within their audience. Instead of openly recognising the profitability of such content, the public's need to know is cited as being the most salient aspect. Whether the need was there in the public domain in the first place or whether it was created by the media is a point of contention. For example, tabloid newspaper coverage would have an uninformed observer believing that the public have an apparently insatiable appetite to hear more about David and Victoria Beckham as well as other popular celebrities. The headlines, column inches and pictures given up to these individuals in many cases far exceed the newsworthiness of their actual exploits. It is as if the public is being offered an extremely limited menu from which to choose from as well as being led to what to access. This is reflected in other media formats such as the heavy scheduling on television of 'reality' shows which proliferate the daily schedules. High ratings are obtained for programmes which place characterless individuals in situations where little of note which is unmanufactured occurs.

There are other reasons for including mental health content such as where individuals have a vested interest in health promotion initiatives or personal therapeutic gain. There has been a steady increase over the past few years in mental health service-user groups becoming involved in a range of media projects and initiatives. The stimulus is provided through the need to promote education and engagement of the general public towards developing less stigmatising and better informed attitudes. From an educational point of view, Internet sites, booklets, fact sheets and television documentaries present

just a small selection of what is available. Engagement is also achieved through creative and expressive forms such as art exhibitions, film festivals (e.g. the Royal College of Psychiatrists' Mind Odyssey) and various dramatic productions. The main stimulus here is provided by the potential change that can be brought about in the receiver. As well as gain for the receiver, there is a potential therapeutic benefit for the creator of a media product. An example can be seen in literature with the ever-increasingly popular autobiographical genre and the approach of *writing as therapy*. The act of writing here provides the author with an opportunity to work through and make sense of individual trauma thereby gaining much personally through the process of writing. There is a duality of purpose here as many autobiographical products reach wide audiences and have a high marketable value. This can be seen with Dave Pelzer's writing about his experience of being abused as a child (beginning with *A Child Called It*) and his subsequent coming to terms with it through a series of hugely popular books.

It is hard therefore to separate out exactly what the catalyst for this process is although we can see from the sender's point of view a number of incentives for the inclusion of mental health material. These incorporate gains for the sender in terms of financial incentives, opportunities for educating the public as well as therapeutic gain through the process of constructing media products.

The consumer's need

The diversity of consumers' needs can be viewed through two separate categories, those of education and entertainment.

Education

A NEED TO BE INFORMED

The importance of the media as a primary communicating agent regarding mental illness is highlighted by Sieff (2003). As consumers, our need for information about mental health issues is stimulated by factors such as personal mental health experience, curiosity about a compelling and fascinating topic, or a need for reassurance. Personal experience of mental health problems will certainly create a desire to seek out information concerning support groups, available treatments and the nature of specific conditions. If we take for instance the example of somebody who has recently been diagnosed with depression a core resource accessed might be the Internet. It is a medium that is proving ever more attractive to mental health service-users because of the ready accessibility and availability of information (Scrivener 2002). Alternatively, they might seek out some of the many self-help books or autobiographical accounts available such as Andrew Solomon's (2002) informative and insightful *The Noonday Demon – an Anatomy of Depression* which

was voted Mind's book of the year in 2002. This publication combines an autobiographical account of the experience of depression along with a critical review of the available evidence, concerning causal factors and treatment approaches. The main issue however relates to the ability that individuals have in selecting from the wide range of resources available, discriminating between what is informative and helpful and what is misleading and potentially harmful.

As well as accessing information for health reasons it is worth also considering the desire of many people to satisfy their own interest or curiosity in what is potentially a compelling and fascinating yet much misunderstood topic. Soap storylines, documentaries, magazine articles, novels and newspaper reports form just a small part of the many different products carrying a mental health theme that are available. In the main they are very popular and marketable, in many cases engaging their audience more for entertainment than for purposes of education.

A NEED FOR REASSURANCE

One of the strands relating to informational needs is governed by feelings of anxiety and discomfort about the mentally ill. It is a need created in part by the media themselves through sensational, explicit and emotive reporting that all serve to unsettle their audience. For example, the saturation coverage of a high-profile crime involving a perpetrator with mental health problems usually evokes a desire for reassurance and understanding. In particular, people seek to find out how such horrific acts might have been prevented. Fears abound centring on aspects such as whether any tell-tale signs were in evidence as to an individual's potential for violence. The apparent demand for information is met in abundance by the media and in some cases involves extraneous fine detail. It seems there is little which is not covered and one often wonders about the degree of insensitivity being shown especially to the families of those concerned. The message being conveyed is that we as a public need to know and want to know all of these intricate details. Because people with mental health problems often do not display any noticeable traits, unlike the traits or characteristics which are often grossly exaggerated within much of the fictional media, it seems that our need for reassurance is enhanced. As the general public are unable to adequately spot who poses a risk to their community, the focus becomes all encompassing. Therefore all those who have the label 'mental illness' applied to them become included within the mass of individuals from whom a general sense of threat is felt.

Entertainment

This covers different elements and may be seen to include a desire for both humorous as well as frightening imagery.

A NEED TO LAUGH

Laughter is important for many reasons including stimulation, stress relief and relaxation. From a mental health point of view the outcast or the fool has historically provided a focus for derision or merriment and can be seen within countless comical depictions. The characterisation ranges from the harmless eccentric (James Stewart's alcoholic character in the film *Harvey*) through to the grossly misrepresented and shameless depictions (Jim Carrey's Hank/Charlie in *Me, Myself and Irene*). We are enticed towards either laughing *with* the character or perhaps in a number of instances laughing *at* them. It is the latter portrayal which is more harmful, undermining much of the work done to combat stigmatising and stereotypical portrayals. Some examples are grossly insensitive and fail to recognise the real seriousness of the subject matter being depicted. A prime example of this is the *Viz* adult cartoon strip character Suicidal Sid, who cheerfully engages in a number of seemingly comic ways to try and kill himself. Unfortunately, the comic clown proves very popular to consumers and appears regularly in derisive imagery and jargonistic language. It shows an overall lack of responsibility by media providers that they are prepared to offer products which are beneficial to them but at the expense of those being ridiculed. Certainly one could argue that many instances contain examples that are simply harmless fun, although they all play a part in developing a global picture that entails those with mental health problems not being taken seriously.

A NEED TO BE SCARED

This need provides the impetus for the increasingly popular horror genre. Films and books of every conceivable quality are produced in order to meet an almost insatiable demand. The principal attraction is the opportunity to experience strong emotions such as terror in a secure and contained environment. We are simultaneously brought into close contact with fearful stimuli as well as retaining a comfortably safe distance. Mental illness adds an extra level of intensity to the fearful scenes being depicted and heightens the experience felt. Mad killers are far more frightening because of their depiction as frenzied or unpredictable. Their ranks include cannibal killers (*The Silence of the Lambs* and *The Texas Chain Saw Massacre*), apparently indestructible killers (*Halloween*), phantom-like killers (*Nightmare on Elm Street* and Freddie Krueger). Perhaps the most frightening are those who are portrayed as apparently normal until their madness becomes apparent. There are two classic Hitchcock examples here involving Norman Bates as the nervy motel owner in *Psycho* and Barry Foster as the affable and confident character in *Frenzy*. A core aspect with these portrayals is the ability the recipient has in putting the book down, leaving the cinema or turning the television off. It is a means of experiencing cathartically strong emotions which we would

be unable to do otherwise. The highly popular nature of this form of entertainment means that many new examples are being created.

Sender

The types of message being packaged and transmitted by media groups are subject to a variety of factors and influences. First, the particular characteristics of a given media provider and the available channel of communication will play a significant part in shaping the message to be sent out. Of particular relevance is the influence exerted by those who hold a controlling influence in a given media type. This is further affected by the degree of control and structuring exerted through regulation and censorship of media products. This may be set up through internal procedures whereby a media provider has a self-regulatory approach or as a response to pressure from outside agencies such as governmental legislation. There are also various types of guidance provided for those working within media organisations from a range of mental health groups (professional and service-user) aimed at achieving a better portrayal of mental health issues.

Ownership

One of the most significant factors influencing the media relates to the concept of ownership. Whether media organisations are set up as profit making or non-profit making ventures or are private or public concerns, the concept of ownership has a strong bearing upon media content (Devereux 2003). If we consider the global picture, mainstream media ownership progressively rests in fewer hands as a consequence of mergers, takeovers, technological change and privatization. This results in a concentration of ownership with a handful of national and multinational corporations dominating the mass communications industry (Bagdikian 1997). At the same time conglomeration has been taking place, with media companies becoming part of larger corporations which in turn grow bigger. A major influencing factor is that in concentrated media ownership the search for profit is seen as key arbiter of what is produced (O'Sullivan, Dutton and Rayner 1994). Croteau and Hoynes (2000) reflect upon the impact of conglomeration in that previously some news media had been sheltered from the full pressure of profit making. This view is supported by Squires (1993), who indicates that corporate takeovers of print media place an emphasis upon entertaining and attracting consumers rather that informing them. All of this has major implications with regard to the reporting of mental health issues as sensitivity and realism are not as appealing from a sales perspective as are the usual stereotypical 'fodder' served up by large sections of the media.

The small number of controlling interests with regard to the mass media results in audiences becoming conditioned to accept a somewhat limited view of the world (McQuail 2005). This picture is changing with the increased

choice currently being offered by the rise and development of new media products and services (cable and satellite, fibre optic technology and computers) and has resulted in a move away from mass broadcast audiences towards smaller, more specialised niche populations. It is a process described by Croteau and Hoynes (2000) as 'narrowcasting' and provides a contrast to the conglomeration of media providers. The implications here are that a greater degree of choice can be offered to consumers concerning the type of media products available. The greater flexibility and choice of media services and products also means that the concept of ownership is increased to include a greater number of individuals and organisations with a vested interest in mental health issues. For example, a brief search for mental health related material on the Internet indicates a wide array of information that has been posted by professional organisations, service-user groups and individuals with an experience of mental health problems.

Censorship

Each media source explored within this book will be examined with a focus upon the constraints or structures that play a fundamental part in shaping the message to be sent out. The pressure brought to bear upon media providers comes from many different sources with varying degrees of authority. We can first look at the process of internal regulation, whereby a degree of control is exerted by the media organisation itself or those working within it, i.e. writers, producers or editors. Second, we can refer to the range of external regulations that are imposed by various authoritative bodies and which include governmental legislation.

One form of regulation is provided through censorship, whereby products are gauged regarding their suitability for public consumption. The term *censorship* has different connotations and can be welcomed on the one hand as a necessary safeguard protecting vulnerable groups in society (i.e. children), or alternatively might be seen as an oppressive and controlling power curtailing freedom of speech. Censorship is applied with the rationale and explanation that it is the public's interest that is being served. Many examples of censorship can be found across different media formats with examples such as the books *Lady Chatterley's Lover* and *Lolita* or the films *Crash* and *The Man with the Golden Arm*. In many instances what is deemed acceptable or unacceptable differs according to the perspective with which a product is viewed. First, we might consider a historical perspective as what is deemed unsuitable in one era may be perfectly acceptable at a later date. A clear example of this is the 1954 Marlon Brando film *The Wild One* which was not screened in Britain until 1968 for the damaging effect it was felt it might have upon young people watching it. Interestingly, by today's standards the mean and moody posturing of Brando's motorcycle gang appears more camp and comedic. Another important aspect is the issue of cultural acceptability as different groups of people hold contrasting views over, for example, religious

or moral grounds. This has been seen in the hostile reception by certain groups to some media products, such as the fatwa ordered over Salman Rushdie's *Satanic Verses* or the viewing of Monty Python's *A Life of Brian* which was regarded as blasphemous and offensive.

A major factor is of course the question as to exactly whose interests are being served through censorship. From a political point of view, curtailing free speech might be regarded as a necessary means of controlling a populace. This can be seen in a number of examples such as during China's Cultural Revolution or in the eastern bloc communist regimes where censorship was applied as a means of silencing particular expressions and controlling people's thoughts and speech. In some cases it was severely applied, in its most drastic forms resulting in imprisonment, exile or even execution. The effects upon those censored are well documented in a number of sources including Jung Chang's powerful autobiographical novel *Wild Swans*, which documents the harsh and restrictive climate that existed within Mao's China.

One might argue that a counter-productive outcome from censorship is that in a number of instances it has the opposite desired effect. It can draw attention to and effectively promote the product it is trying to restrict. In other words, censorship instils a sense of power and attractiveness in products that may not have been there in the first place. The perhaps short-sighted approach of banning radio air time to the Sex Pistols' *God Save the Queen* or Frankie goes to Hollywood's *Relax* made both of these records instant hits. Another example can be seen in the huge sales of D.H. Lawrence's novel *Lady Chatterley's Lover* that immediately followed its initial banned publication.

Clearly censorship has different applications pertinent to the place and media type. In England for example, there is no direct censorship of the written word although any publication can be challenged in the courts 'after the event'. Published work could be challenged for instance by legislative acts relating to issues of obscenity, blasphemy or racial hatred. Therefore in labelling a book as obscene one would need to show that it tended to 'deprave' or 'corrupt' the reader. This clearly though relates to the targeted audience as what might not be an obscene publication for an adult might easily be held to be obscene and tasteless if made available to children. As far as mental health issues go, it is far less clear and it seems that there is no clear legislation protecting this group. Using the previous example, what is deemed to be stigmatising and harmful by those experiencing mental health problems might differ considerably from the views or perceptions of the general public. The difficulty in changing this picture lies in the attractiveness and appeal that the topic of *madness* has for media providers and consumers alike. Products that are grossly offensive or harmful provide greater opportunities for seeking redress from their instigators, although the large numbers that are 'merely' insensitive or misleading are harder to tackle.

Media regulations and guidelines

Depending upon the media format type, there are different sets of guidelines and regulatory standards that govern the type of message to be sent out. Television, for example is heavily regulated with particular advice regarding mental health content provided initially by the Broadcasting Standards Commission *Codes of Guidance* (1998) and the Independent Television Commission *Programme Code* (2002), but now assumed by Ofcom. With regard to 'the Press', the *Code of Practice* of the Press Complaints Commission (UK) (2005) and the National Union of Journalists (1999) *Code of Conduct* highlight the need for journalists to ensure accuracy and fairness in their writing and to avoid discrimination. The cinematic world is influenced by bodies such as the British Board of Film Classification (BBFC) and the Motion Picture Association of America (MPAA) that have a role in classifying films regarding their suitability to various audience groups. Even largely unregulated 'new media' formats such as the Internet are beginning to create indicators of quality (such as the Hon Code), which include approved evidence based sites. Ofcom, the regulator for the UK communication industries has been given responsibility for 'maintaining content standards in the electronic media'. Guidance even extends to the world of advertising where the Advertising Standards Authority (ASA) administers the various Codes of Advertising across a range of broadcast and non-broadcast media. The Disability Discrimination Act (1995), although including the term *mental impairment*, does not feature strongly with regard to mental health issues as there is little evidence of it being applied in instances other than those concerning physical impairment.

One mental health theme in particular, around which a considerable range of guidelines have been produced, is that of suicide. The Department of Health (2002) has produced a consultation document *National Suicide Prevention Strategy for England*, which sets out a number of goals to improve the reporting of suicidal behaviour in the media. This builds upon evidence that the reporting of suicide can increase the rate especially among those already at risk (DOH 2002). It is stated that: 'By limiting some aspects of the reporting of suicide and by portraying it in ways which may discourage imitation, the media can make an important contribution to suicide prevention.' (DOH 2002:19).

Other bodies such as the Samaritans (1997) set out a structure for guidance on suicide coverage in the media which includes:

- Avoid sensationalism and remove positive messages about suicide
- Avoid reference to suicide
- Increase the prominence given to responsible reports on suicide prevention
- Include facts about suicide
- Influence the training of journalists to ensure that they report on mental illness and suicidal behaviour in an informed and sensitive manner

- Establish a method of ensuring that such training is repeated in a rolling programme

Perhaps one of the most striking features is that despite each media provider having its own set of guidelines that regulate against the employment of discriminating or stigmatising imagery, there seem to be only small movements being made to reduce the steady stream of negative and stigmatising depictions. It seems that the incentives for producing ever-more impactful and commercially enticing products in many instances prove stronger than those of respecting and adhering to available regulatory guidelines.

Training and media involvement

A notable development over recent years has been the gradual increase in direct involvement that health care professionals and mental health service-user groups have fostered with various media providers. This particularly relates to the broadcast and print media and encompasses a variety of roles such as the offering of comment and consultancy services or through direct involvement with production. As a consequence, many professional and service-user groups now offer training and advice to their members who are wishing to become more proactively engaged with the media. It has been furthered through initiatives such as the Department of Health's (2001) Mindout for Mental Health's (2001a) Mindshift campaign and the Royal College of Psychiatrists' (2001) Changing Minds campaign that have targeted the need to reduce stigmatising media coverage of mental health issues and include recommendations for the development of greater collaboration between mental health groups and media providers. The importance of this type of liaison cannot be overestimated as it means that media personnel are provided with informed guidance and are called upon to question what they are producing. One notable example is the collaborative *Guide for Journalists and Broadcasters Reporting on Schizophrenia* produced, among other parties, by the Royal College of Psychiatrists and the National Union of Journalists.

Berlo

Berlo (1960) identifies 4 factors within the source which play a part in increasing the fidelity of the communication process: Communication skills, attitudes, knowledge level, and position within a socio-cultural system.

Communication skills

The type of communication utilised within the media is influential here and may take many forms including those of a written, narrative, visual or sound base. The expressiveness and complexity of a message will clearly be increased

through the use of multiple forms. Also, the recipient's favoured mode of address needs to be borne in mind.

Attitudes

The attitudes of the sender towards self, subject matter and the receiver all play a significant part here. One of the main strands would be the relationship that media personnel have with the issue of mental illness. For example, the message sent out from someone with personal experience of mental health problems may be shaped much more sensitively than from somebody with little or no awareness. Media personnel clearly have some expectations as to what the perceived consumer's needs are and will gear presentations towards specific recipient groups. An example of this can be seen in the press and the type of language used as well as the way in which news stories are constructed and formatted.

Knowledge level

Berlo states that:

> One cannot communicate with maximum effectiveness content material that one does not understand. On the other hand if the source knows too much, if he is overspecialized, he might err in that his particular communication skills are employed in so technical a manner that his receiver cannot understand him.
>
> (Berlo 1960: 48)

This statement raises a number of issues which can be addressed with regard to the handling of information by the media. The first part of this statement certainly does not deter a lot of misleading and erroneous presentation that can be found within numerous media products, much of which would seem to suggest that the originator of the message does not indeed know much about the subject they are portraying. It may be that media providers in some instances are acting in good faith with the information they are presenting, although they are unable to recognise that their sources of knowledge are flawed. As Wahl (1995) points out, misconceptions that abound in the general public are shared by those involved with the media. The second strand, that of over-specialism, may be true of some examples, such as Internet sites or some health promotional material, although the question here would relate to appropriateness of different information types to their intended audience.

Position within a socio-cultural system

This category addresses all the influences upon one's perception of the world around us. The way we structure and interpret mental health issues may be

borne out of personal experience or attitudinal aspects and expectations of the various groups we belong to. This includes the ways in which group pressure can play a part in the modification and distortion of judgement (Asch 1961).

Message

Message framing

One of the core features of the communicating process involves the particular way in which a message has been shaped or presented. Framing can be defined as the means by which media information is organised, presented and subsequently interpreted (Sieff 2003). This can be explored through frameworks, such as Hall's (1974a) encoding/decoding model, that address the codes and conventions employed by media professionals in the construction of messages and their subsequent decoding by audience members. These features are also outlined by Berlo (1960) who highlights the factors of:

- Message code – a group of symbols structured in a way that is meaningful to another person i.e. language, music, painting, dance
- Message content – the material in the message which provides structure
- Message treatment – the decisions which the communication source makes in selecting and arranging both codes and content. It includes what is deemed interesting to the receiver

Clearly, frequently negative frames contribute towards the public's unfavourable attitudes to issues of mental health. This may be out of context with actual reality, as outlined by Philo:

> The media are highlighting a tiny minority of cases relative to the very large number of people with mental health problems, and that in doing so media accounts are distorting public perceptions of the whole area of mental health.
>
> (Philo 1996b: xii)

This statement is disturbing in that the core message being carried by the media as a whole is incorrect and misleading. The educative and evidence based information is submerged within a larger mass which means that in many cases they will be missed or, as with Broadbent's (1958) filter theory, the weight of what is transmitted is diluted by the plethora of competing messages.

The means of communication will obviously vary according to the media type selected although broadly can be seen as comprising those of imagery, narrative and sound.

Imagery

Mental health imagery has a powerful resonance with those accessing it and often evokes strong emotions. The imagery is frequently negative with the mentally ill being portrayed as being bizarrely different or violent and dangerous. This reflects Wahl's (1995) notion of those with mental health problems being segregated and treated as 'a breed apart'. The continued need for this type of representation is perhaps reinforced because of the psychologically self-protective function it serves. In a sense this means that individuals can discriminate more simply between the mentally ill and the mentally well and therefore take steps towards what is felt to be a safe distance.

When considering the nature of images it is important to note the various ways in which they are encountered or created through both pictures and words. The essence perhaps is of audience perception as in some cases the recipient is guided towards very specific interpretations and in others might be confused by ambiguous messages and left to form much of their own understanding. Visual imagery is powerfully depicted within the media of film and television and can present viewers with pictures of what is happening within a character's internal world or what is external and observable by others. An example of the former can be seen in Polanski's *Repulsion* where the cracks appearing in the walls form symbolic representations of the principal character's fragmenting mental health state. The more commonly portrayed imagery, though, seems to be located in the second element, that of external impressions and characterisations. The predominant presentation here is of individuals who look different, such as David Helfgott's dishevelled looking character in the film *Shine* or the scary intensity of Anthony Hopkins as Hannibal Lecter.

Mental health imagery is impactful and compelling and can serve to engage the receiver in a very powerful way. These images are often negative and portray the mentally ill through a number of stereotypes such as appearing violent, socially inadequate or eccentric (Wilson *et al.* 1999). Children's media in particular abounds with stereotypical caricatures, either that of the evil madman or the drooling idiot (Wahl 2003a; Wilson *et al.* 2000). In many cases these images permeate our thinking and feelings about those we regard as mentally ill, leaving us with associations that in some instances bear little resemblance to what the reality actually is. The audience are provided with positive imagery as well although the violent and scary images are often the more potent with images of Norman Bates or Hannibal Lecter superseding other, softer ones such as Judy Dench's emotive role in the film *Iris*.

Imagery is also used to portray factors other than characterisation and includes background features such as the settings within which care is delivered. A wide contrast is presented here from the stark and sterile environment in *One Flew over the Cuckoo's Nest* and *Girl Interrupted* to the cluttered yet comfortable psychotherapists' offices in *Ordinary People* or *Good Will Hunting*. In most of these cases the environment within which

scenes take place act as a secondary means of communication conveying to the audience member a feeling of mood which resembles the style of care being offered – either impersonal and severe or warm and secure. The particular choice of setting is not always apparent although we might suppose that suspenseful or dramatic engagement play a part. The film *Gothika*, for example, features a high-security mental health institution which is on reflection rather unnecessary as well as misleading. The high level of security conveys to the viewer a feeling of potential danger from those imprisoned and serves to perpetuate the age-old association between mental illness and violence potential.

Imagery is also created through the written word whereby the reader creates their own pictures from the text in front of them. In a number of cases the reader is led towards formulating their impressions through direct cues provided by the author. For example, in the book *Harry Potter and the Goblet of Fire* the madness of Mr Crouch is described to the reader through drawing attention to his dishevelled appearance and odd behaviour – 'He looked utterly mad. His eyes were rolling and bulging, and a trickle of spittle was sliding down his chin.' The image portrayed is not a positive one and connects the reader very quickly to many classic stereotypes regarding the mentally ill. The written word also creates symbolic imagery that is representative of other related aspects. Kafka's *Metamorphosis* for instance powerfully conveys the reaction of others towards disease or human suffering through the symbolic of portrayal of Gregor Samsa's plight at finding himself transformed overnight into a beetle.

Narrative

A core distinction with regard to narrative style relates to whether or not those with mental health problems are referred to by an external narrator or through first-person accounts. The former applies to much of what readers might get from newspapers or literature. The printed word can be very evocative and can build up a damning picture of individuals through a few select words such as 'psycho', 'mental' or 'schizo'. The type of words chosen may be misleading, inaccurate and damaging yet at the same time favoured by a media provider because of their ability to achieve dramatic impact. Take for instance the headlines 'Freed Cannibal Killer Ate Brain of One of his Victims' (*Daily Mirror* online version), '*Silence of the Lambs* Maniac Freed to Kill' (*Today*) and 'A Psychotic on the Loose in Suffolk' (*Guardian*). These use words in very emotive and disparaging ways that are morbidly appealing to their potential readers. It conjures up, though, very unfavourable stereotypes maintaining a range of negative associations such as that of mental illness and the potential for violence. The continued use of stereotypes is explained by Salter (2003) in that people prefer certainties and that stereotypes reduce the uncertainty accompanying new and novel stimuli.

Madness as a topic is commercially attractive and appealing to readers and

the medium of literature includes numerous books which include mental health themes as a means of engagement. The predominant presentation is through third-person narratives that generally feature those with mental health problems for their interest or entertainment value. In a number of instances their inclusion represents an external threat and thereby aids the building of tension especially when we are concerned about the safety of central characters. The lurking, psychopathic presence somewhere outside helps to build the suspense to an almost unbearable tension as in books such as Patricia Cornwell's *Body of Evidence* or Ian McEwan's *Enduring Love*.

Alternatively, there is a growing body of journalistic writing and auto-biographical literature in which the author takes us beyond the surface into the thoughts and feelings of those experiencing mental health problems. In these instances words lead us on a guided tour through someone else's inner world and provide the reader with a glimpse of that person's thoughts, feelings and beliefs. It is a type of presentation that is seen frequently within magazines with articles such as 'My Drugs Hell' or 'Surviving Depression'. It has also over recent years become extraordinarily popular within the genre of autobiographical writing and often features strongly within best-selling book lists. They are written mainly from a position of survival with authors having 'come through' sometimes appalling experiences, yet they provide feelings of optimism and hope for the future. David Pelzer for example has written four extremely successful books about his experience of child abuse and the way in which he has been able to foster a healthy relationship with his own son. First-person narratives are also employed within fiction as a means of connecting the reader more closely with the inner world of characters who are experiencing mental health problems. It is a journey that is not always comfortable and can be extremely unsettling as with narratives that keep the reader engaged for an entire book within disordered (*Briefing for a Descent into Hell*) or psychopathic (*American Psycho*) worlds.

Sound

The previous two parts are concerned with the ways in which we engage with the media and interpret messages through what we see. A further powerful strand of communication can be seen in terms of what we hear, experience through music, exclamations and the spoken word. First, we can look at the use of music as a means of generating feelings among the receiver, be it peacefulness and tranquillity or a sense of imminent danger. When connected with a visual medium such as film or television, sound and music act as a vital mode of communication, informing the receiver for instance when a powerful moment is occurring and guiding them towards a particular emotional response (Turner 1999). It also has a function of amplifying the mood or atmosphere connected with a particular scene as can be seen in Hitchcock's shower scene in the film *Psycho* where the sense of danger and suspense are powerfully evoked through the unnerving and shrieking violin strings

(Carroll 1996). The type of music played in some cases provides cues to the receiver as to the underlying psychological states of characters (Prendergast 1992). Bobker (1969) provides a clear example of this in the film *Through a Glass Darkly* where the fragmentation between the music and the film scenes not quite fitting together reveal something of the daughter's schizophrenic world.

The advent of film, radio and television has brought new channels for carrying the spoken voice. It was previously left to the domain of dramatic stage productions to entertain their audience with spoken narrative regarding mental illness. There is a rich historical base here including a number of plays by Shakespeare (e.g. *King Lear* or *Macbeth*) and we can look even further back in time to the Greek tragedies such as the Euripidean dramas of *The Bacchae* and *Heracles*. The spoken word carries expressiveness that is not present in the written word with tone, inflexion, volume and pitch all being employed to convey specific meanings. There are many examples to be found in the media although unfortunately they seem predominantly to feature disparaging and stereotypical representations. For example, the viewer might be alerted towards a character's fragmented or distorted mental health state through their maniacal laughter, sudden exclamations or delusional speech. It is a much-employed stereotype often used within the genre of comedy such as with Inspector Clousseau's long-suffering boss in the Pink Panther films, clearly informing the viewers that he is having a breakdown. There are normally sharp distinctions made between the language of wellness and the language of illness. As with Wahl's (1995) concept of the mentally ill being featured as *a breed apart*, they not only look different but they also sound different. The film *Me, Myself and Irene* for instance highlights this aspect with the definite changes in vocal presentation from the well state (sensitive and quiet) to the ill state (loud and abusive). Stigmatising messages are also given through the words used by others in connection with mentally ill characters, often with demeaning and rejecting words being used. It is indeed very common to come across words such as 'fruit cake', 'nutter', 'schizo' and 'loony'. These types of portrayal perhaps stand out more forcibly from the number of examples that demonstrate a more favourable and accepting approach towards the mentally ill and fit the general stereotype and expectations of many of their audience.

Medium (channel)

Channel types

The channel of communication relates to the mode by which messages are carried between sender and receiver. Obviously attention is given to the qualities or restrictions connected with each channel type when determining how a message is to be constructed. Media channels almost exclusively cater for the senses of sight and sound, collectively covering a broad expanse of types

of sensation. The visual media is experienced as pictures and words whereas sound media is conveyed predominantly through the forms of music and speech. Both cover a broad expanse of media types and are employed either as single modes of communication or are integrated to combine various stimuli more powerfully together into a unified message. The manner in which these aspects are conveyed to their audience is to a large degree determined by the type of channel they are carried by.

As media services and products continue to change so does the make up of their audience. The expanding range of media types is resulting in an audience's attention being dispersed over a number of different products and the concept of 'mass' audience is becoming more of a fragmented entity (McQuail 1997). People will belong to several different potential audiences at the same time influenced by the characteristics and attractiveness of a particular media channel. Of particular significance is the accessibility and suitability of a given channel type as it fits in with a person's daily routine. For example, one might choose to listen to the radio while driving to work or watch the television at the same time as carrying out household chores. An understanding of their audience's needs and mode of engagement is used directly by some media providers to shape and develop the product being carried. For example, the narrative form of soap operas has been linked to some of the typical features of a housewife's daily routine (fragmented and distracted) that prevent continuous attention (Geraghty 1991). Media providers therefore have in mind their audience's preference to a channel type as well as their mode of engagement with it.

The choice or selection of channel types and specific products is governed by a number of factors including those of availability, accessibility, cost implications and personal preferences. Channel sources are selected in part for what they offer over other types. For example, the Internet might be chosen instead of newspapers and books as a source of information because of the immediate access to an almost unlimited array of sites. One of the prime considerations reflects Berlo's (1960) view that communication modes are approached with a 'what's in it for me' attitude. It can also be seen in the work of Palmgreen and Rayburn (1985) that highlighted the significance of audience gratification for continued use of a particular media type. McQuail *et al.* (1972) identified a number of media–person interactions with regard to television and radio that highlight the reasons for engaging with this medium and include factors such as relaxation, diversions and companionship. There are certainly a number of aspects here that help to explain the addition of mental health content for its capacity for drama and impactful engagement, or simply as a means of drawing audience members in. This reinforces Biocca's (1988) focus upon affective arousal in that the more an audience member is 'caught up' or 'engrossed' the more they are likely to retain their engagement with a selected media type.

Media channels are also carefully chosen by those wishing to have their products carried. For instance, organisations concerned with health

promotion will have a number of factors to consider concerning which channels offer the greatest exposure. This of course is partly determined by the financial constraints connected with each type. The expansion of new media services and the enhanced capacity to convey a greater number of products more cheaply is good news for mental health organisations. Traditionally, the electronic media had proved fairly prohibitive in terms of cost although has now opened up considerably through the financially accessible media such as the Internet and community television channels (offered through digital and cable television packages). The problem still exists that these more productive and positive messages are still swamped by the plethora of stigmatising and derogatory portrayals carried by the same channel types.

Receiver

Making sense of the media

An important framework for considering the communication between a media provider and receiver is Hall's (1974b) encoding/decoding model. In order to understand how a media message works or doesn't, there is a need to explore the codes and conventions employed by media professionals in the construction of a message and the subsequent decoding by audience members. Hall (1974b) focuses upon four main codes:

- Dominant/hegemonic code
  The interpretation or decoding of messages by audience members in accordance with intended or preferred meaning.

- Professional code
  Conventions that media professionals use to encode meaning within media messages incorporating production techniques used to tell a story in a particular way.

- Negotiated code
  An audience member might accept the broad thrust of a specific media message yet either adapt or reject elements of the overall message because it does not fit with their own immediate experience of the world.

- Oppositional code
  The capacity of audience members to reject outright the preferred or intended meaning of a media message.

The essence of Hall's (1974b) encoding/decoding model is that a message is constructed by a sender prior to its transmission. It is subsequently deconstructed by the receiver although may be decoded by individual audience members in very different ways. This is supported by Anderson (2003) who states that some audiences will read the sender's intended meaning while others will establish a new meaning of their own. Goffman's (1974) frame

analysis looks at the individualised nature of organising experience and the view that what one person has of what is going on is quite different from that of another. The meaning derived from media content is very dependent upon the perceptions, experiences and social location of audience members (Philo *et al.* 1994; Jensen 1988). It means in a number of cases the message encoded by the receiver is not the same as that sent out and explains to some degree the overwhelming evidence for poor or faulty understanding of news (Gunter 1987).

These aspects are reflected very aptly by White's (1990) detailing of five different people's rereading of the novel *Great Expectations*, five years after first reading it.

Reader 1: 'I loved it then, it seemed so lifelike; but now that I've studied literature I see it as a myth about bourgeois guilt about money.'

Reader 2: 'I didn't like it then, but I've seen the film since, and that made me more interested because I could visualise the scenes.'

Reader 3: 'I once found it really funny, full of macabre jokes – now it seems a complete tragedy.'

Reader 4: 'I can see more in it now – Miss Havisham is just like my aunty.'

Reader 5: 'I hated it then and I hate it now, no difference.'

White summed this up with the statement: 'On each occasion of reading, a person is a different reader bringing to the work a new set of "meanings" which he/she wants to find.' (White 1990: 250). He concludes that instead of looking for a plurality of meaning in texts we can instead look for the plurality that exists in each individual reader. Each reader therefore plays a significant part in creating the 'meaning' which they find in any given media product. This is also supported by Umberto Eco who states that: 'Every reception of a work of art is both an interpretation and a performance of it, because in every reception the work takes on a fresh perspective for itself' (Eco 1989: 4).

Another core issue for the recipient relates to their perception of a set of messages and their understanding of the context within which messages are framed. One issue relates to a person's expectations as these will clearly influence what is noticed or selected from the huge plethora of stimuli exposed to. This may entail a fair degree of wastage as most communication receives only a small fraction of its potential attention and impact (Clausse 1968). The overwhelming range of media messages sent out presents the receiver with an unmanageable supply of stimuli with which to deal. This is illustrated by Broadbent's (1958) filter theory in that what is retained by the recipient measures only a small fraction of all that is accessed. This fact clearly leads those involved in media production towards creating products that stand out from the background and gain maximum impact from their targeted audience. Mental health themes in particular can be seen as an ideal choice for inclusion because of their potential for dramatic, engaging and impactful presentations. This reflects the concept of *figure and ground* in that

different interpretations can be derived from the same set of stimuli (King and Wertheimer 2005). This depends largely upon what is placed into the foreground and what is therefore relegated to the background. The illustration in Figure 2.2 may be seen either as two black silhouetted faces or a white goblet in the centre while the image in Figure 2.3 can be perceived in two very different ways, seeing either an old or young woman. Of significance here is the receiver's perspective as, for example, the impression gained of media coverage by those with first-hand experience is likely to be different from those with little or no experience.

It is also worth acknowledging the media effects model, an approach that has been used to measure the impact and influence that media products have upon those exposed to them. One of the most prominent studies is that of Bandura (1986) who illustrated the concept of social learning and how a group of children exposed to violent images developed imitative behaviour. The effects model is one that has been criticised by a number of media analysts because of its overly restrictive and linear focus which, it is felt, does not address all of the potential influencing factors (Rogers 1986). We might consider facts such as the amount of distracting 'noise' that is sent out alongside main messages or the fact that messages are open to checking through other contacts (McQuail 2005). Violent or negative images may also be responded to in alternative ways, for example being perceived as cathartic (Wolfenstein and Leites 1970; Feshbach and Singer 1971).

Figure 2.2 Figure and ground.

Figure 2.3 Old woman/young woman.

Feedback

Approval

This is the rounding off part to the communication cycle and one that helps to shape the ways in which messages are subsequently framed by media providers. Feedback may be received directly in the form of complaints or commendations, or indirectly through means such as box office receipts and sales figures. Perhaps the most significant factor regarding the continuation of a particular media type relates to its commercial appeal. There may in a number of instances be some discrepancy between the types of feedback received with negative comments being received alongside a product's popular receipt by large numbers of people. For example, the tabloid news press is widely regarded as having the most detrimental and stigmatising coverage of mental health issues (Mind 2000) yet at the same time receives a large percentage of the newsprint sales circulation outselling the broadsheets by far. Approval through sales in many cases appears to override the regulatory guidance and negative feedback that may be received as media types continue to produce poor representations of mental illness.

The commercial aspects are perhaps the most striking and media providers obviously have a keen eye on potential sales, ratings and box office takings. These factors first represent the continued survival of a product type but also influence aspects such as continued marketability and potential advertising revenue. High ratings and product uptake has a direct impact upon the way in which media products are constructed. The television ratings war, for example, has led to ever more dramatic storylines being developed within the popular soaps, of which mental health themes have proven very popular i.e. 'Mad Maya' in *Coronation Street*. The commercial appeal has also resulted in numerous sequels being made within the 'Psycho-killer' genre such as with the films *Nightmare on Elm Street* and *Friday the 13th*, finally bringing their murderous perpetrators together in the 2003 film *Freddy vs Jason*.

Approval is also granted for a product's content and the positive depiction of mental health issues. The annual Mental Health Media awards and the Mind Awards for the best coverage of mental health themes is one example. These highlight and showcase examples where mental health is being positively promoted. Direct feedback has been enabled through the close liaison links that have been developed by a number of media groups and mental health organisations.

Disapproval

Most media organisations provide mechanisms for complaints about their products which can be sent directly to the media body concerned or through its own specific regulatory body. For example, if concerned about items presented by the broadcast media (radio and television), individuals might contact the station or Ofcom (the office of communications). Other media with their own regulatory body include newsprint (Press Complaints Commission), the Internet (Internet Watch Foundation) and non-broadcast adverts (Advertising Standards Authority). Further guidance is provided by mental health service-user organisations or charitable groups such as Media Wise, which provides advice and guidance concerning media complaints. This process is vital as it might be argued that certain stigmatising images persist because of the lack of consumer feedback (Wahl 1995). Clearly, the outcome depends upon the credibility of the individual or organisation expressing dissatisfaction or the number of complaints received. This can have an almost instant response as can be seen with *The Sun* newspaper's withdrawal of their first edition coverage ('Bonkers Bruno') of Frank Bruno's hospitalisation for depression following a barrage of complaints.

The worst in media coverage is also showcased through Mind's annual *bigot of the year* awards with examples such as *The Sun*'s Paul Gilfeather and his article about Home Secretary Jack Straw's plans to introduce new powers of detention for people diagnosed with personality disorders with the headline of '600 Psychos to be Locked up'. The need for continued feedback concerning negative coverage is evidenced by the findings that the 'mentally

ill' represent one of the most stigmatized conditions (Bloch and Singh 1997). They have traditionally been poorly protected unlike those in the categories of ethnic minorities, disabled and gender related who are supported through a wide range of legislation. It is therefore heartening to note the number of initiatives and campaigns (e.g. Mindshift and Changing Minds) that are currently helping to challenge the negative depiction of mental health themes and bring about a sense of change and optimism for the future.

Conclusion

To conclude this section, Berlo's model can be regarded as a cycle of communication with numerous factors and influences playing a core part through each stage of this process. People's attitudes and thoughts about mental health issues are not generated through a single cycle but can be regarded as the product of numerous revolutions with regard to a wide variety of media sources. It is a continuous process of bombardment by countless competing stimuli, carrying a full spectrum of messages both positive and negative. These issues are all addressed in depth within the following chapters which focus upon different media types and the influences and issues connected with them.

3 Stigma, labelling and the media: the negative representation of mental health issues

This chapter is concerned with the depiction within the media of negative stereotypes and stigmatising imagery relating to mental health issues. Negative representation is the predominant message being relayed and can be found in all media source types from the print media, film, TV and radio, through to the new electronic media. These negative messages are reinforced through countless examples which can be located both in historical and current media types. The degree to which stigmatising mental health imagery is reflected in the media is outlined in a number of current publications and reports such as the Mindout for Mental Health's (2001a) *Mindshift: a Guide to Open-Minded Coverage of Mental Health*, the Royal College of Psychiatrists' (2001) *Changing Minds: Every Family in the Land* and Mind's (2000) *Counting the Cost* report. These look at the extent of negative coverage of mental health issues and the effects upon the individual experiencing psychological problems. The significance of the predominantly negative portrayal is the maintenance and influence of stigmatising attitudes within societal and individuals' views. As Sieff (2003) identifies, the frequently negative frames deployed by the mass media contribute towards the persistence of the public's negative attitudes regarding the mentally ill. This sets up a cyclical relationship whereby negative perceptions are reinforced.

As identified by Bloch and Singh (1997), mental disorder and mental ill-health stand worldwide as being one of the most stigmatised of all human conditions. This is an alarming statement especially given the difficulty that may be experienced by many individuals within this group of representing themselves. There has been a shift over recent years towards a greater social awareness, enhanced advocacy and a greater 'voice' being developed (as well as perhaps permitted) regarding those experiencing mental health problems. This is complemented by campaigns and initiatives that promote positive mental health messages and challenge some of the commonly held myths and misrepresentations. Certainly with some stigmatised groups there has been a wealth of movement towards fostering a new culture of change and acceptance. The mentally ill have been left behind somewhat without the same level of sustained interest or concern and the negative representation of mental illness continues with representations that would be widely deemed as

thoroughly unacceptable if associated with other marginalised groups. Indeed, as Wahl (1995) states, in the age of political correctness, people with mental illnesses are one of few remaining groups to be subject to such consistently thoughtless labelling. This process reflects the insidious and perpetuating nature of stigma whereby certain negative strands and assumptions are continuously reinforced.

As a starting place it is worth looking at definitions of stigma, defined by *The Oxford English Dictionary* as: 'A mark of disgrace or infamy; a sign of severe censure or condemnation, regarded as impressed on a person or thing; *a brand*' (*Oxford English Dictionary* 2005). A number of words stand out from this definition. First, those of *mark* and *brand* which both indicate some kind of distinguishing feature highlighting a sense of difference between the individual and others within their wider societal group. It is something which is easily identifiable and categorises the stigmatised as, to use Wahl's (1995) words, 'a breed apart'. It is interesting to note the origin of the term stigma, which related to a physical mark or brand made on Greek slaves to prevent their running away. It is perhaps this word *brand*, which more clearly evokes a sense of mental illness as a product of societal discrimination. It signifies an intentional process of creating some kind of mark that distinguishes the *mentally ill* from the *mentally well*. Individuals themselves may present with certain features that set them apart from others such as through what is observable by their appearance or behaviour. Whether these are deemed acceptable or not by various societal factions relates to the degree of stigmatising attitudes held by each specific group.

Another strand of the term stigma is the concept of labelling. As Becker (1963) stresses, once a label such as child molester or rapist is applied to someone, all actions that individual performs or has performed are interpreted in light of that label. Thomas Scheff (1974) proposed that the label *schizophrenic* activates stereotypes of mental illness learned in childhood from friends, family and the media. Certainly, mental illness references in children's media are common (Wilson *et al.* 2000) although are more often negative than positive with portrayals that typically disparage and ridicule (Wahl 2003a). An example from the *Beano* (16 August 2003) has the character Calamity James being chased around a park, first by a sabre wielding pirate ('Short John Saliva') and second by a First World War German pilot ('The Black Baron'). Their mentally ill status is made very clear both through their bizarre looks and violent behaviour, reinforced by Calamity James' final statement while running away: 'Waah! This park is chock full of loonies.' It is this type of exposure that leads us from an early age to see the mentally ill as being different.

One of the consequences of labelling is influencing the way in which people perceive themselves. Cooley's *The Looking Glass Self* stresses that one's identity and view of oneself is built primarily as a result of how others act and respond towards us (Cohen 1982). This is borne out by surveys such as Mind's (2000) *Counting the Cost* report which shows that individuals have

had their self-esteem and confidence affected through negative media reporting. While some people have the power to reject a negative label, many are unable to and therefore have to seek ways to cope with it (Becker 1963). This obviously presents potentially insurmountable obstacles for those who are already under-confident and psychologically vulnerable. Each label brings with it a set of expectations that foster responses such as dependence behaviour or accentuated eccentricity in those so categorised. Goffman (1963) refers to this process as *spurious interaction*, where the use of diagnostic labels has a profoundly negative effect on the very behaviour of the patient. One such effect is the individual becoming in a sense a product of their label. This is reflected by Scheff (1974) and Kitwood (1997) with the view that an individual's illness behaviours are produced in part by the expectations placed upon them.

It is also worth noting that there is a negative effect on the behaviour of those people around them resulting in the labelled person being treated as 'sick' (Roediger *et al.* 1991). Once a person is labelled, professional carers will attach particular frames to an individual's conversation and actions. For example, a person's agitated behaviour might be regarded predominately as a result of their underlying psychopathology instead of their feelings of frustration or irritation at how powerless they are made to feel. This then picks up on other parts of the definition with words such as *condemnation* and *censure* that highlight the negative appeal and dismissive approach evoked. The term stigma has in common usage come to refer to any undesirable trait of an individual or group that devalues them and evokes negative or punitive responses (Susman 1994; Miles 1981). This view concurs with Goffman's (1963) view of stigma being socially discrediting, permanent and affecting the perception of the person as a whole. One issue here would relate to the identity of the person or group who does the branding, whether it is something that is applied by society or the media. A common media response to criticism of its predominantly negative portrayal of mental illness is that it is merely reflecting the current picture in society, the brands therefore they would argue have already been applied.

One of the most commonly held misrepresentations is the association of violence and unpredictability with mental illness (Nairn *et al.* 2001; Wahl 1995). It is a representation that tends on the whole to be generalised more towards the psychotic disorders. Williams and Taylor (1995) report on a study that carried out a content analysis of 83 newspaper articles over a two-year period. The coverage was overly negative and reinforced the stereotypical perception of the mentally ill as aggressive and unpredictable. Another study by Crisp *et al.* (2000) set out to determine the opinions of the British adult population (n = 1737) regarding their responses to seven types of mental disorder (severe depression, panic attacks, schizophrenia, dementia, eating disorders, alcoholism, drug addiction). The view that 'those with mental illness are dangerous' is held mostly with regard to schizophrenia, drug dependence and alcoholism. There was a widely held opinion

that those experiencing mental health problems are hard to talk to, feel different from the way that we do and are unpredictable, which obviously accounts for some of the social distancing and isolation that is experienced.

Why do we stigmatise?

Wahl (1995) illustrates a number of potential reasons as to why such inaccurate representations of mental illness exist that include profit, ignorance, history, socialisation, psychological reassurance and lack of consumer feedback.

Profit

Profit provides a major incentive towards the continued use of stigmatising associations. As Salter and Byrne (2000) state, media is a business, its output driven by an overriding need to gain and sustain attention. It seems that the more dramatic the representation of *madness* the greater impact and selling potential it has. There is therefore a tendency among investors to repeat what has proved profitable in the past.

Ignorance

There is much that media personnel apparently do not know about mental illness. This is fuelled through common misconceptions held by members of the general public but are also shared by those working within media organisations. Recently, there have been attempts to challenge this through education of media personnel and liaison with professional or mental health service-user groups although many inaccurate and misrepresented portrayals continue to be used.

History

Images in today's mass media reflect conceptualisations and representations that have been around for centuries. This can be seen, for example, in the colloquial use of language that draws upon mental health terminology from a previous era, i.e. the regular featuring within tabloid headlines of words such as 'Lunatic' or 'Mental patient'. There are also representations that play upon the *possessed* theme evoking an earlier time where madness was seen as a visitation by divine forces.

Socialisation

The mass media can be regarded as the storytellers of today, acting as a primary socialising agent and passing on to their members the knowledge of the world. The significance here perhaps concerns which items out of the

multitude available are selected and framed by media providers as being salient and appropriate for public consumption. Obviously, commercial considerations play a big part here and may result in fairly insignificant items being given a much higher priority than those having greater and farther-reaching consequences.

Psychological reassurance

Presenting the ill as different or dangerous may serve as a psychologically self-protective function. One reason is to do with predictability since being able to easily identify who is mentally ill means that members of the public can more easily take measures to protect themselves. There is also a polarisation process that takes place whereby the mentally ill are separated out and distanced from those who, by comparison, are deemed to be mentally well. The impression gained from many tabloid style depictions with their many stereotypes is that they are predominantly aimed at an audience who would wish to consider themselves as being mentally well.

Lack of consumer feedback

One of the historical problems resulting in the perpetuation of stigmatising portrayals has been the scarcity of feedback given to media providers. Another consideration is the weight or degree of reliability afforded those providing feedback, as more credibility is obviously afforded recognised groups over that of individuals. In recent years, though, campaigning and health promotion initiatives have meant that feedback about media depictions is taken on board far more strongly by those producing the various products on offer.

Maintaining stigma

It is interesting to consider factors that maintain the need for stigmatising or stereotypical representations. The need for media stereotypes can be seen as a way of presenting the receiver with reference points in what is experienced as a relentless stream of messages. As Valenti (2000) asserts, we are constantly bombarded by new information and stimuli and are not capable of an in-depth and instantaneous analysis of every aspect we encounter. The only way to manage this is through classifying and grouping according to familiar patterns. This is highlighted by Broadbent's (1958) filter theory which suggests we cope with a prolific amount of incoming stimuli by passing information through a filter. Haghighat (2001) looks at the pressure which the brain is under to respond to the proliferation of incoming stimuli and which copes with the increased demand by processing faster. He outlines that it may not therefore be as efficient to find out whether a person has qualities over and above what the name of their illness implies. This view is supported by

Rothbart *et al.* (1978) who indicate that when the brain is overloaded with data it is likely to treat examples of the behaviour of a single person as relatable to the behaviour of their group. Therefore examples of violence by mentally ill individuals tend to be generalised and transferred over to the wider grouping of those with mental health problems. Stigmatising messages therefore are pervasive, have lasting impact and devalue a lot of the mileage gained through campaigning and presentation of alternative, positive imagery. The greater impact from negative messages is indicated by the study of Kanouse and Hanson (1972) who have shown that the brain weights negative evaluations in preference to positive ones. The implications here are that positive health promotion and campaigning on their own are not enough and, for lasting change to occur, must be coupled with a dramatic reduction of negative and stigmatising presentations.

There are a number of factors which maintain the placing of the mentally ill as a group within a deviant category. One reinforcing aspect originates in societal intolerance and a fear of mental illness. This might transcend all attempts to educate the public as to the '*real*' facts concerning those with mental health problems and, for instance, their actual lower than expected potential for violence (DOH 1999). An interesting comparison is indicated by Laurance (2003) who points out that we actually show greater tolerance to what are much more lethal behaviours such as dangerous driving and alcohol abuse which are shown to kill or maim a larger number of people. This brings up the notion of societal *scapegoating*, with the mentally ill presenting easier targets on whom to visit all of our unwanted or negative feelings. It highlights Foucault's (1961) notion of madness being a constructed entity and something that we prefer to externalise onto others. The sense of distancing and separation shown here between the mentally well and the mentally ill is strongly found throughout the institutional era with the purging of *madness* from within families and society. It is a process that can also be found within therapeutic environments as shown by Kantor and Gelineau's (1965) study that observed staff members actually stimulating continued symptom expression among patients in subtle ways. Although they were not aware of this dynamic, the influences behind this behaviour were felt to be concerned with maintaining a clear and psychologically needed distinction between patient and helper. It is interesting therefore to note the view that deviance is not a quality of the act the person commits, but rather a consequence of the application by others of rules and sanctions (Becker 1963).

Clearly one of the main reasons for the inclusion of stigmatising and stereotypical mental health portrayals by the media is the dramatic impact that they have upon their audience. This results in aspects regarding the mentally ill often being distorted and exaggerated in order to make products more appealing to their audience (Nunnally 1981). Despite some very detailed sets of guidelines concerning media content (i.e. the Broadcasting Standards Commission 1998; Independent Television Commission 2002; and the National Union of Journalists 1999), it seems that in many cases the

advice given is ignored in favour of a sensational or eye-catching approach. It is evident that madness as a topic is very commercially appealing and that this in many cases overrides the degree of sensitivity being shown to those who are stigmatised.

The effects of stigma

The most impactful factors affecting those who are stigmatised concerns an individual's critical self-perception as well as the distancing and rejecting response experienced from others. Stigma therefore can be seen as a process that is either generated from a process of internal or external feedback (see Figure 3.1). These elements are echoed in Scambler's (1998) aspects of stigma concerning felt stigma and enacted stigma.

Felt stigma (internal stigma)

The frequent bombardment of derogatory language such as 'mentals', 'nutters', 'lunatics' and 'psycho', as well as the frequent use of unflattering and unrealistic imagery cannot help to engender good feelings in those with mental health problems. The first issue here is the felt experience and the issue of self-stigmatisation concerning how individuals come to reappraise their experience in light of media coverage. This is illustrated by Gilbert (2003) with regard to the process of external and internal shame. The *external* shame might include the feeling that 'others see me as unattractive' which results in a sense of *internal* shame in that 'I see myself as unattractive'. The shame and

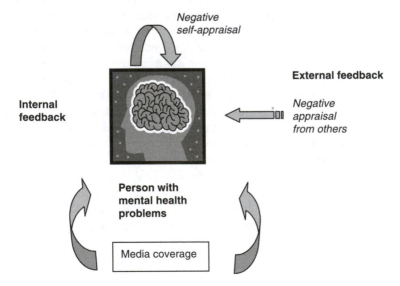

Figure 3.1 Stigma and negative appraisal.

expectation of discrimination prevents people from talking about their experiences and discourages them from seeking help. An individual's concept of self is affected through stigma with enhanced feelings of hopelessness, low self-worth and increased social withdrawal (Gray 2002). The prejudice and discrimination experienced can compound the distress felt and interfere further with personal coping skills already affected as a result of mental health problems (Johnstone 2001). These features are all reflected in Mind's (2000) *Counting the Cost* report which details the negative impact that media coverage has upon those experiencing mental health problems. The cycle of disadvantage is illustrated by the Social Exclusion Unit (2003) in that once mental health problems develop, they can often have a negative impact on employability, housing, income and opportunities to access services and social networks, potentially leading to severe economic deprivation and social isolation. Indeed, studies conducted in the late 1990s illustrate that only 13 per cent of those with long-term mental health problems were actually working compared to 35 per cent among the physically disabled (Sayce 2000). As is stressed by Link *et al.* (2001), a major consequence of reducing stigma is to improve the self-esteem of those with mental illnesses. It is worth mentioning, however, that not all of those who are stigmatised will be unable to respond or cope with the deluge of negative imagery and representations in the media. This is illustrated in Camp *et al.*'s (2002) study of women with chronic mental health problems who, although being aware of societal responses and attitudes and the effects it had on their lives, did not accept these representations as valid and rejected them as applicable to themselves.

A number of those experiencing mental health problems indicate the extreme feelings of anxiety felt regarding their 'coming out'. As Sayce (2000) states, for some this can be a liberating experience yet for others it can be hard to reconcile the different aspects of themselves such as competent researcher and mental health survivor. Certainly, the liberating process is reflected upon in a number of autobiographical accounts, as demonstrated by the footballer Tony Adams writing in the book *Addicted* about his coping with alcoholism. The 'coming out' by notable individuals is in some cases greeted favourably by the public as exampled by Norwegian Prime Minister Mr Bondevik's decision to take time off with depression, an action applauded by the public and even his political opponents. Another notable example was the revelation by Princess Diana about her struggles with the eating disorder bulimia. The importance of sharing such experiences publicly cannot be overestimated as it means that the taboo surrounding certain mental health states is reduced and the featured condition is afforded degrees of acceptance, thereby facilitating others talking about and sharing related issues. This all plays a major role in reducing the sense and feeling of felt stigma experienced by those with mental health problems.

Enacted stigma (external stigma)

Essentially what stereotypical and stigmatising portrayals do is to objectify and distance those with mental illness from others in society. A large percentage of media portrayals tend to offer us representations of mental illness which show little regard for the actual person and their felt experience. The predominant perspective is one that outlines the potential threat posed to the rest of society by those deemed to be mentally unfit. Responsibility for perpetuating stereotypes is to a large extent attributed to the media, although this is largely rejected with the claim that they are merely mirroring the values and beliefs held already within society (Bolton 2000). The origin of stigma is a topic that evokes considerable debate although it can certainly be regarded as a cyclical process whereby both societal attitudes and media portrayals strongly influence each other. This can be reflected in the view that what we learn about mental health issues is largely generated by what is picked up from the media (Philo 1996a). The media subsequently develop products that are regarded as appealing and reflecting the needs and interests of their audience.

A major problem affecting the mentally ill through the process of stigmatisation is that of social exclusion, which this is well documented in a number of studies such as Mind's (2000) *Counting the Cost* report and the Social Exclusion Unit's (2003) project. Recent attempts to tackle this include the setting up of the Social Exclusion Unit, which initiated a project in 2003 to tackle the barriers to opportunity faced by adults with mental health problems. This is a governmental initiative with the core aims of investigating what can be done to enable more adults with mental health problems to enter and to retain work, as well as having the same opportunities for social participation and access to services as the general population. Such schemes are vital in helping tackle both the impact upon the person with mental health problems as well as the rejecting and distancing attitudes held by others towards them. These attitudes have also been noted with regard to care delivery where services are driven to some degree by fear and where risk reduction through containment is the norm. At the same time that mental health service-users are calling for greater empowerment and autonomy, care services are responding with an authoritarian risk-reduction approach (Laurance 2003). This has in part been influenced by media coverage of well publicised incidents of homicides, violence and suicide where policy measures which have been introduced in response to public concerns have only served to impose additional constraints on those with mental health problems (Hallam 2002). It fits in with Linné and Warfella's (1998) view of *moral panics*, the effects that are supposed to emerge when the media consistently represent a subgroup or subculture as being dangerous or deviant.

Courtesy stigma

The power of stigma is such that it does not reside alone with the mentally ill but can be widened to include others such as families, friends and carers (Östman and Kjellin 2002). Stigma by association or 'courtesy stigma' relates to the problems whereby the family of a 'mentally ill' individual may share some of the discredit of their stigmatised relative (Angermeyer *et al.* 2003). This then widens the example to encompass the family as a dysfunctional unit and to some degree explains the desire by some family groups to safeguard their own interests by 'expelling' the sick member. The aspect of how stigma affects and envelops others close to and involved with the mentally ill has been paid little attention by researchers. The concept of family burden has been looked at although not specifically with regards to the concept of stigma. Wally Lamb's fictional novel, *I Know This Much is True*, provides a vivid account of the impact that mental illness has on other members of the family. This book centres upon Thomas's experience of schizophrenia and the psychological suffering and burden of guilt endured by both his twin brother Dominick and his stepfather Ray. It is a powerful narrative that highlights the need to understand how mental health issues and associated stigma affects family members and their subsequent requirements from psychiatric services.

The concept of courtesy stigma can also be widened to encompass those treating the mentally ill. This is particularly illustrated within the cinema through numerous films depicting the professional carers every bit as, if not more, disturbed than those they are treating (Clare 2001). One of the messages being portrayed here, as conveyed very strongly through the film *Shock Corridor*, is of contamination through becoming too intimately involved with madness. Another aspect concerns the attractiveness of the psychiatric professions to psychologically disturbed individuals, as with the murderous psychiatrists Hannibal Lecter in *The Silence of the Lambs* and Dr Robert Elliot in *Dressed to Kill*. It is certainly alarming to witness such depictions involving those we place our trust in when at our most vulnerable.

What's bad about . . .?

This section focuses upon a selection of media types and features some of the more prominently negative characteristics or examples portrayed. The sources covered are those of film, TV, Internet, press and literature.

. . . Film

Characterisation

A character's appearance conveys some very strong messages to the audience. From a mental health perspective numerous stereotypes are employed

whereby selected individuals are framed through their looks, speech or behaviour as being different. There may be a fair degree of deliberation in the casting of characters that fit some of the typical notions as to what the mentally ill look like. An example here can be seen in the typecasting of Peter Lorre who, because of his distinctively odd appearance, was chosen to play the deranged killer in a succession of films. Their portrayal is often aided by a number of accompanying cues, which highlight factors such as the dangerousness of the character (Hannibal Lecter's wildly excessive collection of restraints), a person's social ineptitude (Geoffrey Rush's dishevelled portrayal of David Helfgott in *Shine*) or the wide gulf between wellness and illness (Jim Carrey's Jekyll and Hyde portrayal in *Me, Myself and Irene*). These characterisations help to perpetuate the societal myth that we can spot those with mental health problems by their appearance and behaviour alone. It serves to further distance those with mental health problems from others and fits Wahl's (1995) classification of 'a breed apart'.

The mentally ill as killers

The stereotypical association between violence and mental health issues is found in prolific quantity within the medium of film. The imagery provided by the showcasing of the mentally ill killer provides the viewer with a heightened sense of tension, drama and excitement. In a number of cases, these types of film also meet individuals' needs for catharthis and curiosity regarding what violent impulses look like (Wolfenstein and Leites 1970). Films within this genre are enormously appealing to audiences and sometimes even receive critical acclaim, factors that help to ensure their continued appearance (Wahl 1995). A major problem with this is the maintenance of the association between mental illness and a person's propensity for violence, leaving the receiver with a feeling of unease and disquiet (Byrne 2001a). These powerful stereotypical messages undermine attempts made at educating the public through various campaigns and health promotion initiatives. The related imagery and language are so pervasive and have permeated our culture to such a degree that words such as '*psycho*' have come to represent homicidal impulses or an unpredictable and deranged mind (Welch and Racine 1999). The peculiar establishment of some of the murderous characters who are featured as cult heroes (such as Hannibal Lecter and Freddy Krueger) only serves to establish the link more fully within our subconscious.

Misrepresentation

A key feature evoking criticism about film portrayals of mental illness relates to the huge number of inaccuracies or misrepresentations being shown. One film in particular that was greeted with a fair amount of critical rebuke for its offensively inaccurate portrayal is that of *Me, Myself and Irene*. This movie

erroneously featured the main character's split personality with the good self being manifested in his mentally well part and the bad self represented by his mentally ill one. The fact that this film proved such a huge success at the box office is a depressing one given the number of people exposed to such negative and misleading facts about mental illness. The scale of misrepresentation within the cinema is huge and even extends towards the 'based upon a true story' type of film. For example, David Helfgott's sister Margaret stressed that her father and the hospital staff treating her brother were not as harsh or oppressive as their portrayal in the film *Shine* suggested (Rosen and Walter 2000). This was clearly built up and exaggerated for the benefit of offering the viewer cues for dramatic engagement. Another example is the film *A Beautiful Mind* which can be regarded as misrepresentative by its omission of certain facts, such as Nash's younger son's diagnosis of schizophrenia, an issue strongly featured within Sylvia Nasar's (1998) biographical work. It is certainly true that condensing a person's life story down into about ninety minutes of film is obviously going to be a difficult task. It may involve over-dramatising certain elements in order to engage and stir the emotions of the audience but it also means that, because of available space, certain features are omitted. The story presented to the audience therefore can be regarded as a construct of the director, scriptwriter and film crew, with commercial and artistic considerations having a major say in how the person's story is told.

... TV

Dramatic licence

As within the cinema, there are many examples whereby those with mental health problems are grossly misrepresented. This was noted in particular by Wilson *et al.*'s (1999) study of prime time television dramas that found a predominantly negative characterisation of mentally ill characters being used. This saw them being depicted as dangerous, simple, unpredictable and socially inept. These examples feature strongly within the hospital dramas and *Holby City* and *Casualty* in particular regularly carry storylines where mentally disturbed characters add an extra spice to the drama being served up. For instance, *Holby City* carried a storyline reminiscent of the Beverly Allitt case with a nurse killing some of her patients. Some clues were given as to the causes of this nurse's psychological disturbance although providing the viewer with another portrayal that associated the concepts of 'mentally ill' and 'dangerous'. The addition of mentally ill characters also occurs in soaps where enhanced audience engagement is desired. It is not coincidental that in many of these cases the television ratings are enhanced. This is particularly true in the case of psychopathically disturbed individuals such as 'Mad Maya' in *Coronation Street* or Sarah in *Eastenders*. It is clearly the case that madness is attractive to viewers and certainly something that adds extra drama or impact to products.

Exploitation

This section relates primarily to the increasingly popular genres of the chat show and reality TV formats. The chat shows range from the sensitive and informative to the grossly exploitative and abusive. The former include shows such as *Esther* and to some degree *Oprah*, which feature some important social issues (i.e. abuse and bereavement) and treat their participants with a degree of respect and sensitivity. There is also an important function here for viewers who can engage in a form of vicarious therapy, connecting with and feeling supported by the experience shared by participants. The latter, though, include examples (such as *Trisha* and J*erry Springer*) where the needs of participants appear to be relegated behind those of providing the audience with an entertaining show. The feeling here is of individuals being deliberately manipulated by the charismatic facilitator towards confrontational situations and displays of distress or anger, the stronger the emotion, it seems, the better. The sense of individuals 'performing' for the audience's pleasure is very strongly conveyed through the numerous *reality TV* shows that dominate our viewing schedules. Some are loosely packaged along the social experiment lines reminiscent of studies such as Zimbardo's 1971 Stanford University prison experiment which placed volunteers in the roles of prisoners and guards. The experiment had to be stopped after six out of the planned fourteen days because of the pathological reactions being displayed by most of the participants, five of whom were released earlier than planned because of depression (Haney and Zimbardo 1998). This then raises an important issue concerning the increasing lack of concern being shown towards those participating within television shows as viewers are regularly entertained by a person's public humiliation or abuse. The lack of respect for participants is also to some degree shared by the audience, illustrated by the level of celebration afforded those involved in abusing others such as *Pop Idol*'s Simon Cowell. It is also reflected in the high viewing figures with shows featuring the abuse of contestants proving very popular, for example the jungle contest *I'm a Celebrity Get Me Out of Here* had various trials where contestants were bitten by snakes, covered in spiders or viciously pecked by emus. All of this aptly sums up Woods' (2002) statement about reality TV as a form of mass voyeurism where a person's dignity no longer matters.

... The Internet

Information overload

One of the biggest strengths of the Internet also provides one of its main problems in that the easy availability and access of vast stores of information causes problems for consumers in terms of sifting through and selecting what is relevant. The almost limitless amount of material retrievable means that those searching the Internet are faced with an overload of information

(Christensen and Griffiths 2000). As Cooke (2001) indicates, this problem is compounded by the way in which many search tools are programmed to retrieve as much as possible of the available material. This poses significant problems in selecting out what is pertinent as well as having the time and ability to process it. Some of these aspects are highlighted by Scrivener (2002) as the mistaking of unrefined data for knowledge; the stockpiling of information; and the failure to appraise information through time mismanagement. This all means that some of the valid and worthy material accessible online remains unseen or unappreciated by many of those at whom it is targeted.

Confusing or harmful material

A brief search of the Internet can prove a bewildering and confusing process as a fair degree of the information accessed appears contrary to that found on other more authoritative sites. Mixed in with all of the educative and supportive health sites are some that can be extremely misleading and harmful. In some cases Internet sites post erroneous material as a result of ignorance or a lack of understanding concerning the aspects being relayed. In other cases poorly evidenced information is very deliberately included for an individual or a group's personal reasons. Their agenda here is not always clear although might be borne out of an individual's own dissatisfying experience of health care. This would in some instances explain the posting within anti-psychiatry sites of information such as 'All psychiatric drugs are harmful'. In most cases no credible evidence is given to support wildly subjective claims such as this and it is common to find information being provided mostly through personal rhetoric. As Thompson (1999) indicates, a major concern relates to the uncertain type of information that desperate people might be exposed to. It is therefore very worrying to reflect upon those Internet sites which advocate self-harmful behaviours and sanitise the very real and distressing nature of suicide through their use of terms such as 'self-deliverance'.

... *The press*

Misinformation

Given that we learn a large percentage of our information from the media, it is perhaps disturbing to consider the degree to which we are actually being misinformed. The reliability of what we are exposed to varies significantly and news can be regarded either as a reflection of what is occurring in society or as a construction by journalists (Potter 2004). Reporting styles have come under much scrutiny over the years and it is interesting to note a Media Bureau (2001) study which indicates that a large percentage (64 per cent) of reporters themselves believe that the coverage of news should be better. The degree to which misleading items are down to the journalists' lack of knowledge or due to the pressures to present a more commercially appealing product is unclear.

One of the most frequently portrayed categories when writing about the mentally ill concerns that of violent behaviour (Philo *et al.* 1996; Nairn *et al.* 2001). Although this association is strongly contended by a wealth of evidence suggesting that the mentally ill present a low risk of harming others (DOH 1999), it continues to be reinforced by many subjective and poorly constructed news items. A more dramatic style of reporting is clearly attractive to readers and helps, despite the various regulations applicable, to maintain poor and misleading journalistic styles.

Stigmatisation

The main thread here is of a negative depiction primarily through words but also to some extent through associated imagery. The public are treated on a regular basis to many examples where stories are presented in sensationalist style with many phrases or words such as 'mental patient', 'psycho killer' or 'patient escaped' being used for dramatic effect. These terms stand out forcibly from the background and are often attached to other well-recognised aspects to heighten their effect, such as '*Silence of the Lambs* Maniac Freed to Kill'. The association with a person's violence potential is complemented by other negative portrayals such as that of mental deficiency or powerlessness. The main types of characterisation used, therefore, are either geared towards evoking feelings of unease and discomfort or those of pity and paternalism. Both of these are stigmatising reactions which place the other person at a distance from us and do not encourage acceptance or empowerment. The three main ingredients for a 'top story', as highlighted by Kalbfleisch (1979), were insanity, unpredictability and victimisation of ordinary people. Clearly, the perpetuation of insensitive and stigmatising depictions is strongly influenced by the fact that they help publications to sell.

Contradictions

There are many examples that can be found within the print media where conflicting or ambiguous messages are presented. This occurs frequently in most of the glossy magazines which showcase and promote various health issues such as stress, body image and eating disorders. While on its own this is laudable enough, in many cases there is a fair degree of competition from conflicting stimuli in the form of pictures and features which pursue perfection or mercilessly expose and attack imperfection through 'Caught on Camera' type features. The newsprint media is an extremely effective channel for conveying health promotion because of its exposure potential and readership by large numbers of people. In a number of cases, though, the potential benefits are outweighed and somewhat confused by the contradictory messages also being relayed. A prime example of this is *The Sun* newspaper's sudden shift towards mental health campaigner in the wake of the widespread criticism and condemnation following their appalling 'Bonkers Bruno'

headlines. However, this did not deter the newspaper from continuing to display less than flattering or ridiculing messages such as the picture of Frank Bruno in pantomime costume.

. . . Literature

Destructiveness to self

There are a number of publications that feature mental illness as a destructive entity with regard to self. This type of writing follows an individual's gradual fragmentation and eventual consumption through their mental health state. A notable example here is that of Malcolm Lowry's *Under the Volcano* depicting the ex-consul Geoffrey Firmin's gradual alienation and destruction through alcoholism. A particular issue is the portrayal of the protagonist as powerless and unable to do much about slowing down or preventing their eventual fate. It also features the helplessness of others who are unable to provide sufficient support. One factor worth highlighting here is the stage in a person's illness when the narrative is written. The book *Catcher in the Rye* features Holden Caulfield's deteriorating mental health state and finishes the narrative with his future progression uncertain. An interesting comparison can be provided through autobiographical accounts that take the reader beyond the time of crisis towards a place of resolution and hope. Without the 'happy ending', stereotypes such as mental illness as an unrecoverable state, are fostered.

Destructiveness to others

The other type of depiction focuses on the destructive potential towards others and can be found within the extremely popular genre of psycho-killer fiction (e.g. Patricia Cornwell's *Body of Evidence* or Ian McEwan's *Enduring Love*). The essence of this type of writing is the placing of the 'mad murderer' as an external threat to the mentally well heroic central figures. This provides the reader with a touch of drama and engagement with the text although again serves to reinforce a negative misassumption concerning mental illness. Another issue is the location of the mentally ill as a destructive or controlling presence in the background. Books such as *Jane Eyre* (Mrs Rochester) and *Cold Comfort Farm* (Aunt Ada) feature characters who, despite being rarely seen, hold a strong controlling influence over central characters. This again promotes mental illness very much in a negative and destructive light.

Negative representations of mental illness

The following section identifies some of the core themes running throughout much of this work where negative representations of mental illness are fostered. These include aspects where the mentally ill are characterised as being

different, the power or language, other related prejudices and images of perfection.

The mentally ill as 'a breed apart'

A predominant feature, as briefly alluded to earlier in the allocation of stigma, is the perception of difference, or as Wahl (1995) determines, identifying the mentally ill as 'a breed apart'. According to a large majority of media portrayals, the mentally ill are portrayed as looking different and acting peculiarly, thereby separating them from what are seen as the 'normal' population. It serves a function of making them easily identifiable and to some degree, as far as the general public is concerned, controllable. These types of representation leave the receiver in little doubt as to which of all the characters shown to them have altered mental health states. *Difference* is made to stand out forcibly and is therefore more readily noticeable as with the Gestalt concept of figure and ground (King and Wertheimer 2005). A predisposition to notice difference is something that is innate to all human (and many animal) groups, since they depend upon the predictable behaviour of their members for their functioning and safety (Smith 2002). However, it is worth clarifying the point that difference can to a large extent be imagined, exaggerated or applied according to one's expectations, as is often the case with regard to mental illness. The characterisation and portrayal of distinct differences in a number of cases makes mental illness a visible entity either through imagery, narrative or terminology. The exaggerated physical characteristics, dramatic and unpredictable behaviour and asocial lifestyles have come to represent what might be regarded as the uniform of the mentally ill. For instance, *Schizophrenic* the debut album by JC Chasez not very imaginatively features the singer in a straight jacket on its cover.

The two core strands of observable difference can be seen as *Looks* and *Behaviour* with the mentally ill being shown to appear and act in ways which signify their altered mental health state. In a number of stereotypical examples, the mentally ill are portrayed as bizarre, ghoulish or deformed. This includes at times a deliberate casting of individuals who are sufficiently 'weird' or 'odd' looking (e.g. Peter Lorre). It also involves those whose screen behaviour and demeanour seem well suited for the part, for instance Jim Carrey in the film *Me, Myself and Irene*. Perhaps over time the extent of exaggeration with regard to visible characteristics has been toned down although is still prominently visible within genres such as horror films or children's television. The horror film incorporates many of the classic stereotypes leaving us in no doubt as to the sense of threat presented by the psychopathic killer, who clearly *looks* dangerous. Even when the killer's physical appearance appears fairly normal, accompanying cues are used to exemplify traits and aspects which we might not otherwise see. For example, the excessive use of restraint used to transport Hannibal Lecter clearly signifies the degree of danger which is present despite any reassurances of safety given.

The portrayal of difference is also prolifically found within children's media and in particular television programmes with the predominant representation of mental illness featuring exaggerated physical attributes and behaviours (Wilson *et al.* 2000). These portrayals present children with a distorted view of the world as well as having a significant impact upon their subsequent attitudes and beliefs (Vooijs and Van der Voort 1993). This theme is not limited to the visible medium and can be found in abundance within the newsprint media and the world of literature where words are used to convey ways in which the mentally ill present as being different. Charlotte Brontë's *Jane Eyre* for example provides a clear example of this with Mrs Rochester being portrayed more as a wild beast than a human being. There are certainly numerous examples to be found within the tabloid press where the violent or socially inadequate mentally ill stereotypes are heavily featured.

It seems that the mentally ill within much of the media are destined to be presented as looking or behaving according to what is expected of them. There have over the past few years been a number of notable attempts to change this and provide media consumers with less stereotypical and more realistic representations. For example, the portrayal of Zoe Tate's schizophrenic breakdown in *Emmerdale* has been covered generally with a greater degree of sensitivity and compassion than most other depictions. The typical representation of mental illness on television generally characterises the individual as violent, bad, a victim or a failure (Signorielli 1989). In contrast to this, the *Emmerdale* example featured a character who was a wealthy businesswoman and successful veterinary surgeon as well as being likeable and fundamentally good. It was disappointing therefore to note the occasions on which her character reverted to stereotype with scenes such as the setting fire to a church, barricading her children in the kitchen of her house or her apparent involvement in the near killing of her daughter's father. Programme makers perhaps have found it too difficult to resist the dramatic potential presented by her illness.

Language and terminology

When debating what is acceptable and what isn't concerning the presentation of mental health themes, we need to view them in the context within which they are presented. First, we have the notion of historical applicability where it can be seen that what is deemed acceptable or unacceptable is forever changing. Indeed, the terminology used in conjunction with mental illness strongly indicates this. An example relates to the language used to denote those who are mentally ill ranging from terms such as *lunatics, mentally deficient, mentally ill,* through to some of the currently used titles such as *mental health service-users* in the UK or s*urvivors* and *consumers* in the US. Equally, the setting within which care is delivered has also been subject to a wide range of definitions including *madhouse, lunatic asylum, psychiatric hospital* and *mental health unit.* Clearly, many other terms could be added to

this list including those used jargonistically or offensively within the media but which have subsequently become fairly mainstream words, for example *psycho* or *mental home*. Whether or not changing terminology does anything to combat stigmatising attitudes is debatable. Often, the wording that was acceptable in a previous era (e.g. *lunatic*) signifies a lack of understanding and care when used in the present context. It is a process highlighted by Haghighat (2001) with regard to the language used within legislation and learning difficulties, each term acquiring the discrediting connotations of the previous one. It is evident that the single approach of changing terminology does little to combat the overall effects of stigmatisation of the mentally ill and that a much more concerted educative and health promotional approach is required.

It is clear that words influence our relationship and feelings towards those with mental health problems. The widespread and prolific use of disparaging terms within the media helps to foster an 'us and them' dynamic. It is very much a distancing process which diminishes the opportunities for actual connection and appreciation of another person's felt experience. The stigmatising power of words is reflected by Sartorius (2002), who highlights in particular the careless use of diagnostic labels. The common misuse of certain terms means that they will be adopted and used more widely by others who do not realise the errors being made. A common misrepresentation is the interchangeable use made of certain terms that includes the association of schizophrenia with that of 'split personality'. Other interchangeably misused terms include those of 'psychotic' and 'psychopathic' as well as 'learning difficulties' and 'mental illness' (Wahl 1995). The exposure to careless, stigmatising and inaccurate references permeates the whole of the media and starts at a very young age. As Wilson *et al.* (2000) worryingly found, there are countless 'mental illness' references being made even within children's media with the vocabulary including many negative and derogatory terms such as 'crazy', 'mad', 'losing your mind', 'wacko', 'cuckoo' and 'loony'.

Pictures of perfection

There are a number of other ways in which negative messages regarding mental illness are conveyed other than the more obvious stigmatising portrayals. It might include media products where positive messages are notably absent or indeed those which 'sell' images of *perfection*. These are found prolifically within large sections of the media and in particular on television and within magazines. The need to address this issue is reflected by the findings that prolonged exposure to images of perfection can have a significantly negative impact upon those receiving them (Durkin 2002; Martinez-Gonzalez *et al.* 2003). The popularity of these types of media product has been noted by a number of sources, and women's magazines in particular attain high levels of exposure with circulation rates in some instances running into millions (Borman 2003).

The overly attentive focus upon beauty issues and the strong conveyance of flawless images all help to draw attention towards the opposite position, that of imperfection. The implications here are that not looking a certain way is subsequently felt as unacceptable and lowers a person's tolerance towards any type of 'flaw'. The huge selling of perfection is complemented by an almost smug, gloating approach which can be found where certain types of imperfection are spotted, for example when celebrities dare to be casually dressed or even worse perhaps display signs of fat. In these cases, any perceived flaw identified is mercilessly and insensitively treated. The choice of words used also compounds this problem with commonly used terms such as 'perfect' regularly found at one end of the spectrum compared to a range of disparaging and insensitive ones being reflected at the other end. For example, *Now* magazine's 'Exclusive Caught on Camera Feature' includes a collection of unflattering pictures of the television presenter Eammon Holmes leaving a cake shop with captions such as 'Laden with an overflowing bag of goodies he can't wait to get home and tuck in'. This ridiculing and abusive approach centres primarily upon his weight and appearance, engaging readers in having a laugh at his expense. It is an extremely insensitive and offensive approach although more accepted by publishers and readers with celebrities being regarded as 'fair game'. The major problem, though, is the impact that these approaches have upon the general population where beauty is venerated and imperfection is regarded as intolerable. It is made worse by the increase of methods to help people in their pursuit of looking younger and more attractive. Magazines frequently carry advertising offering products and treatments such as cosmetic surgery and liposuction. The need to resort to some of these methods is stimulated further by a host of television programmes demonstrating the 'marvellous' transformation from frumpy to attractive before our eyes. This is achieved through a number of methods such as rigorous dieting, hairdressing, make-up, clothing, as well as certain surgical techniques. We are also shown the humiliating and demeaning processes that participants go through as they are manipulated towards change in a very forthright and critical fashion. For example, in *What Not to Wear*, Trinny and Susannah maintain a running commentary on the featured person's appearance letting them know in no uncertain terms if they are making a poor choice with regard to what they are wearing. This all appears fairly mild when compared to shows such as *10 Years Younger* where the treatment of the participant is often offensive and humiliating, being paraded in front of the public by the presenter Nicky Hambleton-Jones in order to initially receive some insulting and critical comments. The purpose of this is for the viewer's benefit to help achieve a feeling of before and after contrast with the subsequent parading in front of the public evoking more complimentary noises and comments. The process of transition though is a harsh one involving invasive physical treatments such as chemical peels and nose surgery. It is interesting therefore to consider the thoughts of the average television viewer who is unable to attain such a

transformation because of financial or other reasons. There is certainly evidence to suggest that exposure to these types of media messages has a detrimental effect upon many people's concept of self and to some degree helps to explain the dramatic uptake in cosmetic surgery over recent years (Wykes and Gunter 2005). Until the message being sent out by the media becomes more balanced, the need by many to strive towards an unattainable goal will be maintained.

Associated prejudice

The sense of stigma may be further heightened when mental illness is linked with other groups which are also marginalised for reasons of race, gender and disability. An alarming consequence of this can be seen in the higher incidence of Afro-Caribbean individuals than expected entering the psychiatric in-patient system (McGovern and Cope 1987) or being diagnosed with schizophrenia at a rate 12–13 times higher than the average number (Harrison *et al.* 1988). As Weiss *et al.* (2001) point out, an understanding of what stigma means involves looking at how it is viewed across cultures as it is not evident that different cultures will regard the same features as salient with regard to stigma.

Negative representations of those with mental health problems are compounded by prejudicial attitudes such as those of a racial nature. In some instances, the reporting of black people with mental health problems uses descriptions or terms which do not adequately reflect the person being reported. Certain descriptors stand out very forcibly and in a sense are used representatively to highlight the essence of the person being reported and to draw us as readers into a particular relationship with them. For example, if we consider headlines such as 'Mum Attacked by Black Mental Patient', we have a way of relating immediately to the subjects contained within the article. Without reading any further, we can feel a sense of pity towards the victim ('mum'), an adverb that signifies qualities of kindness, caring and nurturing. On the other hand, the 'Black Mental Patient' is used to convey a sense of threat, complemented by the commonly applied reading of 'big, black and dangerous'. What these types of portrayals do is to depersonalise the individual and reduce them to a collection of catch phrases. It is a point reflected by Wilson (1997) who states that when newspapers turn a black man who has committed a violent crime into a 'psycho killer', 'schizophrenic killer', or 'Beast of Belgravia', they endlessly obliterate the person behind the label.

It is interesting, therefore, to note the National Union of Journalist's (1999) *Code of Conduct* Clause 10 which affirms that:

A journalist shall only mention a person's race, colour, creed, illegitimacy, marital status (or lack of it), gender or sexual orientation if this information is strictly relevant. A journalist shall neither originate nor

process material which encourages discrimination, ridicule, prejudice or hatred on any of the above-mentioned grounds.

(NUJ 1999)

Instead of adhering to this code, there is at times an almost blatant disregard shown to individuals or groups of people through the references which are made. Numerous adjectives have been used to describe a person experiencing mental health problems, many of them far from flattering. One of the core problems with prejudicial and discriminatory attitudes is the sense of marginalisation and distance created between separate groups. As illustrated by Van Dijk (1987) these negative views are kept alive by the central role that these beliefs play in the symbolic world of the majority, allowing them to form a comfortable in-group identity. In this instance, negative associations are applied to the stigmatised groups and externalised from those who deem themselves to be mentally well.

Tackling stigma

Corrigan and Penn (1999) suggest three basic ways in which groups can confront stigma – through 'Protest', 'Education' and 'Contact'. These issues are covered in more detail in the following chapter although will be briefly addressed here.

Protest

Priebe (2003) confirms the picture that efforts to achieve more positive attitudes are operating within the background of a predominantly negative coverage of mental health issues. Changing attitudes or confirming positive stereotypes according to Rothbart and Park (1986) requires a larger number of positive examples and fewer contrary examples to disconfirm it. It also needs a sustained level of critical feedback concerning portrayals that are less than accurate or flattering. Over the past few years a number of organisations representing governmental, heath professional and service-user groups have become very active in campaigning against stigmatising coverage of mental health issues in the media. Critical feedback to media providers about their coverage linked with education and guidance has helped to reduce some of the stereotypical content found across all media types. It appears though that the response to protest is exceedingly slow and perhaps instances of change and response are due in large part to worries over the potential commercial implications. This was highlighted strongly with *The Sun* newspapers surprising U-turn with regard to their coverage of the Frank Bruno story from insensitive and stigmatising to staunch mental health advocate.

Education

While often perpetrating negative stereotypes, if properly harnessed the media may be used to combat stigma (Salter and Byrne 2000). Crisp *et al.*'s (2000) study found that in most instances stigmatising opinions are based upon factors other than a general lack of knowledge about mental disorder. It follows here that destigmatising campaigns have to do more than simply educate and increase knowledge. This viewpoint is shared by Haghighat (2001) who indicates that people need more than logic, as providing rational evidence that refutes a schizophrenic individual's propensity for violence does not necessarily combat their already conditioned autonomic circuit of arousal, fear and anxiety. This reflects Bodenhausen's (1993) findings that it is the feeling rather than the cognitive component of attitudes that determines people's social judgement. Destigmatising approaches therefore clearly need to address the emotional content and enable people with means of ventilating and understanding associated anxiety.

Contact

The importance of contact with the mentally ill as a destigmatising approach is also outlined by Penn *et al.* (1994). This helps individuals to appreciate something of the reality experienced by people with mental illness, thereby countering many stereotypical notions. A degree of contact is also provided through media examples such as autobiographical accounts and television documentaries which highlight the actual lived and felt experience of mental illness. For example, the documentary programme *Inside my Head: Michael* featured a 16-year-old boy with two severe schizophrenia episodes already behind him. His frank and exposing honesty in the face of abuse and worsening symptoms provided the viewer with a strong opportunity for connection and understanding of the condition of schizophrenia. These types of example importantly foster connecting and empathic approaches, something sadly lacking in the majority of media depictions.

4 Selling mental health (positive health promotion)

Introduction

As has been illustrated in the previous chapter, there is a predominantly negative portrayal of mental health issues to be found within the media as a whole. This is illustrated through various reports and studies that have initiated a number of campaigns and recommendations aimed at reducing stigmatising media coverage (Mind 2000; Mindout for Mental Health 2005; RCP 2001; Media Bureau 2001; DOH 1999). Advocacy initiatives, developments in liaison, campaigning and health promotion are all playing a significant part in raising awareness and challenging negative attitudes. The media organisations themselves are responding with subtle changes in their portrayals including better informed reporting, more likeable and realistic characterisations and an increase in the utilisation of biographical style accounts. Some of these initiatives have led towards subtle yet important shifts in reporting styles such as the reduced association between mental illness and violence found by some researchers (Health Education Authority 1999; Francis *et al.* 2004). These developments all offer hope that a better representation of mental health issues can be achieved.

Definition of *positive*

The term *positive* might generally be regarded as relating to portrayals that challenge traditional stigmatising and stereotypical associations; those which educate and inform the receiver; and those which enable a sense of connection to be made with the person experiencing mental health problems. From a different perspective, *positive* might refer to a sense of personal or organisational gain. If we consider Berlo's (1960) communication model and the referent or stimulus for a particular message then the way in which *positive* is defined might perhaps be contested by different groups. Each group naturally will have their own needs and expectations that in turn impact upon the way in which messages are decoded and understood. The interpretation of media messages for example as being sensitive and supporting or patronising and unhelpful can be seen as being shaped by an individual's particular

predisposition. Therefore, as with Jastrow's image (Figure 4.1), what we actually see, whether it be a duck or a rabbit, depends upon a range of influencing factors. How we see this image is governed in part by what we expect to see and what we want to see. Our orientation to a particular stimulus is fostered and influenced by our past experience and learning. We need also to consider the cues which are present, for example the labels or narrative content that help with comprehension. With the image in Figure 4.1, for instance, the title *rabbit* accompanied with a comment upon its long ears will help to focus the receiver's direction of engagement with it. It may at times, though, require extra coaxing to guide receivers away from particular readings of stimuli that are more familiar to them. From a mental health perspective, this can be seen in relation to the presentation of the message that the mentally ill do not pose a significant threat to the general public, a view that runs contrary to popular belief.

With regard to examples of positive mental health portrayal, it is worth clarifying what the term *positive* actually means as it may denote a number of different aspects dependent upon who is sending the message and who is receiving it. This is addressed in the following sections concerning the different groups of media provider, the mentally ill, and the mentally well. The terms mentally ill and mentally well are used here to provide a direct contrast with each other and the heading mentally well can be taken as referring to those who might perceive themselves to be free of mental health problems.

Media providers

We can look first at the media providers and what they might deem to be *positive* with regard to mental health portrayals. The most obvious factor here relates to the fact that 'madness' is an extremely attractive topic to media groups because of its selling potential. Commercial success will help to pacify and please the various stakeholders involved and perhaps ensure the continuation of a product. Mental health depictions are appealing and impactful and can have a major influence upon factors such as box office takings, television

Figure 4.1 Duck/rabbit (Jastrow).

ratings, book sales, newspaper circulation and Internet site visitors. There are obvious pressures here to continue to use certain characterisations and terminology that have on past occasions proven successful. This is not to say that the use of overly dramatic or stereotypical representations is all bad as the high level of exposure achieved can play an important role in raising awareness if supported by opportunities for subsequent discussion and processing of issues. An example of this can be seen within the medium of television and the provision of information and contact details for self-help groups following the dramatisation of topics such as family abuse or self-harm.

The mentally ill

The issues of prime importance as regarded by those experiencing mental health problems concern those of accuracy, sensitivity and likeability. These messages are to be found within the media's vast output and have been stimulated by the growing recognition of the mental health service-user's voice and progress made through active campaigning, liaison with media groups and opportunities for direct expression through the media. The importance here is of providing the general public with a more realistic and accurate picture of the lived and felt experience of those with mental health problems. It also entails the portrayal of messages that are more normalising of mental illness as opposed to the generally depicted stereotypes of 'oddness', 'violence' or 'imbecility'. The importance here is of challenging age-old assumptions and associations and engaging the receiver with new and more productive ways of thinking. This helps to break down the 'us and them' barrier often found and fosters a greater feeling of connectedness. Magazine articles, television documentaries, autobiographical accounts and self-help Internet sites all include examples whereby the 'voice' of those experiencing mental health problems can be heard and whereby more informed and accurate role models are made accessible. Taking a slightly different approach, *positive* might also be regarded as relating to mental health media products that do not reflect negative connotations. Although not necessarily promoting positive associations either, the mere absence of a negative reinforcer can be seen as an improvement upon the generally found misleading portrayals. Although it is unlikely that sufficient numbers will exist for the process outlined by Skinner (1974) of extinction of the public's conditioned response to occur, it can certainly be perceived as a more welcome approach.

The mentally well

The term mentally well is used here to refer to those in the general population who deem themselves to be at the present time without mental health problems and is more of a perceptual opinion than anything based in fact. Two areas of importance for those in this category are education and

entertainment. From an educative point of view, certain media products might be regarded as positive because of their potential to provide recipients with desired information. On the one hand, this might relate to an individual's need to learn more about the facts of mental illness because of genuine altruistic feelings. On the other hand, information might be sought as a means of coping with the anxiety and fear felt concerning the mentally ill or as a means of satisfying one's morbid curiosity about a fascinating and compelling topic. What is interesting, though, is the degree to which these recipients might accept various products as *positive* irrespective of the authority and accuracy of the information being provided. The other core strand includes media portrayals that are regarded as entertaining either because of their humorous or dramatic portrayals. These types of portrayal are certainly impactful and engaging and include some hugely popular examples such as the films *The Silence of the Lambs* and *Me, Myself and Irene*. While being applauded by many movie-goers as hugely entertaining and enjoyable they are at the same time rounded upon by mental health advocacy groups as being damaging and misrepresentative of those with mental health problems.

Altered thinking and creativity

When defining what is positive concerning the subject of mental illness it is important also to consider the degree to which altered states particularly within the domain of arts have been courted and even to some degree venerated. Whether it be through mental illness or chemical inducement, the changes in a person's thinking can be seen as helpful in providing direct access to untold expanses of creative thought normally unavailable to them. The sense of liberation created by altered thought processes and the productive drive provided by some mental health states are the main areas being focused upon here.

The evidence

A fair amount has been written about the links between mental illness and creativity although the evidence remains particularly uncertain. While there are a number of studies and reviews supporting a causal association between these two themes, they are not without their critics. Ludwig's (1995) study of 1,004 'eminent' people in creative professions found them to have higher rates of mental illness than those in the general population or eminent people in other walks of life. Another piece of research by Andreasen (1987) examined 30 creative writers finding a higher rate of mental illness than matched control subjects, a feature also true of the writers' first-degree relatives. Post (1994) investigated the backgrounds of 291 world famous men finding certain pathological personality characteristics and tendencies towards depression and alcoholism being causally linked to various types of creativity. These themes have also been studied in some depth by Jamison (1996) who

demonstrated that mood disorders and artistic creativity tend to co-occur. The available evidence is fairly substantial although not without its detractors who view the research with concerns about methodology and lack of scientific evidence (Lauronen *et al.* 2004; Schlesinger 2002a; Waddell 1998). Another point of criticism is provided by Wright (1997) who contends that what the evidence mainly demonstrates is a more specific link between creativity and bipolar disorder and not the wider picture encompassing other mental health states. Schlesinger's (2002b) view is that the desire for a link between madness and creativity is in part generated through the idea that great talent coming from special suffering is romantic and thrilling. Despite the criticisms levelled at the available research, there are certainly grounds for considering the significance of this link: first, the wealth of historical and personal accounts that assert the importance that a person's altered states of thinking have upon the products being created; second, we might consider the desire of some within artistic spheres to actively seek altered states of cognition through psychotropic means in order to achieve a sense of creative expressiveness. Furthermore, we might also look at the significance that understanding the cognitive changes common to manic, depressive and creative states has in lessening the stigma of mental illness (Jamison 1989).

Jamison's (1993) study of living artists and writers revealed that most of them had high periods (mood changes) that were documented as coming on just prior to a productive period. This is supported elsewhere by theories that address dimensions of personality such as psychoticism, incorporating the two parts of thymotypy (working mainly through the mood) and schizotypy (working mainly through divergent thought). This, as Nettle (2001) states, facilitates the speed and range of imagination deemed so important for creative originality. It also provides the enormous energy required to drive on through a task in the absence of immediate rewards, especially in what are essentially solitary occupations and where critical feedback about a particular piece of work may be absent or only arrive years later. The periods of productivity following mood changes have been found in a number of creative and artistic people, for example Virginia Woolf who wrote that:

> one thing, in considering my state of mind now, seems to me beyond dispute; that I have at last, bored down into my oil well, and can't scribble fast enough to bring it all to the surface . . . I have never felt this rush and urgency before.
>
> (Woolf 1953: 74)

There are many instances where artists and writers have had access to divergent thought processes either as a consequence of their mental health state or as something induced through chemical means. It is perhaps the sense of disassociation and creative freedom that has been deliberately sought after by some, such as the writers Carlos Castenada and Aldous Huxley or the musician Syd Barrett. The feeling of cognitive liberation and creative

expressiveness is a strong enticement and helps to explain why individuals such as William Blake are said to have actively embraced and even rejoiced in their madness. This is reflected by the degree to which Blake's madness allowed him to distance himself from the restrictions of worldly rationalism and embrace a new way of seeing the world around him. The notion being addressed here concerns the channels of expressiveness and lateral vision that are being opened up and are normally denied the majority. It reflects the views held by the avant-garde in Paris, of Flaubert, Baudelaire, Verlaine and Rimbaud, that true art sprang from the morbid and pathological. Furthermore it reflects the romantic notion that suffering and illness fired and liberated the spirit and that works of genius were in a sense hammered out on the '*anvil of pain*' (Nettle 2001). A number of classic works can be linked to this such as Malcolm Lowry's *Under the Volcano* or Sylvia Plath's *The Bell Jar* where these works of literature were in a sense directly fuelled by the authors' own personal experience of mental distress. A number of themes are related here including that of the creative genius suffering for their art. This is where great artists are drained and consumed by their talent, giving their all in the production of immense masterpieces. Certainly examples such as the composer Schumann and the legendary dancer Nijinsky fit this profile with their most productive periods being borne out of phases of mental illness and being in a sense eventually consumed by their art.

Just as the pyramids of Giza might be admired as a monumental achievement despite the extreme cost in human suffering, the admiration of great works of artistic or literary endeavour may take place in the absence of any real consideration for the toll exacted upon those behind them. It is a point reflected by Elizabeth Wurtzel in her book about depression, *Prozac Nation*. She writes:

> Forget about the scant hours in her brief life when Sylvia Plath was able to produce the works in Ariel. Forget about that tiny bit of time and just remember the days that spanned into years when she could not move, couldn't think straight, could only lie in a hospital bed, hoping for the relief that electro convulsive therapy would bring . . . think about living in depression from moment to moment, and know it is not worth any of the great art that comes as its by-product.
>
> (Wurtzel 1994: 260)

This is one facet relating to the concept that is mental illness but as expressed by Liz Sayce: 'It [Madness] is not irredeemably awful but mixed: at times tragic, wasteful, frustrating, boring, life denying; at other times extraordinary in the ways that contribute both to users' lives and to those around them' (Sayce 2000: 29).

Despite the various points addressed above, the association between madness and creativity is one that fascinates people and has not surprisingly proven an attractive lure to film-makers, something that is apparent in a

number of recent films such as *Shine, A Beautiful Mind* and *Iris*. In these films we have a range of creative individuals whose talent provides the audience member with a strong point of contact overriding potential difficulties they might experience with that person's mental health state. Emotions are stirred within the receiver, such as feelings of sadness at the plight of John Nash (*A Beautiful Mind*) and Iris Murdoch (*Iris*) who are denied through their respective illnesses the talents that are most important to them. Likewise with the film *Shine*, the viewer is left with the uncertainty as to what extent David Helfgott's prodigious musical talent could have been developed further in the absence of his illness. What these types of portrayal importantly offer the receiver is a point of recognising the serious impact that mental illness can have on the lives of those affected. It takes the viewer to a position where they actually care about a person's experience and which generates a much greater sense of acceptance and awareness than might be otherwise achieved.

What's good about . . .?

As with the previous chapter, a variety of core media types have been selected with brief comments provided as to their positive potential with regards to the conveyance of mental health issues.

. . . *Film*

Connectedness

Film as a medium has the capacity to enable viewers to temporarily suspend their ordinary existence and to some degree become immersed in a new experience (Wedding and Boyd 1999). This experience sometimes involves entering the world of others and to a degree living and feeling experiences as if being directly involved. It might include gaining a sense of how altered states of cognition are perceived by the mentally ill but perhaps more importantly something of their felt experience. Some films, encourage a sense of connectedness and appreciation of a person's inner world, engaging the viewer with sensations such as hallucinations that are normally unseen. Polanski's *Repulsion*, for example, gives a very symbolic and observable representation of Catherine Deneuve's fragmenting world. Another example can be found with the film *A Beautiful Mind* where the viewer is presented with the same difficulty experienced by its principal character John Nash in spotting the distinction between reality and fantasy. The significance here is of the medium of film allowing what is normally unseen to be seen and what is unheard to be heard. Essentially, it enables the viewer to grasp something of what it might feel like to experience cognitive impairment and to subsequently foster more caring and nurturing feelings towards those concerned.

Caring treatment

Despite the number of films where treatment is depicted as a punitive or oppressive process there are some which show mental health care as a competent and caring process. These examples provide the viewer with a counter to the many negative stereotypes available and offer a sense of hope and reassurance in a system which individuals might approach with some trepidation. What is desired by many is the feeling that care is governed by the needs of the individual concerned and not by the system as is destructively shown in the film *One Flew over the Cuckoo's Nest*. Films such as *The Prince of Tides* and *Ordinary People* serve as positive advertisements for therapy by portraying an insightful and connected carer, someone who really does care. On a critical note, some of these films can be challenged for their lack of realism as they perhaps play into another stereotype with their dramatic and cathartic scenes. What does come across very strongly, though, is the message of recovery, that mental health problems can be overcome. This is aided in part by the concerned and caring helper or, as in the case of Dr Malcolm Sayer (as played by Robin Williams) in the film *Awakenings*, a tireless activist, prepared to risk all in the interests of their patients. What we get from films such as these is a sense of faith and optimism in mental health care that strongly contrasts against the showing of treatment as a destructive or punitive process.

Positive role models

The presentation of positive and likeable role models helps to counteract the usual association of unattractive and 'flawed' characterisations. The largely negative portrayal of the mentally ill as looking different or unattractive is similar to that of the disabled. Attractive or charismatic stars add a fresh appeal and foster a better climate for liking characters and in developing an enhanced sense of concern regarding their plight. Even fairly disagreeable or cantankerous characters such as Melvin Udall in *As Good As It Gets* come across in a favourable light. It is helped to some degree because we as an audience largely admire the actor Jack Nicholson and his character's warm side begins to emerge, enabling a more positive attraction to be formed. Other examples can be seen with the casting of Russell Crowe in *A Beautiful Mind* or Judy Dench in *Iris*, both attractive and popular stars. The importance for the viewer is in having aspects that help to develop feelings of attraction for mentally ill characters and subsequently help with acceptance of the 'whole' person.

... *Television*

Vicarious therapy

An important facet provided by the medium of television is its ability to help viewers feel supported and connected with others albeit vicariously. The television schedules are packed with shows that enable viewers to observe and learn from the problems encountered by participants or other viewers. Day-time television and the magazine-style formats offered by various stations include features about selected health matters, complete with phone-ins and 'your questions answered' by studio doctors such as Dr Hilary Jones. There are also a number of talk shows available to the viewer, some offering appalling examples of exploitation and participant abuse while others handle themes more sensitively and responsibly. To some degree, the latter type of example could be regarded as an on-air self-help group providing viewers who have experienced similar issues with a powerful sense of connectedness. This is usefully accompanied at the end of many such shows with contact details for related links and further information.

Education

The ability to inform an audience as well as entertain them about mental health issues is something that is strongly featured within the medium of television. This is achieved through a range of programme types such as news, documentaries, chat shows and features within breakfast and day-time TV shows. The public are offered different types of information depending upon the style of the show but these might include reports, case-study style information (as with documentaries), advice from health care professionals, or direct statements from television show participants about their experience of mental health problems. Television stations periodically place a strong focus upon education regarding mental health issues with short series of dedicated programmes, for example the BBC's *States of Mind* or Channel 4's *Inside My Head*. Short featured items with phone-ins and professional advice are regularly shown within the morning television schedules although these might be criticised for not adequately reflecting the full spectrum of mental health difficulties. The bias tends towards highlighting individuals whose plight is more sympathetically reviewed by the public as opposed, for instance, to the less comfortable subjects such as schizophrenia. An educatory function is also offered through programme types that, although being primarily geared towards drama and entertainment, carry enlightening mental health storylines.

Identification

Another regular means of engagement through the medium of television comes via what Horton and Wohl (1956) describe as parasocial relations and refers to a process of emotional identification whereby the audience relates to the experience of characters viewed on screen. This is found in particular with the prime-time dramas and soaps which regularly carry storylines with characters suffering from stress, emotional and psychological difficulties as well as relationship problems. Because many of these characters are so familiar to most of their audience, the feeling when watching them is that they are actually known to us. This is positive in that the sense of connectedness already felt with characters means that a greater understanding of and compassion for their distress can be achieved. The viewer can in a sense enter the world of the television character and to some degree connect with their experience, for example the emotional distress endured by Marlon in *Emmerdale* following the death of his wife or Sonia's emotional turmoil in *Eastenders* following the forced adoption of her baby. The significance, as illustrated by Livingstone (1998), is that viewers recognise and identify with the characters and experience them as real people, almost as if they were part of their family. It therefore puts us in touch with the lived experience and the feelings of those enduring mental health difficulties. These shows are on the whole extremely popular and achieve a large range of exposure.

. . . Literature

Inside looking out

Perhaps one of the most significant factors within the world of literature is the opportunity provided to enter the world of those experiencing mental health problems. This takes the reader into a position of connecting with a person's thoughts and feelings as opposed to the more familiar stance of observing them from a detached distance. This is achieved primarily through formats such as autobiographical writing or first-person narratives. To a certain degree we can regard autobiographical styles of writing as providing us with some of the most insightful and clear prose concerning issues of mental health. One might argue that it is the writing about mental illness by those who best understand the material being handled, having experienced aspects first-hand. These types of publication are currently highly popular and regularly feature as best sellers and include books such as Julie Gregory's *Sickened* (surviving Munchausen's syndrome by proxy) or Richard McCann's *Just a Boy* (learning to cope following his mother's murder by the Yorkshire Ripper). They also include publications that have won various awards, such as David Solomon's (2002) *The Noonday Demon: Anatomy of Depression* which was the Mind book of the year 2002. An extra feature provided by first-person narratives in fictional pieces of work is the ability to access places

we would not normally be able to go, for example the emotional detachment experienced within the thoughts of the psychopathic killer (*American Psycho*) or the disordered and fragmented thinking within altered mental health states (*Briefing for a Descent into Hell*). These types of narrative provide the reader with a brief glimpse at the inner world of the person with mental health problems and consequently a greater appreciation and understanding.

Survival

In contrast to many media depictions where the person with mental health problems is either consumed by their condition or destructive towards others, is the sense of hope and optimism that comes through survival. These are found in abundance within both autobiographical and fictional types and provide a refreshing change to the often-found stigmatising alternative. The writing within autobiographical texts at times displays an immense degree of honesty and openness, as portrayed within Tony Adams' account of recovering from alcoholism (*Addicted*) or Paul Gascoigne's frank account of his personal problems (*Gazza: My Story*). This is also the case within a number of fictional accounts where featured individuals succeed in finding ways of coping with extreme life stressors that threaten to consume them (*White Oleander, I Know This Much is True*). Accounts focusing upon survival through adversity and hardship also focus upon collective experiences such as Mao's Cultural Revolution – two notable examples here being Jung Chan's *Wild Swans* and Hong Ying's *Daughter of the River*. These accounts are at times hard to read because of the extreme suffering being recounted although at the same time provide some very heartening images regarding the strength found to cope with extreme hardship and adversity.

... The press

Exposure

The degree of exposure offered through the newsprint media, aided by the high circulation some titles achieve, is an important factor with regard to positive health promotion. The significance of this is highlighted by the findings that newspapers provide us with most of our information about mental illness (Mason 2003). Although a fair degree of material accessed is neither positive nor accurate, there are a number of examples where care is taken to develop better and more productive messages. This is aided through various promotional campaigns as well as health information provided through featured articles, personal accounts, health advice and even to some degree the 'Agony Aunt' columns. The focus upon health promotion features very strongly within certain types of publication which include the better women's and men's magazines. There is a strong contrast found within newspaper types between tabloid and broadsheets as the former employs an overly

stereotypical and sensational style of reporting whereas the latter features well within annual mental health awards for positive mental health coverage. Further exposure is gained when particular mental health issues are brought to the public's attention through the problems experienced by noted celebrities. Although not always sensitively handled, the better coverage provides others struggling with similar difficulties with feelings of connection and acceptance.

Liaison

The strongest liaison between media providers and mental health advocates has perhaps been developed within the newsprint media. The importance of increased involvement with those who better understand the nature and implications relating to mental health issues is reflected by various anti-stigmatising campaigns (*Changing Minds: Every Family in the Land; Mindout*; and *Shift*). Until recent years most liaison involved mental health professionals and the picture is now changing to encompass a variety of mental health service-user organisations. The significance of this is reflected in the Media Bureau's (2001) study *Mental Health and the Press* which found that only 6.5 per cent of all articles analysed included the voice of current or former mental health service-users. Many service-user organisations (e.g. Rethink, Mind, Zito Trust, Media Bureau) now actively prepare their members for getting involved with the media providing them with guidance, support and training days. Rethink in particular run a media volunteer scheme that puts journalists and broadcasters in touch with 'real experts' from a base of over 200 volunteers with direct experience of severe mental illness. These types of initiative help in directing journalistic personnel towards developing more sensitive and informed portrayals regarding mental illness.

... Internet

Accessibility

One of the most important qualities of the Internet is the ready availability of information on offer and the ease with which individuals can retrieve it. Recipients are presented with a vast storehouse of knowledge with material being posted from every conceivable viewpoint. This includes legislative material by the Department of Health, information about various conditions and treatments by health professional groups (e.g. the Royal College of Psychiatry) and supportive links by user–carer groups. This resource also offers immediacy with up-to-date material instantly available which is important concerning issues that need updating on a regular basis.

Empowerment

A core feature of the Internet is the opportunity afforded for those experiencing mental health problems in taking a more active role in their care. As individuals are able to seek out their own health information they are subsequently better informed and thereby come to health care professionals with a clearer understanding of their condition (Thede 1999). This has a number of implications upon the patient–practitioner relationship helping to foster shared decision making and the creation of a real partnership (Bauer 2002; Winker *et al.* 2000). It places a degree of power with the patient who is thereby better informed and more able to decide between available modes of treatment being offered.

Universality

The concept of *universality* can be understood as a process felt strongly by participants of group psychotherapy – feeling connected with others (Yalom 1995). The essence here is the sense of 'I'm not alone', as comfort and support can be obtained from the understanding that similar symptoms and difficulties are also being experienced by others. The Internet provides this facility both directly and indirectly. Direct support can be obtained through Internet support groups and various discussion room facilities whereby participants are provided with a vehicle for sharing and working through particular issues (Lamberg 2003). The feeling of connectedness can also be gained vicariously, by reading some of the many postings left by individuals and organisations concerning specific issues. This facility is particularly important for individuals who are experiencing difficulties in seeking help and may use this resource as an initial point of sharing or as a supplemental means of support (Oravec 2000).

Role models

An important contribution to the positive promotion of mental health issues is provided by the example of role models who share their distress and conflicts within a public arena and thereby remove some of the stigma attached. Such role models might mainly include well-known people although can also encompass non-celebrities who have a powerful experience to relate. Notable examples here include the revelations by Princess Diana about her problems with bulimia, of the Arsenal and England footballer Tony Adams concerning his addiction to drink, or even Kelly Holmes' account of her self-harming behaviour. Such examples as these reflect Bandura's (1986) social learning theory whereby learning can take place through observing another person modelling certain behaviours. It means that individuals who might be experiencing similar problems can gain heart from having a positive and powerful role model with whom to relate. In these instances, the public are provided

with somebody expressing openly and honestly issues that are both deeply distressing as well as humiliating. What these examples significantly offer is a raised level of understanding and acceptance concerning the featured condition as well as a granting of permission to others to talk about and share their own experience. This is especially important with regard to topics that might otherwise be regarded as taboo, such as childhood abuse, so that many individuals do not deny themselves vital and much-needed support. The more certain aspects are shared, the more the climate is able to change to accommodate expression by others on related experiences. This can be seen in the steady increase in autobiographical accounts dealing with childhood trauma and abuse that now regularly feature on supermarket shelves and best-selling lists.

The way in which we respond to those in the public eye exhibiting mental health problems to a large degree relates to the affinity we already have for them. It is also interesting to note the sense of relish that may be exhibited by some concerning an individual's downfall, although it seems that this is mainly generated by the perspective from which their tale is told. If the individual concerned has direct access to the receiver then a more empathic and connected relationship can be achieved. The difficulty occurs when problems are related by an unconcerned third party (e.g. tabloid newspapers) with more interest in the 'scoop' obtained than the sensitivities of the person involved. The particular mental health state involved may also play a significant part with the more socially accepted forms of drug and alcohol abuse being treated more favourably than others such as schizophrenia. The type of coverage given by the media also plays a core role in helping the public appreciate and understand what a person's experience of distress actually entails. The largely detached and matter-of-fact reporting style reflected when, for example, stars book into a clinic for their next course of detoxification does not convey the desperation, isolation or humiliation endured by real people in real distress. It is mainly when the person is able to recount issues from their own perspective that public feeling becomes more sympathetic and understanding, which can again be illustrated by the case of Tony Adams who received a fair degree of media condemnation before finally being able to recount the story from his viewpoint.

The sense of acceptance provided by positive role models is also encompassed within the sense that mental health problems really can affect anyone. They are not conditions reserved solely for the obviously strange or more expected choice of individual but can literally affect anybody irrespective of their status. The famous role model, attractive, successful and adored provides a strong alternative to the classic stereotype of the mentally ill person and helps to challenge fixed views held by large sections of the public. This is aided through campaigns and initiatives engaged in by celebrities who help to promote positive associations of mental health. One example here is the collaboration between famous people who have endured mental health problems and health professionals to write what are essentially self-help books offering support and advice to others, for example Spike Milligan and

Anthony Clare's *Depression and How to Survive It* or John Cleese and Robin Skynner's *Families and How to Survive Them*. Other examples can be seen with their involvement in media initiatives such as the Headspace campaign, an exhibition by Mindout for Mental Health (2001b) where stars including Sting, Daniel Bedingfield, Romeo and Liberty X open up about personal difficulties they have suffered themselves or seen in others.

Positive role models provide those accessing media products with a much needed counter to the many negative role models whose destructive lifestyles have in some instances come to be admired or even venerated. This is especially true with regard to the destructive 'Rock and Roll' lifestyle that advocates a policy of living hard, and where dying young is a potential and accepted consequence. Many famous individuals within the music world have succumbed to this legend and the casualty list is littered with high profile stars such as Jim Morrison, Brian Jones, Janis Joplin and Jimi Hendrix. These are chaotic and tormented individuals who have tragically been consumed by their difficulties as an adoring yet fairly unconcerned public watches on. In more recent years the Nirvana singer Kurt Cobain successfully committed suicide after a number of failed attempts. Another tortured musician was the Manic Street Preachers' guitarist Ritchie Edwards who disappeared a number of years ago. He had a history of self-harming behaviour and would even cut his arms on stage accompanied by the cheers of fans. This in a sense illustrated something of the rock and roll myth, the legend that self-destructive and hard living behaviours are to some degree expected or even demanded by their fans. What are needed instead are role models who illustrate and portray something different, expressing the true nature of problems without glamorising them and advocating support-seeking instead of self-destruction as the way forward. This is why, for example, Tony Adams stands as a much more vital and productive role model than, for instance, the footballer George Best.

Service-user expression

In recent years there have been numerous developments and initiatives aimed at promoting the artistic expression of those affected by mental health problems. This importantly recognises the right and need of anyone affected by mental health difficulties to have access to various channels through which to communicate their experience. It also provides others with valuable opportunities to gain greater awareness and insight into the thoughts and feelings concerning a person's felt experience of psychological distress. It is in a sense the learning about mental health issues from those who best understand them (Rogers *et al.* 1993). Another core feature here is the fact that creative expression is encouraged and accessible, in principle, to anyone affected by mental health problems and not something that is reserved solely for the artistic genius. This is matched by the public's growing acceptance of and interest in the personal reflections of 'ordinary people' as reflected in the

huge popularity of autobiographical narratives that are steadily attracting both critical as well as commercial acclaim. One of the most significant factors concerning a person's involvement with creative or artistic expression is the potential therapeutic value that is gained. This is highlighted by a number of authors who state that the very act of writing has proven beneficial in helping them to work through and resolve personal issues (Pegler 2003; Lott 1997). Writing has an extremely powerful therapeutic potential as illustrated by McArdle and Byrt's (2001) study that employed the medium of literature with mental health service-users and reported some positive treatment outcomes. It is also worth noting that there are now some specific publishers such as Chipmunkapublishing that cater specifically for individuals who are survivors of mental health problems and wish to promote better attitudes towards mental illness.

There are a number of national and local initiatives and projects that have encouraged and even celebrated service-user expressions. One initiative of particular significance has been the Royal College of Psychiatrists' (2001b) *A Mind Odyssey*, launched in 2001 to help inspire both mental health care professionals and service-users in expressing their creativity through various forms of the arts (RCP 2005). This has led on to the creation of a range of locally organised exhibitions including the 'A Mind Odyssey: Diversity' programme of events offered across the city of Leeds in October 2003. The sheer diversity of expressive types is illustrated through the wide range of activities covered including the forms of art, photography, dance, drama, writing, music, poetry and film. These events were organised and led by a variety of individuals from the voluntary sector and the National Health Service and involved people who have used or worked in mental health services.

The encouragement and development of service-user modes of expressions are importantly helping to normalise the experience of mental illness with the message that anybody can experience psychological distress. The provision of direct access to a person's thoughts and feelings means that what has traditionally proven a frightening and to some degree avoided topic can now be better addressed and understood. Historically, the societal approach was to distance and rid itself of madness by segregating and removing those designated as being so afflicted. The present climate of community care and high media exposure means that different approaches are needed including better education and to some degree a process of desensitisation. Service-user expression offers countless benefits to both those experiencing mental health problems as well as others who are better able to connect with and understand them. It also helps to reduce some of the stigma involved by creating a more open and accepting climate in which people are more able to talk about and share experiences without the fear of being rejected, ridiculed or alienated.

Promoting mental health

When looking at the dynamics and processes involved with mental health promotion certain core features stand out. Changing people's attitudes towards a more accommodating and understanding approach requires a certain degree of education. This is vital if individuals are to be helped to make better sense of the messages they are exposed to including the ability to discriminate between positive and stigmatising material. As well as addressing a person's requirement for accurate information is the need to tackle the emotional aspects (e.g. fear and anxiety) that keep people with mental health problems segregated and at a distance. This means developing greater feelings of connectedness with not only the person but also the topic of mental illness. One of the main problems facing those involved in health promotion is how to most effectively produce and disseminate their material to make it as widely accessible as possible. This involves getting their material noticed, certainly something that is important given the wealth of stimuli they have to compete against. Therefore two major issues which health promotion needs to address are those of education and exposure.

Education

A prime factor in helping to shift misconceptions and inaccuracies regarding mental health issues is the exposure to reliable sources of information and messages that inform people about what is actually occurring. This is recognised by various campaigns and strategies such as the Royal College of Psychiatrists' Changing Minds: Every Family in the Land campaign or the Mindout for Mental Health's (2001a) *Mindshift: A Guide to Open-minded Media Coverage of Mental Health* which both, among their various targets, seek to promote a better understanding of the real nature of mental illness. Among the various anti-stigmatisation approaches being employed are projects specifically geared towards better education. One such scheme is the Mental Health Awareness in Action programme of educational workshops set up in West Kent schools to help tackle stigma and discrimination (Pinfold 2003). The main aims of the workshops were the promotion of the messages that:

- We all have mental health
- Mental health problems are common
- Mental health problems are different to learning difficulties
- People can recover from mental health problems
- The discrimination that people with mental health problems feel is damaging and hurtful
- Any link between mental health problems and violent behaviour is a myth

The emphasis of these workshops was on discussion and engagement with these issues as opposed to a simple reception of imparted information. Prior to the workshops most information that participants had received regarding mental health issues were cited as being primarily from the various media sources or their parents. There was a significant change in attitude noted as a result of this programme in that the language used to describe the mentally ill replaced derogatory phrases and stigmatising terms with more sensitive and accepting words. This scheme in particular illustrated the fact that raising awareness and improving understanding about mental illness helps to facilitate and accommodate better attitudes being developed towards mental illness. The success of workshop-like events such as this is illustrated by Haghighat (2001) as being largely due to the opportunity for individuals to ventilate their anxieties and feelings. This is an important point and worth noting as informing people about the low risk in reality posed by those with mental health problems may on its own be insufficient. Many people need the opportunity to express and understand what their fears are actually based upon if they are to be able to accommodate and consider this point properly.

The liaison between mental health advocates and media groups is another core approach that is helping to tackle misrepresentations and promote more accurate messages. It involves media groups working directly with mental health professionals and those who have experienced psychological distress. These links have steadily developed with both service-user organisations and mental health professional groups providing training and support for their members who wish to get involved. These initiatives have on the whole been widely welcomed although in some instances are viewed with concern. In particular, Persaud (2000) reflects upon the involvement of service-users and questions how in touch some of the media's favourite pressure group leaders might be with medical research and practice. He also criticises the fact that they are in some instances called upon for comment before medical practitioners with considerable experience. This argument perhaps plays down the very real importance of allowing the public to be addressed directly by those who it might be argued have real expertise to speak upon topics concerning mental illness. The point in question here concerns who is regarded as having the most authority and expertise to speak about a mental health condition – those with years of professional experience or those with years of personal experience. The main issue, however, is to achieve the right balance with both health care professionals and service-users being employed by various providers of media services. Persaud (2000) raises an interesting question concerning the ways in which spokespersons among service-users are selected. It is, though, an aspect that relates equally to health care professionals. Obviously media personnel will have their own favourites, a choice that is assisted by accessibility or the particular mental health topic being addressed. While mental health advocates are steadily developing their liaison role, Cuenca (2002) feels that health care professionals need to recognise the power of the media and to increase their involvement from that of isolated individuals to

that of a collective group. The continued development of these relationships should help to foster more positive and less distorted messages about mental illness and mental health professionals. This relationship also involves to a certain degree of educating and challenging the attitudes held by those within the media because, as Salter (2000) points out, informing the public is not necessarily the journalistic profession's primary motive. Clearly, financial considerations and the dramatic and impactful potential provided by the topic of mental illness will also feature strongly.

As well as educating the public about aspects of mental health the media also provides a function for educating health care professionals. This is illustrated by Wall and Rossen (2004) who highlight the potential for developing critical thinking skills through using the media as a teaching strategy. This is done by enhancing students' sensitivity to the personal experiences of mental health service-users and broadening their understanding of mental illness and its treatment.

Exposure

One of the greatest difficulties facing those involved in mental health promotion concerns the issue as to how to make their message stand out and get it noticed. Certain media channels and products gain high exposure rates and would be ideal vehicles for positive health messages but they may prove prohibitive in terms of access. Austin and Husted (1998) reviewed the experience of developing media programmes through several broadcast and print formats and found a number of restrictions in terms of cost effectiveness and space available to carry messages. New media products such as the Internet provide wonderful opportunities for making wide ranges of material easily accessible and are commercially viable options to develop. It is a means that enables material to be disseminated and available to people instantly across the world, although this obviously relies upon those searching the Internet being able to find the site.

The issue of exposure relates to the number of people who have access to messages being sent out. In terms of developing awareness and understanding of mental health issues, the initial input could be of a positive or negative type, the importance being a person's noticing of the material and the opportunity to challenge and reflect upon it. This means that even products such as television soaps that rely upon dramatic and stereotypical imagery can be potentially beneficial if this leads to an eventual raising of awareness. Another useful example is provided by Lars von Trier's film *The Idiots* which could be regarded as offensive and insulting or alternatively can be viewed as challenging and thought provoking, depending upon how it is understood. This film focuses upon a group of people who deliberately present themselves as being mentally handicapped in order to evoke a reaction from the public and who purposely use stereotypical presentations including the word 'spass' as a means of provocation and confrontation. It is a powerful film that

challenges the audience members to consider their own discriminatory attitudes and potential feelings of discomfort relating to behaviours that are
'strange' and 'embarrassing'. This relates to a major theme involved within
health promotion, that of social exclusion, and the extent to which we might
play a part in its perpetuation. The exposure provided by blatantly negative
exposure could also be productive if followed up by immediate protest or
comment as seen, for example, by *The Sun*'s U-turn following the complaints
received regarding their initial appalling coverage of the news that Frank
Bruno had been involuntarily admitted to hospital for depression. The
importance here is the exposure that more productive messages can subsequently achieve as well as the opportunity for the public to be informed that
what it was initially in receipt of was actually incorrect.

A degree of exposure is necessary in order to help positive imagery stand
out and be noticed amidst the vast array of negative and stereotypical messages. As illustrated by Broadbent's (1958) filter theory, the amount of information passing along the input channels (sensory system) is far too much and
would overload the brain with too much information to assimilate. A filter is
followed by a bottleneck (limited capacity channel) that selects some of the
incoming messages for processing by the brain to regulate the intake (Figure
4.2). There is a short-term storage facility for input not initially selected,
although these impulses become weaker with time if not accessed.

What is important here is the extent to which particular messages stand
out as obviously some will attract more attention than others and increase
their likelihood of passing into the brain for processing. A difficulty facing
those engaged in health promotion concerns the simple fact that positive
images on the whole are far less appealing and impactful than their negative
and dramatic counterparts. The high degree of impact evoked through the
sensationalist reporting of a high profile news event such as the Soham

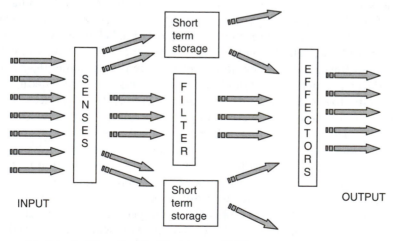

Figure 4.2 Adapted Broadbent's filter theory (1958).

murders is hard to match for sheer emotional intensity. The steady diet of negative reporting along with the periodically dramatic 'Psycho Killer' type of headlines is unnerving and unsettling. It is subsequently hard to put ones fears and uncertainties to the side even when confronted with information to the contrary. The messages mostly portrayed within the media would seem to suggest that those with mental health problems are on the whole unpredictable, potentially violent, unsuccessful, asocial or eccentrically odd. The fact that some individuals fit this profile does not equate with the erroneous assumption that all of those with mental health problems must do so as well. The problem here is of regarding the mentally ill as a unified 'mass' instead of a collection of unique individuals with their own individual sets of experiences. In some cases it is only when people get to hear first-hand of an individual's experience of psychological trauma that their attitudes about mental health issues start to shift. It is perhaps still a very slow process with those 'telling their story' being separated out from the 'mass' rather than any real reorganisation of attitudes and beliefs taking place. This is because of the pervasive and insidious power that the steady drip of negative imagery and messages has upon our values and beliefs. It might be interesting to view the public's relationship with mental health issues via the following equation:

1 High profile media story $= x$ (media campaigns + positive storylines)

The value for x is the aspect needing to be determined although it can generally be regarded as being greater than 1. This all means that health promotional campaigns have to create products which are able to compete against and challenge messages that on the whole have a greater intensity and emotional resonance. The way forward is obviously a combination of approaches working at both challenging and questioning negative media messages while at the same time promoting more realistic and productive alternatives. It means helping to educate people but at the same time tackling the fears and anxieties that restrict any real attitudinal change. Getting messages noticed through dramatic means is proving useful, something for example portrayed within television soaps that are first engaging their audiences through entertainment and dramatic means and then taking the opportunity to present new associations and educative messages. Even though some of these are still far from perfect because of the unrealistically rapid shifts between illness and wellness the overall degree of exposure and ability for viewers to engage *with* the mentally ill character is a positive achievement. This coupled with helplines and contact information helps to make the coverage of mental health themes more favourable. This forms in part the essence of positive mental health promotion, which involves: normalising mental health topics and encouraging people to talk about them; presenting more of the person's lived and felt experience thereby making their actions and behaviours more understandable and consequently less

frightening; educating people as to what is fact and what is fiction. These types of approach will help to reduce some of the distance felt between those with mental health problems and those who deem themselves to be mentally well thereby reducing some of the painful and alienating consequences of social isolation.

5   The news media

Introduction

This chapter focuses upon the medium of news reporting and the way in which mental health issues are reflected in newspapers and magazines. The emphasis is placed here upon the printed news medium as other formats such as those provided by television and the Internet will be addressed in subsequent chapters. The significance and importance of news information is illustrated by the view that television and newspapers come ahead of family and friends or other sources of information when it comes to influencing opinion about mental illness (Mason 2003). While television news is seen as being characteristically thin in content (McNair 2003), exposure to information in newspapers enables a lasting impression on memory to be obtained (Robinson and Levy 1986). The printed news medium therefore offers scope for greater depth of coverage as well as acting as a reinforcing agent for stimuli accessed through other sources.

It is interesting to consider the issue as to how we learn about the world around us as well as the range of sources accessed from which we derive our news. In the current era of multimedia, *news* is accessed whenever we pick up a newspaper or magazine, turn on the TV or radio or log on to the Internet. This process is added to by what we learn through social interaction from others who have been exposed to these sources. The *Oxford English Dictionary* defines *news* as 'newly received information about recent events or matters of topical, local, or personal interest' (OED 2005). It is through this process of inputting incoming stimuli that our understanding and learning about the world around us is obtained. These stimuli carry messages which may be regarded as single information chunks or collectively as news. The printed news media is accessed in conjunction with other media formats and may involve minimal amounts of time compared to our use of television, the radio or the Internet. A study into how we engage with different media types found the 'average' person in Britain spends about 20 minutes per day reading a paper as opposed to 3.8 hours watching TV and 3 hours listening to the radio (Kent 1994). This obviously raises the question as to which media type is the most influential with regard to developing attitudes concerning the topic of mental illness.

One of the first issues related to accessing the news concerns that of choice and deciding upon which information sources to select from. Almost 200 years after the invention of printing, the first recognisable form of newspapers became distinguishable from the pamphlets and newsletters of the sixteenth and seventeenth centuries (McQuail 2000). Since then the range of publication types has developed into an almost limitless array of titles to choose from. In the case of newspapers, choice is offered initially by national and local press and then by broadsheet and tabloid style presentations. The presentation of news in the printed format is widened further with the large availability of women's and men's magazines, specialist interest publications and professional journals. Readers are drawn towards particular titles by virtue of their attractiveness, informational value and appeal. Choice is influenced by a range of issues such as the style of presentation used, the political or social stance reflected, accessibility and the degree of influence exerted towards certain titles by peers and family members. While most readers retain a regular choice of newspaper or magazine, some are periodically swayed by the coverage of big news stories and the captivating titles and images displayed prominently on the front pages of other publications.

The way in which news items are packaged is influenced by the needs and expectations of a publication's target market. A clear contrast can be found between broadsheets that carry a more detailed and sober style of reporting and the more simplistic and moralistic tabloid style. The largest selling types of magazine available are women's magazines with different interest groups and ages being catered for by separate publication types. While the predominant focus appears to be upon glamour and fashion, other main themes include lifestyle issues such as cookery and comfort-living, 'people' stories and health matters. There are also the 'coffee-table' type publications that attract their readers with promises of the latest celebrity stories and dramatic features of coping with trauma and hardship. There are also a growing number of magazines aimed at a teen and pre-teen market that use attractive and popular television and music stars as their main selling point. A further strand of news is obtained from specialist titles with most interest groups being represented within the spheres of leisure and sport, social issues (e.g. *The Big Issue*) or professional groups.

The above publication types provide the reader with a vast range of presentation styles with their various means of attracting attention and meeting the requirements of their readership. For example, a clear contrast can be noted between the dramatic, sensational and easily accessible tabloid style and the more contemplative and less subjective broadsheet approach. What we learn in terms of news can be regarded as being heavily dependent upon the source accessed and the manner in which information is relayed. This information will vary widely as regards degrees of accuracy and detail of reporting. This all raises particular concerns around whether or not the more reliable items of news can be extracted from the overall mass as well as the degree to which it is interpreted and understood correctly.

The current picture

There have been numerous reports highlighting the fact that coverage of mental health issues within the press is predominantly of a negative nature with many age-old stereotypes being reinforced (Health Education Authority 1999; Mind 2000; Mindout 2001; Day and Page 1986). A study of 1,999 newspapers in terms of mental health coverage revealed dangerousness to be the most common aspect covered and it was rare to find stories of accomplishment or recovery (Wahl 2003). Calls for the reporting of mental health issues to be improved have been made by many parties and indeed a study carried out by the Media Bureau (2001), *Mental Health and the Press*, found that many journalists themselves (64 per cent) believed that coverage should be better.

One of the main problems resulting from negative coverage is the effect upon those experiencing and living with mental health problems. The Mind (2000) *Counting the Cost* report surveyed 515 people with mental health problems living in England. Over half of these said that negative media depictions made their mental health problems worse. A third said they felt more anxious and depressed as a result of bad press and one in twelve said that they felt suicidal as a consequence. The key messages emerging from this report highlighted that press coverage is poorly balanced, reinforces stigmatising portrayals, has a negative effect on individuals' mental health and perpetuates social exclusion. The sensationalising of news items does not demonstrate adequate sensitivity or responsibility to many concerned, a point strongly illustrated by Richard McCann in his book *Just a Boy* about his struggle to cope with the newspaper coverage of his mother's murder by the Yorkshire Ripper.

What comes across strongly from these studies and reports is the overwhelmingly negative coverage of mental health issues reflected through news stories. It is especially disconcerting when considering that this source generates most of our learning about mental illness (Mason 2003). A bit of comfort perhaps can be derived from the subtle shift demonstrated in recent years with a small increase in positive imagery and educative messages being shown (Health Education Authority 1999). The broadsheet newspapers and certain women's and men's magazines in particular have devoted space to articles and features relating to the active promotion of mental health matters.

Regulation and guidelines

With regard to the world of publishing, the issue of ownership is a significant factor as owners have a major influence upon the presentation of news stories and features (Hetherington 1985). From a mental health perspective, therefore, it is discouraging to note McNair's (2003) assertion that the ownership of the British national press continues to be concentrated in the hands of a few publishing organisations. Unlike other news sources such as 'new media'

and the Internet, the overall degree of impartiality or freedom within the print media is restrictive with fewer perspectives being represented. At times, it is questionable as to whose interests are best being served by particular news stories. While writers might maintain that the interests of their readers are being served, there are clearly also commercial considerations that have to be addressed in order for a publication type to remain operational. This raises the issue as to what control or checks are in place to maintain a sense of balance between the interests of these two parties. On occasion, when reading headlines which 'scream out' such terms as 'Mad Psycho' or '*Silence of the Lambs* Maniac Freed to Kill', one might be forgiven for assuming that newsprint was a totally unregulated media where subjective opinion was the accepted norm. The reality is that journalists work within what is mainly a self-regulating industry and have various sets of guidelines that advise against these styles of reporting.

The first Royal Commission on the press introduced voluntary self-regulation in the form of the Press Council in 1947. This was established in part as a response to public and parliamentary criticism of declining press standards (Calcutt 1990). It was not particularly successful and the failure of the Press Council seemed to be related to the fact that it had no formal code of practice as to what the press should and should not be doing, nor any legal powers of enforcement (McNair 2003). The main thrust of the Calcutt Committee's report (1990) was for continuing self-regulation by the press and the replacement in 1991 of the Press Council by the Press Complaints Commission (Snoddy 1993). As Petley (1999) indicates, the PCC is regarded as being largely ineffective as we only need to immerse ourselves in the daily, debased reality of a large amount of the British press to understand why the PCC cannot be taken too seriously as a regulatory body.

Previous versions of the *Code of Practice* of the PCC have been replaced with the newly revised (2005) code which has added a few extra clauses and altered the wording from *should* to *must* in an attempt to strengthen their members' compliance. Selected clauses from the PCC indicate the huge gulf that exists between the ideal and the reality of press reporting as illustrated by Clause 1 (*Accuracy*) and Clause 12 (*Discrimination*).

Clause 1 – Accuracy
(i)   The Press must take care not to publish inaccurate, misleading or distorted information, including pictures.
(ii) A significant inaccuracy, misleading statement or distortion, once recognised must be corrected, promptly and with due prominence, and where appropriate an apology published.
(iii) The Press, while free to be partisan, must distinguish clearly between comment, conjecture and fact.
(iv) A publication must report fairly and accurately the outcome of an action for defamation to which it has been a party, unless an agreed settlement states otherwise, or an agreed statement is published.

If we consider the impact that certain types of presentation may have, one might argue that the damage is not so easily undone. An apology may seem fairly insignificant when compared with the destructive nature of stereotypical terminology or imagery often used. An aspect pointed out by those experiencing mental health problems is that of feeling stigmatised and alienated by the predominantly disparaging reporting styles used. This has a marked impact upon individuals' self-esteem and confidence, significantly affecting numerous aspects of their lives. It is questionable, therefore, as to how much the damage is redressed by the offering of an apology.

One of the issues here depends upon the perspective from which we are viewing material. Although potentially offending a number of readers, from an editor's point of view, subjective, emotive and stereotypical language may be seen as justified. A headline such as 'MAD PSYCHO KILLER ON THE LOOSE' emerges forcibly from the page and demands immediate attention. Such a presentation leaves the reader with a sense of unease that may be fully out of context with the actual threat posed. For a start, headlines are in larger font and placed in a predominant eye-catching position on the front of the newspaper. Any resultant apologies may be placed somewhere inside the newspaper in small font, in a place which is very easy to miss or ignore. What is needed perhaps is to create a similar impact with a newspaper having to give up their headlines to: 'NEWSPAPER PRINTS INSENSITIVE AND MISLEADING MENTAL HEALTH STORY'. This ideally would then be followed up with a new, balanced and sensitive article promoting a more accurate and positive mental health view. As it stands, particularly in the case of tabloid reporting, this is unlikely to change much as commercial considerations continue to strongly influence and dictate styles of reporting.

Clause 12 – Discrimination
  (i) The Press must avoid prejudicial or pejorative reference to an individual's race, colour, religion, sex or sexual orientation or to any physical or mental illness or disability.
  (ii) Details of an individual's race, colour, religion, sexual orientation, physical or mental illness or disability must be avoided unless genuinely relevant to the story.

This clause appears to be frequently ignored with the continuation of stereotypical and stigmatising notions such as the association between the concepts of *mad* and *violent*. The term mental illness is also, as Philo (1996a) and Wahl (1995) indicate, used as a metaphor to represent features that include helplessness, violence or mental handicap.

A regulatory aspect, although perhaps loosely linked, is libel law which protects a person's right to reputation against defamatory allegations. This was defined by Lord Atkin in 1936 as: 'Any publication which tends to lower the plaintiff in the estimation of right-thinking members of the public generally' (Petley 1999). However, this raises the question as to what opinion

'right-minded' people hold about the theme of mental illness, especially in light of Bloch and Singh's (1997) assertion that it represents one of the most stigmatised conditions worldwide. Therefore, the frequent discriminatory and unrealistic portrayals offered by the press seem to match the overall picture found in society. A core issue then concerns the opportunities that those in this group have of representing themselves and of speaking out against defamatory and misleading statements. Traditionally the mentally ill were regarded as a group of individuals who did not have a collective voice or sufficiently strong advocates who were willing to act on their behalf. Fortunately this picture is starting to change with many instances of editors and writers being challenged, about stories they have written, by professional and voluntary organisations such as Leeds Media Minders, a group of service-users and mental health workers who actively encourage liaison with and feedback to media providers.

Other guidelines have been developed within the journalistic industry to guide its members such as the National Union of Journalists' *Code of Conduct* (NUJ 1999). Clause 3 of this code states that: 'A Journalist shall strive to ensure that the information he/she disseminates is fair and accurate, avoid the expression of comment and conjecture as established fact and falsification by distortion, selection or misrepresentation' (NUJ 1999). This reflects the sentiments as expressed by the PCC with terms here such as 'accuracy', 'falsification' and 'misrepresentation' standing out. We can again challenge these points particularly considering the regular distortion and misrepresentation that takes place within the print media. One highly misleading issue in particular relates to the widely held view that the mentally ill pose a significant risk of violence to the general community. As a number of studies indicate, there is no significant risk posed by this group and they are far more likely to harm themselves than they are to harm others (DOH 1999). The public's general unease about mental illness is firmly highlighted by the fact that they are more at risk from young men under the influence of alcohol (DOH 2001) or those using recreational drugs (Repper *et al.* 1997) than they are from those experiencing mental health difficulties. Another significant issue relates to the question as to what accuracy actually means. There are many ways in which misconceptions may be fuelled by an insensitive choice of subjective and slang terminology. Consider, for instance, *The Sun*'s 'Bonkers Bruno . . .' headline regarding the boxer Frank Bruno's hospitalisation for depression. This understandably was met with a severe backlash from the general public and a number of mental health organisations. No direct apology was given for their coverage of a story that appears to contravene Clauses 1 and 12 of the PCC *Code of Practice* (2005). *The Sun* newspaper did, however, respond quickly with a subsequent edition of their paper carrying the headline 'Sad Bruno in Mental Home' and a day later initiating their fund for mental health charities. While the newspaper can be commended for acting swiftly upon this matter, the second headline seems hardly an improvement and their mental health fund might be viewed from a cynical point of view to be geared more

towards protecting their readership than in addressing the feelings of Frank Bruno or others who might be affected.

One aspect influencing poor reporting of mental health issues is concerned with a writer's lack of understanding or experience regarding the reality of mental illness. In an attempt to address this, various guides aimed specifically at journalists have been produced. An example of this is the *Guide for Journalists and Broadcasters Reporting on Schizophrenia* (NUJ/RCP 1999). This has been developed in collaboration between the NUJ and other bodies such as the Royal College of Psychiatrists and Schizophrenia Ireland. It is an informative and well-presented guide challenging some of the widely held misconceptions such as the association between schizophrenia and split personality as well as the much-misrepresented connection between mental illness and violence. Another example is the booklet *Severe Mental Illness Explained – A Guide for Journalists* (DOH/Rethink 1999). This guide was developed by Rethink (a leading mental health charity) in collaboration with the Department of Health. This guide similarly explores and challenges some of the stereotypical and stigmatising attitudes towards mental illness and provides factual information regarding schizophrenia and personality disorder as well as challenging violence myths and concludes with the section 'Reporting without Stigma'. These types of guides are extremely valuable and highlight the developing collaboration between media providers and mental health advocates.

Liaison

When looking at a number of poorly constructed or overly dramatic stories we might be forgiven for thinking that nobody of any experience or reliability has been consulted and that the story's sensationalism has been preferred over that of accuracy. This is despite the steady increase in involvement between media personnel and professional organisations or service-user groups. While the longer-established links are with health care professionals there is a growing voice among those who have experienced first-hand mental health problems. Besides complaining and offering feedback about negative media coverage, service-users are becoming more active in liaising with media providers and involving themselves more directly with broadcasting and publication initiatives. This challenges the historical trend of the mentally ill being treated as if they have little of credibility or value to offer. It means that journalists are encouraged to look beyond the tried and trusted health care professionals, the people who might be generally regarded as being able to supply more reliable information. As Potter (1998) highlights, most are chosen on appearance of their expertise and their willingness to tell a good story. Official sources, such as professional organisations, are often preferred as journalists and editors believe that they have important things to say and accept the information provided as factual, thereby eliminating the need to double and triple check facts (Paletz and Entman 1981). Reliability is

obviously a core factor but it also points towards a lack of trust in the voice of experience by the mentally ill.

A study by the Media Bureau (2001) *Mental Health and the Press* found only 6.5 per cent of all articles analysed include the voice of current or former mental health service-users (either individual or group). Most journalists said that the main barrier to contacting people with mental health problems was that they were not sure who to contact or didn't include their perspective because a number of individuals didn't want to be named or photographed. There are two core issues here, that of preparing news personnel to access service-users and that of preparing service-users to involve themselves with media groups. First, we might consider the pro-activeness or the accessibility of service-user groups in coming forward and making contact with news agencies. It also involves training and preparation for members and their involvement. The Media Bureau's (2001) study found that the biggest barrier for service-user groups getting involved with local or national newspapers was in not knowing who to contact and a fear of negative coverage. Only half of the individuals who made contact had their views published although most were pleased with the results and the accuracy shown by journalists. This applied more so to the national than to the local or regional press. This involvement will hopefully develop further and has been made a priority by a variety of service-user organisations such as Rethink, Mind, the Zito Trust and the Media Bureau who actively prepare their members for working with media providers by offering guidance, support, workshops and training days. This reflects the strong moves being made by professional groups such as the Royal College of Psychiatrists and British Psychological Association that recognise the importance of preparing their members for a greater involvement with the media.

The best and the worst of news reporting

The type of message being transmitted through the print media will evoke a corresponding reaction in its readers. With regard to mental health content, this may fall somewhere on the *connecting–distancing* continuum reflecting perhaps the largely polarised portrayals of mental illness, either depicted as a survivable condition or as a destructive force. The latter view is clearly the predominant depiction, that of mental illness as a negative, deteriorating or destructive condition. The opposite pole from this presents a more hopeful aspect where we may be heartened by astonishing tales of courage and survival or simply provided with accurate facts about mental health issues. It is not always clear as to which type of message is being transmitted as there may be a confusing plethora of ambiguous sub-texts and images, all of which serve at the same time to educate and mislead their readers.

Mental illness as a destructive force

The core theme here relates to the destructive nature of mental illness either to the individuals themselves by self-harm and neglect or to others through violence and intimidation. Although various studies actually highlight the fact that those with mental health problems are significantly at risk themselves from the public or actually pose a greater risk to themselves than to others (DOH 1999), the predominantly reported association is of the mentally ill representing a threat to other people (Philo *et al.* 1996). This is reinforced by the findings of Nairn *et al.* (2001), with mental illness depictions being predominantly negative and consistently linked with the characteristics of violence, failure and unpredictability.

These are very strongly held views with a sense of threat and unpredictability being attached to the mentally ill irrespective of the nature of their actual condition. This point is highlighted by Wahl who asserts that:

> It is not simply that the image of people with mental illness as violent and criminal appears so often and in so many different sources that troubles mental health advocates, it is that this image is characteristic of media portrayals . . . When one sees or reads about a person with a mental illness in the media, it is more likely that the person will be shown as criminal or dangerous than in any other way.
>
> (Wahl 1995: 65)

An interesting example of this can be illustrated by the *Daily Mail*'s article concerning the murder of a young American artist in a London park and their headlines 'Four Hundred Care in the Community Patients Live near the Murder Park.' In the middle of a lengthy report was a brief statement by the officer in charge of the case stating 'there was no evidence yet that Muller was attacked by a person with mental health problems and that police were keeping an open mind on the motive' (Main 2003).

Some of the responsibility for the media amplification and public panic, according to Morrall (2000b), rests with the psychiatric disciplines for not acknowledging the gravity of the problem and failing to offer the public appropriate reassurance. This is an important point as in a sense the public need to be debriefed and helped to place high profile murders in context. The typical media scrimmage that followed the conviction of Ian Huntley over the Soham murders appeared to highlight the public's perceived desire for every scrap of information possible. This is a familiar process that has been seen in other devastating high profile events such as the Hungerford massacre or the Dunblane tragedy. Clearly, public attitudes are influenced and hardened towards the mentally ill following such traumatic public events and Appleby and Wessely (1988) noted following the Hungerford massacre a significant increase in agreement with the statement 'people who commit horrific crimes are likely to be mentally ill'. It also assists in placing the mentally ill into a

separate category from 'normal' murderers, being construed as double trouble, *mad* and *bad* (Morrall 2000a).

There are a number of negative consequences presented by unbalanced media reporting that focus strongly upon the risks that individuals with mental health problems pose to themselves and others. The publicity connected with these has contributed to an unbalanced policy debate and measures introduced in response to public fears have served to impose additional constraints on people with mental health problems (Hallam 2002). Aided by such coverage, the public and politicians are led to believe that unless people with mental disorders are segregated from the general public the streets will not be safe. This misassumption is aptly summed up by Taylor and Gunn's (1999) analogy that the odds of being killed by a mentally ill person are the same as those of winning the National Lottery.

There is certainly a wealth of evidence to suggest that the effect of reading newspaper articles reporting violent crimes committed by those with mental health problems has a particularly destructive influence upon people's attitudes (Mason 2003). Howlett (1998), however, provides a contrasting view, analysing data from a 1997 MORI national survey of attitudes towards mentally disordered offenders and mental health services. He argues that media focus on homicide and violence by mentally disordered offenders does not increase stigmatisation and that, on the whole, both positive and negative imagery are presented within the media. While there is some support for this argument it perhaps fails to recognise the impact that may be created by a single negative storyline that has a more pervasive and impactful effect than a number of other educative and health promotional messages.

There is a need to maintain the subtle modifications in reporting styles which have been noted over recent years. Wahl, Wood and Richards (2002) examined changes in newspaper articles between the years of 1989 and 1999 and although noting that dangerousness was still the most commonly reported theme in 1999, the incidence portrayed was less than that of a decade earlier. It is also helped by first-person accounts addressing the reality of living with a mental illness. The journalist Ingrid O'Gunleye writes in *The Independent on Sunday*: 'It does not help that most people have the wrong idea about a psychotic person, often accompanied with screaming tabloid headlines. I am only a danger to myself and not to other people' (2003: 1). It is an extremely open and frank account that in a sense stresses the sensitivity that needs to be demonstrated by those responsible for carelessly portraying mental illness. Poor reporting styles serve to add to the sense of alienation and persecution felt which in turn influence negative outcomes such as self-harming behaviour.

While destructiveness displayed by the mentally ill towards others is greeted with fear and trepidation, when it is turned inwards the reaction is generally very different. The reporting here may be largely absent unless detailing the plight of a noted celebrity. Witnessing the downfall of famous individuals appears in some cases as a type of *schadenfreude* (joy at the

misfortune of others), something that is almost gleefully celebrated by the media and the public, especially when linked to a sex scandal. In other cases, where individuals are universally liked, the reaction may be geared more towards emotions such as sorrow and pity. This is exacerbated by the use of words or phrases that evoke sympathy such as the term 'sad', as featured in the headlines concerning the plight of Frank Bruno 'So Sad' (*Daily Mirror*) or Kerry McFadden's hospitalisation for depression towards the end of 2004 'Sad Kerry in Clinic' (*The Sun*). While an improvement upon other styles of reporting, the tendency in some cases leans towards reporting styles that employ past-tense phrases and regard the person as 'pathetic'.

A further issue concerns the over-selling of glamour and the unattainable goal of perfection sold prolifically through large sections of the media. The disturbing nature of associated learning is reflected in a number of studies that focus upon body image perceptions following exposure to various magazines. Martinez-Gonzalez *et al.*'s (2003) study reported disturbing findings of a higher risk of incidents of eating disorder from those having a high exposure to girls' magazines. This reflects the findings by Hamilton and Waller (1993) which showed that acute exposure to media images can increase body dissatisfaction in anorexics and bulimics. Similarly, studies by Cash *et al.* (1983), Stice and Shaw (1994) and Durkin (2002) revealed that participants exposed to idealised female images in magazines demonstrated a reduction in body satisfaction and an increase in levels of depression, shame, insecurity and guilt. The unrealistic sense of self is also promoted within men's magazines with the creation of the fantasy of modern men who can work long hours, develop new and satisfying relationships with women and children while preserving their bodies against ageing and decay (Jackson *et al.* 2001). These types of portrayal foster the same kind of problems found with women's and teen magazines with unrealistic and unattainable goals being offered up and a subsequent infusing of anxiety and critical self-approval with regard to one's own presentation. The steady diet of enticing, glamorous and largely unattainable messages has an insidious and detrimental effect upon many individuals' self-perception. As illustrated by Wykes and Gunter this is largely caused through the internalisation of socio-cultural messages reflecting that: 'The ideal self-image may be considered as either an "internal ideal" or a "societal ideal" resulting from the dictates of the surrounding cultural and societal environment as to what constitutes the perfect body' (Wykes and Gunter 2005: 4).

Mental illness as a survivable condition

A significant contrast to the recognition of mental illness as a destructive entity can be found in a number of publications presenting a positive alternative. This is where mental health problems are seen as being survivable and where a more sensitive and realistic portrayal is demonstrated. These types of depiction highlight the fact that anyone might succumb to the pressures and

stresses of life and experience mental health problems. They include detailed and informative articles, inspirational and heart-warming tales of survival, frank and honest accounts of problems experienced as well as features and advice concerning health issues. These types of presentation encourage better responses towards the subject of mental illness by encouraging feelings of connectedness with another person's lived experience and by offering a contrasting point of view to the wealth of misleading messages encountered elsewhere.

Within the newsprint media, *survival* stories are largely found within magazines and feature both celebrities as well as unknown members of the public. They include examples such as:

- The comedian Hugh Laurie's account of his experience of depression and how he overcame it with the aid of psychotherapy (*Woman*, 15 July 2002).
- The Irish actor Colin Farrell recounting how he was assisted by his psychiatrist to cope with his drug problem (*Best*, 16 December 2003).
- TV chat show host Trisha's history of personal and family mental health problems and related problems of panic attacks and depression (*Now*, 12 March 2003).

Survival stories can be heartening and it is encouraging to note the extent to which people are able to cope with extensive amounts of trauma, heartache and distress and yet still appear to have a reserve of strength and optimism with which to face the future. For some readers this will provide them with role models they can identify with and from whom they gain some inspiration towards discovering and developing their own means of coping. These features are usually brief and contain a 'happy ending', written at a point when individuals are beginning to overcome their difficulties, have come to a sense of resolution and are subsequently able to rebuild their lives. The celebrity articles in particular are important in reducing some of the stigma associated with mental illness. A number of campaigners hope that the increasing willingness of stars to talk about their mental health problems will help lift the taboo surrounding mental illness which is a strong aim of Mindout for Mental Health's (2001b) Headspace campaign. The difficulty faced here concerns the polarisation of attitudes, noted by some mental health charities, concerning different types of mental illness, notably with young people hardening in their views towards patients with schizophrenia or serious mental illness yet sympathising with those who are depressed or distressed (Rethink 2004).

Dramatic, emotive and stereotypical reporting stirs up the public's passions and helps with sales. The same can be true of positive mental health reporting but perhaps with a very different set of feelings being evoked. In place of fear, outrage and concern we have those of pity, sympathy and hope. While negative coverage has an all-pervasive distancing quality that

marginalizes and segregates those experiencing mental health problems, positive coverage can be defined primarily by material that increases understanding and acceptance. It enables the reader to engage in a brief feeling of connection with the individual involved either through sympathy for their plight or through being heartened by their struggle and survival. These types of article can be received in a different light although it needs to be recognised that for a number of individuals the pitying and sympathetic coverage will be felt as patronising and disempowering.

Magazines present us with a variety of information types, with fashion, feature articles and health issues perhaps predominating. This is borne out by a content review of teen magazines which found fashion topics to be the dominant subject (35 per cent), followed by an emphasis on feature articles (interpersonal relations), self-esteem issues, special problems, beauty, entertainment and special recurring columns that offer tips and advice (Evans *et al.* 1991). There is some room for optimism with regard to the coverage of mental health issues in popular periodicals which over recent years have demonstrated both an increase in articles featured as well as changes in terminology with less stigmatising terms being used (Wahl and Kaye 1992). This is a welcome aspect especially when coupled with the high exposure attained by some publication types such as women's magazines with circulation rates that can be measured in millions (Borman 2003). Certain regular features such as health sections, featured articles and even agony aunt columns provide the reader with optimistic and supportive messages relating to mental health issues.

A number of magazines carry regular features and pages offering health advice which is listed under headings such as 'Mind, body and soul' (*Prima*) or 'Beauty and health' (*Elle*). These include information such as 'Stress-busters', *Marie Claire's* top ten techniques for tackling stress. They are usually presented in a very reader-friendly format with language very much geared towards their targeted audience, for example 'Sorting out the Mr rights from Mr wrongs can take its toll on your time and energy . . .' Other versions include the case-study article, questionnaire-type format and 'agony aunt' advice column. The 'agony aunt' column has undergone a fair degree of change over the years with some now offering much more constructive and supportive advice including links to self-help groups and organisations. For example, while *New* magazine's Jane O'Gorman's advice is fairly general in nature she importantly offers a variety of links to specialised agencies, such as women's aid helplines, self-harm organisations, Cruse and Relate, for further contact and support. This reflects Winship's (1987) assertion that the modern day 'agony aunts' support rather than blame women, encouraging them to be self-assertive about their needs. The total range of advice offered covers the spectrum from insensitive and careless through to the supportive and helpful. Another issue for the reader to consider concerns the qualifications of the person giving advice as in some cases few credentials are indicated. Where recognised professional qualifications are provided the reader is

offered a measure of reassurance, for example *Prima*'s Dr Sarah Brewer who is listed as a GP and specialist in complementary medicine and herbal medicines.

There are a number of positive presentations found within feature articles, for example *New Woman* magazine's (May 2004) focus upon three women with mental illness that carries the introductory comment: 'They're young, attractive and successful. But Liz, Emma and Sharon all share the same problem. They all suffer from a mental illness' (*New Woman* May 2004). Another example from *Prima* (May 2004) helps reduce some of the stigma attached to mental health problems by showing three 'ordinary women living normal lives'. What these types of representation do is to reflect either attractive and successful role models or those that are simply 'normal', a far cry from the often-employed unattractive and unsuccessful stereotypes. Features such as this go a long way to normalising mental health problems as well as challenging the myth that once diagnosed one can never completely recover. The essence being portrayed is not necessarily that of complete cure but one of learning to accept and cope with particular difficulties. It is perhaps a more powerful message than the illness–wellness polarisation and brings us into a closer proximity with mental illness and an understanding that psychological distress can co-exist with coping and wellness, and that the mentally well can experience mental health difficulties and that the mentally ill can experience wellness.

News framing

Clearly, the format or packaging of news is geared towards the perceived needs of the audience. As Murdock states:

> Having selected an event for presentation as news, newsmen face the problem of placing it within a context that will render it meaningful to the majority of their audience. Necessarily therefore news presentations must work with meanings and imagery which are both widely available and generally understood.
>
> (Murdock 1998: 208)

This perhaps explains the narrow language base used by the tabloid press or the clear similarities in presentation found between various titles.

Another factor concerns the positioning of news articles within a publication where a sense of imbalance may be apparent. The Glasgow Media Group's study of press content found that negative mental health images tended to receive headline treatment while positive items were largely 'back page' in their profile (Philo 1996c, 1999). As Kress and Leeuwen (1998) highlight, newspaper front pages provide different degrees of salience and framing to material and thereby endow them with particular values. This can distort the actual newsworthiness or significance of particular stories as their

importance is reflected in the number of column inches taken up, the font size employed or their placing within a paper. We can already reflect that:

> Of the millions of events which occur every day in the world, only a tiny proportion ever become visible as 'potential news stories'; and of this proportion only a small fraction are actually produced as the day's news in the news media.
>
> (Hall 1981: 234)

Therefore, the irresponsible front-page coverage that alarms the reader with the sensationalised association between mental illness and violence places the whole issue out of its real context. With mental health issues, the difficulty for many readers lies with their lack of experience and knowledge and their subsequent difficulty in discriminating between what is factual and what is not. With regard to front-page coverage, there are a number of instances where featured items are clearly not the most important or newsworthy item, as can be illustrated by the extreme focus within the tabloid press upon David Beckham's broken metatarsal prior to the 2002 World Cup.

A further issue relates to that of noticeability and which stories in particular stand out from the wealth of news items being covered. From a perceptual point of view the most apparent item might be that which is placed forcibly before our consciousness by virtue of its front-page treatment or through the inclusion of striking images or of emotive language. As many people's reading habits might be fleeting and passive, reporters and editors find attention-grabbing techniques very appealing. This poses a difficulty for those concerned with mental health promotion which is unlikely to gain the same impact as that of a tabloid style headline such as 'Cannibal Psycho Killer on the Loose'. People are drawn towards the dramatic, the scary and the sensational, all of which tend to perpetuate their continued use by the press. It is certainly evident that normalised stories concerning mental illness are almost invisible by contrast.

Informing or misinforming?

The reporting of news can be regarded either as a reflection of what is occurring in society or as a construction by journalists. News, according to Potter is: 'a creation resulting from the active selecting and interweaving of images into a processed reality. . . . they [journalists] are strongly influenced by elements outside the event, such as their deadlines, space limitations, and their own news sense' (Potter 1998 : 111).

The process of news construction includes aspects such as selecting what gets covered, deciding upon what will become the focus of the story (or the hook to interest people), as well as determining how the story is to be told. In some cases this involves manipulating reality, which according to Shoemaker and Reese (1996) involves the media emphasising certain behaviours or

including stereotypes. It can further be illustrated with the inclusion of factual inaccuracies, such as that observed by Crepaz-Keay (1996) that over the 18 months of the Boyd inquiry into homicides and suicides by discharged mentally ill patients, the actual reported frequency of such deaths was doubled by nearly all newspapers. There have been a number of calls for greater responsibility to be shown in reporting with even 64 per cent of reporters themselves noting that it should be better (Media Bureau 2001). Allan (1999) echoes this with the statement that journalism should be committed to truth and upholding the various codes of newsworthiness. There is an issue here, though, concerning what exactly the term *truth* means and whose *truth* is being told. Hall *et al.* (1978) argue that news organisations do not merely report events but are active agents in constructing the sociopolitical environment that frames those events. Journalists therefore contribute significantly to the process of where and how problems are defined. Other writers indicate a deviancy amplification model whereby public indignation or moral panic concerning a type of 'deviancy' may be fanned (McNair 2003). Much of this is heavily influenced by commercial considerations with publishers very mindful of what generates the largest audience with the presentation of deviance proving attractive and newsworthy (Potter 1998). The bottom line for many, therefore, is the fact that no newspaper can achieve adequate sales and survive unless it has a clear concept of what will interest its readers. A paper is packaged or presented in ways that will attract attention and hold its audience (Hetherington 1985), a factor that picks up Kalbfleisch's (1979) three basic ingredients for a 'top story' of insanity, unpredictability and victimisation of ordinary people. Indeed, the pressures to get the best story are aptly reflected by Belsey who states: 'The doctor who exploits a vulnerable patient for sexual favours can be struck off . . . an accountant who steals from a client can be sent to prison, but a journalist who misbehaves may get a scoop and a promotion' (Belsey 1998: 5).

Reading the news

A person's understanding of news items is influenced significantly by the way in which material is packaged and formatted. We can regard the style of news presentation being subject to a range of considerations not least the type of publication and audience expectations. For example we can look at titles such as *The Times, The Sun, Hello* magazine, *Cosmopolitan* and *The Big Issue*, as having a diversely different readership and consequently varied formats. Clearly, each publication type will have a view as to the distinct needs and desires of their readers, an important consideration linked to subsequent sales. In order to briefly reflect upon these differences, the comparison of publication types will centre around three different titles, *The Times* (broadsheet), *The Sun* (tabloid) and *Now* (popular magazine) with regard to their coverage of Frank Bruno's involuntary hospitalisation for depression in September 2003. The main focus is upon the tabloid and broadsheet style

with the magazine example being included as a further point of interest. These articles will be reflected upon in relation to the messages conveyed through headlines, images and narrative.

Headlines

On the whole tabloids favour eye catching, jargonistic or humorous headlines, whereas broadsheets opt for a more objective and informative style. The tabloid approach is one of quickly engaging the reader, rousing their curiosity to want to learn more of the dramatic and engrossing tale promised by the headline. The headlines are often enriched with adjectives usually associated with mental health problems and some of the references made seem almost incidental, in a number of cases having little relevance to the story being recounted (Vousden 1989). Emotive or dramatic words stand out and the intention is clearly one of attracting readers who might be perusing the various titles on offer. In sharp contrast, the broadsheets present succinct terms that serve to a greater degree to alert the readers concerning some of the information to follow.

When considering the range of headlines depicting news of Frank Bruno's distressing condition, the most obviously damaging and insensitive headlines were provided by *The Sun* with their first edition headline 'Bonkers Bruno Locked Up'. This naturally resulted in a fierce outcry and condemnation from many parties and a statement by the mental health charity SANE read:

> It is both an insult to Mr Bruno and damaging to the many thousands of people who endure mental illness to label him as 'bonkers' or a 'nutter' and having to be put in a mental home ... we call upon newspapers involved to apologise to Mr Bruno and to all those who experience the stigma such attitudes inflame.
>
> (SANE 2003)

A fair degree of criticism centred upon the paper's headline which was roundly condemned for its insensitivity and poor choice of words. The paper's initial concession was a rapid change of headline within later editions of the paper to the perhaps equally bad 'Sad Bruno in Mental Home'. Along with the paper's subsequent launching of a mental health fund were printed comments that alluded to the interest and concern that they have afforded Frank Bruno throughout his career (*The Sun* comment, 24 September 2003). From a cynical point of view this appears to be a blatant attempt at bolstering the paper's image in light of its badly calculated choice of words. Tucked away within this piece is the line '*To us he's one of the family*'. It comes across almost as a desperate attempt at reassuring their readers that the paper, like millions of their readers, really does care about Frank Bruno after all.

A quick glance at other tabloid headlines illustrates the fact that a lack of sensitivity and stigmatising language was also being displayed by others in this newspaper type:

* 'Bruno Put in Mental Home' (*Daily Express*)
* 'So Sad' (*Daily Mirror*)
* 'Sick Bruno in Siege Drama' (*Daily Star*)

These headlines provoke misleading interpretations and serve to reinforce a number of classic stereotypes with words such as 'Mental Home' (associations such as *mentally defect or learning disability*), 'Siege' (*drama, crisis and danger*) and 'Sad' (*an object of pity or someone pathetic*). Some of these terms reflect Bagnall's (1993) reference to the language used within the tabloid press as *popspeak*, having a strong ritual flavour and using a small stock of recognisable words.

Interestingly, although using very different language, the broadsheets appear to have their own small collection of words and phrases to choose from. This is illustrated by the following:

* ' "Depressed" Bruno sectioned under Mental Health Act' (*The Times*)
* 'Depressed Frank Bruno is sectioned under Mental Health Act' (*Independent*)
* 'Frank Bruno Admitted for Psychiatric Treatment at Hospital' (*Guardian*)
* 'Frank Bruno is Sectioned under Mental Health Act' (*Telegraph*)

These headlines collectively inform the reader as to the essence of the story – that of Frank Bruno being involuntarily committed for mental health care owing to depression. Further information is provided by *The Times*' use of inverted commas around the term depression implying that his diagnosable mental health state has not yet been publicly confirmed.

Surprisingly though one of the most positive headlines was provided by *Now* magazine with 'Frank's Biggest Battle Yet'. This headline is both positive and optimistic, alluding to the fact that mental health problems can be overcome. He is also affectionately referred to by his first name only, reinforcing the personhood of the individual within this story and reflecting something of the degree of affection with which he is held by a large majority of the population. This seems to be more in tune with *The Sun*'s claim of 'To us he's one of the family'. When addressing the impact upon the general public we have the contrast between, on the one hand, messages that tend to work by provoking an emotional reaction and, on the other, those that are objective and informative. As tabloid newspapers reach a much wider readership we can infer that many stereotypical associations will be perpetuated and accepted by a largely unquestioning audience.

Images

The stories and narrative accounts being conveyed within the print media are complemented by the inclusion of pictures that further develop the overall set of messages that are to be sent out. The perceptual receipt of these images can be understood though a semiotic approach whereby aspects within a visual array have particular meaning for the observer (Harris and Lester 2002). The publication types under discussion used some very different types of imagery, each leading the reader towards a particular set of messages or associations. *The Sun* for example chose to include as its most prominent picture a photograph of Frank Bruno in pantomime costume holding the glove puppet Sooty. This, in relation to the story being conveyed is at best a poorly chosen one and at worst an attempt to see him because of his mental health problems as an object of ridicule or derision. It does not in any way convey the true seriousness of mental illness and only serves to reduce his credibility further. Other images featured by *The Sun* show his wife Laura looking stressed and upset, an ambulance leaving his home, a boxing ring he had installed in his garden and a final picture of Frank the World Boxing Council (WBC) champion. Some of these images seem almost randomly selected or chosen to specifically highlight his eccentricity, as with the case of the boxing ring and pantomime shots. The ambulance is shown for no real purpose other than the dramatic nature of Bruno being taken away from his home. This seemingly random assortment of images has been carefully selected reflecting some of the qualities of visual stimuli identified by Berlyne (1960), that elicit attention from their recipients: intensity, contrast, change, movement, novelty and incongruity.

In contrast to this, *The Times* chose a single picture on their front page, that of Frank holding aloft the WBC belt after having triumphed in his fight against Oliver McCall in September 1995. This depicts Frank simply as the popular hero, in sharp contrast to *The Sun*'s depiction of clown. *The Times* followed this up in the next day's paper with a collection of shots far more sensitively chosen than those appearing in *The Sun*. The first two featured his wife Laura looking worried and drawn and Frank with his hand to his head as if in exasperation. This was followed by a collection of eight images, all of them, apart from one (victorious in the ring and disbelieving), of a smiling Frank. It is in a sense a greatest-hits montage of photos charting his personal and professional triumphs. These pictures tell their own story and highlight the great affection held by the public for Frank the *person*.

The personal view also featured very strongly in *Now* magazine where he is pictured in a suit after a night out. This is not Frank the public persona (boxing hero or clown), but simply Frank the person doing ordinary things. The picture is accompanied by the caption 'Frank looked drawn on a recent night out in London'. It is a well-chosen image, which evokes feelings of sympathy for the person that is Frank Bruno.

Narrative

Some of the fundamental differences between broadsheet and tabloid news-papers may be reflected in the view that broadsheet readers seek new ideas to make them sit up and think whereas popular paper readers want stories that fit their current conception of the world and not one that will disturb it. As Allan (1999) states, British tabloids provide varying degrees of depth regard-ing straight news although each places a premium upon entertaining as opposed to informing the reader. The preferred modes of address are straight talking, snappy headlines and everyday vernacular to enhance popular appeal. Pursehouse's (1991) analysis of interviews with British tabloid readers indi-cated that the tabloids are regarded as offering respite or distraction from tasks that require concentration. They were not seen necessarily as a reliable source of balanced reporting with most readers looking towards the medium of television for their 'real news'.

A number of these issues are reflected in *The Sun*'s article which says very little about the nature of mental illness other than reinforcing a number of stereotypes. In particular, phrases are included from unclear sources includ-ing how he at times slept in a boxing ring or tent in his garden as well as the statement, 'At the weekend it was claimed that he had started believing he was racing legend Frankie Dettori'. No information is given as to who it was claimed by and it seems only to have been included because it fits the classic popular behaviour patterns of the mentally ill. The notion of source is an interesting one, and *The Sun* primarily seeks boxing personnel for comment. The only medical source is a retired neuropathologist asked for comment to help make the weak link between brain damage caused by boxing and Frank's mental health state. No real information about the true nature of mental illness is given and it amazingly takes the boxing promoter Frank Warren to provide any thoughts as to diagnosis.

All of this seems contrary to the National Union of Journalists *Code of Conduct* (1999) Clause 3 with regards to accuracy. *The Sun*, along with other tabloid titles has rightly in this instance met with broad condemnation over their handling of this story and a number of statements were released by mental health charity and advocacy groups over the handling of this story: 'The shameful tabloid media treatment of Frank Bruno is unfortunately reflected in the day to day experience of 630,000 people with a severe mental illness who are too often shunned by society' (Cliff Prior, Chief Executive of Rethink 2003). Richard Brook, the Chief Executive of Mind, issued an open letter to the Editor of *The Sun* newspaper stating:

> Despite recent improvements ... your news reporting has historically been an area of grave concern and has often caused a flood of complaints into Mind. *The Sun*'s reporters have been short-listed or awarded Mind's Bigot of the Year Award more times than any other national newspaper. Only a long-term overall editorial commitment will address this. Failure

to do so will suggest that the paper's actions on Monday evening, to change the headline, were forced by embarrassment rather than representative of journalistic integrity.

(Brook 2003)

This last point is certainly one worth addressing. The backlash from readers and mental health advocacy groups will have certainly caused some discomfort prompting them, a day later, to launch their own campaign for mental health titled '*The Sun*'s Fund for Bruno'. This fund was promoted with emotive terms such as 'Dig deep . . . like Bruno did for Britain' and cynically perhaps kicked off with a £10,000 donation. This response might reflect what Eric Berne (1964) refers to as *good games*, that of being helpful to others but with an ulterior motive. In this instance the change of moralistic stance from 'Bonkers Bruno' to staunch mental health advocate is certainly helped by protecting their commercial interests.

In contrast to the tabloid style, the broadsheet coverage has been less sensational and more concerned with presenting the facts in a more concise and objective style. Unlike the tabloid presentation, this story was not the main feature in any of the broadsheet newspapers and in the case of 'The *Guardian* did not even make the front page. *The Times* article uses words sparingly and avoids using the titillating details included by other papers. It is a more sober piece of reporting which informs the readers succinctly as to the nature of 'sectioning', Frank's boxing career, family problems and something of the wide-ranging affection felt for him by others. Bias in the tabloids is blatant and unashamed, bombarding the reader with emotive words and phrases whereas bias in the broadsheets may consist of omission of certain facts or selected quotes (Bagnall 1993). The broadsheet language used is kinder, such as the phrase 'Two uniformed officers . . . spent four hours persuading Bruno to go for treatment', whereas the same detail was reported in *Now* magazine as 'police took three hours to remove him'. The *Now* magazine style incorporates elements of the tabloid style with a number of stereotypical details, such as Frank believing he was Frankie Dettori and a comment from a nightclub owner stating that, 'we knew as soon as he spoke that he'd lost it'. These are unnecessary details other than to dismiss the experience of those experiencing mental health problems. This article, though, does include a significant comment from the mental health charity Mind that appears a welcome inclusion and in part challenges some of the stigmatising messages addressed elsewhere in this article.

In sharp contrast to the quality broadsheets that are widely regarded as being more informative, the reporting style in the popular press focuses more upon emotive and sensational content omitting a fair degree of contextual evidence (Chalaby 1998). The style of presentation employed reflects the informational requirements of their targeted readership as people obviously differ in their generalised motivations for learning and their willingness to confront new messages. As Slattery *et al.* (2001) indicate, the broadsheets are

aimed at those at the higher end; the active seekers who are interested in all kinds of information whereas the lower end is geared towards those exhibiting a low level of interest in accessing new learning. To some degree, the issue affecting those at the lower motivational end can be reflected in Chalaby's (1998) view that they may not be aware that they are particularly missing anything and consequently do not feel the desire to seek out added information. The concern here relates to the fact that most of the information actually accessed contains a large degree of inaccurate and misleading content. As with the perceptual image in Chapter 2 (Figure 2.3) of the *old woman/ young woman*, unless alerted to the presence of another way of interpreting this picture the observer may not feel the need to search further, retaining solely their initial perception.

Engaging with news

With regard to news accounts, at the heart of the process of inclusion and exclusion are 'frames' or 'principles of organisation' which work to impose order on the multiple happenings of the social world so as to render them into a series of meaningful events (Goffman 1974). Critiques of news coverage include the metaphor of a mirror being held up to reflect the social world and the amount to which distortions have been allowed to creep into the reporting process, coupled with vast numbers of 'blind spots' (Allan 1999). This clearly highlights the importance relating to the writer's background and the particular version of events we are subsequently exposed to. It might be illustrated on a large scale by the circulation of propaganda messages within, for example, the communist bloc regimes and the deliberate extent to which the public might be misinformed of events occurring in the wider world. A subtler example could be seen in the reporter's lack of knowledge about mental health issues and the inclusion of inaccuracies within their writing. Readers might take for granted that what they read in their chosen newspaper or magazine has a good degree of accuracy because of the strict regulatory structures that are available to govern what is written. Information and advice are received generally in good faith with few opportunities to stop and challenge it or to find out how credible the writer's base of experience is. Readers might be particularly interested to note the extent, or even lack of research, consultation and personal experience that have played a part in informing the writer as to the facts being reported. The negative association with mental health issues is heavily reflected in styles of reporting across all newsprint formats and includes broadsheet as well as tabloid reporting. One study in particular focused upon the print media in three countries (UK, USA and Australia) and reviewed 118 articles over a one-year period, accessing two broadsheets from each country. The predominant tone relating to mental health issues in all three countries was negative, more so in the UK (Priebe 2003). The tabloid format, however, contains more stigmatising messages than their broadsheet counterparts (Peters 2002). This is also borne out by

Mind's (2000) *Counting the Cost* report with regard to the best and worst coverage of mental health issues within different publication types where respondents saw the best coverage being employed by the broadsheets and the worst by the tabloids.

Our concept of news or what is regarded as *reality* can be seen as being created through the social process of communication sent out by the mass media (Johnson-Cartee 2005; Nimmo and Combs 1983). The stream of messages received are filtered through an individual's own perceptual screen and developed further through discussion with others. The chain of communication from sender to receiver is fraught with difficulties influencing the overall fidelity of this process. Some journalists and writers refute notions of subjectivity in their accounts and support the 'mirror on society' approach by arguing that a number of journalists in a room together will all produce the same story (Chibnall 1981). McNair (1998), however, argues that many journalists fail to recognise that in their selection of facts and in their contextualising of them, they are creating news by giving such facts 'meaning and context' when they are transformed into a story or narrative. It is also perhaps hard to ignore the fact that many will also have an eye on how the final product will be received and engaged with by their targeted audience. This helps to explain the divergence in reporting styles whereby journalists writing for different publication types address their readers with an appropriate level of linguistic complexity and sophistication (McNair 1998) as well as degrees of emotive and dramatic engagement. Although being influenced significantly by the sender, the reader brings their own personal interpretive diversity from which to decode facts. As McQuail (1997) states, this depends to a large degree upon the social position and outlook of the receiver who subsequently fits the facts accessed into personal frames of interpretation and relevance. This process is supported by Potter (2004) who outlines the process of filtering that is applied to the process of reading whereby individuals screen out material that is deemed as irrelevant for their purposes. The primary need, though, is for media providers to change in their reporting styles towards a more sensitive and responsible style of coverage. There are some indications that this is starting to shift, as outlined earlier, with a number of initiatives being employed. These include campaigning, liaison with media providers, health promotion schemes and educative messages. Progress is minimal, although there are small signs of change as indicated by the Health Education Authority (1999) as well as Mind's (2001) inclusion of fewer articles in their annual shortlist for bigot of the year.

Conclusion

The overall picture with regards to news reporting of mental health issues suggests a slight positive shift over recent years in what remains though a largely negative style of coverage. Various initiatives have aided in the promotion of better mental health coverage such as the developing collaboration

and liaison between news personnel and mental health advocates. This has resulted, in some instances, in a better-informed and more thoughtful style of reporting. It is concerning however, that the strides taken with regards to the positive coverage of mental health issues found within the broadsheet press is not reflected by what is produced by their tabloid counterparts. As the tabloid press have a much higher sales circulation it could be assumed that the majority of readers are still exposed to regular messages that report upon mental health issues in a sensationalist and emotive style, with a common usage of stereotypical representations. A problem facing those involved with the promotion of mental health concerns the attractiveness of certain styles of coverage both to press personnel and their readers. It takes a case such as *The Sun's* temporary transformation to mental health campaigner (following complaints received about their coverage of the Frank Bruno story) to suggest that the overall picture can change. The main factor here however related to the fact that this was a much liked and widely respected figure. There is also the issue regarding the type of mental health problem reported to consider as a diagnosis perhaps of schizophrenia would not arouse the same degree of sympathy and concern. It seems that a major change in societal attitudes is still needed before sufficient pressure is brought to bear upon those producing the news.

6 Literature

The medium of literature

The medium of literature offers something uniquely different to other media sources such as television or film. While these other types of media communicate through the combined modes of narrative, imagery and sound, literature provides us with messages primarily through the narrative format. It is in a sense left to the reader to construct their own perceived images and understanding from the text laid out before them. The writer acts as a guide, evoking feelings and creating meaning through the richness of their narrative. It is a medium that has limitless potential, constrained only by the limitations of the writer's craft or the reader's imagination. The literary genre has the potential for a deeper level of engagement with characters than that offered by other media formats. This is achieved through the ability to take the reader directly into a person's inner world connecting with their thoughts and feelings. While other media types rely primarily upon external cues to achieve this, the world of literature has the ability to take the receiver more directly into that person's world. Film and television, for example, provide glimpses of the inner world through facial gestures and expressiveness of speech, leaving the viewer in many instances to form their own interpretation of what a person's experience might be. Aspects such as frustration, rage or upset might be conveyed clearly enough although without all the intricacies and ambiguities of individual thoughts and feelings. The style of writing utilised (e.g. first or third person narrative) plays a significant role in the ways in which readers engage with the theme of mental illness and will be explored later in this chapter, paying particular attention to the type of relationship fostered, either of a connecting or distancing kind.

The themes of 'mental illness' or 'madness' have appeared within all the varied forms of writing (e.g. prose, poetry and drama) for thousands of years. The examples generally signify something of the varied societal attitudes relating to the historical era of their production. It is a popular choice of topic aided by the view that:

Portrayals of madness convey in symbolic form human beings'

preoccupation with their own mental functioning . . . in literature, as in daily life, madness is the perpetual amorphous threat within and the extreme of the unknown in fellow human beings.

(Feder 1980: 4)

The vast body of literature available to readers reflects the theme of mental illness from every conceivable angle ranging from negative, stigmatising types to positive, engaging ones. One appeal for writers concerning the inclusion of mental health content regards the enhanced degree of drama or spice that it lends to their narrative. It is something found in abundance within the horror and thriller genres, prolifically involving the full range of misleading and inaccurate stereotypes. Another attraction involving the more sensitive and informed writing concerns the author's desire to look specifically at the lived experience of mental health problems and to educate their readership accordingly.

Historical aspects

The medium of literature provides us with depictions of 'madness' that date back to the Ancient Roman and Greek writings of Homer and Virgil. The appeal of mental health content is reflected in Salkeld's statement that: 'Tales of madness are unsettling. They have a strange and enduring power to fascinate, amuse and appal beyond the limits of their own historical moment' (Salkeld 1993: 8). When reading texts from a different time, it is important to recognise something of the contextual views pertinent to the era of their publication. This means therefore utilising a 'historicist' approach as madness in ancient texts, for example, can only properly be understood by acknowledging ancient opinions about madness (Hershkowitz 1998).

Madness in Ancient Greek and Roman cultures was seen as the result of divine intervention or sickness (Padel 1995; Hershkowitz 1998). The Greek epics in particular portrayed the individual's struggle with various forms of trial while the tragedies dealt with passions and emotions of an *extreme kind*; fear, anger, hate, madness, jealousy and love in *extreme circumstances*; murder, suicide, incest, rape and mutilation (Barlow 1996). The belief that madness is caused and can only be cured by divine intervention continued to proliferate through the middle ages to the fourteenth and fifteenth centuries and included the views that madness resulted either in death and damnation or served as a test leading towards self-knowledge, confession and reform (Feder 1980). The combination of destructiveness and self-discovery-type messages are still evident within later centuries as illustrated within the dramatic work of Shakespeare. In *King Lear*, for example, the experience of madness provides the king with a new awareness of the suffering and injustice that can be found in society. Another common depiction within Shakespearian plays portrayed madness as a terrible and agonising experience of suffering.

The late eighteenth and nineteenth centuries included a number of extra-ordinarily popular stories about women who go mad when they lose their lovers. This represented a significant shift from the image of the madman in chains towards the woman whose insanity was regarded as an extension of her female condition (Small 1996). The depiction of 'mad woman' was also used in some instances to signify a destructive and malevolent background presence as illustrated with Mrs Danvers in Daphne de Maurier's *Rebecca* or Mrs Rochester in Charlotte Brontë's *Jane Eyre*.

The era of asylum care and incarceration provides some powerful examples such as *One Flew over the Cuckoo's Nest, Faces in the Water* and *The Bell Jar*. Interestingly, these accounts sit alongside the growing realisation that emerged in the late 1950s and early 1960s (Goffman 1961; Barton 1976; Scheff 1974) of the detrimental and depersonalising effects of institutional care. The trend of exploring expanded thought by authors such as Carlos Castaneda and Aldous Huxley helped to stimulate interest into the perceived world of altered cognition, although to a large extent this mirrored the trend for experimentation with drugs already being carried out by many in society. Lastly, the current era of community care and the greater visibility of mental health issues have contributed towards the steady increase in autobiograph-ical first-person accounts concerning psychological distress that now feature regularly on best-selling lists.

Writer influences

The inclusion of mental health themes and content within written works is influenced significantly by the intention of the writer and may be the prime focus of the work or merely a part of the whole. The reasons why mental health content is addressed may be reflected in the type of narrative being written including:

- Autobiography (*what the act of writing gives to the author*)
  Deriving therapeutic value from the process of writing.
- Semi-autobiography (*what the experience of mental health problems gives to the art of writing*)
  Connectedness borne out of personal experience.
- Fiction (*what the inclusion of mental health material gives to the reader*)
  Lending dramatic impact to the narrative.

These three different types of writing offer a wide range of mental health perspectives. At one end of the spectrum we have the insightful, expressive and connected forms of writing that enable the reader to engage with those being depicted. At the other end we have the stereotypical and misleading portrayals where the driving factors of financial rewards and personal gain override other sensitivities.

Autobiography (therapeutic value)

To a certain degree autobiographical writing provides us with the most insightful and clear prose concerning issues of mental health. One might argue that it is the writing about 'mental illness' by those who best understand the material being handled. Although dating back over the centuries with examples such as George Trosse's *The Life of the Reverend Mr George Trosse* in 1693 and Bunyan's *Grace Abounding to the Chief of Sinners* in 1666, it is only over the past decade or so that there has been a significant increase in autobiographical writing centring upon personal distress and coping with traumatic experience. This type of writing has been notably gaining a greater acceptance in mainstream literature mirroring trends in society (e.g. the advent of community care) and its depiction within other media formats. It perhaps already has a proven track record in the popularity of many *coffee-table* magazines with their many varied stories of survival and coping with personal trauma. The need to understand, connect with or catch a glimpse of others' lives and problems, albeit a degree voyeuristically, appeals to a large number of the public. In contrast to the dramatic fictional portrayal, we have here the dramatic factual tale, in some cases every bit as suspenseful and compelling as their fictional counterparts. These publications include best-sellers and award winners such as David Solomon's (2002) *Noonday Demon: An Anatomy of Depression* (Mind book of the year 2002); Tim Lott's (1997) acclaimed *The Scent of Dried Roses* and the international best selling trilogy by Dave Pelzer (1995, 1997, 1999) of *A Child Called It, The Lost Boy* and *A Man Named Dave*.

Many of these accounts are both distressing as well as uplifting. In many cases they recount experiences of individuals who have endured a lifetime's suffering or, because of certain life events, have hit rock bottom, survived and dragged themselves back up. A notable example is the book *Addicted* by the footballer Tony Adams (1998) which recounts his recovery from alcoholism. Within the plethora of footballer autobiographies this one carries comments such as: 'So good, so scorchingly honest and revealing . . .'; and 'An impressive and candid memoir . . . it's hard to recall another book in which the author has spoken with such self-lacerating honesty.' It is a painfully honest account of his personal fragmentation although provides a very strong sense of connecting with a real person. A less honest narrative, for example a more typically macho account, would lose much of this book's very real appeal.

A major influencing factor concerning this type of writing concerns the therapeutic value afforded both the author from the process of writing and the reader from the sharing of their experience. A significant part of the process for the author is in the working through and making sense of traumatic experience. This is clearly illustrated by Anne Deveson in her account *Tell Me I'm Here*, relating to her search for a cure and understanding for her schizophrenic son through his illness and ultimately his suicide:

I needed to write this book: to lay before myself the richness of the experience and the bleakness. I needed not to deny the bad aspects because these were a part of the whole and, for me, serenity rests in the whole. I still feel distress when I think of the terrors that Jonathan endured. I miss him. But I no longer feel despair.

(Deveson 1992: 259)

A sense of resolution and acceptance is also illustrated by Tim Lott in *A Scent of Dried Roses*. This book attempts to make sense of and understand both his mother's suicide and his own feelings of depression. He concludes that he subsequently feels detached from suffocating feelings of guilt and:

I cannot ever know if I am guilty, but if I am, I no longer have difficulty forgiving myself, I have decided that I would rather not be such a super-naturally good person – as my mother fantasised herself, finally to be, that it involves me killing myself, or living a life of despair, in order to prove it.

(Lott 1997: 263)

Similarly, David Pelzer's trilogy beginning with the book *A Child Called It* can be seen as a search for understanding and reconciling his own experience of being abused and neglected as a child. He writes about horrific cruelty from the perspective of a survivor although with a healthy and positive outlook for the future.

The steady increase in autobiographical work concerning mental health issues is complemented by publishers such as Chipmunkapublishing, whose core purpose is to publish work by individuals who have experienced or been touched by mental distress. Two of their publications in particular continue the writing as therapy theme. Jason Pegler, commenting upon writing about his experience of manic depression (*A Can of Madness*), said: 'Writing saved my life. It was the only way that I could rationally come to terms with the humiliation that I felt from being labelled with a mental illness' (Pegler 2003: 31).

Likewise, another author, Dolly Sen, stated about the writing of *The World is Full of Laughter*, a book about her experience of depression: 'I say of my book that it started out as a suicide note and ended as a celebration of life . . . for me creativity gave me control in a world where because of a diagnosis, I had no control' (Sen 2003: 31).

The *writing as therapy* theme is certainly one that needs encouragement and avenues for further development. Indeed, many mental health promotional initiatives such as that run by Leeds Mind (*Including Us*) encourage writing as a means of expression and sharing. The main strength of this process is the opportunity for making sense of personal experience and gaining a degree of resolution and control over one's life. It aids the process of survival and the act of writing itself allows the author to ventilate and share

their thoughts and feelings initially in a way that feels safe. What perhaps is unclear is the degree of guidance or pressure that those writing such accounts might feel under, particularly with the commercial value of highly traumatic and distressing revelations proving so attractive to publishers and readers alike.

Autobiographical accounts by celebrities proliferate and fill the best-seller shelves of bookshops. They are written with wide-ranging degrees of skill and ability, some apparently very hurriedly to meet public demand. Some of these include accounts of dealing with mental health issues, for example Geri Halliwell's (2003) *Just for the Record*, Robbie Williams' (2002) *Somebody Someday* and Paul Gascoigne's (2005) *Gazza: My Story*. An interesting account is provided by the accomplished New Zealand writer Janet Frame with her book *An Angel at My Table*. This publication details her treatment and hospitalisation for mental health problems including her fortunate reprieve from psychosurgery. It is notable that critical receipt of this work centred upon the 'autobiographical' label as reducing the impact of the book's intellectual content as it emphasised her experience more than her ideas (Unsworth 1995). This is an extremely restrictive viewpoint that diminishes the powerful and connecting nature of this expressive and highly insightful narrative.

What is interesting today is the widening appeal and accessibility of autobiographical writing, a form of expression that was previously conceived as the lifetime reflections of highly prominent individuals (Chamberlain and Thompson 1998). This genre has now widened to encompass previously unknown authors who have 'a story to tell'. Celebrity writers are more commonly found within mainstream publishing and are helping to lead the way in making this form of narrative more acceptable and accessible. It even includes collaborative works that marry the credibility and authority of mental health professionals with the popular appeal of noted celebrities such as *Depression and How to Survive It* (Spike Milligan/Anthony Clare 1994) and *Families and How to Survive Them* (Robin Skynner/John Cleese 1993). The professional voice adds a further dimension here and Professor Kay Jamison's (1997) excellent autobiographical account (*An Unquiet Mind*) of her own battles with manic-depression presents an insightfully written account supported by clear scientific evidence.

For the reader, the attraction of this type of work may be generated either by curiosity or a desire to achieve a sense of connectedness and identification with the mental health experience. As Miller (2002) illustrates, the proximity of shared experience might apply where an individual reads a text and feels that it has been written especially for them. This highlights a self-help feature of many of these accounts whereby readers gain a sense of shared experience as well as a degree of hope and optimism through another's narrative. The point at which they are written is important as they generally reflect a picture of survival and resolution, not one of hopelessness and unresolved conflict. Nonetheless they are not necessarily easy to read and the awfulness and

distress of what is being narrated can be unbearable at times; for example, the tormenting cruelty suffered by David Pelzer as a child at the hands of his abusive, alcoholic mother and his neglecting, ignorant father.

The rather astonishing popularity of this genre of writing is illustrated by their regularly featuring within top-selling book lists. A recent glance at the *Sunday Times* (13 February 2005) best-selling non-fiction book list illustrates this point with the top two selling hardback books *A Brother's Journey* by Richard Pelzer and *The Little Prisoner* by Jane Elliott, both being about childhood abuse. Similarly, the 'top ten' paperback list contained five such entries that included:

- *Sickened* / Julie Gregory (Munchausen's by proxy)
- *One Child* / Torey Hayden (childhood abuse – a biographical account written by a therapist)
- *The Privilege of Youth* / Dave Pelzer (childhood abuse)
- *To Die For* / Carol Lee (anorexia)
- *My Story* / Dave Pelzer (childhood abuse)

These types of narrative are obviously extremely popular and it is unclear as to the types of pressure or coercion that might be exerted upon authors to include material they feel uneasy or uncertain about revealing. Also uncertain is the extent to which the commercial value of these products plays a part in their writing. Richard Pelzer's *A Brother's Journey*, for example, was written following his brother David's astonishing success with his series of auto-biographical works detailing childhood abuse. While in all probability having his own reasons for writing this book there is perhaps the danger of com-mercial considerations overtaking those of therapeutic ones. Nevertheless, the valuable sense of exposure cannot be overestimated especially where taboo topics such as child abuse are brought out of the shadows and into the public arena thereby enabling others so affected to feel encouraged about expressing and sharing their own experiences.

Semi-autobiography (connectedness)

> When a writer draws on his own experience of insanity as the subject or emotional source of his work, what is of most interest is his adaptation of delusion, dissociation, or other aberrations to the creation of a unique view of his society, his art and his own mind.
>
> (Feder 1980: 9)

Clearly, experience of mental distress provides authors with a degree of expression both useful in writing directly about that experience or using it as a base from which to draw upon. Themes of personal trauma, distress or difficulty are written about with greater insight and are more elaborately and expressively laid down in the main text. In a sense, one's own personal

experience breathes life into the body of writing. This approach to writing is regarded as semi-autobiographical and has many examples within classical and contemporary literature. Perhaps the earliest clear example is Goethe's *The Sorrows of Young Werther* (*Die Leiden des Jungen Werthers*) which was originally published in 1774. This piece of writing is modelled upon Goethe's own personal experience of frustrated love as well as the suicide of his close friend Karl Wilhelm Jerusalem. It is very vivid and expressive prose describing how Werther is progressively driven to more fevered and tortured thoughts of despair because of an unattainable love, longing for suicide as his only release. The power of this piece of work and the degree to which readers identified with Goethe's Werther is illustrated in the outcry which followed its publication with assertions that it led a number of people to take their own lives. The increased rate in suicide across Europe following its publication saw the book banned in a number of countries (Pirkis and Blood 2001).

There may be a contrast between semi-autobiographical writing and autobiographical in terms of the author's intention and the resultant impact their work has upon them. In some cases it seems the art of writing is an all-consuming process that has a destructive effect upon the author. Consigning one's emotions into written words can, as has been addressed above, leave some with a feeling of resolution and clarity although at the same time can leave others drained and spent, having given all for their art. Two prominent names in the world of literature who are recognised as 'suffering through their art' are Sylvia Plath and Malcolm Lowry. Sylvia Plath committed suicide a few months after the publication of *The Bell Jar*, a piece of work directly related to her own illness and experience of mental health treatment. It is a piece of writing rich in prose, symbolism and imagery, all of which can be traced directly back to Plath's own mental anguish. The sense of creative expression being borne out of inner torment is related by her former husband, the poet Ted Hughes who states: 'The root system of her talent was a deep and inclusive inner crisis . . . She used details from [her outer upheavals and her preoccupation] as a matter of course for images to develop her X-Rays' (Hughes 1985). The essence here is the direct channel provided between the author's own felt experience of distress and the words which are subsequently placed down on paper.

Another author who is regarded as writing from personal experience is the writer Malcolm Lowry. *Under the Volcano* (1947), widely regarded as his best work, is a semi-autobiographical novel with the main character Geoffrey Firmin's destructive alcoholism mirroring Lowry's own. The many links with Lowry's own life include alcoholism, depression, murderous attacks on his wife and a number of suicide attempts before his eventual death after a drinking bout (Bradbrook 1974). Lowry's own experience no doubt provided a rich depth of understanding that is reflected within the narrative itself. There is a hallucinatory quality to the writing borne out in a narrative style that is full of symbolism and metaphor. Grace (1982) regards the writing of this book, which took ten years to complete, as having a detrimental impact

upon its author, exhausting his genius in the creation of a single masterpiece, his other fiction being neglected and relatively unknown.

> Indeed the words of Lowry himself in the short poem '*After publication of Under the Volcano*' supports this. Commencing with the line: 'success is like some horrible disaster,' he continues to elaborate upon the damaging toll exacted upon himself through stark terms such as ruination and damnation. He finishes the poem by rueing the sense of acclaim afforded this publication and wishing that he had been '. . . left in darkness forever to founder and fail'.
>
> (Birney 1962).

Another writer worthy of a mention here includes the New Zealand writer Janet Frame whose experience is very different from that of Lowry and Plath as she regarded writing as a way to survive (Hannah 1978). She has written a number of books which are clearly in part informed through her own experiences of mental health problems such as *Faces in the Water, Scented Gardens for the Blind* and *Owls do Cry*. In particular, many parallels have been drawn between her own experience within psychiatric hospitals and those of Istina Mavet, the principal character in her novel *Faces in the Water* (Ferrier 1995), although Janet Frame herself refutes suggestions that it is directly about her but under a different name (Penny 1992). Where writing has a strong foundation within direct experience the distinction between fiction and reality is not always easy to define as some of the imagery and messages being presented can be extremely persuasive. For example, a degree of alarm was caused by the widespread belief that Frame's *Owls do Cry* was an autobiographical account, in response to which she managed to convince a doctor, who had read the book, that this was not so by demonstrating the absence of leucotomy scars. As she aptly summed up: 'Not every aspiring writer has such a terrifying but convincing method of displaying to others "proof" that she has been writing fiction' (Bruce 1975: 148).

A core component therefore of the semi-autobiographical category relates to the fact that despite the strength and expressiveness of this form of writing, there can be very different consequences for the writer, with some finding it a painful and consuming process whereas others feel liberated and supported by it.

Fiction (dramatic impact)

There is little doubt that mental health issues have a curiosity appeal and can be compelling for the reader of literature. They add a degree of attractiveness that may be intentionally or unintentionally manipulated in order to engage the reader. This voyeuristic quality is not too dissimilar to the historical pastime of visiting psychiatric institutions where madness was presented as the prime exhibit. It is, as Ingram (1991) asserts, the dramatic equivalent of

the literary or actual sightseeing tour of lunacy. Adding mental health themes to a narrative may be seen as a purposeful attempt at manipulating the reader's engagement with the material accessed. It may be the subject which sells the book or which helps to maintain focus where interest may be flagging. From an attentional perspective, influential factors include stimuli that are novel, engage curiosity and stand out by virtue of their intensity (Child 2004), all of which are stimulated by the inclusion of mental health content. These lend products a touch of drama and impact, serving to draw the reader in and to keep them engaged. Wally Lamb's book *I Know This Much is True* (2000), for example, commences with Dominick Birdsey's schizophrenic twin brother cutting off his hand in a public library as a result of delusional thought processes. This occurs right at the beginning of a fairly long publication (912 pages) and serves to instantly engage the reader and hook them into the narrative. What follows, though, is a degree of more sensitive writing detailing the impact that mental illness has upon a family.

A consequence of the significant impact created by mental health content is the potential for wide-ranging exposure and enhancing the popularity of books that perhaps would not otherwise gain as wide a circulation. Selling books and reaching a wide audience is good when the messages being transmitted are positive and sensitive. The problem lies, however, in the wealth of popular literature that sensationalises mental health issues and which is often misleading and inaccurate. In order to look at the fictional representation it is perhaps a useful exercise to compare the handling of particular themes within different literary genres. For the purposes of this comparison, the topic of child abuse will be looked at as portrayed by Virginia Andrews' (1979) fictional novel *Flowers in the Attic* and David Pelzer's (1995) autobiographical narrative *A Child Called It*. Although based upon a similar theme, the way in which this extremely delicate topic has been handled and the overall message being transmitted is vastly different. Pelzer's account is much more sensitively handled and portrays an overall message of survival and hope, whereas *Flowers in the Attic* seems more interested in dramatically engaging its readers with its bleak message of destruction. Unlike *A Child Called It*, the fictional narrative is written from a position of bitterness and a desire for revenge. It is unforgiving in tone:

> I find every word I put down, I put down with tears, with bitter blood, with sour gall, well mixed and blended with shame and guilt ... The tempest of rage that once stormed within me has simmered down so I can write I hope with truth and with less hatred and prejudice.
>
> (Andrews 1979: 7)

The message throughout the book is one of destructiveness and pain, the surviving characters leaving the house of their confinement battered and seeking revenge. In contrast to this, Pelzer's autobiographical account is optimistic and hopeful despite the appalling nature of some of the experiences

being related and at the end of the book he writes: 'I believe it is important for people to know that no matter what lies in their past, they can overcome the dark side and press on to a brighter world' (Pelzer 1995: 145). He also goes on to describe the supportive and healthy relationship he has with his son and his hope for the future. It is a book that has been written with forgiveness and understanding and with a clear indication that the cycle of child abuse can be broken, unlike that of the tale being told by *Flowers in the Attic* and its sequels where the cycle of abuse is perpetuated. Although the packaging of these books obviously changes with subsequent reprints, they are still significantly different in overall appearance. With regard to the editions accessed, *A Child Called It* is very simply presented with a bright, white cover featuring a black and white photo of an innocent-looking young child. It is appealing in a way that is starkly different from that of *Flowers in the Attic* which is synonymous with many horror books with its dark, Gothic style cover displaying a pair of haunted-looking eyes gazing out over the top of a shadowy silhouetted mansion. What is evident from both of these publication types is that the fictional version appears primarily concerned with a dramatic engagement of readers and a selling of books rather than in showing any real sensitivity towards the topic concerned. The autobiographical account, on the other hand, demonstrates a greater concern about the overall message and the support and help that can be gained by others reading it.

Perhaps the most negative and careless mental health references are made within the genre of horror or thriller writing. While a good deal of these seem to pay little obvious attention to actual facts, others achieve a blend of drama and impact along with a more thoughtful exploration of themes, for example *The Wasp Factory* or *American Psycho*. A common representation within the fictional domain is the mentally ill killer whose portrayal, as illustrated by Thomas Harris's Hannibal Lecter character, seems rarely true to life. This characterisation, according to Ressler and Schachtman (1992), combines attributes of several different sorts of killers, with a range of personality dynamics that would be highly unlikely to coexist in any one person in the real world. It is borne out by Wahl's (1995) assertion that, despite their apparent popularity, the psychotic psychopath is a very unrealistic and misleading characterisation. It is a compelling one, though, and one that proliferates in numerous accounts by popular writers within this genre (e.g. Patricia Cornwell) wherein accuracy is displaced by the need for exciting and dramatic prose. An interesting example, however, is demonstrated by Jeffery Deaver's *Praying for Sleep*, a thriller about a schizophrenic man who has escaped from a hospital for the criminally insane and is apparently pursuing the woman who testified against him. This novel cleverly uses the public's inaccurate understanding and preconditioned feelings about the mentally ill to deliver its biggest surprise at the end of this work when it is revealed that he is actually completely innocent of all the violent crimes attributed to him. These revelations cause the character to undergo a complete transformation

in the eyes of the reader from a dangerous and clever manipulator to a vulnerable and caring person.

Regulation and censorship

Literature unlike other media sources such as the press or television has far fewer restrictions or regulations governing what is presented. There is a fair deal of freedom presented to authors in what can be written although some degree of restriction or censorship is imposed by the publishers or external organisations. It is normally left to individual publishers to review work prior to its publication and place restrictions where it is deemed necessary in order to comply with governmental legislation and specific acts concerned with copyright, defamation, racism and sexism, disability, human rights and obscene publications.

Some notable publications have met with fierce condemnation from various groups and have had various sanctions placed upon them. In September 2002, the publisher Gallimard bowed to legal threats and decided not to resupply bookshops with *Rose Bonbon* by Nicolas Jones-Gorlin, the story of a murderous paedophile. Another novel, *Satanic Verses*, earned its author Salman Rushdie a *fatwa* (death sentence) from the Ayatollah Khomeini in Iran. While censorship is geared towards restricting publication there are notable examples where the opposite has happened, such as in the case of D.H. Lawrence's *Lady Chatterley's Lover*, which sold 200,000 copies in a day following Penguin's triumph following its acquittal from prosecution under the Obscene Publications Act. An important aspect regarding censorship relates to the organisation or group imposing sanctions and it is normally the view of a group that holds overall power and influence which determines what is deemed acceptable or not. In some cases this is deemed a protective measure, generally agreed upon and supported by the majority of people. Alternatively, it might be viewed as a means of stifling individual expression, something that is enforced through extreme measures. There are many historical examples of this with authors forced to write in exile, their writing deemed unacceptable in their own country, for example the Russian authors Solzhenitsyn (*Gulag Archipelago*) and Boris Pasternak (*Doctor Zhivago*).

The censorship argument with books generally relates to what is deemed unacceptable by certain groups or societies. Clearly this may differ from one individual or culture to another and what tends to matter is how powerful the dissenting voice is. Traditionally, the mentally ill have been poorly represented and have been given little *voice* with which to make their displeasure known. Currently, a number of mental health service-user groups are taking a much more active stance with media providers in terms of collaboration, campaigning and offering feedback. The difficulty with the medium of literature is the huge wealth of existing literature of a stigmatising kind already in circulation, including well-established or critically well-received texts as well as

books that have enjoyed a huge commercial appeal. In order for censorship to be applied properly to the stigmatisation of mental illness, there needs to be a consensus from a powerful enough collective voice that such stigmatisation is deemed unacceptable. Although the newsprint and broadcast media have come under significant scrutiny from mental health advocates it seems that in the world of literature, with a few minor exceptions, little has been done.

Riddell (2002) argues that while there is a place for regulation in the arts, censorship does not take account of readers' ability to detach themselves from what they are reading, and the fact that they are not all impressionable people easily swayed by what they encounter. It may be true to a point that reading about violence or self-destructiveness does not necessarily influence one's own personal behaviour. The continued reinforcement of stereotypical mental health content, however, has an insidious effect upon the public who may have limited access to more productive and accurate material. Because of the difficulties in restricting the negative portrayals of mental health themes it seems that the best counter is provided through education. This in particular helps individuals to understand what they are reading and to discriminate better between positive and negative messages located within a narrative. It is greatly helped by autobiographical work and initiatives that promote and celebrate positive mental health writing such as the Mind book awards that identify some of the best texts covering mental health themes with previous winners including David Solomon's (2002) factual/autobiographical text on depression (*The Noonday Demon*) and Bernlef's (1988) first-person narrative detailing the experience of a man with dementia (*Out of Mind*).

The 'inner world' (*inside looking out*)

One of the most powerful aspects of literature is its ability to travel with significant depth into the 'inner world' of characters and directly connect with another's thoughts and feelings, seeing the world from their perspective. It is a process of identification where we might develop a sense of connectedness with others and for a while suspend our own lives and travel with them along the particular journey they are taking. The main style of writing providing this type of direct contact is the use of first-person narrative. It can help by taking the reader directly into the fragmented and confused thought processes experienced within a number of acute mental health states and thereby prove an enlightening and educating experience, helping to develop one's sensitivity towards those experiencing mental health problems. It can also, though, be an immensely discomforting and scary process as felt, for example, when the experience of a person's ordered world becomes more chaotic and fragmented. An example of this can be seen in Hannah Green's *I Never Promised You a Rose Garden*:

She saw the doctor's mouth moving, and imagined that it was spewing

questions and accusations. She began to fall, going with Anterrabae through his fire-fragmented darkness into Yr. This time the fall was far. There was utter darkness for a long time and then a greyness, seen only in bands across the eye. The place was familiar; it was the pit. In this place gods and Collect moaned and shouted, but even they were unintelligible. Human sounds came, too, but they came without meaning. The world intruded, but it was a shattered world and unrecognisable.

(Green 1964: 34)

Reading through this passage and others in the book we are given a very strong sense of Deborah's feelings of disassociation, anxiety and powerlessness. This perspective (*inside looking out*) is uniquely different from the external one which might describe a person's odd behaviour without the reader gaining any sense or understanding as to what is going on within.

Connecting with an individual's felt experience can be related to the psychotherapeutic term empathy, which is regarded as the ability to sense another person's world as if it were one's own (Rogers 1951; Cassedy and Cutliffe 1998). From a therapeutic perspective, a potential problem within this process involves the therapist having too great an emotional reaction and subsequently moving away psychologically from their client (Gladstein 1983). If this is true then of the trained therapist, it is highly likely that the reader will also experience significant problems in connecting with distressing and uncomfortable emotions. An important issue here relates to the fact that readers will differ in their ability or even their desire to get closer to certain characters encountered within literature. This is perhaps true with Doris Lessing's *Briefing for a Descent into Hell* where the text itself is extremely difficult to stay with. The book's narrative focuses primarily upon the fragmented and confused thoughts of Charles Watkins and is written in a largely unstructured and rambling prose, occasionally 'surfacing' to catch fragments of dialogue before again returning to his delusional world. As the story progresses, the narrative becomes more ordered and less chaotic. Sentences become generally shorter than those that at times last for a number of pages and the content becomes more tuned into the prime character's surroundings, noticing more of the world outside of his internal one. It is a strongly and creatively written piece of work that depicts very vividly the feelings of disconnectedness and confused thought processes operating within certain psychotic states. The form of expression conveyed here is reflected in other examples that also use what could be described as the language of madness. Publications such as these lend a degree of credibility to the expression by those deemed to be mentally ill and include some notable examples including Jonathan Swift's (1704) *Tale of a Tub*, a narrative that gradually reveals the fact that the narrator was once an inmate of Bedlam (Hawes 1996), and *Lucida Intervalla*, James Carkesse's 1679 text that is perhaps the first collection of verse published in England by an inmate of an asylum. Accounts such as these have helped to develop a new climate of expressive communication

and, as Maclennan (1992) highlights, allow the experience of madness to become available in literature for the production and expression of subjective meaning.

The disturbing nature of remaining within the direct world of madness is perhaps aptly illustrated by the novel *American Psycho* which provides the reader with an insightful yet unsettling connection with the thoughts of a psychopathic killer. Patrick Bateman's sense of emptiness and cold detachment is aptly illustrated by the first-person narrative used and the reader is maintained throughout the book at a disturbingly close proximity to the inner world of this killer as he emotionlessly dispatches victim after victim. His only real sense of insight is acknowledged towards the end of the book, as shown in the following passage:

> There is no real me, only an entity, something illusory, and though I can hide my cold gaze and you can shake my hand and feel flesh gripping yours and maybe you can even sense our lifestyles are comparable : I am simply not there . . . my conscience, my pity, my hopes disappeared a long time ago if they ever did exist . . . my pain is constant and sharp and I do not hope for a better world for anyone. In fact I want my pain to be inflicted on others. I want no one to escape.
>
> (Easton-Ellis 1991: 377)

This book provides an unsettling experience for the reader and it is at times extremely difficult to stay with, perhaps more so because we are led towards an unfamiliar vantage point. Our perspective within horror or thriller books is normally somewhere close to the thoughts and feelings of the person being pursued. This text connects us with the inner world of the predator allowing the reader to see not only the horror of his actions but also the horror of his thoughts. The way in which these types of work are handled and the opportunity to educate the public as to the 'greater picture' is important because of the tendency to stereotype and apply isolated examples to the entire collective known as 'the mentally ill'.

First- versus third-person narrative

Genette (1980) identifies two main types of writing: external focalisation, where the recounting is carried out by an observer focusing on a character, and internal focalisation where a narrative is told through the consciousness of a character. These narrative styles (in essence third and first person) lead the reader into very different relationships with the characters being portrayed and strongly influence the sense of identification and connectedness they have with them. This is outlined by Lothe (2000) who indicates that within first-person narratives the reader is active within the plot as opposed to third-person writing of being located outside or above it. An example of the significance of this can be illustrated by the following two extracts taken

from Mary Shelley's (1818) *Frankenstein* and J.K. Rowling's (2000) *Harry Potter and the Goblet of Fire.*

- Internal focalisation – *Frankenstein*:

They are kind – they are the most excellent creatures in the world; but unfortunately they are prejudiced against me. I have good dispositions; my life has been hitherto harmless and in some degree beneficial; but a fatal prejudice clouds their eyes, and where they ought to see a feeling and kind friend they behold a detestable monster.

The old man [replied] . . . 'I am blind but cannot judge of your countenance, but there is something in your words which persuades me you are sincere.'

. . . At that instant the cottage door was opened, and Felix, Safie and Agatha entered. Who can describe their horror and consternation on beholding me? Agatha fainted, and Safie unable to attend to her friend, rushed out the cottage. Felix darted forward and with supernatural force tore me from his father, to whose knees I could have torn him limb from limb, as the lion rends the antelope. But my heart sunk within me as with bitter sickness, and I refrained . . .

. . . Cursed, cursed creator! Why did I live? Why I that instant, did I not extinguish the spark of existence which you had so wantonly bestowed? I know not: despair had not yet taken possession of me; my feelings were those of rage and revenge. I could with pleasure have destroyed the cottage and its inhabitants, and have glutted myself with their shrieks and misery.

(Shelley 1818)

- External focalisation – *Harry Potter and the Goblet of Fire* (2000), 'The madness of Mr Crouch':

Next moment a man had staggered out from behind a tall oak. For a moment, Harry didn't recognise him . . . then he realised it was Mr Crouch. He looked as though he had been travelling for days. The knees of his robes were ripped and bloody; his face scratched; he was unshaven and grey with exhaustion. His neat hair and moustache were both in need of a wash and a trim. His strange appearance, however, was nothing to the way he was behaving. Muttering and gesticulating, Mr Crouch appeared to be talking to someone that he alone could see. He reminded Harry vividly of an old tramp he had seen once when out shopping with the Dursleys. That man, too, had been conversing wildly with thin air . . . 'I've done . . . stupid . . . thing . . .' Mr Crouch breathed. He looked

utterly mad. His eyes were rolling and bulging, and a trickle of spittle was sliding down his chin.

(Rowling 2000)

The first extract from Mary Shelley's classic text depicts the creature's sense of longing for companionship. It is essentially the tale of a child who wants to be loved but instead receives rejection and abuse, subsequently becoming rejecting and abusive towards others. The impact upon the reader can be seen as being in stark contrast to the following extract that presents a very different message with phrases such as: 'He [Mr Crouch] looked utterly mad'. Mr Crouch no doubt presents his observers with a similarly foreboding appearance to that of the creature as seen by Felix, Safie and Agatha. We are not given the benefit here of accessing Mr Crouch's thoughts and perhaps experiencing some of his fear and confusion. Instead, he is presented as an image of unpredictability and somebody from whom we might seek to distance ourselves. This latter extract portrays the stereotypical view of madness being a visible entity, borne out by Mr Crouch's responding to voices, facial grimaces and his overall state of dishevelment. A core difference therefore between these examples is the vantage point from which each person is viewed. With Mr Crouch, we are located on the *outside looking in*, registering from the same perspective as Harry Potter, his wild behaviour and unkempt appearance. With the first extract, however, we are on the *inside looking out*, gaining a sense of connection with the creature's inner world and as a consequence responding in a different way to the cottage's inhabitants who see a monster instead of a being in need of loving care. As with Jastrow's duck/rabbit image (see Figure 4.1), our understanding of what we are exposed to can change dramatically if looked at from an alternative perspective. The important point perhaps concerns the degree to which readers are actually alerted to the presence of an alternative viewpoint. From a mental health perspective the significance is in recognising the person who exists within a condition or diagnosis, and reflecting the person-centred approach as advocated strongly through the humanist school (Rogers 1961; Maslow 1971). Essentially, the more that individuals are able to connect with and understand another's felt experience regarding mental health issues, the more they will be able to challenge and question common stereotypes, starting to see the person in a new and more productive light.

Survival versus destruction

The portrayal of mental health content in literature covers a wide spectrum that can be seen as lying on a continuum somewhere between the polarised positions of *survival* and *destruction*. The *survival* category demonstrates an ability to cope with mental health problems and offers hope whereas the *destruction* one portrays various conditions as all-consuming and destructive for self or others.

Survival

This category focuses upon mental illness as a survivable condition and features strongly throughout autobiographical accounts as well as within a range of fictional narratives. The main message being conveyed here regards individuals developing ways of coping with various mental health conditions, aided in part by support from others and particular treatments offered. The primary messages are those of re-emergence from one's struggles with mental health difficulties as well as learning to live with and accept them. These accounts are to a large degree inspirational and heartening, providing the reader with a sense of hope and optimism relating to specific psychological difficulties. This message is strongly demonstrated in Janet Fitch's (1999) *White Oleander*, a book that relates the tale of a young girl, Astrid, and her search for meaning in her life following a series of rejections and abuse as well as her mother's imprisonment. It conveys very powerfully her ability to overcome extreme physical and emotional trauma through her incredibly strong will to survive. Another novel, *I Know This Much Is True* (Lamb 2000), shifts the attention onto family members and reflects upon how they learn to cope with their own feelings of helplessness and suffocating feelings of guilt. It is a sensitively written narrative that strongly conveys the impact that mental illness has upon the whole family as well as the support mechanisms used by them to cope.

Examples of individuals re-emerging from a distorted state can be found as far back as the Ancient Greek times as illustrated in the tale of Heracles' awakening following his murderous rage:

> Ah, I am still breathing and I see all I should see, the sky, the earth and the sun's shafts. I was swamped somehow by a terrible confusion of mind and my breath comes hot and unsteady from my lungs, not calm at all. But look, why am I anchored like a ship with ropes around my powerful chest and arms? Why am I sitting against the broken stone pillar with corpses all around me? . . . Is there some friend of mine anywhere who could cure my ignorance?
>
> (Simon 1978: 99)

This example depicts the picture of Heracles' distorted cognitive state being transient in nature showing him becoming lucid and aware of his surroundings even though he is in this instance greeted with the appalling consequences of his actions. While a renewed sense of clarity is met here with despair, many other accounts portray a different picture, that of awakening to the joys of life as shown in Tim Lott's autobiographical novel *The Scent of Dried Roses*:

> I begin to take them [anti-depressant medication] every day. I have absolutely no faith that they will work. . . . Since the tablets supposedly take

three weeks to work, that day I estimate will be 28 December 1987 . . .
[On] 28 December I awake, unusually first thing in the morning. I am
alone. I have an odd perception. There is a pigeon cooing on the balcony
outside my bedroom window. It is pleasant and soothing. I haven't
noticed birdsong for a long time . . . I feel strange in that I feel normal,
average . . . As if by magic, all my thoughts about sin and redemption,
God and the devil, have disappeared. It occurs to me that the desire to
kill myself is utterly ridiculous. Why would I want to kill myself? I know,
quite clearly and calmly now, like a camera suddenly finding focus, that I
really have been ill, and equally that I have begun to recover.

(Lott 1997: 245)

The message of re-emergence is similarly covered in other narratives such
as Sylvia Nasar's (1998) biographical account (*A Beautiful Mind*) of the
gifted mathematician John Nash and his survival from a debilitating set of
experiences with schizophrenia. Nash's recovery is topped off in the fairy-tale
style of triumph over adversity through being awarded the Nobel Prize for his
seminal work with game theory.

The concept of survival is heavily featured within the autobiographical
novel with numerous examples now available involving those that centre upon
an individual's personal experience or others that feature a shared collective
trauma. The collective accounts are written by individuals about experiences
that are shared such as social deprivation, poverty or political oppression. A
number of examples can be illustrated here including the book *Angela's
Ashes* which portrays Frank McCourt's astonishing ability to emerge from
what reads as an appalling catalogue of tragedy and hardship (McCourt
1996). Another account, Alexander Solzhenitsyn's (1963) *One Day in the Life
of Ivan Denisovich*, conveys a message familiar to a number of people struggling with conditions such as alcoholism or depression; that of coping 'one
day at a time'. This narrative centres upon life in a Siberian labour camp and
the way in which the central character and others discover various means to
survive within the stark and punishing hardships they have to endure. Perhaps a more astonishing account is written by Tadeusz Borowski (1959), an
Auschwitz survivor whose book *This Way for the Gas, Ladies and Gentleman*
demonstrates the will to survive (mainly through numbness and detachment)
found among those who had to endure the unendurable. This does not mean
to say that they are able to actually overcome such trauma, a point aptly
illustrated by the author's suicide in 1951. Lastly, there are a number of
excellent accounts detailing the experience of living through Chairman
Mao's cultural revolution in China including Jung Chan's *Wild Swans* and
Hong Ying's *Daughter of the River*. These books aptly sum up the restrictive-
ness, fear and privations that formed part of daily life, although also illustrate
the determination and strength found by many to overcome these and survive.

The steady increase in written accounts reflecting the survivable side of
mental health difficulties or psychological trauma is both positive and

encouraging. The popularity of these types of account is perhaps reflected in the *human interest* theme (Cortazzi 1993), although we can also consider the dramatic nature of the tale being recounted. It seems as if the greatest impact is created where a person's suffering seems unimaginable yet a will to survive still exists. The appeal that these types of narrative have for publishers and readers alike does present a problem in that what might be regarded as more 'ordinary' accounts of mental illness are consequently not as sought after. What is needed perhaps are avenues for airing experiences of coping with mental health problems that do not need to involve the worst forms of trauma or distress and are also representative of large numbers of people who are not at present being covered.

Destructiveness

The theme of destructiveness with regard to mental illness can be looked at from a number of perspectives involving negative consequences for the persons concerned or for those around them. The 'violence to others' view is perhaps the more popular and one that unsettles the reader especially when linked to accounts that portray victims as innocent and unsuspecting. It is the random and unpredictable nature of many of the portrayed attacks and the victim's complete innocence and vulnerability that make these more frightening to readers, raising the idea that the sporadic violence of madmen can reach anyone, even people like them (Wahl 1995). The degree of drama and suspense related here make mental illness as a theme a very appealing and attractive choice for writers. Indeed, books about psychopathic killers such as Thomas Harris' series of books about Hannibal Lecter, Bret Easton-Ellis' *American Psycho* and Iain Banks' *The Wasp Factory* have all proven extraordinarily popular

The *destructiveness to self* theme is aptly conveyed either directly as a consequence of a person's mental health difficulties or as a process visited on them by others. The former demonstrates the negative and all-consuming nature of a person's condition which they are unable to cope with or overcome. One example of this is provided by Malcolm Lowry's (1947) *Under the Volcano* which deals with the subject of alcoholism and the principal character Geoffrey Firmin's progressive absorption within a world of despair, resignation and isolation. Despite the available care and support of his wife Yvonne and friend Hugh, he is unable to help himself or take heart from their optimism and concern, instead feeling contemptible and unworthy. The narrative follows his progressive downward spiral through his steady absorption with alcohol, alienation from those who care for him, defilement with a prostitute and eventual death.

The sense of destruction, as briefly alluded to above, is something that can be visited upon an individual by other people. This is portrayed within a number of texts as a consequence of the controlling and abusive regime of care encountered. Perhaps the most well-known account of this is Ken

Kesey's *One Flew over the Cuckoo's Nest* that viewed the needs and interests of the institution coming firmly before those of the patients, and where non-compliance was treated brutally and harshly. The overriding sense of power-lessness and impotence experienced by those who are mentally ill is also illustrated in other accounts such as Janet Frame's *Faces in the Water* show-ing patients waiting meekly and passively for treatments such as ECT. This process is taken a stage further in Marge Piercy's *Woman on the Edge of Time* with an illustration of the terrifying concept of social control:

> 'That's Alice Blue Bottom,' Sybil hissed. 'Look what they've done to her!'
> 'What is it? Did she have an accident ?' . . . 'It looks like they busted her head. Maybe she tried to get away.'
> . . . Skip shook his head 'They did a kind of operation. They stuck needles in her brain.'
> . . . Connie called out 'Is it true you got needles stuck in your . . . head?'
> 'No lie electrodes they call them'
> '. . . Alice, if they're electrodes where are the wires?' Sybil asked cautiously.
> 'You old fashion. No wires. They use a little radio, and they stick that inside too.'
> . . . 'But what for?'
> 'Control. To turn us into machines so we obey them,' Sybil whispered.'
>
> (Piercy 1976: 202)

These types of account all help to reinforce the feelings of powerlessness and lack of importance that fit the popular view of the mentally ill. It is especially borne out by narratives that see patients as objects for psychiatric professions to experiment upon as illustrated by the above extract or the following from Patrick McGrath's book *Asylum* concerning the doctor's view:

> Now that I had her here in the female wing I relished the prospect of stripping away her defences and opening her up, seeing what that psyche of hers really looked like. I understood of course that she would resist me but we had time.
>
> (McGrath 1996: 208)

It is clear that these examples only serve to build up the sense of scariness that the topic mental illness represents for both the sufferer and those around them. For the individual concerned there will be a fair amount of trepidation involved in seeking help or in disclosing their problems to others for fear of rejection or abuse. From the other perspective, the feeling of dangerousness posed by the mentally ill serves to reinforce and perpetuate the degree of distancing and exclusion subsequently encountered.

Making sense of literature

When reading a printed narrative, there are a number of factors which play a part in the final message that is taken away. First, we can look at the intention of the author as well as their ability to guide us towards a certain understanding that includes their narrative style and use of imagery and symbolism. Second, the readers themselves play a significant part in determining meaning by encoding a text in a specific way. The degree to which meaning is generated by a text is influenced to a large degree by the craft and intention of the author. As Sartre illustrates: 'The writer can guide you and, if he describes a hovel, make it seem the symbol of social injustice and provoke your indignation' (Sartre 1967: 3). This view states that it is the style of narrative which infuses life and depth to what is being related, guiding the reader towards the real significance of what is being recounted. It may also reflect Baudelaire's *double simultaneous postulation* where each word refers to two contexts, two forces being applied simultaneously to each phrase. Examples of this can be seen with allegorical narratives such as Joseph Heller's *Catch 22* or Franz Kafka's *Metamorphosis. Catch 22*, for example, can be read as a metaphorical account of madness, complete with its absurd logic and implied sense of impotence. The story *Metamorphosis* begins with the line: 'As Gregor Samsa awoke one morning from uneasy dreams he found himself transformed in his bed into a gigantic insect' (Kafka 1933: 9). It is a narrative that can also be read as a parable on human reaction to suffering and disease and the response of many towards mental illness. The significance of metaphorical and symbolic imagery is that the reader is required to suspend their rational thought and use their imagination in order to make sense of texts, thereby having new and provocative ways of exploring and understanding certain concepts and ideas.

Foucault (1979) questions the notion of the author being the presiding authority for the understanding of a text. This view reflects the concept of reception theory which states that a piece of writing cannot make sense independently but requires the intervention of an interpreting reader (Livingstone 1998; Holland 1980), which brings in the sense of collaboration between writer and reader, aptly illustrated by Sartre:

> On the one hand, the literary object has no substance but the reader's subjectivity . . . But on the other hand, the words are there like traps to arouse our feelings and to reflect them towards us . . . the work exists only at the exact level of his [the reader] capacities; while he reads and creates, he knows that he can always further in his reading, can always create more profoundly, and thus the work seems to him as inexhaustible . . . Thus the writer appeals to the reader's freedom to collaborate in the production of his work.
>
> (Sartre 1967: 31)

Readers hold a measure of power relating to the control of a story's flow, for

example through reading a narrative in instalments (Armes 1994), as well as the understanding and comprehension they take away. This is illustrated by Young who asserts that: 'Meaning . . . is not stable or fixed . . . although authors may have intentions when they write, once they have written they cannot control and fix the meaning of any reading' (Young 1991: 238). This is borne out by the interpretative diversity brought by readers who have their own set of experiences and expectations from which to engage a particular text (Martin 1986). The notion of the interpretative reader limits the overall control that writers have as they can guide but they have no assurance as to what final meaning is taken away. It is an issue that can prove extremely frustrating for writers especially when their texts are misinterpreted, a fact bemoaned by Herman Hesse regarding his classic novel *Steppenwolf* (Hesse 2001). The role of the reader is highlighted by Bennett and Royle who illustrate two contrasting styles:

> Is reading simply something that happens to a text as if by chance, something which leaves a text fundamentally unaltered? If so, then the role of reader would appear to be determined by the text itself: each literary text would be like a set of instructions, a kind of recipe for how it should be read. By contrast, the text may be understood as fundamentally incomplete, to be constructed in the act of reading. In this case the text is remade in every reading.
>
> (Bennett and Royle 1999: 16)

While some writing provides very clear guidance for the reader, other forms present a more open text with a plurality of potential interpretations (Barthes 1972). Opportunities are left for the reader to construct the meaning of a text and form their own interpretations. Another strand to consider is that of the reader undergoing changes between subsequent re-readings of a text, bringing with them a different mood and awareness of what happens next, resulting in an altered reading and a perceiving of new patterns (Martin 1986). We can see this process being influenced by a person's exposure to other media formats where new 'readings' or access to visual cues cause them to reinterpret what they know, for instance returning to Ken Kesey's *One Flew Over the Cuckoo's Nest* with an image of Jack Nicholson's charismatic screen character in their minds. Another factor influencing a reader's engagement concerns their level of engagement with parts of a text either as an active or passive participant. It is a type of engagement that is not always constant and, as schema and script theories suggest, readers may alternate between the two. Augoustinos and Walker (1995) indicate that the existence of well-established representational knowledge structures favour a passive type of processing, in which the person does not perceive anything which contradicts their preconceptions and merely retraces former steps, reruns old experiences and treats the novel as familiar. Therefore, once a person has seen what they expect to see they may not challenge or question further. This reflects something of

the mentally ill stereotype being accessed within a text without one really standing back and questioning the authenticity of the message being relayed. This concern can be matched by the uncertain degree of authority attached to many authors concerning the topic they are writing about. Having limited knowledge or insight into what one is writing was identified by Lothe (2000) as a major factor that makes a narrator unreliable. A brief look within the thriller and horror genres would appear to demonstrate that a large number of writers are unreliable sources when it comes to mental health content, opting for dramatic engagement of their readers over accurate portrayals.

The understanding that is taken away from works of literature is therefore subject to a variety of factors including both the intentions of the author as well as the particular interpretive framework applied by the reader. The importance from a health promotional point of view is to encourage further development of writing that presents mental illness from a better informed position as well as helping recipients to become more discerning and questioning about what they are reading.

Conclusion

The medium of literature has the ability to engage the reader more powerfully with the theme of mental illness than perhaps is achievable through other media sources. Of core significance here is the ability that this source has to engage the reader directly with the inner world (thoughts and feelings) of those involved, particularly through first-person narratives or autobiographical accounts. This medium provides a communication type that is rich in imagery, symbolism and narrative illustration, guiding those accessing it to construct their own pictures and understanding of the text before them. As has been illustrated above, the reader is provided with some very distinct associations concerning mental illness; on the one hand an all destructive process and on the other a survivable condition. The understanding about mental health issues gleaned from books is clearly to a large extent determined by the type of literary genre accessed. The dramatic potential that mental illness can bring to a text and its subsequent appeal for readers is perhaps too enticing for some authors to avoid. This means that the misleading, stereotypical and unrealistic forms of representation will continue to flourish. On a heartening note however, the increasingly popular reception of autobiographical accounts of distress is a welcome process in communicating more of the lived experience. Perhaps it should be noted that these predominantly feature mental health themes (i.e. abuse, eating disorders, alcoholism or surviving tragedy) that frame the person as *victim*, evoking feelings of sympathy and sorrow among their readers. It would be good to see this type of reception mirrored in other less-accepted mental health states such as schizophrenia, thereby helping the public to appreciate the reality of certain conditions more, and forming a base from which to challenge the many poorly-constructed representations accessible.

7 Film

The medium of film

For over a hundred years now viewers have been able to engage with the hugely appealing and attractive medium of film. Although not as popular today, at the beginning of the twentieth century moviegoers would queue in vast numbers to catch the latest releases. The cinema audience has progressively become more fragmented declining from 1,585 million in 1945 to 72 million in 1985 before rising to 140 million in 1999 (British Film Institute 2005). The overall fall in numbers is in part explained by increased competition from other developing media services, beginning perhaps with the advent of television in the 1950s and then the accessibility of film on video in the 1970s. In recent years the diversity of available products has widened further with cable and satellite services as well as new digital technology providing an almost overwhelming array of products to select from.

The medium of film has created a new channel for artistic and creative expression and has opened a new world of imagination by projecting the fantasies of writers and film-makers onto the screen (Bloom 1993). Prior to this, the mode of visual expression belonged predominantly to the world of art and the domain of stage production. Creative expression, utilising means such as drawing, painting or sculpture has for thousands of years been employed either as a means of recording and reporting or as a mode of stimulating and challenging creative thought. Hogarth's *Rake's Progress*, for example, documented the conditions and experiences of the mentally ill incarcerated within Bedlam hospital. Stage productions provided many features that were to later be captured and developed by the medium of film. Mood and atmosphere were first created by the presentation of the stage sets within which the drama took place. Against this background, the story was acted out using numerous visual and auditory modes of expression to enable audience members to engage with the overall set of messages being conveyed. It is a mode of storytelling that dates back over centuries, with a number of notable examples relaying mental illness themes to the audiences of their era. For example, the ancient Greek view of madness being manifested by the gods was reflected in a number of plays such as *The Bacchae* and *Heracles*.

There is also, of course, the important body of work produced by Shakespeare with numerous mental health references being found throughout his work in plays such as *King Lear* and *Macbeth*.

The innovation of reproductive imagery began at the beginning of the nineteenth century with developments of early photographic products such as the heliograph and the daguerreotype. This was matched by the creation of the moving image initially through various devices including the kineto-scope and the zoöpraxiscope but later, at the end of nineteenth century, with films by Thomas Eddison (*Fred Ott's Sneeze* 1894) and the Lumière brothers (*Workers Leaving the Lumière Factory* 1895). Sound recording initially presented difficulties with regard to synchronisation, although found partial success through methods involving the tri-ergon process (a means of record-ing sound directly onto film), de Forest's phonofilm (using light as a method for writing and reading sound) and the vitaphone (a method of recording sound directly onto a disc). Clearly, these early initiatives seem primitive by comparison with modern film-making techniques but it is important to recognise how they might have been received by a fascinated public eager to enter more fully into the world created by the medium of film.

The ways in which we as an audience watch film is influenced by numer-ous lifestyle factors such as available time, cost issues and access to various technology and services. Films can be watched in the cinema as well as on television and computer screens, although it is in the cinema that viewers are presented with the most powerful engagement with the medium of film. This particular environment heightens the experience through reducing peri-pheral distracting stimuli and attracting the viewer more strongly towards what is presented before them. The reduction of external lighting and the large screen size means that our scope of vision is taken up exclusively with the film images projected before us. This is accompanied by a dominant volume of sound that helps to forcibly place us within the action being depicted. Our engagement with film is further influenced by audience mem-bers who share this experience with us and in a way act as guides towards particular emotional reactions that we might have in response to various scenes.

As Wedding and Boyd observe:

> When someone is watching a movie, an immediate bond is set up between the spectator and the film, and all the technical apparatus involved with the projection of the film becomes invisible as the images from the film pass into the spectator's consciousness. With the best films the viewer experiences a sort of dissociative state in which ordinary existence is temporarily suspended.
>
> (Wedding and Boyd 1999: 1)

The camera in a sense becomes what Metz (1982) refers to as our own viewing perspective as we collapse the distinction between our eyes and the projec-

tion apparatus. Unlike stage productions, the medium of film provides a more reliable means of ensuring that the viewer is looking where they ought to be looking (Carroll 1996). The importance of the visual stimuli engaged in by viewers is enhanced by the placing of a frame around it (Braudy 2002), and the methods used, including close-up shots and camera movement, are some of the many techniques used to guide an audience's attention and to provoke certain reactions. The final scene in Hitchcock's *Psycho*, for example, leads the viewer towards Norman Bates' eyes in order to draw them slowly and uncomfortably towards his disturbed and frightening world.

The medium of film engages audience members in various ways as Lothe states:

> Many film theorists have found that film, like music, works through atmosphere, resonance and rhythm. Film communication differs greatly from verbal language in that film is a language without a code and that understanding inferences etc. from a single camera shot may vary to the point of infinity.
>
> (Lothe 2000: 13)

The complexity of film as a communicating agent relates to the fact that it is much more than a set of observable cues, with a duality of sensory modes being employed. In essence, it covers the *auditory channel* (relating to noise, voice and music) as well as the *visual channel* that combines a range of camera and editing techniques (Chatham 1990). The issues outlined above highlight the intricacy of the messages being received through film and the multitude of stimuli to which we are exposed. As illustrated by Gestalt theory, film as an entire entity can be seen as being constructed from the intricate relationship of all its component parts. It is perhaps easier to understand the collective 'whole' by first exploring the various ways in which messages are transmitted. The depiction of mental health issues will be looked at with regard to imagery, narrative and sound (see Figure 7.1).

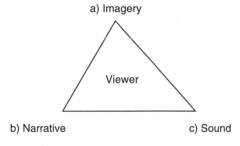

Figure 7.1 Film communication.

Film as a visual medium: imagery

As a visual medium, film provides a number of mental health representations that cover the whole spectrum from the sensitive and subtle through to the insensitive and grossly exaggerated. It is the latter type of depiction, though, that creates the greater impact and which is more memorable for the viewer. This can be reflected through the notion within perceptual theory of *figure and ground* whereby our attention is drawn towards a specific detail and, by focusing upon it, causes it to emerge from the background (King and Wertheimer 2005). Because film is not a static medium, the concept of what is figure and what is ground is constantly shifting as certain camera techniques cause our focus to move from one item to another. This then builds up a collective understanding as our glimpses of the background carry the context within which principal subjects are placed.

Characters/main subjects

Perhaps the first clue we are given regarding somebody's mental health state relates to the way in which they appear to us. The characterisation of mental illness is usually achieved through various stereotypical cues that leave the audience with little difficulty in discriminating between those who have mental health problems and those who do not. Wahl (1995) refers to this as the portrayal of the mentally ill as '*a breed apart*', made different by virtue of their looks and behaviour. One of the more deliberate ways of presenting mental illness is through the casting of actors who look odd or different. A notable example of this was the selection of Peter Lorre who played a series of 'mad' and deranged characters. His build, facial features, large eyes and 'creepy' Eastern European accent provided film-makers with what has been described as a textbook illustration of schizophrenia (Wahl 1995). Another example of intentionally casting people who look 'mad' can be seen in the film *One Flew over the Cuckoo's Nest* where some actors were selected because their appearance fitted stereotypical notions of the mentally ill. One choice in particular was the casting of Michael Berryman as the tall bald patient. He was already a 1970s horror genre icon because of his distinctive features, a rare medical condition resulting in him having no hair, fingernails or teeth. A counter perhaps to the many typically unattractive characterisations of the mentally ill is provided by a variety of more engaging and charismatic ones such as Jack Nicholson as the obsessive compulsive Melvin Udall in the film *As Good As It Gets*, Russell Crowe as John Nash in *A Beautiful Mind* and Judy Dench as Iris Murdoch in the film *Iris*. A further issue linked with characterisation relates to the presence of accompanying cues that serve to provide clues as to a person's mental health state, highlighting certain features such as dangerousness. The excessive use of restraint devices for Hannibal Lecter in the film *The Silence of the Lambs* and Freddy Krueger's (*Nightmare on Elm Street*) cadaverous look and bladed gloves all help to exacerbate the sense of threat posed.

Background

There are a number of the ways in which mood or complementary under-standing is created by virtue of the background within which scenes are enacted upon. In some cases, the exterior setting acts almost as a mirror, providing the viewer with a visual enactment of specific characteristics or elements being covered. This is observed by Bobker (1969) in relation to the film *Through a Glass Darkly* where the character of the sunlight (flat, grey and totally lacking in warmth) can be seen as an external projection of the internal conflicts and hopelessness felt with regard to the daughter's schizo-phrenia. Another example can be seen in the film *One Flew over the Cuckoo's Nest* where the dull, colourless and impersonal background perfectly reflects the overall climate of care. It is also interesting to note the way in which the chaotic world of madness is depicted in the artistic, stage-type sets employed in the silent German film *The Cabinet of Dr Caligari*. This is helped by the angular, asymmetrical and unfinished aspect of the scenery that serves to unsettle and disorient the viewer.

Film as an auditory medium: narrative and sound

Narrative

The style of narrative found within films reflects something of the prevailing attitudes towards the topic of mental illness. It is at times sensitive, thought-ful and funny and at other times offensive, cruel and uninformed. To some degree it relates to the film as a whole and the type of reaction that film-makers are trying to evoke in their audience. The impact that specific words have is not solely down to what is said but also relates strongly to the context within which they appear. For example, the film *One Flew over the Cuckoo's Nest* includes a number of seemingly derogatory and stigmatising statements including McMurphy's: 'We're nuts, we're in the mental defectives league.' However, the prevailing attitude from McMurphy towards his fellow patients is respectful and caring and the words used come across less as insults and more as self-parody. This can also be reflected in some of the language in the film *Arsenic and old Lace* concerning the highly 'eccentric' Brewster family: 'Madness doesn't run in our family it gallops.' While these examples are more of the benevolent kind, the same cannot be said of *Me, Myself and Irene* and the use of terms such as 'You've got a screw loose', 'psycho' and 'schizo'. This film also displays a marked change in vocal style between the split person-alities of Hank and Charlie, with Hank, for example, adopting a menacing Clint Eastwood style drawl. These references are unashamedly used with little consideration being shown for the offence they might cause. Fortunately there are films that provide examples of a softer and more caring dialogue as shown by Suzanna's (*Girl Interrupted*) statement: 'Crazy isn't being broken, it's just me and you amplified.' The range of examples therefore found within the

medium of film is very mixed and deciding whether they are positive or negative depends upon the 'global' characterisation of mental illness being depicted.

Sound

The purpose of film music is reflected in the broad functions outlined by Prendergast (1992); these include:

- Creating atmosphere
- Underlining the psychological states of characters
- Providing neutral background fillers
- Building a sense of continuity
- Sustaining tension and then rounding it off with a sense of closure

As illustrated by these characteristics, film scores are evocative of mood and music can generate feeling, be it peacefulness and tranquillity or imminent danger. As Devereaux and Hillman state: 'Music can seek to represent in sound a written text' (Devereaux and Hillman 1995:183). As an example, they cite Hitchcock's 1943 film *Shadow of a Doubt* and the choice of the Merry Widow waltz (a piece of music embellished with horror harmonies) for a story concerning a homicidal maniac with a penchant for widows. In another film, *Through a Glass Darkly*, there is a sense of fragmentation between the film scenes and music which do not quite synchronise, both being allowed in a sense to go their own way. This, according to Bobker (1969), accompanied by the bleak, dark character of Bach's Cello Suite number 2, reveals something of the daughter's schizophrenic world.

Sound and music act as a powerful communicator telling us, for instance, when a significant moment is happening and indicating what we should feel about it (Turner 1999). This is supported by Frith who states: 'Music amplifies the mood or atmosphere and also tries to convey the emotional significance of a scene' (Frith 1986: 65). A notable example here is Hitchcock's shower scene from *Psycho* where the sense of danger and suspense are powerfully evoked through the unnerving and shrieking violin strings that appear cruel, painful and murderous when matched with the descending knife (Carroll 1996). There is also the significance of certain screen characters having their own signature tune, or *leitmotif*, when a particular recurring style of music is played in order to help characterise a person.

Lastly, when considering the importance of sound it is worth reflecting upon its absence and the deliberate use of silence. As has been addressed above, a disturbing and frightening feeling can be evoked in the audience member by the use of loud music, fragmented orchestration and screeching violin strings. An equally disturbing mood can be created by removing sound or reducing volume, thereby leaving viewers with either a confused auditory experience or a feeling of agonising suspense. The film *Psycho* provides a

vivid example of this where immediately preceding the detective's murder, the volume is reduced to a very quiet state in order to unsettle and discomfort the viewer who is thereby alerted in a different way to what is expected (music becoming louder) and to the imminent presence of danger.

The sender

While the text of a novel can be regarded as a complete entity in itself, the scriptwriter provides a text that is designed to serve as a stimulus to the actors who, under the guidance of a director, offer a personal interpretation of each character (Armes 1994). The performance, therefore, that reaches the spectator is not purely the version offered by the scriptwriter but one that contains interpretations and influences from a number of others. It is also subject to change owing to related regulations and issues of censorship. A point made by the British Film Institute (2005) is that the moving image is subject to far greater censorship than any other artistic medium, with film and video releases in Britain being among the most tightly regulated in the Western world. Indeed, there are a variety of legislative and regulatory processes governing the medium of film, the first piece of British legislation being the Cinematograph Act (1909) which provided for the licensing of exhibition premises and the safety of audiences. This was followed by a number of cinematograph acts before these were all eventually replaced by the 1985 Films Act. A further piece of legislation relating to the release of film on video was provided by the Video Recordings Act (1984) which was set up to control and restrict the amount of obscene material, sex and violence included. The focus on screen content has been reflected in a number of acts covering a range of subjects including cruelty to animals (Cinematograph Films (Animals) Act 1937), obscenity (Obscene Publications Act 1959 – extended to cover films in 1977), indecent images of children (Protection of Children Act 1978), freedom of expression (Human Rights Act 1998), as well as various types of criminal activity (Criminal Justice Act 1994).

Two major organisations concerned with film classification are the aptly named British Board of Film Classification (BBFC) (formerly British Board of Film Censors), and the Motion Picture Association of America (MPAA). Neither of these organisations has any legal status with regard to film censorship but they carry out their regulatory role in collaboration with local authorities. The local authorities hold the main power and may decide to ignore the board's decisions as, for example, with the banning of the films *A Clockwork Orange* and *Crash* despite their gaining BBFC approval. Both the BBFC and MPAA provide ratings as to who watches what although there is little direct reference made to mental health themes. The BBFC provide classification relating to the themes of:

- Language
- Nudity

- Sex
- Violence
- Imitable techniques
- Horror
- Drugs

The MPAA covers similar themes and it is surprising to note that besides drug abuse and aspects concerning suicide and self-harm, no direct reference is made to mental health content. This appears to be an ongoing problem dating back to the earliest days of film regulation. Indeed, the British Board of Film Censors covered 43 aspects within their 1913–1915 annual report as satisfying grounds for deletion, covering nothing about disability or mental health issues besides a single reference to 'The drug habit'. The theme of drug addiction is one that causes considerable concern and one that was listed as the most concerning topic by the public in a BBFC (2005) report. An example from the United States relates to the 1955 film about drug addiction, *The Man with the Golden Arm*. This was initially banned by the Maryland State Board of Censors but later released by the Court of Appeals with the ruling that the film did not advocate the use of narcotics and was likely to act as a deterrent. However, a 30-second scene showing Frank Sinatra preparing heroin in a spoon was required to be deleted (Grazia and Newman 1982). Within the British Board Film of Classification (2000) publication *Sense and Sensibilities: Public Opinion & the BBFC Guidelines*, a small majority (52 per cent) agreed that films should be allowed to portray drug use in a realistic manner although there were mixed views regarding the portrayal of method. Calls have been made for film-makers to demonstrate a social responsibility in the messages and themes they are portraying with anti-drug portrayals being regarded as preferable to pro-drug ones (Valenti 2000). It is a point that could be debated with regard to the receipt of film content by different audience members using as illustration the film *Trainspotting* which could be viewed either as a glamorisation of drug culture or as a powerful anti-drug message.

Despite there being few references made concerning the portrayal of mental health content it is perhaps surprising to note that in 1928 the BBFC wanted to ban Robert Wiene's *Cabinet of Dr Caligari*, afraid that the asylum scenes might upset people in the cinema audience who had relatives in mental health hospitals (Film Education 2005). Other films with mental health content that have met with the BBFC's disapproval include Roman Polanski's *Repulsion* and Samuel Fuller's *Shock Corridor*. The BBFC's consultant, Dr Stephen Black, expressed concerns about *Repulsion*'s fantasy rape scenes (shown as part of Catherine Deneuve's delusional and paranoid mental state) although the film was passed uncut. *Shock Corridor* however was banned in 1963 for suggesting that residency in a mental hospital could induce insanity. The BBFC refused to grant a certificate saying that depiction of conditions in an American mental asylum bore no comparison with hospitals in Britain. It

was also stated that the film might frighten cinemagoers who had relatives in mental institutions (Mathews 1994). This is an interesting response although the emergent views about the detrimental effects of long-term institutional care expressed by Goffman (1961), Barton (1976) and Scheff (1974) are perhaps far more alarming than the images depicted in film. What is not lost, though, is the degree of sensitivity and concern being demonstrated by the BBFC in these instances concerning the potential negative impact of mental health themes being depicted. However the laudability of this type of response is let down by the overall level of inconsistency shown as many other misleading and sometimes appalling examples, such as *Me, Myself and Irene*, are passed unchallenged. There has long been a culture of depicting the disabled and mentally ill in a negative and unproductive light and such destructively stigmatising messages can in the long term prove exceedingly damaging to those with mental health problems and their families. What is required is a much more direct focus being applied within the regulatory guidelines concerning the topic of mental illness.

The historical picture

Film has been described by some as a mirror, whereby the images of insanity presented bear a unique relationship with fluctuations in psychological theory and practice (Flemming and Manvell 1994). The extent to which cinematic images either reflect societal attitudes or in some cases create them is open to debate. Certainly, there are some very powerful and impactful film depictions that still resonate many years after their first screening. The film *Psycho*, for instance, has left us with a negative term of reference and association that is still very much in evidence within everyday speech and newspaper headlines (Welch and Racine 1999).

Starting with early cinematic releases at the beginning of the twentieth century we can see examples such as *The Escaped Lunatic* (1904), *Dr Dippy's Sanitarium* (1906), or even the Stan Laurel film *Nuts in May* (1917). The titles alone present a very disparaging and ridiculing view creating the feeling that 'mad' people belong in institutions. This was an era when the population of institutions was on the increase, maintaining the largely held view that incarceration was beneficial both to society as well as the mentally ill. These early portrayals depicted the mentally ill either as monsters or as comically insane seemingly little bothered about the feelings or experiences of those concerned.

The 1930s and 1940s provided a contrast to the preceding era with a degree of ridicule extending towards those treating mental illness and the portrayals were often of comic figures treating sane individuals. In the 1940s and 1950s Hollywood turned its attention to the social problem film (e.g. *The Man with the Golden Arm* and drug addiction) covering many different issues and including themes relating to mental illness (Gabbard and Gabbard 1999). The late 1950s and early 1960s could be seen as the 'Golden Age' with an idealised view of psychiatry being represented. It reflected the growing conviction that

psychiatrists were the authoritative voices of reason, adjustment and well-being. It was also interestingly an era that heralded the introduction of a major new product within the domain of mental health care, namely pheno-thiazine medication, thus further strengthening the power and authority afforded the medical practitioner. The mid- to late 1960s and the 1970s was denoted by Gabbard and Gabbard (1999) as the 'Fall from Grace', corresponding with a growing disillusionment with psychiatric care as the detrimental effects of institutional care became more apparent. These aspects are clearly outlined in a number of films including Milos Forman's *One Flew over the Cuckoo's Nest* and Mark Robson's *Bedlam*.

The shift towards community care and the enhanced visibility of mental health problems in society has culminated in the growing trend of showing the viewer more of an individual's felt experience of mental health problems. Films such as *A Beautiful Mind* and *Iris* present us with characters with whom viewers can readily form an emotional attachment, feeling compassion and sorrow for their sense of loss and experience of fragmenting worlds. It is a welcome change from other contemporary films that perpetuate stereo-typical notions of the mentally ill as violent (Hannibal Lecter series) or schizophrenia as a split personality (*Me, Myself and Irene*).

The message

This section addresses two core themes, that of the cinematic depiction of mental illness as well as the portrayal of treatment. The ways in which mental illness is depicted within the medium of film can be viewed via a number of different categories. For the purposes of this book the chosen areas are *the mentally ill* as the killer, the afflicted genius and the comic/eccentric. These are adapted from the themes portrayed in Radio 4's *Back Row* programme (4th May 2002) concerning the portrayal of mental illness and learning disabilities in the cinema.

The killer

Cinematic history contains countless examples of portraying the mentally ill as killers. There is an extra chilling edge added to the mentally ill killer as a consequence of their uncertain state of mind, and they are often shown as being deranged, frenzied or detached. It seems that over the decades, sub-sequent films each go a stage further in dispatching their victims in an ever more grisly fashion, with increased carnage and ferocity being depicted. These characters range in presentations from those whose altered psycho-logical state is merely seen as a transient phase to others who are deemed hopelessly insane and who will never recover, for example the psychopathic killer Michael Myers in the film *Halloween*.

The continued association between violence and mental illness is one that is heavily influenced by its popularity as well as the enhanced level of

excitement or drama it adds. Many of these types of film attract large audiences and sometimes even critical acclaim, responses that help to ensure their continued appearance (Wahl 1995). The ongoing success of 'slasher' films perhaps relates to a societal desire for 'monsters' and the cathartic needs which are met through watching certain films. This is highlighted by Wolfenstein and Leites who state that: 'It is a perennial function of drama and literature to present images of what violent impulses, usually restrained in life, might look like if more fully expressed' (Wolfenstein and Leites 1970: 175). We are thus able to quench our curiosity and confront the 'monsters' that lurk in society while in what is perceived to be a safe and contained environment. At the end of the film we can leave the cinema or switch off the television and return to a feeling of secure normality. A problem with this is that some of these disturbing images and associations remain with us. As demonstrated through the process of classical conditioning and the reinforcement of associated stimuli (Pavlov 1958), the continued link between mental health problems and violence only serve to perpetuate the dangerousness myth. As Byrne (2001a) states, many films reinforce two misconceptions, mental illness as violence and the belief that every mentally ill person harbours one 'great dark secret'. Despite all the educative messages to the contrary that the general public are exposed to, this continued association leaves the viewer with a general feeling of unease. One consequence of this is a desire of some to place distance (physically and psychologically) between themselves and those with mental health problems. It is not surprising therefore to hear of the opposition by certain local communities towards plans for the placing of those with mental health problems within their midst, with the misassumption that they pose a significant threat of danger.

A number of grossly misrepresented facts permeate our collective body of knowledge and become integrated to a large extent within our culture and language. This is illustrated by Welch and Racine (1999) who point out that the term 'psycho' has become a byword for terrifying, homicidal impulses, or the unpredictability of a deranged mind. Cinema creates a number of lasting and dramatic impressions that are readily accepted by those who wish to add extra spice to reported events as shown in the newspaper headline '*Silence of the Lambs* Maniac Freed to Kill' (*Today*). It seems that the power of these images is such that they extend beyond the confines of their original film. The stereotypical killer may be ridiculous, farcical and totally exaggerated although some such as Hannibal Lecter and Freddy Krueger have managed to achieve a wide degree of popularity, even a type of cult hero status.

It is interesting to note the variation in type of character selected to represent the mentally deranged killer and their relationship to the victims. Two broad types of representation include the murderer as somebody known to the victim and someone who is not. The first category features the unsettling representation of the killer who is already in our midst. It is the individual who is trusted and liked and perhaps the least suspected by their unfortunate victim. It may be a friend ('Good old Bob' – the serial killer in *Frenzy*); the

family man who goes berserk (as with Jack Nicholson in *The Shining*), or even a trusted health care professional (the cannibalistic and nightmarish Hannibal Lecter in *The Silence of the Lambs* or Michael Caine as the murderous transvestite in *Dressed to Kill*). The impact of these types of portrayal is the sense that no matter how rational or well-presented those with mental health problems seem, there is a feeling they may perhaps be a 'ticking time bomb', slowly winding up towards their murderous and frenzied explosion. This illustrates the insidious nature of stigmatisation whereby certain views and connections are strongly held irrespective of any messages that are presented to the contrary. It highlights the feeling of unsettlement and mistrust which can be attached to those who are unfortunate enough to be labelled mentally ill, even family members and friends who, pre-diagnosis, were regarded in a wholly different light.

The second type of categorisation signifies the threat posed should our safe and secure world come into contact, however chance or random, with those who are mentally unstable. This meeting however fleeting is portrayed in a number of films (e.g. *Enduring Love, Play Misty for Me* or *Fatal Attraction*) as having murderous consequences. Other films depict the random slaying of whoever happens, unluckily, to be in the wrong place at the wrong time. These killers often use excessive savagery and ferocity in the dispatch of their hapless victims such as that seen in *Natural Born Killers* or *The Texas Chainsaw Massacre*. Despite educative messages to the contrary, such as that provided by the Department of Health's (1999) Safer Services report, the desire for security and safety leaves a number of individuals desiring a sense of distance from the mentally ill.

Afflicted genius

This is a fascinating category as it engages strong sympathetic feelings and affords opportunities to get closer to the individual concerned. To a large extent it depends upon the way in which they are portrayed as, on one side of the spectrum, we have the deranged, power-mad individuals, whereas, on the other, are the struggling genius types hampered by their mental health state. The former group are shown as obsessively driven towards their goal, be it the creation of life (*Frankenstein, The Island of Dr Moreau*) or the striving for power (as for instance with most of the James Bond villains). The more sensitive portrayal centres on the talented individual who has become handicapped by their fragmenting state of mind. The feeling evoked in the audience might be one of pity for their plight or a real sense of loss for their declining abilities. The core theme here is of the central figure striving to cope with their affliction. A number of recent films have created a sense of attraction by focusing upon 'based upon a true story' scripts and by choosing charismatic and popular actors to play the main parts. All of these aspects help to create a real sense of emotional connectedness in the viewer and a liking for the main characters. The '*real story*' theme means that their talent is not simply

imagined and is an approach that stirs stronger feelings of sympathy within their audience. For example, in the film *Iris* we follow the writer Iris Murdoch on her painfully distressing journey as she loses what is most important to her and her prodigious talent: words. One scene painfully depicts Iris struggling through a cognitive assessment, unable to name even the simplest of items such as a spoon or a tennis racquet. It is a heartbreaking and tragic process to witness, and reflects a process that is also played out in other films featuring gifted individuals as seen with the brilliant mathematician John Nash (*A Beautiful Mind*).

From a cynical point of view these films might be criticised for their lack of realism regarding the ordinary person who is most represented within mental health problem statistics. Taking a different stance we might consider Landesman's remark regarding the disability film *The Sea Inside* that: 'Somewhere in the world there must be a disabled person who is boring. Someone who has no talent for writing, maths or science; who is not brave and witty, but has bad breath and cracks terrible jokes' (Landesman 2005: 19). Obviously this could also refer to the mentally ill, many of whom do not possess a remarkable talent. The focus upon genius or gifted ability, while helping to distance a film from the many made-for-television 'true life stories', is perhaps the prime factor being offered in terms of providing the audience with a vehicle for acceptance. These individuals' special talents transgress their fragile mental health states and allow them as a consequence to be better accommodated by the audience. A scene in the film *Shine* gives a very vivid example of this as the shabby and dishevelled David Helfgott shuffles into a posh bar and moves through an unsettled crowd towards the piano. The jeering calls do not deter him and a few chords into his playing of Rachmaninov's *Third Piano Concerto* brings about an almost hushed reverence. His outstanding performance is greeted with loud applause and he is promptly installed as their resident pianist, all previous doubts about him apparently dismissed. In a sense his talented genius transforms and reclassifies his mentally ill status into that of the more tolerable and accepted one of 'eccentric'. It reflects the criticism levelled at this film that: 'If mentally ill, you can only make it in society, or are acceptable if you are a genius, or famous or on the path to fame' (Rosen and Walter 2000: 239). Likewise, John Nash (*A Beautiful Mind*), because of his prodigious mathematics talent, is accommodated and accepted by many on campus despite his increasingly bizarre and erratic behaviour.

There is obviously a gulf between the experience of mental illness depicted in these types of films and the reality felt by many so-called 'ordinary' people. The showcasing of a talented individual provides the audience member perhaps with an added level of appeal. This is complemented by the intriguing and compelling focus upon that person's fragmented mental health state. It is an issue raised by Rosen and Walter (2000) who state that if you are mentally ill, and talented, the audience will only take an interest if they can gawk voyeuristically at your bizarre antics, no matter how interested they are in your talent. This statement illustrates further the attractiveness of this dramatic

subject matter to both film-makers and audience members and reflects one of the prime reasons why a person's illness is given so much prominence over other aspects of their life which are largely ignored.

Despite the problems inherent in this type of film, there is a valuable opportunity afforded to establish a degree of understanding regarding the lived experience of mental health problems. The biographical focus enables us as viewers to follow the person showcased and develop an interest and even a feeling of caring about their life. John Nash's desperate struggles, for example, convey the serious impact his mental health state has on his ability to function and the distressing consequences for his family. The close relationship formed between audience member and principal character means that the viewer will have specific feelings aroused by the events unfolding before them on the screen. It might involve an appreciation of the sense of fear and frustration felt or simply an understanding of the alienation and rejection experienced by many of those encountering mental health problems and their families.

Comic/eccentric

It is evident that in most instances within the comic/eccentric categorisation the principal focus is upon entertaining the audience to the detriment of actually highlighting the reality of the experience being portrayed. Perhaps one of the crucial factors relating to the comedic portrayal of mental illness concerns the audience's engagement with characters and whether they are laughing with them or at them. On the negative side, viewers are provided with opportunities to be amused and entertained by the bizarre and 'clownish' antics of the mentally ill with many stereotypes being employed. These depictions generally present characters for the audience to laugh *at*, an approach that does not foster feelings of concern for their welfare. On the positive side, there are some engaging portrayals featuring characters who are on the whole liked by the audience. A core difference here relates to the enticement of the audience to laugh *with* screen characters, in a number of instances recognising aspects familiar in their own lives.

One type of depiction in this category is of the harmless eccentric, something in sharp contrast to that of the 'mentally ill as killer' classification. Two vivid examples of this can be seen with James Stewart as Elwood P. Dowd, the jovial and hallucinating alcoholic (*Harvey*), and Uncle Teddy, who believes he is Teddy Roosevelt (*Arsenic and Old Lace*). The characters illustrated here are not people to be scared of, as with the 'killer' category, but rather to be pitied, tolerated or amused by. The pursuit of incarceration for each of the examples raised here are less about removing them for the protection of others but seem to be more generated by feelings of benevolence. Both Elwood and Teddy are reasonably well tolerated and accepted by their families despite their fairly unusual behaviours. Elwood has an imaginary friend, a large white rabbit named Harvey, whom only he can see, whereas Teddy

believes he is the president of the United States and is busy building the Panama Canal in his basement. The insistence that Teddy is 'unwell' and will be 'happy at Happydale' seems more farcical because it appears as if the entire Brewster family is in need of help. The film *Arsenic and Old Lace* provides an interesting collection of representations of madness with both the comic killer and the harmless eccentric being portrayed alongside each other. As well as the aforementioned Uncle Teddy, Cary Grant puts in an exhaustively manic performance as Mortimer Brewster, another apparently harmless eccentric. On the other hand, the comedic killer is depicted by the surgically disfigured brother Jonathan, a murderer on the run with his plastic surgeon sidekick (played by Peter Lorre), as well as Aunts Abby and Martha who have been poisoning gentleman visitors and burying them in the cellar. It is perhaps made more ludicrous with the singling out of Teddy, on whom the family's madness is projected, as the sole person in need of treatment. This wonderfully illustrates the process of displacement as seen with the old asylum culture whereby certain individuals were designated as mentally ill and removed from their families for treatment.

The comedic representation is not always a benign one as it also offers up offensive characterisations or portrayals that evoke a sense of ridicule and disparagement. It is here that the entertainment needs of the audience are placed securely before any considerations being shown concerning the mentally ill. A prime example of this is the film *Me, Myself and Irene* which shows the character played by Jim Carrey struggling between his distinct states of wellness and illness. There are many classic stereotypes being played out here including those of the depiction of schizophrenia as a split personality. Charlie represents the mentally well state and is a caring although submissive person, whereas Hank, the mentally ill one, is loud, abrasive and abusive. It is a film that has been largely criticised by mental health groups such as Mind (2000) for its harmful reinforcement of a number of stereotypes concerning mental illness. This film differs significantly from those illustrated above in that there is nothing likeable about Jim Carrey's Hank. While the audience might laugh at the absurdity of the scenes being relayed, it is actually a disturbing and deeply offensive portrayal that does much to harm society's developing attitudes and awareness towards the mentally ill.

A further aspect engaging the audience in a laughing *with* response concerns the depiction of the neurotic. This representation is perhaps the closest and most easily identifiable representation for many audience members. It presents a form less associated with severe psychiatric disturbance and something more aligned to the quirkiness of individual characters. To a large extent those centred upon are likeable characters with their neuroses providing the audience with moments for amusement as well as sympathetic concern. A prime example here can be seen with the angst ridden character played by Woody Allen in a number of his films such as *Annie Hall* and *Play it Again Sam*. Another good example is reflected by the ridiculous sense of incongruity provided by the film *Analyze This* as the neurotic mobster boss (Robert

DeNiro) seeks treatment for anxiety. It presents a stark contrast when compared with the usual screen portrayal of a mobster as fearless and ruthless. What is interesting about many of the neurotic representations is the sense of connectedness fostered with the audience member. As with Woody Allen's agitated mannerisms and ceaseless pacing before landing a date in the film *Annie Hall*, it is perhaps easy for many to identify with the excruciating intensity felt when asking somebody out on a first date. Although the intensity of experience might be different to that being depicted on the screen, the audience are still offered a number of points of engagement whereby difficulties and problems shown are understood.

Audience response

The categories listed above of killer, afflicted genius and comic/eccentric all lead the viewer towards a distinctly different way of relating to the mentally ill. First, we can regard the depiction of the psychopathic killer as leading the viewer towards a position of fear and unsettlement. Second, the categorisation of afflicted genius serves to engage pitying and sympathetic reactions. This is mainly evoked by highlighting a person's plight and the sense of the tragedy regarding what they have lost or are consequently unable to do. The third categorisation of comic/eccentric engenders feelings of amusement through laughing directly *at* characters or *with* them. The implications here for learning about mental health issues are to a large degree dependent upon the type of characterisations that individuals are exposed to as each has the capacity to evoke very different feelings and attitudes. Individuals will therefore be drawn towards certain responses and understanding by virtue of which genres they select for viewing although further reinforcers will also be obtained from other media sources that individuals are exposed to. Particular characterisations such as 'the killer' could be regarded as having a greater influence than the others because of the fear factor involved and the general absence of likeable traits. This is to some degree countered by the latter two groups which on the whole include the more likeable and identifiable representations, more of which are certainly needed.

Mental health treatment

Cinematic history contains a wide array of examples demonstrating mental health treatment and the individuals who offer it. There is on the whole an overrepresentation of talking cures and hypnosis within films and an under-representation of pharmacotherapy or medical approaches such as electro-convulsive therapy (ECT), unless included for dramatic social control effects or as a form of punishment. These depictions appear polarised and from the earliest days of cinema, films either idealised or degraded the mental health profession (Greenberg and Gabbard 1990). This may vary from the sense of awe and omnipotence afforded to psychiatrists in their so-called

golden era (Gabbard and Gabbard 1999) to a general discreditation through the serving up of harsh, uncaring and controlling approaches. It is a view supported by Clare who states that: 'Psychiatrists as seen through the eyes of filmmakers are at one and the same time omnipotent and useless, progressive and reactionary, compassionate and destructive, perceptive and blind' (Clare 2001: ch. 2, sec. 4). Alternatively, this variation can be summed up in the categories identified by Schneider (1987) of Dr Dippy, Dr Evil and Dr Wonderful. A further issue concerns the confusion as to the background of those who are actually providing care because of the tendency to merge together the different professions portrayed (Tam 2002). This point is further highlighted by Gabbard and Gabbard (1992) who state that Hollywood portrayals often do not distinguish between psychiatrists, psychoanalysts and psychologists.

The confusing plethora of messages found within the medium of film reflects that presented by other media providers. The type of material exposed to and the way in which it is portrayed will no doubt influence expectations and feelings about treatment. As indicated by Gabbard and Gabbard: 'Psychiatric patients come to the consulting room with expectations of how a psychiatrist should behave based on what they see in the movies' (Gabbard and Gabbard 1999: 177). Dependent therefore on which films have been seen, individuals will have very different feelings about mental health treatment. This is demonstrated by the extreme range of examples on offer as there are, for instance, the oppressive and regimented care as depicted in *One Flew Over The Cuckoo's Nest*, the paternalistic asylum approach in *Quills*, the comic/ ineffective approach in *The Couch Trip*, the sensitive, tireless and determined help in *Awakenings* and the murderous, psychopathic approach in *The Silence of the Lambs* or *Dressed to Kill*. The impact that film can have upon attitudes towards mental illness was illustrated by Domino's (1983) study concerning the film *One Flew over the Cuckoo's Nest* that observed a less positive attitude being demonstrated by those who had seen the film. Although this study was questioned by Secker and Platt (1996) because of what they identified as research design weaknesses it nonetheless raises some very important questions concerning the potential impact of film upon resultant attitudes. This is illustrated by Tim Lott in his autobiographical work *A Scent of Dried Roses* where he states that: 'The idea of tablets and treatments remains beyond the pale; they [his parents] too have seen *One Flew over the Cuckoo's Nest*' (Lott 1997: 238). It is easy therefore to understand the extra sense of trepidation felt when seeking care or even avoiding it altogether given the depersonalising and brutal treatment regime portrayed very powerfully in this particular film.

The positive side of care is illustrated by appealing role models like the psychologist Sean Maguire (Robin Williams) in *Good Will Hunting* or Dr Berger (Judd Hirsch) in the film *Ordinary People*. They provide us with a glimpse of the sort of carer we would perhaps hope to encounter if we were feeling vulnerable and in need of support as both of them present as

jargon-free, approachable, caring and unpretentious. Films containing positive and caring role models who are properly able to connect with those they are treating stand as a positive advertisement for mental health care. They also help to challenge the wealth of negative examples accessible and are encouraging for those who are uncertain about seeking help. While presenting us with a very desirous image of carers who actually do seem to care, potential problems may be caused for individuals whose own experience falls short of any subsequently held expectations. This is especially illustrated by Clare's (2001) observation that positive role models tend towards idealised interpretations and include the common portrayal of psychoanalysts as an amalgam between Sherlock Holmes and Sigmund Freud. Another unrealistic representation is the tireless activist who is prepared to risk all in the interests of their patients, a portrayal strongly conveyed in the film *Awakenings*. It follows the familiar tradition of the police action film depicting the hero improbably risking his badge and his life in the pursuit of justice. The image of the idealised carer is contrasted by a number of examples portraying them in a far from perfect light. As Gabbard (2001) indicates, the denigration of psychiatrists neutralises something of their perceived omniscience and shows they have the same human frailties as everyone else. This can be seen in a number of films such as *High Anxiety* or *The Couch Trip* where it becomes questionable as to who is most in need of therapy, those giving it or those receiving it.

The screen image can be extremely evocative and engaging as shown in the final cathartic breakthrough and tearful hug with Dr Berger in *Ordinary People* where the guilt held over Conrad's brother's death is finally laid to rest. The cathartic breakthrough is usually included in scenes towards the end of films and is the culmination of a difficult and at times fraught process. A criticism that could be levelled at such scenes involves the over-dramatisation of the therapeutic process and the presentation of a number of inaccuracies. Such misrepresentations not only prove confusing for those receiving care but can also lead to therapists encouraging cathartic interventions when it is not what the client has come for (Jinks 2000). Another common cinematic portrayal is the sudden recovery of repressed memories, an aspect recognised by Freud as in itself not being curative. As Gabbard and Gabbard state: 'If filmmakers have studied the history of the psychoanalytic movement, it would seem that they stopped reading Freud's work at this particular historical point' (Gabbard and Gabbard 1999: 28). It seems therefore that film-makers are more concerned with enticing and engaging their viewers with dramatic scenes than in presenting accuracy. This is particularly illustrated by *The Three Faces of Eve* (1957), where it remains a mystery for viewers as to how finally remembering childhood trauma actually cures her illness.

Although it is heartening to note the number of films depicting mental health care in a positive light they are perhaps outnumbered by those carrying a negative message. Physical treatments in particular are much maligned providing the film-maker with opportunities for visually dramatic scenes. One

such method is ECT which, although initially shown in films such as the 1948 film *The Snake Pit* as a severe but helpful remedy for personal distress, has become progressively portrayed as a more negative and cruel treatment, leaving the impression of a brutal and abusive treatment that has little therapeutic benefit (McDonald and Walter 2001; Hodgkinson 1986). This is evidenced within the film *One Flew over the Cuckoo's Nest* where a crowd of people await McMurphy as he enters the treatment room suggesting to the viewer that there is no room for refusal. The scene in itself makes this particular treatment method appear cruel and uncaring, more concerned with issues of social control than of benevolent care. The themes of control and punishment are strongly reinforced throughout this film ending with McMurphy being lobotomised as a final attempt to control his 'disruptive' behaviour. The problem with such powerfully negative stereotypes of care is that it may lead those seeking or receiving mental health care to expect that they will somehow also be violated or abused (Gabbard and Gabbard 1999). Even though individuals are also exposed to other sources of information, examples such as these convey very powerful messages that can be hard to overcome.

Lastly, it is worth mentioning here a popular theme among film-makers, that of an individual recovering through the power of love (Byrne 2001b). It is a theme occurring in numerous films such as *Crazy People, As Good As It Gets* and *Shine* providing salvation for an individual who is struggling with issues of mental distress. The suggestion that love can be sufficiently powerful to overcome one's psychological difficulties could in some instances be regarded as trivialising the serious nature of mental illness. It does however help to stress a crucial component of the therapeutic relationship that relates to the Rogerian concept of feeling connected with and cared for (Rogers 1961). It also reflects the recognition that feelings of separation, disconnectedness and isolation have a significant impact upon one's mental well-being (Maslow 1971; Kitwood 1997; Social Exclusion Unit 2003).

Making sense of film

An interesting concept here is the influence that movie images have upon our understanding and subsequent perception of mental illness. Norden (1994), focusing upon physical disability in the cinema, illustrates how the movie industry has perpetuated or initiated a number of stereotypes. These stereotypes are regarded as being so durable and pervasive that they have become mainstream society's perception of disabled people and have obscured if not outright supplanted disabled people's perception of themselves. The immense chasm that exists therefore between disabled and screen counterparts is clearly also applicable to a mental health perspective which is reinforced through numerous stereotypes. As Kolker states: '[film] substitutes images and sounds for "real" experience, and with those images and sounds communicates to us and manipulates particular feelings, ideas and perspectives on reality' (Kolker 1988: 14). It can therefore be difficult to determine which aspects viewers are

exposed to on the screen actually reflect the real facts regarding mental illness. Further discrimination is provided by viewers who bring their own individual perspective from which they interpret the inputted stimuli. While producers and film-makers might be seen as encoding a single 'meaningful message' to be read by viewers, a sense of polysemic or textual openness applies so that texts are open to more than one possible reading (Moores 1993). There are a variety of factors affecting a viewer's perception here including their prior knowledge and experience that lead to certain viewing perspectives being adopted.

Another core factor concerns the audience member's type of engagement with film and their ability to suspend reality. As Armes states:

> When we watch a film, we make a conscious decision to enter a world of fiction and make believe . . . and place ourselves under the illusory guidance of a maker of narratives. We are not duped or deceived in the sense that we believe we are still in the world of everyday reality, but we do desire to have our emotions aroused and our thoughts provoked.
>
> (Armes 1994: 48)

Allen (1995) refers to this process as *projective illusion* in that viewers know that what they are watching is only an impression of reality yet actively participate in the illusion that cinema affords. This is further argued by Lothe (2000) in the view that fictional film shows us an illusory real world that resembles to the point of confusion the world we know ourselves, a world into which we are free to peep for a couple of hours without participating. The core thread being highlighted here is that of an active spectator voluntarily entering the film world as opposed to a passive viewer having images imposed upon them. It also addresses the notion of a *conscious spectator*, an individual who is able to determine what is real and what isn't. Some of the less obvious fantasy-based material may be harder to determine as manufactured reality. This is especially true when relating to attitudinal qualities or stereotypical content. The problems are caused here when viewers do not have a contrasting point of reality from which to question or challenge what they are exposed to within a particular film. For example, the statistics and facts concerning mentally ill killers do not tie in with the messages being offered by their psychopathic screen counterparts. It is a point made by Gabbard and Gabbard (1999) who indicate that without knowing what the customary behaviour is, the audience has no standard by which to judge the appropriateness of what it witnesses on the screen. In general, the audience member is offered a variety of stereotypical portrayals that fit the popular view concerning mental illness. They are therefore not alerted in many instances to look for different interpretations. An illustration of this can be given with the Necker cube (Figure 7.2), whereby the position of the grey dot changes from the front to the rear of the cube. If not alerted to this fact the viewer can easily miss this dynamic, seeing only one interpretation and not looking further for others.

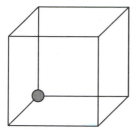

Figure 7.2 The Necker cube.

A further issue here concerns the way in which viewers engage on an emotional level with the medium of film. This is highlighted by Kolker (1988: 14) who states that particular feelings, ideas and perspectives on reality are manipulated through the illusory images that viewers are exposed to. It is certainly the case that what we might challenge on a rational level can be overtaken by what we feel on an emotional one. A classic example of this is the radio broadcast in 1938 by Orson Welles of *War of the Worlds*. The illusory sense of reality created was so powerful that a number of listeners fled their homes for fear of an incoming Martian invasion. The engagement of powerful emotions and subsequent influences upon a recipient's behaviour can also be reflected upon with regard to Brown's (2000) illustration of imitative behaviour in homicides relating to the film *Natural Born Killers* and Russian Roulette deaths relating to the *Deerhunter*. Another consideration is the fact that the sense of trepidation and fear experienced as Freddy Krueger (*Nightmare on Elm Street*) and Michael Myers (*Halloween*) dispatch their victims in grisly fashion can be hard to shake off. It leaves the viewer feeling uneasy and uncertain concerning the real violence potential of the mentally ill, a point not helped by the steady reinforcement through the tabloid media and television drama.

Attraction (connecting with mental health issues)

Of major significance here is the way in which we engage with mental health issues and those portrayed as having mental health problems who generally are not depicted as likable or appealing to the viewer. Our ability to connect with and engage with screen characters is influenced by a number of features that create feelings of attraction. These are illustrated by Hoffner and Cantor (1991) as:

- Liking
- Perceived similarity
- Desire to be like a character

These factors relate to the desirability of the personal characteristics

associated with an individual and relate to those that hold positive attributes, are kind and helpful, display positive social and non-verbal behaviours, are successful in coping with threats, and are competent and resourceful. The concept of *liking* is important as it plays a significant part in the type of emotional response evoked in the viewer such as feelings of concern for their welfare. It also engages in the viewer a tendency to feel similar emotions to those experienced on screen (Zillmann 1980). The cinematic world is littered with examples of both likeable and unlikeable mentally ill characters although it is predominantly the latter who seem to be portrayed. Some of those who are liked by viewers can be quite surprising as they even include anti-hero types such as Hannibal Lecter or the murderous Jack Torrance (Jack Nicholson) in *The Shining*. It is heartening, though, to note the greater use of charismatic and attractive stars such as Russell Crowe or Judy Dench who provide the audience with attractive mentally ill role models, a far cry from the stereotypical choices that have proliferated in films of the past. The qualities and characteristics afforded individuals seen on screen are influenced by their perceived attractiveness to the viewer. This is a point addressed by Hatfield and Sprecher (1986) who indicate that physically attractive people are seen as possessing more socially desirable personality traits than unattractive individuals. It is important therefore to present the viewer with a greater number of positive characterisations, thereby helping overall to present a more balanced representation including the portrayal of mentally ill people maintaining relationships, looking *normal* and being engaged with *ordinary* activities.

The sense of engagement with film characters is also strongly influenced by the degree to which we as viewers are able to catch a glimpse of that person's inner world. There are two distinct perspectives that can be taken including:

- *Inside looking out* (internal viewing)
- *Outside looking in* (external viewing)

The first example, *inside looking out*, takes the viewer into the mind of the screen character, offering them a sense of how the world appears from their distinct perspective, whereas the second one, *outside looking in*, locates the viewer firmly at a position external to the character. The ability of film to engage with both of these perspectives is outlined by Rothman who states that: 'Film is a medium limited to surfaces, to the outer, the visible . . . [and yet film is] a medium of mysterious depths, of the inner, the invisible' (Rothman 1988: xv).

There are a number of films presenting directly to us the altered reality of those experiencing mental health problems. An example is the 1960s film *Repulsion* where we are led progressively into a world that is becoming more fragmented and disturbed. It is portrayed very vividly with the hallucinatory imagery of cracks appearing accompanied by strange distorted

sounds. As viewers, we are led into experiencing something of Carol's (Catherine DeNeueve) confused world which proves a disconcerting and unnerving experience. Another film, *A Beautiful Mind*, takes the audience member on a journey whereby it becomes unclear as to what is reality and what isn't. It is only later in the film that viewers become aware of the fact that a collection of characters they have been watching are in fact a product of Nash's hallucinatory perspective and are not seen by other people in the film. Ron Howard's direction of this material is cleverly and sensitively handled helping to bring about various feelings in the audience such as confusion, frustration and loss, no doubt similar to those felt by Nash himself. The importance of these types of engagement is the sense of entering into the empathic process of seeing the world from another person's perspective. According to Carl Rogers, accurate empathic understanding means that an individual is completely at home in the universe of another person, sensing that person's inner world of private personal meanings as if it were their own (Kirschenbaum and Henderson 1990). When relating this process to film characters, it is clear that it is a process that will not always be a comfortable one for the viewer and that it will at times prove unsettling and disturbing, especially where a distorted sense of reality is being presented.

The distorted world, however, is not always presented as frightening and destructive as evidenced by the film *Don Juan de Marco*. Here it is depicted as something preferable to the stale and restrictive state that marks reality for a number of people. As viewers we are invited to engage with the fantasy created by Don Juan's (Johnny Depp) world and, along with the psychiatrist Dr Mickler (Marlon Brando), have an opportunity of appraising our own lives and considering the benefits offered by the fantasy existence. This can be considered with regard to Flemming and Manvell's statement that:

> 'Madness . . . provokes fundamental questions about our place in, and understanding of the world. It makes us look more closely at our definitions of the nature of things and at our expectations of what we should follow. Madness, therefore has profound implications for our interpretation of ourselves and of our environment and eventually leads us to question who we are and what we are.'
>
> (Flemming and Manvell 1985: 17)

Film as a medium has much to offer and can provide an extremely impactful engagement with various characters, themes and concepts. Because of this, film has been used for both therapeutic as well as educative purposes. Chaudhuri (2002) illustrates the notion of *Cinematherapy* as a form of self-help in that identifying with characters in films provides the viewer with inspiration as well as opportunities for validation. It relates to the process of vicarious learning through watching someone else encounter similar emotions and experiences. The *film as therapy* theme is further illustrated by Gabbard and Gabbard (1999) who indicate that movies might serve as a

'once-removed' analogue allowing a person to express transference longings that are difficult to verbalise, for example with a phrase such as 'I liked the closeness between therapist and patient in the film'. This makes it therefore an attractive point of reference that can be brought into the therapeutic environment and discussed between client and therapist thereby aiding understanding and insight development. A further application of film is seen in teaching where a comprehension of complex dynamics and issues can be better explored through the use of cinematic examples. This is illustrated by Frisch who asserts that: 'There is no better way to understand nursing clients and their varied psychiatric conditions and diagnoses than by entering into their lives through reading literature or by turning down the lights and experiencing the magic world of film' (Frisch 2001: 782).

There are also a number of educational benefits that can be gained by health care professionals through making film recommendations to students as a means of developing understanding about specific mental health topics (Hyler and Morre 1996; Bhugra 2003). These aspects can be understood in relation to Bandura's (1986) Social Learning Theory in that a complex range of issues can be more easily made sense of by observing them through the behaviour of others. This highlights some of the beneficial qualities offered by the medium of film which, combined with a further development of more realistic and less stigmatising portrayals and a greater involvement with mental health advocates, points the way forward.

Conclusion

As illustrated above, the medium of film impacts upon the viewer through a variety of modes such as imagery, narrative and sound. These, at times, engage their audience in very powerful ways and for a film's duration may deter the actual realisation that what is being viewed is fiction or fantasy. This highlights the potential for engagement with characters, storylines and experiences that in many cases last longer than the ninety minutes or so of a films' screening. The film *Psycho* for example, directed in Hitchcock's inimitable style, has provided a particular way of comprehending and relating to mental illness that enhances our instinctive and primitive fears about difference or the unknown. The association of madness with violence and unpredictability permeates the collective understanding about mental health issues and despite countless heath promotion initiatives over the years, survives as an overall assumption, fuelled by tabloid headlines and colloquial language ('*Psycho*') heard within the media or by one's peers. The cinematic world perhaps in a number of instances is only reflecting the comparative societal view of mental illness as can be seen by looking at historical examples. It does though have the capacity to promote better depictions and views of mental health as demonstrated by films such as *A Beautiful Mind* and *Iris*. This reflects a desire and interest by the public to learn and understand more about the theme of mental illness. As with *A Beautiful Mind*,

there may be a touch of voyeurism behind its appeal, although the positive messages being conveyed (attractive role model, the overall sense of survival and conveyance of experience from a felt perspective) all help to construct an overall message that is better suited to educate and develop real understanding about mental illness. While the destructive, psycho-killer type of film will obviously still be produced, the more high-profile positive examples there are to challenge this and reduce the distance felt between the audience member and the topic of mental illness the better.

8   Television

Introduction

One of the core issues concerning the power of television as a communicating medium is the ready accessibility on a daily basis of programmes targeting all interest and age groups. Indeed the range and scope of programmes seem almost limitless, boosted further in recent years with the addition of cable and satellite television providers. There appears to be something for everybody with specific time schedules and programme types geared towards different audiences. There are numerous factors playing a part in how we interact with TV and the subsequent understanding taken away. It may depend to a large extent upon whether we are seeking to be entertained or educated, our levels of interest, as well as the type of programme genre we are watching. Our viewing habits will also play a part with programmes being watched either with full or partial attention. We may be selective, choosing programmes which appeal to us be it one-off shows or serialisations, or alternatively leaving the television on in the background to accompany mundane household chores.

Amidst the myriad of themes or messages portrayed on television are a number of references relating to mental health issues. These references have varying degrees of intention and can be found in even the most surprising genres such as children's TV. There are a substantial number of positive examples to be found although the overall picture reflects that observed in other media sources of having to compete with a mass of stereotypical and stigmatising portrayals. It illustrates the concerns being raised about the predominantly negative portrayal of mental health issues within the media by bodies such as Mind (2000), the Royal College of Psychiatrists (2001) and the Mindout for Mental Health (2001a).

The sender

Influences

When considering the medium of television it is important to examine the influences encountered at the varying stages in a programme's production.

For the purposes of this work, those having an influence over television programmes and the development of messages that are to be transmitted can be regarded as 'shapers'. Invariably the large number of individuals and organisations who have an interest in television programmes presents the potential for conflict because of the differing needs of political, media, health professional and voluntary groups. Each group has its own range of concerns, interests and pressures regarding how particular themes or issues should be depicted. This section focuses upon these 'shapers' and includes the following: political agencies, programme makers, professional groups and service-user groups.

Political agencies

Television programming is subject to a variety of regulatory bodies governing or influencing the way in which they are run. From a European perspective, of particular influence is the European Union (2001) 'Television without Frontiers' directive. Nationally, Ofcom (the regulator for the UK communication industries) has a prime role within the sphere of broadcasting regulation. The Broadcasting Acts of 1990 and 1996 have had a significant impact with the subsequent setting up of the Broadcasting Standards Commission (BSC) and the Independent Television Commission (ITC), both having a regulatory role that concerned matters of taste, decency, fairness and privacy. The BSC, among other things, provided codes of guidance regarding what is covered on television. There is particular reference made to people with disabilities or mental health problems with the statement:

> People with mental health difficulties are [liable to be stereotyped], while words like 'loony', 'nutter' and 'schizo' may cause great offence. Care should be taken not to propagate myths nor to stigmatise. Programme makers should also take care not to add a stereotype, for example to suggest that black people with a schizophrenic illness are invariably black or dangerous. Programmes should seek to avoid stereotypes by consulting with people with mental health difficulties through the production process whenever appropriate.
>
> (BSC 1998: 19)

It is interesting to note that despite these guidelines a large number of programmes subsequently were still found to be carrying negative portrayals of mental health issues. These are invariably defended by programme makers with comments relating to issues such as creative freedom, dramatic appeal or audience expectations. The section within the ITC guidelines concerned with mental health issues stated:

> There is a danger of offence in the use of humour based on physical, mental or sensory disability, even where no malice is present. Reference

to disability should be included only where necessary to the content and patronising expressions replaced by neutral terms.

(ITC 2002: 12)

This is not always clear cut, especially when what is regarded as offensive is defended by programme makers. Notable examples of this include *Brass Eye*'s coverage of a paedophilia storyline and the 'offensive' and insensitive references made to the mentally ill on the *11 O'clock Show*. The programme makers supported their portrayal by pointing out that the show was intended to be satirical and provocative (Brindle 2000).

Both the BSC and the ITC have now had their responsibilities taken up by Ofcom, the body charged by parliament to set standards for the content carried by broadcast media. What is interesting is the relative lack of specific focus upon mental health matters featured within Ofcom's Broadcasting Code (2005) as compared with those created by the BSC (1998) and the ITC (2002). Although carrying statements concerning the coverage of substance abuse and suicide, as well as brief references to 'discriminatory treatment' and 'disability' relating to offensive material, there is little particular emphasis upon mental health issues.

A number of guidelines have been made concerning the coverage of suicide. The Department of Health (2002) in their consultation document *National Suicide Prevention Strategy for England*, set out a number of goals to improve the reporting of suicidal behaviour in the media. This reflected upon evidence that the reporting of suicide can increase the rate especially among people already at risk (Schmidtke and Schaller 2000). One of the main recommendations states that:

'By limiting some aspects of the reporting of suicide and by portraying it in ways which may discourage imitation, the media can make an important contribution to suicide prevention' (DOH 2002: 19). Likewise, Ofcom's Broadcasting Code (2005) stresses the need for methods of suicide and self harm to be excluded from programmes except where they are justified by content. These are welcome statements geared towards a more responsible coverage of suicide through the media. While Pirkis and Blood (2001) found the evidence for a causal association between television portrayal of suicide in fictional programmes and subsequent completed or attempted suicide being only of a moderate consistency, Hawton *et al.*'s (1999) findings were more conclusive indicating that a paracetamol overdose storyline in the hospital drama *Casualty* resulted in an increase of self-poisoning incidents in the following two weeks. They concluded that as well as being associated with an increase in self-harming behaviour, media portrayals also have an influence over the choice of method.

The National Union of Journalists (NUJ) (1999) produced a guide for journalists and broadcasters on the reporting of schizophrenia. This provides a concise, educative guide covering some of the factual elements including the assertion that there is little evidence to support the schizophrenia–violence

link. It also calls for the need for accurate reporting and the using of correct terminology. The NUJ (1999) code of conduct Clause 3 states that: 'A Journalist shall strive to ensure that the information he/she disseminates is fair and accurate, avoid the expression of comment and conjecture as established fact and falsification by distortion, selection or misrepresentation' (NUJ 1999). The television news format perhaps is less prone to 'tabloid style' reporting although messages may be distorted through associated cues and the attention given to specific details. Factual news reporters are also targeted through particular campaigns such as the Royal College of Psychiatry's *Changing Minds* and the Department of Health's Mindout for Mental Health (2001a) *Mindshift – a Guide to Open-minded Media Coverage of Mental Health*. These are important and much needed initiatives that call upon the media to shift towards a more productive and less stigmatising portrayal of mental health themes.

Programme makers

Writers involved with television programmes have in mind a structure or a message that will be portrayed once the final production has been completed. They are hampered, though, by a number of factors which play a part in shaping the final message. One of these is what Henderson (1996) refers to as 'narrative pace', where restrictive timescales and the need to meet audience expectations means that characters move more swiftly between illness and health than is realistic. This is a criticism which has been levelled at the soaps as this programme format requires rapidly developing and not static story-lines. Another difficulty facing television writers is the fact that the visual portrayal of mental well-being may not be regarded as particularly interesting. Crisis situations can be depicted very powerfully creating maximum impact within storylines. The soaps contain many examples here of mental ill-health adding a touch of spice to storylines such as Jimmy Corkhill's erratic and violent behaviour (*Brookside*/manic depression), Zoe Tate's setting fire to a church and attempted murder (*Emmerdale*/schizophrenia) and Joe Wicks barricading himself in his room as a result of paranoid thoughts (*Eastenders*/schizophrenia). The expectation that this is what the audience want to see is reinforced by McQuail's (1997) view that media organisations and those who work in them develop stereotypes concerning the interests, expectations and cultural tastes of their regular or intended audience and seek to match these stereotypes with appropriate content.

Another core issue regards the extent to which writers engage in research (this term is used very loosely here) in order to find out about the themes being addressed. Arguments in support of researching topics indicate that it affords valuable insights into the material being presented whereas those against maintain it contaminates the act of writing. A more honest excuse perhaps concerning the absence of research is given by a *Brookside* writer who points to the tedious, boring process of attending to factual and technical

details (Henderson 1996). This obviously has an influence over the degree of sensitivity and understanding shown towards the subject area being covered. A recent series of Channel 4 drama programmes including *Black Dog* and *Insight in Mind* have been written by individuals who have experienced mental health problems. This brings about an important and refreshing change as topics are handled by individuals who arguably have the greatest levels of insight and understanding.

As regards TV production, what we finally see on TV is the culmination of a complex negotiation process and a multitude of competing pressures. Perhaps the most significant factor influencing the degree of responsibility shown to subjects covered is that of ratings. This is borne out by a *Brookside* producer who says that there is no point in producing challenging storylines unless audiences watch them (Henderson 1996). A major concern facing those involved in producing television programmes is that audiences may switch off, a factor that will no doubt greatly govern the way in which issues are portrayed. Commercial pressures therefore may lead to an increase in dramatic portrayal and a reduction in realism connected to mental health storylines. Another problem within programme making relates to potential bias of the particular perspective of those involved. The type of message sent out is largely dependent upon the predominant view of mental illness among those involved in programme production. This is an important point to note as even the documentary format can be regarded to a certain extent as being constructed and contrived by those making them (Collins 1990). What we are exposed to, therefore, can be seen as having been filtered through the programme makers' view of the world with varying degrees of sensitivity consequently being shown.

Professional groups

When making programmes which involve mental health themes it is interesting to look at the degree of involvement of mental health professionals. Those participating may be chosen either to help with research or to provide 'expert' opinion. As with other subject areas there are a number of familiar faces who have regular involvement with the medium of television. Bourdieu (1996) reflects upon this and the fact that a number of those who speak regularly on television will be virtually on call. Indeed it may be that having known and trusted faces who can be contacted spares researchers a great deal of trouble in locating an appropriate source. Organisations such as the Royal College of Psychiatrists even list topics under which their media experts are listed.

Alongside the BSC (1998) guidelines for contributors (see Figure 8.1), a number of professional bodies such as the Royal College of Psychiatrists and the British Psychological Association (2002) have developed guidelines for their members who appear in the media. Those most sought after to provide comment are seen as the special thinkers, who can think and communicate

Contributors should:

- Be told what the programme is about

- Be given a clear explanation of why they were contacted by the programme

- Be told what kind of contribution they are expected to make – i.e. interview or part of a discussion

- Be informed about the areas of questioning and, wherever possible, the nature of other likely contributions

- Be told whether their contribution is to be live or recorded; and if recorded whether it is likely to be edited

- Not be coached or pushed or improperly induced into saying anything which they know not to be true or do not believe to be true

- Whenever appropriate be made aware of any significant changes to the programme as it develops which might reasonably affect their original consent to participate, and cause material unfairness

- If offered an opportunity to preview the programme, be given clear information about whether they will be able to effect any change in the programme

Figure 8.1 Broadcasting Standards Commission (1998) *Codes of Guidance.*

effectively in these conditions where no one else can do so (Bourdieu 1996). Unfortunately this has meant in most instances selecting health care professionals over service-user groups perhaps demonstrating prejudicial and stereotypical attitudes. This obviously raises a number of issues as those who have experienced mental health problems may be stigmatised against regarding the trustworthiness afforded their accounts.

From a professional perspective, there are a number of well-known faces and voices who have appeared regularly on television and radio speaking about or presenting programmes which have a mental health content. Take for instance Raj Persaud, consultant psychiatrist and programme presenter / 'resident expert' whose popularity within the media has even included appearances on shows such as Channel 4's *Countdown*. In the past, notable 'celebrities' have included Clare Rayner, nurse and agony aunt, as well as the psychiatrist Anthony Clare, who had his own television and radio series *In the Psychiatrist's Chair*. We can see therefore the reassuring nature of turning to these respected and trusted figures for guidance on anxiety provoking stories concerning the mentally ill. In a sense it is a bit like going to the family GP for advice on health matters as they represent an authority we trust in and feel secure with.

The professionals are found in abundant supply on daytime TV (e.g.

Dr Hilary) providing timely advice to callers, viewers and even those present in the studio. Other programmes such as the 'talk shows' usually have a resident expert on hand whose purpose ranges from the provision of sensitive and reassuring comments through to that of promoting their new book which *'fortunately'* they have with them in the studio. Professional 'experts' are even included in reality TV shows such as *Big Brother* where a psychologist's view is offered to help viewers understand the interpersonal dynamics they have been witnessing. An alternative view is that this seems more about trying to convince their audience that these types of show are more than an exploitation of participants for their viewers' entertainment but really can be regarded as valid forms of social experimentation.

Service-user groups

There has been a wealth of criticism directed towards the media concerning the under involvement of a service-user perspective compared to the involvement of professional groups. There is still a stark difference, perhaps because the 'professional voice' is seen to carry greater weight and earns greater respect and trust. However, the need for greater realism in the portrayal of mental health issues has seen service-users (both individuals and groups) having an increased involvement within the media, be it providing 'expert' comment or more directly through programme making as with the aforementioned Channel 4 programmes *Black Dog* and *Insight in Mind*.

An area in which the service-user groups and voluntary organisations are particularly active is in producing guidelines or reports for the media. A significant example of this is the media booklet provided by the Samaritans (1997) relating to the reporting of suicide. Mind in particular has been particularly active in campaigning and research and has compiled the important *Counting the Cost* report (Mind 2000) which highlights stereotypical coverage of mental health issues in the media. Rethink (formerly the National Schizophrenia Fellowship) stresses that the best way to improve media portrayal is to broadcast or print people's direct experience of it (Rethink 2002). A number of its media volunteers have appeared on TV in programmes such as *Newsnight* and *Sky News*. The Zito Trust is also involved in a number of initiatives attempting to enlighten the media regarding the need to respect patients and provide the best kind of therapeutic care possible. The organisation Mental Health Media offers media skills training and information material for users of mental health services and mental health workers (Mental Health Media 2002).

It is interesting to note the link which television stations have with service-user groups. For example, Alison Walsh the Disability Adviser at Channel 4 liaises with programme makers and encourages producers to hire researchers who are disabled or have experience of the issues being covered in the programme. Walsh (2002) stresses that production companies might also show rough cut versions of programmes to service-user groups in order to gauge

their reaction and obtain feedback. The initiatives outlined above are very welcome and clearly play a vital part in tempering the more dramatic and unrealistic portrayals which are regarded as more audience pleasing.

The message

As previously addressed, there are a wide range of factors which influence the messages which are to be transmitted. The packaging and shaping of the message to be sent out is largely governed by the particular programme format and its intended audience. It may help to understand this by categorising television programmes into their various types. From a broad perspective we can see programmes either having a fictional or factual base. To some degree this may determine the aim of the message sent out, whether it be to educate or to entertain. Programmes will therefore fall somewhere along the education–entertainment spectrum, either separately or in some instances addressing both poles.

The following section explores a range of fictional and factual programme genres looking at the contrasting ways in which mental health images are portrayed. It focuses in particular upon issues such as characterisation, words and language used as well as the core focus upon either positive or negative imagery.

Factual

News

TV news offers us immediacy and can have a powerful impact upon attitudes with the pictures it brings into our lives. This is starkly illustrated by the stirring and harrowing pictures of starving children, abused and desperate war refugees, bemused and lost survivors of a natural disaster, or the unforgettable horror of the pictures relating to the terrorist attacks on 11 September 2001. These images are so forceful that we are left haunted by them and either feel helpless or compelled to act in some way. We are moved both by the visual cues as well as the emotive words and tone used. This perhaps marks the main distinction between television news and the printed format as stories are brought with greater impact into our living space. As demonstrated within perceptual theory, issues that are brought more forcibly to the forefront of our attention are subsequently harder to relegate to the background (Köhler 1929).

The overly negative and stereotypical coverage of mental health issues is influenced by the placing of emphasis or type of associations made. The predominant message which emerges seems to be that of the mentally ill being an unpredictable and violent group. An example of this can be found in the coverage of high profile murder cases where the perpetrator is later found to be suffering from some form of mental illness. As demonstrated by

Pavlov's (1958) process of classical conditioning, an association between the themes of violence and psychological disorder is made and reinforced on a continued basis thereby evoking a new learned response – that the mentally ill are dangerous. We see the individual with mental health problems primarily in the role of *perpetrator* and not the more appropriate one of *victim*, a fact supported by Mind's (2000) *Counting the Cost* report and the Department of Health's (1999) *Safer Services: National Inquiry into Suicide and Homicide by People with Mental Illness*. It is perhaps the case, therefore, that the difficulties and problems experienced by the mentally ill are not so easily depicted or regarded as being particularly newsworthy. This helps to reinforce the barrier and sense of distance felt from those with mental health problems and it seems that despite the move towards care in the community, many present-day attitudes remain firmly rooted in the past with our fears fuelling a desire to remove 'madness' from society. It is vital that news broadcasters have an appreciation of the total effect generated by their coverage and work towards a more balanced style of reporting promoting the topic *mental health* in equal proportion to that of their own show. News programmes will feel the same commercial pressures as those experienced by the newsprint media, being drawn towards 'audience grabbing' styles of presentation, and the danger is of television genres starting to merge together. This is where the need to entertain and gratify the audience overtakes considerations for educating them, as illustrated recently by the way in which the verdicts in the Michael Jackson trial were shown on Sky News. To all extents and purposes the viewer could have been waiting expectantly to see who would be voted off in the latest reality game show, all sensitivities towards the seriousness of the topic concerned momentarily suspended for a dramatic and suspenseful piece of TV.

Documentary

Documentaries were among those programme types found to be dealing most extensively and sympathetically with mental illness (Wober 1991). They are largely educative in nature geared towards bringing about a greater understanding and acceptance of themes covered. Documentary making is a far from easy process which is highlighted by Bourdieu's (1996) statement that there is nothing more difficult to convey than reality in all its ordinariness. This raises the concern that what we see is not necessarily a genuine representation as programme makers and editors have a vested interest in making documentaries more interesting and appealing to their targeted audience.

There have been a large number of documentaries on television (both single programmes and series) covering mental health issues. Notable series include the BBC's *States of Mind* and *A Living Hell*, Channel 4's *Inside My Head* and *Young Minds*, as well as Channel 5's *Driving Mum Crazy*. What the documentary format importantly allows us is a view of how individuals and

their family experience mental health difficulties. It is a connecting experience in that the audience are helped towards a more empathic understanding of the issues being portrayed. For example, *Inside My Head: Michael* depicted a 16-year-old with schizophrenia. The surprise potentially for viewers was in seeing an eloquent, brave and expressive teenager who, despite his worsening condition, continued to express what he was experiencing and feeling. What was shown here reflected a very real glimpse of the suffering not only endured by Michael but also by his family. From an attentional perspective we can see a range of factors being employed within the documentary genre such as the engagement of curiosity and interest as a recipient's desire for greater understanding is stimulated (Child 2004). The style of presentation is important as it has the capacity to either draw us into the role of detached voyeur or that of engaged and compassionate viewer. The former might be evoked through the choice of mental health issues such as body dysmorphic disorder or Tourette's syndrome that entice the viewer to gawk at those featured in a manner reminiscent of the carnival freak show. The latter style, however, provides opportunities to hear the *sufferer*'s story and for viewers to gain a greater awareness and understanding not only of the condition being highlighted but something of the lived experience as well.

Docu-soaps / reality TV

Over the past few years there has been a rise in the number of programmes shown which fit the docu-soap / reality TV label. This incorporates all the 'fly on the wall' experimental type programmes that provide us with regular glimpses of people going about their daily lives. Whether these 'daily lives' are naturally occurring or in part constructed for them varies. The focus for these shows might be profession based (*Driving School* and *Vets in Practice*), situation based (*Life Laundry, What Not to Wear*), experiment based (*Prisoner: the Experiment*) or game show based (*Big Brother* and *I'm a Celebrity Get Me out of Here*). The impression given from these shows is that the participants do not seem to really matter, and they are coaxed into performing solely for our amusement and entertainment. It is as Woods states, a form of mass voyeurism: 'reality television, a strange land where dignity no longer lives or matters' (Woods 2002).

There are many parallels which can be drawn here with the historical pursuit of visiting the old asylums in order to observe the 'antics' of the insane. It includes observing the conflicts and emotions that real people endure and either connecting with them through an empathic sharing of effect or remaining distanced but entertained by their potentially humiliating experiences. The general impression given by many of these shows is that participants are seen less as feeling people but more as objects to be manipulated and controlled for our entertainment. It conjures up images of *The Truman Show*, a film where the main character's whole life was being directed and manipulated, unbeknown to him, by the television company. These types of

show are generally justified on two counts involving entertainment and social experimentation. The concept of entertainment is perhaps a more honest and satisfying explanation than the social study angle, as looking at how people behave in certain situations appears to have no discernible purpose other than to attract viewers. Indeed, *Prisoner: the Experiment* set out to recreate Zimbardo's 1970s social research study which separated volunteers into the roles of prisoners and warders even though the original study was halted after a few days because of the psychological distress encountered by those taking part. Even the entertainment angle does not sufficiently address the issues of active manipulation and public humiliation that are part of this process. Some shows even have a gladiatorial feel with the audience and panel of 'experts' having the power to decide contestants' fates. Examples here include *Pop Idol* and *The X Factor* which show us the visible degradation, ridicule and distress endured by the participants who are voted off, in some cases with extremely unnecessary and hurtful personal remarks being made. We have other shows such as the *Life Laundry* where, fortunately perhaps for the programme makers, participants cry mostly on cue when challenged with the need to throw away objects they have held onto that relate to a deceased relative. Although in part having a connecting quality relating to the audience's opportunity to identify with participants, shows such as these tend to breed a sense of indifference towards the distress of others. The discomfort and suffering of others is presented in a sanitised and detached way with the commercial needs of programme makers and the entertainment needs of the audience taking priority over those of the participants.

Another type of programme worth considering is that concerned with improvement of appearance, lifestyle and environment. The problem with the proliferation of these types of programme is the implied message that we the viewers are satisfying ourselves with imperfection and consequently need to change. As discussed in Chapter 5, the need to strive towards perfection that is reinforced by large sections of the media has a negative and detrimental effect upon many people's self-esteem and body image satisfaction. For example, the resonance caused by Trinny and Susannah's (*What Not to Wear*) critical and caustic scolding of their participant's choice of clothing is perhaps hard to detach from for a number of viewers who subsequently have these remarks reverberating within their own thoughts when selecting items to wear. The very real damage from shows such as these is reflected in a number of studies that demonstrate the impact of television exposure upon body image distortions and the development of an internalised ideal body concept (Myers and Biocca 1992; Martin and Kennedy 1993; Borzekowski *et al.* 2000).

Talk shows

There is currently a proliferation of talk shows on TV, the quality of which varies greatly and certainly covers the full education–entertainment spectrum.

First, we have the more focused and informative subject-based shows such as *Esther* that display a degree of sensitivity towards those taking part who are sharing emotive and vulnerable issues. We also have the studio debate format covering topical issues as seen with shows such as the now defunct *Kilroy*. Perhaps the most popular version, though, is the problem–relationship type show such as *Ricki Lake, Oprah* and *Jerry Springer*. A core feature of all of these shows is the charismatic presenter after whom it is named, clearly informing us the viewer who the most important person is. They demonstrate greatly varied facilitation styles that range from the sensitive and understanding through to the exploitative and abusive.

The exploitation of participants may be regarded almost with a sense of *schadenfreude* where viewers can delight in the mess that those taking part seem to make of their relationships and personal lives. It might be that participants' partners reveal illicit affairs, pregnant lovers or the fact that they are actually trans-sexual. Indeed, shows such as *Ricki Lake* even disclose the results of paternity tests live on air. Apart from a few isolated examples, people's personal and relationship difficulties are served up to the audience in a predominantly unconcerned and insensitive manner. As with the docu-soap/reality TV format the overall impression given is that the needs of those taking part is less important than the entertainment needs of the audience. It is uncertain exactly what the attraction is for those taking part although a study by Rene Diekstra, professor of clinical psychology at Leiden University, suggested that appearing on TV could be regarded as therapy itself (Sheldon 1996). This research has resulted in the Foundation for Mental Health giving advice to programme makers about providing those taking part with written details about the nature of their participation (Sheldon 1996). The extent to which this is carried out or followed up to ensure that details are understood is debatable. Our doubts are perhaps strengthened by the awareness of how important ratings are to the show and the incentives for programme makers to perhaps coerce participants towards levels of disclosure that they are unprepared for. Even within a therapeutic context, disclosing intimate details will feel unsettling and can leave individuals feeling exposed and vulnerable. What then of being led towards this point not at one's own pace but within the time constraints of a television show's schedule, in front of countless numbers of viewers and with the rather false sounding assurance of 'don't worry you'll be offered counselling after the show' ringing in one's ears? It is a shame, therefore, that the therapeutic and educational potential of this format is overshadowed by its entertainment value. If handled sensitively the potential is for these shows to act as on-air self-help groups with those taking part feeling supported and those watching being made more aware of certain issues such as bullying, eating disorders or coping with disability and learning, albeit vicariously by observing those taking part. This promotes the concept referred to by Yalom (1995) as *Universality*, where viewers feel that they are not alone with particular problems and are empowered to seek help. This is complemented by the

offering of advice about available resources such as the helpline shown at the end of programmes.

Fictional

Drama

There is an abundance of TV drama shows (particularly police or hospital based) covering mental health issues and providing a mixture of positive and negative portrayals. The depiction though as with many other genres seems to be overwhelmingly negative with many stereotypical characterisations being made. This is highlighted in particular by a study carried out by Wilson *et al.* (1999) exploring the depiction of the mentally ill in prime-time drama (see Figure 8.2). Concerns were raised by the authors that unpleasant, aggressive and antisocial actions are sourced in the characters' mental illness. Persons with a mental illness were constructed as abnormal and unattractively different from the viewer, for example as failures/unproductive, asocial and outcast. This concurs with the findings of Signorielli (1989) who found that characters in prime-time drama portrayed as mentally ill were more likely to be depicted as violent or as victims than any other character. They were also more likely to be portrayed as bad and least likely to be portrayed as good, most being depicted as failures. It is a process that is strongly reflected within labelling theory where the 'deviant' is characterised alongside a set of stereotypical assumptions (Moore 1988).

A drama show that was actually set in a mental health hospital in Glasgow (*Psychos*) attracted a fair degree of criticism concerning its title and portrayal of mental illness. The opening episode highlighted a range of negative associations including the mental illness–violence link, a general detachment between staff and patients, as well as the dubiously unclear psychological state of professional staff involved. One scene which depicts a patient vehemently

---

- Dangerousness-aggressive
- Simple/childlike
- Unpredictability
- Failures/unproductive
- Asocial
- Vulnerability
- Dangerousness-incompetence
- Untrustworthy
- Caring/empathic
- Social outcast

Features listed in order of priority with highest frequency examples placed above

---

Figure 8.2 The depiction of the 'mentally ill' in prime-time drama (Wilson *et al.* 1999).

stressing his rationality but being dismissed by staff members is reminiscent of Rosenhan's (1973) study; 'On Being Sane in Insane Places'. Disappointingly perhaps the patient later returns to stereotype announcing in a ward round, 'I am the rightful King of England'. Popular drama series such as *Casualty* frequently include storylines that involve mental health themes and this hospital drama currently features a mental health nurse as one of the staff team. The dramatic potential of mentally ill characters is perhaps too good to avoid and storylines are often stereotypical and misleading. For example, one episode in particular centred on a mental health group home and highlighted the plight of their tormented neighbour who was unable to sell his home. This in itself would be bad enough but the story continued with some of the group home's residents managing to blow up their house while another committed suicide by laying down on a set of train tracks. Such coverage is obviously geared towards viewers' entertainment and attracting higher ratings. This does not support the statement made in the BBC's (2005) production guidelines that: 'We aim to reflect fully and fairly all of the United Kingdom's people and cultures in our services. Content may reflect the prejudice and disadvantage which exist in our society but we should not perpetuate it' (BBC 2005).

A more balanced and informed coverage of mental health issues is clearly needed as demonstrated through programmes such as Channel 4's drama *Losing it*. This programme located mental health issues within everyday 'normal' experiences presenting characters whom the audience could relate to and identify with. It clearly demonstrated that viewers can be engaged and entertained without having to resort to misleading and incorrect stereotypes.

Soaps

As with the television drama there are many examples where mental health issues have been included within the soaps and it seems as if each show has carried one or more storylines, for example: Shelley Unwin's depression and agoraphobia in *Coronation Street*; Zoe Tate's schizophrenic breakdown in *Emmerdale*; Jimmy Corkhill's manic-depressive episodes in *Brookside*; and Joe Wick's paranoid, psychotic behaviour in *Eastenders*. There is generally a tried and tested soap format although with some differences in the approach. This is observed by Henderson (1996) in relation to the more popular soaps with *Coronation Street* and *Eastenders* being character-driven (not issue-led) whereas *Brookside* is driven by social issues with the aim of provoking debate. Naturally these aspects will play a part in how mental health issues are characterised in the programmes while also being influenced by commercial factors and the intense pressure of developing storylines to maintain existing audiences and attract new ones.

The soaps in particular present us with an array of attractive role models, easily identifiable by the target audience which may have positive as well as negative associations. An example of this can be related to the self-harming

storyline in *Hollyoaks* as experienced by the glamorous character Lisa. It is unclear, though, exactly what assumptions or associations might be made here with both positive (glamorous and attractive characterisation) and negative (self-harming behaviour) connections being made leaving viewers to form their own interpretation based upon personal knowledge and experience. This process is highlighted by Livingstone:

> Soap operas cannot offer clear and singular solutions to the personal and moral problems portrayed . . . the complexity and multiplicity of the text invites the viewer to impose a certain order or closure according to his or her own notions of what is likely or desirable or meaningful.
>
> (Livingstone 1998: 52)

The narrative and structure of soaps offer a contrast to traditional shows, which offer a beginning, middle and end, by serving up an endless middle, with narratives weaving in and out of each other, remaining unfinished and full of potential for future development (Livingstone 1998). This is complemented by the presence of between four and seven sub-plots per episode, all relatively independent of each other (Gripsrud 2002). This has a profound influence upon the degree of realism being presented especially in terms of the rapid shift observed between states of wellness and ill health. This is frequently seen with those who are ill either disappearing or making dramatically swift recoveries. What is not often depicted, apart from rare instances such as the wheelchair-user Chris Tate in *Emmerdale*, is a character's prolonged living with disability or illness. This is especially true in the case of mental health problems where characters fluctuate between states of wellness and illness but are not generally shown as learning to adapt and cope with their difficulties. The unrealistic and sensational portrayal of mental illness can in part be put down to the constraints of time and character type, as well as the need to keep viewers engaged by ending on a dramatic note (Livingstone 1998).

Comedy

A study by Wober (1991) found that mental illness was seldom portrayed through comedy shows although, when it did, the depiction was rarely sympathetic. Certain programmes such as *Brass Eye* and the *11 O'clock Show* have been heavily publicised and criticised for what were seen as offensive or insensitive references. It seems that there is scant evidence of positive characterisation in comedy although, on a rare note, the TV sit-com *Takin' Over the Asylum* was praised by mental health service-users as a reasonably accurate and balanced portrayal, depicting psychiatric patients as articulate and humorous (Henderson 1996). This differs from the usual fare which is commonly served up such as the 'escaped from the asylum' situational comedy characterisation. This is the tired old stereotypical format which is used

to raise a few laughs as illustrated by Victor Meldrew's plight at being shaved for a hernia operation by an escaped 'mental patient' in the comedy sit-com *One Foot in the Grave*. It seems that another tried and tested formula in comedy shows features characters fearing for their own state of mind. A notable illustration of this can be seen in an episode of *Fawlty Towers – The Psychiatrist* which shows Basil Fawlty's increasingly eccentric and frustrated behaviour when attempting to convince a psychiatrist of his healthy mental health state. This is another example where what is essentially a serious and distressing theme is treated in a casual and dismissive way. Basil Fawlty's desperate need to assert his wellness seems merely to reflect something of the societal need in distancing oneself as far as possible from the scary and unsettling topic of mental illness.

Other depictions seem to highlight notions of craziness or insanity with characters exhibiting zany, eccentric and unpredictable behaviour. These portrayals are mainly stereotypical with depicted behaviour being all too predictable and fitting the expected type. There are many examples of this in classic comedy shows such as Spike Milligan's *Q* series or *Monty Python's Flying Circus*, which famously featured a sketch about 'loony party' election candidates. As discussed in Chapter 7, a major issue with regard to whether or not a comedic representation is offensive or not concerns the way in which audience members are engaged, either laughing *at* or *with* those being depicted. An interesting example here concerns an ongoing sketch running through consecutive episodes of the comedy show *Little Britain*. This featured Anne, a care in the community patient whose clearly inappropriate behaviour (e.g. urinating in ponds and throwing unwrapped loaves of bread at ducks) allied with the total lack of awareness by her accompanying psychiatrist seemed to poke as much fun at those with mental health problems as it did to the system set up to care for them. The culmination of these sketches seemed to illustrate that Anne's eccentric and bizarre behaviour was assumed, perhaps reflecting Thomas Scheff's (1968) assertion of the mentally ill behaving according to expectation. What is clear is that viewers will have their own individual thoughts about what they are watching. The perspective from which material is viewed will help determine how characters are engaged with, and, for example, whether or not we are amused by the strange antics of the mentally ill or alerted to the overly stigmatising societal response or the deficits in care.

Children's TV

A study by Wilson *et al.* (2000) found 46 per cent of children's television programmes surveyed containing references to mental illness. These references particularly related to vocabulary and characterisation with words including terms such as 'crazy', 'mad', 'losing your mind', 'wacko', 'cuckoo' and 'loony'. They noted in particular the opening song to Tiny Toon adventures which begins: 'We're tiny, we're toony, we're all a little loony . . .' The characterisation

was interesting with individuals being placed into two sets: the comic character, displaying illogical and irrational actions; and the evil villain, determined and obsessive. Their physical attributes and behaviours were commonly exaggerated, denoting and marking these characters as being different. What is surprising is the extent of programming within this particular genre that carries content relating to mental health issues. This reaffirms the findings of Scheff (1968) who sees our stereotyped imagery of mental health issues being learned in early childhood and continually reaffirmed inadvertently in ordinary social interaction. It is the predominance of negative and misrepresentative characterisation that is particularly disturbing and which clearly signals the need for a greater number of positive and more realistic imagery. Children therefore are frequently exposed to the message that mental illness either represents a threat or is an object of ridicule. This helps to create a negative mindset which serves to obstruct the receipt or perception of messages dealing with mental illness in a more accurate and sympathetic way. As identified in educational workshops run as part of the Mental Health Awareness in Action programme, a significant degree of learning about mental health issues comes from the media (Pinfold 2003). Potentially, what is needed is an increase in programmes that feature more productive examples and present role models with whom viewers are able to identify, such as the storylines in *Grange Hill* covering issues of teenage pregnancy and bullying. It is this type of portrayal that is important, holding difficult issues up for closer inspection and tackling aspects that may otherwise remain largely unexpressed.

The recipient

Making sense of television

A number of theoretical approaches such as personal construct theory, Gestalt theory and schema theory address our predisposition to learn and interpret messages in specific ways. From a personal construct theory perspective we each have a unique way of seeing the world around us which is governed by our own personal constructs. These constructs are borne out of past experience and are constantly being tested out, refined and revised in light of subsequent experience (Epting 1984). Gestalt theory looks at how incoming sensory stimuli are processed and organised into what is regarded as a meaningful and unified whole (King and Wertheimer 2005). Alternatively our base of understanding and interpretation may be related to our cognitive schemas. Schemas can be understood as patterns which are imposed on a complex reality or experience in order to assist in explaining it (Piaget 1958). These schemas are constructed in relation to a stock of shared social experiences (Shore 1996) and include attitudes and emotions (Höijer 1998).

What the above theoretical approaches have in common is the influence that past experience has in predisposing us to interpret stimuli from a certain

perspective and how this affects the way we subsequently make sense of things. For example, the Gestalt process of closure relates to the way in which we take what is initially incomplete and fill in the gaps, rounding off messages to create our own understanding (Hamlyn 1957). There are a number of issues which predispose us to see things from a particular perspective. A study by Gunter and Wober (1992) illustrates how our cultural base may influence our perception and cites examples of how American and British audiences differed in terms of viewing scenes on television either negatively or positively. From these arguments the inference seems to be that the actual framing of the transmitted message is a secondary issue to the individual's own base for understanding things from a certain perspective. This is supported by Livingstone who states that: 'The active viewer makes sense of programmes relatively unconstrained by the structure of the text, drawing instead upon his or her interests, knowledge and experience' (Livingstone 1998: 37).

Philo (1990) contests the view that what we see and understand is conditioned by pre-existing assumptions. He argues that our beliefs may have contradictory elements in them and that our perception is not insulated against the processes by which people try to win our consent to see the world in a given way. In Philo's (1990) study, the extent to which subjects believed in the television version of the world depended on several factors, particularly on whether they had access to alternative accounts. This is an important point which is reflected in Höijer's (1998) research where meaning is seen as being created by a network of relations between the text, audience, social reality and other texts seen or due to be seen. The sense we make of television is very much an individual experience, largely influenced by the unique way in which we, as individuals, think and the ways in which we perceive the world around us. Murdock (1998) highlights the significant difference between fiction and news genres when it comes to how well texts are understood. In particular she found that the reception of news events is often quite brief and sketchy, sometimes fragmentary and not as coherent and elaborate as the reception of fiction. What is particularly unsettling about this is the assertion that television news is our main source of information for national and international events (Philo 1990). Murdock (1998) postulates that it may be the case that fiction is easier to interpret because it is closer to the narrative mode – a story-based mode that deals with a sequence of events, characters and happenings. These have dramatic qualities (and some moral point) whereas news follows the more difficult paradigmatic mode, based on a more scientific way of thinking in which logical reasoning and concept formation play important roles.

Naturally television presents us with a rich medium for receiving messages and subsequently testing out and revising assumptions, thoughts or ideas. The proliferation of negative characterisation and stigmatising imagery presents a depressing picture regarding potential change. Audience reception research, though, has shown people's ability to challenge incoming messages.

As Kitzinger (1999) states, people can consume different messages and may also challenge one representation by drawing on another. This ability to discriminate and challenge what is being presented relies upon the availability and accessibility of more positive imagery. The ability to discriminate perhaps lies at variance with the statement in the Newson report (Barker 2001) that 'The principle that what is experienced vicariously will have some effect on some people is an established one and is the reason why millions of pounds are spent on advertising' (Barker 2001).

It is a stance which is contended by Barker and Petley (2001), who point out that the assumption from campaigners, that because TV has some influence it must be the influence they ascribe to it, does not take heed of the myriad of influences which make us laugh or cry, those which interest us or those which prove thought provoking. Television has a responsibility here in what M. Bragg (2001) highlights as a key issue, that of helping people orient towards and understand what it is they are encountering. This should be applied to both negative and positive portrayals of mental health issues and understanding what it is that makes this imagery productive or destructive. An example of this can be related to *The 11 O'clock Show*, a satirical comedy programme which was branded as offensive particularly because of a reference made to 'mentals sitting in their own shit'. The point where perhaps satire misses the mark is summed up by the director of the training and support group Mental Health Media who stated that:

> It is high time that self styled satirists paused for thought. Satire and irony are based on the fact that the majority of people understand you are not being serious, but public understanding of mental health problems is not yet at the level that it is clear that . . . it is satire.
>
> (Brindle 2000)

The message here is that ignorance and lack of awareness provide a ready supply of fuel for discriminating and stigmatising approaches and that what is needed is a greater attention upon education and awareness-raising. This certainly fits in with initiatives such as the Mindout and Changing Minds media awareness campaigns.

Interaction with TV

An important factor influencing our understanding of messages being transmitted is the way in which we interact with television. On the one hand Hobson (1988) asserted that viewers were active rather than passive during viewing, that they were involved and not bored by programmes, and that they were critical rather than mindlessly accepting them. In contrast Barwise and Ehrenberg (1988) describe television as a 'low involvement' medium involving passive activity, mainly watched as a *filler* when we have nothing better or more important to do. They saw the degree of attention required for television

viewing as being at a comfortable level. These contrasting viewing styles are outlined by Rubin (1984) who categorised different possible motivations for viewing into broadly active/instrumental (seeking knowledge, reality orientation, social utility) and passive/ritualised (habitual, mindless viewing). Our motivation for active viewing is influenced by our desire for information. This can be seen in particular following a high profile news event such as an abduction and murder case and our desperate need to make sense of what has happened. This need is driven by wanting to understand something of the murderer's mental health state and has the effect of actively 'tuning' us in to what is being presented. We can also reflect upon dramatic storylines covered in the soaps, for example Joe Wick's psychotic breakdown in *East-enders* or Lisa's self-harming behaviour in *Hollyoaks* which grab viewers' attention moving them from passive to active viewing. This is clearly summed up by Nelson:

> The very best in TV drama makes you think. It stops viewers in their tracks, drawing their attention away from the knitting, the newspaper, the distractions of domesticity, to command attention. After the event it plays on people's minds. By coming from an angle different from the regular perspective, by framing things just off-centre, it demands that viewers see something afresh and perhaps to recognise that their accustomed mythologies are inadequate accounts of the world.
>
> (Nelson 1997: 156)

Another issue worthy of consideration is the degree of interaction which viewers have with characters on television. Rosengren and Windahl (1989) distinguished a number of different kinds of 'television relations' including:

- *Interaction* – having the feeling of interacting with actors on the screen
- *Identification* – variable degree of involvement with media figure

Indeed, this can be viewed in terms of parasocial relations where viewers experience interactions between characters as if they themselves were participants, retaining their identity and playing against the characters, taking sides, answering back and reacting emotionally (Horton and Wohl 1956). Livingstone (1998) sees this occurring strongly in drama and soap operas where the relationship is one of connection and of having the feeling of engaging with real people. The importance here is the ability to relate meaningfully with characters, experiencing understanding and sympathy for them. Viewers recognise and identify with the characters and experience them as real people, almost as if they were part of their family (Livingstone 1998). It is this relationship with familiar television characters that Gauntlett and Hill (1999) focus upon when documenting the findings of a five-year British Film Institute project exploring respondents' lives, their television watching and the relationship between the two. In particular, for some respondents, television

was seen to bring 'friends' to their living space or indeed even 'one of the family'. It was not seen as just a piece of furniture but meant a lot to respondents, offering information, entertainment and engagement with presenters or actors. Our levels of engagement with characters will be dependent on the type of characterisation being portrayed. Trevor Jordache's abusive and violent character in *Brookside* will no doubt have a significantly different impact on viewers compared to the schizophrenic breakdown of Zoe Tate observed in *Emmerdale*. A major difference here is that Trevor Jordache was depicted from the beginning as a brutal and unlikable character whereas Zoe Tate was somebody whom audiences had first seen and got to know and connect with in a well state.

The way in which we identify with television characters has an affective component as well as a cognitive one. Feshbach and Feshbach (1997) point out that there may be a blurring of the distinction between drama and real experience and that an emotion-arousing event happening to another person will elicit a similar feeling in an observer. On a positive note, this vicarious sharing of affect can help to develop empathy with characters. It has the impact of 'tuning' viewers in to the feelings of those we are watching. From a more critical perspective, we can consider the voyeuristic and exploitative quality of a number of programmes such as the talk shows *Jerry Springer* and *Trisha* having a questionably less than caring approach to those taking part. This can also be applied to documentaries such as the *Driving Mum Crazy* Channel 5 series which was criticised by McClure (2000) as being poorly balanced, suggesting that the purpose of the series was to shock viewers with severe examples of juvenile behaviour. He questions whether this series simply facilitated voyeurism, stating the need to get the balance between informing and entertaining. Likewise, Channel 4's *Witness: 'Valkenberg'* presented a 'fly on the wall' view of the wards in a South African hospital. As McKenzie (1994) states, there was only a superficial coverage of issues and this documentary became more of a voyeuristic process and was always likely to descend into a Victorian freak show.

From this viewpoint, we can see the relationship of television with mental health issues as being a predominantly negative one. Clearly what is needed are stronger and more realistic role models whom we are able to connect with and relate to. For instance the admission by Princess Diana about her struggles with bulimia led to a greater understanding and acceptance of the condition. From a social learning perspective (Bandura 1986), we can see the public was presented with a role model whom they not only could relate to but, in particular, with somebody they had a desire to help and understand. Television drama and soaps in particular present viewers with role models whom they can get to know and identify with. There is a considerable potential here for understanding and awareness raising of mental health issues, although much depends upon the degree of realism and sensitivity being employed. The importance of having access to specific experiences through the medium of television is outlined by Berry and Asamen (1993) who

observe that few non-disabled people know individuals with disabilities well enough for information to be shared with them as intimate as that revealed by those on screen. This highlights the educative potential of television as well as the degree of responsibility that programme makers need to demonstrate as there are many examples where the public are actually misinformed through ambiguous and inaccurate depictions.

Television and behavioural change

A great deal of research has been carried out into investigating media effects, focusing upon the impact that television content has upon the subsequent behaviour of viewers. In particular a number of studies have focused upon the link between television content and its subsequent impact upon violent behaviour (Gauntlett 2001). As Livingstone (1998) observes, as well as looking at resultant behaviour, media effects are also concerned with thoughts, emotions, social interactions and attitudes. The media effects model itself has met with considerable criticisms including the implied presumption that the media presents one singular and clear-cut message which viewers are not able to respond differently to or come up with their own interpretations (Gauntlett 1995). Gauntlett further states that the effects model can only really make sense to people who consider popular entertainment to be a set of very basic propaganda messages flashed at the audience in the simplest terms. In Comstock *et al.*'s (1978) model, the act or behaviour seen on television will have an impact on the individual viewer, depending on the degree of positive value attached to the act and on the degree to which it is shown to be close to real life. Therefore, the further removed from reality a television portrayal is, the less likely it is seen to have relevance to the viewer (McQuail and Windahl 1993). Whether or not the viewer perceives portrayals to be unrealistic is debatable as familiar stereotypes or recognisable screen characters may be taken as true to life.

We may regard the link between the media and society as a cyclical one, as each in turn plays a part in shaping the views and behaviour of the other. Television is a particularly influential media source which not only portrays societal trends but can have a direct effect upon individual or societal attitudes. This is highlighted by S. Bragg (2001) who states that television is not so much a window on the world as a mirror and in some ways the maker of society, enforcing attitudes, manners and fashions. This view is also supported by Fiske and Hartley (1978) who indicate that our attitudes are in part shaped by the environment of significance that we have collectively produced. They see part of that environment as comprising the constant stream of 'secretions' that emanate from the small screen. In this sense television can be regarded as being firmly entwined with changes and developments in society.

What perhaps has not been sufficiently addressed is the individual's reaction to media coverage as influenced by personal experiences of mental health problems. Scheff (1968) looks at the extent to which the behaviour of people

who are labelled mentally ill is influenced by stereotypical expectations and may be modelled upon characterisations learned through the media. The overwhelmingly negative portrayal of mental health issues in the media plays a part in highlighting the 'deviance' element and reinforcing the effects of labelling. The effects upon the individual and how they perceive themselves can be reflected in the term 'The looking glass self' which illustrates how identity is built primarily as a result of how others act towards and respond to us (Moore 1988). This obviously plays a central part in how individuals experiencing mental health problems subsequently behave. A further consequence is the reaction of others and a failure to adequately connect with the lived experience, treating the individual's actions in light of their underlying psychopathology (Goffman 1963). As illustrated in the Changing Minds campaign (RCP 2001), people with mental health problems have been locked away from society for centuries, but today negative attitudes lock them out more subtly but just as effectively. This all fuels the negative, downward spiral whereby those who are labelled mentally ill embark upon what Becker (1964) describes as a deviant career. Television depictions of mental health issues as a whole play a central role in this process by perpetuating and reinforcing negative, unrealistic and stereotypical imagery.

Modifications in attitudes are governed by the degree of personal motivation we have to change. As Petty and Priester (1994) state, information will only be successful in producing enduring changes in attitude and behaviour if people are motivated and able to process the information, and if this processing results in favourable thoughts and ideas. From a mental health perspective people influenced may lack the necessary skills or self-confidence to translate new attitudes into action. The Dutch critical viewing project explored the influence of television on children's attitudes and beliefs (Vooijs and Van der Voort 1993). The suggestion made was that TV offers a distorted view which can be corrected by comparing it with what happens in real life. This may prove difficult, though, especially where fears or fantasies may be involved. Fears and fantasies can be played upon, for instance as expressed in the comment 'I know that the mentally ill do not pose a significant risk but I still wouldn't allow my children near them'. This is where our primitive instincts prove stronger than our cognitive understanding of reality. Philo's (1990) study found that the fear generated by media accounts was such that it could overwhelm direct experience in formation of beliefs. An example given was the extreme anger shown by the public towards the nanny in *Coronation Street*, Carmel, a character who was sexually obsessed with Martin, the baby's father. The level of emotion aroused seemed to relate to a real event experienced by the viewer and not a fictional account that was observed on screen.

Future needs

What has been highlighted by the above are the many competing and contradictory factors which play a part in what we take away from the messages

we are exposed to on television. It seems that despite the multitude of guide-lines directed towards television programming there is still an overwhelm-ingly negative and stereotypical portrayal being used. The vast number of issues covered are presented through a variety of television genres which have a factual or fictional base. The potential for education and awareness-raising is not always realised as entertainment and the pressure of ratings play a significant part. What is clearly needed is a greater input into follow-ing up the themes and issues raised. Having brought mental health issues to the public's attention and awareness there is then a great opportunity to 'fill in the gaps' and educate viewers in a meaningful way. Whether the pro-gramme has a factual or a dramatic base should not deter it from following up with various messages relating to education or support giving. This has been well applied in soaps, drama programmes and talk shows covering sensitive issues such as sexual abuse, bullying and specific mental health conditions.

There is a need to help viewers discriminate between what are productive and healthy mental health images and what are not. Importantly this is already being done through the increasing recognition which is now being given to the positive and sensitive handling of mental health issues (e.g. the mental health media awards) and the attention drawn towards stigmatising media depictions by Mind's (2000) *Counting the Cost* report or the Royal College of Psychiatrists' (2001) Changing Minds campaign. A welcome add-ition is also the greater voice and representation being given to mental health user groups/organisations, not only through their direct media involvement but also through their increased influence on mental health legislation. The more that media depictions of mental health issues are shaped by those who best understand them, the greater the opportunity that attitudes and awareness will be changed for the better.

Conclusion

As with print media, it seems that the most popular products offered by the medium of television carry portrayals that on the whole are stigmatising, unrealistic and misleading. This can be seen with genres that have a prime function of entertainment such as soaps, drama and comedy. The job of informing and educating the public about mental health issues remains largely within the news and documentary formats. There have been some welcome attempts over recent years though to marry the educational to the entertaining which bring a number of benefits in the promotion of better understanding and awareness concerning the reality about certain mental health issues. The success of some of these ventures, notably the improved coverage within some of the more popular soaps, has been greeted with praise by mental health advocates and recognised by various mental health awards. Critics might point though towards overly dramatic scenes or depictions that are still present as being on the whole, unrepresentative of the mental health

state concerned. At the same time, programme makers might defend this as gearing their material to the needs and desires of their targeted audience, a fact supported by the increase in ratings following a particularly dramatic storyline. This is in a sense sold as the '*pay off*', the price for using their high-profile vehicle (television programme) to carry a particular message. Because the potential benefits are so valuable (high exposure, better education and understanding, a sense of identification with known and liked characters, clear comprehension of the felt and lived experience concerning certain mental health states, feelings of connection with others and further contact information), it is an area where continued development is evidently required. In order to facilitate this, further liaison between programme makers and mental health advocates needs to be fostered. This would help to provide television personnel with clear and definite information, not only of the reality concerning different mental health states but also the impact that poor coverage has upon the lives of those involved. The core message to convey to those involved within television is that coverage need not be totally purged of dramatic content or made so blandly unappealing that mental health issues are no longer showcased. The greater sensitivity now being afforded other historically stigmatised groups (i.e. race / physical disability) is something that needs to be matched by the way in which the mentally ill are treated. Progress has been made although ongoing attention to the promotion of better mental health coverage is clearly required.

9   The Internet

The Internet: the medium

The advent of new media and the Internet offers a rich and valuable resource
from which to obtain information. The almost limitless scope of material
available and instantaneous access make it an extremely effective source for
updating. Evidence-based information, contact details, chat rooms, e-mail,
self-help organisations and online therapy are only a few services offered
through this new medium. Indeed, it offers a valuable resource not only to
health care professionals but also to mental health service-users and other
interested parties. From a mental health perspective there is a rich array of
resources to choose from. This encompasses a vast selection of Internet sites
provided by an extremely diverse selection of organisations and individuals.
While this multi-perspective presents those accessing information with a
greater selection of choice, it can also make it a bewildering and confusing
process. The quality of information varies dramatically from site to site; from
credible to unreliable, helpful to harmful and informative to misleading.
Although there are various guides and indicators as to which are the more
productive sites, the difficulty in distinguishing between the good and poor
ones is a matter of some concern. Those accessing the Internet may struggle,
therefore, to authenticate the information they find. There are no guarantees
regarding the intention or credibility of many individuals or organisations
posting information, and in a number of cases this has proved to be harmfully
misleading or actively encouraging self-destructive behaviour. Searching the
Internet does on the whole present individuals with what could be regarded
as a storehouse of treasure although the 'trinkets' clearly have to be sifted out
from the piles of accompanying junk. These difficulties are further reinforced
by information overload caused by the almost limitless supply of material
available.

The Internet does provide a number of benefits and advantages over other
information systems. One of the attractions of this new medium is the potential for increased access to health care information for both professionals and
health care consumers (Hebda *et al.* 1998; Tomaiuolo 1995; Christensen and
Griffiths 2000). It is a fast, accessible and relatively cheap medium that as well

as educating offers the potential for empowering mental health service-users. The importance of the Internet as a vehicle for accessing health information is endorsed by the findings that this is one of the most common reasons for using the Internet (Powell and Clarke 2002). It is also an excellent resource for obtaining up-to-date information (Hebda *et al.* 1998), which gives it a clear advantage over that of books. New postings on the Internet replace existing material, whereas new editions of books are brought out while older versions are still available (Scrivener 2002). The currency and speed of updating information online has a great advantage over books which are, in a sense, out of date even before they are published (Booth 2002). Overall, it is a medium that has numerous attractions as well as limitations although these are largely dependent upon the nature of the person accessing material online.

Beginnings

From its conception, there was little indication that the Internet would become as successful and as significant a means of mass communication as it has clearly become. One current estimate reflects that over 10 per cent of the world's population and over half the population of the Western nations now use the Internet (European Information Society Group 2004). In a sense the heralding in of the Internet reflects the experience of cinema in the early nineteenth century and television in the 1950s in the excitement surrounding the huge potential of a new and exciting communicating medium. Its origins date back to the 1960s and the development of packet-switching technology, which entailed breaking strings of data down into small pieces or packets which were then reassembled at their destination (LaBruzza 1997). It was originally used as a US military communications system and was later extended into the world of academia (Graham 1999). Initially, it was limited to just four networked computers joined together but was boosted by the development of a 'hyper-text link' by scientific researchers in Switzerland, allowing an indefinite number of computers to be interconnected electronically. By January 2001, up to 110 million host computers were connected to the Internet with almost 28 million websites accessible (Cooke 2001). A recent study by Ofcom (2004) has estimated that 50 per cent of homes in the UK have Internet access. This trend is set to continue with ongoing developments in technology and enhanced accessibility through means such as mobile phones or television sets.

Regulation and guidance

There is a certain degree of censorship applied to material found on the Internet, for example with content that is deemed to be harmful to children, inciting racial hatred, pornographic or overly violent. Despite some of these initiatives, the Internet remains a largely unregulated medium with numerous

perspectives of all quality types finding representation. In some instances an element of self-regulation will be applied, as the organisations or bodies posting material (for example the Royal College of Psychiatrists or the Nursing and Midwifery Council) provide information that is acceptable within the bounds of their specific professional codes of conduct. The majority of sites accessible over the Internet are offered by largely unknown or uncertain sources, a number of which do not come under any external regulation. Some of the problems with regulating the Internet medium are found in the sheer scale and size of this resource. As McQuail (2005) indicates, the Internet is comprised of a network of internationally, interconnected computers and, unlike other media sources, is not owned, controlled or organised by any single body. This means that any attempt at censoring or limiting what can be expressed is met with a sizeable degree of opposition including organisations that advocate freedom of speech. Part of the reason why the Internet has flourished with a minimum of regulation is due to its place of origin: the United States, a country that provides specific constitutional protection for freedom of speech (House of Commons 2001). The globalisation of Internet resources has added further difficulties in censoring or regulating material as what might be banned in one country can be easily distributed from another where such activity is not illegal (Christensen and Griffiths 2003). The mechanics of banning material can be a crude process and the blocking of material that carries sexual content, for instance, can also result in impeding health information concerned with sexually transmitted diseases. As a consequence of the size, easy accessibility and diversity of material available on the Internet, policing this medium is an extremely complex and problematic process. It means that the large discrepancy regarding the reliability and credibility of information posted will be maintained and that alongside many excellent sites will be those that contain misinformation and are potentially dangerous (Morahan-Martin and Anderson 2000).

The British government believes that a distinct regulatory approach to the Internet is required and proposals were made within the Communications Act (2003) to give Ofcom (the regulator for the UK communication industries) the responsibility for 'maintaining content standards in the electronic media'. Ofcom, the Office of Communications is a body set up to regulate the telecommunications services and is becoming progressively involved with the regulation of Internet content. This is much needed, especially with a medium where so many diverse and different types of quality are available. Certainly, various pieces of legislation aid this process, for example the Protection of Children Act (1978), the Sex Offences Act (2003) and the Obscene Publications Act (1964). This picture is complemented by the range of services and resources that guide Internet users as to the 'quality' or 'reliability' of online material. One such method is the provision of kitemarks, logos or seals of quality. An example of this is the Internet Content Rating Association (ICRA), which is an international, non-profit organisation of Internet leaders working to make the Internet safer for children while respecting the rights

of content providers. Application of the ICRA label to suitable sites provides them with a 'mark' of acceptable content.

Those searching for health care information have a number of available resources to help guide them towards various products. As with conducting a search through other sources such as academic journals and books, reviewers gain confidence from the type of publication accessed and its academic credibility. To some degree the reliability of sources may be identified through the Journal Citation Reports (an essential, comprehensive and unique resource tool for journal evaluation) or whether the publishers of the books are respected in the field of academic publishing. From a health care perspective, certain titles like the *British Medical Journal* or the *Advanced Journal of Nursing* reassure readers that the articles contained will be quality ones because both are highly respected peer reviewed academic journals. What those searching the Internet require is some means of evaluating the significance or credibility of information being looked at. To some degree this is aided through the association with recognised and credible names, bodies and organisations. For example, if looking for information concerning suicide, one might feel more secure with material found on sites posted by the Samaritans, Department of Health or Royal College of Psychiatry than that located within personal sites or unknown organisations.

Other means exist to select and recognise quality pieces of information such as the availability of evidence-based search tools or the application of kitemarks. While this is to be applauded, the global accessibility of information and the fact that different countries have their own approaches to health care means that there will be potential problems with regard to regulating kitemarks. This is indicated by Thede (1999) who observes that what is appropriate in one country may not be in another. It raises the question as to who would be able to regulate properly the various kitemarks applied, with the WHO (World Health Organisation) being put forward as a potential choice. Some recent developments have moved to provide those searching the Internet with a guide to those sites where information posted has a degree of reliability and can be supported by relevant evidence. Examples of this include the European project WRAPIN (Worldwide Online Reliable Advice to Patient and Individuals). This project provides checks on the reliability of documents posted against established benchmarks and provides evidence if information exists in published literature. The Internet Service Providers Association (ISPA) was established in 1995 and is the UK's trade association for providers of Internet services. As a trade association, membership is voluntary but the companies who choose to become members of ISPA must abide by their UK *Code of Practice* if they are to be able to gain the ISPA UK logo as a mark of commitment to good business practice. The ISPA *Code of Practice* (2002) covers various aspects including legality and decency with regard to content. While there are no specific references to disability discrimination or mental illness, Clause 2.4 (Honesty) could be related to material that is misrepresented or inaccurate:

2.4.1 Members shall use their reasonable endeavours to ensure Services (excluding Third Party Content) and Promotional Material are not of a kind that are likely to mislead by inaccuracy, ambiguity, exaggeration, omission or otherwise.

The MedCIRCLE and MedCERTAIN projects are complementary semantic web projects with the overall objective of developing and promoting technologies able to guide consumers to trustworthy health information on the Internet. The aim is for consumers to be able to 'filter' accessed material more effectively and therefore positively select high quality health information on the web. Further regulation is offered by the Swiss Health on the Net foundation (HON) for the provision of authoritative, trustworthy web-based medical information. The Health on the Net Code of Conduct (Hon Code) was issued in July 1996 to help standardise the reliability of medical and health information available on the worldwide web. This code defines a set of voluntary rules designed to help a website developer practise responsible self-regulation and to make sure a reader always knows the source and the purpose of the information he or she is reading. These guidelines cover the following:

1) *Authority*
Any medical or health advice provided and hosted on this site will only be given by medically trained and qualified professionals unless a clear statement is made that a piece of advice offered is from a non-medically qualified individual or organisation.

2) *Complementarity*
The information provided on this site is designed to support, not replace, the relationship that exists between a patient/site visitor and his/her existing physician.

3) *Confidentiality*
Confidentiality of data relating to individual patients and visitors to a medical/health Web site, including their identity, is respected by this Web site. The Web site owners undertake to honour or exceed the legal requirements of medical/health information privacy that apply in the country and state where the Web site and mirror sites are located.

4) *Attribution*
Where appropriate, information contained on this site will be supported by clear references to source data and, where possible, have specific HTML links to that data. The date when a clinical page was last modified will be clearly displayed (e.g. at the bottom of the page).

5) *Justifiability*
Any claims relating to the benefits/performance of a specific treatment, commercial product or service will be supported by appropriate, balanced evidence in the manner outlined above in principle 4.

6) *Transparency of authorship*
The designers of this Web site will seek to provide information in the clearest possible manner and provide contact addresses for visitors that seek further information or support. The Webmaster will display his/her E-mail address clearly throughout the Web site.

7) *Transparency of sponsorship*
Support for this Web site will be clearly identified, including the identities of commercial and non-commercial organisations that have contributed funding, services or material for the site.

8) *Honesty in advertising & editorial policy*
If advertising is a source of funding it will be clearly stated. A brief description of the advertising policy adopted by the Web site owners will be displayed on the site. Advertising and other promotional material will be presented to viewers in a manner and context that facilitates differentiation between it and the original material created by the institution operating the site.

Some of the aspects identified in the Hon Code are important as they help provide those accessing particular sites with a degree of assurance. Core points raised here relate to transparency of authorship and sponsorship as it may be unclear as to who is actually posting information and what their credentials are. For example, one might feel more reassured in accepting advice about treatment options from a recognised medical practitioner. It is also important to recognise the potential influence from other parties providing sponsorship such as that from pharmaceutical companies. It is particularly alarming, however, to note the number of sites which do not post relevant details. A study by Hersch, Gorman and Sacharek (1998) investigating the quality of health information via the web found that over 80 per cent gave no authorship credentials, 69 per cent were without any indication of author and less than 18 per cent provided the date of posting or upgrading. While checklists, kitemarked sites and evidence-based lists provide those searching for information with a helpful guide, there are some difficulties and limitations involved. Of the many checklists and rating tools available, there are few details about how they have been developed and the criteria used in rating sites. Jadad and Gagliardi (1998) examined 47 instruments used to rate health information websites and concluded that many incompletely developed instruments exist on the Internet and that it is unclear if these tools measure what they intend to measure or whether they cause more harm than good.

With regard to material concerning mental health, there are a number of other useful search bases that include:

Cochrane library (http://www.cochrane.org/index0.htm)
The Cochrane Collaboration is an international non-profit and independent organisation, dedicated to making up-to-date and accurate information

about the effects of health care readily available worldwide. It produces and disseminates systematic reviews of health care interventions and promotes the search for evidence in the form of clinical trials and other studies of interventions. It includes several systematic reviews on mental health topics.

NeLH (National Electronic Library for Health) http://libraries.nelh. nhs.uk/mentalHealth/
This is a mental health specialist library website that only includes information which is deemed reliable, unbiased and relevant. It contains the best available evidence to support people who are making mental health care related decisions. At present this includes NICE guidelines and technology appraisals, Cochrane systematic reviews, and a range of best practice articles (including clinical evidence chapters and WHO guidelines for mental health in primary care).

CEBMH (Centre for Evidence Based Mental Health) (http:// www.cebmh.com/)
This organisation promotes and supports the teaching and practice of evidence-based mental health care. Information is provided to consumers about the centre's research activities, educational events and a gateway to various NHS websites on depression, schizophrenia and suicide as well as other high quality sources of mental health evidence.

NHS direct online (http://www.nhsdirect.nhs.uk)
This website provides high quality health information and advice for individuals within the UK. It is supported by a 24-hour nurse advice and information helpline providing details about various treatment methods available. The information is accessed from *Clinical Evidence*, the British Medical Journal's worldwide survey of the best and most up-to-date medical research.

Healthfinder (www.healthfinder.gov)
This website was developed for consumers in the USA. It provides those searching for information on specific health issues with material from a range of carefully selected websites posted by over 1,700 health-related organisations.

TRIP (Turning Research into Practice) (www.tripdatabase.com)
This is a meta-resource which provides access to high quality medical literature from a wide range of sources. The TRIP database's content is reviewed monthly and new material (approximately 300–400 new articles) from the publications covered is added to the site. The TRIP database is separated into a number of categories providing extensive material covering evidence-based information, clinical guidelines, query-answering services, medical images, e-textbooks, patient information leaflets and peer-reviewed journals.

Complaining about new media

To conclude, it is worth mentioning the avenues open to those who are dissatisfied by what they are accessing on the Internet. An important body concerned with complaints is the self-regulatory body the Internet Watch Foundation. This organisation works in partnership with the government, Internet Service Providers (ISP), telecommunication agencies and the police with regard to developing initiatives to minimise the availability of illegal content, such as child abuse images, available on the Internet. If the content is believed to be illegal, it can be reported to the self-regulatory body the Internet Watch Foundation. Illegal material includes that which contravenes national security, protection of minors, protection of human dignity, economic security, information security, protection of privacy, protection of reputation and intellectual property.

The message

Providing misinformation (quackery)

As already discussed, one of the main concerns regarding information accessed via the web relates to its questionable degree of accuracy or reliability. Kiley (1999) writes about this as 'Quackery on the web', relating to medical misinformation, and indicates the following categories: cure-all remedies, inaccurate information and biased information

Cure-all remedies

Many wild, misleading or inaccurate claims are made about health issues on the Internet. These are not always easily verifiable and may be hard to ignore especially for those desperately seeking information, support or treatment. One of the more disturbing trends includes the posting of miracle cures, inaccurate information and unverified claims as evidenced by Bower (1996) such as the acclamation of shark cartilage as a means of strengthening the body's immune system and inhibiting tumour growth and the development of cancer. While these claims may be instantly discredited by some users, others may be swayed by their level of desperation and anxiety about missing potentially life-saving treatments.

From a mental health perspective, a quick search of the Internet provides a range of impressive sounding as well as very dubious sounding remedies and treatments. Some of these are supported, in the absence of any empirical data, by a range of seemingly impressive claims and testimonials from satisfied customers. One site in particular, alternate-health, claims that a number of types of schizophrenia are caused by sugar-handling problems and that orthomolecular therapy can offer impressive rates of cure. Another site, vedicwisdom, states firmly that depression is caused by a

fungus infection and goes on to say that it can be healed easily and permanently, urging people to send 105 dollars for two months supply of what essentially sounds like a foot balm. Naturally, no real evidence-base is given in support of the information that is offered in these examples with such assurance. Neither, in most cases are the credentials of the people providing this type of service identified. It is a shame that these points are not as easily determined by the site visitor as the ways in which payment can be made.

Inaccurate information

The problem with a number of Internet sites is the unverifiable nature of many of the claims being made, coupled with the delivery of misleading and potentially harmful information. This was highlighted in Culver, Gerr and Frumkin's (1997) investigation of Internet sites offering information about painful hand and arm conditions which found many providing misleading, unsubstantiated or inaccurate advice. Another area of concern relates to the increased range of material posted on the Internet by drug manufacturers, including a number of wild and unchecked claims about their products (Brannon 1999). Furthermore, a study by Lissman and Boehnlein (2001) reviewing the quality of Internet information about depression found that, overall, the quality of information posted was poor, with only half of the sites mentioning any diagnostic symptoms. They also found that half of the sites made no mention of medication, psychotherapy or professional consultation as suggested treatments for depression.

There may be an assumption that with the Internet we have a vast storehouse of knowledge, but it is clear that a lot of what we are exposed to can be regarded as misinformation. The problem is that those accessing the Internet infuse this technological medium with a greater sense of credibility than many other sources. When questioning this material, however, it becomes evident that it derives from every type of source imaginable, from the highly credible and verifiable to the overly subjective and unsupported. The knowledge accessed can only be judged reliable if it holds up against standard benchmarks. A significant proportion of the general public though do not have the ability or experience to discriminate effectively between good and poor information. It is particularly worrying where health information is being sought and inaccurate material is posted. Erbele *et al.* (2002) conducted a study to evaluate the reliability and validity of consumer drug-information sites on the Internet. They identified sites with an 'ask the pharmacist' option and found that fewer than 70 per cent of the sites answered the drug information question correctly, concluding that the information being communicated might be unreliable. Similarly, Bessel *et al.*'s (2003) study found that the overall quality of information provided by e-pharmacies on the Internet was poor. This is worrying news for consumers who are using the Internet as a means of empowering themselves and becoming more engaged and proactive

with regard to caring for their own health, as they are exposed to material whose accuracy is hard for them to determine.

Biased information

A particular area of concern facing those searching the Internet for information about mental health issues relates to the degree to which they might be misled by biased information. This is where those posting material on the Internet have a vested interest in the message sent out, either for personal or commercial reasons, and as a consequence do not relate material from an objective point of view. As opinions and philosophies concerning the treatment of mental illness have for countless years invited fiercely opposing views it is hardly surprising that the range of information available on the Internet is so varied. It is like a market place where every type of viewpoint and perspective has representation although some are more prominent and better packaged. An example here relates to the sponsoring of Internet sites by pharmaceutical companies who offer financial incentives to organisations who otherwise would be unable to offer their information to consumers via this electronic resource. The extent to which posted information is geared to the needs of the sponsoring group clearly varies from the carrying of a brand mark or logo through to a more direct selling of the sponsor's product. Another example relates to companies that sponsor their sites with particular search engines thereby achieving a greater prominence. The first site that appears when entering the term 'manic depression' on the Altavista search engine is for an organisation selling a product entitled 'Serenity'. On this particular search there were 107,996 sites listed although these were preceded by a number of sponsored sites that included the one for Serenity. The site itself includes glittering praise for Dr Nieper, the product's creator and includes a number of testimonials from individuals who have used the product and who claim to have had their lives fully restored. There is no actual indication given though as to Dr Nieper's actual qualifications or experience to treat conditions such as manic depression. The site itself is very sales-oriented and includes many pictures of attractive smiling people. The ease with which this product can be purchased online and the lack of medical consultation means that customers are placed in the position of self-prescribing, swayed more by sales rhetoric than by an in-depth knowledge of mental health treatments. The examples listed above highlight the difficulty faced by the inexperienced or desperate person seeking the Internet for support. Distinguishing between the very varied messages and trying to extract what is most helpful seems a veritable minefield and individuals are therefore drawn towards those that are easily locatable and have glowing testimonials and effective-sounding credentials.

Searching the Internet

The issues discussed above highlight some of the problems facing the person using the Internet as an informational resource. Clearly, people have their own particular needs when searching the Internet for mental health information either perhaps as health care professionals or service-users. An illustration of the daunting and sometimes bewildering process facing the Internet user can be seen in the following example which considers a person seeking information after learning of a family member's diagnosis of schizophrenia. Obviously the initial instinct is to feel scared and shocked, wanting reassurance and information. There are a number of places we might go in order to find out about this condition such as to the GP, the library or the Internet. The first choice facing the Internet user concerns which of the many available search engines to use. If, for example, we type in the word 'schizophrenia', Altavista, Google and Yahoo all return over 5 million sites, whereas Ask Jeeves has 1,400,000 and Lycos only 680,000. The sheer scale of sites available makes it extremely unlikely that more than a fraction will be visited. We may, therefore, never reach those further down the list that potentially include valuable and helpful information which is therefore missed. Ideally the key is in knowing what to look for or having particular 'brand' names to try and locate. This includes the names of organisations such as Mind, Rethink or the Royal College of Psychiatry.

The service-user and professional groups are proving enormously helpful with regard to searching the Internet as they provide informative advice about various mental health conditions as well as links to related sites. This includes information about specific conditions, the various modes of treatment available as well as information about how to go about seeking help. A list of some of the core professional and service-user sites is included in Appendix 1. When assessing the quality of particular information sources there are certain aspects that need to be considered. A number of individuals such as Cooke (2001) have provided guides to assist in evaluating Internet sites. These are useful although perhaps need a few extra elements adding when specifically engaging with sites offering mental health content. These are provided in Appendix 2.

Suicide and the Internet

One subject in particular that has raised grave concerns regarding its coverage within the Internet is that of suicide. On the one hand there are many excellent, sensitive and informative sites such as those provided by the Samaritans and the BBC offering visitors practical advice and support in gaining help. These represent the responsible and better-regulated spheres of information obtainable. On the reverse side there are a number of poorly constructed, misleading, irresponsible and actively harmful bodies of information. This in part is due to the lack of regulation and means that very vulnerable

individuals are able to access sites that actively encourage or instruct them in methods for self-harm and suicide (Alao *et al.* 1999). While some of these sites represent so-called pro-euthanasia organisations (e.g. the End of Life Choices, formerly the Hemlock society), others are posted by individuals whose motives are far from clear. The worst sites provide very graphically illustrative material such as copies of suicide notes, death certificates and colour photographs or, as in the case of the 'Church of Euthanasia', the inclusion of a telephone hotline with an A–Z of suicide techniques available. This disturbing picture is reflected by other sites that provide information on 'how to . . .', which relate to every conceivable method of suicide including hanging, electrocution or even snakebite. Product information via the Internet is also available in the book *Beyond Final Exit*, one of the many irresponsible resources obtainable. It is a book that is advertised with a fair amount of jargon and sanitising of terms, with 'self-deliverance' and 'departing drugs', for example, replacing the more stark terminology of 'suicide' and 'death'. It is advertised with classic 'sales-pitch' jargon attempting to make the product appear more desirable with phrases like; 'Common questions about poisonous plants – if you're optimistic about these, be warned of the side effects first!' These are appalling examples although, sadly, not isolated ones and they are perhaps surpassed by the availability of suicide kits (e.g. poison packs of potassium cyanide) that have reportedly been purchased from some Internet sites (BBC 2000). Just as alarming as this are the reported instances of suicide pacts that have been made over the Internet or individuals killing themselves online, apparently goaded by site visitors. The fact that these types of site are so freely accessible by confused and vulnerable people is a cause for grave concern (Thompson 1999). Andrew Solomon (2002), in his excellent account *The Noonday Demon*, aptly sums up the state of mind that people are experiencing when contemplating suicide. It reflects the sense of hopelessness experienced and the overriding feeling that others don't care, compounded by the fact that a person's capacity to recognise supportive gestures is restricted. The significance of this then relates to the type of views that vulnerable and desperate individuals are exposed to, whether it be supportive and containing helpful material, or uncaring and destructive. The worst types of site can for some seem very persuasive, reinforcing feelings of helplessness with the message that no salvation will be forthcoming and the only realistic option open to them is that of suicide. The overly pessimistic and negative rhetoric with which much of this material is presented might provide the only sense of acknowledgement and feeling of understanding from others that some individuals receive. These feelings of connection, although of a detrimental and unhelpful type, can prove extremely powerful in influencing vulnerable and desperate people or leading them towards certain actions. Those who are fortunate enough however to have located other resources such as the Samaritans' website will have a very different experience, with even the most desperate perhaps finding a degree of comfort and support from the feeling that others care and that various forms of help can be

obtained. When accessing the Samaritans' homepage, visitors are initially greeted with the message:

> 'I was going through a really tough time last year. I didn't want to be a downer for my friends so I didn't talk to them. So I called the Samaritans. They gave me the time I needed. Now I can get on with my life.'

(Samaritans 2005)

This is complemented by a variety of easily accessible and navigable links that include details of how to contact them as well as information and audio examples about what to expect after calling. A new and important facility is now provided by the opportunity to use e-mail as a means of contact. What is important about the better type of site such as this one is the opportunity to feel acknowledged and supported by those who wish one well. It means being directed towards resources where a person can feel listened to and heard by others, considerably different to the sites that are more interested in presenting their own views or selling their products than in actually listening and showing concern for others. There are a number of implications here for health care providers including the need to be aware of the range of Internet resources accessible if they are to properly help those in extreme distress (Baume *et al.* 1998). This means directing individuals towards information that is supportive and emotionally containing, as well as helping them to express themselves and talk about the destructive material which they might also have come across. Because of the difficulties inherent in regulating or policing the Internet, these harmful and misleading sites continue to exist. Policing the Internet has resulted in various types of material, such as obscene and pornographic material, being barred or removed although it needs to be applied as strongly to material that encourages self-destructive behaviour. This should be aided by the creation of a greater range of sites that are supportively geared towards the topic of suicide prevention thereby combating the variety of poorly constructed ones (Mehlum 2000). One such example is the *Internet and Suicide Prevention* site, hosted by the suicide research and prevention unit at the University of Oslo in Norway. This organisation is dedicated to preventing suicidal behaviour, alleviating its effects and providing a forum for discussion between academics, mental health professionals, crisis workers, volunteers and suicide survivors. There are a number of other positive links obtainable through the professional and service-user organisations. An example includes the informative online booklet *How to Help Someone who is Feeling Suicidal* available from Mind's website (Mind 2004b). These resources provide a more positive outlook and will help to some degree meet the targets and recommendations for suicide reduction outlined by *The Health of the Nation* (DOH 1992), the governmental White Paper *Saving Lives: Our Healthier Nation* (DOH 1999a), the *National Suicide Prevention Strategy for England* (DOH 2002), the *National Service Framework for*

Mental Health (DOH 1999b) and the *National Confidential Inquiry into Homicides and Suicides: the Safety First Report* (DOH 2001).

Lastly, it is perhaps worth noting the pressure currently being brought to bear upon Internet companies to stop them hosting websites and chat-rooms that appear to encourage suicide. It is a move firmly backed by anti-suicide campaigners, mental health advocates and press agencies such as *The Yorkshire Post* (McGee and Whitehouse 2005). This is a welcome move that hopefully will begin to limit some of the most destructive and distressing material accessible online.

Online therapy

Building upon the rise in computer use a significant development over the past few years has been the availability of therapy over the Internet, aided in part by the current boom in e-mailing and text messaging that has heralded in an era of written electronic communication. The diversity and scope of what can be offered through this new medium is almost limitless and it seems that psychotherapy and counselling have not escaped its potential. It is a process that is referred to in a number of different ways and includes e-therapy, cybertherapy and online counselling.

Most of the better-designed sites make prominently clear to prospective clients that this type of therapy is inappropriate for anyone who is suicidal or has violent thoughts (Landau 2001). While this may be the case for online counselling there are plenty of sites 'selling' therapy through courses, work-shops or tapes without any reference being made concerning its suitability or any possible contraindications. Landau (2001) raises the ethical issues involved with online therapy, namely those involving a practitioner's training, credentials and licensing relating specifically to online work. Accessing a good site may appear a lottery to those without experience to recognise what so-called qualifications actually mean. The title of Dr, for instance, might be highlighted without any indication of a person's actual experience or speciality. This reflects Maheu and Barry's (2000) findings that there is a distinct lack of information about the qualifications of individuals offering mental health services via the Internet. Clearly, when credentials can be assured, those seeking therapy can choose with a greater sense of assurance that they may be helped, particularly as Lange *et al.*'s (2003) study showed that those who benefited most from online counselling and showed significant improvement were those who had accessed online therapists with recognised grounding and training in psychodynamic work.

There are a number of aspects that make online counselling an attractive option for both therapists and those using this service. Increasing waiting lists for face-to-face contact coupled with levels of urgency for help may make this an appealing alternative. Online counselling also proves attractive to many individuals who are physically unable to meet with mental health professionals or are in need of supplementary support outside of counselling

sessions (Oravec 2000). It is a service therefore that can be offered to anyone with Internet access irrespective of location and most types of physical disability or illness.

A number of issues can be raised when comparing Internet therapy with face-to-face work. Cohen and Kerr (1998) found no difference in the effectiveness of computer mediated and face-to-face counselling when treating clients suffering from excessive anxiety. Detractors might point to the absence of many cues that aid the therapeutic process, notably non-verbal communication and the limited expression of affect. Alleman (2002), though, notes that emphasis can still be achieved via certain modes including the use of capital letters or exclamation marks. While this is true in the case of intentional forms of expression, it does not encompass the many aspects a person may be unaware of and are expressed unconsciously. There may also be a strong sense of incongruity between what a person expresses verbally or in writing and what is communicated through their body language. Online work therefore presents a number of barriers to understanding that can be picked up and worked upon in face-to-face contact. The type of engagement between therapist and client may be affected by a person's choice of therapeutic mode as illustrated by Alleman's (2002) findings that higher levels of personal information are disclosed sooner on a computer as opposed to during face-to-face work. While in some cases this might be advantageous it remains unclear as to the extent to which people who have disclosed too much too quickly might be left feeling overly vulnerable and exposed.

A matter of some concern regarding the offering of therapy over the Internet relates to the degree of security and privacy afforded (Oravec 2000; Campbell 1996). In response to this a number of major mental health organisations have issued ethical guidelines for online counselling including encryption and the identification of those having access to patient records. As well as protecting clients there are also issues relating to safeguarding the interests of the therapist, as there are no guarantees against their replies to clients being printed, circulated or published (Cohen and Kerr 1998). While a therapist's professional body or insurance company provides a certain level of security the need for caution in what is written is evident. This has implications with therapists feeling stifled because of concerns about potential litigation or being less expressive and spontaneous because of feeling overly aware about what they might be communicating. These considerations can have a profound impact upon the way in which the therapist–client relationship subsequently develops.

Offered alongside the range of one-to-one work available over the Internet are a range of self-help and support groups. These, according to Lamberg (2003), are proving attractive to people with depression and other mood disorders who are turning to Internet Support Groups (ISGs) as a safe place to bring their concerns. They allow patients to discuss the impact that their illness has on daily life, relate the experiences they have with clinicians and hospitals, share the benefits and drawbacks of particular treatments, review

new research, as well as encourage people to seek help. The effectiveness of these types of therapeutic group is highlighted by Houston, Cooper and Ford (2002) who noted considerable benefits being identified by the participants. The main problems encountered were in finding the most appropriate ISG and the fact that some users were faking their disorders. Internet groups have also been found to be useful in suicide prevention (Mehlum 2000), especially for those who feel isolated and lack the necessary support in their available social networks. ISGs provide them with opportunities to ventilate their feelings and obtain help and containment from others.

As illustrated above there are a number of advantages and disadvantages offered by the online medium that will suit some while proving unattractive to others. It might also complement face-to-face work through offering a holding role for those waiting for available therapists or in providing an immediate crisis response service. A potential problem, however, is raised by Gold (1998), with some not choosing to seek out the necessary therapy or treatment needed while in the comfortable anonymity of cyberspace. Despite its limitations the Internet serves to widen the choice of what is on offer to those in need of psychological support with a number of types of services available. An interesting example of online support can be seen with the brief Internet consultations or 'web chats' offered by *Good Morning* television's Dr Hilary. These provide a type of live 'agony aunt' approach whereby individuals are offered consoling words and urged to seek further help. Opportunities for diagnosis are obviously severely limited through lack of face-to-face contact and only patchy symptomatic details are available. What this does offer, though, is a feeling of connection with others experiencing similar issues and an impetus to seek help. Even if the only benefit obtainable from this type of service is in helping people gain the confidence to seek help, then it is a worthy and necessary venture.

Anti-psychiatry sites

Although representing only one of a number of perspectives, the anti-psychiatry movement is worth mentioning here because of the potential significant impact upon those accessing various sites that argue against the use of traditional mental health treatments. Some of the anti-psychiatry sites strongly condemn conventional methods yet in many cases offer little or no viable alternatives. The language used is often persuasive or frightening, conjuring up images of *One Flew Over the Cuckoo's Nest* and the abusive and oppressive use of treatment. The Say No To Psychiatry site, for example, offers a very stark warning: 'All psychiatric treatments are harmful.' This precedes a long and rambling account warning others of the dangers and evils of psychiatric treatment yet lacking any real substance or direction. While we would hope that most individuals accessing this site would instantly note the complete absence of authorship details and overall absence of any clear arguments or alternatives being offered, it is possible that a number of

individuals looking at this site might be swayed. This includes those who are already fearful of or disillusioned with traditional psychiatry, either because of the stigmatising way in which it is reported or a general lack of support or supervision demonstrated in their own experience of care. The problem is that the wild and fanciful sites that lack any real credibility undermine those that actually make valid claims against the misuse of psychiatry. The worst types are generally vitriolic and abusive of the mental health system, clearly representing the views of dissatisfied and disillusioned consumers. Their opinions, though, are not helpful to the multitude of individuals who can be aided and supported by some of the many good packages of care available. Although in general, questioning and challenging the care on offer can be seen as a productive pursuit, being influenced to avoid all practical help and being left to cope unaided with acute and distressing symptoms is not productive. For example, those accessing the site for the Antipsychiatric Coalition are greeted with the bold heading: 'Why psychiatric drugs are always bad'. The extra degree of stress provided by the word *always* indicates that there is no room for any alternative viewpoints. It is in massive contrast to the active encouragement of drug therapy for the treatment of manic depression posted by organisations such as the Manic Depressive Fellowship (a national user-led organisation and registered charity for people whose lives are affected by manic depression). It has to be mentioned that not all the anti-psychiatry sites reflect such degrees of unsubstantiated rhetoric although they do commonly argue against various modes of treatment. Commonly, no alternatives are offered which is a shame as the process of questioning and challenging the traditions of mental health care is not without its merits. A more balanced and considerate view can be found within many of the service-user sites such as Mind, Rethink, Sane or Together: Working for Wellbeing.

Accessing the Internet

The way in which information on the Internet is received is to a large extent determined by who is doing the searching. It is also affected by what the recipient is intending to get or the particular state of mind of those searching the Internet for information. For example, the stressed and overloaded health care professional or the desperate and suicidal person will not have much time to peruse the huge number of sites available. Locations that are hard to navigate around or those appearing further down a search engine's listed postings may consequently be disregarded. This makes a search of the Internet a bit of a lottery concerning those sites that are accessed and those that remain undiscovered. It also means that those searching the Internet are as likely to be directed towards supportive and informative locations as they are to misleading and potentially harmful ones. Although those searching the Internet come from a wide range of different categories and groupings, the categories focused on below are those of health care professionals and mental health service-users.

Mental health carers/professionals

It appears that mental health professionals are steadily embracing and engaging with new technologies despite Lukoff's (1999) concerns a few years ago that they were behind in learning Internet skills. Recent reports though are more encouraging highlighting the establishment of an increasingly 'mental health literate' community (Christensen and Griffiths 2003). The steady development and utilisation of new media resources while having much of value to offer also present problems in information overload, poor quality material, potential harm and lack of scientific evaluation (Christensen and Griffiths 2000). This in part is reflected by Scrivener's assertion that: 'The Internet is bringing a cornucopia of resources to our desktops. However it is simultaneously threatening to unleash an epidemic of information overload' (Scrivener 2002: 4). The problems with information overload are compounded by the configuration of many search tools that are programmed to retrieve as much as possible of the material available (Cooke 2001). The Internet is to all intents and purposes a maze, and it is very easy to become disoriented and lost. Indeed, the diverse range of sources and content concerning health care information highlights the need to establish the validity and currency of what is posted. As Hebda, Czar and Mascara (1998) argue, there is a need for health care professionals and lay consumers to evaluate online resources using the same criteria as applied to other sources of information. These include the credentials of the source, the accuracy of information accessed, the date of issue or revision, as well as the potential bias of the posting organisation or person. It is clearly impractical and disconcerting for the over-worked health care professional who has a limited amount of time and a seemingly infinite array of resources to consider. Scrivener (2002) identifies a number of the problems created through information overload including mistaking unrefined data for knowledge, using short cuts, stockpiling and failure to appraise information and time mismanagement.

Mistaking unrefined data for knowledge

Clearly when pressured and unable to sufficiently review the material accessed, some information may initially seem informative and appealing. On a more careful and detailed scrutiny certain questions or concerns might be raised about the absence of any clear evidence base for the knowledge provided. Unrefined, raw and unverifiable data may be taken on board by the overloaded health care professional and disseminated as knowledge to colleagues and patients. This might then be received by others as reliable information because of the credentials of the person relaying the message to them.

Using short cuts

The taking of short cuts is influenced by the time constraints a person has to operate within, as experienced, for example, by the GP accessing material between consultations. As a consequence the most easily locatable sites will attract a larger number of visitors. Another consideration relates to which search tool is favoured by those searching the Internet as those offering fewer but more definite 'hits' might be preferred. This is also obviously affected by the abilities and experience of those searching the Internet and their knowledge of particular guidance available such as that provided by the National Institute for Clinical Excellence (NICE).

Stockpiling

This is another problematic feature where the pursuit and collection of data becomes an end in itself. Printouts and saved files fill numerous folders without much sense of purpose or opportunity for critical perusal and reflection. Obviously this problem is compounded by the amount of material that can also be stored electronically.

Failure to appraise information and time mismanagement

The ability to collect huge amounts of information and to store it may well outgrow a person's ability to critically appraise and disseminate it. This is particularly so in light of all the new information that is becoming available on a continuous basis. Therefore, before a person is able to review all previously stored material they will already have a new amount of information to sift through.

If we look at the above features and the already overstretched practitioners, it is interesting to look at how information is shared among the clinical team. Dawkins (1976) coined the term 'memes' to describe self-replicating patterns of information (or misinformation) that behave like viruses. Information is passed from one person to another gaining authority with each new person. This is in a sense a form of 'Chinese whispers' where a message progressively changes with each recitation. It is also the case with a number of Internet sites that recycle data and material from other sites and pass it on electronically with little evidence, in some cases, as to its original source. In a number of cases the authors themselves may believe in the authenticity of what they are posting because of their confidence in the Internet as a reliable source

Mental health service-users

The development of the Internet as an information resource has dramatically transformed the role of the health care recipient to one that is more

empowered and informed. The reasons why service-users are choosing to use the Internet as an informational resource is illustrated by Brown (2002) as including:

- Seeking a second opinion
- More time to interrogate source
- Wide variety of resources available
- Dissatisfaction with traditional health care provider
- Convenient to user (continuous access 24 hours per day)
- Privacy, especially with embarrassing issues.

The points reflected here suggest that individuals are wishing to become more proactive within their care and better informed about the treatment options available to them as well. The Internet is regarded as a valuable and informative resource regarding a wide range of subject areas and a MORI poll conducted in February 2001 revealed that 60 per cent of people who accessed the Internet would use it to seek help for mental health problems. The fact that only a small proportion (9 per cent), believed that the information they were accessing might be unreliable suggests that for most people it is felt to be a trustworthy source. The attractiveness of this resource is aided by its convenience and accessibility as well as the degree of anonymity afforded. The continuous, 24-hour access to sites makes it a very user-friendly location from which to obtain information especially for those whose personal or work commitments makes accessing other places, such as libraries, a more problematic venture. The sense of anonymity is extremely important especially where topics or subjects sought after are potentially embarrassing or individuals are worried about the possible degree of stigma attached. If a family member has suffered a stroke or heart attack, for instance, it is generally felt easier to speak with others about this than it is if they are experiencing mental health problems. This makes the Internet and its available support networks an increasingly valuable resource. Information can be obtained instantly and easily from a multitude of sites without the initial concerns about how one might be judged or critically received by others.

Another advantage offered by the Internet is that of connectedness and a sense of *universality* The process of *universality* is a concept highlighted by Yalom (1995) – a sense or feeling of one's problems and experiences being shared by others. Therefore, through the Internet, an individual has the opportunity to feel part of a worldwide group, connected with others experiencing similar problems, and thereby feels less isolated. This is vital for a number of reasons as a sense of shame or stigma may prevent individuals from seeking assistance through other channels and the feeling of connectedness achieved through this electronic resource might provide the catalyst for seeking further help.

The ready accessibility of information on the Internet means that those in need of help are better informed and aware of the various forms of treatment

on offer. It means that they can have a greater involvement with their care, acting more as participants than of passive recipients of care. The vast range of pharmaceutical information and services available on the Internet also allows individuals to self-prescribe from a certain range of products. To some, this is a positive move forwards enhancing the trend towards consumer empowerment (Dupuits 2002). A number of problems can be seen with this, though, as those accessing these types of services may not fully understand the implications of what they are presented with, being influenced by the sales pitch, biased and misleading information and impressive sounding credentials. A study by Graber and Weckmann (2002) looked at nine pharmaceutical company Internet sites as sources of information about antidepressant medications marketed by the company. All of the websites were found to contain information of an advertising and emotive nature. None of them indicated the cost of their products and there was scant mention of adverse effects. They concluded that the information presented was limited and that it was consequently difficult for prospective consumers to adequately compare products. These are worrying findings, especially for those who have opted to obtain medication over the Internet and who have been misled or only partially informed about these products. In some instances it might also mean that some are getting ineffective or harmful treatment and subsequently being denied products and services that would actually help them.

The caring relationship

The Internet has the potential to create the conditions necessary for transforming the patient–physician relationship to that of a real partnership involving shared decision making (Bauer 2002; Winker *et al.* 2000). One of the core aspects of this is the encouragement and development of patient empowerment and autonomy. Thede (1999) states that this brings a number of practice improvements as patients subsequently come to health care professionals with a more thorough understanding of their condition. The view of the empowered and informed patient is one that raises as many concerns perhaps as it does attractions. For a start we can consider the potential conflict to the patient–practitioner relationship where both parties disagree strongly as to the best course of treatment available. In some cases this might result in care being refused because the patient does not believe it to be in their best interests, a stance that might be based upon a reliable grounding or a set of erroneous messages obtained from the Internet. The degree to which patients are either informed or misinformed by the Internet presents a number of implications, therefore, for this relationship. There is also the issue to consider that almost every conceivable type of perspective is represented as mental health issues are offered through viewpoints as diverse as medical, psychological, social, religious or anti-psychiatry. While this is to be welcomed in many ways, there is also a large potential for confusion and misinformation. Patients may challenge treatment options on the grounds of misleading

or conflicting information that has no reliable evidence base. There is also the issue of desperate individuals seizing upon every potential new treatment method posted on the Internet and finding them unavailable through their practitioners. An example of this concerns the reporting of a trialled treatment for multiple sclerosis using goat serum. It would no doubt prove distressing to read in the *Sunday Times* (25 January 2004) about the dramatic improvement in their condition of those taking part yet reading on the Multiple Sclerosis Society (MSS) website that the drug is not available to the general public. The MSS were more guarded in their claims stating that 'The strong anti-inflammatory component of the serum is thought by researchers to be "potentially useful" in the treatment of MS.' While the information brought by patients might be treated with some scepticism or rejected as lacking in scientific evidence it clearly alerts practitioners to also review these resources themselves for new and updated material. In this manner the practitioner and patient learn together and the person experiencing mental health problems is regarded as having something to offer. In some cases the patient will be better informed and more critically aware of their condition than the person charged with treating them. In others they might be hopelessly misinformed or exploited by some of the many poor sites available. The informed patient, though, is for a number of reasons welcomed by the health care professional who is already struggling with increasing caseloads, time constraints and limited resources. It can also, in some cases, limit the amount of time required for face-to-face consultations as patients can be directed towards various online resources. As well as the 'informed' patient it is worth considering the benefits brought by the 'informed' practitioner to the caring relationship. This can be seen within Galanter *et al.*'s (1998) online educational course in addiction psychiatry. They found that a large number of respondents were psychiatrists, the majority of whom indicated that it helped them understand a 'good deal' about the management of alcoholism.

Conclusion

The virtual explosion into the public sphere of new media technology has to a large extent revolutionised the communication potential of the media. The instant access to an almost limitless array of material is as exciting as it is daunting to the consumer. On the positive side, the availability of information concerning every conceivable viewpoint means that service-users and their families can feel more empowered and included within the process of care. It also means that practitioners can more easily update themselves on a regular basis. On a negative note, the lack of regulation and the proliferation of harmful and misleading material on the Internet continue to cause considerable concern. Of particular note is the difficulty that many consumers have in discerning between what is beneficial and what is detrimental to their well-being, particularly as the language and presentation of some of the worst sites appear to be deliberately geared towards the vulnerable,

mistrustful or disillusioned (i.e. 'All psychiatric care is harmful and oppressive'). It is essential therefore that various initiatives are employed in order to tackle these problems including changes in regulation and a policing of the worst sites such as those that openly advocate suicide. This should be matched by the further promotion of the more productive and positive ones, as illustrated by the Samaritans' recent large billboard advertising initiative. The importance for health care practitioners is in being aware of the range of information available over the Internet which include the negative as well as the positive. Therefore, as well as being able to direct individuals towards the better sites (i.e. Mind or the Alzheimer's Society), practitioners are also aware of the potential range of harmful or misleading material that others might be exposed to. This helps health care professionals where necessary to begin to counteract and deal with some of the often very persuasive and harmful content that is so easily accessible, thereby enabling individuals to be directed towards getting the most supportive help for themselves.

10 And . . .

This book has looked in depth at the way in which attitudes and feelings about mental illness are influenced and shaped through the range of portrayals across a range of media sources. The resultant view is largely dependent upon a number of factors that include a person's prior experience and degree of knowledge with regard to mental health issues. It is also influenced by the potency of messages attached to various media products and the type of engagement an individual has with them. One of the main concerns relates to the types of message accessible and the sense of imbalance that is apparent with predominantly negative portrayals being found. The overly dramatic and sensational style of depiction found in many media examples has an insidious and unsettling effect upon those exposed to them and might be hard to shake off, even following access to educational and health promotional material. One of the core problems here is that mental health promotional material appears on the surface far less enticing or dramatically engaging compared to that which carries stigmatising or stereotypical content. Our reading of messages is therefore heavily influenced by negative depictions as accurate and realistic portrayals are undermined by the more familiar stereotypes that link mental illness with aspects such as violence or eccentric behaviour. In order to tackle this, initiatives or approaches are needed to challenge and restrict the range of negative products on offer and to replace them with a greater selection of realistic and accurate examples.

The ongoing proliferation of negative examples within the media indicates that regulatory mechanisms in place across the different media types are not really working. This can be seen in particular within the formats of television and the newsprint media which, despite being very tightly regulated as well as having clear guidelines (BSC 1998; ITC 2002; PCC 2004; NUJ 1999) denouncing the inclusion of stereotypical and stigmatising mental health content, are still regularly found to be acting against them. This is strongly influenced by commercial pressures that urge producers and editors on towards ever more dramatic and audience-pleasing depictions. The fact that many examples appear to go unchallenged is a particular cause for concern and can be seen as relating to either a lack of critical feedback or the relative ineffectiveness of the regulatory bodies concerned to bring about any change.

A glance at the Press Complaints Commission website illustrates this point as very few instances are noted where negative coverage of mental health issues has resulted in any consequent action being taken. One interesting example concerns a complaint made to the PCC about an article printed in the *Daily Star* on the 4 April 2000 carrying the headline 'Beast Chops out Jail Pals Liver'. It was subsequently followed by another article a day later headlined 'Mental Hospital Set Lector Fiend Free'. The complaint was made by the victim's sister concerning breaches of Clauses 5 (intrusion into grief and shock) and 1 (accuracy) of the *Code of Practice*. The complaint was upheld and the newspaper offered to print an apology and send some flowers to the complainant's mother although this was rejected. It is clear, however, that the number of complaints considered does not match the large number of examples that seem to openly flaunt the regulations as evidenced by items that are regularly found within the tabloid media. But it is also worth being reminded of instances when significant movement has been observed following the critical public receipt of certain media products, such as *The Sun* newspaper's sudden emergence as a mental health campaigner following the widespread criticism received for their poorly chosen coverage of Frank Bruno's hospitalisation for depression. This demonstrated the fact that mental health coverage could be handled in a more productive way if it was perceived to be in the best interests of those concerned to do so. It also illustrates the point that the overall picture concerning what mental illness is perceived to be can be influenced by a number of sources, particularly media personnel, health care professionals or service-user groups. The following section outlines briefly some of the core approaches being employed in an attempt to challenge negative opinion and work towards creating a better-informed and more caring public when it comes to the topic of mental illness. The three main areas being addressed are: connecting (*distancing*), educating (*entertaining*) and exposure (*exploitation*). These themes have been focused upon at different stages throughout this book and reflect the positive end of the spectrum, in sharp contrast to their negative counterparts that are included within the brackets.

Connecting

In order for attitudes and feelings about the mentally ill to alter fundamentally there needs to be a greater sense of caring and concern for their felt and lived experience. As has been seen in the case of individuals whom the public care about (e.g. Frank Bruno), the media can be forced to rescind their current stance and a level of informed debate and exposure can follow. There are many different types of portrayal that take the receiver into a close proximity with the topic or theme of mental illness. As suggested previously, this is not always a comfortable or pleasant process for the recipient as an unpleasant or uncomfortable state might be aroused. This is, on occasions, a deliberate effect as certain media providers seek to arouse strong feelings like

fear or suspense for the purposes of entertainment. The value of connecting portrayals is that they allow receivers to catch glimpses of another's world, an experience that might appear strange and something they would not have been able to imagine or conceive of. It seems that the inner world of every conceivable illness type is able to find representation within the media as a whole although featured heavily within literature. This can be briefly illustrated by the following examples that cover a range of conditions including depression (*The Bell Jar, Prozac Diary*), psychosis (*I Never Promised you a Rose Garden, Briefing for a Descent into Hell*), Munchausen's syndrome by proxy (*Sickened*), dementia (*Out of Mind*) and alcoholism (*Under the Volcano*). The sense of connectedness is strongly employed by the use of techniques such as first-person narrative styles that take readers directly into the thought processes of those involved. It is also achieved with some potency within the visual media of film and television through scenes that illustrate something of the person's inner world. This is done by the utilisation of various approaches including narrative voice-overs illustrating to the recipient what a person might be thinking or feeling. An example here can be seen in the final scene of Hitchcock's *Psycho* where the audience is finally granted access to Norman Bates's disturbed and frightening inner world. Another approach is through the use of visual cues that allow observers to see what a person's hallucinatory content looks and feels like, as cleverly conveyed in the film *A Beautiful Mind*. These can be extraordinarily powerful experiences helping to generate a real sense of understanding and awareness as to what is actually being experienced by the individual with mental health problems.

A sense of connectedness with mental health issues is also aided through the process of identification. This incorporates Horton and Wohl's (1956) concept of *parasocial relations* whereby observers feel a sense of relationship and engagement with particular characters placed in front of them. Clearly, the type of connectedness established is influenced a great deal by the extent to which we actually like or admire characters being portrayed and relates strongly to the types of attitude subsequently developed. It is interesting therefore to note the types of characterisation that are most admired by audiences and include those that are kind and helpful, display positive social and non-verbal behaviours, are successful in coping with threats and are competent and resourceful (Hoffner 1991). It is sadly evident that these qualities are rarely applied to those depicted as having mental health problems who are instead commonly shown as ineffective, odd and menacing, in contrast to those who are seen as belonging to the 'normal' population. The importance of creating a wider range of likeable mentally ill representations relates to the enhanced level of concern that is thereby evoked for their welfare. It means helping to move the recipient away from the more familiar position of detached and unconcerned observer towards one that is more concerned and caring. Another significant feature concerns the range of qualities associated with a person in light of their perceived attractiveness. It is worth considering Hatfield and Sprecher's (1986) findings that physically

attractive people are regarded as possessing more socially desirable personality traits than unattractive individuals. As the mentally ill have traditionally been portrayed as odd and unappealing, it makes a welcome change to note the wider selection of attractive characterisations that are currently being employed such as Judy Dench in the film *Iris* or Lisa in the television soap *Hollyoaks*. This provides audience members with more realistic and identifiable role models than the monstrous, strange and scary representations usually on offer. The concept of role model is an important one and prominent individuals who are universally liked can go a long way in facilitating a shift in entrenched or uninformed attitudes. The degree of desire that a person has to understand something of another's lived experience is important and this inclination can be seen as being generated by different types of catalyst. On the one hand this might be simply a means of satisfying morbid curiosity whereas, on the other, it might be that genuine and altruistic feelings are being acted upon. To a certain extent, these approaches are influenced by the type of mental health problem being experienced, differing significantly, for example, between neurotic and psychotic states. At the neurotic end of the spectrum, the response is more likely to be sympathetic, understanding and caring while the opposite pole, that of the psychotic representation, generates feelings of fear and hostility. This to a large extent is dependent upon the way in which these issues are portrayed, a difference that is starkly seen in the way stories are presented by the tabloid media. Depression, for example, is on occasions highlighted with words such as 'sad' appearing prominently in the headlines (e.g. 'Sad Kerry', a report about Kerry McFadden's experience of depression that appeared in *The Sun*). The word '*sad*' can be regarded from two perspectives, either drawing the reader into a sympathetic and concerned response or alternatively carrying implications of 'pathetic' and helpless. It is, though, in direct contrast to the way in which psychotic states are regularly covered with familiar stereotypical terms such as 'psycho' or 'nutter' being employed. The essence of this concerns the type of reaction being encouraged by the style of coverage which plays a large part in the type of response engaged in the recipient, be it sympathetic and caring or unconcerned and dismissive. The essence therefore of the connecting approach is of allowing those experiencing psychological difficulties to be better understood, leading to a greater sense of acceptance and inclusion by others.

Educating

Allied to the process of connecting with another's felt and lived experience is that of helping media consumers to appreciate the real facts about mental illness. This means providing recipients with accurate information as well as helping them to become more discerning and questioning regarding the authenticity of what they are exposed to. The need for clear and factual education is aptly illustrated by the many misleading and inaccurate portrayals of mental illness found in abundance across all media types. In

order to combat this, a number of initiatives have been developed to help in the education of media providers as well as those accessing their products. This is aided through a number of major campaign initiatives targeted at tackling stigma and discrimination concerning mental health issues including the Mindout for Mental Health's Mindshift campaign, the Royal College of Psychiatry's Changing Minds: Every Family in the Land and Shift, a 5-year campaign run by the National Institute for Mental Health in England.

Because of the vast informational reach of the mass media, it is vital that those involved in communicating mental health messages are actually sending material out that is both accurate and realistic. It is important therefore to ensure that media personnel are updated and more fully aware about the content carried within their products. In order to achieve this, the development of good working relationships between media providers and mental health advocates is essential. In total it incorporates what can be seen as a tri-partite relationship (see Figure 10.1) with service-user, health care professional and media groups all working together. There are a number of benefits that can be gained through closer ties between these groups and that can result in the creation of products such as the *Guide for Journalists and Broadcasters Reporting on Schizophrenia*, a venture including consultation between the National Union of Journalists and the Royal College of Psychiatry. Liaison with the media is seen as a vital step in the fight against stigmatisation and discrimination by both professional and service-user groups. As a consequence, most of these groups actively train or advise their members about getting involved with media personnel. In a number of instances the result is a media product that reflects a sense of collaboration between those who understand mental health issues and those who understand the communicating power of a specific media source. An example is the Media Action Group for Mental Health, a West Midlands based group that puts together local stories for journalists reflecting a more honest and accurate and positive perspective on mental health.

Another approach relates to the educative potential that the media itself

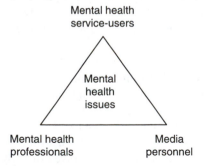

Figure 10.1 Media liaison and the tri-partite relationship.

has in helping individuals understand various aspects connected with mental illness. It includes projects or events that utilise examples from various media sources such as literature, film and music in order to enhance students' sensitivity to the personal experiences of psychiatric patients and to broaden their understanding of mental illness and the various methods used in its treatment (Wall and Rossen 2004). This is reflected in other successful studies by Frisch (2001), Bhugra (2003) and Hyler and Morre (1996) that employ cinematic examples as a means of developing students' awareness and understanding about specific mental health topics. The media with its multifaceted range of examples both positive and negative, historical and current, provides an enormous resource to dip into and examine the diversity of ways in which the topic of mental illness is represented. On a number of occasions the author of this book has devised and run a taught module (Mental Health Issues and the Media) that encourages students to examine the influence that particular mental health media messages have upon one's resultant attitudes. Student comments and evaluations have indicated significant shifts in approach with subsequent media engagement being carried out in a much more critical and questioning manner. One student in particular mentioned that she had initially been greatly amused and entertained by the film *Me, Myself and Irene* although on watching it again during the course of the module had a far greater appreciation as to how insensitive and offensive much of the content actually is.

Educating and changing a person's attitudinal approach is difficult and clearly does not rely upon information alone. Knowing that the majority of mentally ill people are not dangerous does not necessarily mean that we will feel safe and comfortable in the presence of those with mental health problems. One scheme in particular, the Mental Health Awareness in Action programme of educational workshops, was set up in west Kent schools in order to help tackle stigma and discrimination. It resulted in a significant change in attitude among those taking part and saw derogatory and stigmatising language being replaced by more sensitive and accepting words (Pinfold 2003). As illustrated by Haghighat (2001), one of the core elements in the success of workshops such as these concerns the opportunity for individuals to ventilate and share their anxieties and feelings. Many people need the opportunity to express and understand what their fears are actually based upon if they are to be properly able to accommodate and accept those with mental health problems.

Running alongside the presentation of clear and unambiguous material is the need to tackle and challenge the range of misinforming messages accessible. As already mentioned, these are plentiful and are strongly influenced by aspects of commercialism that encourage their continued appearance. As highlighted within a study by the Media Bureau (2001), the majority of journalists themselves observed that their reporting about mental health should be better. It is interesting to note that even those who are involved directly in producing stigmatising and stereotypical material would like to improve it

but are swayed by pressures from other departments such as editors and production staff. It is therefore at all levels within media organisations that liaison needs to be developed.

A further approach concerns the provision of direct feedback to media providers regarding what is seen as either commendable or unacceptable coverage of mental health issues. This feedback is given in order to encourage the continued appearance of positive content as well as prompting media personnel to look at the potential harm that might be caused by poor reporting or inaccurate representations. Of course, some of the poorer styles of coverage are completely intentional and are unlikely to be swayed by persuasive arguments to the contrary. This is where the appropriate regulatory body can be engaged, with complaints directed to bodies such as Ofcom or the Press Complaints Commission (see Appendix 2 for fuller range of information). The importance of this is outlined by Philo (1996a) who states that those involved in creating media products should be more aware of the problems they are creating. Demands for change should not be left to mental health professionals but members of the public, service-users and their families should also be encouraged to get involved.

Exposure

Education and connection are both vital approaches although they are largely reliant upon the degree of exposure that various media products are able to achieve. As with the newsprint media, it is worth acknowledging the distinction between the tabloid and broadsheet styles, with the less accurate and more stigmatising format (tabloid) reaching a far more extensive audience. This is reflected across other media types where the dramatic and sensational is witnessed by a greater number of individuals. The challenge facing those involved with mental health promotion, therefore, relates to the uncomfortable fact that, for many, mental ill-health is far more exciting and appealing than mental well-health. The stereotypical and the stigmatising is the type of material that fascinates or shocks people and encourages them to buy into various products, enticed in part by the sense of dramatic content to be found within. Gaining maximum exposure for health promotional material means attending to the packaging of products and looking at the various ways in which audience appeal can be enhanced. In some cases this involves the offering up of products that are both entertaining and educative in order to get them noticed. This can be reflected in the effect achieved by some of the television dramas and soaps that combine somewhat unrealistic or overly dramatic material with opportunities to understand something of a person's experience. This is at times complemented by the provision of helplines and other contact details at the end of programmes for those interested in seeking support or needing to talk about issues raised.

The theoretical notions of perception and Gestalt theory have been addressed previously, focusing upon the attributes that help certain messages

stand out from the background and be noticed. From a health promotional point of view, there is a strong need to investigate the particular characteristics of the channel selected for carrying a message. If, for example, the Internet is being used as a vehicle to transmit information, it is important to look at the various ways by which potential consumers are made aware of the existence of particular sites. This might be achieved through advertising or the range of content words entered when registering sites which are locatable through various search engines. The Samaritans organisation has helped to direct attention towards the existence of their electronic resources through advertising including a range of billboards carrying slogans such as: 'When was the last time anyone overheard an e-mail?' and 'The trouble with talking about things over the phone is the words don't always come out the way right' (Samaritans 2005).

Another factor helping to gain exposure for certain media products concerns the degree of intensity attached to content material. This can be achieved through the type of experience being recounted, as evidenced by the high popularity of autobiographical accounts dealing with appalling personal experiences such as child abuse or the murder of family members. Some of these accounts are linked to experiences that have already achieved a high level of exposure within the news media. They are ostensibly written as a means of putting the tragedy of personal experience into some sense of order and in gaining a degree of therapeutic value through the process of writing. There is also a significant degree of value on offer to others who have encountered related experiences and who are emboldened to share their feelings with others.

As has been seen above, the intensity of a mental health experience can cause it to stand out and gain greater attention. Maximum exposure is also achieved where particular psychological issues are associated or connected with individuals who themselves regularly gain widespread public attention. This can be seen where celebrities convey powerful messages to their audience, either of a self-destructive or of a self-nurturing kind. There is a long history, particularly within the music industry, of self-destructive behaviour being glamorised, even to some extent admired, and a person's tragic downfall helping to cement their iconic status, such as with Janis Joplin, Jim Morrison and Kurt Cobain. On a more refreshing note, there are a range of celebrities who are prepared to openly reveal and talk about their problems, allowing others to glimpse something of their vulnerable side. The current climate perhaps makes this a more accepted process than in previous years and includes a number of popular celebrities such as Geri Halliwell (bulimia/ depression) and Paul Gascoigne (alcoholism). The crucial message being sent out by these individuals is that of survival as well as the sense of optimism in that help is obtainable. Readers are hopefully emboldened by the courage taken to reveal what appear to be excruciatingly painful and embarrassing details. This process is aided and complemented by various initiatives such as the Mindout for Mental Health's (2001b) Headspace campaign whereby a

number of music stars have spoken out about their own personal experiences of mental distress or that of people close to them. It can be illuminating and enlightening, therefore, for others to hear of the pain and distress that others have experienced and, in some cases, the identity of the person speaking out can be very surprising. It does help to demystify something about the nature of mental illness, certainly the fact that anybody, irrespective of background or social status, can experience psychological distress. This incorporates even those people who in the general public might pass off as having 'everything going for them' and therefore impervious to mental distress. It is a point raised by Geri Halliwell in her autobiographical account *Just for the Record*, stating how difficult it is to be met by such a misunderstanding attitude.

It is also worth mentioning here the exposure achieved by initiatives such as the World Federation for Mental Health's (2005) annual World Mental Health day, now being held each October as a means of publicising mental health issues and promoting better awareness among the general public.

Lastly, there is huge mileage to be gained in events that encourage and celebrate mental health expression and provide a sustained focus upon the topic of mental illness. This helps by gathering various products and modes of expression together and promoting them as a collective package, thereby gaining maximum exposure. An example of this can be seen with the Royal College of Psychiatry's Mind Odyssey programme of events that included multiple forms of expression such as film, art, dance, writing and music. This importantly provided both a means for creative expression as well as opportunities to question what those accessing these products were exposed to. Some of the films shown, for example, were followed by discussion panels (comprising health care personnel and service-user representatives) thereby providing a forum for exploration.

The way forward

The three issues identified above (connecting, educating and exposure) all help in the development of more adaptive images as well as looking at ways in which recipients engage with them. It is clear that the process of liaison is significant in helping to develop better relationships between mental health advocates and media personnel as well as enhancing the flow of communication between them. The maintenance and development of further health promotion/education initiatives will help in changing the 'total' picture of mental illness that is picked up by the receiver. It is this sense of the 'whole' that is important, as stigmatising and stereotypical depictions will never be completely eradicated owing to their attractiveness and commercial potential. The key, therefore, is in complementing the attention focused upon the media provider with a corresponding degree of attention upon the receiver. This means helping to develop the 'discerning' and 'interpretive' receiver as an individual who is able to thoughtfully question what it is they are exposed to. It might even represent the audience member who enjoys watching the film

Me, Myself and Irene yet is able to correctly distance Jim Carrey's facial contortions, exaggerated mannerisms and abusive behaviour with the 'collective group' regarded as experiencing mental health problems. It means partly starting the process of education at a young age, helping children to understand that the stereotypical characteristics they are exposed to are not representative of the 'total' group. Another aspect explored regards the process of perception and the type of 'filter' that messages might be passed through as a result of prior knowledge and experience. The space for people to express and make sense of what their fears and anxieties about the mentally ill are goes a long way in reducing the subsequent degree of discriminatory attitudes demonstrated as well as making people more receptive to factual information. Changing attitudes is not easy although certainly not impossible. If we relate back to Jastrow's duck and rabbit image (as seen in Figure 4.1) we can consider the issue that perhaps, for some, the duck is the stronger interpretation because it appears as a more exciting and attractive representation. Bringing another representation in front of the public's gaze is the main challenge although once we fully appreciate that there are two different interpretations we can move with greater ease between the two images. This, therefore, is the 'discerning' recipient, a person who is aware of the proximity of competing stimuli and is more thoughtful about the overall message taken away. The way forward for mental health campaigners is not a journey without difficulties although there have been some positive responses to various aspects that they should take heart from. If *The Sun* newspaper, for example, can be transformed, albeit very briefly, into a staunch mental health campaigner then one might believe that anything is possible.

Appendix 1 Internet sites – professional and service-user locations

Professional organisations

There are some very well constructed and clearly laid out sites aimed specifically at members of various professional bodies who deal with those with mental health problems. A selection of these is provided below:

Royal College of Psychiatrists (http://www.rcpsych.ac.uk/)
This site provides extensive material covering professional and practice issues. Information is offered about a wide range of mental health problems, various treatment options available and details of current initiatives such as the Changing Minds and Partners in Care campaigns. It also has links with published research, related articles and press releases. Specific information is also provided for professionals with regards to training courses or updating sessions available.

British Association of Social Workers (http://www.basw.co.uk/)
A range of articles, books and current news reports are accessible through this site. It also provides those accessing this site with links to other related sites. Professional advice and representation details are also given for its members.

British Association of Occupational Therapists (http://www.cot.co.uk/)
This site includes separately accessible material for its members and general members of the public who are directed to different home pages. A small range of mental health material is accessible via the 'public' site concerning legislation, treatment and certain conditions.

British Psychological Society (http://www.bps.org.uk/index.cfm)
This site is informative, is well laid out and very accessible. It has many links, press releases training and development, as well as information about finding a psychologist or making complaints. Careers and development, events and conferences, press and media releases, publications. Its accessibility is enhanced with the inclusion of a service for visually impaired users.

Royal College of Nursing (http://www.rcn.org.uk)
Some mental health information is provided although it is only accessible to members of the RCN. It includes the Mental Health Zone, which is billed as a one-stop shop for mental health nurses. This provides resources, policy initiatives, links and current news concerning mental health issues. Online journals, current news items, campaign initiatives and a discussion forum are also accessible.

Nursing and Midwifery Council (http://www.nmc-uk.org)
A range of research reports, legislative items and current news items are available through this site. It also includes specific professional advice for its members, various press release statements as well as links to related sites.

Mental health charities/user groups

Mind (http://www.mind.org.uk/)
The purpose of Mind is to challenge discrimination, influence mental health policy, as well as provide a voice and advance the views of those affected with mental health problems. Their Internet site is an informative location that offers a range of resources including online booklets, information sheets, newsroom items and details of policies and campaigns. It is easy to navigate around with good links provided.

RETHINK **(formerly the National Schizophrenia Fellowship)**
(http://www.rethink.org/)
The aim of RETHINK is to help those affected by severe mental illness, including schizophrenia, to *recover* a better quality of life. Their site is uncluttered and provides a number of good resources such as the 'How mentally fit are you?' quiz as well as links and advice for other services (e.g. the Samaritans, 'contacting your GP'). Of particular interest within their main site is the @ease site, which is geared towards a younger readership encountering stress through issues such as exams, leaving home or starting work.

Samaritans (http://www.samaritans.org.uk/)
This is a well laid out and very inviting site including statements such as: 'It doesn't matter who you are – if you are in crisis, despairing or suicidal, it can make all the difference to talk about how you are feeling. You can speak in total confidence with one of our volunteers about anything that is troubling you. We will not judge you; we will not tell you what to do; but we will try to help you think things through. With Samaritans, you get the time and the space to find a way through.' It includes an audio clip resource that details what happens if you call.

Mentality (http://www.mentality.org.uk/)
Mentality is a national charity dedicated solely to the promotion of mental health. They work with the public and private sector, user and survivor groups and voluntary agencies to promote the mental health of individuals, families, organisations and communities. Their Internet site is an easy to access location providing a range of mental health promotional material, campaign information, news reports and related publications.

Sainsbury Centre for Mental Health (http://www.scmh.org.uk)
The Sainsbury Centre for Mental Health (SCMH) is a registered charity that aims to improve the quality of life for people with severe mental health problems. This organisation provides an excellent Internet resource that covers an extensive amount of information including practice issues, conference details, key discussion points, training material, as well as access to methods and tools for service review, evaluation and audit.

Maca (http://www.maca.org.uk/index.asp)
This is one of the country's leading national charities supporting people with mental health problems. They work in partnership with other organisations, such as primary care trusts and local authorities, to run a wide range of mental health services of which a good deal of material is provided on their website such as advocacy work, respite care and a range of therapeutic approaches. They also cover campaign information, current news items and have a range of downloadable publications.

Mental Health Foundation (http://www.mentalhealth.org.uk/)
The Mental Health Foundation bill themselves as the biggest website on mental health (and mental illness) in the UK. This claim is suitably reflected by the considerable amount of informative material and detailed resources concerning mental health issues available. They include information on problems, treatments as well as strategies for living with mental distress. This is complemented by related policy and published material, links with other sites and current news items.

Zito Trust (http://www.zitotrust.co.uk/)
The Zito Trust is a registered mental health charity seeking to highlight issues relating to mental illness and the care of those who are affected by it. They include information about treatment and prescribing issues as well as policy issues and inquiry reports. Their website includes some interesting resources such as a press office section, with access to press materials and an interview request mechanism for journalists to contact experts and patients with experience of schizophrenia.

SANE (http://www.sane.org.uk/)

SANE is one of the UK's leading charities concerned with improving the lives of everyone affected by mental illness. They include material concerning fund-raising and research, and have a discussion group facility as well as a section providing links to other related sites. An extensive selection of mental illness literature is available and they also interestingly include a selection of artwork painted by those with mental health problems.

Appendix 2 Evaluating Internet sites

The following provides a guide to those accessing various Internet sites as to the validity of the information posted. It relates specifically to sites carrying mental health material and the extent to which this either promotes or denigrates, informs or misleads, and is helpful or harmful. Prompts and areas for further consideration are provided by the text in italics.

Internet site
- What is the specific purpose of this site?
  (*Education, entertainment, campaigning or a selling of products*)
- Who is the targeted audience?
  (*Service-user, mental health professional or lay public*)
- How easily accessible is this source?
  (*Position on search engine list, links from other sites, published/advertised URL*)

Currency
- How up to date is the information provided?
  (*This can be weighed up against other sources. Are there any major omissions?*)
- Are dates provided indicating when the information has been posted?
  (*Home page, index or within the main body*)
- Is the information updated as new material becomes available?
  (*Some sites clearly list dates and provide site visitors with indications of this*)

Ownership
- Who has posted this information?
  (*e.g. Governmental agency, professional group, service-user organisation, media provider, pharmaceutical company or personal*)
- Is it a recognised organisation or group?
  (*e.g. Mind, Royal College of Psychiatry, Department of Health, BBC*)
- What are the credentials of those offering this site?
  (*e.g. Professional, personal experience, affiliation to user-carer group*)

- What possible bias could be present?
  (*e.g. Drug sponsorship or personal experience of care*)
- Have those posting information had any material published or presented elsewhere?
  (*Journal articles, books, official publications, television or radio programmes*)

Mental health promotion
- To what extent are mental health issues being positively promoted?
  (*Accurate and realistic messages, support and acceptance, campaigning*)
- To what extent could this material prove harmful?
  (*Inaccuracies, dissuasion re various treatment types*)
- Is any stereotypical or stigmatising content present?
  (*Imagery, terminology, overall content*)
- Does this site provide any links with other related sites?
  (*Range and quality*)

Presentation and site layout
- How easy is it to orientate around the site and retrieve information?
  (*Clarity of navigation, site maps, links to home page, index*)
- Is the information provided supported by any suitable evidence-base?
  (*e.g. Links to legislation and governmental acts, research material*)
- How accessible is the language used with regards the targeted audience?
  (*User-friendliness, jargonistic or technical terms, use by adolescent visitors*)

Appendix 3 Complaining about the media

Broadcast media

BBC
Tel: 08700 100222 (information line); e-mail: info@bbc.co.uk
Website: www.bbc.co.uk (includes contact details for specific producers)
Address: Head of Programme Complaints, BBC Broadcasting House,
London W1A 1AA.

Channel 4
Tel: 020 73068333 (viewer enquiries); e-mail: righttoreply@channel4.co.uk
Website: www.channel4.com
Address: Channel 4 Television, 124 Horseferry Road, London SW1.

Channel 5
Tel: 08457 050505 (duty office); e-mail: customerservices@five.tv
Website: www.fivetv
Address: Duty Office, Channel 5 Broadcasting Ltd, 22 Long Acre, London
WC2E 9LY.

ITV
Tel: 020 78438000 (programme complaints); e-mail: dutyoffice@itv.co.uk
Website: www.itv.co.uk
Address: Network Limited, 200 Gray's Inn Road, London WC1X 8HF.

Ofcom (The Office of Communications)
Tel: 0845 4563000; e-mail: contact@ofcom.org.uk
Website: www.ofcom.org.uk
Address: Ofcom, Riverside House, 2a Southwark Bridge Rd, London
SE1 9HA.

The Internet

Internet Watch Foundation
Tel: 01223 237 700; e-mail: media@iwf.org.uk
Website: www.iwf.org.uk
Address: The Internet Watch Foundation, East View, 5 Coles Lane,
Oakington, Cambridge CB4 5BA.

Advertising (non broadcast)

Advertising Standards Authority
Tel: 020 7580555 (Complaints Department); e-mail: inquiries@asa.org.uk
Website: www.asa.org.uk (online complaints form)
Address: Advertising Standards Authority, 2 Torrington Place, London
WC1 7HW.

Newsprint media

Press Complaints Commission
Tel: 020 73533732; e-mail: pcc@pcc.org.uk
Website: www.pcc.org.uk
Address: Press Complaints Commission, 1 Salisbury Square, London
EC4 8JB.

National and local press
Complainants can either contact the editor of a particular newsprint title or
the journalist responsible for the story in question. Alternatively, correspondence can be sent to the letters page marked 'for publication'.

Advice for those wishing to make complaints

For advice or information about the style and content of complaints, e.g.
what to include and how to phrase it, the following are useful contacts:

Manic Depression Fellowship – www.mdf.org.uk (Tel: 020 77932600)
MediaWise – www.presswise.org.uk (Tel: 0117 941 5889)
Mental After Care Association – www.maca.org.uk (Tel: 020 74366194)
Mental Health Foundation – www.mentalhealth.org.uk (Tel: 020 78020300)
Mental Health Media – www.mhmedia.com (Tel: 020 77008171)
Mind – www.mind.org.uk (Tel: 020 85192122)
Rethink – www.rethink.org (Tel: 020 73309100)

Bibliography

Adams, T. (1998) *Addicted*. London: Collins Willow.

Alao, A., Yolles, J. and Armenta, W. (1999) Cybersuicide: The Internet and Suicide. *The American Journal of Psychiatry*, 156(11): 1836–1837.

Allan, S. (1999) *News Culture*. Buckingham: Open University Press.

Alleman, J. (2002) Online Counselling: The Internet and Mental Health Treatment. *Psychotherapy: Theory, Research, Practice, Training*, 39(2): 199–209.

Allen, R. (1995) *Projecting Illusion*. Cambridge: Cambridge University Press.

Alternate Health. *Schizophrenia*. Available at <http://www.alternate-health.com/schizo.html> (Accessed 12 March 2005).

Anderson, M. (2003) 'One Flew over the Psychiatric Unit': Mental Illness and the Media. *Journal of Psychiatric and Mental Health Nursing*, 10, 297–306.

Andreasen, N. (1987) Creativity and Mental Illness: Prevalence Rates in Writers and their First Degree Relatives. *American Journal of Psychiatry*, 144(10): 1288–1292.

Andrews, V. (1979) *Flowers in the Attic*. London: HarperCollins.

Angermeyer, M., Schulze, B. and Dietrich, S. (2003) Courtesy Stigma – a Focus Group Study of Relatives of Schizophrenia Patients. *Social Psychiatry and Psychiatric Epidemiology*, 38(10): 593–602.

Antipsychiatric Coalition. *The Antipsychiatry Coalition*. Available at <www.antipsychiatry.org> (Accessed 16 March 2005).

Appleby, L. and Wessely, S. (1988) Public Attitudes to Mental Illness: The Influence of the Hungerford Massacre. *Medicine, Science & the Law*, 28(4): 291–295.

Armes, R. (1994) *Action and Image – Dramatic Structure in Cinema*. Manchester: Manchester University Press.

Asch, S. (1961) Effects of Group Pressure upon the Modification and Distortion of Judgement. In Henle, M. (ed.) *Documents of Gestalt Theory*. Los Angeles: University of California Press.

ASH (2005) Available at <http://www.ash.org.uk/html/press/990528.html> (Accessed 22 March 2005).

Augoustinos, M. and Walker, I. (1995) *Social Cognition: an Integrated Introduction*. London: Sage.

Austin, L. and Husted, K. (1998) Cost Effectiveness of Television, Radio, and Print Media Programs for Public Mental Health Education. *Psychiatric Services*, 49(6): 808–811.

Bagdikian, B. (1997) *The Media Monopoly* (5th edn). Boston: Beacon Press.

Bagnall, N. (1993) *Newspaper Language*. Oxford: Focal Press.

Bandura, A. (1986) *Social Foundations of Thought and Action: a Social Cognitive Theory*. Englewood Cliffs: Prentice Hall.

Banks, I. (1984) *The Wasp Factory*. London: Abacus.

Barker, M. (2001) The Newson Report. In Barker, M. and Petley, J. *Ill Effects – the Media/Violence Debate* (2nd edn). London: Routledge, pp. 27–46.

Barker, M. and Petley, J. (2001) *Ill Effects – the Media/Violence Debate* (2nd edn). London: Routledge.

Barlow, S. (1996) *Heracles*. Warminster: Aris and Phillips.

Barthes, R. (1972) *Mythologies*. St Albans: Paladin.

Barton, R. (1976) *Institutional Neurosis* (3rd edn). Bristol: J Wright.

Barwise, P. and Ehrenberg, A. (1988) *Television and its Audience*. London: Sage.

Bauer, K. (2002) Using the Internet to Empower Patients and to Develop Partnerships with Clinicians. *World Hospitals & Health Services*, 38(2): 2–10.

Baume, P. Rolfe, A. and Clinton, M. (1998) Suicide on the Internet: a Focus for Nursing Intervention? *Australian and New Zealand Journal of Mental Health Nursing*, 7(4): 134–141

Becker, H. (1963) *Outsiders: Studies in the Sociology of Deviance*. New York: The Free Press.

Becker, H. (1964) *The Other Side: Perspectives on Deviance*. New York: The Free Press.

Belsey, A. (1998) Journalism and Ethics: Can they Co-exist? In Kieran, M. (ed.) *Media Ethics*. London: Routledge, pp.1–14.

Bennett, A. and Royle, N. (1999) *Introduction to Literature, Criticism and Theory*. (2nd edn). London: Prentice Hall.

Berlo, D. (1960) *The Process of Communication*. San Francisco: Reinhart Press.

Berlyne, D. (1960) *Conflict Arousal and Curiosity*. New York: McGraw Hill.

Berne, E. (1964) *Games People Play*. Middlesex: Penguin.

Bernlef, J. (1988) *Out of Mind*. London: Faber and Faber.

Berry, G. and Asamen, J. (1993) *Children and Television: Images in a Changing Socio-cultural World*. London: Sage.

Bessell, T., Anderson, J., Silagy, C. Sansom, L. and Hiller, J. (2003) Surfing, Self-Medicating and Safety: Buying Non-Prescription and Complementary Medicines via the Internet. *Quality and Safety in Health Care*, 12(2): 88–92.

Bhugra, D. (2003) Teaching Psychiatry through Cinema. *Psychiatric Bulletin*, 27, 429–430.

Biocca, F. (1988) Opposing Conceptions of the Audience. In Anderson, J. (ed.) *Communication Yearbook*. Newbury Park: Sage, pp. 51–80.

Birney, E. (ed.) (1962) *Selected Poems of Malcolm Lowry*. San Francisco: City Lights Books.

Bloch, S. and Singh, B. (1997) *Understanding Troubled Minds: a Guide to Mental Illness and its Treatment*. Melbourne: Melbourne University Press.

Bloom, V. (1993) The Darker Forces: Freud and the Movies. *Journal of the American Academy of Psychoanalysis*, 21(1): 33–44.

Bobker, L. (1969) *Elements of Film*. New York: Harcourt, Brace and World Inc.

Bodenhausen, G. (1993) Emotion, Arousal and Stereotypic Judgement: a Heuristic Model of Affect and Stereotyping. In Mackie, D. and Hamilton, D. (eds) *Affect, Cognition and Stereotyping: Interactive Processes in Group Perception*. San Diego: Academic Press Inc., pp. 13–37.

Bolton, J. (2000) Mental Illness and the Media: the 13th Royal College Christmas Lecture for Young People. *Psychiatric Bulletin*, 24: 345–346.

Booth, A. (2002) Accessing Evidence-Based Practice. In McKenzie, B. (ed.) *Medicine and the Internet* (3rd edn.) Oxford: Oxford University Press, pp. 87–101

Borman, J. (2003) Depression in Women's Magazines. *Journal of the American Psychiatric Nurses Association*, 9(3): 71–76.

Borowski, T. (1959) *This Way for the Gas, Ladies and Gentlemen*. London: Penguin.

Borzekowski, D., Robinson, T. and Killen, J. (2000) Does the Camera add 10 pounds? Media Use, Perceived Importance of Appearance and Weight Concerns Among Teenage Girls. *Journal of Adolescent Health*, 26(1): 36–41.

Bourdieu, P. (1996) *On Television and Journalism*. London: Pluto Press.

Bower, H. (1996) Internet sees Growth in Unverified Health Claims. *British Medical Journal*, 313(7054): 381.

Bradbrook, M. (1974) *Malcolm Lowry*. Cambridge: Cambridge University Press.

Bragg, M. (2001) The Media and the Message. Edward Boyle Memorial Lecture 2001. University of Leeds.

Bragg, S. (2001) Just What the Doctors Ordered: Media Regulation, Education, and the 'Problem' of Media Violence. In Barker, M. and Petley, J. *Ill Effects – the Media/ Violence Debate* (2nd edn). London: Routledge. pp. 87–100.

Brannon, L. (1999) Regulating Drug Promotion on the Internet. *Food & Drug Law Journal*, 54(4): 599–621

Braudy, L. (2002) *The World in Frame – What we see in Films*. The University of Chicago Press: London.

Brindle, D. (2000) Ticking off at 11 O'clock. *The Guardian*. Wednesday, 4 October.

British Board of Film Classification (2000) *Sense and Sensibilities: Public Opinion & the BBFC guidelines*. BBFC September 2000.

British Board of Film Classification (2005) *BBFC*. Available at <http://www.bbfc. co.uk/> (Accessed 5 May 2005).

British Broadcasting Corporation (2000) *bbc.co.uk: HOME*. Available at <bbc.co.uk> (Accessed 6 September 2004).

British Broadcasting Corporation (2005) *BBC Guidelines*. Available at <http:// www.bbc.co.uk/guidelines/> (Accessed 20 July 2005).

British Film Institute (2005) *Screenonline*. Available at <http://www.screenonline. org.uk/film/id/790199/> (Accessed 16 May 2005).

British Psychological Association (2002) *Media Training Days*. Available at http:// www.bps.org.uk/about/bandc1.cfm (Accessed 14 May 2005).

Broadbent, D. (1958) *Perception and Communication*. London: Pergamon.

Broadcasting Standards Commission (BSC) (1998) *Broadcasting Standards Commission Codes of Guidance. Available* at http://www.bsc.org.uk/pdfs/research/ bsccode.pdf (Accessed 15 December 2002).

Brontë, C. (1983) *Jane Eyre*. London: Everyman.

Brook, R. (2003) *Mind Statement*. Available at <http://www.mind.org.uk/index.htm> (Accessed 24 September 2003).

Brown, H. (2002) Information for Patients. In McKenzie, B. (ed.) *Medicine and the Internet* (3rd edn.) Oxford: Oxford University Press, pp. 169–177

Brown, L. (2000) Entertainment in Our Extended World. In Valenti, F. *More than a Movie: Ethics in Entertainment*. Colorado: Westview Press, pp. 9–19.

Bruce, M. (1975) *Janet Frame: an Annotated Bibliography of Autobiography and Biography*. Wellington: National Library of New Zealand.

Byrne, P. (2001a) Imagining the Nineties: Mental Illness Stigma in Contemporary Cinema. Chapter 2, Part 4. *Every Family in the Land*. Available at http://www.stigma.org/ (Accessed 15 January 2005).

Byrne, P. (2001b) The Butler(s) DID it – Dissociative Identity Disorder in Cinema. *Medical Humanities*, 27(1): 26–29.

Calcutt, D. (1990) *Report of the Committee on Privacy and Related Matters*. London: HMSO.

Camp, D., Finlay, W. and Lyons, E. (2002) Is Low Self-Esteem an Inevitable Consequence of Stigma? An Example from Women with Chronic Mental Health Problems. *Social Science and Medicine*, 55(5): 823–834.

Campbell, L. (1996) How Secure is the Internet for Healthcare Applications? *Radiology Management*, 18(1): 28–32.

Carroll, N. (1996) *Theorizing the Moving Image*. Cambridge: Cambridge University Press.

Cash, T., Cash, D. and Butters, J. (1983) Mirror Mirror on the Wall . . .? Contrast Effectors and Self-Evaluations of Physical Attractiveness. *Personality and Social Psychology*, 9, 359–364.

Cassedy, P. and Cutliffe, J. (1998) Empathy, Students and the Problems of Genuineness. *Mental Health Practice*, 1(9): 28–33.

Chalaby, J. (1998) *The Invention of Journalism*. Basinsgstoke: Macmillan.

Chamberlain, M. and Thompson, P. (1998) Genre and Narrative in Life Stories. In Chamberlain, M. and Thompson, P. (eds) *Narrative and Genre*. London: Routledge, pp. 1–22.

Chan, J. (1993) *Wild Swans*. London: Flamingo.

Chatham, S. (1990) *Coming to Terms: the Rhetoric of Narrative in Fiction and Film*. Ithaca: Cornell University Press.

Chaudhuri, A. (2002) Why Weepy films are Good for You. Lifestyle Magazine, *Sunday Times*, 21 April.

Chibnall, S. (1981) The Production of Knowledge by Crime Reporters. In Cohen, S. and Young, J. (eds) *The Manufacture of News: Social Problem, Deviance and the Mass Media*. California: Sage, pp. 75–97.

Child, D. (2004) *Psychology and the Teacher* (7th edn). London: Continuum.

Christensen, H. and Griffiths, K. (2000) The Internet and Mental Health Literacy. *Australian & New Zealand Journal of Psychiatry*, 34(6): 975–979.

Christensen, H. and Griffiths, K. (2003) The Internet and Mental Health Practice. *Evidence Based Mental Health*, 6, 66–69.

Clare, A. (2001) Contemporary Images and the Future. Cinematic Portrayals of Psychiatrists. Chapter 2, Part 4. *Every Family in the Land: Understanding Prejudice and Discrimination against People with Mental Illness*. Available at <http://www.stigma.org/everyfamily/aclare.html> (Accessed 17 May 2005).

Clausse, R. (1968) The Mass Public at Grips with Mass Communication. *International Social Science Journal*, 20(4): 625–643.

Cohen, G. and Kerr, B. (1998) Computer-Mediated Counselling: an Empirical Study of a New Mental Health Treatment. *Computers in Human Services*, 15(4): 13–26.

Cohen, M. (1982) *Charles Horton Cooley and the Social Self in American Thought*. New York: Garland.

Collins, R. (1990) *Television – Policy and Culture*. London: Unwin Hyman.

Comstock, G., Chaffee, S., Katzman, N., McCombs, M. and Roberts, D. (1978) *Television and Human Behaviour*. New York: Columbia University Press.

Cooke, A. (2001) *A Guide to Finding Quality Information on the Internet: Selection and Evaluation Strategies* (2nd edn). London: Library Association Publishing.

Corrigan, P. and Penn, D, (1999) Lessons from Social Psychology on Discrediting Psychiatric Stigma. *American Psychologist*, 54, 765–776.

Cortazzi, M. (1993) *Narrative Analysis*. London: The Falmer Press.

Crepaz-Keay, D. (1996) A Sense of Perspective: the Media and the Boyd Inquiry. In Philo, G. (ed.) *Media and Mental Distress*. London: Longman, pp. 37–44.

Crisp, A., Gelder, M., Rix, S., Meltzer, H. and Rowlands, O. (2000) Stigmatisation of People with Mental Illnesses. *British Journal of Psychiatry*, 177, 4–7.

Croteau, D. and Hoynes, W. (2000) *Media Society: Industries, Images and Audiences* (2nd edn). London: Pine Forge Press.

Cuenca, O. (2002) Mass Media and Psychiatry. In Sartorius, N. and Gaebel, W. (eds) *Psychiatry in Society*. New York: Wiley and Sons, pp. 263–279.

Culver, J., Gerr, F. and Frumkin, H. (1997) Medical Information on the Internet: a Study of an Electronic Bulletin Board. *Journal of General Internal Medecine*, 12(8): 466–470.

Dawkins, R. (1976) *The Selfish Gene*. Oxford: Oxford University Press.

Day, D. and Page, S. (1986) Portrayal of Mental Illness in Canadian Newspapers. *Canadian Journal of Psychiatry*, 31(9): 813–817.

Deaver, J. (1994) *Praying for Sleep*. London: Coronet.

Department of Health (1990) *National Health Service and Community Care Act*. Available at <http://www.opsi.gov.uk/acts/acts1990/ukpga_19900019_en_1.htm> (Accessed 5 July 2005).

Department of Health (1992) *The Health of the Nation*. London: Department of Health.

Department of Health (1995) *Disability Discrimination Act*. Available at <www.direct.gov.uk> (Accessed 5 June 2005).

Department of Health (1999) *Safer Services: National Inquiry into Suicide and Homicide by People with Mental Illness*. London: Department of Health.

Department of Health (1999) *Saving Lives: Our Healthier Nation*. London: Department of Health.

Department of Health (1999) *National Service Framework for Mental Health. Standard One: Health Promotion*. London: Department of Health

Department of Health (2002) *National Suicide Prevention Strategy for England – Consultation Document*. London: Department of Health.

Department of Health (2004) *Draft Mental Health Bill*. Available at <http://www.dh.gov.uk/PolicyAndGuidance/HealthAndSocialCareTopics/MentalHealth/MentalHealthArticle/fs/en?CONTENT_ID=4089593&chk=t9P0rz> (Accessed 16 July 2005).

Department of Health/Rethink (1999) *Severe Mental Illness Explained – a Guide for Journalists*. London: Department of Health.

Devereaux, L. and Hillman, R. (eds) (1995) *Fields of Vision*. London: University of California Press.

Devereux, E. (2003) *Understanding the Media*. London: Sage.

Deveson, A. (1992) *Tell Me I'm Here*. London: Penguin.

Dictionary.com (2005) Available at <http://dictionary.reference.com/> (Accessed 19 July 2005).

Domino, G. (1983) Impact of the Film One Flew over the Cuckoo's Nest on Attitudes to Mental Illness. *Psychological Reports*, 53, 173–182.

Dupuits, F. (2002) The Effects of the Internet on Pharmaceutical Consumers and Providers. *Disease Management & Health Outcomes*, 10(11): 679–691.

Durkin, S. (2002) Predictors of Vulnerability to Reduced Body Image Satisfaction and Psychological Wellbeing in Response to Exposure to Idealized Female Media Images in Adolescent Girls. *Journal of Psychosomatic Research*, 53(5): 995–1005.

Easton-Ellis, B. (1991) *American Psycho*. Basingstoke: Picador.

Eco, U. (1989) *The Open Work*. London: Hutchinson.

Elliott, J. (2005) *The Little Prisoner*. London: Harper Element.

Epting, F. (1984) *Personal Construct Counselling and Psychotherapy*. Chichester: John Wiley.

Erbele, S., Riggins, J., Williams, C. and Heck, A. (2002) Evaluating Internet Drug Information. *Hospital Pharmacy*, 37(2): 141–145.

European Information Society Group. (2004) *Current Internet Regulation Issues*. Available at <http://www.eurim.org/briefings/IWF_eurim2.htm> (Accessed 8 February 2005).

European Union (2001) *Television Without Frontiers Directive*. Available at <http://www.dentonwildesapte.com/assets/T/TVWithoutFrontiersDirective_Nov2001.pdf> (Accessed 21 July 2005).

Evans, E., Rutberg, J., Sather, C. and Turner, C. (1991) Content Analysis of Contemporary Teen Magazines for Adolescent Females. *Youth and Society*, 23(1): 99–120.

Feder, L. (1980) *Madness in Literature*. Princeton: Princeton University Press.

Ferrier, C. (1995) *The Janet Frame Reader*. London: Women's Press.

Feshbach, N. and Feshbach, S. (1997) Children's Empathy and the Media: Realizing the Potential of Television. In Kirschner, S. and Kirschner, D. (eds) *Perspectives on Psychology and the Media*. Washington: American Psychological Association, pp. 3–27.

Feshbach, S. and Singer, R. (1971) *Television and Aggression: an Experimental Field Theory*. San Francisco: Jossey Bass.

Film Education (2005) *Film Education*. Available at <http://www.filmeducation.org/secondary/concept/film-real/docs/real6.html> (Accessed 16 May 2005).

Fiske, J. and Hartley, J. (1978) *Reading Television*. London: Routledge.

Fitch, J. (1999) *White Oleander*. London: Virago Press.

Flemming, M. and Manvell, R. (1985) *Images of Madness: The Portrayal of Insanity in the Feature Film*. Cranbury NJ: Associated University Press.

Flemming, M. and Manvell, R. (1994) Through a Lens Darkly. In Rieger, B. (ed.) *Dionysus in Literature: Essays in Madness*, pp. 49–57.

Foucault, M. (1961) *Madness and Civilisation*. London: Routledge.

Foucault, M. (1979) What is an Author? In Harari, J. (ed.) *Textual Strategies: Perspectives in Post Structuralist Criticism*. London: Methuen, pp. 145–148.

Frame, J. (1961) *Faces in the Water*. London: The Women's Press.

Frame, J. (1980) *Scented Gardens for the Blind*. London: The Women's Press.

Frame, J. (1984) *An Angel at my Table*. London: Paladin.

Frame, J. (2002) *Owls do Cry*. London: The Women's Press.

Francis, C., Pirkis, J., Blood, R., Dunt, D., Burgess, P., Morley, B., Stewart, A. and Putnis, P. (2004) The Portrayal of Mental Health and Illness in Australian Non-Fiction Media. *Australian and New Zealand Journal of Psychiatry*, 38(7): 541–546.

Frisch, L. (2001) Friday Night at the Movies. In Frisch, N. and Frisch, L. (eds) *Psychiatric Mental Health Nursing*. Albany, NY: Delmar Publishers, pp. 779–799.

Frith, S. (1986) Hearing Secret Harmonies. In McCabe, C. (ed.) *High Theory/Low Culture: Analysing Popular Television and Film*. Manchester: Manchester University Press, pp. 53–70.

Gabbard, G. (2001) Psychotherapy in Hollywood Cinema. *Australasian Psychiatry*, 9(4): 365–369.

Gabbard, G. and Gabbard, K. (1992) Cinematic Stereotypes Contributing to the Stigmatisation of Psychiatrists. In Fink, P. and Tasman, A. *Stigma and Mental Illness*. Washington, DC: American Psychiatric Press, pp. 113–126.

Gabbard, G. and Gabbard, K. (1999) *Psychiatry and the Cinema* (2nd edn). London: American Psychiatric Press.

Galanter, M., Keller, D., Dermatis, H. and Biderman, D. (1998) Use of the Internet for Addiction Education. Combining Network Therapy with Pharmacotherapy. *American Journal on Addictions*, 7(1): 7–13.

Gascoigne, P. (2005) *Gazza: My Story*. London: Headline Book Publishing.

Gauntlett, D. (1995) *Moving Experiences*. London: John Libbey.

Gauntlett, D. (2001) The Worrying Influence of Media Effects Studies. In Barker, M. and Petley, J. *Ill Effects – the Media/Violence Debate* (2nd edn). London: Routledge, pp. 47–62.

Gauntlett, D. and Hill, A. (1999) *TV Living: Television, Culture and Everyday Life*. London: Routledge.

Genette, G. (1980) *Narrative Discourse*. Oxford: Blackwell.

Geraghty, C. (1991) *Women and Soap Opera*. Cambridge: Polity Press.

Gilbert, P. (2003) Shame, Stigma and the Family: 'Skeletons in the Cupboard' and the Role of Shame. In Crisp, A. *Every Family in the Land: Understanding prejudice and discrimination against people with mental illness*. Available at <http://www.stigma.org/> (Accessed 6 May 2005).

Gladstein, G. (1983) Understanding Empathy. Integrating Counselling, Developmental and Social Psychology Perspectives. *Journal of Counselling Psychology*, 30(4): 467–482.

GMTV (2004) *Dr Hilary's Web Chats*. Available at <http://www.gmtv.co.uk/index.cfm?articleid=2144&pageNumber=2> (Accessed 9 September 2004).

Goffman, E. (1961) *Asylums*. Middlesex: Pelican.

Goffman, E. (1963) *Stigma: Notes on Management of Spoiled Identity*. Harmondsworth: Penguin.

Goffman, E. (1974) *Frame Analysis*. London: Penguin.

Gold, J. (1998) Mental Health and the Internet. *Computers in Nursing*, 16(2): 85–6, 89.

Graber, M. and Weckmann, M. (2002) Pharmaceutical Company Internet Sites as Sources of Information about Antidepressant Medications. *CNS Drugs*, 16(6): 419–423

Grace, S. (1982) *The Voyage That Never Ends*. Vancouver: University of British Columbia Press.

Graham, G. (1999) *The Internet: a Philosophical Inquiry*. London: Routledge.

Gray, A. (2002) Stigma in Psychiatry. *Journal of the Royal Society of Medicine*, 95(2): 72–76.

Grazia, E. and Newman, R. (1982) *Banned Films*. London: R. R. Bowker.

Green, H. (1964) *I Never Promised You a Rose Garden*. London: Pan.

Greenberg, H. and Gabbard, K. (1990) *Reel Signification: an Anatomy of Psychoanalytic Film Criticism*, 77(1): 89–110.

Gregory, J. (2003) *Sickened*. London: Arrow.

Gripsrud, J. (2002) *Understanding Media Culture*. London: Arnold.

Gunter, B. (1987) *Poor Reception*. Hillsdale NJ: Lawrence Erlbaum.

Gunter, B. and Wober, M. (1992) *The Reactive Viewer: a Review of Research on Audience Reaction Measurement*. London: John Libbey.

Haghighat, R. (2001) A Unitary Theory of Stigmatisation. *British Journal of Psychiatry*, 178, 207–215.

Hall, S. (1974a) *Encoding and Decoding in the Television Discourse*. Centre for Contemporary Cultural Studies, Stencilled Occasional Paper No. 7. Birmingham: University of Birmingham.

Hall, S. (1974b) The Television Discourse: Encoding and Decoding. *Education and Culture*, 25, 8–14.

Hall, S. (1981) The Determinations of News Photographs. In Cohen, S. and Young, J. (eds) *The Manufacture of News*. London: Constable, pp. 226–243.

Hall, S., Critcher, S., Jefferson, T., Clarke, J. and Roberts, B. (1978) *Policing the Crisis*. London: Macmillan.

Hallam, A. (2002) Media Influences on Mental Health Policy: Long Term Effects of the Clunis and Silcock Cases. *International Review of Psychiatry*, 14(1): 26–33.

Halliwell, G. (2003) *Just For the Record*. London: Ebury Press.

Hamilton, K. and Waller, G. (1993) Media Influences of Body Size Estimation in Anorexia and Bulimia: an Experimental Study. *British Journal of Psychiatry*, 162, 837–840.

Hamlyn, D. (1957) *The Psychology of Perception: a Philosophical Examination of Gestalt Theory and Derivative Theories of Perception*. London: Routledge and Kegan Paul.

Haney, C. and Zimbardo, P. (1998) The Past and Future of U.S. Prison Policy: Twenty Five Years after the Stanford Prison Experiment. *American Psychologist*, 53(7): 709–727.

Hannah, D. (1978) Faces In the Water: Case History or Work of Fiction? In Delbaere, J. (ed.) *Bird, Hawk, Bogie: Essays on Janet Frame*. Denmark: Dangaroo Press, pp. 45–52.

Harris, C. and Lester, P. (2002) *Visual Journalism: a Guide for New Media Professionals*. London: Allyn and Bacon.

Harrison, G., Owens, D., Holton, A., Neilson, D. and Boot, D. (1988) A Prospective Study of Severe Mental Disorder in Afro-Caribbean Patients. *Psychological Medicine*, 11, 289–302.

Hatfield, E. and Sprecher, S. (1986) *Mirror, Mirror . . . The Importance of Looks in Everyday Life*. New York: State University of New York Press.

Hawes, C. (1996) *Mania and Literary Style*. Cambridge: Cambridge University Press.

Hawton, K., Simkin, S., Deeks, J., O'Connor, S., Keen, A., Altman, D., Philo, G. and Bulstrode, C. (1999) Effects of a Drug Overdose in a Television Drama on Presentations to Hospital for Self Poisoning: Time Series and Questionnaire Study. *British Medical Journal*, 318, 972–977.

Hayden, T. (2004) *One Child*. London: Element Books.

Health Education Authority (1997) *Mental Health and the National Press*. London: Health Education Authority.

Health Education Authority (1999) *Media Mentality: How the Print and Broadcast Media Treat Mental Health Issues*. London: Health Education Authority.

Health on the Net. *Honcode*. Available at <http://www.hon.ch/> (Accessed 22 July 2005).

Hebda, T., Czar, P. and Mascara, C. (1998) *Handbook of Informatics for Nurses and Health Care Professionals*. Reading: Addison Wesley.

Heller, J. (1961) *Catch 22*. London: Vintage.

Henderson, L. (1996) Selling Suffering: Mental Illness and Media Values. In Philo, G. (ed.) *Media and Mental Distress*. London: Longman, pp. 18–36.

Hersch, W. Gorman, P. and Sacharek, L. (1998) Applicability and Quality of Information for Answering Clinical Questions on the Web. *Journal of the American Medical Association*, 280(15): 1244–1245.

Hershkowitz, D. (1998) *The Madness of Epic*. Oxford: Clarendon Press.

Hesse, H. (2001) *Steppenwolf*. London: Penguin.

Hetherington, A. (1985) *News, Newspapers and Television*. London: Macmillan.

Hobson, D. (1988) *Crossroads. The Drama of a Soap Opera*. London: Methuen.

Hodgkinson, J. (1986) Disney's Return to Oz, and ECT. *Biological Psychiatry*, 21(5–6): 578.

Hoffner, C. and Cantor, J. (1991) Perceiving and Responding to Mass Media Characters. In Bryant, J. and Zillman, D. (eds) *Responding to the Screen: Reception and Reaction Process*. New Jersey: Lawrence Erlbaum, pp. 63–101.

Höijer, B. (1998) Social Psychological Perspectives in Reception Analysis. In Dickinson, R., Harindranath, R. and Linné, O. (eds) *Approaches to Audiences*. London: Arnold, pp. 166–183.

Holland, N. (1980) Unity Identity Text Self. In Tompkins, J. (ed.) *Reader-Response Criticism From Formalism to Post Structuralism*. Baltimore: John Hopkins University Press. pp. 118–133.

Horton, D. and Wohl, R. (1956) Mass Communication and Para-Social Interaction. *Psychiatry*, 19, 215–229.

House of Commons (2001) *Culture, Media and Sport – Second Report (7 March 2001)* Available at <http://www.parliament.the-stationery-office.co.uk/pa/cm200001/cmselect/cmcumeds/161/16108.htm> (Accessed 14 June 2005).

Houston, T., Cooper, L. and Ford, D. (2002) Internet Support Groups for Depression: A 1- Year Prospective Cohort Study. *American Journal of Psychiatry*, 159(12): 2062–2068.

Howlett, M. (1998) *Medication, Non-Compliance and Mentally Disordered Offenders: The Role of Non-Compliance in Homicide by People with Mental Illness and Proposals for Future Policy*. London: The Zito Trust.

Hughes, T. (1985) Ariel Ascending. In Alexander, P. (ed.) *Sylvia Plath and her Journals*. New York: Harper and Row, pp. 153–154.

Hyler, S. and Morre, J. (1996) Teaching Psychiatry? Let Hollywood Help! Suicide in the Cinema. *Academic Psychiatry*, 20(4): 212–219.

Independent Television Commission (2002) *The ITC Programme Code January 2002*. Available at <http://www.ITC.co.uk> (Accessed 12 December 2002).

Ingram, A. (1991) *The Madhouse of Language: Writing and Reading Madness in the Eighteenth Century*. London: Routledge.

Internet Service Providers Association. *ISPA*. Available at <http://www.ispa.org.uk/html/index3.html?frame=http%3A//www.ispa.org.uk/html/about_ispa/index.html> (Accessed 14 June 2005).

Internet Watch Foundation. *IWF*. Available at <www.iwf.org.uk> (Accessed 23 May 2005).

Jackson, P., Stevenson, N. and Brooks, K. (2001) *Making Sense of Men's Magazines. Men's Health Magazines*. Cambridge: Polity Press.

Jadad, A. and Gagliardi, A. (1998) Rating Health Information on the Internet; Navigating to Knowledge or to Babel. *Journal of the American Medical Association*, 279(8): 611–614.

Jamison, K. (1989) Mood Disorders and Patterns of Creativity in British Writers and Artists. *Psychiatry*, 52(2): 125–134.

Jamison, K. (1993) *Touched with Fire: Manic Depression and the Artistic Temperament*. New York: The Free Press.

Jamison, K. (1996) Mood Disorders, Creativity and the Artistic Temperament. In Schildkraut, J. and Otero, A. (eds) *Depression and the Spiritual in Modern Art: Homage to Miro*. Oxford: John Wiley, pp. 15–32.

Jamison, K. (1997) *An Unquiet Mind: Memoirs of Moods and Madness*. London: Picador.

Jensen, K. (1988) News as a Social Resource. *European Journal of Communication*, 3(3): 275–301.

Jinks, G. (2000) Therapeutic Skills and Clinical Practice. In Feltham, C. and Horton, I. (eds) *Handbook of Counselling and Psychotherapy*. London: Sage, pp. 122–151.

Johnson-Cartee, K. (2005) *News, Narratives and News Framing*. Oxford: Rowman and Littlefield.

Johnstone, M. (2001) Stigma, Social justice and the Rights of the Mentally Ill: Challenging the Status Quo. *Australian, New Zealand Journal of Mental Health Nursing*, 10(4): 200–209.

Kafka, F. (1933) *Metamorphosis and Other Stories*. London: Penguin.

Kalbfleisch, P. (1979) *The Portrayal of the Killer in Society: A Comparison Study*. PhD Dissertation. Department of Communication, Michigan State University.

Kanouse, D. and Hanson, L. (1972) Negativity in Evaluations. In Jones, E., Kanouse, D., Kelley, H., Nisbett, R., Valins, S. and Weiner, B. (eds) *Attribution: Perceiving the Causes of Behaviour*. Morristown, NJ: General Learning Press, pp. 1–16.

Kantor, D. and Gelineau, V. (1965) Social Processes in Support of Chronic Deviance. *International Journal of Social Psychiatry*, 11, 280–289.

Kent, R. (1994) Measuring Media Audiences: the Way Ahead. In Kent, R. (ed.) *Measuring Media Audiences*. London: Routledge.

Kesey, K. (1962) *One Flew over the Cuckoo's Nest*. London: Picador.

Kiley, R. (1999) *Medical Information on the Internet: a Guide for Health Professionals* (2nd edn). Edinburgh: Churchill Livingstone.

King, D. and Wertheimer, M. (2005) *Max Wertheimer and Gestalt Theory*. London: Transaction.

Kirschenbaum, H. and Henderson, V. (eds) (1990) *Carl Rogers: Dialogues: Conversations with Martin Buber, Paul Tillich, B.F. Skinner, Gregory Bateson, Michael Polanyi, Rollo May, and Others*. London: Constable.

Kitwood, T. (1997) *Dementia Reconsidered: the Person Comes First*. Buckingham: Open University Press.

Kitzinger, J. (1999) A Sociology of Media Power: Key Issues in Audience Reception Research. In Philo, G. (ed.) *Message Received*. Harlow: Addison Wesley Longman, pp. 3–20

Köhler, W. (1929) *Gestalt Psychology*. New York: H. Liveright.

Köhler, W. (1947) *Gestalt Psychology – an Introduction to New Concepts in Modern Psychology*. London: New English Library.

Kolker, R. (1988) *A Cinema of Loneliness* (2nd edn). Oxford: Oxford University Press.

Kress, G. and Leeuwen, T. (1998) Front Pages: (The Critical) Analysis. In Bell, A. and Garrett, P. (eds) *Approaches to Media Discourse*. Oxford: Blackwell, pp. 186–219.

LaBruzza, A. (1997) *The Essential Internet: a Guide for Psychotherapists and other Mental Health Professionals*. London: Jason Aronson.

Laing, R. (1990) *The Divided Self: an Existential Study in Sanity and Madness*. Harmondsworth: Penguin.

Lamb, W. (2000) *I Know This Much is True*. London: HarperCollins.

Lamberg, L. (2003) Online Empathy for Mood Disorders: Patients Turn to Internet Support Groups. *Journal of the American Medical Association*, 289(23): 3073–3077.

Landau, B. (2001) Psychotherapy Online in 2001: For Psychotherapists new to the Internet. *Journal of Mental Imagery*, 25(1–2): 65–82.

Landesman, C. (2005) The Sea Inside. *Sunday Times Culture Magazine*, 13 February, p. 19.

Lange, A., Rietdijk, D., Hudcovicova, M. van de Ven, J., Schrieken, B. and Emmelkamp, P. (2003) Interapy: A Controlled Randomised Trial of the Standardized Treatment of Posttraumatic Stress through the Internet. *Journal of Consulting and Clinical Psychology*, 71(5): 901–909.

Laurance, J. (2003) *Pure Madness: How Fear Drives the Mental Health System*. London: Routledge.

Lauronen, E., Veijola, J, Isohanni, I., Jones, P., Nieminem, P. and Isohanni, M. (2004) Links Between Creativity and Mental Disorder. *Psychiatry*, 67(1): 81–98.

Lawrence, D.H. (1972) *Lady Chatterley's Lover*. New York: Viking Press.

Lee, C. (2005) *To Die For*. London: Arrow.

Lessing, D. (1971) *Briefing for a Descent into Hell*. St Albans: Panther.

Link, B., Struening, E., Neese-Todd, S., Asmussen, S. and Phelan, J. (2001) The Consequences of Stigma for the Self-Esteem of People with Mental Illnesses. *Psychiatric Services*, 52(12): 1621–1626.

Linné, O. and Warfella, E. (1998) In Dickinson, R., Harindranath, R. and Linné, O. (Eds.) *Approaches to Audiences*. London: Arnold.

Lissman, T. and Boehnlein, J. (2001) A Critical Review of Internet Information about Depression. *Psychiatric Services*, 52(8): 1046–1050.

Livingstone, S. (1998) *Making Sense of Television – the Psychology of Audience Interpretation* (2nd edn). London: Routledge.

Lothe, J. (2000) *Narrative in Fiction and Film*. Oxford: Oxford University Press.

Lott, T. (1997) *The Scent of Dried Roses*. London: Penguin.

Lowry, M. (1947) *Under the Volcano*. London: Penguin.

Ludwig, A. (1995) *The Price of Greatness: Resolving the Creativity and Madness Controversy*. New York: Guildford Press.

Lukoff, D. (1999) The Mental Health Internet. *Health Care on the Internet*, 3(2): 3–17.

McArdle, S. and Byrt, R. (2001) Fiction, Poetry and Mental Health: Expressive and Therapeutic Uses of Literature. *Journal of Psychiatric and Mental Health Nursing*, 8(6): 517–524.

McCann, R. (2004) *Just a Boy*. London: Ebury Press.

McClure, I. (2000) Driving Mum Crazy. *British Medical Journal*, 320, 388.

McCourt, F. (1996) *Angela's Ashes*. London: Harper Collins.

McDonald, A. and Walter, G. (2001) The Portrayal of ECT in American Movies. *Journal of ECT*, 17(4): 264–274.

McGee, S. and Whitehouse, P. (2005) *Internet Firms Face More Pressure on Suicide Sites*. Available at <http://www.yorkshiretoday.co.uk/ViewArticle2.aspx?

242   *Bibliography*

SectionID=55&ArticleID=1218182> (Accessed 4 December 2005).

McGovern, D. and Cope, R. (1987) The Compulsory Detention of Males of Different Ethnic Groups with Special Reference to Offender Patients. *British Journal of Psychiatry*, 150, 505–512.

McGrath, P. (1996) *Asylum*. London: Penguin.

McKenzie, K. (1994) Spot the Loony. *British Medical Journal*, 309, 1588.

McNair, B. (1998) *The Sociology of Journalism*. London: Arnold.

McNair, B. (2003) *News and Journalism in the UK* (4th edn). London: Routledge.

McQuail, D. (1992) *Media Performance: Mass Communication and the Public Interest*. London: Sage.

McQuail, D. (1997) *Audience Analysis*. London: Sage.

McQuail, D. (2000) *McQuail's Mass Communication Theory* (4th edn). London: Sage.

McQuail, D. (2005) McQuail's Mass Communication Theory (5th edn). London: Sage.

McQuail, D. and Windahl, S. (1993) *Communication Models: for the Study of Mass Communications* (2nd edn). London: Longman.

McQuail, D., Blumler, J. and Brown, J. (1972) The Television Audience, a Revised Perspective. In McQuail, D. (ed.) *Sociology of Mass Communication*. Beverly Hills: Sage, pp. 135–164.

Maclennan, G. (1992) *Lucid Interval*. Leicester: Leicester University Press.

Maheu, M. and Barry, G. (2000) Counselling and Therapy on the Internet. *Professional Psychology: Research and Practice*, 31(5): 484–489.

Main, L. (2003) Scare in the Community. *Mental Health Today*. July/August, 8–9.

Manic Depression Fellowship. *MDF the bipolar organisation*. Available at <http://www.mdf.org.uk/bipolar/treatments.html> (Accessed 17 February 2005)

Martin, W. (1986) *Recent Theories of Narrative*. London: Cornell University Press.

Martin, M. and Kennedy, P. (1993) Advertising and Social Comparison: Consequences for Female Preadolescents. *Psychology and Marketing*, 10, 513–530.

Martinez-Gonzalez, M., Gual, P., Lahortiga, F., Alonso, Y., De Irla-Estevez, J. and Cervera, S. (2003) Parental Factors, Mass Media Influences, and the Onset of Eating Disorders in a Prospective Population-Based Cohort. *Pediatrics*, 111(2): 315–320.

Maslow, A. (1971) *The Farther Reaches of Human Nature*. Harmondsworth: Penguin.

Mason, G. (2003) News Media Portrayal of Mental Illness: Implications for Public Policy. *American Behavioural Scientist*, 46(12): 1594–1600.

Mathews, T. (1994) *Censored*. London: Chatto and Windus.

Maurier, D. Du (1992) *Rebecca*. London: Arrow.

Medcircle. *Collaboration for Internet Rating, Certification, Labelling and Evaluation of Health Information*. Available at <www.medcircle.org> (Accessed 12 July 2005).

Media Bureau (2001) *Mental Health and the Press*. Available at <http://www.mhmedia.com/training/report.html. (Accessed 21 July 2005).

Mehlum, L. (2000) Crisis: The Internet, Suicide, and Suicide Prevention. *The Journal of Crisis Intervention and Suicide Prevention*, 21(4): 186–188.

Mental Health Media (2002) *MHM*. Available at www.mhmedia.com (Accessed 21 July 2005).

Mental Health Media (2004) *Mental Health Media's Anti-Discrimination Toolkit*. Available at <http://www.openuptoolkit.net/take_action/the_bill.php> (Accessed 14 July 2005).

Metz, C. (1982) *The Imaginary Signifier: Psychoanalysis and the Cinema*. Bloomington: Indiana University Press.

Miles, A. (1981) *The Mentally Ill in Contemporary Society: a Sociological Introduction*. Oxford: Martin Robertson.

Miller, N. (2002) *But Enough about Me*. New York: Columbia University Press.

Milligan, S. and Clare, A. (1994) *Depression and How to Survive it*. London: Arrow.

Mind (2000) *Counting the Cost: a Survey of the Impact of Media Coverage on the Lives of People with Mental Health Problems*. London: Mind Publications.

Mind (2001) *Mind: for better Mental Health*. Available at <www.mind.org.uk> (Accessed 17 March 2005).

Mind (2004a) *Mind Statement on Draft Mental Health Bill Announcement*. Available at <http://www.mind.org.uk/News+policy+and+campaigns/Press/MHBstate.htm> (Accessed 15 October 2004).

Mind (2004b) *How to Help Someone who is Suicidal*. Available at <www.mind.org.uk> (Accessed 11 July 2005).

Mindout for Mental Health (2001a) *Mindshift: a Guide to Open-Minded Coverage of Mental Health*. Available at <http://mindout.clarity.uk.net/p/mindshift.pdf> (Accessed 11 November 2005).

Mindout for Mental Health (2001b) *Headspace*. Available at <http://www.mindout.net/headspace/lx.asp> (Accessed 20 October 2004).

Mindout for Mental Health (2005) *Mindout for Mental Health*. Available at <http://mindout.clarity.uk.net/iwi/iC2-Camp-info.asp> (Accessed 12 August 2005).

Moore, S. (1988) *Investigating Deviance*. London: Collins Educational.

Moores, S. (1993) *Interpreting Audiences: The Ethnography of Media Consumption*. London: Sage.

Morahan-Martin, J. and Anderson, C. (2000) Information and Misinformation Online: Recommendations for Facilitating Accurate Mental Health Information Retrieval and Evaluation. *Cyberpsychology and Behaviour*, 3(5): 731–746.

Mori (2001) *Mori Poll: Nearly 3 out of 5 Internet Users Would Seek Help for Mental Health Problems on the Net*. Available at <www.mori.com/polls/2001/zeus.shtml> (Accessed 22 July 2005).

Morrall, P. (2000a) *Madness and Murder*. London: Whurr.

Morrall, P. (2000b) Madness and Murder. *Mental Health Practice*, 4(1): 8–10.

Motion Picture Association of America (2003) *Motion Picture Association of America*. Available at <http://mpaa.org/about/content.htm> (Accessed 27 November 2003).

Murdock, G. (1998) Mass Communication and the Construction of Meaning. In Dickinson, R., Harindranath, R. and Linné, O. (eds) *Approaches to Audiences*. London: Arnold, pp. 205–217.

Myers, P. and Biocca, F. (1992) The Elastic Body Image: the Effect of Television Advertising and Programming on Body Image Distortion in Young Women. *Journal of Communication*, 42 (3): 108–133.

Nairn, R., Coverdale, J. and Claasen, D. (2001) From Source Material to News Story in New Zealand Print Media: a Prospective Study of the Stigmatising Processes in Depicting Mental Illness. *Australian and New Zealand Journal of Psychiatry*, 35, 654–659.

Nasar, S. (1998) *A Beautiful Mind*. London: Faber and Faber.

National Patient Safety Agency (2001) Safety First, National Confidential Inquiry into Suicide and Homicide by People with Mental Illness, five-year report of the National Confidential Inquiry.

National Union of Journalists (1999) *Code of Conduct*. Available at <http://www.nuj.org.uk/inner.php?docid=59> (Accessed 12 July 2005).

National Union of Journalists/Royal College of Psychiatry (1999) *Guide for Journalists and Broadcasters Reporting on Schizophrenia*. Dublin: Lilly Neuroscience Bureau.

Nelson, R. (1997) *TV Drama in Transition – Forms, Values and Cultural Change*. London: Macmillan.

Nettle, D. (2001) *Strong Imagination: Madness Creativity and Human Nature*. Oxford: Oxford University Press.

Nimmo, D. and Combs, J. (1983) *Mediated Political Realities*. New York: Longman.

Noble, G. (1973) Effects of Different Forms of Filmed Aggression on Children's Constructive and Deconstructive Play. *Journal of Personality and Social Psychology*, 26, 54–59.

Norden, M. (1994) *The Cinema of Isolation*. New Jersey: Rutgers University Press.

Nunnally, J. (1981) Mental Illness: What the Media Present. In Cohen, S. and Young, J. (eds) *The Manufacture of News: Deviance, Social Problems and the Mass Media*. Beverly Hills: Sage, pp. 186–196.

O'Connor, J. and Seymour, J. (1990) *Introducing Neurolinguistic Programming. Psychological Skills for Understanding and Influencing People*. London: Aquarian.

Ofcom. *Office of Communications*. Available at <www.ofcom.org.uk> (Accessed 14 June 2005).

Ofcom. (2004) *The Ofcom Internet and Broadband Update*. Available at <http://www.ofcom.org.uk/research/telecoms/reports/bbresearch/int_bband_updt/may2004/#content> (Accessed 24 November 2005).

Ofcom (2005) *Ofcom Broadcasting Code*. Available at <http://www.ofcom.org.uk/tv/ifi/codes/bcode/ofcom-broadcasting-code.pdf> (Accessed 6 December 2005).

O'Gunleye, I. (2003) My Descent into Psychosis. *The Independent on Sunday*, 26 October, pp. 1–2.

Oravec, J. (2000) Online Counselling and the Internet: Perspectives for Mental Health Care Supervision and Education. *Journal of Mental Health*, 9(2): 121–135.

Östman, M. and Kjellin, L. (2002) Stigma by Association. Psychological Factors in Relatives of People with Mental Illness. *British Journal of Psychiatry*, 181, 494–498.

O'Sullivan, T., Dutton, B. and Rayner, P. (1994) *Studying the Media: An Introduction*. London: Arnold.

Oxford English Dictionary (2005) Available at <www.oed.com> (Acccessed 19 July 2005)

Padel, R. (1995) *Whom Gods Destroy*. Princeton NJ: Princeton University Press.

Paletz, D. and Entman, R. (1981) *Media, Power, Politics*. New York: Free Press.

Palmgreen, P. and Rayburn, J. (1985) An Expectancy-Value approach to Media Gratification. In Rosengren, K., Palmgreen, P. and Wenner, L. (eds) *Media Gratification Research: Current Perspectives*. Beverly Hills: Sage, pp. 61–73.

Pasternak, B. (1978) *Doctor Zhivago*. London: Collins.

Pavlov, I. (1958) *Experimental Psychology and Other Essays*. London: Peter Owen.

Pegler, J. (2003) Mad Memoirs of the 21st Century. *Mental Health Today*, November, 31–33.

Pelzer, D. (1995) *A Child Called It*. London: Orion.

Pelzer, D. (1997) *The Lost Boy*. London: Orion.

Pelzer, D. (1999) *A Man Named Dave*. London: Orion.

Pelzer, D. (2004) *My Story*. London: Orion.

Pelzer, D. (2005) *The Privilege of Youth*. London: Penguin.

Pelzer, R. (2005) *A Brother's Journey*. London: Time Warner.

Penn, D., Guynan, K., Daily, T., Spaulding, W., Garbin, C. and Sullivan, M. (1994) Dispelling the Stigma of Schizophrenia: What sort of Information is Best? *Schizophrenia Bulletin*, 20(3): 567–574.

Penny, J. (1992) *I Have What I Gave: the Fiction of Janet Frame*. Wellington: Daphne Brassell Associates Press.

Peplau, H. (1988) *Interpersonal Relations in Nursing: a Conceptual Frame of Reference for Psychodynamic Nursing*. Basingstoke: Macmillan Education.

Persaud, R. (2000) Psychiatrists Suffer from Stigma too. *Psychiatric Bulletin*, 24, 284–285.

Peters, C. (2002) Doctor's Bad Press Depends on Type of Newspaper. *British Medical Journal*, 324, 241.

Petley, J. (1999) The Regulation of Media Content. In Stokes, J. and Reading, A. (eds) *The Media in Britain*. New York: St Martin's Press, pp. 143–157.

Petty, R. and Priester, J. (1994) Mass Media Attitude Change: Implications of the Elaboration Likelihood Model of Persuasion. In Bryant, J. and Zillman, D. (eds) *Media Effects: Advances in Theory and Research*. New Jersey: Lawrence Erlbaum, pp. 91–122.

Philo, G. (1990) *Seeing is Believing: The Influence of Television*. London: Routledge.

Philo, G. (1996a) The Media and Public Belief. In Philo, G. (ed.) *Media and Mental Distress*. London: Longman, pp. 82–104.

Philo, G. (1996b) Introduction. In Philo, G. (ed.) *Media and Mental Distress*. London: Longman, pp. xi–xv

Philo, G. (1996c) Users of Services, Carers and Families. In Philo, G. (ed.) *Media and Mental Distress*. London: Longman, pp. 105–118.

Philo, G. (1999) Media and Mental Illness. In Philo, G. (ed.) *Message Received*. Harlow: Addison Wesley Longman, pp. 54–61.

Philo, G., McLaughlin, G. and Henderson, L. (1996) Media Content. In Philo, G. (ed.) *Media and Mental Distress*. London: Longman, pp. 45–81.

Philo, G., Secker, J. and Platts, S. (1994) Impact of the Mass Media on Public Images of Mental Illness: Media Content and Audience Belief. *Health Education Journal*, 53, 271–281.

Piaget, J. (1958) *The Growth of Logical Thinking from Childhood to Adolescence*. London: Routledge.

Piercy, M. (1976) *Woman on the Edge of Time*. London: The Women's Press.

Pinfold, V. (2003) Awareness in Action. *Mental Health Today*, July/August, 24–25.

Pirkis, J. and Blood, R. (2001) Suicide and the Media: Part II: Portrayal in Fictional Media. *Crisis: The Journal of Crisis Intervention and Suicide Prevention*, 22(4): 155–162.

Plath, S. (1963) *The Bell Jar*. London: Faber and Faber.

Porter, R. (2002) *Madness: a Brief History*. Oxford: Oxford University Press.

Post, F. (1994) Creativity and Psychopathology: A Study of 291 World-Famous Men. *British Journal of Psychiatry*, 164, 22–34.

Potter, W. (1998) *Media Literacy*. London: Sage

Potter, W. (2004) *Theory of Media Literacy: a Cognitive Approach*. London: Sage.

Powell, J. and Clarke, A. (2002) The www of the World Wide Web: Who What and Why.? *Journal of Medical Internet Resources*, 4: E4 ⊏medline⊐.

Prendergast, R. (1992) *Film Music: a Neglected Art: a Critical Study of Music in Films* (2nd edn). London: Norton.

Press Complaints Commission (2000) *Past Decisions*. Available at <http://www.pcc.org.uk/reports/details.asp?id=56> (Accessed 18 July 2005).

Press Complaints Commission. (2005) *Code of Practice*. Available at <http://www.pcc.org.uk/cop/cop.asp> (Accessed 12 July 2005).

Priebe, S. (2003) Media Coverage of Mental Health Care in the UK, USA and Australia. *Psychiatric Bulletin*, 27, 331–333.

Prior, C. (2003) *Shocked Sun readers show national anti-stigma campaign needed.* Available at <http://www.rethink.org/news%2Bcampaigns/press_releases/frank-bruno.htm> (Accessed 24 September 2003).

Pursehouse, M. (1991) Looking at *The Sun*: into the Nineties with a Tabloid and its Readers. *Cultural Studies at Birmingham*, 1, 88–133.

Repper, J., Sayce, L., Strong, S., Wilmot, J. and Haines, M. (1997) *Tall Stories from the Backyard*. London: Mind.

Ressler, R. and Schachtman, T. (1992) *Whoever Fights Monsters*. New York: St Martin's Press.

Rethink (2002) *Severe Mental Illness*. Available at <www.rethink.org> (Accessed 20 May 2005).

Rethink (2004) *Severe Mental Illness*. Available at <http://www.rethink.org/> (Accessed 15 November 2004).

Riddell, M. (2002) The Fiction of New Fiction. *Observer Sunday*, 22 September.

Robinson, J. and Levy, M. (1986) *The Main Source*. London: Sage.

Roediger, H., Rushton, J., Capaldi, E. and Paris, S. (1991) *Psychology* (3rd edn). New York: HarperCollins.

Rogers, C. (1951) *Client Centred Therapy: its Current Practice, Implications and Theory*. London: Constable.

Rogers, C. (1961) *On Becoming a Person: a Therapist's View of Psychotherapy*. Boston: Houghton Mifflin.

Rogers, E. (1986) *Communication Technology*. New York: Free Press.

Rogers, A., Pilgrim, D. and Lacey, R. (1993) *Experiencing Psychiatry: User's Views of Services*. London: Macmillan.

Rosen, A. and Walter, G. (2000) Way out of Tune: Lessons from Shine and its Expose. *Australian and New Zealand Journal of Psychiatry*, 34, 237–244.

Rosengren, K. and Windahl, S. (1989) *Media Matter: TV use in Childhood and Adolescence*. Norwood NJ: Ablex.

Rosenhan, D. (1973) On Being Sane in Insane Places. *Science*, 179, 250–258.

Rothbart, M. and Park, B. (1986) On the Confirmability and Disconfirmability of Trait Concepts. *Journal of Personality and Social Psychology*, 50, 131–142.

Rothbart, M., Fulero, S. and Jensen, C. (1978) From Individual to Group Impressions: Availability Heuristics in Stereotype Formation. *Journal of Experimental Social Psychology*, 14, 237–255.

Rothman, W. (1988) *The 'I' of the Camera: Essays in Film Criticism, History and Aesthetics*. Cambridge: Cambridge University Press.

Rowling, J. K. (2000) *Harry Potter and the Goblet of Fire*. London: Bloomsbury.

Royal College of Psychiatrists (2001) *Changing Minds: Every Family in the Land*. Available at http://www.stigma.org/everyfamily/everycontentsnew.html (Accessed 21 July 2005).

Royal College of Psychiatrists (2005) *2001: A Mind Odyssey*. Available at http://www.rcpsych.ac.uk/campaigns/2001/ (Accessed at 18 June 2005).

Rubin, A. (1984) Ritualised and Instrumental Television Viewing. *Journal of Communication*, 34(3): 67–77.

Rushdie, S. (1994) *The Satanic Verses*. London: Vintage.

Salkeld, D. (1993) *Madness and Drama in the Age of Shakespeare*. Manchester: Manchester University Press.

Salter, M. (2003) Psychiatry and the Media: from Pitfalls to Possibilities. *Psychiatric Bulletin*, 27, 123–125.

Salter, M. and Byrne, P. (2000) The Stigma of Mental Illness: How You can Use the Media to Reduce it. *Psychiatric Bulletin*, 24, 281–283.

Samaritans (1997) *Media Guidelines on Portrayals of Suicide*. Online booklet, Available at <www.samaritans.org.uk> (Accessed 12 July 2005).

Samaritans (2005) *Samaritans*. Available at <http://www.samaritans.org.uk/> (Accessed 22 July 2005).

SANE (2003) *SANE*. Available at http://www.sane.org.uk/ (Accessed 24 September 2003).

Sartorius, N. (2002) Iatrogenic Stigma of Mental Illness: Begins with Behaviour and Attitudes of Medical Professionals, Especially Psychiatrists. *British Medical Journal*, 324(7352): 1470–1471.

Sartre, J. P. (1967) *What is Literature*. London: Methuen.

Say No To Psychiatry. *Say No To Psychiatry*. Available at <http://www.sntp.net/> (Accessed 12 May 2005).

Sayce, L. (2000) *From Psychiatric Patient to Citizen*. London: Macmillan.

Scambler, G. (1998) Stigma and Disease: Changing Paradigms. *Lancet*, 352, 1054–1055.

Scheff, T. (1968) The Role of the Mentally Ill and the Dynamics of Mental Disorder. In Spitzer, S. and Denzin, N. *The Mental Patient*. London: McGraw Hill, pp. 8–22.

Scheff, T. (1974) The Labelling Theory of Mental Illness. *American Sociological Review*, 39, 444–452.

Schlesinger, J. (2002a) Issues in Creativity and Madness Part One: Ancient Questions, Modern Answers. *Ethical Human Sciences & Services*, 4(1): 73–76.

Schlesinger, J. (2002b) Issues in Creativity and Madness Part Two: Eternal Flames. *Ethical Human Sciences & Services*, 4(2): 139–142.

Schmidtke, A. and Schaller, S. (2000) The Role of Mass Media in Suicide Prevention. In Hawton, K. and van Heeringen, K. (eds) *The International Handbook of Suicide and Attempted Suicide*. New York: Wiley, pp. 675–697.

Schneider, I. (1987) The Theory and Practice of Movie Psychiatry. *American Journal of Psychiatry*, 144(8): 996–1002.

Scrivener, R. (2002) *Mapping Health on the Internet*. Abingdon: Radcliffe Medical Press.

Seale, C. (2002) *Media and Health*. London: Sage.

Secker, J. and Platt, S. (1996) Why Media Images Matter. In Philo, G. (ed.) *Media and Mental Distress*. London: Longman, pp. 1–17.

Sen, D. (2003) Mad Memoirs of the 21st Century. *Mental Health Today*, November, pp. 31–33.

Serenity. Available at <http://www.findserenitynow.com/uk/index.html> (Accessed 29 April 2005).

Shakespeare, W. (1972) *King Lear* (9th edn). London: Methuen.

Sheldon, T. (1996) Public Therapy. *British Medical Journal*, 313, 238 (27 July).

Shelley, M. (1818) *Frankenstein*. London: Penguin.

Shoemaker, P. and Reese, S. (1996) *Mediating the Message: Theories of Influences on Mass Media Content* (2nd edn). London: Longman.

Shore, B. (1996) *Culture in Mind. Cognition, Culture and the Problem of Meaning*. New York: Oxford University Press.

Sieff, E. (2003) Media Frames of Mental Illnesses: The Potential Impact of Negative Frames. *Journal of Mental Health*, 12(3): 259–269.

Signorielli, N. (1989) The Stigma of Mental Illness on Television. *Journal of Broadcasting and Electronic Media*, 33(3): 325–31.

Simon, B. (1978) *Mind and Madness in Ancient Greece. The Classical Roots of Modern Psychiatry*. London: Cornell University Press.

Skinner, B. (1974) *About Behaviourism*. New York: Alfred Knopf.

Skynner, R. and Cleese, J. (1993) *Families and How to Survive Them*. London: Mandarin.

Slattery, K., Doremus, M. and Marcus, L. (2001) Shifts in Public Affairs Reporting on the Network Evening News: A Move to the Sensational. *Journal of Broadcasting and Electronic Media*, 45, 290–292.

Small, H. (1996) *Love's Madness. Medicine, the Novel and Female Insanity 1800–1865*. Oxford: Clarendon Press.

Smith, M. (2002) Stigma. *Advances in Psychiatric Treatment*, 8, 317–325.

Snoddy, R. (1993) *The Good, The Bad and the Unacceptable*. London: Faber and Faber.

Social Exclusion Unit (2003) *Mental Health and Social Exclusion. Consultation Document*. Available at <http://www.socialexclusionunit.gov.uk/downloaddoc.asp?id=44> (Accessed 20 July 2005).

Solomon, A. (2002) *The Noonday Demon: an Anatomy of Depression*. London: Vintage.

Solzhenitsyn, I. (1963) *One Day in the Life of Ivan Denisovich*. London: Penguin.

Solzhenitsyn, I. (1974) *The Gulag Archipelago*. New York: Viking.

Squires, J. (1993) *Read all about it! The Corporate Takeover of America's Newspapers*. New York: Times Books.

Stevenson, N. (2002) *Understanding Media Cultures* (2nd edn). London: Sage.

Stice, E. and Shaw, H. (1994) Adverse Effects of the Media Portrayed Thin-Ideal on Women, and Linkages to Bulimic Symptoms. *Journal of Social and Clinical Psychology*, 13, 288–305.

Susman, J. (1994) Disability, Stigma and Deviance. *Social Science & Medicine*, 38(1): 15–22.

Szasz, T. (1992) The Myth of Mental Illness. In Miller, R. (ed.) *The Restoration of Dialogue: Readings in the Philosophy of Clinical Psychology*. Washington: American Psychological Association, pp.175–182.

Tam, P. (2002) Psychiatry and the Cinema. *Australasian Psychiatry*, 10(2): 178.

Taylor, P. and Gunn, J. (1999) Homicides by People with Mental Illness: Myth and Reality. *British Journal of Psychiatry*, 174, 9–14.

Thede, L. (1999) *Computers in Nursing*. New York: Lippincott.

Thompson, S. (1999) The Internet and its Potential Influence on Suicide. *Psychiatric Bulletin*, 23 (8): 449–451.

Tomaiuolo, N. (1995) Accessing Nursing Resources on the Internet. *Computers in Nursing*, 13(4): 159–164.

Turner, G. (1999) *Film as Social Practice* (3rd edn). London: Routledge.

Unsworth, J. (1995) Why Does an Author who Apparently Draws so Much on Autobiography seem Committed to Alienating the Reader? In Swindells, J. (ed.) *The Uses of Autobiography*. London: Taylor & Francis, pp. 24–29.

Valenti, M. (2000) *More than a Movie: Ethics in Entertainment*. Oxford: Westview Press.

Van Dijk, T. (1987) *Communicating Racism: Ethnic Prejudice in Thought and Talk*. Newbury Park: Sage.

Vedic Wisdom. *Vedic Wisdom*. Available at <http://www.vedicwisdom.com/decure.html> (Accessed 24 June 2005).

Von Goethe, J. (1989) [1774]. *The Sorrows of Young Werther*. Trans Michael Hulse. London: Penguin.

Vooijs, M. and Van der Voort, T. (1993) Learning about Television Violence: the Impact of a Critical Viewing Curriculum on Children's Attitudinal Judgements of Crime Series. *Journal of Research and Development in Education*, 26(3): 133–142

Vousden, M. (1989) 'Loony Lefties' and 'Mad Mullahs'. *Nursing Times*, 85(28): 16–17.

Waddell, C. (1998) Creativity and Mental illness: Is there a Link? *Canadian Journal of Psychiatry*, 43(2): 166–172.

Wahl, O. (1995) *Media Madness: Public Images of Mental Illness*. New Brunswick, NJ: Rutgers University Press.

Wahl, O., Wood, A. and Richards, R. (2002) Newspaper Coverage of Mental Illness: Is it Changing? *Psychiatric Rehabilitation Skills*, 6(1): 9–31.

Wahl, O. (2003a) Depictions of Mental Illness in Children's Media. *Journal of Mental Health*, 12(3): 249–258.

Wahl, O. (2003b) News Media Portrayal of Mental Illness: Implications for Public Policy. *American Behavioural Scientist*, 46(12): 1594–1600.

Wahl, O. and Kaye, A. (1992) Mental Illness Topics in Popular Periodicals. *Community Mental Health Journal*, 28(1): 21–28.

Wall, B. and Rossen, E. (2004) Media as a Teaching Tool in Psychiatric Nursing Education. *Nurse Educator*, 29(1): 36–40.

Walsh, A. (2002) *E-Mail Correspondence*. Channel 4 Disability Advisor. 5th June 2002.

Wedding, D. and Boyd, M. (1999) *Movies and Mental Illness*. Boston, MA: McGraw Hill Education.

Weiss, M., Sushrut, J., Raguram, R., Vounatsou, P. and Littlewood, R. (2001) Psychiatric Stigma across Cultures: Local Validation in Bangalore and London. *Anthropology and Medicine*, 8(1): 71–87.

Welch, M. and Racine, T. (1999) A Psycho for Every Generation. *Nursing Inquiry*, 6(3): 216–219.

White, R. (1990) The Birth of the Reader. In McGregor, G. and White, R. (eds) *Reception and Response – Hearer Creativity and the Analysis of Spoken and Written Texts*. London: Routledge, pp. 242–259.

Williams, M. and Taylor, J. (1995) Mental Illness: Media Perpetuation of Stigma. *Contemporary Nurse*, 4(1): 41–46.

Williams, R. (2002) *Somebody Someday*. London: Ebury Press.

Wilson, C., Nairn, R., Coverdale, J. and Panapa, A. (1999) Mental Illness Depictions in Prime-Time Drama: Identifying the Discursive Resources. *Australian and New Zealand Journal of Psychiatry*, 33, 232–239.

Wilson, C., Nairn, R., Coverdale, J. and Panapa, A. (2000) How Mental Illness is Portrayed in Children's Television. *British Journal of Psychiatry*, 176, 440–443.

Wilson, M. (1997) Printing it in Black and White. *OpenMind*, 85, May/June, 16–17.

Wing, J. (1978) *Reasoning about Madness*. Oxford: Oxford University Press.

Winker, M., Flanagin, A., Chi-Lum, B., White, J., Andrews, K., Kennett, R., DeAngelis, C. and Musacchio, R. (2000) Guidelines for Medical and Health Information Sites on the Internet: Principles Governing AMA Web Sites. *Journal of the American Medical Association*, 283(12): 1600–1606.

Winship, J. (1987) *Inside Women's Magazines*. London: Pandora.

Wober, J. (1991) *Television and Mental Ill Health*. London: Independent Television Commission Research Monographs.

Wolfenstein, M. and Leites, N. (1970) *Movies: A Psychological Study* (2nd edn). New York: Atheneum.

Woods, R. (2002) The Death of Dignity. *Sunday Times*, 21 July.

Woolf, L. (ed.) (1953) *A Writer's Diary: Virginia Woolf*. London: Hogarth Press.

World Federation for Mental Health (2005) *World Mental Health Day*. Available at <http://www.wfmh.org/wmhday2005.htm> (Accessed 6 December 2005).

Wright, T. (1997) Creativity and Bipolar Disorder. *Medical Problems of Performing Artists*, 12(3): 89–92.

Wurtzel, E. (1994) *Prozac Nation*. London: Quartet Books.

Wykes, M. and Gunter, B. (2005) *The Media and Body Image*. London: Sage.

Yalom, I. (1995) *The Theory and Practice of Group Psychotherapy* (4th edn). New York: Basic Books.

Ying, H. (1999) *Daughter of the River*. London: Bloomsbury.

Young, R. (1991) Poems that Read Themselves. *Tropismes*, 5, 233–261.

Zillmann, D. (1980) Anatomy of Suspense. In Tannebaum, P. (ed.) *The Entertainment Functions of Television*. New Jersey: Lawrence Erlbaum.

Zito Trust (2005) *The Zito Trust*. Available at <http://www.zitotrust.co.uk/> (Accessed 12 July 2005).

Index